The Most Current Text Available

This edition includes the latest media trends and developments and coverage of the political, economic, and cultural issues affecting the mass media and our culture today:

▲ A new Extended Case Study, "Analyzing Coverage of the Financial Crisis," provides critical analysis of how the media covered the 2008 economic downturn (pages 524–531)

▲ Analysis of the 2008 presidential campaigns and election (pages 2–4)

▲ How the new open access wireless spectrum will affect the mobile phone industry (pages 42–44)

▲ How Radiohead became the poster-band for the "pay what you wish" experiment in music (pages 70–72)

▲ A discussion of the switch to digital television (page 149) and the emerging popularity of watching TV online (pages 170 and 177)

▲ The challenges facing print newspapers including declining readerships, blogs, and the move to online distribution (pages 270–275)

▲ How Google went from Internet start-up to a major advertising company (pages 342–344)

▲ A discussion of how journalism functions in China, giving a global perspective to the news industry (page 457)

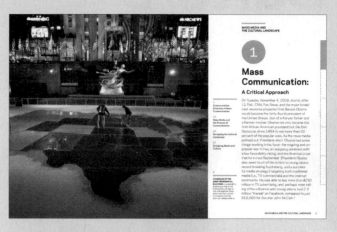

Online resources are also available. For more information, please see the inside back cover or visit **bedfordstmartins.com/mediaculture/catalog**.

Praise for Media & Culture

I am extremely impressed with *Media & Culture.*

LAURIE FLUKER,
*TEXAS STATE
UNIVERSITY*

Media & Culture is the best survey text of the current crop. The writing is well-constructed and does not to talk down to the students.

STEVE MILLER,
RUTGERS UNIVERSITY

Media & Culture's critical approach to the history, theory, economy, technology, and regulation of the various mass media helps students become critical users of the media.

SHIO NAM,
UNIVERSITY OF NORTH FLORIDA

This is one of the most up-to-date texts I've ever seen, and students certainly recognize this too.

KAREN PITCHER,
UNIVERSITY OF IOWA

I think the Campbell text is out-standing. It is a long-overdue media text that is grounded in pressing questions about American culture and its connection to the techniques and institutions of commercial communication. It is, indeed, an important book. At the undergraduate level, that's saying something.

STEVE M. BARKIN,
UNIVERSITY OF MARYLAND

Media & Culture offers a readable, insightful, and comprehensive look at a complicated subject.

ROBERT BLADE,
FLORIDA COMMUNITY COLLEGE

The Critical Perspective has enlightened the perspective of all of us who study media, and Campbell has the power to infect students with his love of the subject.

ROGER DESMOND,
UNIVERSITY OF HARTFORD

I will switch to Campbell because it is a tour de force of coverage and interpretation, it is the best survey text in the field hands down, and it challenges students. Campbell's text is the most thorough and complete in the field. . . . No other text is even close.

RUSSELL BARCLAY,
QUINNIPIAC UNIVERSITY

This book is an outstanding contribution to the field. It allows students to build upon their own experiences with various media they use, to see the ways in which those media are active constructors of culture.

JOHN PANTALONE,
UNIVERSITY OF RHODE ISLAND

The feature boxes are excellent, and are indispensable to any classroom.

MARVIN WILLIAMS,
KINGSBOROUGH COMMUNITY COLLEGE

Media & Culture

An Introduction to Mass Communication

Seventh Edition

Richard Campbell
Miami University

Christopher R. Martin
University of Northern Iowa

Bettina Fabos
University of Northern Iowa

BEDFORD/ST. MARTIN'S
Boston • New York

For Bedford/St. Martin's

Executive Editor for Communication: Erika Gutierrez
Developmental Editor: Noel Hohnstine
Editorial Assistant: Emily Cavedon
Senior Production Editor: Bill Imbornoni
Senior Production Supervisor: Dennis J. Conroy
Marketing Manager: Adrienne Petsick
Art Director: Lucy Krikorian
Text and Cover Design: TODA (The Office of Design and Architecture)
Copy Editor: Denise Quirk
Indexer: Kirsten Kite
Photo Research: Sue McDermott
Composition: Nesbitt Graphics, Inc.
Printing and Binding: RR Donnelley & Sons

President: Joan E. Feinberg
Editorial Director: Denise B. Wydra
Director of Development: Erica T. Appel
Director of Marketing: Karen R. Soeltz
Director of Editing, Design, and Production: Marcia Cohen
Assistant Director of Editing, Design, and Production: Elise S. Kaiser
Managing Editor: Shuli Traub

Library of Congress Control Number: 2008943128

Manufactured in the United States of America.

4 3 2 1 0 9
f e d c b a

For information, write: Bedford/St. Martin's, 75 Arlington Street,
Boston, MA 02116 (617-399-4000)

ISBN-10: 0-312-48546-8
ISBN-13: 978-0-312-48546-7

"WE ARE NOT ALONE."
For my family — Chris, Caitlin, and Dianna

"YOU MAY SAY I'M A DREAMER,
BUT I'M NOT THE ONLY ONE."
For our daughters — Olivia and Sabine

About the Authors

Richard Campbell, director of the journalism program at Miami University, is the author of *"60 Minutes" and the News: A Mythology for Middle America* (1991) and coauthor of *Cracked Coverage: Television News, the Anti-Cocaine Crusade, and the Reagan Legacy* (1994). Campbell has written for numerous publications, including *Columbia Journalism Review, Journal of Communication*, and *Media Studies Journal*, and he is on the editorial boards of *Critical Studies in Mass Communication* and *Television Quarterly*. He holds a PhD from Northwestern University and has also taught at the University of Wisconsin-Milwaukee, Mount Mary College, the University of Michigan, and Middle Tennessee State University.

Bettina Fabos, an award-winning video maker and former print reporter, is an assistant professor of visual communication and interactive media studies at the University of Northern Iowa. She is the author of *Wrong Turn on the Information Superhighway: Education and the Commercialized Internet* (2003). Her areas of expertise include critical media literacy, Internet commercialization, the role of the Internet in education, and media representations of popular culture. Her work has been published in *Library Trends, Review of Educational Research*, and *Harvard Educational Review*. Fabos has also taught at Miami University and has a PhD from the University of Iowa.

Christopher R. Martin is an associate professor of journalism at the University of Northern Iowa and author of *Framed! Labor and the Corporate Media* (2003). He has written articles and reviews on journalism, televised sports, the Internet, and labor for several publications, including *Communication Research, Journal of Communication, Journal of Communication Inquiry, Labor Studies Journal*, and *Culture, Sport, and Society*. He is also on the editorial board of the *Journal of Communication Inquiry*. Martin holds a PhD from the University of Michigan and has also taught at Miami University.

Brief Contents

Preface

◢ WHEN WE FIRST PUBLISHED *MEDIA AND CULTURE* in 1997, our goal was to create a new kind of introduction to mass communication textbook, one that went beyond basic facts, names, dates, and events. We wanted to create a book that would provide students with a critical and cultural perspective on the media to help them think deeply about the media messages that surround them and understand better the complex relationship between the mass media and our shared culture. And because we wanted to create a book that would have wide appeal, we focused on connecting with students through the media they already know well and through an approach based on storytelling.

In the ensuing years, we were pleased to find that this approach struck a chord with hundreds of instructors and thousands of students across the United States and North America. We were especially elated to learn that after a few editions, *Media and Culture* had become not only widely admired but also the best-selling introductory text for this course. It was so encouraging to know that our original vision had truly connected with students and instructors. And we are excited to continue the tradition of bringing students and instructors coverage of the most pressing developments and issues in the world of the media.

Since *Media and Culture* was first published, we have seen the Internet morph from a relatively new medium to the center of much of our media consumption, watched a tide of deregulation dramatically alter the landscape of media ownership, and witnessed the emergence of abundant new forms of expression—from blogs and podcasts to social networking and digital filmmaking—that have ushered in a new world of storytelling and participatory media. Given these profound changes, we recognized that this new edition provided a perfect opportunity to create a deep and thorough revision that would refocus on the book's original vision while still keeping up with furious and fast-paced change. If we did this job right, we knew that we would make the new edition an even better resource than ever before.

In starting to think about this revision, we first looked at core content. Over the last decade, so much has happened in media that we felt it was time to go through every chapter—paragraph by paragraph and line by line—and streamline the text to refocus only on the most essential concepts and key historical coverage. We also revised the headings throughout to highlight main points and to provide students with clearer signposts at every step. The result? We cut the book's text by almost 15 percent while still giving students all the necessary facts, contemporary coverage, and compelling stories they need.

Beyond the core content, we also wanted to help students see the big picture on how various aspects of the media connect. New media ownership snapshots now go beyond simply listing what a company owns: To help students understand the *impact* of major media conglomerates, these snapshots show students how media ownership issues affect not only the world at large but also their daily lives. In addition, the new Common Threads feature in the end-of-chapter reviews helps students connect each chapter's content to the book's recurring themes as explained in Chapter 1.

As always, we have also added new examples and stories throughout, keeping the book up-to-date with the most important media developments and trends, including a new Extended Case Study on the recent financial crisis. And as ever, we are excited to continue the tradition of bringing students and instructors coverage of the most pressing developments in the world of the media. Finally, to match these significant changes and revisions in features and content, we also redesigned the book's interior for the first time in several editions. We enlisted the acclaimed design studio TODA (The Office of Design and Architecture) to give the text a bold new look and help us capture student attention.

We would like to take a moment and express our gratitude to all the teachers and students who have supported *Media and Culture* over the years. We continue to be enthusiastic about—and humbled by—the chance to work with the amazing community of teachers that has developed around *Media and Culture*, helping us not only to stay current but also to take the project in important new directions—with fresh examples and practical experience from those using the book in the classroom. We are also grateful for the opportunity to help so many students become media literate. We believe that the critical and cultural perspectives we present in *Media and Culture* help students understand the media and their role in the larger ebb and flow of everyday life. We hope the text enables students to become more knowledgeable media consumers and more fully engaged citizens with a critical stake in shaping our world. In the seventh edition, we believe that instructors will find the content they have always relied on but with a direction more focused than ever.

The past decade has been an honor, and we are excited to bring you the best of *Media and Culture* for another ten.

The Best and Broadest Introduction to the Mass Media

- **A critical approach to media literacy.** *Media and Culture* introduces students to five stages of the critical thinking and writing process: description, analysis, interpretation, evaluation, and engagement. The text uses these stages as a lens for examining the historical context and current processes that shape mass media as part of our culture. This framework informs the writing throughout, including the Media Literacy and the Critical Process boxes in each chapter.
- **A cultural perspective.** The text consistently focuses on the vital relationship between mass media and our shared culture—how cultural trends influence our mass media and how specific historical developments, technical innovations, and key decision makers in the history of the media have affected the ways our democracy and society have evolved.
- **Comprehensive coverage.** The text gives students the nuts-and-bolts content they need to understand each media industry's history, organizational structure, economic models, and market data.
- **An exploration of media economics and democracy.** To become more engaged in our society and more discerning as consumers, students must pay attention to the complex relationship between democracy and capitalism, between the marketplace of ideas and the global consumer market. To that end, *Media and Culture* addresses the significance of the dramatic rise in multinational media systems. It invites students to explore the implications of the 1996 Telecommunications Act and other deregulation resolutions. Additionally, it looks critically at the global picture and encourages students to participate in the debates over ownership. Each chapter ends with a discussion of the effects of various mass media on the nature of democratic life.
- **Compelling storytelling.** Most mass media—whether news, prime-time television, magazines, film, paperback novels, digital games, or advertising—make use of storytelling to tap into our shared beliefs and values, and so does *Media and Culture*. Each chapter presents the events and issues surrounding media culture as intriguing and informative narratives rather than as a series of unconnected facts and feats as it maps the uneasy and parallel changes in consumer culture and democratic society.
- **The most accessible book available.** Learning features in every chapter help students find and remember the information they need to know: chapter-opening outlines give students a roadmap to main points, annotated timelines offer powerful visual guides that highlight key events and refer to more coverage in the chapter, Media Literacy and the Critical Process boxes model the five-step process, and the Chapter Reviews help students study and review.

New to This Edition

- **Renewed focus and streamlined coverage.** With the fast-paced changes and developments in the media today, it can seem overwhelming to try to study and understand the broad history and cutting-edge events that surround each medium. In the seventh edition, we have streamlined the text (about 15 percent shorter) to focus on key coverage and added more headings to provide signposts for students and help them get a handle on the past, present, and future of the media industries.

- **Helping students see the big picture.** The new edition helps students take the pieces that they learn about individual media industries and issues and put them together to see the bigger picture of today's mass media. By understanding how the industries intersect—especially via media convergence and diminishing ownership laws—students will see how media affect our culture and our daily lives.

  - **A new look at media ownership** expands beyond simply listing the properties owned by the major media conglomerates. New media ownership snapshots now consist of two parts: first, a "What Do They Own?" list highlights a given corporation's holdings across multiple media industries; second, the new "What Does This Mean?" section puts ownership into context for students by exploring the real-world implications of the given company's ownership pattern.

  - **The new Common Threads feature,** at the end of each chapter, discusses how the chapter content connects with the book's recurring themes, such as the developmental stages of mass media, the commercial nature of media industries, the role the media play in democracy, cultural expression and storytelling, and critical analysis of the media.

  - **A new "Extended Case Study: Analyzing Coverage of the Financial Crisis"** guides students through a critical analysis of how the media covered the economic downturn that began in 2008. By exploring and critiquing the role of the media, students can judge how the media performed as a watchdog for society, how well they told the story of the crisis, and how students can lend their voices to the media landscape.

- **Always the most current book available.** Studying and analyzing the media means keeping on top of the latest developments. We always work to include the most recent issues and trends in *Media and Culture,* and the seventh edition is no exception. Coverage of everything from the 2008 economic crisis and presidential election to the transition to digital television and the success of Hulu.com and Radiohead's "pay what you wish" experiment will keep students attentive and engaged while they are learning.

- **A new interior design.** *Media & Culture* has a fresh new look and helps capture student attention through a stunning visual program of over 300 photos and images and informative captions.

Student Supplements

Book Companion Site at bedfordstmartins.com/mediaculture

Free study aids on the book's Web site help students gauge their understanding of the text material through chapter summaries with study questions, visual activities that combine images and critical thinking analysis, and pre- and post-chapter quizzes to help students assess their strengths and weaknesses and focus their studying. Students can also keep current on media news with streaming headlines from a variety of news sources and can use the Media Portal to find the best media-related sites on the Web.

Media and Culture e-Book at bedfordstmartins.com/mediaculture

The *Media and Culture e-Book* is an online, interactive, and inexpensive version of the print text. Further enhancing students' learning experience, the e-book allows students to highlight portions of the text, add notes to any page, search the e-book and the Internet, and link to the book's glossary. Instructors can customize the e-book by adding their own material or by omitting or reordering chapters, making this the ideal book for your course. To order the e-book packaged **free** with the print book, use ISBN-10: 0-312-57126-7; ISBN-13: 978-0-312-57126-9. To order the e-book **stand-alone** use ISBN-10: 0-312-54348-4; ISBN-13: 978-0-312-54348-8.

Media Career Guide: Preparing for Jobs in the 21st Century, Seventh Edition

James Seguin, *Robert Morris College*; Sherri Hope Culver, *Temple University*; ISBN-10: 0-312-56082-6; ISBN-13: 978-0-312-56082-9

Practical, student-friendly, and revised with recent statistics on the job market, this guide includes a comprehensive directory of media jobs, practical tips, and career guidance for students considering a major in the media industries. To order the *Media Career Guide* packaged **free** with the print book, use ISBN-10: 0-312-59254-X; ISBN-13: 978-0-312-59254-7.

Instructor Supplements

VideoCentral at bedfordstmartins.com/mediaculture

This new video resource from acclaimed videographer and teacher Peter Berkow features short clips (three to five minutes) of working media professionals. Issues such as the future of print media, net neutrality, media convergence, and the deregulation of media ownership are discussed by a wide variety of professionals across the industries who are working on both national and local levels, such as Anne Rice, Clarence Page, Charles Osgood, Amy Goodman, and even student journalists at the award-winning *Orion* student newspaper at California State University-Chico. These short videos are great as in-class lecture launchers or for students to use outside of class to explore media issues further. This resource is available for students and instructors. Learn more at **bedfordstmartins.com/mediaculture/catalog**.

About the Media: Video Clips DVD to Accompany *Media and Culture*

ISBN 0-312-45173-3; ISBN-13: 978-0-312-45173-8

This unique instructor's resource includes more than fifty media clips, keyed to every chapter in *Media and Culture*. It provides historical and contemporary footage as well as excerpts from critical pieces about the media. The DVD is available upon adoption of *Media and Culture*; please contact your local sales representative.

Instructor Resources at bedfordstmartins.com/mediaculture

In addition to access to all student resources, the site offers instructors PowerPoint presentations for each chapter, the Instructor's Resource Manual, and student quiz tracking. And Clicker Questions for every chapter help integrate the latest personal response systems (PRS) into the classroom and get instant feedback on students' understanding of course concepts as well as their opinions and perspectives.

Instructor's Resource Manual at bedfordstmartins.com/mediaculture

Bettina Fabos, *University of Northern Iowa*; Christopher R. Martin, *University of Northern Iowa*; and Richard Campbell, *Miami University*

This manual improves on what has always been the best and most comprehensive instructor teaching tool available for the introduction to mass communication course. Every chapter offers teaching tips and activities culled from dozens of instructors who use *Media and Culture* to teach thousands of students. In addition, this extensive resource provides a range of teaching approaches, tips for facilitating in-class discussions, writing assignments, outlines, lecture topics, lecture spin-offs, critical process exercises, classroom media resources, and an annotated list of more than two hundred video resources.

Test Bank

Bettina Fabos, *University of Northern Iowa*; Christopher R. Martin, *University of Northern Iowa*; Computerized Test Bank ISBN-10: 0-312-54212-7; ISBN-13: 978-0-312-54212-2; Print Test Bank ISBN-10: 0-312-54214-3; ISBN-13: 978-0-312-54214-6

A complete testing program is available both in print and as software formatted for Windows and Macintosh, with multiple choice, true/false, fill-in-the-blank, and short and long essay questions.

Content for Course Management Systems

Instructors can access content for course management systems such as WebCT and Blackboard. Visit **bedfordstmartins.com/cms** for more information.

The Bedford/St. Martin's Video Resource Library

A wide selection of contemporary and historical media-related videos is organized around the issues explored in *Media and Culture*. Qualified instructors are eligible to select videos from the resource library upon adoption of the text. Please contact your local sales representative for more information.

Media Presentations CD-ROM

ISBN-10: 0-312-25045-2; ISBN-13: 978-0-312-25045-4

CD-ROM technology and PowerPoint software let you build classroom presentations around three case studies: "Popular Music and Freedom of Expression," "Newspapers: From Print to the Web," and "Photojournalism, Photography, and the Coverage of War." These case studies include visual and textual material that instructors can use as is for lectures or customize with additions from the Web or other sources.

Acknowledgments

We are very grateful to everyone at Bedford/St. Martin's who supported this project through its many stages. We wish that every textbook author could have the kind of experience we had with these people: Chuck Christensen, Joan Feinberg, Denise Wydra, Erika Gutierrez, Erica Appel, Adrienne Petsick, and Simon Glick. We also collaborated with superb and supportive developmental editors: Noel Hohnstine, Linda Stern, and Bruce Cantley, and editorial assistant Emily Cavedon. We particularly appreciate the tireless work of Shuli Traub, managing editor, who oversaw the book's extremely tight schedule; William Imbornoni, senior project editor, who kept the book on schedule while making sure we got the details right; Dennis J. Conroy, senior production supervisor; and the designers at TODA, whose new design gives the book a fresh look. We are especially grateful to our research assistant, Susan Coffin, who again functioned as a one-person clipping service through the process.

We also want to thank the many fine and thoughtful reviewers who contributed ideas to the seventh edition of *Media and Culture*: Robert Blade, *Florida Community College*; Lisa Boragine, *Cape Cod Community College*; Joseph Clark, *University of Toledo*; Richard Craig, *San Jose State University*; Samuel Ebersole, *Colorado State University-Pueblo*; Brenda Edgerton-Webster, *Mississippi State University*; Tim Edwards, *University of Arkansas at Little Rock*; Mara Einstein, *Queens College*; Lillie M. Fears, *Arkansas State University*; Connie Fletcher, *Loyola University*; Monica Flippin-Wynn, *University of Oklahoma*; Gil Fowler, *Arkansas State University*; Donald G. Godfrey, *Arizona State University*; Kristin Watson Hatem, *Metropolitan State University*; Patricia Homes, *University of Louisiana at Lafayette*; Daniel McDonald, *Ohio State University*; Connie Hicks McMahon, *Barry University*; Steve Miller, *Rutgers University*; Siho Nam, *University of North Florida*; David Nelson, *University of Colorado-Colorado Springs*; Zengjun Peng, *St. Cloud State University*; Deidre Pike, *University of Nevada-Reno*; Neil Ralston, *Western Kentucky University*; J. Michael Reed, *Saddleback College*; David Roberts, *Missouri Valley College*; Donna

Simmons, *California State University-Bakersfield*; Marc Skinner, *University of Idaho*; Michael Stamm, *Michigan State University*; Bob Trumpbour, *Penn State University*; James Weaver, *Virginia Polytechnic and State University*; David Whitt, *Nebraska Wesleyan University*.

For the sixth edition: Boyd Dallos, *Lake Superior College*; Roger George, *Bellevue Community College*; Osvaldo Hirschmann, *Houston Community College*; Ed Kanis, *Butler University*; Dean A. Kruckeberg, *University of Northern Iowa*; Larry Leslie, *University of South Florida*; Lori Liggett, *Bowling Green State University*; Steve Miller, *Rutgers University*; Robert Pondillo, *Middle Tennessee State University*; David Silver, *University of San Francisco*; Chris White, *Sam Houston State University*; and Marvin Williams, *Kingsborough Community College*.

For the fifth edition: Russell Barclay, *Quinnipiac University*; Kathy Battles, *University of Michigan*; Kenton Bird, *University of Idaho*; Ed Bonza, *Kennesaw State University*; Larry L. Burris, *Middle Tennessee State University*; Ceilidh Charleson-Jennings, *Collin County Community College*; Raymond Eugene Costain, *University of Central Florida*; Richard Craig, *San Jose State University*; Dave Deeley, *Truman State University*; Janine Gerzanics, *West Valley College*; Beth Haller, *Towson University*; Donna Hemmila, *Diablo Valley College*; Sharon Hollenback, *Syracuse University*; Marshall D. Katzman, *Bergen Community College*; Kimberly Lauffer, *Towson University*; Steve Miller, *Rutgers University*; Stu Minnis, *Virginia Wesleyan College*; Frank G. Perez, *University of Texas at El Paso*; Dave Perlmutter, *Louisiana State University-Baton Rouge*; Karen Pitcher, *University of Iowa*; Ronald C. Roat, *University of Southern Indiana*; Marshel Rossow, *Minnesota State University*; Roger Saathoff, *Texas Tech University*; Matthew Smith, *Wittenberg University*; Marlane C. Steinwart, *Valparaiso University*.

For the fourth edition: Fay Y. Akindes, *University of Wisconsin-Parkside*; Robert Arnett, *Mississippi State University*; Charles Aust, *Kennesaw State University*; Russell Barclay, *Quinnipiac University*; Bryan Brown, *Southwest Missouri State University*; Peter W. Croisant, *Geneva College*; Mark Goodman, *Mississippi State University*; Donna Halper, *Emerson College*; Rebecca Self Hill, *University of Colorado*; John G. Hodgson, *Oklahoma State University*; Cynthia P. King, *American University*; Deborah L. Larson, *Southwest Missouri State University*; Charles Lewis, *Minnesota State University-Mankato*; Lila Lieberman, *Rutgers University*; Abbus Malek, *Howard University*; Anthony A. Olorunnisola, *Pennsylvania State University*; Norma Pecora, *Ohio University, Athens*; Elizabeth M. Perse, *University of Delaware*; Hoyt Purvis, *University of Arkansas*; Alison Rostankowski, *University of Wisconsin-Milwaukee*; Roger A. Soenksen, *James Madison University*; Hazel Warlaumont, *California State University-Fullerton*.

For the third edition: Gerald J. Baldasty, *University of Washington*; Steve M. Barkin, *University of Maryland*; Ernest L. Bereman, *Truman State University*; Daniel Bernadi, *University of Arizona*; Kimberly L. Bissell, *Southern Illinois University*; Audrey Boxmann, *Merimack College*; Todd Chatman, *University of Illinois*; Ray Chavez, *University of Colorado*; Vic Costello, *Gardner-Webb University*; Paul D'Angelo, *Villanova University*; James Shanahan, *Cornell University*; Scott A. Webber, *University of Colorado*.

For the second edition: Susan B. Barnes, *Fordham University*; Margaret Bates, *City College of New York*; Steven Alan Carr, *Indiana University/Purdue University, Fort Wayne*; William G. Covington Jr., *Bridgewater State College*; Roger Desmond, *University of Hartford*; Jules d'Hemecourt, *Louisiana State University*; Cheryl Evans, *Northwestern Oklahoma State University*; Douglas Gomery, *University of Maryland*; Colin Gromatzky, *New Mexico State University*; John L. Hochheimer, *Ithaca College*; Sheena Malhotra, *University of New Mexico*; Sharon R. Mazzarella, *Ithaca College*; David Marc McCoy, *Kent State University*; Beverly Merrick, *New Mexico State University*; John Pantalone, *University of Rhode Island*; John Durham Peters, *University of Iowa*; Lisa Pieraccini, *Oswego State College*; Susana Powell, *Borough of Manhattan Community College*; Felicia Jones Ross, *Ohio State University*; Enid Sefcovic, *Florida Atlantic University*; Keith Semmel, *Cumberland College*; Augusta Simon, *Embry-Riddle Aeronautical University*; Clifford E. Wexler, *Columbia-Greene Community College*.

For the first edition: Paul Ashdown, *University of Tennessee*; Terry Bales, *Rancho Santiago College*; Russell Barclay, *Quinnipiac University*; Thomas Beell, *Iowa State University*; Fred Blevens, *Southwest Texas State University*; Stuart Bullion, *University of Maine*; William G. Covington Jr., *Bridgewater State College*; Robert Daves, *Minneapolis Star Tribune*; Charles Davis, *Georgia Southern University*; Thomas Donahue, *Virginia Commonwealth University*; Ralph R. Donald, *University of Tennessee-Martin*; John P. Ferre, *University of Louisville*; Donald Fishman, *Boston College*; Elizabeth Atwood Gailey, *University of Tennessee*; Bob Gassaway, *University of New Mexico*; Anthony Giffard, *University of Washington*; Zhou He, *San Jose State University*; Barry Hollander, *University of Georgia*; Sharon Hollenbeck, *Syracuse University*; Anita Howard, *Austin Community College*; James Hoyt, *University of Wisconsin-Madison*; Joli Jensen, *University of Tulsa*; Frank Kaplan, *University of Colorado*; William Knowles, *University of Montana*; Michael Leslie, *University of Florida*; Janice Long, *University of Cincinnati*; Kathleen Maticheck, *Normandale Community College*; Maclyn McClary, *Humboldt State University*; Robert McGaughey, *Murray State University*; Joseph McKerns, *Ohio State University*; Debra Merskin, *University of Oregon*; David Morrissey, *Colorado State University*; Michael Murray, *University of Missouri at St. Louis*; Susan Dawson O'Brien, *Rose State College*; Patricia Bowie Orman, *University of Southern Colorado*; Jim Patton, *University of Arizona*; John Pauly, *St. Louis University*; Ted Pease, *Utah State University*; Janice Peck, *University of Colorado*; Tina Pieraccini, *University of New Mexico*; Peter Pringle, *University of Tennessee*; Sondra Rubenstein, *Hofstra University*; Jim St. Clair, *Indiana University Southeast*; Jim Seguin, *Robert Morris College*; Donald Shaw, *University of North Carolina*; Martin D. Sommernes, *Northern Arizona State University*; Linda Steiner, *Rutgers University*; Jill Diane Swensen, *Ithaca College*; Sharon Taylor, *Delaware State University*; Hazel Warlaumont, *California State University-Fullerton*; Richard Whitaker, *Buffalo State College*; Lynn Zoch, *University of South Carolina*.

Special thanks from Richard Campbell: I would also like to acknowledge the number of fine teachers at both the *University of Wisconsin-Milwaukee* and *Northwestern University* who helped shape the way I think about many of the issues raised in this book, and I am especially grateful to my former students at the *University of Wisconsin-Milwaukee, Mount Mary College,* the *University of Michigan, Middle Tennessee State University,* and my current students at *Miami University.* Some of my students have contributed directly to this text, and thousands have endured my courses over the years—and made them better. My all-time favorite former students, Chris Martin and Bettina Fabos, are now essential coauthors, as well as the creators of our book's Instructor's Manual, Test Bank, and the *About the Media* DVD. I am grateful for Chris and Bettina's fine writing, research savvy, good stories, and tireless work amid their own teaching schedules and writing careers, all while raising two independent and spirited daughters.

I remain most grateful, though, to the people I most love: my son, Chris; my daughter, Caitlin; and, most of all, my wife, Dianna, whose editing skills, daily conversations, shared interests, and ongoing support are the resources that make this project go better with each edition.

Special thanks from Christopher Martin and Bettina Fabos: We would also like to thank Richard Campbell, with whom it is always a delight working on this project. We also appreciate the great energy, creativity, and talent that everyone at Bedford/St. Martin's brings to the book. From edition to edition, we also receive plenty of suggestions from *Media and Culture* users and reviewers and from our own journalism and media students. We would like to thank them for their input and for creating a community of sorts around the theme of critical perspectives on the media. Most of all, we'd like to thank our daughters, Olivia and Sabine, who bring us joy and laughter every day, and a sense of mission to better understand the world of media and culture in which they live.

Please feel free to e-mail us at **mediaandculture@bedfordstmartins.com** with any comments, concerns, or suggestions!

Contents

SOUNDS AND IMAGES

WORDS AND PICTURES

THE BUSINESS OF MASS MEDIA

DEMOCRATIC EXPRESSION AND THE MASS MEDIA

◤Media & Culture

1

Mass Communication:

A Critical Approach

◀

**COVERAGE OF THE
2008 PRESIDENTIAL
ELECTION** included NBC's
projecting a map of the
United States on the ice
rink at Rockefeller Plaza,
which was then colored
in as results from the
electoral college came in.

On Tuesday, November 4, 2008, shortly after
11 P.M., CNN, Fox News, and the major broadcast networks projected that Barack Obama
would become the forty-fourth president of
the United States. Son of a Kenyan father and
a Kansan mother, Obama not only became the
first African American president but the first
Democrat since 1964 to win more than 50
percent of the popular vote. As the news media
pointed out, President-elect Obama had some
things working in his favor: the ongoing and unpopular war in Iraq, an outgoing president with
a low favorability rating, and the financial crisis
that hit in mid-September. President Obama
also owed much of his victory to young voters,
record-breaking fundraising, and a successful media strategy targeting both traditional
media (i.e., TV commercials) and the Internet
community. He was able to buy more than $250
million in TV advertising, and, perhaps most telling of his influence with young voters, had 2.3
million "friends" on Facebook, compared to just
610,000 for Senator John McCain.[1]

During the 2008 elections, the news media played a major role in helping us get to know the candidates and understand their platforms. How well, then, did the news media help Americans understand the complex issues raised during the national election? The media — as they did in 2000 and 2004 — continued to overemphasize polls, which often reduced the story of the election to a two-dimensional "who's winning/who's losing" racehorse narrative, obscuring complex policy issues like economic recovery, the war in Iraq, and environmental threats. This narrative was encouraged by the proliferation of presidential polls and Internet sites that tracked polls (e.g., realclearpolitics.com) and critiqued polling data (e.g., pollster.com, fivethirtyeight.com). At the time, the public editor of the *New York Times*, Clark Hoyt, reported that of the 270 political articles published in the *Times* during the last few months of the election, just "a little over 10 percent were primarily about policy substance." These figures were similar to election coverage for much of mainstream media. Hoyt noted that other studies reported that in fall 2008 the vast majority of election stories were about "the horse race, political tactics, polls, and the like."[2]

Sometimes overlooked amid the poll stories was the record $3 billion the candidates, the major parties, and their supporters spent on political advertising through the primaries and presidential election season. However, most of the money went to TV stations in ten or so "battleground" states — like Indiana, North Carolina, Colorado, Nevada, Ohio, and Missouri — where either presidential candidate had a chance to win. In Missouri alone, TV stations took in more than $50 million in 2008 and aired nearly 115,000 political ads from party

primaries through the final election.[3] More significantly, the narratives offered in most of these ads also functioned at a two-dimensional level, pitting the "good" ideas or character of one candidate against the "bad" ideas or character of the other. However, these kinds of ads may no longer be as effective; the proliferation of independent online "fact checkers" (such as factcheck.org) and the Web sites of most mainstream media instantly responded to misrepresentations in the ads and circulated this information throughout the news media to help keep voters informed.

In a democracy, we depend on news media to provide us with information that helps us make decisions about our political leaders. As citizens, therefore, we should expect that the TV and cable stations — who earn so much money through political advertising — use a portion of that revenue to investigate the main issues of the day and serve as a counterpoint to the often one-sided political TV ads. However, as critics rightly point out, little of that money was used to hire more journalists to analyze major issues. Instead, in 2008 mainstream journalism continued to slash jobs in the face of their own economic crisis. Despite the limitations of our news media, their job of presenting the world to us is enormously important. But we also have a job to do that is equally important. We must point a critical lens back at the media and describe, analyze, and interpret the stories that we hear, watch, and read daily to arrive at our own judgments about the media's performance. This textbook offers a map to help us all become more media literate, critiquing the media not as detached cynics but as informed audiences with a stake in the outcome.

◢ SO WHAT EXACTLY ARE THE ROLES AND RESPONSIBILITIES OF THE MEDIA

in the wake of the 2008 election, the economic crisis, and the war in Iraq? In such times, how do we demand the highest standards from our media? In this book, we take up such questions, examine the history and business of mass media, and discuss the media as a central force in shaping culture within our democracy. After all, the media have an impact beyond the reporting of news stories. At their best, in all their various forms, from mainstream newspapers to radio talk shows to blogs, the media try to bring understanding to events that affect all of us.

But, at their worst, the media's appetite for telling and selling stories leads them not only to document tragedy but also to misrepresent or exploit it. Many viewers and social critics disapprove of how media, particularly TV and cable, seem to hurtle from one event to another, often dwelling on trivial, celebrity-driven content. They also fault media for failing to remain detached from reported events—for example, by uncritically using government-created language such as "shock and awe" (the military's term for the early bombing strikes on Baghdad in the Iraq war). In addition, the growth of media industries, commercial culture, and new converging technologies—fiber-optic cable, handheld computers, digital television—offers a challenge to all of us. If we can learn to examine and critique the powerful dynamics of the media, we will be better able to monitor the rapid changes going on around us.

In this chapter, we examine key concepts and introduce critical processes for investigating media industries and issues. In later chapters, we probe the history and structure of media's major institutions. In the process, we develop an informed and critical view of the influence these institutions have had on community and global life. The goal is to become *media literate*— more critical as consumers of mass media institutions and more engaged as participants who accept part of the responsibility for the shape and direction of media culture.

Culture and the Evolution of Mass Communication

One way to understand the impact of the media on our lives is to explore the cultural context in which the media operate. Often, culture is narrowly associated with art, the unique forms of creative expression that give pleasure and set standards about what is true, good, and beautiful. Culture, however, can be viewed more broadly as the ways in which people live and represent themselves at particular historical times. This idea of culture encompasses fashion, sports, architecture, education, religion, and science, as well as mass media. Although we can study some cultural products, such as novels or songs from various historical periods, culture itself is always changing. It includes a society's art, beliefs, customs, games, technologies, traditions, and institutions. It also encompasses a society's modes of **communication**: the creation and use of symbol systems that convey information and meaning (for example, languages, Morse code, motion pictures, and one-zero binary computer codes).

Culture is made up of both the products that a society fashions and, perhaps more importantly, the processes that forge those products and reflect a culture's diverse values. Thus, **culture** may be defined as the symbols of expression that individuals, groups, and societies use to make sense of daily life and to articulate their values. According to this definition, when we listen to music, read a book, watch television, or scan the Internet, we are not asking, "Is this art?" but are instead trying to identify or connect with something or someone. In other words, we are assigning meaning to the song, book, TV program, or Web site. Culture, therefore,

is a process that delivers the values of a society through products or other meaning-making forms. For instance, the American ideal of "rugged individualism" has been depicted for decades through a tradition of westerns and detective stories on television, in movies and books, and even in political ads.

Culture links individuals to their society, providing both shared and contested values, and the mass media help circulate those values. The **mass media** are the cultural industries—the channels of communication—that produce and distribute songs, novels, newspapers, movies, Internet services, and other cultural products to large numbers of people. The historical development of media and communication can be traced through several overlapping eras in which newer forms of technology disrupted and modified older forms.

These eras, which all still operate to greater or lesser degrees, are oral, written, print, electronic, and digital. The first two eras refer to the communication of tribal or feudal communities and agricultural economies. The last three phases feature the development of **mass communication**: the process of designing cultural messages and stories and delivering them to large and diverse audiences through media channels as old as the printed book and as new as the Internet. Hastened by the growth of industry and modern technology, mass communication accompanied the shift of rural populations to urban settings and the rise of a consumer culture.

THE MEDIA, in all their varied forms from television news to online advertising, function as part of our larger shared culture.

Oral and Written Eras in Communication

In most early societies, information and knowledge first circulated slowly through oral traditions passed on by poets, teachers, and tribal storytellers. As alphabets and the written word emerged, however, a manuscript, or written, culture began to develop and eventually overshadow oral communication. Documented and transcribed by philosophers, monks, and stenographers, the manuscript culture served the ruling classes. Working people were generally illiterate, and the economic and educational gap between rulers and the ruled was vast. These eras of oral and written communication developed slowly over many centuries. Although exact time frames are disputed, historians generally consider these eras as part of Western civilization's premodern period, spanning the epoch from roughly 1000 B.C.E. to the mid-fifteenth century.

Early tensions between oral and written communication played out among ancient Greek philosophers and writers. Socrates (470-399 B.C.E.), for instance, made his arguments through public conversations and debates. Known as the Socratic method, this dialogue style of communication and inquiry is still used in college classrooms and university law schools. Many philosophers who supported the superiority of the oral tradition feared that the written word would threaten public discussion by offering fewer opportunities for the give-and-take of conversation. In fact, Socrates' most famous student, Plato (427-347 B.C.E.), sought to banish poets, whom he saw as purveyors of ideas less rigorous than those generated in oral, face-to-face, question-and-answer discussions. These debates prefigured similar discussions in the twentieth century regarding the dangers of television and the Internet. Do aspects of contemporary culture, such as TV talk shows and anonymous online chat rooms, cheapen public discussion and discourage face-to-face communication?

The Print Revolution

While paper and block printing developed in China around 100 C.E. and 1045, respectively, what we recognize as modern printing did not become practical in Europe until the middle of the fifteenth century. At this time, Johannes Gutenberg's invention of movable metallic type and the printing press in Germany ushered in the modern print era. Printing presses and publications spread rapidly across Europe in the late 1400s and early 1500s. Early on, many books were large, elaborate, and expensive. It took months to illustrate and publish these volumes, and they were usually purchased by wealthy aristocrats, royal families, church leaders, prominent merchants, and powerful politicians. Gradually, however, printers reduced the size and cost of books, making them available and affordable to more people. Books thus became the first mass-marketed products in history.

The printing press combined three elements necessary for this mass-market innovation. First, machine duplication replaced the tedious system in which scribes hand-copied texts. Second, duplication could be done rapidly, so large quantities of the same book could be produced. Third, the faster production of multiple copies brought down the cost of each unit, which made books more affordable to less affluent people.

Since mass-produced printed materials could spread information and ideas faster and farther than ever before, writers could use print to disseminate views counter to traditional civic doctrine and religious authority–views that paved the way for major social and cultural changes, such as the Protestant Reformation and the rise of modern nationalism. People started to resist traditional clerical authority and also to think of themselves not merely as members of families, isolated communities, or tribes, but as part of a country whose interests were broader than local or regional concerns. While oral and written societies had favored decentralized local governments, the print era marked the ascent of more centralized nation-states.

Eventually, the machine production of mass quantities that had resulted in a lowered cost per unit for books was also an essential factor in the mass production of other goods, which led to the Industrial Revolution, modern capitalism, and the rise of consumer culture in the twentieth century. With the revolution in industry came the rise of the middle class and an elite business class of owners and managers who acquired the kind of influence once held only by the nobility or the clergy. Print media became key tools used by commercial and political leaders to distribute information and maintain social order.

As with the Internet today, however, it was difficult for a single business or political leader, certainly in a democratic society, to gain total control over printing technology (although the king or queen did control printing press licenses in England until the early nineteenth century, and even today governments in many countries worldwide control presses, access to paper, and advertising and distribution channels). Instead, the mass publication of pamphlets, magazines, and books helped democratize knowledge, and literacy rates rose among the working and middle classes. Industrialization required a more educated workforce, but printed literature and textbooks also encouraged compulsory education, thus promoting literacy and extending learning beyond the world of wealthy upper-class citizens.

Just as the printing press fostered nationalism, it also nourished the ideal of individualism. People came to rely less on their local community and their commercial, religious, and political leaders for guidance. By challenging tribal life, the printing press "fostered the modern idea of individuality," disrupting "the medieval sense of community and integration."[4] In urban and industrial environments, many individuals became cut off from the traditions of rural and small-town life, which had encouraged community cooperation in premodern times. By the

EARLY BOOKS
Before the invention of the printing press, books were copied by hand in a labor-intensive process. This beautifully illuminated page is from an Italian Bible from the early 1300s.

mid-nineteenth century, the ideal of individualism affirmed the rise of commerce and increased resistance to government interference in the affairs of self-reliant entrepreneurs. The democratic impulse of individualism became a fundamental value in American society in the nineteenth and twentieth centuries.

The Electronic and Digital Eras

In Europe and America, the impact of industry's rise was enormous: Factories replaced farms as the main centers of work and production. During the 1880s, roughly 80 percent of Americans lived on farms and in small towns; by the 1920s and 1930s, most had moved to urban areas, where new industries and economic opportunities beckoned. The city had overtaken the country as the focus of national life.

The Electronic Age

In America, the gradual transformation from an industrial, print-based society to one grounded in the Information Age began with the development of the telegraph in the 1840s. Featuring dot-dash electronic signals, the telegraph made four key contributions to communication. First, it separated communication from transportation, making media messages instantaneous—unencumbered by stagecoaches, ships, or the pony express.[5] Second, the telegraph, in combination with the rise of mass-marketed newspapers, transformed "information into a commodity, a 'thing' that could be bought or sold irrespective of its uses or meaning."[6] By the time of the Civil War, news had become a valuable product. Third, the telegraph made it easier for military, business, and political leaders to coordinate commercial and military operations, especially after the installation of the transatlantic cable in the late 1860s. Fourth, the telegraph led to future technological developments, such as wireless telegraphy, the fax machine, and the cell phone, which ironically resulted in the telegraph's demise: In 2006, the Western Union telegraph offices sent their final messages.

The rise of film at the turn of the twentieth century and the development of radio in the 1920s were early signposts, but the electronic phase of the Information Age really began in the 1950s and 1960s with the arrival of television and its dramatic impact on daily life. Then, with the coming of the latest communication gadgetry—ever smaller personal computers, cable TV, DVDs, DVRs, direct broadcast satellites, cell phones, PDAs, and e-mail—the Information Age passed into its digital phase.

The Digital Age

In **digital communication**, images, texts, and sounds are converted (encoded) into electronic signals (represented as varied combinations of binary numbers—ones and zeros) that are then reassembled (decoded) as a precise reproduction of, say, a TV picture, a magazine article, a song, or a telephone voice. On the Internet, various images, texts, and sounds are all digitally reproduced and transmitted globally.

New technologies, particularly cable television and the Internet, have developed so quickly that traditional leaders in communication have lost some of their control over information. For example, starting with the 1992 presidential campaign, the network news shows (ABC, CBS, and NBC) began to lose their audiences to MTV, CNN, MSNBC, Fox News, Comedy Central, and radio talk shows; by the 2004 national elections, Internet **bloggers**—people who post commentary on personal-opinion Web sites—had become a key element in news.

Moreover, e-mail—a digital version of oral culture—has assumed some of the functions of the postal service and is outpacing attempts to control communications beyond national borders. A professor sitting at her desk in Cedar Falls, Iowa, sends messages routinely to research scientists in Moscow. Yet as recently as 1990, letters between the United States and former communist states might have been censored or might have taken months to reach their destinations.

The Age of Convergence

The electronic and digital eras have fully ushered in the age of **media convergence**. And *media convergence* today has two very different meanings. First, it refers to the technological merging of content in different mass media–for example, magazine articles and radio programs are also accessible on the Internet, and songs, TV shows, and movies are now available on iPods and cell phones.

Such technical and media content convergence is not entirely new. For example, in the late 1920s, the Radio Corporation of America (RCA) purchased the Victor Talking Machine Company and introduced machines that could play both radio and recorded music. Then in the 1950s, the recording and radio industries (as deejays played records) united again during the emergence of television. However, contemporary media convergence is much broader than the simple merging of older and newer forms. In fact, the various eras of communication are themselves reinvented in this "age of convergence." Oral communication, for example, finds itself reconfigured, in part, as e-mail and instant messaging. And print communication is re-formed in the thousands of newspapers now available online. Also, keep in mind the wonderful ironies of media convergence: The first major digital retailer, Amazon.com, made its name by selling the world's oldest mass medium–the book–on the world's newest mass medium–the Internet.

A second definition of media convergence–sometimes called **cross platform** by media marketers–describes a business model that involves consolidating various media holdings, such as cable connections, phone services, television transmissions, and Internet access, under one corporate umbrella. The goal is not necessarily to offer consumers more choice in their media options, but to better manage resources and maximize profits. For example, a company that owns TV stations, radio outlets, and newspapers in multiple markets–as well as in the same cities–can deploy a reporter or producer to create three or four versions of the same story for various media outlets. So rather than having each radio station, TV station, newspaper, and online news site generate diverse and independent stories about an issue vital to a community, a media corporation employing the convergence model can use fewer employees to generate multiple versions of the same story. Such a company needs fewer reporters, producers, and editors–not more. Ultimately, fewer stories are generated from fewer perspectives, which means that consumers have less choice in news coverage.

The convergence business model offers more profits to those companies that downsize–or converge–their workforce while increasing their media holdings in many markets. But while it's easy to see the benefits for media owners, this model offers serious disadvantages for society. In addition to limiting the range of perspectives from which stories are told, another consequence is that the owners' biases and interests–for example, in culture, politics, and economics–are

possibly more influential. Also, the apparent need for fewer journalists means the employment of fewer journalists, possibly from a narrower array of racial and ethnic backgrounds. Contributions from a range of journalistic voices are often diminished. (See Chapter 2 for more about media convergence.)

Mass Media and the Process of Communication

The mass media constitute a wide variety of industries and merchandise, from documentary news programs about famines in Africa to infomercials about vegetable slicers or mind readers. The word *media* is, after all, a Latin plural form of the singular noun *medium*, meaning an intervening material or substance through which something else is conveyed or transmitted. Television, newspapers, music, movies, magazines, books, billboards, radio, broadcast satellites, and the Internet are all part of the media; and they each are quite capable of either producing worthy products or pandering to society's worst desires, prejudices, and stereotypes. Let's begin by looking at how mass media develop, and then at how they work and are interpreted in our society.

The Evolution of a New Mass Medium

The development of most mass media is initiated not only by the diligence of inventors, such as Thomas Edison, but also by social, cultural, political, and economic circumstances. For instance, both telegraph and radio evolved as newly industrialized nations sought to expand their military and economic control and to transmit information more rapidly. The phonograph emerged because of the social and economic conditions of a growing middle class with more money and leisure time. Today, the Internet is a contemporary response to new concerns: transporting messages and sharing information more rapidly for an increasingly mobile and interconnected global population.

Typically, media innovations emerge in three stages. First is the *novelty,* or *development, stage,* in which inventors and technicians try to solve a particular problem, such as making pictures move, transmitting messages aboard ships, or sending mail electronically. Second is the *entrepreneurial stage,* in which inventors and investors determine a practical and marketable use for the new device. For example, early radio relayed messages to and from places where telegraph wires could not go, such as military ships at sea. Part of the Internet also had its roots in the ideas of military leaders, who wanted a communication system that was decentralized enough to survive nuclear war or natural disasters.

The third phase in a medium's development involves a breakthrough to the *mass medium stage.* At this point, businesses figure out how to market the new device as a consumer product. Although the government and the navy played a central role in radio's early years, it was commercial entrepreneurs who pioneered radio broadcasting and quickly reached millions of people. In the same way, Pentagon and government researchers developed the prototype for the Internet, but commercial interests extended the Internet's global reach and business potential.

The Linear Model of Mass Communication

Now that we know how the mass media evolve, let's look at two particularly influential models for how a mass medium actually communicates messages and meanings. In one of the older and more enduring explanations about the way media communicate, mass communication is conceptualized as a *linear process* of producing and delivering messages to large audiences. **Senders** (authors, producers, and organizations) transmit **messages** (programs, texts, images, sounds,

CIVIL RIGHTS
In the 1950s, television images of early civil rights struggles visually documented the inequalities faced by black citizens. In 1957, the governor of Arkansas refused to allow black students like Elizabeth Eckford to enter Little Rock's Central High School, even though racial segregation had been outlawed by the Supreme Court in 1954. In response, President Dwight Eisenhower sent in the army to integrate the school and control angry white mobs. Think about the ways in which TV images can make events "real" to us.

and ads) through a **mass media channel** (newspapers, books, magazines, radio, television, or the Internet) to large groups of **receivers** (readers, viewers, and consumers). In the process, **gatekeepers** (news editors, executive producers, and other media managers) function as message filters. Media gatekeepers make decisions about what messages actually get produced for particular audiences. The process also allows for **feedback**, in which citizens and consumers, if they choose, return messages to senders or gatekeepers through letters-to-the-editor, phone calls, e-mail, Web postings, or talk shows.

The problem with the linear model is that in reality media messages do not usually move smoothly from a sender at point A to a receiver at point Z. Words and images are more likely to spill into each other, crisscrossing in the flow of everyday life. Media messages and stories are encoded and sent in written and visual forms, but senders often have very little control over how their intended messages are decoded or whether the messages are ignored or misread by readers and viewers.

A Cultural Approach to Mass Communication

A second model for understanding media takes a *cultural approach* to mass communication. This concept recognizes that individuals bring diverse meanings to messages, given factors such as gender, age, educational level, ethnicity, and occupation. In this model of mass communication, audiences actively affirm, interpret, refashion, or reject the messages and stories that flow through various media channels. For example, when controversial filmmaker Michael Moore released the 2007 documentary *Sicko*, which calls for a universal nonprofit health-care system, regular filmgoers and health insurance company executives often had very different interpretations of the story that the movie told. Some executives saw the documentary's support for universal health

care as an indictment of capitalism and the "American way," while many ordinary people read the film as advocating a commonsense solution for providing health care to uninsured individuals and lowering soaring health-care costs.

People also reacted with a range of complex views when they learned through the media about Iranian President Mahmoud Ahmadinejad's invitation and subsequent visit to Columbia University in September 2007. Many thought inviting Ahmadinejad to speak at a major U.S. university helped legitimize an "evil" regime. Others felt the invitation reflected the university's commitment to encouraging free speech and to promoting dialogue about important issues. Still others objected to the invitation, but then also objected to a perceived incivility on the part of Columbia University's president, who called the Iranian leader "a petty and cruel dictator" in his introduction.

While the linear model may demonstrate how a message gets from a sender to a receiver, the cultural model suggests the complexity of this process and the lack of control "senders" (i.e., media executives, creative writers, news editors, ad agencies, etc.) often have over how audiences receive messages and the meanings the senders may have intended. Sometimes producers of media messages seem to be the active creators of communication while audiences are merely passive receptacles. But as the *Sicko* and Ahmadinejad examples illustrate, consumers also shape media messages to fit or support their own values and viewpoints. This phenomenon is known as **selective exposure**: People typically seek messages and produce meanings that correspond to their own cultural beliefs, values, and interests. For example, studies have shown that the people with political leanings toward the left or the right tend to seek out blog sites that reinforce preexisting views.

Stories: The Foundation of Mass Communication

Despite selective exposure, the stories of mass communication can shape a society's perception of events and attitudes. Throughout the twentieth century and during the recent wars in Afghanistan and Iraq, for instance, courageous journalists covered armed conflicts, telling stories that helped the public comprehend the magnitude and tragedy of such events. In the 1950s and 1960s, television news stories on the Civil Rights movement led to crucial legislation that transformed the way many white people viewed the grievances and aspirations of African Americans. In the late 1960s to early 1970s, the persistent media coverage of the Vietnam War ultimately led to a loss of public support for the war. In the late 1990s, stories about the President Clinton-Monica Lewinsky affair sparked heated debates over private codes of behavior and public abuses of authority.

More recently, in 2005, news media stories about the federal government's inadequate response to the devastation of the Gulf Coast by Hurricane Katrina prompted the resignation of Michael Brown as head of the Federal Emergency Management Agency. From 2005 into 2008, news reports about the Bush administration's secret domestic spying operation and the CIA's destruction of videotapes of prisoner interrogations sparked debates about terrorism, privacy rights, torture, and the ongoing war in Iraq. By the 2008 election, overall support for the war had eroded substantially in public opinion polls. In each of these instances, the stories mass media told played a key role in changing individual awareness, cultural attitudes, and even public policy.

To take a cultural approach to mass communication is to understand that our media institutions are basically in the **narrative**—or storytelling—business. Media stories put events in context for us, helping us to better understand both our daily lives and the larger world. As psychologist Jerome Bruner argues, we are storytelling creatures, and as children we acquire language to tell those stories that we have inside us. In his book *Making Stories*, he says, "Stories, finally, provide models of the world." *The common denominator, in fact, between our entertainment and information cultures is the narrative.* It is the media's main cultural currency—whether it's Oliver Stone's quasi-fictionalized *JFK*, a Dixie Chicks ballad, a Fox News "exclusive," a *New York Times* article, or a television commercial. The point is that the popular narratives of our culture are complex and varied. Roger Rosenblatt, writing in *Time* magazine during the polarizing 2000 presidential election, made this

"We tell ourselves stories in order to live."

JOAN DIDION, *THE WHITE ALBUM*

"Stories matter, and matter deeply, because they are the best way to save our lives."

FRANK MCCONNELL, *STORYTELLING AND MYTHMAKING*, 1979

observation about the importance of stories: "We are a narrative species. We exist by storytelling–by relating our situations–and the test of our evolution may lie in getting the story right."[7]

The Power of Media in Everyday Life

The earliest debates, at least in Western society, about the impact of cultural narratives on daily life date back to the ancient Greeks. Socrates, himself accused of corrupting young minds, worried that children exposed to popular art forms and stories "without distinction" would "take into their souls teachings that are wholly opposite to those we wish them to be possessed of when they are grown up."[8] He believed art should uplift us from the ordinary routines of our lives. The playwright Euripides, however, believed that art should imitate life, that characters should be real, and that artistic works should reflect the actual world–even when that reality is sordid.

In *The Republic*, Plato developed the classical view of art: It should aim to instruct and uplift. He worried that some staged performances glorified evil and that common folk watching might not be able to distinguish between art and reality. Aristotle, Plato's student, occupied a middle ground in these debates, arguing that art and stories should provide insight into the human condition but should entertain as well.

The cultural concerns of classical philosophers are still with us. At the turn of the twentieth century, for example, newly arrived immigrants to the United States who spoke little English gravitated toward cultural events (such as boxing, vaudeville, and the emerging medium of silent film) whose enjoyment did not depend solely on understanding English. Consequently, these popular events occasionally became a flash point for some groups, including the Daughters of the American Revolution, local politicians, religious leaders, and police vice squads, who not only resented the commercial success of immigrant culture but also feared that these "low" cultural forms would undermine what they saw as traditional American values and interests.

In the United States in the 1950s, the emergence of television and rock and roll generated several points of contention. For instance, the phenomenal popularity of Elvis Presley set the stage for many of today's debates over hip-hop lyrics and television's negative influence, especially on young people. In 1956 and 1957, Presley made three appearances on the *Ed Sullivan Show*. The public outcry against Presley's "lascivious" hip movements was so great that by the third show the camera operators were instructed to shoot the singer only from the waist up. In some communities, objections to Presley were motivated by class bias and racism. Many white adults believed that this "poor white trash" singer from Mississippi was spreading rhythm and blues, a "dangerous" form of black popular culture.

Today, with the reach of print, electronic, and digital communications and the amount of time people spend consuming them (see Table 1.1), mass media play an even more controversial role in society. Many of us have become increasingly critical of the quality of much contemporary culture and are concerned about the overwhelming amount of information now available.

TABLE 1.1

HOURS PER PERSON PER YEAR USING CONSUMER MEDIA

Source: Veronis Suhler Stevenson Communications Industry Forecast.

Total hours includes time spent with recorded music, consumer magazines, consumer books, home video/DVD, box office, interactive TV, and wireless content, and time spent media multitasking—using media simultaneously.

Estimates.

Year	Total TV	Broadcast & Satellite Radio	Newspaper	Consumer Internet	Video Games	Total*
1999	1,427	939	205	65	58	3,280
2002	1,519	991	194	147	70	3,430
2004	1,546	986	188	176	77	3,480
2006	1,555	975	179	190	82	3,499
2009	1,562	984	165	203	96	3,555**
Five-Year Change						
1999-2004	+119	+47	-17	+111	+19	+200
2004-2009	+16	-2	-23	+27	+19	+75

EXAMINING ETHICS

Covering the War

Back in 2006—with the war in Iraq about to begin its fourth year—then-President George W. Bush criticized the national news media for not showing enough "good news" about U.S. efforts to bring democracy to Iraq. Bush's remarks raised ethical questions about the complex relationship between the government and the news media during times of war: How much freedom should the news media have to cover the war? What topics should they report on? How much control should the military have over the media's reports on the war? Are there topics that should not be covered?

These kinds of questions have also created ethical quagmires for local TV stations that cover war and its effects on communities where soldiers have been called to duty and then injured or killed. Some station managers—out of fear of alienating viewers—encourage their news division not to seem too critical of war efforts, wanting the station to appear "patriotic." In one extreme 2004 case, the nation's largest TV station owner—Sinclair Broadcast Group— would not air the ABC News program *Nightline* because it devoted an episode to reading the names of all U.S. soldiers killed in the Iraq war up to that time. Here is an excerpt from a *New York Times* account of that event:

> *Sinclair Broadcast Group, one of the largest owners of local television stations, will preempt tonight's edition of the ABC News program "Nightline," saying the program's plan to have Ted Koppel [who then anchored the program] read aloud the names of every member of the armed forces killed in action in Iraq was motivated by an antiwar agenda and threatened to undermine American efforts there.*
>
> *The decision means viewers in eight cities, including St. Louis and Columbus, Ohio, will not see "Nightline." ABC News disputed that the program carried a political message, calling it in a statement "an expression of respect which simply seeks to honor those who have laid down their lives for their country."*
>
> *But Mark Hyman, the vice president of corporate relations for Sinclair, who is also a conservative commentator on the company's newscasts, said tonight's edition of "Nightline" is biased journalism. "Mr. Koppel's reading of the fallen will have*

How much freedom should the news media have to cover the war?

no proportionality," he said in a telephone interview, pointing out that the program will ignore other aspects of the war effort.

The company's reaction to "Nightline" is consistent with criticism from some conservatives, who are charging ABC with trying to influence opinion against the war.

Mr. Koppel and the producers of "Nightline" said earlier this week that they had no political motivation behind the decision to devote an entire show, expanded to 40 minutes, to reading the names and displaying the photos of those killed. They said they only intended to honor the dead and document what Mr. Koppel called "the human cost" of the war.[1]

Given such a case, how might a local TV news director today—under pressure from the station's manager or owner—formulate guidelines to help negotiate such treacherous ethical territory? While most TV news divisions have ethical codes to guide journalists' behavior in certain situations, could ordinary citizens help shape ethical discussions and decisions? Following is a general plan for dealing with an array of ethical dilemmas that face media practitioners and for finding ways in which nonjournalists might insert themselves into this decision-making process.

Arriving at ethical decisions is a particular kind of criticism involving several steps. These include (1) laying out the case; (2) pinpointing the key issues; (3) identifying the parties involved, their intent, and their competing values; (4) studying ethical models and theories; (5) presenting strategies and options; and (6) formulating a decision or policy.[2] As a test case, let's look at how local TV news directors might establish ethical guidelines for war-related events. Following the six steps above, our goal is to make some ethical decisions and to lay the groundwork for policies that address TV images or photographs used for war coverage (for example, protesters, supporters, or memorial/funeral images). (See Chapter 14, page 435, for details on confronting ethical problems.)

Examining Ethics Activity

As a class or in smaller groups, design policies that address at least one of the issues raised above. Start by researching the topic; find as much information as possible. For example, you can research guidelines that local stations already use by contacting local news directors and TV journalists.

Do they have guidelines? If so, are they adequate? Are there images they will not show? How are protesters and supporters of war treated? Finally, if time allows, send the policies to various TV news directors and/or station managers; ask for their evaluations and whether they would consider implementing the policies. ◢

Many see popular media culture as unacceptably commercial and sensationalistic. Too many talk shows exploit personal problems for commercial gain, reality shows often glamorize outlandish behavior and sometimes dangerous stunts, and television research has once again documented a connection between aggression in children and violent entertainment programs. Children, who watch nearly forty thousand TV commercials each year, are particularly vulnerable to marketers selling junk food, toys, and "cool" clothing. Even the computer, once heralded as an educational salvation, has created confusion. Today, when kids announce that they are "on the computer," parents wonder whether they are writing a term paper, playing a video game, chatting with "friends" on Facebook, or peeking at pornography.

Yet how much the media shape society—and how much they simply respond to existing cultural issues—is still unknown. Although media depictions may worsen social problems, research has seldom demonstrated that the media directly cause our society's major afflictions. For instance, when a middle-school student shoots a fellow student over a designer jacket, should society blame the ad that glamorized the clothing and the network that carried the ad? Or are parents, teachers, and religious leaders failing to instill strong moral values? Or are economic and social issues involving gun legislation, consumerism, and income disparity at work as well? Even if the clothing manufacturer bears responsibility as a corporate citizen, did the ad alone bring about the tragedy, or is the ad symptomatic of a larger problem?

With American mass media industries earning more than $200 billion annually, the economic and societal stakes are high. Large portions of media resources now go toward studying audiences, capturing their attention through stories, and taking their consumer dollars. To increase their revenues, media outlets try to influence everything from how people shop to how they vote. Like the air we breathe, the commercially based culture that mass media help create surrounds us. Its impact, like the air, is often taken for granted. But to monitor that culture's "air quality"—to become media literate—we must attend more thoughtfully to diverse media stories that are too often taken for granted. (For further discussion, see "Examining Ethics: Covering the War" on pages 14-15.)

Surveying the Cultural Landscape

Some cultural phenomena gain wide popular appeal, and others do not. Some appeal to certain age groups or social classes. Some, such as rock and roll, jazz, and classical music, are popular worldwide; other cultural forms, such as Tejano, salsa, and Cajun music, are popular primarily in certain regions or communities. Certain aspects of culture are considered elite in one place (opera in the United States) and popular in another (opera in Italy). Though categories may change over time and from one society to another, two metaphors offer contrasting views about the way culture operates in our daily lives: culture as a hierarchy, represented by a skyscraper metaphor, and culture as a process, represented by a map metaphor.

Culture as a Skyscraper

Throughout twentieth-century America, critics and audiences took for granted a hierarchy of culture placing supposedly superior products at the top and inferior ones at the bottom. This can be imagined, in some respects, as a modern skyscraper. In this metaphor, the top floors of the building house **high culture**, such as ballet, the symphony, art museums, and classic literature. The bottom floors—and even the basement—house popular or **low culture**, including such icons as soap operas, rock music, radio shock jocks, and video games (see Figure 1.1). High

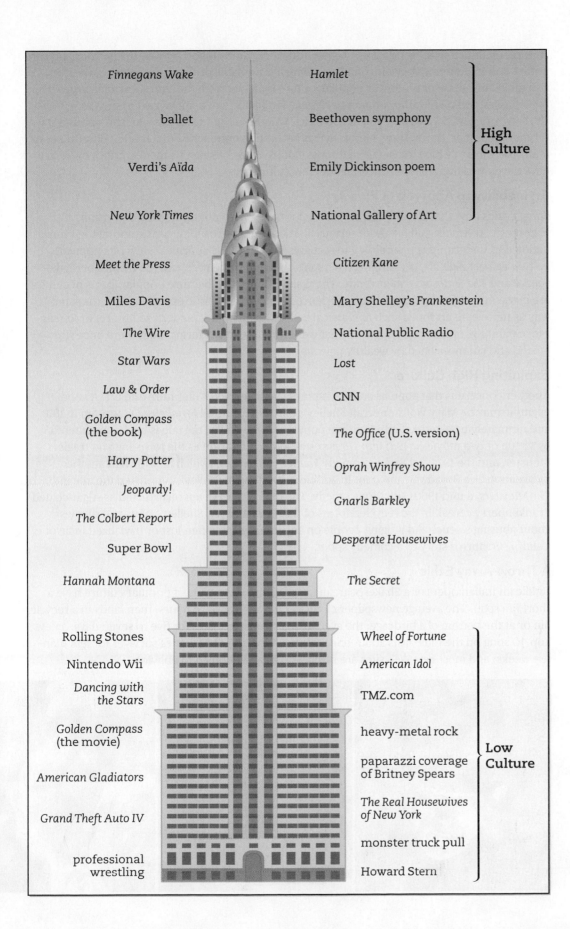

Finnegans Wake

Hamlet

ballet

Beethoven symphony

Verdi's Aïda

Emily Dickinson poem

New York Times

National Gallery of Art

High Culture

Meet the Press

Citizen Kane

Miles Davis

Mary Shelley's Frankenstein

The Wire

National Public Radio

Star Wars

Lost

Law & Order

CNN

Golden Compass (the book)

The Office (U.S. version)

Harry Potter

Oprah Winfrey Show

Jeopardy!

Gnarls Barkley

The Colbert Report

Super Bowl

Desperate Housewives

Hannah Montana

The Secret

Rolling Stones

Wheel of Fortune

Nintendo Wii

American Idol

Dancing with the Stars

TMZ.com

Golden Compass (the movie)

heavy-metal rock

American Gladiators

paparazzi coverage of Britney Spears

Grand Theft Auto IV

The Real Housewives of New York

Low Culture

monster truck pull

professional wrestling

Howard Stern

◀

FIGURE 1.1

CULTURE AS A SKYSCRAPER

Culture is diverse and difficult to categorize. Yet throughout the twentieth century, we tended to think of culture not as a social process but as a set of products sorted into high, low, or middle positions on a cultural skyscraper. Look at this highly arbitrary arrangement and see if you agree or disagree. Write in some of your own examples.

Why do we categorize or classify culture in this way? Who controls this process? Is control of making cultural categories important— why or why not?

culture, identified with "good taste," higher education, and support by wealthy patrons and corporate donors, is associated with "fine art," which is available primarily in libraries, theaters, and museums. In contrast, low or popular culture is aligned with the "questionable" tastes of the "masses," who enjoy the commercial "junk" circulated by the mass media, such as reality TV, celebrity gossip Web sites, and action films. Whether or not we agree with this cultural skyscraper metaphor, the high-low hierarchy has become so entrenched that it often determines or limits the ways in which we view and discuss culture today.[9] Using this model, critics over time have developed five areas of concern about low culture.

An Inability to Appreciate Fine Art

Some critics note that popular culture, in the form of contemporary movies, television, and rock music, distracts students from serious literature and philosophy, thus stunting their imagination and undermining their ability to recognize great art.[10] This critical view pits popular culture against high art, discounting a person's ability to value Bach and the Beatles or Shakespeare and *The Simpsons* concurrently. The assumption is that because popular forms of culture are made for profit, they cannot be experienced as valuable artistic experiences in the same way as more elite art forms such as classical ballet, Italian opera, modern sculpture, or Renaissance painting (even though many of what we regard as elite art forms today were once supported and commissioned by wealthy patrons).

Exploiting High Culture

Another concern is that popular culture exploits classic works of literature and art. A good example may be Mary Wollstonecraft Shelley's dark Gothic novel *Frankenstein*, written in 1818 and ultimately transformed into multiple popular forms. Today, the tale is best remembered by virtue of two movies: a 1931 film version starring Boris Karloff as the towering and tragic monster, and the 1974 Mel Brooks comedy *Young Frankenstein* (which in 2007 had another incarnation as a Broadway musical). In addition to the movies, television turned the tale into *The Munsters*, a mid-1960s situation comedy. The monster was even resurrected as sugar-coated Frankenberry cereal. In the recycled forms of the original story, Shelley's powerful themes about abusing science and judging people on appearances are often lost or trivialized in favor of a simplistic horror story or a comedy spoof.

A Throw-Away Ethic

Unlike an Italian opera or a Shakespearean tragedy, many elements of popular culture have a short life span. The average newspaper circulates for about twelve hours, then lands in a recycle bin or at the bottom of a birdcage; the average magazine circulates for five to seven days; a new Top 40 song on the radio lasts about one month; a typical new TV series survives for less than ten weeks; and most new Web sites are rarely visited and doomed to oblivion.

EXPLOITING HIGH CULTURE

Mary Shelley, the author of *Frankenstein*, might not recognize our popular culture's mutations of her Gothic classic. First published in 1818, the novel has inspired numerous interpretations, everything from the scary—Boris Karloff in the classic 1931 movie—to the silly—the Munster family in the 1960s TV sitcom and the lovable creature in the 1974 movie *Young Frankenstein*. Can you think of another example of a story that has developed and changed over time and through various media transformations?

Although endurance does not necessarily denote quality, in the view of many critics, so-called better or "higher" forms of culture have more staying power. In this argument, lower or popular forms of culture are unstable and fleeting; they follow rather than lead public taste. Known in the television industry in the 1960s and 1970s as the "least objectionable programming," this tactic meant that network executives pandered to mediocrity by airing bland, disposable programming that a "normal" viewer would not find objectionable or disturbing.

A Diminished Audience for High Culture

Some observers also warn that popular culture has inundated the cultural environment, driving out higher forms of culture and cheapening public life.[11] This concern is supported by data showing that TV sets are in use in the average American home for more than seven hours a day, exposing adults and children each year to thousands of hours of trivial TV commercials, violent crime dramas, and superficial "reality" programs. According to one story critics tell, the prevalence of so many popular media products prevents the public from experiencing genuine art. Forty or more radio stations are available in large cities; cable systems with hundreds of channels are in place in 60 percent of all U.S. households; and Internet services and DVD players are in more than 90 percent of U.S. homes. In this scenario, the chances of audiences finding more refined forms of culture supposedly become very small, although critics fail to note the choices that are also available on such a variety of radio stations, cable channels, and Internet sites. (For an alternate view, see "Case Study: The Sleeper Curve" on pages 20-21.)

Inhibiting Political Discourse and Social Change

Another cautionary story, frequently recounted by academics, politicians, and TV pundits, tells how popular culture, especially its more visual forms (such as TV advertising and daytime talk shows), undermines democratic ideals and reasoned argument. According to this view, popular media may inhibit not only rational thought but also social progress by transforming audiences into cultural dupes lured by the promise of products. A few multinational conglomerates that make large profits from media products may be distracting citizens from examining economic disparity and implementing change. Seductive advertising images, for example, showcasing the buffed and airbrushed bodies of professional models frequently contradict the actual lives of

FAMILY GUY
Building on the longevity and success of Fox's *The Simpsons*, the animated comedy *Family Guy* was canceled twice by Fox in 2000 and 2002. But Fox revived the show in 2005 because of strong DVD sales and a loyal audience that tuned in to early syndicated episodes of the series on cable's Cartoon Network. Like *The Simpsons*, this irreverent program satirizes other forms of culture, including its own network.

The Sleeper Curve

In the 1973 science fiction comedy movie *Sleeper*, the film's director, Woody Allen, plays a character who reawakens two hundred years after being cryogenically frozen (after a routine ulcer operation had gone bad). The scientists who "unfreeze" Allen discuss how back in the 1970s people actually believed that "deep fat," "steaks," "cream pies," and "hot fudge" were unhealthy. But apparently in 2173, those food items will be good for us.

In his 2005 book, *Everything Bad Is Good for You*, Steven Johnson makes a controversial argument about TV and culture based on the movie. He calls his idea the "Sleeper Curve" and claims that "today's popular culture is actually making us smarter."[1] Johnson's ideas run counter to those of many critics who worry about popular culture and its potentially disastrous effects, particularly on young people. An influential argument in this strain of thinking appeared twenty years ago in Neil Postman's 1985 book, *Amusing Ourselves to Death*. Postman argued that we were moving from the "Age of Typology" to the "Age of Television," from the "Age of Exposition" to the "Age of Show Business."[2] Postman worried that an image-centered culture had overtaken words and a print-oriented culture, resulting in "all public discourse increasingly tak[ing] the form of entertainment." He pointed to the impact of advertising and how "American businessmen discovered, long before the rest of us, that the quality and usefulness of their goods are subordinate to the artifice of their display."[3] For Postman, image making has become central to choosing our government leaders, including the way politicians are branded and packaged as commodity goods in political ads. Postman argued that the TV ad has become the "chief instrument" for presenting political ideas, with these results: "that short simple messages are preferable to long and complex ones; that drama is to be preferred over exposition; that being sold solutions is better than being confronted with questions about problems."[4]

Now that we are somewhere between the Age of Television and the Age of the Internet, Johnson's argument offers an opportunity to assess where our visual culture has taken us. According to Johnson, "For decades, we've worked under the assumption that mass culture follows a path declining steadily toward lowest-common-denominator standards, presumably because the 'masses' want dumb, simple pleasures and big media companies try to give the masses what they want. But, the exact opposite is happening: the culture is getting more cognitively demanding, not less."[5] While Johnson shares many of Postman's 1985 concerns, he disagrees with the point from *Amusing Ourselves to Death* that image-saturated media is only about "simple" messages and "trivial" culture. Instead, Johnson discusses the complexity of video and computer games and many of TV's dramatic prime-time series, especially when compared with less demanding TV programming from the 1970s and early 1980s.

As evidence, Johnson compares the plot complications of Fox's CIA/secret agent thriller *24* with *Dallas*, the prime-time soap opera that was America's most popular TV show in the early 1980s. "To make sense of an episode of *24*," Johnson maintains, "you have to integrate far more information than you would have a few decades ago watching a comparable show. Beneath the violence and the ethnic stereotypes, another trend appears: to keep up with entertainment like *24*, you have to pay attention, make inferences, track shifting social relationships." Johnson argues that today's audience would be "bored" watching a show like *Dallas*, in part "because the show contains far less information in each scene, despite

Lost (2004–)

Dallas (1978–1991)

the fact that its soap-opera structure made it one of the most complicated narratives on television in its prime. With *Dallas*, the modern viewer doesn't have to think to make sense of what's going on, and not having to think is boring."

In addition to *24*, a number of contemporary programs offer complex narratives, including *Desperate Housewives, Lost, House, Grey's Anatomy*, and *CSI*, which air on the traditional broadcast networks; and *The Sopranos, Big Love*, and *Curb Your Enthusiasm* on cable's HBO. Another example, *Dexter*—about an L.A. police department blood spatter expert who moonlights as a serial killer (of bad guys)—premiered on cable's Showtime in 2005 and was edited for broadcast on CBS beginning in 2008. Johnson says that in contrast to older popular programs like *Dallas* or *Dynasty*, contemporary TV storytelling layers "each scene with a thick network of affiliations. You have to focus to follow the plot, and in focusing you're exercising the parts of your brain that map social networks, that fill in missing information, that connect multiple narrative threads." Johnson argues that younger audiences today—brought up in the Age of the Internet and in an era of complicated interactive visual games—bring high expectations to other kinds of popular culture as well, including television. "The mind," Johnson writes, "likes to be challenged; there's real pleasure to be found in solving puzzles, detecting patterns or unpacking a complex narrative system."

In countering the cultural fears expressed by critics like Postman and by many parents trying to make sense of the intricate media world that their children encounter each day, Johnson sees a hopeful sign: "I believe that the Sleeper Curve is the single most important new force altering the mental development of young people today, and I believe it is largely a force for good: enhancing our cognitive faculties, not dumbing them down. And yet you almost never hear this story in popular accounts of today's media."

Steven Johnson's theory is one of many about media impact on the way we live and learn. Do you accept Johnson's Sleeper Curve argument that certain TV programs—along with challenging interactive video and computer games—are intellectually demanding and are actually making us smarter? Why or why not? Are you more persuaded by Postman's 1985 account—that the word has been displaced by an image-centered culture and, consequently, that popular culture has been dumbed down by its oversimplified and visual triviality? As you consider Postman, think about the Internet: Is it word based or image based? What kinds of opportunities for learning does it offer?

In thinking about both the 1985 and 2005 arguments by Postman and Johnson, consider as well generational differences. Do you enjoy TV shows and video games that your parents or grandparents don't understand? What types of stories and games do they enjoy? What did earlier generations value in storytelling, and what is similar and dissimilar about storytelling today? Interview someone who is close to you but from an earlier generation about media and story preferences. Then discuss or write about both the common ground and the cultural differences that you discovered.

"The Web has created a forum for annotation and commentary that allows more complicated shows to prosper, thanks to the fan sites where each episode of shows like *Lost* or *Alias* is dissected with an intensity usually reserved for Talmud scholars."

– Steven Johnson, 2005

> "TV is a genre of reruns, a formulaic return to what we already know. Everything is familiar. Ads and old programs are constantly recycled. It's like mythology, like the Homeric epics, the oral tradition, in which the listener hears passages, formulae, and epithets repeated over and over again. There is a joy in repetition, as children know when they say, 'Mommy, tell me that story again.'"
>
> CAMILLE PAGLIA,
> SOCIAL CRITIC,
> *HARPER'S*, 1991

people who cannot hope to achieve a particular "look" or may not have the money to obtain high-end cosmetic products offered on the market. In this environment, art and commerce have become blurred, restricting the audience's ability to make cultural and economic distinctions. Sometimes called the "Big Mac" theory, this view suggests that people are so addicted to mass-produced media menus that they lose their discriminating taste for finer fare, and, much worse, their ability to see and challenge social inequities.

Culture as a Map

The second way to view culture is as a map. Here, culture is an ongoing process—rather than a vertically organized hierarchy—and allows us to better account for our diverse and individual tastes. Maps represent large, unwieldy spaces that extend in all directions. Maps highlight main highways and familiar urban centers, but they also include side roads and small towns, directing our focus to unexplored areas. This metaphor depicts culture in a more complex way—spreading out in more directions—than the skyscraper model does. An individual guided by the cultural map can pursue many connections from one cultural point to another and can appreciate a range of cultural experiences without necessarily ranking them.

Cultural phenomena—such as the stories we read in books or watch at the movies—offer plenty of places to go that are conventional, recognizable, stable, and comforting. Yet at the same time, our culture's narrative storehouse contains other stories that tend toward the innovative, unfamiliar, unstable, and challenging. Most forms of culture, however, demonstrate both tendencies. For example, we may buy the CD of a favorite artist or watch our favorite TV programs for both their innovation *and* their familiarity. We may listen to an old song or see a new film to complement a mood, to distance ourselves from problems, or to reflect critically on the song's lyrics or the movie's meanings.

The Comfort of Familiar Stories

The appeal of culture is often its familiar stories, pulling audiences toward the security of repetition and common landmarks on the cultural map. Consider, for instance, early television's *Lassie* series, about the adventures of a collie named Lassie and her owner, young Timmy. Of the more than five hundred episodes, many have a familiar and repetitive plot line: Timmy, who arguably possessed the poorest sense of direction and suffered more concussions than any TV character in history, gets lost or knocked unconscious. After finding Timmy and licking his face, Lassie goes for help and saves the day. Adult critics might mock this melodramatic formula, but many children find comfort in the predictability of the story. This quality is also illustrated when night after night children ask their parents to read the same book, such as Margaret Wise Brown's *Good Night, Moon* or Maurice Sendak's *Where the Wild Things Are*, or watch the same DVD, such as *Snow White* or *The Princess Bride*.

Innovation as Direction for Personal Growth

Like children, adults also seek comfort, often returning to an old Beatles or Motown song, a William Butler Yeats or Emily Dickinson poem, or a TV rerun of *Seinfeld* or *Andy Griffith*. But we also like cultural adventure. We may stray from a familiar film on cable's American Movie Classics to discover a new movie from Iran or India on the Independent Film Channel. We seek new stories and new places to go—those aspects of culture that demonstrate originality and complexity. For instance, James Joyce's *Finnegans Wake* (1939) created language anew and challenged readers, as the novel's poetic first sentence illustrates: "riverrun, past Eve and Adam's, from swerve of shore to bend of bay, brings us by a commodius vicus of recirculation back to Howth Castle and Environs." A revolutionary work, crammed with historical names and topical references to events, myths, songs, jokes, and daily conversation, Joyce's novel remains a challenge to understand and decode. His work demonstrated that part of what culture provides is that impulse to explore new places, to strike out in new directions, searching for something different that may contribute to our own growth.

A Range of Maps and Messages

We know that people have complex cultural tastes, needs, and interests based on different backgrounds and dispositions. It is not surprising, then, that our cultural treasures—from blues music and opera to comic books and classical literature—contain a variety of messages. Just as Shakespeare's plays—popular entertainments in his day—were packed with both obscure and popular references, TV episodes of *The Simpsons* have included allusions to the Beatles, Kafka, *The Adventures of Ozzie & Harriet,* Tennessee Williams, talk shows, Aerosmith, *The X-Files,* Freud, and *Citizen Kane.* In other words, as part of an ongoing process, cultural products and their meanings are "all over the map," spreading out in diverse directions.

Challenging the Nostalgia for a Better Past

Some critics of popular culture assert—often without presenting supportive evidence—that society was better off before the latest developments in mass media and resist the idea of re-imagining an established cultural hierarchy as a map. The nostalgia for some imagined "better past" has often operated as a device for condemning new cultural phenomena. In the nineteenth century, in fact, a number of intellectuals and politicians worried that rising literacy rates among the working class might create havoc: How would the aristocracy and intellectuals maintain their authority and status if everyone could read?

Throughout history, a call to return to familiar terrain, to "the good old days," has been a frequent response to new, "threatening" forms of popular culture. Yet over the years many of these forms, including the waltz, silent movies, ragtime, and jazz, have themselves become cultural "classics." How can we tell now what the future holds in store for such cultural expressions as comic books, rock and roll, soap operas, fashion photography, heavy metal, hip-hop, tabloid newspapers, "reality" television programs, and Internet blogs?

Cultural Values of the Modern Period

To understand how the mass media have come to occupy their current cultural position, we need to trace significant changes in cultural values from the modern period until today. In general, scholars think of the **modern** period in the United States as having its roots in the Industrial Revolution of the nineteenth century and extending until about the mid-twentieth century. Although there are certainly many ways to conceptualize what it means to be "modern," we will focus on four major features or values that resonate best with changes across media and culture: efficiency, individualism, rationalism, and progress.

Working Efficiently

In the business world, modernization involved captains of industry using new technology to create efficient manufacturing centers, produce inexpensive products to make everyday life better, and make commerce more profitable. Printing presses and assembly lines made major contributions in this transformation, and then modern advertising spread the word about new gadgets to American consumers. In terms of culture, the modern mantra has been "form follows function." For example, modern skyscrapers made of glass, steel, and concrete replaced the supposedly wasteful decorative and ornate styles of premodern Gothic cathedrals. This new value was replicated or echoed in journalism, where a front-page style rejected decorative and ornate adjectives and adverbs for "just the facts," requiring reporters to ask and answer the questions: who, what, when, where, and why. To be lean and efficient, modern news de-emphasized description, commentary, and historical context.

Cultural responses to and critiques of modern efficiency often manifested themselves in the mass media. For example, Aldous Huxley, in *Brave New World* (1932), created a fictional world in which he cautioned readers that the efficiencies of modern science and technology posed a threat to individual dignity. Charlie Chaplin's film *Modern Times* (1936), set in a futuristic manufacturing plant, also told the story of the dehumanizing impact of modernization and machinery. Writers and artists, in their criticisms of the modern world, have often pointed to technology's ability to

alienate people from one another, capitalism's tendency to foster greed, and government's inclination to create bureaucracies whose inefficiency oppressed rather than helped people.

Celebrating the Individual

The values of the *premodern period* (before the Industrial Revolution) were guided by strong belief in a natural or divine order, placing God or Nature at the center of the universe. But becoming modern meant elevating individual self-expression to a more central position. Scientific discoveries of the period allowed modern print media to offer a place for ordinary readers to engage with new ideas beyond what their religious leaders and local politicians communicated to them. Along with democratic breakthroughs, however, modern individualism and the Industrial Revolution triggered new forms of hierarchy in which certain individuals and groups achieved higher standing in the social order. For example, those who managed commercial enterprises gained more control over the economic ladder, while an intellectual class of modern experts—masters of specialized realms of knowledge on everything from commerce to psychology to literature—gained increasing power over the nation's economic, political, and cultural agendas.

Believing in a Rational Order

To be modern also meant to value the capacity of logical, scientific minds to solve problems by working in organized groups, both in business and in academic disciplines. Progressive thinkers maintained that the printing press, the telegraph, and the railroad, in combination with a scientific attitude, would foster a new type of informed society. At the core of this society, the printed mass media, particularly newspapers, would educate the citizenry, helping to build and maintain an organized social framework.[12]

A leading champion for an informed rational society was Walter Lippmann, who wrote the influential book *Public Opinion* in 1922. Later a major newspaper columnist, Lippmann believed that the world was "altogether too big, too complex, and too fleeting for direct acquaintance." He distrusted both the media and the public's ability to navigate such a world and to reach the rational decisions needed in a democracy. Instead, he called for "an independent, expert organization" for making experience "intelligible to those who have to make decisions." Driven by a strong belief in science and rationality, Lippmann advocated a "machinery of knowledge" that might be established through "intelligence bureaus" and staffed by experts. While such a concept might look like the modern "think tank," Lippmann saw these as independent of politics, unlike think tanks today, such as the Brookings Institute or Heritage Foundation, which have strong partisan ties.[13]

Rejecting Tradition/Embracing Progress

Although the independent bureaus never materialized, Walter Lippmann's ideas were influential throughout the twentieth century and were a product of the **Progressive Era**—a period of political and social reform that lasted roughly from the 1890s to the 1920s. Presidents Teddy Roosevelt and Woodrow Wilson were prominent national figures associated with this era. On both local and national levels, Progressive Era reformers championed social movements that led to constitutional amendments for both women's suffrage and Prohibition, political reforms that led to the secret ballot during elections, and economic reforms that ushered in the federal income tax to try to foster a more equitable society. In journalism, the muckraking period (see Chapter 9) represented media's significant contribution to this era. Working mostly for reform-oriented magazines, *muckrakers* were journalists who exposed corruption, waste, and scandal in business and politics. Like other Progressives, muckraking journalists shared a belief in the transforming power of science and technology. And they (along with Lippmann) sought out experts to identify problems and develop solutions.

Influenced by the Progressive movement, the notion of being modern in the twentieth century meant throwing off the chains of the past, breaking with tradition, and embracing progress. Many Progressives were skeptical of religious dogma and sought answers in science. For example, in architecture the differences between a premodern Gothic cathedral and a modern skyscraper are startling, not only because of their different "looks," but also because of the cultural values these building types represent: the former symbolizing the past and tradition, the latter standing for efficiency and progress. Similarly, twentieth-century journalists, in their quest for modern efficiency, became captive to the reporting of timely and immediate events. Newly standardized forms of front-page journalism that championed "just the facts" and current events that "just happened yesterday" did help reporters efficiently meet tight deadlines. But, realizing one of Walter Lippmann's fears, modern newspapers often failed to take a historical perspective or to analyze sufficiently the ideas and interests underlying these events.

Shifting Values in Postmodern Culture

For many people, the changes occurring in the contemporary, or **postmodern**, period—from roughly the mid-twentieth century to today—are identified by a confusing array of examples: music videos, remote controls, Nike ads, shopping malls, fax machines, e-mail, video games, blogs, *USA Today*, YouTube, *TRL*, hip-hop, and reality TV. Some critics argue that postmodern culture represents a way of seeing—a new condition, or even a malady, of the human spirit. Chiefly a response to the modern world, controversial postmodern values are playing increasingly pivotal roles in our daily lives. Although there are many ways to define the postmodern, this textbook focuses on four major features or values that resonate best with changes across media and culture: populism, diversity, nostalgia, and paradox (see Table 1.2).

Celebrating Populism

During the 2008 presidential race, Democratic and Republican candidates as well as political pundits associated certain campaigns with populism. As a political idea, **populism** tries to appeal to ordinary people by highlighting or setting up a conflict between "the people" and "the elite." For example, populist politicians often tell stories and run ads that criticize big corporations and political favoritism. Meant to resonate with working- and middle-class values and regional ties, such narratives generally pit Southern or Midwestern small-town "family values" against the supposedly coarser urban lifestyles associated with big cities and the privilege of East or West Coast "high society."

In postmodern culture, populism manifests itself in many ways. For example, artists and performers, like Chuck Berry in his 1950s rock and roll anthem "Roll Over Beethoven," blur the border between high and low culture. In the visual arts, following Andy Warhol's popular 1960s style, advertisers borrow from both fine art and street art, while artists borrow from commerce

TABLE 1.2
TRENDS ACROSS HISTORICAL PERIODS
▼

	Premodern (pre-1800s)	Modern Industrial Revolution (1800s–1950s)	Postmodern (1950s–present)
Work hierarchies	peasants/merchants/rulers	factory workers/managers/national CEOs	temp workers/global CEOs
Major work sites	field/farm	factory/office	office/home/"virtual" or mobile office
Communication reach	local	national	global
Communication transmission	oral/manuscript	print/electronic	electronic/digital
Communication channels	storytellers/elders/town criers	books/newspapers/magazines/radio	television/cable/Internet/multimedia
Communication at home	quill pen	typewriter/office computer	personal computer/laptop/cell phone
Key social values	belief in natural or divine order	individualism/rationalism efficiency/anti-tradition	anti-hierarchy/skepticism (about science)/diversity/multiculturalism/irony & paradox
Journalism	oral & print-based/partisan/decorative/controlled by political parties	print-based/objective/efficient/timely/controlled by publishing families	TV-Internet based/opinionated/conversational/controlled by entertainment conglomerates

FILMS OFTEN REFLECT THE KEY SOCIAL VALUES of an era—as represented by the modern and postmodern movies pictured. Charlie Chaplin's *Modern Times* (1936, above) satirized modern industry and the dehumanizing impact of a futuristic factory on its overwhelmed workers. Similarly, Ridley Scott's *Blade Runner* (1982, above, right), set in futuristic Los Angeles in 2019, questions the impact on humanity when technology overwhelms the natural world. As author William Romanowski said of *Blade Runner* in *Pop Culture Wars*, "It managed to quite vividly capture some postmodern themes that were not recognized at the time. . . . We are constantly trying to balance the promise of technology with the threats of technology."

and popular art. In magazines, arresting clothing or cigarette ads combine stark social commentary with low-key sales pitches. At the movies, populist themes in films like *Fargo* (1996), *Little Miss Sunshine* (2006), and *Juno* (2008) fuse the comic and the serious, the ordinary and the odd. Even film stars, like Angelina Jolie and Richard Gere, often champion oppressed groups while releasing movies that make the actors wealthy global icons of consumer culture.

Other forms of postmodern style blur modern distinctions not only between art and commerce, but also between fact and fiction. For example, television vocabulary now includes *infotainment* (*Entertainment Tonight, Access Hollywood*) and *infomercials* (fading celebrities selling anti-wrinkle cream). On cable, MTV's reality programs–such as *Real World* and *The Hills*–blur boundaries between the staged and the real, mixing serious themes with comedic interludes and romantic spats; Comedy Central's fake news programs, *The Daily Show with Jon Stewart* and *The Colbert Report*, combine real, insightful news stories with biting satire of traditional broadcast and cable news programs.

Diversifying and Recycling Culture

Closely associated with populism, another value (or vice) of the postmodern period emphasizes diversity and fragmentation, including the wild juxtaposition of old and new cultural styles. In a suburban shopping mall, for instance, Waldenbooks and Gap stores border a Vietnamese, Italian, and Mexican food court, while techno-digitized instrumental versions of 1960s protest music play in the background to accompany shoppers.

Part of this stylistic diversity involves borrowing and transforming earlier ideas from the modern period. In music, hip-hop deejays and performers sample old R&B, soul, and rock classics to reinvent songs. Borrowing in hip-hop is often so pronounced that the original artists and record companies have frequently filed for copyright infringement.

Critics of postmodern style contend that such borrowing devalues originality, emphasizing surface over depth and recycled ideas over new ones. Throughout the twentieth century, for example, films were adapted from books and short stories. Now, films often derive from popular TV series: *The Brady Bunch, Mission Impossible, Charlie's Angels,* and *Transformers,* to name just a few. In 2007, *The Simpsons Movie* premiered–"18 years in the making," its promotional ads read, a reference to the long TV series run on Fox. Meanwhile, the public radio program *This American Life*, hosted by Ira Glass, became a television program on Showtime, starting in 2006.

Questioning Science and Revering Nostalgia

Another tendency of postmodern culture is to raise doubts about scientific reasoning. Rather than seeing science purely as enlightened thinking, some postmodern artists and analysts criticize it for laying the groundwork for bureaucratic problems. They reject rational thought as *"the* answer" to every social problem, revealing instead nostalgia for premodern values of small communities, traditional religion, and mystical experience. For example, since the late 1980s, a whole host of popular TV programs—such as *Twin Peaks, Northern Exposure, The X-Files, Buffy the Vampire Slayer, Charmed, Angel, Lost, Medium*—emerged to offer the mystical and supernatural as responses to the "evils" of our daily world and the limits of the purely rational. Both major political parties also spent time and energy establishing religious credentials for candidates in the 2008 election.

In other areas of contemporary culture, Internet users are reclaiming lost conversational skills and letter-writing habits in instant messaging and e-mail. Even the current popularity of radio and TV talk shows, according to a postmodern perspective, partly represents an attempt to recover lost aspects of oral traditions. Given the feelings of powerlessness and alienation that mark the contemporary age, one attraction of the talk-show format—with its populist themes—has been the way it encourages ordinary people to participate in discussions with celebrities, experts, and one another.

Acknowledging Paradox

A key aspect of our postmodern time is the willingness to accept paradox. While modern culture emphasized breaking with the past in the name of progress, postmodern culture stresses integrating retro styles with current beliefs: At the same time we seem nostalgic for the past, we embrace new technologies with a vengeance. Although some forms of contemporary culture raise questions about science, still other aspects of postmodern culture warmly accept technology. Blockbuster films such as *Jurassic Park, The Matrix*, and the Harry Potter series do both, presenting stories that challenge modern science but that depend on technology for their execution.

During the modern period, artists and writers criticized the dangers of machines, pointing out that new technologies often eliminate jobs and physically isolate us from one another. While postmodern style often embraces new technology, there is a fundamental paradox in this alliance. Although technology can isolate people, as modernists warned, new technologies can also draw people together to discuss politics on radio talk shows, in electronic town-hall meetings, on Facebook, or on iPhones, as postmodern society proves. Our lives today are full of such incongruities.

Critiquing Media and Culture

In contemporary life, cultural boundaries are being tested; the arbitrary lines between information and entertainment have become even more blurred. Consumers now read newspapers on their computer screens. Media corporations do business across vast geographic boundaries. We are witnessing media convergence, in which satellite dishes, TV screens, cable or computer modems, and cell phones easily access new and old forms of mass communication. For a fee, everything from magazines to movies is channeled into homes through the Internet and cable or satellite TV.

Considering the diversity of mass media, to paint them all with the same broad brush would be inaccurate and unfair. Yet that is often what we seem to do, which may in fact reflect the distrust many have of prominent social institutions, from local governments to daily newspapers. Of course, when one recent president lies about an extramarital affair with a young White House intern and another leads us into a long war based on faulty intelligence that mainstream news failed to uncover, our distrust of both government and media is understandable. It's ultimately more useful, however, to replace a cynical perception of the media with an

"A cynic is a man who, when he smells flowers, looks around for a coffin."

H. L. MENCKEN

Media Literacy and the Critical Process

1 **DESCRIPTION.** If we decide to focus on how well the news media serve democracy, we might critique the fairness of several programs or individual stories from *60 Minutes* or the *New York Times*. We start by describing the programs or articles, accounting for their reporting strategies, and noting what persons are featured as interview subjects. We might further identify central characters, conflicts, topics, and themes. From the notes taken at this stage, we can begin comparing what we have found to other stories on similar topics. We can also document what we think is missing from these news narratives—the questions, viewpoints, and persons that were not included—and other ways to tell the story.

2 **ANALYSIS.** In the second stage of the critical process, we isolate patterns that call for closer attention. At this point, we decide how to focus the critique. Because *60 Minutes* has produced thousands of hours of programs, our critique might spotlight just a few key patterns. For example, many of the program's reports are organized like detective stories, reporters are almost always visually represented at a medium distance, and interview subjects are generally shot in tight close-ups. In studying the *New York Times*, on the other hand, we might limit our analysis to social or

It is easy to form a cynical view of the stream of TV advertising, talk shows, rock stars, and news tabloids that floods the cultural landscape. But cynicism is no substitute for criticism. To become literate about media involves striking a balance between taking a critical position (developing knowledgeable interpretations and judgments) and becoming tolerant of diverse forms of expression (appreciating the distinctive variety of cultural products and processes).

A cynical view usually involves some form of intolerance and either too little or too much information. For example, after enduring the glut of news coverage and political advertising devoted to the 2004 and 2008 presidential elections, we might easily have become cynical about our political system. However, information in the form of "factual" news and knowledge about a complex social process such as a national election are not the same thing. The critical process stresses the subtle distinctions between amassing information and becoming media literate.

political events in certain countries that get covered more often than events in other areas of the world. Or we could focus on recurring topics chosen for front-page treatment, or the number of quotes from male and female experts.

3 **INTERPRETATION.** In the interpretive stage, we try to determine the meanings of the patterns we have analyzed. The most difficult stage in criticism, interpretation demands an answer to the

"So what?" question. For instance, the greater visual space granted to *60 Minutes* reporters—compared with the close-up shots used for interview subjects—might mean that the reporters appear to be in control. They are given more visual space in which to operate, whereas interview subjects have little room to maneuver within the visual frame. As a result, the subjects often look guilty and the reporters look heroic—or, at least, in charge. Likewise, if we look again at the *New York*

attitude of genuine criticism. To deal with these shifts in our experience of our culture and the impact that mass media have on our lives, we need to develop a profound understanding of the media—what they produce and how they work.

Media Literacy and the Critical Process

Developing **media literacy**—that is, attaining knowledge and understanding of mass media—requires following a **critical process** that takes us through the steps of description, analysis, interpretation, evaluation, and engagement (see "Media Literacy and the Critical Process" above). We will be aided in our critical process by keeping an open mind, trying to understand the specific cultural forms we are critiquing, and acknowledging the complexity of contemporary culture.

Developing a media-literate critical perspective involves mastering five overlapping stages that build on each other:

- *Description*: paying close attention, taking notes, and researching the subject under study
- *Analysis*: discovering and focusing on significant patterns that emerge from the description stage
- *Interpretation*: asking and answering the "What does that mean?" and "So what?" questions about one's findings
- *Evaluation*: arriving at a judgment about whether something is good, bad, or mediocre, which involves subordinating one's personal taste to the critical assessment resulting from the first three stages
- *Engagement*: taking some action that connects our critical perspective with our role as citizens to question our media institutions, adding our own voice to the process of shaping the cultural environment

Let's look at each of these stages in greater detail.

Times, its attention to particular countries could mean that the paper tends to cover nations in which the United States has more vital political or economic interests, even though the *Times* might claim to be neutral and evenhanded in its reporting of news from around the world.

4 EVALUATION. The fourth stage of the critical process focuses on making an informed judgment. Building on description, analysis, and interpretation, we are better able to evaluate the fairness of a group of *60 Minutes* or *New York Times* reports. At this stage, we can grasp the strengths and weaknesses of the news media under study and make critical judgments measured against our own frames of reference—what we like and dislike as well as what seems good or bad about the stories and coverage we analyzed.

This fourth stage differentiates the reviewer (or previewer) from the critic. Most newspaper reviews, for example, are limited by daily time or space constraints. Although these reviews may give us important information about particular programs, they often begin and end with personal judgments—"This is a quality show" or "That was a piece of trash"—which should be the final stage in any substantial critical process. Regrettably, many reviews do not reflect such a process; they do not move much beyond the writer's own frame of reference.

5 ENGAGEMENT. To be fully media literate, we must actively work to create a media world that helps serve democracy—the fifth stage of the critical process. In our *60 Minutes* and *New York Times* examples, engagement might involve something as simple as writing a formal or e-mail letter to these media outlets to offer a critical take on the news narratives we are studying.

But engagement can also mean participating in Web discussions, contacting various media producers or governmental bodies like the Federal Communications Commission (FCC) with critiques and ideas, organizing or participating in public media literacy forums, or learning to construct different types of media narratives ourselves—whether print, audio, video, or online—to participate directly in the creation of mainstream or alternative media. The key to this stage is to challenge our civic imaginations, to refuse to sit back and cynically complain about the media without taking some action that lends our own voices and critiques to the process.

Just as communication is not always reducible to the linear sender-message-receiver model, many forms of media and culture are not easily represented by the high-low metaphor. We should, perhaps, strip culture of such adjectives as *high, low, popular,* and *mass.* These modifiers may artificially force media forms and products into predetermined categories. Rather than focusing on these worn-out labels, we might instead look at a wide range of issues generated by culture, from the role of storytelling in the mass media to the global influences of media industries on the consumer marketplace. We should also be moving toward a critical perspective that takes into account the intricacies of the cultural landscape.

A fair critique of any cultural form, regardless of its social or artistic reputation, requires a working knowledge of the particular book, program, or music under scrutiny. For example, to understand W. E. B. Du Bois's essays, critics immerse themselves in his work and in the historical

GLOBAL VILLAGE

Bedouins, Camels, Transistors, and Coke

Upon receiving the Philadelphia Liberty Medal in 1994, President Václav Havel of the Czech Republic described postmodernism as the fundamental condition of global culture, "when it seems that something is on the way out and something else is painfully being born." He described this "new world order" as a "multicultural era" or state in which consistent value systems break into mixed and blended cultures:

For me, a symbol of that state is a Bedouin mounted on a camel and clad in traditional robes under which he is wearing jeans, with a transistor radio in his hands and an ad for Coca-Cola on the camel's back. . . . New meaning is gradually born from the . . . intersection of many different elements.[1]

Many critics, including Havel, think that there is a crucial tie between global politics and postmodern culture. They contend that the people who overthrew governments in the former Yugoslavia and the Soviet Union were the same people who valued American popular culture—especially movies, rock music, and television—for its free expression and democratic possibilities.

As modern communist states were undermined by the growth and influence of transnational corporations, citizens in these nations capitalized on the developing global market, using portable video, digital cameras and phones, and audio technology to smuggle out recordings of atrocities perpetrated by totalitarian regimes.

Thus it was difficult for political leaders to hide repressive acts from the rest of the world. In *Newsweek*, former CBS news anchor Dan Rather wrote about the role of television in the 1989 student uprising in China:

Television brought Beijing's battle for democracy to Main Street. It made students who live on the other side of the planet just as human, just as vulnerable as the boy on the next block. The miracle of television is that the triumph and tragedy of Tiananmen Square would not have been any more vivid had it been Times Square.[2]

At the same time, we need to examine the impact on other nations of the influx of popular culture (movies, TV shows, music, etc.)—the second biggest American export (after military and airplane equipment). Has access to an American consumer lifestyle fundamentally altered Havel's Bedouin on the camel? What happens when CNN or MTV is transported to remote African villages that share a single community TV set? What happens when Westernized popular culture encroaches on the mores of Islamic countries, where the spread of American music, movies, and television is viewed as a danger to tradition? These questions still need answers. A global village, which through technology shares culture and communication, can also alter traditional customs forever.

To try to grasp this phenomenon, we might imagine how we would feel if the culture from a country far away gradually eroded our own established habits. This, in fact, is happening all over the world as U.S. culture has become the world's global currency. Although newer forms of communication such as instant messaging and cell phone texting have in some ways increased citizen participation in global life, in what ways have they muted the values of older cultures?

Our current postmodern period is double-coded: It is an agent both for the renewed possibilities of democracy and for the worldwide spread of consumerism and American popular culture.

context in which he wrote. Similarly, if we want to develop a meaningful critique of TV's *Dexter* (where the protagonist is a serial killer) or Rush Limbaugh's radio program or gossip magazines' obsession with Britney Spears, it is essential to understand the contemporary context in which these cultural phenomena are produced.

To begin this process of critical assessment, we must imagine culture as more complicated and richer than the high-low model allows. We must also assume a critical stance that enables us to get outside our own preferences. We may like or dislike hip-hop, R&B, pop, or country, but if we want to criticize these musical genres intelligently, we should understand what the various types of music have to say and why their messages appeal to particular audiences. The same approach applies to other cultural forms. If we critique a newspaper article, we must account for the language that is chosen and what it means; if we analyze a film or TV program, we need to slow down the images in order to understand how they make sense.

Benefits of a Critical Perspective

Developing an informed critical perspective and becoming media literate allow us to participate in a debate about media culture as a force for both democracy and consumerism. On the one hand, the media can be a catalyst for democracy and social progress. Consider the role of television in spotlighting racism and injustice in the 1960s; the use of video technology to reveal oppressive conditions in China and Eastern Europe or to document crimes by urban police departments; the way in which hip-hop, as a commercial product mostly of African Americans, draws attention to social injustice; and how the TV coverage of the government's slow response to Hurricane Katrina victims in 2005 impacted people's understanding of the event. The media have also helped to renew interest in diverse cultures around the world and other emerging democracies (see "Global Village: Bedouins, Camels, Transistors, and Coke" on page 30).

On the other hand, competing against these democratic tendencies is a powerful commercial culture that reinforces a world economic order controlled by fewer and fewer multinational corporations. For instance, when Poland threw off the shackles of the Soviet Union in the late 1980s, one of the first things its new leadership did was buy and dub the American soap operas *Santa Barbara* and *Dynasty*. For some, these shows were a relief from sober Soviet political propaganda, but others worried that Poles might inherit another kind of indoctrination—one starring American consumer culture and dominated by large international media companies.

This example illustrates that contemporary culture cannot easily be characterized as one thing or another. Binary terms such as *liberal* and *conservative* or *high* and *low* have less meaning in an environment where so many boundaries have been blurred, so many media forms have converged, and so many diverse cultures coexist. Modern distinctions between print and electronic culture have begun to break down largely because of the increasing number of individuals who have come of age in what is *both* a print *and* an electronic culture.[14] Either/or models of culture, such as the high/low approach, are giving way to more inclusive models, including the map metaphor for culture discussed earlier.

What are the social implications of the new, blended, and merging cultural phenomena? How do we deal with the fact that public debate and news about everyday life now seem as likely to come from *The View,* Jon Stewart, David Letterman, or bloggers as from the *New York Times, NBC Nightly News*, or *Newsweek*?[15] Clearly, such changes challenge us to reassess and rebuild the standards by which we judge our culture. The search for answers lies in recognizing the links between cultural expression and daily life. The search also involves monitoring how well the mass media serve democratic practices and involve a rich variety of people, not just as educated consumers but as engaged members of society. A healthy democracy requires the active involvement of everyone. Part of this involvement means watching over the role and impact of the mass media, a job that belongs to every one of us—not just the paid media critics and watchdog organizations. ▶

CHAPTER REVIEW

REVIEW QUESTIONS

Culture and the Evolution of Mass Communication

1. Define *culture, mass communication,* and *mass media,* and explain their interrelationships.

2. What are the key technological breakthroughs that accompanied the transition to the print and electronic eras? Why were these changes significant?

Mass Media and the Process of Communication

3. Explain the linear model of mass communication and its limitations.

4. In looking at the history of popular culture, explain why newer forms of media seem to threaten status quo values.

Surveying the Cultural Landscape

5. Describe the skyscraper model of culture. What are its strengths and limitations?

6. Describe the map model of culture. What are its strengths and limitations?

7. What are the chief differences between modern and postmodern values?

Critiquing Media and Culture

8. What are the five steps in the critical process? Which of these is the most difficult and why?

9. What is the difference between cynicism and criticism?

10. Why is the critical process important?

QUESTIONING THE MEDIA

1. Using music or television as an example, identify a performer or program you once liked but grew away from as you got older and your tastes changed. Why do you think this happened? Do you think your early interests in popular music or television have had an impact on shaping your identity? Explain.

2. From your own experience, cite examples in which the media have been accused of unfairness. Draw on comments from parents, teachers, religious leaders, friends, news media, etc. Discuss whether these criticisms have been justified.

3. Pick an example of a popular media product that you think is harmful to children. How would you make your concerns known? Should the product be removed from circulation? Why or why not? If you think the product should be banned, how would you do it?

4. Make a critical case either defending or condemning Comedy Central's *South Park,* a TV talk show, professional wrestling, a hip-hop group, a soap opera, or TV news coverage of the U.S. occupation of Iraq. Use the five-step critical process to develop your position.

5. Although in some ways postmodern forms of communication, such as e-mail, MTV, and CNN, have helped citizens participate in global life, in what ways might these forms harm more traditional or native cultures?

For review quizzes, chapter summaries, links to media-related Web sites, and more, go to bedfordstmartins.com/mediaculture.

COMMON THREADS

In telling the story of mass media, several plotlines and major themes recur and help provide the "big picture"—the larger context for understanding the links between forms of mass media and popular culture. Under each thread that follows, we pose a set of questions that we will investigate together to help you explore media and culture:

- **Developmental stages of mass media.** How did the media evolve, from their origins in ancient oral traditions to their incarnation on the Internet today? What discoveries, inventions, and social circumstances drove the development of different media? What roles do new technologies play in changing contemporary media and culture?

- **The commercial nature of mass media.** What role do media ownership and government regulation play in the presentation of commercial media products and serious journalism? How do the desire for profit and other business demands affect and change the media landscape? What role should government oversight play? What role do we play as ordinary viewers, readers, students, critics, and citizens?

- **The role that media play in a democracy.** How are policy decisions and government actions affected by the news media and other mass media? How do individuals find room in the media terrain to express alternative

(non-mainstream) points of view? How do grassroots movements create media to influence and express political ideas?

- **Mass media, cultural expression, and storytelling.** How is our culture shaped by the mass media? What are the advantages and pitfalls of the media's appetite for telling and selling stories? As we reach the point where almost all media exist on the Internet in some form, how has our culture been affected?

- **Critical analysis of the mass media.** How can we use the critical process to understand, critique, and influence the media? How important is it to be media literate in today's world?

At the end of each chapter, we will examine the historical contexts and current processes that shape media products. By becoming more critical consumers and engaged citizens, we will be in a better position to influence the relationships among mass media, democratic participation, and the complex cultural landscape that we all inhabit.

KEY TERMS

The definitions for the terms listed below can be found in the glossary at the end of the book. The page numbers listed with the terms indicate where the term is highlighted in the chapter.

communication, 5
culture, 5
mass media, 6
mass communication, 6
digital communication, 8
bloggers, 8
media convergence, 9
cross platform, 9
senders, 10
messages, 10
mass media channel, 11
receivers, 11

gatekeepers, 11
feedback, 11
selective exposure, 12
narrative, 12
high culture, 16
low culture, 16
modern, 23
Progressive Era, 24
postmodern, 25
populism, 25
media literacy, 28
critical process, 28

Extended Case Study:

Video Games and Storytelling

By 2007, the soaring appeal of intuitive, motion-activated video games meant that a "gamer" no longer had to master twenty-three control buttons and devote lots of youthful energy to play. Bridging the generation gap and appealing to the broader public, the new wave of video games—from Nintendo's Wii system to the popular *Guitar Hero* game—also offered opportunities for social interaction. Today it's not unusual for older people to gather in retirement communities to play Wii's bowling and tennis games, while college students and young profes- sionals meet in dorm rooms and lunch rooms to play "in" their favorite bands. *Guitar Hero* took in more than $1 billion in 2007, while Nintendo could not keep up with Wii demand, despite pro- ducing 1.8 million units a month in 2008 (each unit costs about $250) and selling 6.3 million units in 2007. This success undermined the long-standing criticisms of digital games that went something like this: "In their 30-plus years, video games have been blamed for everything from childhood obesity to school shootings, from moral corruption to antisocial behavior. At best, they were considered a harmless waste of time."[1] Demonizing new popular media forms—particularly those that appear to threaten children—has occurred in music, television, and even books. In Great Britain, the British Police Federation described *Grand Theft Auto* as "sick, deluded and beneath contempt."[2] (In 2007, the British Board of Classification refused to rate *Manhunt 2*, making it illegal, while many U.S. child advocacy groups urged parents not to buy the game.) That didn't discourage fans; by 2008, the different versions of *Grand Theft Auto* had sold more than sixty-five million copies worldwide.

According to a 2007 University of Michigan study that tracked subjects over fifteen years, exposure to violent images in movies, television, and video games increased the risk that "the viewer or player will behave aggressively in both the long and short term." L. Rowell Huesmann, a senior research scientist at Michigan's Institute for Social Research, reported: "This is the first study that shows a relation between childhood exposure to violent TV, playing violent video games, seeing violent movies, and behaving violently enough to be incarcerated as a delinquent."[3] In addition to violence concerns, other experts "believe children who frequently play video games have no time for socializing, and may become isolated."[4]

However, the game industry and other researchers make claims for the positive cultural impact of digital games, citing studies about improved levels of eye-hand coordination. Fans of the *SimCity* computer game praise the knowledge of basic government, tax systems, and population control required to skillfully simulate the construction of a fictional city. In his book *Everything Bad Is Good for You*, Steven Johnson reported that games stimulate interactivity and problem solving, drawing players into complex situations that require difficult choices in order to reach workable solutions. In 2008, Nintendo even introduced *Wii Fit*, which allows players to exercise to a video game. In fact, a 2007 Mayo Clinic study found that playing physically oriented video games helped children fight obesity.

These competing narratives can be explored by using the critical process to discover possible uses and influences of video games.

"We had no interest in video games until the Wii came along. Now I think we're addicted."

EARL DAVIS, RETIRED MARINE SERGEANT MAJOR (AGE 73), 2007

▲ *DIGITAL GAMES AND GAME SYSTEMS* are a massive media-related industry that earned $19 billion in the United States alone in 2007. Beyond the violence and isolation issues or the potential benefits, perhaps the most powerful allure of video games is the opportunity that games provide for players to tell their own complicated stories. Their cultural influence is also complicated. Although critics argue that games like the highly popular Sims franchise offer "some of the voyeuristic kicks of a reality TV show" and overcelebrate "the brutal rules of free-market capitalism,"[5] young people interviewed about the pleasure (and frustration) of playing digital games emphasize the intricate and detailed stories that game players construct and control. Therefore, this Extended Case Study explores the dynamic relationships and disagreements among the digital game industry, popular tastes and cultural interests, adult responsibilities for supervising youth culture, and the ideals of free expression.

As developed in Chapter 1, a media-literate perspective involves mastering five overlapping critical stages that build on each other: (1) description, (2) analysis, (3) interpretation, (4) evaluation, and (5) engagement. (See "Media Literacy and the Critical Process" on pages 28–29 for an explanation of each stage.) In illustrating the value of the critical process, we put forward several important questions: First, who are the major players in the lucrative digital game business, and how do they figure out what attracts and holds players? Second, how are video and computer games like and unlike older mass media forms (such as books or television), and what are the ramifications of these games for the larger culture? Third, what kinds of stories do digital games tell, to whom do these stories appeal, and how central is storytelling to their allure? Fourth, what are our responsibilities as students of the media—with a stake in the quality of the cultural environment—in the creation, consumption, and circulation of digital games?

VIDEO GAMES, TODAY AND TOMORROW
Grand Theft Auto IV, played on Xbox 360 (left), represents the traditional way video games are played with joysticks and control pads. But the new Emotiv Systems headset (above) lets you operate a video game by picking up electrical impulses from the brain and translating them into on-screen commands. In other words, the system reads your mind. This system uses the same experimental technology that has allowed monkeys to manipulate prosthetic arms with their thoughts.

Step 1: Description

Using video and computer games as our subject for study, let's examine aspects of the up- and downsides of games through the lens of the critical process. The idea here is to take notes on the influence of such games and make critical assessments of the relationships among technology, business, culture, and storytelling. First, for the description phase, we might study a variety of crucial topics, such as the ways in which digital games are similar to and different from other mass media technologies. We might also note the companies that manufacture games, scholars who research games, and stories that games tell.

Next, let's focus on what gets said: What kinds of narratives dominate video and computer games? Interview male and female gamers whose ages vary (they can be relatives, friends, or strangers). Ask them why they play digital games and ask them to describe the storytelling that unfolds in those games. Remember that most of us make sense of the world through stories—from the song lyrics we enjoy, to the novels we read, to the news reports we view, to the movies and TV shows we watch. And the cultural industries that produce games pay lots of attention to these types of stories. In this descriptive phase of the critical process, identify central characters, conflicts, topics, and themes that emerge in the games under study. Limit your focus to two or three selected games. From your notes, document particular kinds of stories and characters that dominate in the games—and note what kinds of stories and characters are not featured. Look at ways in which games draw on our familiarity with older media storytelling forms, such as serialized children's books, Hollywood films, and network or cable television. For example, look at the influence of digital games like *Tomb Raider* on the movie business or the impact of the latest *Madden NFL* on pro football and how that sport is presented to fans (who also might play the video game).

Finally, consider some of the larger cultural discussions surrounding these types of games. State legislators in California, Florida, Michigan, Illinois, and Minnesota have passed laws that restrict video and computer game sales, although the game industry is challenging most of these laws. Specifically, the California bill, championed by the state's governor, tried to ban games that "depict serious injury to human beings in a manner that is especially heinous, atrocious or cruel."[6] But a judge ruled that the law violated the First Amendment rights of the game industry. (In 2008, California was still appealing the decision.) Ironically, California's governor, former

POPULAR VIDEO GAMES
According to the Entertainment Software Association, some of the best-selling video game genres in 2007 include: Action (22.3 percent), Sports (14.1 percent), Family Entertainment (17.6 percent), and Shooter (12.1 percent). What is the compelling narrative behind games in each of these genres? (For example, pictured from left: *Grand Theft Auto, Halo,* and *The Sims.*)

body builder and movie star Arnold Schwarzenegger, had to condemn the "new ultra-violent video game" *Conan,* based on the 1982 movie that made him a star–*Conan the Barbarian.*[7]

As a counterpoint, the video and computer game industry's main trade group, the Entertainment Software Association (ESA), reported in 2005 that gamers devoted 23.4 hours per week "to exercise, playing sports, volunteering in the community, religious activities, creative endeavors, cultural activities, and reading," compared with just 6.8 hours per week playing games.[8] In 2008, ESA also reported that the average age of a gamer was 35, and that "26 percent of Americans over age 50 played video games; this is a 9 percent increase from 1999."[9]

Step 2: Analysis

In the analysis phase we are looking for patterns or themes that emerge from the games under study. In this second stage of the critical process, we isolate those patterns that call for closer attention. For example, a 2008 study from the *Journal of Psychiatric Research* found that generally males like video games more than females because "a part of the [male] brain involved in feelings of reward and addiction becomes more activated than it does in women."[10] How do your findings compare with this comment? Is it possible to say what kinds of stories male and female game players prefer?

Other areas of interest may include: What types of games are the most popular among the people you interviewed? Why? In what ways do games in various genres differ–for example, how are strategy games different from storytelling games? How is the storytelling in games like the kinds of stories found on television or in movies? How are the stories different? Do the stories that unfold in the selected games feature lone heroic individuals as the main characters, or do they require team or group solutions? What kinds of stories do younger players like compared with older players? For this analysis, focus on two or three of the above questions. Or, based on what was uncovered in the description phase of the study, suggest other patterns or themes that emerged and are worthy of study and focus.

Step 3: Interpretation

In the interpretation stage, we try to determine the meanings of the patterns or themes we analyzed. What's the bigger picture here? What do your findings mean? For example, what does it mean that certain kinds of stories tend to dominate video and computer games? A possible interpretation may be found in the central value that emerges from so much of our popular storytelling: the ideal of individualism, or the notion that one person can stand in for all of us and make a difference in our lives. Of course, one of the limits of narrative is that our lives don't usually play out like fictional stories. In fact, most progress–whether it is small cultural change at work or big political shifts that affect our legal or military system–often results from collective action. Rather than the initiative of one heroic person (which does happen) as played out in television, movies, video games, and other mainstream narratives, communities and societies often move forward because a group of people—a number of individuals—work together to make such movement possible.

If we find patterns of storytelling that celebrate the adventurous hero versus stories that require teamwork, what does this mean? Do we need both kinds of stories? What kinds of video and computer games come to light that either support or resist the mainstream cultural myths of the powerful hero character? And, what does all this mean in light of the new interest in social, rather than individual, games like *Guitar Hero* or those designed for Wii systems?

There are, of course, other possible interpretations and other patterns that can be investigated as part of this particular phase of the critical process. For example, do digital games that involve complicated strategy and calculation fit into conventional ideas of narrative? If male and female players seem to prefer different kinds of stories in their games of choice, what does that mean? Do the interactive sports games created for the Wii have any appeal as storytelling? In what ways, if any, are sports structured as narratives? Do narrative and character types surface in games that celebrate something other than heroic individualism or the benefits of team play? Are there alternative video and computer games that are sharply different from most of the games that circulate in our popular culture? If so, what does that suggest?

Step 4: Evaluation

The evaluation stage of the critical process focuses on making informed judgments. Building on description, analysis, and interpretation, we are better able to evaluate the place of games in society and their impact on our culture. At this stage, we try to make judgments on what

VIDEO GAMES ADAPTED FOR FILM
Hollywood has traditionally used books and theatrical productions as the basis for movie projects. With the rising popularity of digital games, Hollywood has discovered a new source for narrative material. For example, the *Lara Croft* and *Resident Evil* movies were based on successful game series. A common challenge in turning a game into a movie is hiring actors who physically resemble the idealized digital heroes. These heroes are often represented as a culture's "ideal" man or woman: extremely fit, muscular, and unrealistically proportioned. How do you think gender roles play into digital representations of these characters? How are these roles transformed or adapted for another medium, such as movies?

the positive and negative impact of the games studied might be. We decide what we like and dislike about the stories told through video and computer games. For our current case study, evaluate the ways in which games celebrate individual character, or the virtues of team play, or social interaction. Are these features positive or negative aspects of the games? Assess the violent or sexual content of some games against the problem-solving skills and narrative imagination needed to play them. Evaluate the different ways men, women, and children are portrayed in the games under study. Evaluate differences and similarities between strategy or sports games and storytelling games.

Step 5: Engagement

The engagement stage invites us to take some action that connects our critical interpretations and evaluations with our responsibility to question the cultural industries that manufacture digital games and the critics who seek to regulate them. In this stage, we add our own voices to the process of shaping the cultural environment. For example, after researching a number of these games, call or e-mail game manufacturers about your findings. Or together with other students, write a letter about your findings and submit it to a newspaper, magazine, radio station, or Web site. Or the class may want to convene a forum on the state of video and computer gaming that raises questions about the cultural contributions and drawbacks of these games. Such a forum might probe the range of storytelling and strategies that exist in digital games or explore the various ways gender, age, authority, politics, economics, or some other issue is portrayed in games. Finally, the class might produce a strategy–or media narrative–that would draw news media attention, offering a competing point of view to the more negative narratives that tend to dominate mainstream media when they tell us about video and computer games.

The Internet and New Technologies:

The Media Converge

In the United States, the future of mobile phones as Internet devices will be built on, oddly enough, the demise of old-fashioned television. When television made its transition from analog to digital broadcasting in 2009, the Federal Communications Commission (FCC) assigned the old broadcast spectrum a new purpose: wireless broadband for the Internet. While the FCC planned the auction for the frequencies, observers expected the two largest cell phone companies, AT&T and Verizon, to be the main bidders. But then a company more famous for its search engine became interested: Google.

Why was Google interested? As it turns out, Google didn't want to build a competing cell phone network but wanted to ensure that the next generation of wireless broadband is *open access*; that is, open to all companies who make cell phones, manufacture other communication devices, or provide wireless Internet content. Google, of course, is involved in providing wireless content (like Google search and YouTube), and it would like to put its wireless content—and sell ads, its chief source of revenue—on the new network.

Google didn't win the auction for the wireless spectrum—Verizon and AT&T did—but it did push bids high enough to meet government conditions for making the new network open access. AT&T or Verizon will manage the new network but will be required to allow other companies' devices and cell phone service resellers to operate on it. Up until this point, the U.S. mobile phone market has been a relatively closed system, with customers forced to buy only cell phones approved by their wireless company and to sign contracts for long-term service plans, often with limited Internet content. Closed mobile phone systems are advantageous for companies like Verizon and AT&T but have slowed innovation in the U.S. mobile telephone market. Google envisions an open access system more like those in Europe, East Asia, and Australia. In those regions, customers can keep their cell phones if they switch to new service providers, applications like text messaging are less expensive, and Wi-Fi is widely available for mobile Internet connections.[1]

Open access in the wireless phone industry could force innovation, similar to what happened with wired telephones. At first, U.S. phone customers were required to rent telephones from the limited selection of AT&T (then the monopoly phone company). The most common telephone for years was the heavy, black, rotary dial desk model. In 1968, the FCC opened access to other telephone makers, and new innovations like answering machines, cordless phones, caller ID, fax machines, dial-up modems, and even novelty phones (like a hamburger or football phone) soon hit the market. Today, Google and other companies hope to create a similar wave of innovations, "bringing the Internet developer model to the mobile space," which serves almost three billion people worldwide.[2]

Now, with the spectrum space dedicated to open access, wireless broadband Internet service is poised to become the third major route to high-speed Internet service—in addition to cable and DSL. And Google hopes to be a significant presence on the wireless broadband network, enabling anyone to Google on the run and increasing its advertising revenue.

▲

"A fresh approach to fostering innovation in the mobile industry will help shape a new computing environment that will change the way people access and share information in the future."

ERIC SCHMIDT, GOOGLE CHAIRMAN AND CEO, 2007

◢ THE INTERNET—the vast network of telephone and cable lines, wireless connections, and satellite systems designed to link and carry computer information worldwide—was initially described as an *information superhighway*. This description implied that the goal of the Internet was to build a new media network, a new superhighway, to replace the traditional media (e.g., books, newspapers, television, and radio), the old highway system. In many ways, the original description of the Internet has turned out to be true. The Internet has expanded dramatically from its initial establishment in the 1960s to the enormous media powerhouse that encompasses—but has not replaced—all other media today.

Even with its tremendous growth, the full impact of the Internet has yet to emerge. Unlike radio, television, cable, and other mass media, the Internet uniquely lacks technological limitations on how large its databases of content can grow and how many people around the globe can be connected to it. Unending waves of new innovations and capabilities appear rapidly online. These advances have presented both challenges and opportunities to virtually every traditional mass medium, including the recording industry, broadcast and cable television, movies, newspapers, magazines, and books. With its ability to transport both personal conversation and multimedia mass communication, the Internet has begun to break down conventional distinctions among various media industries and between private and public modes of communication.

As governments, corporations, and public and private interests vie to shape the Internet's continuing evolution, answers for many questions remain ambiguous. Who will have access to the Internet, and who will be left behind? Who or what will manage the Internet? What are the implications for the future and for democracy? The task for critical media consumers is to sort through competing predictions about the Internet and new technology, analyzing and determining how the "new and improved" Information Age can best serve the majority of citizens and communities.

This chapter will explore the many dimensions of the Internet, including its evolution, its current structure, its convergence with other forms of media, and its critical issues: ownership, free speech, security, and access. Why discuss the Internet before the many traditional forms of media—books, radio, television, etc.—that both preceded and shaped it? The answer is simple: We are all witnesses and participants in the emergence of this dynamic medium. Because of this unique vantage point, we are able to gain firsthand understanding of the factors that cause a medium to evolve over time, and we can apply that understanding to the older, more established media we'll talk about in later chapters.

YOUTUBE is one of the most popular Web sites, with more than twenty-five million hits a day. Its videos challenge traditional broadcast and cable television.

The Evolution of the Internet

From its humble origins as an attack-proof military communications network in the 1960s, the Internet became increasingly interactive by the 1990s, allowing immediate two-way communication and one-to-many communication. By the 2000s, the Internet was a multimedia source for both information and entertainment as it quickly became an integral part of our daily lives. For example, in 2000, about 50 percent of American adults were connected to the Internet; by 2008, 75 percent of American adults used the Internet.

> "The dream behind the Web is of a common information space in which we communicate by sharing information. Its universality is essential: the fact that a hypertext link can point to anything, be it personal, local, or global, be it draft or highly polished."
>
> TIM BERNERS-LEE,
> INVENTOR OF THE
> WORLD WIDE WEB,
> 2000

The Birth of the Internet

The Internet originated as a military-government project, with national security as one of its goals. Begun in the late 1960s by the Defense Department's Advanced Research Projects Agency (ARPA), the original Internet–called **ARPAnet** and nicknamed the Net–enabled military and academic researchers to communicate on a distributed network system (see Figure 2.1 on page 47). The distributed network system differed from the centralized telephone system of the time, offering two security advantages. First, because multiple paths linked computers to each other, communications "traffic" would be less likely to get clogged at a single point. Second, because the network was distributed across so many paths, it offered a communication system that was more impervious to technical problems, natural disasters, or military attacks than a centralized system.

In developing one of the prototypes for the military, the Rand Corporation, a national security think tank, conceptualized a communications network that had no central authority and no hierarchical structure. Ironically, one of the most hierarchically structured and centrally organized institutions in our culture–the national defense industry–created the Internet, possibly the least hierarchical and most decentralized social network ever conceived. Each computer hub in the Internet has similar status and power, so nobody can own the system outright and nobody has the power to kick others off the network. There isn't even a master power switch, so authority figures cannot shut off the Internet, although as we will discuss later, some nations and corporations have attempted to restrict access for political or commercial benefit.

To enable military personnel and researchers involved in the development of ARPAnet to better communicate with each other from separate locations, an essential innovation during the development stage of the Internet was **e-mail.** E-mail was invented in 1971 by computer engineer Ray Tomlinson, who developed software to send electronic mail messages to any computer on ARPAnet. He decided to use the @ symbol to signify the location of the computer user, thus establishing the "login name@host computer" convention for e-mail addresses.

▼ **The Internet and New Technologies: The Media Converge**

Microprocessors
These miniature computer circuits, developed in 1971, enable personal computers to be born. PCs become increasingly smaller, cheaper, and more powerful (p. 48).

1940	1950	1960	1970

Digital Technology
In the late 1940s, images, texts, and sounds are first converted into "binary code"—ones and zeros— vastly improving the rate at which information is stored and reproduced (p. 51).

ARPAnet
The U.S. Defense Department begins research in the late 1960s on a distributed communication network—the groundwork for the Internet (p. 46).

E-mail
The process by which electronic messages are sent from computer to computer on a network is first developed in the early 1970s, revolutionizing modes of communication (p. 46).

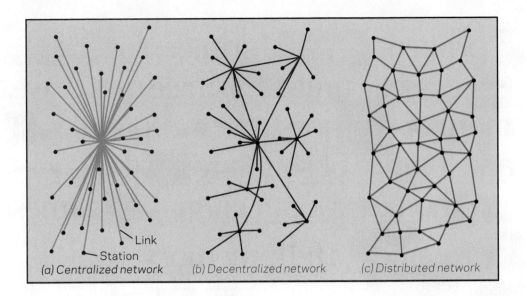

Link
Station
(a) Centralized network　　(b) Decentralized network　　(c) Distributed network

FIGURE 2.1

DISTRIBUTED NETWORKS

Paul Baran, a computer scientist at the Rand Corporation during the Cold War era, worked on developing a national communication system that could survive a nuclear attack. Centralized networks (a) are vulnerable because all the paths lead to a single nerve center. Decentralized networks (b) are less vulnerable because they contain several main nerve centers. In a distributed network (c), which resembles a net, there are no nerve centers; if any connection is severed, information can be immediately rerouted and delivered to its destination. But is there a downside to distributed networks when it comes to the circulation of network viruses?

Source: Katie Hafner and Matthew Lyon, Where Wizards Stay Up Late (New York: Simon & Schuster, 1996).

At this point in the development stage, the Internet was primarily used by universities, government research labs, and corporations involved in computer software and other high-tech products to exchange e-mail and to post information on computer *bulletin boards,* sites that listed information about particular topics such as health issues, computer programs, or employment services. As the use of the Internet continued to proliferate, the entrepreneurial stage quickly came about.

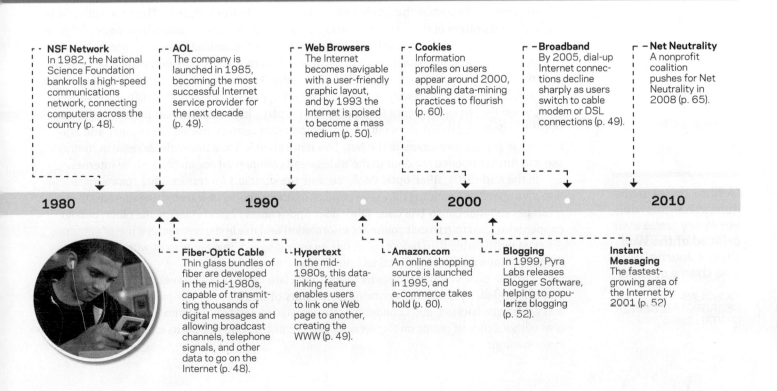

NSF Network
In 1982, the National Science Foundation bankrolls a high-speed communications network, connecting computers across the country (p. 48).

AOL
The company is launched in 1985, becoming the most successful Internet service provider for the next decade (p. 49).

Web Browsers
The Internet becomes navigable with a user-friendly graphic layout, and by 1993 the Internet is poised to become a mass medium (p. 50).

Cookies
Information profiles on users appear around 2000, enabling data-mining practices to flourish (p. 60).

Broadband
By 2005, dial-up Internet connections decline sharply as users switch to cable modem or DSL connections (p. 49).

Net Neutrality
A nonprofit coalition pushes for Net Neutrality in 2008 (p. 65).

1980　　　　**1990**　　　　**2000**　　　　**2010**

Fiber-Optic Cable
Thin glass bundles of fiber are developed in the mid-1980s, capable of transmitting thousands of digital messages and allowing broadcast channels, telephone signals, and other data to go on the Internet (p. 48).

Hypertext
In the mid-1980s, this data-linking feature enables users to link one Web page to another, creating the WWW (p. 49).

Amazon.com
An online shopping source is launched in 1995, and e-commerce takes hold (p. 60).

Blogging
In 1999, Pyra Labs releases Blogger Software, helping to popularize blogging (p. 52).

Instant Messaging
The fastest-growing area of the Internet by 2001 (p. 52)

About the only thing the Commodore 64 doesn't have is any serious competition.

"A fiber the size of a
human hair can deli-
ver every issue ever
printed of the *Wall
Street Journal* in
less than a second."

NICHOLAS
NEGROPONTE, *BEING
DIGITAL*, 1995

The Net Widens

From the early 1970s until the late 1980s, a number of factors, both technological and historical,
brought the Net from the development stage, in which the Net and e-mail were first invented, to
the entrepreneurial stage, in which the Net became a marketable medium.

The first signal of the Net's marketability came in 1971 with the introduction of **microprocessors,** miniature circuits that could process and store electronic signals. This innovation facilitated the integration of thousands of transistors and related circuitry into thin strands of silicon
along which binary codes traveled. Using microprocessors, manufacturers were eventually able
to introduce the first *personal computers* (*PCs*), which were smaller, cheaper, and more powerful
than the bulky computer systems that occupied entire floors of buildings during the 1960s. With
personal computers now readily available, a second opportunity for marketing the Net came in
1986, when the National Science Foundation developed a high-speed communications network
(NSFNET) designed to link university research computer centers around the country and also
encourage private investment in the Net. This innovation led to a dramatic increase in Internet
use and further opened the door to the widespread commercial possibilities of the Internet.

In the mid-1980s, **fiber-optic cable** became the standard for transmitting communication data speedily. Featuring thin glass bundles of fiber capable of transmitting thousands of
messages simultaneously (via laser light), fiber-optic cables began replacing the older, bulkier
copper wire used to transmit computer information and made the commercial use of computers even more viable than before. With this increased speed, few limits exist with regard to the
amount of information that digital technology can transport.

With the dissolution of the Soviet Union in the late 1980s, the ARPAnet military venture
officially ended. By that time, a growing community of researchers, computer programmers, amateur hackers, and commercial interests had already tapped into the Net, creating
tens of thousands of points on the network and the initial audience for its emergence as a
mass medium.

Web 1.0: The World Begins to Browse

The introduction of the World Wide Web and the first web browsers, Mosaic and Netscape, in the 1990s helped to prompt the mass medium stage of the Internet. That first decade of the Web is now often referred to as Web 1.0.

Prior to the 1990s, most of the Internet's traffic was for e-mail, file transfers, and remote access of computer databases. The **World Wide Web** (or the Web) changed all of that. Developed in the late 1980s by software engineer Tim Berners-Lee at the CERN particle physics lab in Switzerland to help scientists better collaborate, the Web was initially a text data-linking system that allowed computer-accessed information to associate with, or link to, other information no matter where it was on the Internet. Known as *hypertext*, this data-linking feature of the Web was a breakthrough for those attempting to use the Internet. **HTML (HyperText Markup Language)**, the written code that creates Web pages and links, is a language that all computers can read, so computers with different operating systems, such as Windows or Macintosh, can communicate easily. The Web and HTML allow information to be organized in an easy-to-use nonlinear way, making way for the next step in using the Internet.

The release of Web **browsers**—the software packages that help users navigate the Web—brought the Web to mass audiences. In 1993, computer programmers led by Marc Andreessen at the National Center for Supercomputing Applications (NCSA) at the University of Illinois in Urbana-Champaign released Mosaic, the first window-based browser to load text and graphics together in a magazine-like layout, with attractive fonts and easy-to-use back, forward, home, and bookmark buttons at the top. In 1994, Andreessen joined investors in California's Silicon Valley to introduce a commercial browser, Netscape. Together, the World Wide Web and Mosaic gave the Internet basic multimedia capability, enabling users to transmit pictures, sound, and video. The Internet experienced extraordinarily rapid growth, and by 1994 the masses had arrived. As *USA Today* wrote that year, this "new way to travel the Internet, the World Wide Web," was "the latest rage among Net aficionados."[3] The Web soon became everyone else's rage, too, as universities and businesses, and later home users, got connected.

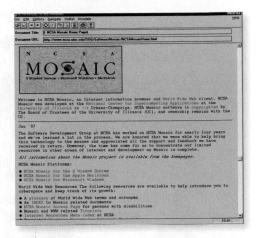

WEB BROWSERS
The GUI (graphical user interface) of the World Wide Web changed overnight with the release of Mosaic in 1993 (*above*). As the first popular Web browser, Mosaic unleashed the multimedia potential of the Internet. Mosaic was the inspiration for the commercial browser Netscape, which was released in 1994.

The Commercial Structure of the Web

As with other mass media forms, the Internet quickly became commercialized, leading to battles between corporations vying to attract the most users. In the beginning, commercial entities were seeking to capture business in four key areas: Internet service, Web browsing, e-mail, and Web directories/search engines.

Internet Service Providers

One of the first ways businesses got involved with the Internet was by offering connections to it. AOL (formerly America Online), which began in 1985 and bought the world's largest media company, Time Warner, in 2001, was for a long time the United States' top **Internet service provider (ISP)**, connecting millions of home users to its proprietary Web system through dial-up access. As **broadband** connections—which can quickly download multimedia content—became more available (about 60 percent of all American households had such connections by 2008), users moved away from the slower telephone dial-up ISP service (AOL's main service) to high-speed service from cable, telephone, or satellite companies. In 2007, both AT&T and Comcast surpassed AOL in numbers of customers. Other national ISPs include Verizon, Time Warner, and Earthlink. These are accompanied by hundreds of local services, many

> "The medium, or process, of our time—electric technology—is reshaping and restructuring patterns of social interdependence and every aspect of our personal life."
>
> MARSHALL MCLUHAN, 1967

offered by regional telephone companies, that compete to provide consumers with access to the Internet.

Web Browsing

In the early 1990s, as the Web became the most popular part of the Internet, many thought that the key to commercial success on the Net would be through a Web browser, since it is the most common interface with the Internet. As discussed earlier, the first browser to come on to the market was the government-funded Mosaic in 1993. The next year, Andreessen and several of his graduate school colleagues from NCSA relocated to Silicon Valley in California and teamed with venture capital firms to release Netscape.

In 1995, Microsoft released its own Web browser, Internet Explorer, and within a few years, Internet Explorer—strategically bundled with Microsoft operating system software—overtook Netscape as the most popular Web browser, and it continues to dominate the Web browser business today. AOL purchased Netscape in 1998, and today Netscape survives only as a minor brand of AOL. Other browsers, such as Safari, Firefox, Opera, and Konqueror, offer alternatives to Internet Explorer.

E-mail

Another area of the Internet on which companies focused their attention was e-mail. Because sending and receiving e-mail is the most popular use of the Internet, major Web corporations such as Yahoo!, AOL, Google, and Microsoft (Hotmail) offer free Web-based e-mail accounts to draw users to their sites, and each now has millions of users. All of the e-mail services also include advertisements in their users' e-mail messages, one of the costs of the "free" e-mail accounts.

Directories and Search Engines

As the number of Web sites on the Internet quickly expanded, companies seized the opportunity to provide ways to navigate this vast amount of information by providing directories and search engines. **Directories** rely on people to review and catalogue Web sites, creating categories with hierarchical topic structures that can be browsed. Yahoo! was the first company to provide such a service. Yahoo! started as a hobby to keep track of all the information on the Web. In 1994, Stanford University graduate students Jerry Yang and David Filo created a Web page—"Jerry and David's Guide to the World Wide Web"—to organize their favorite Web sites, first into categories, then into more and more subcategories as the Web grew. At that point, the entire World Wide Web was almost manageable, with only about 22,000 Web sites (today there are more than 110 million sites). The guide made a lot of sense to other people, and soon enough Yang and Filo renamed it the more memorable "Yahoo!" and started what would become a very profitable corporation and an important player in the Web's continuing development.

Search engines, meanwhile, offer a different route to finding content by allowing users to enter key words or queries to locate related Web pages. Some of the first search engines were Yahoo!, which searched information in its own directory catalogs, and Alta Vista and Inktomi, which were the first *algorithmic search engines* (searching the entire Web and looking for the number of times a key word shows up on a page). Soon search results were corrupted by Web sites that tried to trick search engines in order to get ranked higher on the results list. One common trick was to embed a popular search term in the page, often typed over and over again in the tiniest font possible and in the same color as the site's background. Although users didn't see the word, the search engines did, and ranked the page higher even if it had little to do with the search term.

Google, released in 1998, became a major success because it introduced a new algorithm that mathematically ranked a page's "popularity" based on how many other pages linked to it. Users immediately recognized Google's algorithm as an improvement, and it became the favorite search engine almost overnight. Even other portals chose to use Google's search engine on their sites. By 2008, Google's market share accounted for about 60 percent of searches in the United States, while Yahoo!'s share was about 23 percent.[4]

The Internet Today: Web 2.0

The hallmark of Web 2.0 is *media convergence*, the technological merging of content in different mass media. Recently, the Internet has been the hub for convergence as content from various mass media is distributed and presented on it. The innovation of **digital communication**—central to the development of the first computers in the 1940s—makes media convergence possible because it enables all media content to be created in the same basic way. In digital technology an image, text, or sound is converted into electronic signals represented as a series of binary numbers—ones and zeros—which are then reassembled as a precise reproduction of an image, text, or sound. Digital signals operate as pieces, or bits (from *BI*nary digi*TS*), of information representing two values, such as yes/no, on/off, or 0/1. For example, a typical compact disc track uses a binary code system in which zeros are microscopic pits in the surface of the disc and ones are represented on the unpitted surface. Used in various combinations, these digital codes can duplicate, store, and play back the most complex kinds of media content.

Aided by faster microprocessors, high-speed broadband networks, and a proliferation of digital content, the Internet has become more than just an information source in its second decade as a mass medium. The second generation of the Internet, known as Web 2.0, is a much more rapid and robust environment, and has become a place where music, television shows, radio stations, newspapers, and movies coexist. It has also moved toward being a fully interactive and collaborative medium with instant messaging, social networking, interactive games, and user-created content like wikis, blogs, YouTube, Flickr, and PhotoBucket. It's the users (especially those in their teens and twenties) who ultimately rule in Web 2.0, sharing the words, sounds, images, and creatively edited mash-up videos that make these Web communities worth visiting.

MEDIA CONVERGENCE enables us to access digital content across an array of devices, including mobile phones, digital music players, and notebook computers.

Instant Messaging

One of the Internet's fastest-growing features since the late 1990s is a cousin of e-mail–**instant messaging**, or IM, which enables users to send and receive real-time computer messages. Users assemble personalized "buddy lists" of friends and can chat with any of their buddies who are also online at a given time. Messages tend to be short and conversational, with one small window assigned to each discussion and users often having multiple conversations at once. Although instant messaging can be used to facilitate conversations among coworkers or family members, its most popular use is as an extended social scene among students, who log on after school and chat for hours with their friends. As such, instant messaging foreshadowed the development of social networking sites, another important development in Web 2.0.

Major IM services–many of which now include voice and video chat capabilities–include AOL Instant Messenger (AIM), Microsoft's MSN Messenger Service, Yahoo!'s Messenger, Apple's iChat, Skype (owned by eBay), Gmail's Chat, and MySpaceIM. Instant messaging is one of the Internet's "stickiest" portal services, with users tending to keep open the same advertising-strewn screen for hours. IM windows also operate as full-service portals, providing buttons linking users to their e-mail, news briefs, and Web search engines. In addition, IM users fill out detailed profiles when signing up for the service, providing advertisers with multiple ways to target them as they chat with their friends.

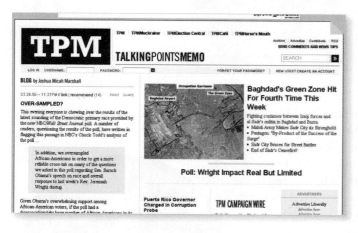

Blogs

The biggest phenomenon in user-created content on the Internet has been Web logs, more commonly known as **blogs**. Blogs are sites that contain articles in chronological, journal-like form, often with reader comments and links to other sites. Ideally, blogs are updated frequently, often with daily posts that keep readers coming back to them. A 2006 study by the Pew Internet & American Life Project found that more than twelve million U.S. adults have created blogs, and 39 percent of Internet users report that they read blogs.[5] Blogs have become personal and corporate multimedia sites, sometimes with photos, graphics, and podcasts that can be played on computers and portable digital devices such as iPods. More recently, *vlogs* have emerged, bringing video to blog pages. Some of the leading blogs include Engadget, Boing Boing, Daily Kos, Talking Points Memo, and the local news/culture "ist" blogs such as *gotham*ist (New York City), *chicago*ist, *la*ist, *dc*ist, *seattle*st, *austin*ist, and *boston*ist.

Wiki Web Sites

Another fairly recent Internet development involves *wiki* (which means "quick" in Hawaiian) technology. **Wiki Web sites** enable anyone to edit and contribute to them. There are several large wikis, such as wikitravel (a global travel guide), WikiMapia (combining Google Maps with wiki comments), and FluWiki (a clearinghouse for influenza pandemic preparation), but the most notable example is Wikipedia: an online encyclopedia that is constantly updated and revised by interested volunteers. All previous page versions of the Wikipedia are stored, allowing users to see how each individual topic develops. The English version of Wikipedia is the largest, containing almost two million articles, but Wikipedias are also being developed in more than one hundred different languages.

Although Wikipedia has become one of the most popular resources on the Web, there have been some criticisms of its open editing model. In 2005, John Seigenthaler Sr., a former editor of the *Nashville Tennessean* newspaper, discovered that the biographical article about him on Wikipedia falsely claimed that he may have played a role in the assassinations of John F.

Kennedy and Robert F. Kennedy. Investigators later identified the man who had posted the false biography content as a joke. While the false copy was corrected, Seigenthaler and many in the mainstream media continue to criticize Wikipedia's open architecture as an invitation to inaccuracies and disinformation.[6] On the other hand, a follow-up study by *Nature* magazine found that Wikipedia's articles were sometimes poorly written but only slightly less accurate than the traditionally edited *Encyclopaedia Britannica*.[7]

Social Networking Sites

The do-it-yourself content of the Internet doesn't end with blogs and wikis. A whole host of **social networking sites** like MySpace, Facebook, Friendster, LiveJournal, Hi5, Bebo, and Xanga are now available. MySpace and Facebook, in particular, have been two of the fastest-growing sites on the Internet. Both sites allow users to create personal profiles, upload photos, create lists of favorite things, and post messages to connect with old friends and to meet new ones.

MySpace, founded in 2003, is the leading social networking site and is one of the leading Web sites in user traffic. In addition to personal profiles, MySpace is known for its music listings, with millions of unsigned, independent, and mainstream artists alike setting up profiles to promote their music, launch new albums, and allow users to buy songs. Its popularity with teens made it a major site for online advertising. That popularity attracted the attention of media conglomerate News Corp., which bought MySpace in 2005 for $580 million. Shortly after, the company announced the formation of MySpace Records, a label that releases compilation recordings from the site with Interscope Records.

Similar to MySpace, Facebook also creates online social networks. Started at Harvard in 2004 as an online substitute to the printed facebooks the school created for incoming freshmen, Facebook was instantly a hit. Originally, access was restricted to college students, but in 2006 the site expanded to include anyone. Soon after, Facebook grew at a rate of more than two million global users a month, and by 2008 had sixty million users, or about half of MySpace's active users. These numbers also attracted a host of potential buyers; Microsoft beat other rivals to buy a small stake (1.6 percent) in Facebook for $240 million in 2007, setting Facebook's total market value at $15 billion.

"In less than three years, the Internet's World Wide Web has spawned some 10 million electronic documents at a quarter million Web sites. By contrast, the Library of Congress has taken 195 years to collect 14 million books."

TIM MILLER,
NEW MEDIA
RESOURCES, 1995

FACEBOOK originated as a social networking site for university users with .edu accounts but by 2006 expanded its base to include anyone with an e-mail address. Classmates, coworkers, and regional network friends can share messages, photos, links, and videos. Users can also limit viewings of their profiles to confirmed friends and people in their networks.

**ONE OF THE MOST
POPULAR MMORPGs,**
World of Warcraft was first
introduced in 1994. Today,
it has ten million subscribers
worldwide and is played in
seven languages.

"The Internet has
now become a
leading source of
campaign news for
young people and
the role of social
networking sites
such as MySpace
and Facebook is
a notable part of
the story. Fully
42% of those ages
18 to 29 say they
regularly learn
about the campaign
from the Internet,
the highest percen-
tage for any news
source."

PEW INTERNET &
AMERICAN LIFE
PROJECT, 2008

Although MySpace and Facebook enable users to limit access to their pages, schools, law-enforcement officials, and parents have voiced concern that online photos and personal information may attract Internet predators. In response to these concerns, both sites have improved their security and launched advertising campaigns to educate users and parents about Internet safety. Public disclosures on social networking sites have also led to real-world consequences. For example, a student at Millersville University was initially denied her teaching degree for "unprofessional" behavior as a result of a photo on her MySpace page.[8]

Massively Multiplayer Online Role-Playing Games (MMORPG)

The newest part of Web 2.0 is the virtual world of online role-playing games. Online role-playing games require users to play through an **avatar**, their online identity. For example, in the fantasy adventure game *World of Warcraft*, the most popular MMORPG with ten million players, users can select from ten different types of avatars, including dwarves, gnomes, night elves, orcs, trolls, and humans. In *Second Life,* a 3D game set in real time, players build human avatars, selecting from an array of physical characteristics and clothing, and then use real money to buy virtual land and trade in virtual goods and services. One of the biggest growth areas is in virtual world games for children. *Club Penguin*, a moderated virtual world purchased by Disney, allows children to play games and chat as colorful penguins. The toy maker Ganz even developed the online *Webkinz* game to revive its stuffed animal sales. Each Webkinz stuffed animal comes with a code for accessing the online game, where players can care for the virtual version of their plush pets.

Online role-playing games have helped to cement the idea of the Internet as a place of convergence—*World of Warcraft*, for example, is now a comic book series, and a movie is in the works. The "massively multiplayer" part of MMORPG also indicates that video games—once designed for solo or small-group play—have expanded to reach large groups at once, similar to traditional mass media.

Web 3.0

There is debate about what the next era of the Web will be like. Certainly it will involve even greater bandwidth for faster, more graphically rich 3D applications. But many Internet visionaries talk about Web 3.0 as the *Semantic Web*, a term that gained prominence after hypertext inventor Tim Berners-Lee and two coauthors published an influential article in a 2001 issue of *Scientific American*.[9] If "semantics" is the study of meanings, then the Semantic Web is about creating a more meaningful–or more organized–Web. To do that, Web 3.0 promises a layered, connected database of information that software agents will sift through and process automatically for us. Whereas the search engines of Web 2.0 generate relevant Web pages for us to read, the software of Web 3.0 will make our lives even easier as it places the basic information of the Web into meaningful categories–family, friends, calendars, mutual interests, location–and makes significant connections for us.

One Web site that already uses some of the principles of Web 3.0 is Freebase.com, a Semantic Web version of Wikipedia. Whereas Wikipedia presents an article for each topic, plus relevant links, Freebase presents a smaller introduction to the topic that is then accompanied by database fields that point a user in relevant directions and to increasingly relevant connections. A Freebase user might link to an article about a film, then to an article about that film's director, then to a list of all the films the director made, then to links to the director's parents and their associations, and so on. In Web 3.0, a computer will generate these logical connections, not a human.

Ownership Issues on the Internet

One of the unique things about the Internet is that no one owns it. But that hasn't stopped some corporations from trying to control it. Since the **Telecommunications Act of 1996**, which overhauled the nation's communication regulations, most regional and long-distance phone companies and cable operators have competed against each other in the Internet access business. However, there is more to controlling the Internet than being the service provider for it. In addition, companies have realized the potential of dominating the Internet business through search engines, software, and, perhaps most importantly, advertising.

Dividing up the Web

By the end of the 1990s and Web 1.0, four companies–Yahoo!, Microsoft, AOL, and Google–emerged as the leading forces on the Internet, each with a different business angle. Yahoo!'s method has been to make itself an all-purpose entry point–or **portal**–to the Internet. Computer software behemoth Microsoft's approach began by integrating its Windows software with its Internet Explorer Web browser, drawing users to its MSN.com site and other Microsoft applications. AOL attempted to dominate the Internet as the top ISP, connecting millions of home users to its proprietary Web system through dial-up access. Finally, Google made its play to seize the Internet with a more elegant, robust search engine, to help users find Web sites.

In order to stay relevant in the fast-moving era of Web 2.0, these four major Internet companies have transformed themselves by buying promising Internet start-ups and changing their business model in hopes of gaining more leverage over their competitors.

AOL

Though it has faced struggles in recent years, AOL (formerly America Online) continues to be one of the nation's leading Internet companies, a position it gained by controlling the ISP portion of the market in the 1990s. AOL's struggles began in 2000 when, despite being the smaller company, it bought Time Warner, the largest media and entertainment conglomerate in the world, for $164 billion and formed a new company, AOL Time Warner. Unfortunately for AOL, the new corporation never made its expected revenue increases, and profitability dropped

"You can never be too rich, too thin, or have too much bandwidth."

WALL STREET JOURNAL HEADLINE, 2000

"One of the more remarkable features of the computer network on which much of the world has come to rely is that nobody owns it. That does not mean, however, that no one controls it."

AMY HARMON, *NEW YORK TIMES*, 1998

TABLE 2.1

TOP 10 INTERNET PARENT COMPANIES IN THE UNITED STATES, 2008

Note: Parent companies can own a number of unique Web sites. For example, Ask Network is owned by InterActiveCorp, whose operations include Ask.com, Citysearch, LendingTree, Evite, and Match.com.

Source: comScore Media Metrix, June 2008.

Parent	Unique Monthly Visitors (in millions)
1. Google Sites	140,163
2. Yahoo! Sites	140,080
3. Microsoft Sites	119,677
4. AOL LLC	110,841
5. Fox Interactive Media	85,998
6. eBay	72,972
7. Amazon Sites	57,002
8. Wikipedia Sites	53,337
9. Ask Network	51,646
10. Apple, Inc.	45,396

drastically by 2002. This caused one of the largest financial losses in American history ($99 billion) and prompted "AOL" to be dropped from the corporate name. In 2006, as its dial-up ISP business continued to decline, AOL reinvented itself by dropping its monthly membership service charge and making its content free to everyone on the Internet. The company's strategy was to gain more customers through free services and generate revenue through advertising, and the effort was successful. Today, AOL's sites–such as AOL Instant Messenger, ICQ, Moviefone, and MapQuest–are among the most visited properties on the Internet. Though its power as an ISP has dwindled, AOL still continues to be a major player in Internet content and services.

Microsoft

Microsoft built a near-monopolistic dominance of the Internet through the merger of its Windows operating systems and its Internet Explorer browser software throughout the 1990s. Because of this, the U.S. Department of Justice brought an antitrust lawsuit against Microsoft in 1997, arguing that it used its computer operating system dominance to sabotage competing browsers. However, Microsoft prevailed in 2001, when the Department of Justice dropped its efforts to break Microsoft into two independent companies. European Union regulators were much more aggressive in their antitrust actions against Microsoft, ruling against the company in 2004 and levying a total of about $2.5 billion in fines against Microsoft through 2008 after it found the company proceeded too slowly in sharing interoperability information with other software makers.[10] Today, Microsoft's presence remains considerable: The company continues to operate the most popular Web browser (Internet Explorer) and also owns one of the leading free Web e-mail services (Hotmail), a top Internet service provider (MSN), a popular instant messaging service (MSN Messenger), and a search engine (Live Search).

Yahoo!

Yahoo! quickly grew into a major Internet property after it was established in 1994 by dominating the Web directory portion of the market and, initially, the search engine portion of the market. Although its directory and search engine were eclipsed by Google's, Yahoo! ranks as the second most popular search site. After acquiring the key algorithmic search indexes Overture and Inktomi in 2003, Yahoo! began to compete directly with Google and to aggressively market to users by including sponsored links with search results. Collectively, Yahoo! sites–which include Yahoo! Travel, Flickr, Rivals, Yahoo! Kids, and HotJobs–are the second-most-visited collective of Internet sites (See Table 2.1). Yahoo! also offers popular e-mail, instant messaging, and shopping services.

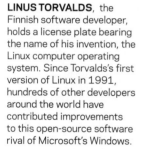

LINUS TORVALDS, the Finnish software developer, holds a license plate bearing the name of his invention, the Linux computer operating system. Since Torvalds's first version of Linux in 1991, hundreds of other developers around the world have contributed improvements to this open-source software rival of Microsoft's Windows.

Google

Google, established in 1998, had instant success with its algorithmic search engine, which now controls about 60 percent of the search market and generates billions of dollars of revenue each year through the pay-per-click advertisements that accompany key-word searches. Google also has branched out into a number of other Internet offerings, including shopping (Froogle), mapping (Google Maps), e-mail (Gmail), blogging (Blogger), and even selling advertising time for Clear Channel radio stations (Google Audio Ads). Google has even begun to challenge Microsoft's Office programs with Google Apps, an online bundle of word processing, spreadsheet, calendar, IM, and e-mail software. Google's most significant recent investments have been its acquisition of YouTube for $1.64 billion and its purchase of DoubleClick, one of the Internet's leading advertising placement companies. (See "What Google Owns" in the margin.)

Advertising on the Internet

In the early years of the Web, advertising took the form of traditional display ads placed on pages. The display ads weren't any more effective than newspaper or magazine advertisements (despite the fact that they would sometimes blink), and because they reached small, general audiences, they weren't very profitable. But in the late 1990s, Web advertising began to shift to search engines. Paid links appeared as "sponsored links" at the top, bottom, and side of a search engine result list and even, depending on the search engine, within the "objective" result list itself. Every time a user clicks on a sponsored link, the advertiser pays the search engine for the click-through. For online shopping, having paid placement in searches can be a good thing. But search engines doubling as ad brokers may undermine the utility of search engines as neutral locators of Web sites (see "Media Literacy and the Critical Process: Search Engines and Their Commercial Bias" on page 59).

Advertising has since spread to other parts of the Internet, including social networking sites, e-mail, and IM—all activities in which computer users reveal something about themselves and their interests. This information has made Internet advertising the most targeted kind of advertising in the history of mass communication. For example, Yahoo! gleans information from search terms, Google scans the contents of Gmail messages, and Facebook uses profile information (age, gender, location, interests, etc.) to deliver individualized ads to users' screens.

For advertisers—who for years struggled with how to measure people's attention to ads— the Internet makes advertising easy to track, effective in reaching the desired niche audience, and relatively inexpensive because ads get wasted less often on the disinterested. Yet, the data collection can sometimes go too far. In 2007, tens of thousands of Facebook users protested when the site began tracking what members bought at affiliated sites (like Travelocity.com) and then alerting their friends about those purchases. Facebook relented, and said it wouldn't release online shopping information anymore without a member's approval.

The unrealized potential of targeted advertising has made Web properties like Google, Yahoo!, MySpace, and Facebook extraordinarily wealthy. In fact, Google and Yahoo! have become advertising powerhouses, spreading their efforts into other advertising platforms, with Google selling radio time and Yahoo! forging an alliance to sell advertising for newspaper Web sites.

Alternative Voices

Independent programmers continue to invent new ways to use and communicate over the Internet. While some of their innovations have remained free of corporate control, others have been taken over by commercial interests. Despite commercial buyouts, however, the pioneering spirit of the Internet's independent early days endures; the Internet continues to be a participatory medium where anyone can be involved. Two of the most prominent areas in which alternative voices continue to flourish are in open-source software and digital archiving.

Search
- Google Web Search
- Google Blog Search
- Google News
- Google Book Search
- Google Scholar
- Google Finance
- Google Maps
- Google Images
- Google Video
- Google Earth
- Google Sky
- Ganji (Chinese language search)

Web Sites and Services
- Blogger
- Gmail
- Postini (security and anti-spam service)
- iGoogle
- YouTube
- Knol
- Picasa/Panoramio

Advertising
- Adwords
- Adsense
- Doubleclick
- Feedburner (ads for blogs and RSS feeds)

Software and Apps
- Google Docs
- Google Calendar
- Google Checkout
- Google Desktop
- Google Glossary
- Google Groups
- Google Talk
- Gapminder's Trendalyzer Software (visualization graphics)

Mobile
- Google Mobile
- Google SMS
- Google Maps Mobile
- GrandCentral Communications (Web-based voicemail integration)
- Zipdash (navigation assistance)

Radio
- dMarc Broadcasting (digital audio systems)
- Maestro (digital audio recording)

Open-Source Software

Microsoft has long been the dominant software corporation of the digital age, but independent software creators persist in developing alternatives. One of the best examples of this is the continued development of **open-source software**. In the early days of computer code writing, amateur programmers developed software on the principle that it was a collective effort. Programmers openly shared program source code and their ideas to upgrade and improve programs. Beginning in the 1970s, Microsoft put an end to much of this activity by transforming software development into a business in which programs were developed privately and users were required to pay for both the software and its periodic upgrades.

However, programmers are still developing noncommercial, open-source software, if on a more limited scale. One open-source operating system, Linux, was established in 1991 by Linus Torvalds, a twenty-one-year-old student at the University of Helsinki in Finland. Since the establishment of Linux, professional computer programmers and hobbyists alike around the world have participated in improving it, creating a sophisticated software system that even Microsoft has acknowledged is a credible alternative to expensive commercial programs. Linux can operate across disparate platforms, and companies such as IBM, Dell, and Sun Microsystems, as well as other corporations and governmental organizations, have developed applications and systems that run on it. Still, the greatest impact of Linux is not seen on the PC desktops of everyday computer users but on the operation of behind-the-scenes computer servers.

Digital Archiving

Librarians have worked tirelessly to build nonprofit digital archives that exist outside of any commercial system in order to preserve libraries' tradition of open access to information. One of the biggest and most impressive digital preservation initiatives is the Internet Archive, established in 1996. The Internet Archive aims to ensure that researchers, historians, scholars, and all citizens have universal access to human knowledge; that is, everything that's digital: text, moving images, audio, software, and more than eighty-five billion archived Web pages reaching back to the earliest days of the Internet. The archive is growing at staggering rates as the general public and partners such as the Smithsonian and the Library of Congress upload cultural artifacts. For example, the Internet Archive stores nearly fifty thousand live music concerts, including performances from Jack Johnson, the Grateful Dead, and the Smashing Pumpkins.

The archive has also partnered with the Open Content Alliance to digitize every book in the public domain (generally, those published before 1922). This book-scanning effort is the nonprofit alternative to Google's "Google Print" program, which, beginning in 2004, has scanned books from the New York Public Library as well as the libraries of Harvard, Stanford, and the University of Michigan despite many books' copyright status. Google pays to scan each book (which can cost up to thirty dollars in labor), and then includes book contents in its search results, significantly adding to the usefulness and value of its search engine. Since Google forbids other commercial search engines from accessing the scanned material, the deal has the library community concerned. "Scanning the great libraries is a wonderful idea," says Brewster Kahle, head of the Internet Archive, "but if only one corporation controls access to this digital collection, we'll have handed too much control to a private entity."[11] Under the terms of the Open Content Alliance, all search engines, including Google, will have access to their ever-growing repository of scanned books. Media activist David Bollier has likened open access initiatives like these as part of an information "commons," underscoring the idea that the public collectively owns (or should own) certain public resources, like airwaves, the Internet, and public spaces (such as parks). "Libraries are one of the few, if not the key, public institutions defending popular access and sharing of information as a right of all citizens, not just those who can afford access," Bollier says.[12]

Media Literacy and the Critical Process

Search Engines and Their Commercial Bias

How valuable are search engines for doing research? Are they the best resources for academic information? To test this premise, we're going to do a search for the topic "obesity," which is prevalent in the news and a highly controversial topic.

1 DESCRIPTION. Here's what we find in the first thirty results from Google: numerous sites for obesity research organizations (e. g., American Obesity Association, Obesity Research, and Obesity-online.com), many of which are government funded. Here's what we find in the top-rated results from Yahoo!: numerous sponsored sites (e.g., Jenny Craig, Bariatric Surgery) and the same obesity research organizations.

2 ANALYSIS. A closer look at these results reveals a subtle but interesting pattern: All the sites listed in the top ten results (of both search engine result lists) offer loads of advice to help an individual lose weight (e.g., change eating habits, exercise, undergo surgery, take drugs). These sites all frame obesity as a disease, a genetic disorder, or the result of personal inactivity. In other words, they put the blame squarely on the individual. But where is all the other research that links high obesity rates to social factors (e.g., constant streams of advertising for junk food, government subsidies of the giant corn syrup food sweetener industry, deceptive labeling practices; see Chapter 11)? These society-level views are not apparent in our Web searches.

3 INTERPRETATION. What does it mean that our searches are so biased? Consider this series of connections: Obesity research organizations manufacture drugs and promote surgery treatments to "cure" obese individuals. They are backed by Big Business, which is interested in selling more junk food (not taking social responsibility), and then promoting drugs to treat the problem. A wealthy site can pay for placement, either directly (via Yahoo!) or indirectly (by promoting itself through various marketing channels and ensuring its popularity–Google ranks pages by popularity). As a result, search results today are skewed toward Big Business. Money speaks.

4 EVALUATION. Commercial search engines have evolved to be much like the commercial mass media: They tend to reflect the corporate perspective that finances them. This does not bode well for the researcher, who is interested in many angles of a single issue. Controversy is at the heart of every important research question.

5 ENGAGEMENT. What to do? Start by including the word *controversy* next to the search term, as in "obesity and controversy." Or, learn about where alternative information sources exist on the Web. A search for "obesity" on the independent media publications AlterNet, MediaChannel, Common Dreams, and Salon, for example, will offer countless other perspectives to the obesity epidemic. Intute (http://www.intute.ac.uk), a powerful subject gateway from Britain; Wikipedia, a collaboratively built encyclopedia; ibiblio; and the National Science Digital Library are other valuable resources that weed out much of the commercial incursions and offer valuable and diverse perspectives.

Security, Appropriateness, and Access

In recent years, three Internet issues have commanded attention: the security of personal and private information, the appropriateness of online materials, and the accessibility of the Internet. Important questions have been raised: Should personal or sensitive government information be private, or should the Internet be an enormous public record? Should the Internet be a completely open forum, or should certain types of communications be limited or prohibited? Should all people have equal access to the Internet, or should it be available only to those who can afford it? With each of these issues there have been heated debates, but no easy resolutions.

Security: The Challenge to Keep Personal Information Private

When you watch television, listen to the radio, read a book, or go to a film, you do not need to provide personal information to others. However, when you use the Internet, whether you are signing up for an e-mail account, shopping online, or even just surfing the Web, you give away personal information, voluntarily or not. As a result, government surveillance, online fraud, and unethical data-gathering methods have become common, making the Internet a potentially treacherous place.

Government Surveillance

Since the inception of the Internet, government agencies around the world have obtained communication logs, Web browser histories, and the online records of individual users who thought their online activities were private. In the United States, for example, the USA PATRIOT Act, which became law about a month after the September 11 attacks in 2001 and was renewed in 2006, grants sweeping powers to law-enforcement agencies to intercept individuals' online communications, including e-mail messages and browsing records. Intended to allow the government to more easily uncover and track potential terrorists and terrorist organizations, many now argue that the Patriot Act is too vaguely worded, allowing the government to probe unconstitutionally the personal records of citizens without probable cause and for reasons other than preventing terrorism. Moreover, searches of the Internet permit law enforcement agencies to gather huge amounts of data, including the communications of people who are not a target of an investigation. For example, a traditional telephone wiretap would intercept only communication on a single telephone line. Internet surveillance involves tracking all of the communications over an ISP, which raises concerns about the privacy of thousands of other users. (To learn more about international government surveillance, see "Global Village: China's Great Firewall" on the next page.)

Online Fraud

In addition to being an avenue for surveillance, the Internet is also increasingly a conduit for online robbery and *identity theft*, the illegal obtaining of personal credit and identity information in order to fraudulently spend other peoples' money. Computer hackers have the ability to infiltrate Internet databases (from banks to hospitals to even the Pentagon) to obtain personal information and to steal credit card numbers from online retailers. Identity theft victimizes hundreds of thousands of people a year, and clearing one's name can take a very long time and cost a lot of money. More than $12 billion worldwide is lost to online fraud artists every year. One particularly costly form of Internet identity theft is known as **phishing.** This scam involves phony e-mail messages that appear to be from official Web sites—such as eBay, PayPal, or AOL—asking customers to update their credit card and other personal information.

Unethical Data Gathering

Another Internet security issue is the unethical gathering of data. Millions of people, despite knowing that transmitting personal information online can make them vulnerable to online fraud, have embraced the ease of **e-commerce**: the buying and selling of products and services on the Internet. What many people don't know is that their personal information may be used without their knowledge for commercial purposes, such as targeted advertising.

One common method commercial interests use to track the browsing habits of computer users is **cookies**, or information profiles that are automatically collected and transferred between computer servers whenever users access Web sites. The legitimate purpose of a cookie is to verify that a user is cleared for access to a particular Web site, such as a library database

China's Great Firewall

Visionaries of the Internet have long heralded the new online world as one without traditional geographic, political, or legal limits. Media theorist Marshall McLuhan wrote in 1972 that "the wired planet has no boundaries and no monopolies of knowledge."[1] William Gibson, the novelist who coined the word *cyberspace* in the 1980s to represent the virtual reality environment of computing networks, similarly argued that "the Internet is transnational. Cyberspace has no borders."[2] And in 2000, Microsoft leader Bill Gates said, "The Internet is a constantly changing global network that knows no borders."[3]

But as the Internet has matured and global communications have grown more widespread, the real, political borders of nations are making themselves known. This trend became most evident with the operation of the Internet in China. Over 162 million Chinese are online, only a fraction of the country's population of 1.3 billion, but with enough Internet users to be second only to the United States. But in rapidly modernizing China, where for decades the Communist Party has tightly controlled mass communication, the openness of the Internet has led to a clash of cultures. As *Washington Post* reporter Philip Pan writes, "The party appears at once determined not to be left behind by the global information revolution and fearful of being swept away by it."[4]

As more and more Chinese citizens take to the Internet, an estimated thirty thousand government censors monitor their use of Web pages, blogs, chat rooms, and e-mails. This surveillance constitutes what some now call the "Great Firewall of China." Internet police give warning calls to people posting material critical of the government,

force Internet service providers to ax unfavorable blogs, and block thousands of international sites. Many Chinese Internet service providers and Webmasters learn to self-censor to avoid attracting attention. For those who persist in practicing "subversive" free speech, there can be severe penalties: Paris-based Reporters without Borders (www.rsf.org) reports that despite China's promise of improved human rights to win the 2008 Olympics, more than eighty cyber dissidents and journalists are in Chinese prisons for writing articles and blogs that criticized the government. Into this regulated environment enter U.S. Internet corporations eager to establish a foothold in the massive Chinese market. Yahoo! Google, and Microsoft are three of the leading U.S. Internet companies, and they have long promoted the liberating possibilities of the Internet—Google's famous corporate motto even states, "Do no evil."

Yet in much-criticized decisions, all three companies are censoring information to appease Chinese authorities. In 2006, Google created a new search engine for the China market, Google.cn, that filters out offending sites, including many relating to Tibetan independence, the Tiananmen Square massacre, the Falun Gong religion, and even BBC News. Moreover, the Google.cn site stripped away e-mail and blog features because they might be used for political protest. According to the Open Net Initiative, Microsoft did much the same,

prohibiting the creation of blogs with politically unacceptable titles (such as "freedom of speech," "democracy," and "human rights"), and deleting Chinese MSN Space blogs that criticized the government.[5] Yahoo! censored Web sites on its Chinese-language search portal, too, and also made a controversial decision: assisting Chinese Internet police in linking computer addresses to the owners of Yahoo! e-mail accounts. Yahoo!'s complicity led to the jailing of at least three cyber dissidents. One of them, journalist Shi Tao, is now serving a ten-year sentence. In March 2008, the Chinese government shut down YouTube.com for one day because the site contained videos showing recent protests against the government for its treatment of Tibet.

China isn't the only country to impose borders on the Internet. As the Open Net Initiative reports, the governments of Burma, Iran, Saudi Arabia, Sudan, Tunisia, United Arab Emirates, Uzbekistan, Vietnam, and Yemen are among those also conducting extensive Internet filtering. While governments may impose virtual borders on the Internet, attempts of any country to block free speech on the medium may ultimately be futile. As major U.S. Internet firms yield to the government's repressive rules, hundreds of thousands of Chinese citizens are bravely evading them, using free services like Hushmail, Freegate, and Ultrasurf (the latter two produced by Chinese immigrants in the United States) to break through China's "Great Firewall."

COOKIES
Several cookies from visiting the *Minneapolis Star Tribune's* Web site will reside on this user's computer until 2023, tracking every subsequent visit to the newspaper Web site unless the user manually removes the cookies.

"These two syllables—'opt in'—strike terror in the hearts of Google, Microsoft, AOL, and everyone else in the interactive marketing fields."

JEFF CHESTER, CENTER FOR DIGITAL DEMOCRACY, 2006

that is open only to university faculty and students. However, they can also be used to create marketing profiles of Web users to target them for advertising. Many Web sites require the user to accept cookies in order to gain access to the site.

Even more unethical and intrusive is **spyware**, information-gathering software which is often secretly bundled with free downloaded software. Spyware can be used to send pop-up ads to users' computer screens, to enable unauthorized parties to collect personal or account information of users, or even to plant a malicious click-fraud program on a computer, which generates phony clicks on Web ads that force an advertiser to pay for each click.

In 1998, the U.S. Federal Trade Commission (FTC) developed fair information practice principles for online privacy to address the unauthorized collection of personal data. These principles require Web sites to (1) disclose their data-collection practices, (2) give consumers the option to choose whether or not their data may be collected and provide information on how that data is collected, (3) permit individuals access to their records to ensure data accuracy, and (4) secure personal data from unauthorized use. Unfortunately, the FTC has no power to enforce these principles, and most Web sites either do not self-enforce them or deceptively appear to enforce them when they in fact don't.[13] As a result, consumer and privacy advocates are calling for stronger regulations, such as requiring Web sites to adopt **opt-in** or **opt-out policies.** Opt-in policies, favored by consumer and privacy advocates, require Web sites to obtain explicit permission from consumers before they can collect browsing history data. Opt-out policies, favored by data mining corporations, allow for the automatic collection of browsing history data unless the consumer requests to "opt out" of the practice.

Appropriateness: What Should Be Online?

The question of what constitutes appropriate content has been part of the story of most mass media, from debates over the morality of lurid pulp fiction books in the nineteenth century to arguments over the appropriateness of racist, sexist, and homophobic content in films and music. Although it is not the only material to be subjected to intense scrutiny, most of the debate about appropriate media content, despite the medium, has centered on sexually explicit imagery.

As has always been the case, eliminating some forms of sexual content from books, films, television, and other media remains a top priority for many politicians and public interest groups. So it should not be surprising that public objection to indecent and obscene Internet content has led to various legislative efforts to tame the Web. Although the Communications Decency Act of 1996 and the Child Online Protection Act of 1998 were both judged unconstitutional, the Children's Internet Protection Act of 2000 was passed and upheld in 2003. This act requires schools and libraries that receive federal funding for Internet access to use software that filters out any visual content deemed obscene, pornographic, or harmful to minors, unless disabled at the request of adult users. Regardless of new laws, pornography continues to flourish on commercial sites, individuals' blogs, and social networking pages. As the American Library Association notes, there is "no filtering technology that will block out all illegal content, but allow access to constitutionally protected materials."[14]

Although the "back alleys of sex" of the Internet have caused considerable public concern, Internet sites that carry potentially dangerous information (e.g., bomb building instructions, hate speech) have also incited calls for Internet censorship, particularly after the terrorist attacks of September 11, 2001, and several tragic school shooting incidents. Nevertheless, many others—fearing that government regulation of speech would inhibit freedom of expression in a democratic society—want the Web to be completely unregulated.

Access: The Fight to Prevent a Digital Divide

A key economic issue related to the Internet is whether the cost of purchasing a personal computer and paying for Internet services will undermine equal access. Coined to echo the term "economic divide" (the disparity of wealth between the rich and poor), the term **digital divide** refers to the growing contrast between the "information haves," those who can afford to purchase computers and pay for Internet services, and the "information have-nots," those who may not be able to afford a computer or pay for Internet services.

Although about 75 percent of U.S. households are connected to the Internet, there are big gaps in access, particularly in terms of age and education. For example, a recent study found that only 37 percent of Americans aged sixty-five and older go online, compared with 72 percent of those aged fifty to sixty-four, 85 percent of those aged thirty to forty-nine, and 92 percent of those aged eighteen to twenty-nine. Education has an even more pronounced effect: only 38 percent of those who did not graduate from high school have Internet access, compared with 67 percent of high school graduates and 93 percent of college graduates.[15]

Another digital divide has developed in the United States as Americans have switched over from slow dial-up connections to high-speed broadband service. By 2007, 71 percent of all Internet users in the United States had broadband connections, but those in lower income households were much less likely to have high-speed service. A Pew Internet & American

NICHOLAS NEGROPONTE, founder of the Media Lab at MIT, began a project to provide $100 laptops to children in developing countries. These laptops, the first supply of which was funded by Negroponte, need to survive in rural environments where challenges include battling adverse weather conditions (dust and high heat) and providing reliable power, Internet access, and maintenance.

A MUNICIPAL WI-FI plan for Philadelphia was first announced in 2004 (right). Despite obstacles such as a lawsuit from Verizon and Earthlink pulling out in 2008, the system is now managed by a private investor group. Only time will determine the viability of such networks.

"[The Internet] is a way for . . . the struggle in our country, and the many other countries where there are a lot of human rights abuses, to be brought out into the open."

JANAL ROBERT ORINA, KENYAN HUMAN RIGHTS WORKER, 1998

Life Project concluded that American adults split into three groups—"the truly offline (29% of American adults); those with relatively modest connections, intermittent users, and non-users who live with Internet users (24%); and the highly-wired broadband elite (47%)."[16]

One way of avoiding the digital divide is to make Internet access available in public libraries. The Bill and Melinda Gates Foundation has been the leading advocate for providing networked computers in libraries since 1997. Now that 99 percent of public libraries in the United States offer Internet access, the main goal is to increase the number of computers in those libraries. Many government documents, medical information, and other research data now exist solely online, so public libraries serve an important public function for assisting all customers and helping to close the digital divide for those who lack Internet access.

Another way to bridge the digital divide is for cities and other municipalities to offer **Wi-Fi**, or wireless Internet access, which enables users of notebook computers and other devices to connect to the Internet wherever they are. Entire cities, such as Corpus Christi, Texas; St. Cloud, Florida; San Francisco; and Washington, D.C., are developing Wi-Fi mesh systems, enabling citizens with Wi-Fi devices to make free or low-cost broadband Internet connections throughout a municipal area. However, some media corporations see municipal Wi-Fi as a threat because Wi-Fi challenges the almost complete control that the cable industry (via cable modems) and telephone companies (through DSL) have over access to broadband Internet service.

In order to bridge the digital divide between rich and poor in one of the nation's largest cities, Philadelphia embarked on building a 135-square-mile Wi-Fi coverage area to blanket the city in low-cost Internet service. But after building 75 percent of the network, the city's commercial ISP partner, Earthlink, withdrew from the project in 2008, halting its operations until a private group bought the system. The project's fate raises questions about how Wi-Fi service

CASE STUDY

Net Neutrality

For every mass medium, there comes a pivotal time when society must decide whether it will be a democratic medium or not. Now is that time for the Internet. The issue is called "net neutrality," and it refers to the principle that every Web site—one owned by a multinational corporation or one owned by you—has the right to the same Internet network speed and access. The idea of an open and neutral network has existed since the origins of the Internet, but it has never been written into law.

But now major telephone companies and cable companies, which control 98 percent of broadband access in the United States (through DSL and cable modem service), would like to dismiss net neutrality and give faster connections and greater priority to clients willing to pay higher rates. The companies that want to eliminate net neutrality, including AT&T, Verizon, Comcast, Time Warner, and Qwest, explain that the money they could make with multitier Internet access will give them the incentive they need to build expensive new networks. Ironically, the telephone and cable companies seem to have had plenty of incentive in the past—they've built profitable and neutral networks for more than a decade. Their current drive to dispose of net neutrality appears to be simply a scheme to make more money by making Internet access less equal.

The cable industry is now trying to confuse the issue with deceptive commercials that have all the charm of negative political ads. With images of wide-eyed, bewildered people, they call net neutrality "Mumbo Jumbo" and falsely claim it will make consumers pay more for Internet service.

One of the main groups in favor of preserving net neutrality is SavetheInternet.com, a nonprofit coalition of more than one million people, mostly bloggers, video gamers, educators, religious groups, unions, and small businesses. Even large Internet corporations like Google, Yahoo!, Amazon.com, eBay, Microsoft, and Facebook support net neutrality, because their businesses depend on their millions of customers having equal access to the Web. SavetheInternet.com outlined some of the threats posed by an Internet without network neutrality rules:

- **Small businesses**—The little guy will be left in the "slow lane" with inferior Internet service, unable to compete.

- **Innovators with the next big idea**—Start-ups and entrepreneurs will be muscled out of the marketplace by big corporations that pay Internet providers for the top spots on the Web.

- **iPod listeners**—A company like Comcast could slow access to iTunes, steering you to a higher-priced music service it owns.

- **Political groups**—Political organizing could be slowed by a handful of dominant Internet providers who ask advocacy groups to pay "protection money" for their Web sites and online features to work correctly.

- **Nonprofits**—A charity's Web site could open at snail-like speeds, and online contributions could grind to a halt if nonprofits don't pay Internet providers for access to "the fast lane."

There is some hope for net neutrality. In December 2006, the Federal Communications Commission approved the $85 billion merger between AT&T and BellSouth with the provision (a bitter pill for AT&T) that the deal preserves network neutrality for at least twenty-four months.

In the meantime, the SavetheInternet.com Coalition is petitioning Congress to make a free and open Internet permanent with the Net Neutrality Act. The movement has bipartisan support, but the telecommunications industry has already spent more than $175 million in lobbying, campaign contributions, and phony grassroots organizations to kill net neutrality, so passage is not a certainty.

should be developed: by existing commercial telephone or cable broadband providers, by fully taxpayer-supported municipal systems, by private investment, or through government-commercial ISP partnerships.

Globally, though, the have-nots face an even greater obstacle crossing the digital divide. Although the Web claims to be worldwide, the most economically powerful countries like the United States, Sweden, Japan, South Korea, Australia, and the United Kingdom account for most of its international flavor. In nations such as Jordan, Saudi Arabia, Syria, and Myanmar (Burma), the government permits limited or no access to the Web. In countries like Argentina, Colombia, Brazil, and Mexico, an inadequate telecommunications infrastructure means that consumers must endure painfully long waits to get online. And in underdeveloped countries, phone lines and computers are almost nonexistent. For example, in Sierra Leone, a nation of about six million in West Africa with poor public utilities and intermittent electrical service, only about ten thousand people—about 0.16 percent of the population—are Internet users.[17]

Even as the Internet matures and becomes more accessible, wealthy users are still able to buy higher levels of privacy, specialty access, and capability than other users. Whereas traditional media made the same information available to everyone who owned a radio or a TV set, the Internet creates economic tiers and classes of service. Policy groups, media critics, and concerned citizens continue to debate the implications of the digital divide, valuing the equal opportunity to acquire knowledge.

The Internet and Democracy

Throughout the twentieth century, Americans closely examined emerging mass media for their potential contributions to democracy. As radio became more affordable in the 1920s and 1930s, we hailed the medium for its ability to reach and entertain even the poorest Americans caught in the Great Depression. When television developed in the 1950s and 1960s, it also held promise as a medium that could reach everyone, including those who were illiterate or cut off from printed information. Despite continuing concerns over the digital divide, many have praised the Internet for its democratic possibilities. Some advocates even tout the Internet as the most democratic social network ever conceived.

The biggest threat to the Internet's democratic potential may well be its increasing commercialization. (See "Case Study: Net Neutrality" on page 65.) Similar to what happened with radio and television, the growth of commercial "channels" on the Internet has far outpaced the emergence of viable nonprofit channels, as fewer and fewer corporations have gained more and more control. The passage of the 1996 Telecommunications Act cleared the way for cable TV systems, computer firms, and telephone companies to merge their interests and become even larger commercial powers. Although there was a great deal of buzz about lucrative Internet start-ups in the 1990s, it has been large corporations such as Microsoft, Time Warner, Yahoo!, and Google that have weathered the low points of the dot-com economy and maintained a controlling hand.

About three-quarters of households in the United States are now linked to the Internet, thus greatly increasing its democratic possibilities but also tempting commercial interests to gain even greater control over it and intensifying problems for agencies trying to regulate it. If the histories of other media are any predictor, it seems realistic to expect that the Internet's potential for widespread use by all could be partially preempted by narrower commercial interests. As media economist Douglas Gomery warns, "Technology alone does not a communication revolution make. Economics trumps technology every time."[18]

However, defenders of the digital age argue that newer media forms—from music distributed as MP3s, to online streaming of films and TV shows, to an array of blogs—allow greater participation than any other medium. **Mass customization**, whereby individual consumers are given the ability by media companies to customize a Web page or other media form, allows the public to engage with and create media as never before. For example, Internet portals such as Yahoo! allow users to personalize their front-page services by choosing their own channels of information—their favorite newspapers or sports teams, local movie listings and weather broadcasts, and many other categories—within the Yahoo! interface. Users of similar services like iGoogle, Facebook, and MySpace get the benefits of creating their own personal Web space—often with their own original content—without having to write the underlying Web code. They are, however, limited to the options, templates, and automated RSS feeds provided by the media company and subject to the company's overall business plan. Such mass customization services blur the boundary between one-to-one communication, which we generally associate with an office conversation or a telephone call, and mass communication, which we associate with daily newspapers or TV programs.

In response to these new media forms, older media are using Internet technology to increase their access to and feedback from varied audiences, soliciting e-mail from users and fostering discussions in sponsored chat rooms and blogs. Skeptics raise doubts about the participatory nature of discussions on the Internet. For instance, they warn that Internet users may be searching out only those people whose beliefs and values are similar to their own. Although it is important to be able to communicate across vast distances with people who have similar viewpoints, these kinds of discussions may not serve to extend the diversity and tolerance that are central to democratic ideals. However, we are still in the early years of the Internet. The democratic possibilities of the Internet's future are still endless. ▶

APPLE'S iPHONE, a hub of convergence featuring phone, Internet, music, video, and gaming capabilities, is also a tool for mass customization—as users can choose and purchase from a wide selection of applications ("apps") to make their iPhones fit their needs and wants.

CHAPTER REVIEW

REVIEW QUESTIONS

The Evolution of the Internet

1. When did the Internet reach the novelty (development), entrepreneurial, and mass medium stages?

2. How did the Internet originate? What does its development have in common with earlier mass media?

3. How does the World Wide Web work? Why is it significant in the development of the Internet?

4. What are the four main features of the commercial structure of the Internet? How do they help users access and navigate the Internet?

The Internet Today: Web 2.0

5. How does media convergence distinguish a different phase in mass media history?

6. How has digital communication made media convergence possible?

7. Why are some Web 2.0 applications like instant messaging and social networking sites attractive to large media corporations?

Ownership Issues on the Internet

8. Who are the major players vying for control of the Internet?

9. How is advertising on the Internet different from all other kinds of advertising in the history of mass communication?

10. What are the major alternative voices on the Internet?

Security, Appropriateness, and Access

11. What are the central concerns about the Internet regarding security?

12. What kind of online content is considered inappropriate, and why have acts of Congress failed in eliminating such content?

13. What is the digital divide, and what is being done to close the gap?

The Internet and Democracy

14. How can the Internet make democracy work better?

15. What are the key challenges to making the Internet itself more democratic?

QUESTIONING THE MEDIA

1. What was your first encounter with the Internet like? How did it compare with your first encounters with other mass media?

2. What possibilities of the Internet's future are you most excited about? Why? What possibilities are most troubling? Why?

3. What are the advantages of media convergence that links televisions, computers, phones, audio equipment, homes, schools, and offices?

4. Do you think virtual communities are genuine communities? Why or why not?

5. As we move from a print-oriented Industrial Age to a digitally based Information Age, how do you think individuals, communities, and nations will be affected?

COMMON THREADS

One of the Common Threads discussed in Chapter 1 is the commercial nature of the mass media. The Internet is no exception, as advertisers have capitalized on its ability to be customized. How might this affect other media industries?

Most people love the simplicity of the classic Google search page. The iGoogle home page builds on that by offering the ability to "Create your own homepage in under 30 seconds." Enter your city and the page's design theme will dynamically change images to reflect day and night. Enter your zip code, and you get your hometown weather information, or local movie schedules. Tailor the page to bring up your favorite RSS feeds, and stay on top of the information that interests you the most.

This is just one form of mass customization—something no other mass medium has been able to provide. (When is the last time a television, radio, newspaper, or movie spoke directly to you?) This is one of the Web's greatest strengths—it can connect us to the world in a personally meaningful way. But a casualty of the Internet may be our shared common culture. A generation ago, students and coworkers across the country gathered on Friday mornings to discuss what happened on NBC's "Must See TV" shows

like *The Cosby Show, Seinfeld, Friends,* and *Will & Grace.* Now they likely engaged with vastly different media the night before. And, if they did share something—say, a funny YouTube video—it's likely they all laughed alone, as they watched it individually.

We have become a society divided by the media, often split into our basic entity, the individual. One would think that advertisers dislike this, since it's easier to reach a mass audience by showing commercials during *American Idol.* But mass customization gives advertisers the kind of personal information they once only dreamed about: your e-mail address, hometown, zip code, and a record of your interests: what Web pages you visit and what you buy online. If you have a Facebook or MySpace profile, they may know even more about you—what you did last night, or what you are doing right now. What will advertisers want to sell to you with all this information? With the mass customized Internet, you may have already told them.

KEY TERMS

The definitions for the terms listed below can be found in the glossary at the end of the book. The page numbers listed with the terms indicate where the term is highlighted in the chapter.

Internet, 45
ARPAnet, 46
e-mail, 46
microprocessors, 48
fiber-optic cable, 48
World Wide Web, 49
HTML (HyperText Markup Language), 49
browsers, 49
Internet service provider (ISP), 49
broadband, 49
directories, 50
search engines, 51
digital communication, 51
instant messaging, 52
blogs, 52

wiki Web sites, 52
social networking sites, 53
avatar, 54
Telecommunications Act of 1996, 55
portal, 55
open-source software, 58
phishing, 60
e-commerce, 60
cookies, 60
spyware, 62
opt-in or opt-out policies, 63
digital divide, 63
Wi-Fi, 64
mass customization, 67

3

Sound Recording and Popular Music

For years the recording industry has been panicking about the file swappers who illegally download songs and thereby decrease recorded music sales. So it struck many in the industry as unusual when the Grammy Award-winning British alternative rock group Radiohead decided to sell their 2007 album *In Rainbows* on the Internet (www.inrainbows.com) for whatever price fans wished to pay, including nothing at all.

Radiohead was able to try this business model because its contract with the record corporation EMI had expired after its previous album, 2003's *Hail to the Thief*. Knowing they had millions of fans around the world, the group turned down multimillion-dollar offers to sign a new contract with major labels, and instead decided to experiment by offering their seventh studio album, *In Rainbows*, online with a "tip jar" approach.

"It's not supposed to be a model for anything else. It was simply a response to a situation," Thom Yorke, the lead singer of Radiohead, said. "We're out of contract. We have our own studio. We have this new server. What the hell else would we do? This was the obvious thing. But it only works for us because of where we are."[1]

Radiohead didn't disclose the sales revenue or numbers of the downloads, but one source claimed at least 1.2 million copies of the album were downloaded in the first two days.[2] In an interview with an Australian newspaper, Yorke mentioned that about 50 percent of the downloaders took the album for free.[3] But a study conservatively estimated that Radiohead made an average of $2.26 on each album download. If that's the case, Radiohead may have made more money per recording than the traditional royalties they might have earned with a release by a major label.[4]

Nevertheless, there remains a market for albums released in compact disc form. In January 2008, Radiohead ended the three-month online availability of *In Rainbows* and released the album as a CD. It immediately became the No. 1 album in both the United States and the United Kingdom, confirming a certain level of viability for the physical CD, even as digital downloads continue to grow in market share. (iTunes became the No. 1 retailer of music in the United States after unseating Wal-Mart in 2008.)

Although Radiohead's Thom Yorke said the online album release experiment was not supposed to be a model for anyone else, it ended up being just that. Hip-hop artist Saul Williams released digital downloads of *The Inevitable Rise and Liberation of Niggy Tardust* (niggytardust.com) for $5, with a "free" option to the first hundred thousand customers. Williams's recording was produced by Trent Reznor of Nine Inch Nails. In March 2008, Nine Inch Nails released *Ghosts I-IV*, a four-album recording with thirty-six songs, at ghosts.nin.com. *Ghost I*, the package of the first nine songs, was available as a free download along with a forty-page pdf file of images to accompany the entire recording. The rest of the songs were available for purchase for only $5. CDs could be ordered for $10, or in a $75 Deluxe Edition Package, or in an Ultra-Deluxe Limited Edition for $300. Despite the no-cost and low-cost options, all twenty-five hundred of the ultra-deluxe packages sold out in just a few days, demonstrating that one part of the future of CDs may be in premium collectors' packages.

RADIOHEAD'S *IN RAINBOWS* WEB SITE

▲ **THE MEDIUM OF SOUND RECORDING** has had an immense impact on our culture. The music that helps shape our identities and comfort us during the transition from childhood to adulthood resonates throughout our lives, and it often stirs debate among parents and teenagers, teachers and students, and politicians and performers, many times leading to social change.

Throughout its history, popular music has been banned by parents, school officials, and even governments under the guise of protecting young people from corrupting influences. As far back as the late 1700s, authorities in Europe, thinking that it was immoral for young people to dance close together, outlawed waltz music as "savagery." A hundred years later, the Argentinean upper class tried to suppress tango music, because the roots of this sexualized dancing style could be traced to the bars and bordellos of Buenos Aires. When its popularity migrated to Paris in the early twentieth century, tango was condemned by the clergy for its allegedly negative impact on French youth. Between the 1920s and the 1940s, jazz music was criticized for its unbridled and sometimes freeform sound and the unrestrained dance crazes (such as the Charleston and the jitterbug) it inspired. Rock and roll from the 1950s onward and hip-hop from the 1980s to today have also added their own chapters to the age-old musical battle between generations.

To place the impact of popular music in context, we begin this chapter by investigating the origins of recording's technological "hardware," from Thomas Edison's early phonograph to Emile Berliner's invention of the flat disk record and the development of audiotape, compact discs, and MP3s. In addition, we study radio's early threat to sound recording and the subsequent alliance between the two media when television arrived in the 1950s. We also examine the content and culture of the music industry, focusing on the predominant role of rock music and its extraordinary impact on mass media forms and a diverse array of cultures, both American and international. Finally, we explore the economic and democratic issues facing the recording industry.

> "If people knew what this stuff was about, we'd probably all get arrested."
>
> BOB DYLAN, 1966, TALKING ABOUT ROCK AND ROLL

The Development of Sound Recording

New mass media have often been defined in terms of the communication technologies that preceded them. For example, movies were initially called motion pictures, a term that derived from photography; radio was referred to as wireless telegraphy, referring back to telegraphs; and television was often called *picture radio*. Likewise, sound recording instruments were initially described as "talking machines" and later as phonographs, indicating the existing innovations, the tele*phone* and the tele*graph*. This early blending of technology foreshadowed our contemporary era, in which media as diverse as newspapers and movies converge on the Internet. Long before the Internet, however, the first major media convergence involved the relationship between the sound recording and radio industries.

From Cylinders to Disks: Sound Recording Becomes a Mass Medium

In the 1850s, the French printer Edouard-Leon Scott de Martinville conducted the first experiments with sound recording. Using a hog's hair bristle as a needle, he tied one end to a thin membrane stretched over the narrow part of a funnel. When the inventor spoke into the funnel, the membrane vibrated and the free end of the bristle made grooves on a revolving cylinder coated with a thick liquid called *lamp black*. De Martinville noticed that different sounds made different trails in the lamp black but he could not figure out how to play back the sound. However, his experiments did usher in the *development stage* of sound recording as a mass medium.

A GRAPHOPHONE and a collection of prerecorded wax cylinders.

In 1877, Thomas Edison had success playing back sound. He recorded his own voice by using a needle to press his voice's sound waves onto tinfoil wrapped around a metal cylinder about the size of a cardboard toilet-paper roll. After recording his voice, Edison played it back by repositioning the needle to retrace the grooves in the foil. The machine that played these cylinders became known as the *phonograph*, derived from the Greek terms for "sound" and "writing."

Thomas Edison was more than an inventor—he was also able to envision the practical uses of his inventions and ways to market them. Moving sound recording into its *entrepreneurial stage*, Edison patented his phonograph in 1878 as a kind of answering machine. He thought the phonograph would be used as a "telephone repeater" that would "provide invaluable records, instead of being the recipient of momentary and fleeting communication."[5] Edison's phonograph patent was specifically for a device that recorded and played back foil cylinders. Because of this limitation, in 1886 Chichester Bell (cousin of telephone inventor Alexander Graham Bell) and Charles Sumner Tainter were able to further sound recording by patenting an improvement on the phonograph. Their sound recording device was known as the *graphophone* and played back more durable wax cylinders.[6] Both Edison's phonograph and Bell and Tainter's graphophone had only marginal success as voice-recording office machines. Eventually, both sets of inventors began to produce cylinders with prerecorded music, which proved to be more popular but difficult to mass-produce and not very durable for repeated plays.

Using ideas from Edison, Bell, and Tainter, Emile Berliner, a German engineer who had immigrated to America, developed a better machine that played round, flat disks, or records. Made of zinc and coated with beeswax, these records played on a turntable, which Berliner called a *gramophone* and patented in 1887. Berliner also developed a technique that enabled

▼ **Sound Recording and Popular Music**

de Martinville
The first experiments with sound are conducted in the 1850s using a hog's hair bristle as a needle; de Martinville can record sound, but he can't play it back (p. 73).

Flat Disk
Berliner invents the flat disk around 1888 or 1889 and develops the gramophone to play it. The disks are easily mass-produced, a labeling system is introduced, and sound recording becomes a mass medium (pp. 74–75).

Radio Threatens the Sound Recording Industry
By 1925, "free" music can be heard over the airwaves (p. 79).

| 1850 | 1860 | 1870 | 1880 | 1890 | 1900 | 1910 | 1920 | 1930 |

Phonograph
In 1877, Edison invents and figures out how to play back sound, thinking this invention would make a good answering machine (p. 74).

Victrolas
Around 1910, music players enter living rooms as elaborate furniture centerpieces, replacing pianos as musical entertainment (p. 75).

him to mass-produce his round records, bringing sound recording into its *mass medium stage*. Previously, using Edison's cylinder, performers had to play or sing into the speaker for each separate recording. Berliner's technique featured a master recording from which copies could be easily duplicated in mass quantities. In addition, Berliner's records could be stamped with labels, allowing the music to be differentiated by title, performer, and songwriter. This led to the development of a "star system," because fans could identify and choose their favorite sounds and artists.

By the early 1900s, record-playing phonographs were widely available for home use. In 1906, the Victor Talking Machine Company placed the hardware, or "guts," of the record player inside a piece of furniture. These early record players, known as Victrolas, were mechanical and had to be primed with a crank handle. The introduction of electric record players, first available in 1925, gradually replaced Victrolas as more homes were wired for electricity; this led to the gramophone becoming an essential appliance in most American homes.

The appeal of recorded music was limited at first because of sound quality. While the original wax records were replaced by shellac discs, shellac records were also very fragile and didn't improve the sound quality much. By the 1930s, in part because of the advent of radio and in part because of the Great Depression, record and phonograph sales declined dramatically. However, in the early 1940s, shellac was needed for World War II munitions production, so the record industry turned to manufacturing polyvinyl plastic records instead. The vinyl recordings turned out to be more durable than shellac records and they were less noisy, paving the way for a renewed consumer desire to buy recorded music.

In 1948, CBS Records introduced the 33 1/3-rpm (revolutions-per-minute) *long-playing record* (LP), with about twenty minutes of music on each side of the record, creating a market for multi-song albums and classical music. This was an improvement over the three to four minutes of music contained on the existing 78-rpm records. The next year, RCA developed a competing 45-rpm record that featured a quarter-size hole (best for jukeboxes) and invigorated the sales of songs heard on jukeboxes throughout the country. Unfortunately, the two new record standards were not technically compatible, meaning they could not be played on each

RECORDS enabled the mass medium stage of sound recording. This recording of the *Star Spangled Banner* was performed by Sousa's Band.

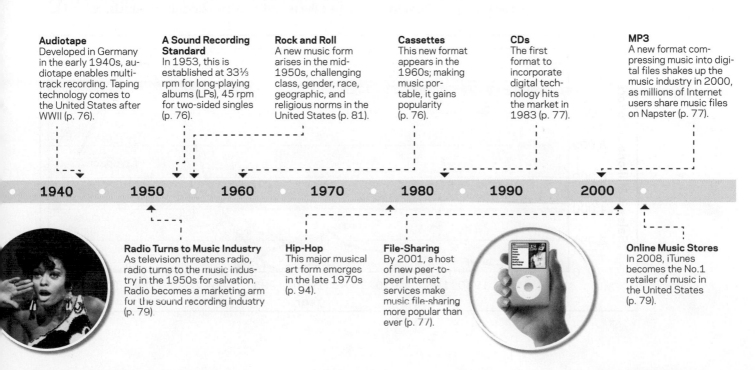

Audiotape
Developed in Germany in the early 1940s, audiotape enables multi-track recording. Taping technology comes to the United States after WWII (p. 76).

A Sound Recording Standard
In 1953, this is established at 33⅓ rpm for long-playing albums (LPs), 45 rpm for two-sided singles (p. 76).

Rock and Roll
A new music form arises in the mid-1950s, challenging class, gender, race, geographic, and religious norms in the United States (p. 81).

Cassettes
This new format appears in the 1960s; making music portable, it gains popularity (p. 76).

CDs
The first format to incorporate digital technology hits the market in 1983 (p. 77).

MP3
A new format compressing music into digital files shakes up the music industry in 2000, as millions of Internet users share music files on Napster (p. 77).

1940	1950	1960	1970	1980	1990	2000

Radio Turns to Music Industry
As television threatens radio, radio turns to the music industry in the 1950s for salvation. Radio becomes a marketing arm for the sound recording industry (p. 79).

Hip-Hop
This major musical art form emerges in the late 1970s (p. 94).

File-Sharing
By 2001, a host of new peer-to-peer Internet services make music file-sharing more popular than ever (p. 77).

Online Music Stores
In 2008, iTunes becomes the No.1 retailer of music in the United States (p. 79).

other's machines. A five-year marketing battle ensued, similar to the Macintosh vs. Windows battle over computer-operating-system standards in the 1980s and 1990s or the mid-2000s battle between Blu-ray and HD DVD. In 1953, CBS and RCA compromised. The LP became the standard for long-playing albums, the 45 became the standard for singles, and record players were designed to accommodate 45s, LPs, and, for a while, 78s.

From Phonographs to CDs: Analog Goes Digital

The invention of the phonograph and the record were the key sound recording advancements until the advent of magnetic **audiotape** and tape players in the 1940s. Magnetic tape sound recording was first developed as early as 1929 and further refined in the 1930s, but it didn't catch on initially because the first machines developed were bulky reel-to-reel devices, the amount of tape required to make a recording was unwieldy, and the tape itself broke or damaged easily. However, owing largely to improvements by German engineers, who developed plastic magnetic tape during World War II, audiotape eventually found its place.

Audiotape's lightweight magnetized strands finally made possible sound editing and multiple-track mixing, in which instrumentals or vocals could be recorded at one location and later mixed onto a master recording in another studio. This led to a vast improvement of studio recordings and subsequent increases in sales, although the recordings continued to be sold primarily in vinyl format, rather than on reel-to-reel tape. By the mid-1960s, engineers had placed miniaturized reel-to-reel audiotape inside small plastic cassettes and developed portable cassette players, permitting listeners to bring recorded music anywhere and creating a market for prerecorded cassettes. Audiotape also permitted "home dubbing": Consumers could copy their favorite records onto tape or record songs from the radio. This practice denied sales to the recording industry, resulting in a drop in record sales, the doubling of blank audiotape sales during a period in the 1970s, and the later rise of the Sony Walkman, a portable cassette player that foreshadowed the release of the iPod two decades later.

Some thought the portability, superior sound, and recording capabilities of audiotape would mean the demise of records. Although records had retained essentially the same format since the advent of vinyl, the popularity of records continued, in part due to the improved sound fidelity that came with stereophonic sound. Invented in 1931 by engineer Alan Blumlein, but not put to commercial use until 1958, **stereo** permitted the recording of two separate channels, or tracks,

FIGURE 3.1

ANNUAL RECORD, TAPE, CD, MOBILE, AND DIGITAL SALES

Source: Recording Industry Association of America, 2007 year-end statistics.

▼

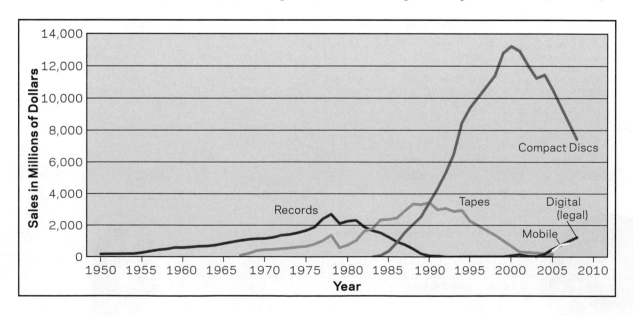

of sound. Recording-studio engineers, using audiotape, could now record many instrumental or vocal tracks, which they "mixed down" to two stereo tracks. When played back through two loudspeakers, stereo creates a more natural sound distribution. By 1971, stereo sound had been advanced into *quadrophonic*, or four-track, sound, but that never caught on commercially.

The biggest recording advancement came in the 1970s, when electrical engineer Thomas Stockham made the first digital audio recordings on standard computer equipment. Although the digital recorder was invented in 1967, Stockham was the first to put it to practical use. In contrast to **analog recording**, which captures the fluctuations of sound waves and stores those signals in a record's grooves or a tape's continuous stream of magnetized particles, **digital recording** translates sound waves into binary on-off pulses and stores that information as numerical code. When a digital recording is played back, a microprocessor translates these numerical codes back into sounds and sends them to loudspeakers. By the late 1970s, Sony and Phillips were jointly working on a way to design a digitally recorded disc and player to take advantage of this new technology, which could be produced at a lower cost than either vinyl records or audiocassettes. As result of their efforts, digitally recorded **compact discs (CDs)** hit the market in 1983.

By 1987, CD sales had doubled LP record album sales (see Figure 3.1). By 2000, CDs rendered records and audiocassettes nearly obsolete, except for DJs and record enthusiasts who continue to play and collect vinyl LPs. In an effort to create new product lines and maintain consumer sales, the music industry promoted two advanced digital disk formats in the late 1990s, which it hoped would eventually replace standard CDs. However, the introduction of these formats was ill-timed for the industry, because the biggest development in music formatting was already on the horizon—the MP3.

From MP3s to the Future: Recordings in the Internet Age

The **MP3** file format, developed in 1992, enables digital recordings to be compressed into smaller, more manageable files. With the increasing popularity of the Internet in the mid-1990s, computer users began swapping MP3 music files online because they could be uploaded or downloaded in a fraction of the time it took to exchange noncompressed music and because they use up less memory.

By 1999, the year Napster's now infamous free file-sharing service brought the MP3 format to popular attention, music files were widely available on the Internet—some for sale, some of them legally available for free downloading, and many traded in violation of copyright laws. Despite the higher quality of industry-manufactured CDs, music fans enjoyed the convenience of downloading and burning MP3 files to CD. Some listeners skipped CDs altogether, storing their music on hard drives and essentially using their computers as stereo systems. Losing countless music sales to illegal downloading, the music industry fought the proliferation of the MP3 format with an array of lawsuits (aimed at file-sharing companies and at individual downloaders), but the popularity of MP3s continued to increase (see "Tracking Technology: The Rise of MP3s and Digital Downloading" on page 78).

In 2001, the U.S. Supreme Court ruled in favor of the music industry and against Napster, declaring free music file-swapping illegal and in violation of music copyrights held by recording labels and artists. It was relatively easy for the music industry to shut down Napster (which has since relaunched as a legal service), because it required users to log into a centralized system. However, the music industry's success against illegal file-sharing was only temporary, as decentralized *peer-to-peer* (P2P) systems, such as Grokster, Limewire, Morpheus, and KaZaA, once again enabled online free music file-sharing. Even with the success of Apple's iTunes and other online music stores, illegal music file-sharing still far outpaced legal downloading in 2008 at a ratio of 20 to 1.[7]

"We've put a lot of work into making the iPod a part of on-the-go living."

STEVE JOBS,
APPLE CEO, 2006

"The real intent of this new focus on students is probably as much about applying pressure on colleges and universities to clean up their networks, as it is about students."

ERIC GARLAND, HEAD OF BIGCHAMPAGNE MEDIA MEASUREMENT, 2007, AFTER THE RIAA TARGETED CAMPUSES FOR ILLEGAL MUSIC DOWNLOADING

TRACKING TECHNOLOGY

The Rise of MP3s and Digital Downloading

By John Dougan

It is a success story that could only have happened in the hyperspeed of the digital age. Since its debut in April 2003, iTunes has gone from an intriguing concept to the No. 1 music retailer (ahead of retail giant Wal-Mart) in the United States. Boasting a customer base of fifty million, a library of six million songs, and sales in excess of four billion dollars, iTunes has conclusively proven that consumers, irrespective of age, have readily and happily adapted to downloading, preferring it to purchasing CDs. Frustrated by escalating CD prices and convinced that most releases contained only a few good songs and too much filler—not to mention the physical clutter created by CDs—digital music sites offer consumers an à la carte menu where they can cherry-pick their favorite tracks and build a music library that is easily stored on a hard drive and transferable to an MP3 player.

Digital downloading has also forever altered locating and accessing non-mainstream music and recordings by unsigned bands. If iTunes resembles a traditional retailer with a deep catalogue, then a competitor such as eMusic (which primarily focuses on artists on independent labels) is the online equivalent of a specialty record store, designed for connoisseurs who are uninterested in mass marketed pop. The success of MySpace (hundreds of millions of members and counting) has made it an important gathering place for virtual communities of fans for thousands of bands in dozens of genres. By capitalizing on the Internet's ability to "marginalize the traditional bodies of mediation between those who make music and those who listen to it,"[1] MySpace (and other online sources such as Facebook, podcasts, and music blogs) makes searching for new music and performers much easier.

The Internet is changing not only how consumers are exposed to music, but how record label A&R (Artist & Repertoire) departments scout talent. A&R reps, who no longer travel as much to locate talent, are searching for acts who do their own marketing and come with a built-in community of fans. MySpace is so powerful in this arena that three of the four major record labels (Universal Music Group, Sony BMG, and Warner Music Group) have joined forces with it to create MySpace Music. This site will offer advertiser-supported music streaming, downloadable files unencumbered by the copy protection software Digital Rights Management (DRM) used by iTunes, and may ultimately branch out into tour merchandise.[2]

The digital age has also, for all intents and purposes, signaled the beginning of the end of the age of the LP. While the technology allows consumers greater and more immediate access to music (as well as an effective method of promoting new acts), aesthetically it harkens back to the late 1950s and early 1960s when the 45-rpm single was dominant and the most reliable indicator of whether a song was a hit. Downloading individual tracks means that consumers build their own collection of virtual 45s that, when taken as a whole, represents what they perceive to be an artist's best work. What is ironic, and disconcerting from the labels' perspective, is that the success of a track does not automatically equate to the success of a CD. The hip-hop track "Low" by Flo Rida became the most popular song of the digital era in 2008, with downloads in excess of three and a half million. This "hit," however, has yielded anemic CD sales of less than 100,000 units.

Now that digital downloading has altered the music industry's long-established methods of production and distribution, record labels are quickly learning to adapt to a present and future where entire music collections will be downloadable, portable, and pieced together. But with fewer acts reliant on record deals to get their music to consumers, and major acts (e.g., Madonna, Nine Inch Nails) self-releasing their latest efforts, the inevitability (and increased speed) of technological change has forced the industry to reexamine itself and contemplate a future where it no longer dictates the terms of purchasing music. ◢

John Dougan is an Associate Professor in the Department of the Recording Industry at Middle Tennessee State University.

The music industry's fight to curb illegal downloading and file-sharing continues. The recording industry fought back in 2002 by increasing the distribution of copy-protected CDs, which could not be uploaded or burned. But the copy-protected CDs created controversy, because they also prevented consumers from legally copying their CDs for their own personal use, such as uploading tracks to their iPods or other digital players. In 2005, P2P service Grokster was fined $50 million by U.S. federal courts and, in upholding the lower court rulings, the Supreme Court reaffirmed that the music industry could pursue legal action against any P2P service that encouraged its users to illegally share music or other media. As a result, the Recording Industry Association of America (RIAA) has filed thousands of lawsuits, with many of its legal efforts targeting university computer network users for copyright infringement. Despite the legal complexities, MP3s are now played on computers, home stereo systems, car stereos, portable devices, and cell phones, establishing MP3s as a leading music format, whether acquired legally or illegally.

Begrudgingly, the music industry realized that it would have to somehow adapt its business to the MP3 format and embraced services like iTunes (launched by Apple in 2003, to accompany the iPod), which has become the model for legal online distribution. By 2008, iTunes had sold more than four billion songs and had become the No. 1 music retailer in the United States, surpassing Best Buy, Target, and Wal-Mart. Even with the success of legal online music retailers like iTunes and Amazon.com, the music industry continues to fight illegal file-sharing.

In some cases, unauthorized file-sharing may actually boost legitimate music sales. Since 2002, BigChampagne.com has tracked the world's most popular download communities and compiled weekly lists of the most popular file-shared songs for clients like the radio industry. Radio stations, in turn, may adjust playlists to incorporate this information and, ironically, spur legitimate music sales.

The Rocky Relationship between Records and Radio

The recording industry and radio have always been closely linked. Although they work almost in unison now, in the beginning they had a tumultuous relationship. Radio's very existence sparked the first battle. By 1915, the phonograph had become a popular form of entertainment. The recording industry sold thirty million records that year, and by the end of the decade, sales more than tripled each year. In 1924, though, record sales dropped to only half of what they had been the previous year. Why? Because radio had arrived as a competing mass medium, providing free entertainment over the airwaves, independent of the recording industry.

The battle heated up when, to the alarm of the recording industry, radio stations began broadcasting recorded music without compensating the music industry. The American Society of Composers, Authors, and Publishers (ASCAP), founded in 1914 to collect copyright fees for music publishers and writers, charged that radio was contributing to plummeting sales of records and sheet music. By 1925, ASCAP established music rights fees for radio, charging stations between $250 and $2,500 a week to play recorded music and causing many stations to leave the air.

But other stations countered by establishing their own live, in-house orchestras, disseminating "free" music to listeners. This time, the recording industry could do nothing, as original radio music did not infringe upon any copyrights. Throughout the late 1920s and 1930s, record and phonograph sales continued to fall, although the recording industry got a small boost when Prohibition ended in 1933 and record-playing jukeboxes became the standard musical entertainment in neighborhood taverns.

The recording and radio industries only began to cooperate with each other after television became popular in the early 1950s. Television pilfered radio's variety shows, crime dramas, and comedy programs and, along with those formats, much of its advertising revenue and audience. Seeking to reinvent itself, radio turned to the record industry, and this time both industries greatly benefited from radio's new "hit songs" format. The alliance between the recording

APPLE'S iPOD, the leading portable music and video player, began a revolution in digital music.

industry and radio was aided enormously by rock and roll music, which was just emerging in the 1950s. Rock created an enduring consumer youth market for sound recordings and provided much-needed new content for radio precisely when television made it seem like an obsolete medium. In the 2000s, though, the music industry turned against radio on the Internet, and it pushed for high royalty charges for online stations streaming music.

> "Music should
> never be harmless."
>
> ROBBIE ROBERTSON,
> THE BAND

U.S. Popular Music and the Formation of Rock

Popular or **pop music** is music that appeals either to a wide cross section of the public or to sizable subdivisions within the larger public based on age, region, or ethnic background (for example, teenagers, Southerners, Mexican Americans). U.S. pop music today encompasses styles as diverse as blues, country, Tejano, salsa, jazz, rock, reggae, punk, hip-hop, and dance. The word *pop* has also been used to distinguish popular music from classical music, which is written primarily for ballet, opera, ensemble, or symphony. As various subcultures have intersected, U.S. popular music has developed organically, constantly creating new forms and reinvigorating older musical styles.

The Rise of Pop Music

Although it is commonly assumed that pop music developed simultaneously with the phonograph and radio, it actually existed prior to these media. In the late nineteenth century, the sale of sheet music for piano and other instruments sprang from a section of Broadway in Manhattan known as Tin Pan Alley, a derisive term used to describe the way that these quickly produced tunes supposedly sounded like cheap pans clanging together. Tin Pan Alley's tradition of song publishing began in the late 1880s with music like the marches of John Philip Sousa and the ragtime piano pieces of Scott Joplin. It continued through the first half of the twentieth century with the show tunes and vocal ballads of Irving Berlin, George Gershwin, and Cole Porter; and into the 1950s and 1960s with such rock-and-roll writing teams as Jerry Lieber-Mike Stoller and Carole King-Gerry Goffin.

At the turn of the twentieth century, with the newfound ability of song publishers to mass-produce sheet music for a growing middle class, popular songs moved from being a novelty to being a major business enterprise. With the emergence of the phonograph, song publishers also discovered that recorded tunes boosted interest in and sales of sheet music. Although the popularity of sheet music would decline rapidly with the introduction of radio in the 1920s, songwriting along Tin Pan Alley played a key role in transforming popular music into a mass medium.

As sheet music grew in popularity, **jazz** developed in New Orleans. An improvisational and mostly instrumental musical form, jazz absorbed and integrated a diverse body of musical styles, including African rhythms, blues, and gospel. Jazz influenced many bandleaders throughout the 1930s and 1940s. Groups led by Louis Armstrong, Count Basie, Tommy Dorsey, Duke Ellington, Benny Goodman, and Glenn Miller were among the most popular of the "swing" jazz bands, whose rhythmic music also dominated radio, recording, and dance halls in their day.

The first pop vocalists of the twentieth century were products of the vaudeville circuit, which radio, movies, and the Depression would bring to an end in the 1930s. In the 1920s, Eddie Cantor, Belle Baker, Sophie Tucker, and Al Jolson were all extremely popular. By the 1930s, Rudy Vallée and Bing Crosby had established themselves as the first "crooners," or singers of pop standards. Bing Crosby also popularized Irving Berlin's "White Christmas," one of the most

LOUIS ARMSTRONG
(1901–1971) transformed jazz with astonishing improvised trumpet solos and scat singing.

covered songs in recording history. (A song recorded or performed by another artist is known as **cover music**.) Meanwhile, the bluesy harmonies of a New Orleans vocal trio, the Boswell Sisters, influenced the Andrews Sisters, whose boogie-woogie style helped them sell more than sixty million records in the late 1930s and 1940s. In one of the first mutually beneficial alliances between sound recording and radio, many early pop vocalists had their own network of regional radio programs, which vastly increased their exposure.

Frank Sinatra arrived in the 1940s, and his romantic ballads foreshadowed the teen love songs of rock and roll's early years. Nicknamed "The Voice" early in his career, Sinatra, like Crosby, parlayed his music and radio exposure into movie stardom. (Both singers made more than fifty films apiece.) Helped by radio, pop vocalists like Sinatra—and many others including Rosemary Clooney, Ella Fitzgerald, Dean Martin, Sammy Davis Jr., Lena Horne, Judy Garland, and Sarah Vaughn—were among the first vocalists to become popular with a large national teen audience. Their record sales helped stabilize the industry, and in the early 1940s, Sinatra's concerts caused the kind of audience riots that would later characterize rock-and-roll performances.

Rock and Roll Is Here to Stay

The cultural storm called **rock and roll** hit in the mid-1950s. As with the term *jazz*, *rock and roll* was a blues slang term for "sex," lending it instant controversy. Early rock and roll combined the vocal and instrumental traditions of pop with the rhythm-and-blues sounds of Memphis and the country twang of Nashville. It was considered the first "integrationist music," merging the black sounds of rhythm and blues, gospel, and Robert Johnson's screeching blues guitar with the white influences of country, folk, and pop vocals.[8] From a cultural perspective, only a few musical forms have ever sprung from such a diverse set of influences, and no new style of music has ever had such a widespread impact on so many different cultures as rock and roll. From an economic perspective, no single musical form prior to rock and roll had ever simultaneously transformed the structure of two mass media industries: sound recording and radio. Many social, cultural, economic, and political factors leading up to the 1950s contributed to the growth of rock and roll, including black migration, the growth of youth culture, and the beginnings of racial integration.

Blues and R&B: The Foundation of Rock and Roll

The migration of southern blacks to northern cities in search of better jobs during the first half of the twentieth century had helped spread different popular music styles. In particular, **blues** music, the foundation of rock and roll, came to the North. Influenced by African American spirituals, ballads, and work songs from the rural South, blues music was exemplified in the work of Robert Johnson, Ma Rainey, Son House, Bessie Smith, Charley Patton, and others. The introduction in the 1930s of the electric guitar—a major contribution to rock music—made it easier for musicians "to cut through the noise in ghetto taverns" and gave southern blues its urban style, popularized in the work of Muddy Waters, Howlin' Wolf, Sonny Boy Williamson, B.B. King, and Buddy Guy.[9]

During this time, blues-based urban black music began to be marketed under the name **rhythm and blues**, or **R&B**. Featuring "huge rhythm units smashing away behind screaming blues singers," R&B appealed to young listeners fascinated by the explicit (and forbidden) sexual lyrics in songs like "Annie Had a Baby," "Sexy Ways," and "Wild Wild Young Men."[10] Although it was banned on some stations, by 1953 R&B continued to gain airtime. In those days, black and white musical forms were segregated: Trade magazines tracked R&B record sales on "race" charts, which were kept separate from white record sales tracked on "pop" charts.

ROBERT JOHNSON (1911–1938), who ranks among the most influential and innovative American guitarists, played the Mississippi delta blues and was a major influence on early rock and rollers, especially the Rolling Stones and Eric Clapton. His intense slide-guitar and finger-style playing also inspired generations of blues artists, including Muddy Waters, Howlin' Wolf, Bonnie Raitt, and Stevie Ray Vaughan. To get a sense of his style, visit The Robert Johnson Notebooks, http://xroads.virginia.edu/~MUSIC/rjhome.html.

DUKE ELLINGTON (1899–1974; top, center) wrote more than fifteen hundred compositions, from pop songs (including the catchy "It Don't Mean a Thing [If It Ain't Got That Swing]") to symphonies and ballets. Most of his work, though, was composed for his sixteen-member dance band, which over fifty years featured many of the greatest talents of jazz.

"Listening to my idol Nat [King] Cole prompted me to sing sentimental songs with distinct diction. The songs of Muddy Waters impelled me to deliver the down-home blues in the language they came from, Negro dialect. When I played hillbilly songs, I stressed my diction so that it was harder and whiter. All in all it was my intention to hold both the black and white clientele."

CHUCK BERRY, *THE AUTOBIOGRAPHY*, 1987

Youth Culture Cements Rock and Roll's Place

Another reason for the growth of rock and roll can be found in the repressive and uneasy atmosphere of the 1950s. To cope with the threat of the atomic bomb, the Cold War, and communist witch-hunts, young people sought escape from the menacing world created by adults. Teens have always sought out music that has a beat–music they can dance to. In Europe in the late 1700s, they popularized the waltz; and in America during the 1890s, they danced the cakewalk to music that inspired marches and ragtime. The trend continued during the 1920s with the Charleston, in the 1930s and 1940s with the jazz swing bands and the jitterbug, in the 1970s with disco, and in the 1980s and 1990s with hip-hop. Each of these twentieth-century musical forms began as dance and party music before its growing popularity eventually energized both record sales and radio formats.

Racial Integration Expands Rock and Roll

Perhaps the most significant factor in the growth of rock and roll was the beginning of the integration of white and black cultures. In addition to increased exposure of black literature, art, and music, several key historical events in the 1950s broke down the borders between black and white cultures. In the early 1950s, President Truman signed an executive order integrating the armed forces, bringing young men from very different ethnic and economic backgrounds together. Even more significant was the Supreme Court's Brown v. Board of Education decision in 1954. With this ruling, "separate but equal" laws, which had kept white and black schools, hotels, restaurants, rest rooms, and drinking fountains segregated for decades, were declared unconstitutional. Thus mainstream America began to wrestle seriously with the legacy of slavery and the unequal treatment of its African American citizens. A cultural reflection of the times, rock and roll would burst from the midst of these social and political tensions.

Rock Muddies the Waters

In the 1950s, legal integration accompanied a cultural shift, and the music industry's race and pop charts blurred. White deejay Alan Freed had been playing black music for his young audiences in Cleveland and New York since the early 1950s, and such white performers as Johnnie Ray and Bill Haley had crossed over to the race charts to score R&B hits. Meanwhile, black artists like Chuck Berry were performing country songs, and for a time Ray Charles even played in an otherwise all-white country band. Although continuing the work of breaking down racial borders was one of rock and roll's most important contributions, it also blurred other long-standing boundaries. Rock and roll exploded old distinctions between high and low culture, masculinity and femininity, the country and the city, the North and the South, and the sacred and the secular.

High and Low Culture

In 1956, Chuck Berry's "Roll Over Beethoven" merged rock and roll, considered low culture by many, with high culture, thus forever blurring the traditional boundary between them with lyrics like: "You know my temperature's risin' / the jukebox is blowin' a fuse . . . Roll over Beethoven / and tell Tchaikovsky the news." Although such early rock-and-roll lyrics seem tame by today's standards, at the time, they sounded like sacrilege. Rock and rollers also challenged music decorum and the rules governing how musicians should behave or misbehave: Berry's "duck walk" across the stage, Elvis Presley's pegged pants and gyrating hips, and Bo Diddley's use of the guitar as a phallic symbol were an affront to the norms of well-behaved culturally elite audiences. Such antics would be imitated endlessly throughout rock's history. In fact, rock and roll's live shows and the legends surrounding them became key ingredients in promoting record sales.

The blurring of cultures works both ways. Since the advent of rock and roll, musicians performing in traditionally high culture genres such as classical have even adopted some of rock and roll's ideas in an effort to boost sales and popularity. Some virtuosos like violinist Joshua Bell and cellist Matt Haimovitz (who does his own version of Jimi Hendrix's famous improvisation of the national anthem) have performed in jeans and in untraditional venues like bars and subway stations to reinterpret the presentation of classical music.

Masculinity and Femininity

Rock and roll was also the first popular music genre to overtly confuse issues of sexual identity and orientation. Although early rock and roll largely attracted males as performers, the most fascinating feature of Elvis Presley, according to the Rolling Stones' Mick Jagger, was his androgynous appearance.[11] During this early period, though, the most sexually outrageous rock-and-roll performer was Little Richard (Penniman), who influenced a generation of extravagant rock stars.

Wearing a pompadour hairdo and assaulting his Steinway piano, Little Richard was considered rock and roll's first drag queen, blurring the boundary between masculinity and femininity (although his act had been influenced by a flamboyant 6½-foot-tall gay piano player named Esquerita, who hosted drag-queen shows in New Orleans in the 1940s).[12] Little Richard has said that given the reality of American racism, he blurred gender and sexuality lines because he feared the consequences of becoming a sex symbol for white girls: "I decided that my image should be crazy and way out so that adults would think I was harmless. I'd appear in one show dressed as the Queen of England and in the next as the pope."[13] Although white parents in the 1950s may not have been concerned about their daughters falling for Little Richard, many saw

ROCK AND ROLL PIONEER
A major influence on early rock and roll, Chuck Berry, born in 1926, scored major hits between 1955 and 1958, writing "Maybellene," "Roll Over Beethoven," "School Day," "Sweet Little Sixteen," and "Johnny B. Goode." At the time , he was criticized by some black artists for sounding white and by conservative critics for his popularity among white teenagers. Today, young guitar players routinely imitate his style.

him as a threat to traditional gender roles and viewed his sexual identity and possible sexual orientation as anything but harmless. Little Richard's playful blurring of gender identity and sexual orientation paved the way for performers like David Bowie, Elton John, Boy George, Annie Lennox, Prince, Grace Jones, and Marilyn Manson.

The Country and the City

Rock and roll also blurred geographic borders between country and city, between the black urban rhythms of Memphis and the white country & western music of Nashville. Early white rockers such as Buddy Holly and Carl Perkins combined country or hillbilly music, southern gospel, and Mississippi delta blues to create a sound called **rockabilly**. Raised on bluegrass music and radio's Grand Ole Opry, Perkins (a sharecropper's son from Tennessee) mixed these influences with music he heard from black cotton-field workers and blues singers like Muddy Waters and John Lee Hooker, both of whom used electric guitars in their performances.

Conversely, rhythm and blues spilled into rock and roll. The urban R&B influences on early rock came from Fats Domino ("Blueberry Hill"), Willie Mae "Big Mama" Thornton ("Hound Dog"), and Big Joe Turner ("Shake, Rattle, and Roll"). Many of these songs, first popular on R&B labels, crossed over to the pop charts during the mid to late 1950s (although many were performed by more widely known white artists). Chuck Berry borrowed from white country & western music (an old country song called "Ida Red") and combined it with R&B to write "Maybellene." His first hit, the song was No. 1 on the R&B chart in July 1955 and crossed over to the pop charts the next month.

Although rock lyrics in the 1950s may not have been especially provocative or overtly political, soaring record sales and the crossover appeal of the music itself represented an enormous threat to long-standing racial and class boundaries. In 1956, the secretary of the North Alabama White Citizens Council bluntly spelled out the racism and white fear concerning the new blending of urban/black and rural/white culture: "Rock and roll is a means of pulling the white man down to the level of the Negro. It is part of a plot to undermine the morals of the youth of our nation."[14] These days, distinctions between traditionally rural music and urban music continue to blur, with older hybrids such as country rock (think of the Eagles) and newer forms like "alternative country," with performers like Ryan Adams, Steve Earle, and Wilco.

The North and the South

Not only did rock and roll muddy the urban and rural terrain, it also combined northern and southern influences. In fact, with so much blues, R&B, and rock and roll rising from the South in the 1950s, this region regained some of its cultural flavor, which (along with a sizable portion of the population) had migrated to the North after the Civil War and during the early twentieth century. Meanwhile, musicians and audiences in the North had absorbed blues music as their own, eliminating the understanding of blues as specifically a southern style. Like the many white teens today who are fascinated by hip-hop (buying the majority of hip-hop CDs on the commercial market), Carl Perkins, Elvis Presley, and Buddy Holly—all from the rural South—were fascinated with and influenced by the black urban styles they had heard on the radio or seen in nightclubs. These artists in turn brought southern culture to northern listeners.

But the key to record sales and the spread of rock and roll, according to famed record producer Sam Phillips of Sun Records, was to find a white man who sounded black. Phillips found that man in Elvis Presley. Commenting on Presley's cultural importance, one critic wrote: "White rockabillies like Elvis took poor white southern mannerisms of speech and behavior deeper into mainstream culture than they had ever been taken."[15]

RICHARD WAYNE PENNIMAN (LITTLE RICHARD) was inducted into the Rock and Roll Hall of Fame in 1986. Little Richard played a key role in getting black music played on white radio stations and sold in mainstream record stores. His flamboyant, gender-tweaking style has been a major influence on many performers—notably Elton John and David Bowie in the 1970s, Culture Club and Prince in the 1980s, and Marilyn Manson and OutKast in the 1990s and 2000s.

"[Elvis Presley's] kind of music is deplorable, a rancid smelling aphrodisiac."

FRANK SINATRA, 1956

"There have been many accolades uttered about [Presley's] talent and performances through the years, all of which I agree with wholeheartedly."

FRANK SINATRA, 1977

The Sacred and the Secular

Although many mainstream adults in the 1950s complained that rock and roll's sexuality and questioning of moral norms constituted an offense against God, in fact, many early rock figures had close ties to religion. As a boy, Elvis Presley dreamed of joining the Blackwoods, one of country-gospel's most influential groups; Jerry Lee Lewis attended a Bible institute in Texas (although he was eventually thrown out); Ray Charles converted an old gospel tune he had first heard in church as a youth into "I Got a Woman," one of his signature songs; and many other artists transformed gospel songs into rock and roll.

Still, many people did not appreciate the blurring of boundaries between the sacred and the secular. In the late 1950s, public outrage over rock and roll was so great that even Little Richard and Jerry Lee Lewis, both sons of southern preachers, became convinced that they were playing the "devil's music." By 1959, Little Richard had left rock and roll to become a minister. Lewis, too, feared that rock was no way to salvation. He had to be coerced into recording "Great Balls of Fire," a song by Otis Blackwell that turned an apocalyptic biblical phrase into a highly charged sexual teen love song that was banned by many radio stations, but nevertheless climbed to No. 2 on the pop charts in 1957. Throughout the rock and roll era to today, the boundaries between sacred and secular music and religious and secular concerns continue to blur, with some churches using rock and roll to appeal to youth, and some Christian-themed rock groups recording music as seemingly incongruous as heavy metal.

Battles in Rock and Roll

The blurring of racial lines and the breakdown of other conventional boundaries meant that performers and producers were forced to play a tricky game to get rock and roll accepted by the masses. Two prominent white disc jockeys used different methods. Cleveland deejay Alan Freed, credited with popularizing the term *rock and roll*, played original R&B recordings from the race charts and black versions of early rock and roll on his program. In contrast, Philadelphia deejay Dick Clark believed that making black music acceptable to white audiences required cover versions by white artists. By the mid-1950s, rock and roll was gaining acceptance with the masses, but rock and roll artists and promoters still faced further obstacles: black artists found that they were often undermined by white cover versions; the payola scandals portrayed rock and roll as a corrupt industry; and fears of rock and roll as a contributing factor in juvenile delinquency resulted in censorship.

White Cover Music Undermines Black Artists

By the mid-1960s, black and white artists routinely recorded and performed each other's original tunes. For example, established black R&B artist Otis Redding covered the Rolling Stones' "Satisfaction" and Jimi Hendrix covered Bob Dylan's "All along the Watchtower," while just about every white rock and roll band established its career by covering R&B classics. Most notably, the Beatles covered "Twist and Shout" and "Money" and the Rolling Stones—whose name came from a Muddy Waters song—covered numerous Robert Johnson songs and other blues staples.

Although today we take such rerecordings for granted, in the 1950s the covering of black artists' songs by white musicians was almost always an attempt to capitalize on popular songs from the R&B "race" charts and transform them into hits on the white pop charts. Often, white producers would not only

ELVIS PRESLEY
Although his unofficial title, "King of Rock and Roll," has been challenged by Little Richard and Chuck Berry, Elvis Presley remains the most popular solo artist of all time. From 1956 to 1962, he recorded seventeen No. 1 hits, from "Heartbreak Hotel" to "Good Luck Charm." According to Little Richard, Presley's main legacy was that he opened doors for many young performers and made black music popular in mainstream America.

LES PAUL
In the 1940s, legendary guitarist Les Paul developed and popularized the solid-body electric guitar, which became a staple of rock and roll.

give co-writing credit to white performers like Elvis Presley (who never wrote songs himself) for the tunes they only covered, but they would also buy the rights to potential hits from black songwriters who seldom saw a penny in royalties or received songwriting credit.

During this period, black R&B artists, working for small record labels, saw many of their popular songs covered by white artists working for major labels. These cover records, boosted by better marketing and ties to white deejays, usually outsold the original black versions. Covers also slowed sales of the original releases and hampered smaller labels. For instance, the 1954 R&B song "Sh-Boom," by the Chords on Atlantic's Cat label, was immediately covered by a white group, the Crew Cuts, for the major Mercury label. Record sales declined for the Chords, although jukebox and R&B radio play remained strong for their original version. As rock critic Ed Ward suggested: "With 'Sh-Boom,' the pop establishment had found itself a potent weapon to use against R&B records—whiten them up and use the corporate might of a major label to get them to places a hapless [small label] caught with a hit on its hands could never reach."[16]

By 1955, R&B hits regularly crossed over to the pop charts, but inevitably the cover music versions were more successful. Pat Boone's cover of Fats Domino's "Ain't That a Shame" went to No. 1 and stayed on the Top 40's pop chart for twenty weeks, whereas Domino's original made it only to No. 10. During this time, Pat Boone ranked as the king of cover music, with thirty-eight Top 40 songs between 1955 and 1962. His records were second in sales only to Presley's. Slowly, however, the cover situation changed. After watching Boone outsell his song "Tutti-Frutti" in 1956, Little Richard wrote "Long Tall Sally," which included lyrics written and delivered in such a way that he believed Boone would not be able to adequately replicate them. "Long Tall Sally" went to No. 6 for Little Richard and charted for twelve weeks; Boone's version got to No. 8 and stayed there for nine weeks.

Overt racism lingered in the music business well into the 1960s. When the Marvelettes scored a No. 1 hit with "Please Mr. Postman" in 1961, their Tamla/Motown label had to substitute a cartoon album cover because many record-store owners feared customers would not buy a recording that pictured four black women. A turning point, however, came in 1962, the last year that Pat Boone, then age twenty-eight, ever had a Top 40 rock-and-roll hit. That year Ray Charles covered "I Can't Stop Loving You," a 1958 country song by the Grand Ole Opry's Don Gibson. This marked the first time that a black artist, covering a white artist's song, had notched a No. 1 pop hit. With Charles's cover, the rock-and-roll merger between gospel and R&B, on one hand, and white country and pop, on the other, was complete. In fact, the relative acceptance of black crossover music provided a more favorable cultural context for the political activism that spurred important Civil Rights legislation in the mid-1960s.

Payola Scandals Tarnish Rock and Roll

The payola scandals of the 1950s were another cloud over rock and roll music and its artists. In the music industry, **payola** is the practice of record promoters paying deejays or radio programmers to play particular songs. As recorded rock and roll became central to commercial radio's success in the 1950s and the demand for airplay grew enormous, independent promoters hired by record labels used payola to pressure deejays into playing songs by the artists they represented.

Although payola was considered a form of bribery, no laws prohibited its practice. However, following closely on the heels of television's quiz-show scandals (see Chapter 5), congressional hearings on radio payola began in December 1959. After a November announcement of the upcoming hearings, stations across the country fired deejays, and many others resigned. The hearings were partly a response to generally fraudulent business practices, but they were also an opportunity to blame deejays and radio for rock and roll's negative impact on teens by portraying it as a corrupt industry.

The payola scandals threatened, ended, or damaged the careers of a number of rock and roll deejays and undermined rock and roll's credibility for a number of years. In 1959, shortly before the hearings, Chicago deejay Phil Lind decided to clear the air. He broadcast secretly taped discussions in which a representative of a small independent record label acknowledged that it had paid $22,000 to ensure that a record would get airplay. Lind received calls threatening his life and had to have police protection. At the hearings in 1960, Alan Freed admitted to participating in payola, although he said he did not believe there was anything illegal about such deals, and his career soon ended. Dick Clark, then an influential deejay and the host of TV's *American Bandstand*, would not admit to participating in payola. But the hearings committee chastised Clark and alleged that some of his complicated business deals were ethically questionable, which hung over him for years.

Congress eventually added a law concerning payola to the Federal Communications Act, prescribing a $10,000 fine and/or a year in jail for each violation. But given both the interdependence between radio and recording and the high stakes involved in creating a hit, the practice of payola persists. In 2005, for example, Sony BMG and Warner Music paid millions to settle payola cases brought by New York State. (See Chapter 4.)

Fears of Corruption Lead to Censorship

Since rock and roll's inception, one of the uphill battles it faced was the perception that it was a cause of juvenile delinquency. In truth, juvenile delinquency was statistically on the rise in the 1950s. Looking for an easy culprit rather than considering contributing factors such as neglect, the rising consumer culture, or the growing youth population, many assigned blame to rock and roll. The view that rock and roll corrupted youth was widely accepted by social authorities, and rock and roll music was often censored, eventually even by the industry itself.

By late 1959, many key figures in rock and roll had been tamed. Jerry Lee Lewis was exiled from the industry, labeled southern "white trash" for marrying his thirteen-year-old third cousin; Elvis Presley, having already been censored on television, was drafted into the army; Chuck Berry was run out of Mississippi and eventually jailed for gun possession and transporting a minor across state lines; and Little Richard felt forced to tone down his image and leave rock and roll to sing gospel music. A tragic accident led to the final taming of rock and roll's first frontline. In February 1959, Buddy Holly ("Peggy Sue"), Richie Valens ("La Bamba"), and the Big Bopper ("Chantilly Lace") all died in an Iowa plane crash—a tragedy mourned in Don McLean's 1971 hit "American Pie" as "the day the music died."

Although rock and roll did not die in the late 1950s, the U.S. recording industry decided that it needed a makeover. To protect the enormous profits the new music had been generating, record companies began to discipline some of rock and roll's rebellious impulses. In the early 1960s, the industry introduced a new generation of clean-cut white singers, like Frankie Avalon, Connie Francis, Ricky Nelson, Lesley Gore, and Fabian. Rock and roll's explosive violations of racial, class, and other boundaries were transformed into simpler generation gap problems, and the music had developed a milder reputation.

PAT BOONE, the squeaky-clean recording artist who topped the charts with many songs that covered black artists' recordings.

RAY CHARLES (1930–2004) merged the sounds of rhythm & blues, gospel, country, jazz, and pop.

A Changing Industry: Reformations in Popular Music

As the 1960s began, rock and roll was tamer and "safer," as reflected in the surf and road music of the Beach Boys and Jan & Dean, but it was also beginning to branch out. For instance, the success of producer Phil Spector's "girl groups," such as the Crystals ("He's a Rebel") and the Ronettes ("Be My Baby"), and other all-female groups, such as the Shangri-Las ("Leader of the Pack") and the Angels ("My Boyfriend's Back"), challenged the male-dominated world of early rock and roll. In addition, rock and roll music and other popular styles went through cultural reformations that significantly changed the industry, including the international appeal of the "British invasion"; the development of soul and Motown; the political impact of folk-rock; the experimentalism of psychedelic music; the rejection of music's mainstream by punk, grunge, and alternative rock movements; and the reassertion of black urban style in hip-hop.

The British Are Coming!

Rock recordings today remain among America's largest economic exports, bringing in billions of dollars a year from abroad. In cultural terms, the global trade of rock and roll is even more evident in exchanges of rhythms, beats, vocal styles, and musical instruments to and from the United States, Latin America, Europe, Africa, Asia, and Australia/New Zealand. The origin of rock's global impact can be traced to England in the late 1950s, when the young Rolling Stones listened to the urban blues of Robert Johnson and Muddy Waters, and the young Beatles tried to imitate Chuck Berry and Little Richard.

Until 1964, rock-and-roll recordings had traveled on a one-way ticket to Europe. Even though American artists regularly reached the top of the charts overseas, no British performers had yet appeared on any Top 10 pop lists in the States. This changed almost overnight. In 1964, the Beatles invaded America with their mop haircuts and pop reinterpretations of American blues and rock and roll. Within the next few years, more British bands as diverse as the Kinks, the Zombies, the Animals, Herman's Hermits, the Who, the Yardbirds, Them, and the Troggs had hit the American Top 40 charts.

Ed Sullivan, who booked the Beatles several times on his TV variety show in 1964, helped promote their early success. Sullivan, though, reacted differently to the Rolling Stones, who were always perceived by Sullivan and many others as the "bad boys" of rock and roll in contrast to the "good" Beatles. The Stones performed black-influenced music without "whitening" the sound and exuded a palpable aura of sexuality, particularly frontman Mick Jagger. Although the Stones appeared on his program as early as 1964 and returned on several occasions, Sullivan remained wary and forced them to change the lyrics of "Let's Spend the Night Together" to "Let's Spend Some Time Together" for a 1967 broadcast. The band complied, but it had no effect on their "dangerous" reputation, and the Stones would go on to enjoy one of the most successful careers in the history of rock music.

With the British invasion, "rock and roll" unofficially became "rock," sending popular music and the industry in two directions. On the one hand, the Stones would influence generations of musicians emphasizing gritty, chord-driven, high-volume rock, including bands in the glam rock, hard rock, punk, heavy metal, and grunge genres. On the other hand, the Beatles would influence countless artists interested in a more accessible, melodic, and softer sound, in genres such as pop-rock, power-pop, new wave, and alternative rock. In the end, the

British invasion verified what Chuck Berry and Little Richard had already demonstrated—that rock-and-roll performers could write and produce popular songs as well as Tin Pan Alley had. The success of British groups helped change an industry arrangement in which most pop music was produced by songwriting teams hired by major labels and matched with selected performers. Even more importantly, the British invasion showed the recording industry how older American musical forms, especially blues and R&B, could be repackaged as rock and exported around the world.

Motor City Music: Detroit Gives America Soul

Ironically, the British invasion, which drew much of its inspiration from black influences, drew many white listeners away from a new generation of black performers. Gradually, however, throughout the 1960s, black singers like James Brown, Aretha Franklin, Otis Redding, Ike and Tina Turner, and Wilson Pickett found large and diverse audiences. Transforming the rhythms and melodies of older R&B, pop, and early rock and roll into what became labeled as **soul**, they countered the British invaders with powerful vocal performances. Mixing gospel and blues with emotion and lyrics drawn from the American black experience, soul contrasted sharply with the emphasis on loud, fast instrumentals and lighter lyrical concerns that characterized much of rock music.[17]

The most prominent independent label that nourished soul and black popular music was Motown, started in 1959 by former Detroit autoworker and songwriter Berry Gordy with a $700 investment and named after Detroit's "Motor City" nickname. Beginning with Smokey Robinson and the Miracles' "Shop Around," which hit No. 2 in 1960, Motown enjoyed a long string of hit records that rivaled the pop success of British bands throughout the decade. Motown's many successful artists included the Temptations ("My Girl"), Mary Wells ("My Guy"), the Four Tops ("I Can't Help Myself"), Martha and the Vandellas ("Heat Wave"), Marvin Gaye ("I Heard It through the Grapevine"), and, in the early 1970s, the Jackson 5 ("ABC"). But the label's most successful group was the Supremes, featuring Diana Ross, who scored twelve No. 1 singles between 1964 and 1969 ("Where Did Our Love Go," "Stop! In the Name of Love").

BRITISH ROCK GROUPS like the Beatles (above, left) and the Rolling Stones first invaded American pop charts in the 1960s. While the Beatles broke up in 1970, each member went on to work on solo projects. The Stones are still together and touring over forty years later.

The Motown groups had a more stylized, softer sound than the grittier southern soul (later known as funk) of Brown and Pickett. Motown producers realized at the outset that by cultivating romance and dance over rebellion and politics, black music could attract a young, white audience.

Folk and Psychedelic Music Reflect the Times

Popular music has always been a product of its time, so the social upheavals of the Civil Rights movement, the women's movement, the environmental movement, and the Vietnam War naturally brought social concerns into the music of the 1960s and early 1970s. Even Motown acts sounded edgy, with hits like Edwin Starr's "War" (1970) and Marvin Gaye's "What's Goin' On" (1971). By the late 1960s, the Beatles had transformed themselves from a relatively lightweight pop band to one that spoke for the social and political concerns of their generation, and many other groups followed the same trajectory.

Folk Inspires Protest

The musical genre that most clearly responded to the political happenings of the time was folk music, which had long been the sound of social activism. In its broadest sense, **folk music** in any culture refers to songs performed by untrained musicians and passed down mainly through oral traditions, from the banjo and fiddle tunes of Appalachia to the accordion-led zydeco of Louisiana and the folk-blues of the legendary Leadbelly (Huddie Ledbetter). Given its rough edges and amateur quality, folk is considered a more democratic and participatory musical form and often inspires its writers and performers to be more socially aware. During the 1930s, folk was defined by the music of Woody Guthrie ("This Land Is Your Land"), who not only brought folk to the city but also was extremely active in social reforms. Groups such as the Weavers, featuring labor activist and songwriter Pete Seeger, carried on Guthrie's legacy and inspired a new generation of singer-songwriters, including Joan Baez; Arlo Guthrie; Peter, Paul, and Mary; Phil Ochs; and—perhaps the most influential—Bob Dylan.

Dylan's career as a folk artist began with acoustic performances in New York's Greenwich Village in 1961, and his notoriety was spurred by his measured nonchalance and unique nasal voice. Significantly influenced by the blues, Dylan identified folk as "finger pointin'" music that addressed current social circumstances. Quickly he became the voice of folk's new wave of social protest. Then, at a key moment in popular music's history, Dylan walked onstage at the 1965 Newport Folk Festival fronting a full, electric rock band. He was booed and cursed by traditional "folkies," who saw amplified music as a sellout to the commercial recording industry. However, Dylan's move to rock was aimed at reaching a broader and younger constituency, and in doing so he inspired the formation of **folk-rock** artists like the Byrds, who had a No. 1 hit with a cover of Dylan's "Mr. Tambourine Man," and led millions to protest during the turbulent 1960s.

Rock Turns Psychedelic

Alcohol and drugs have long been associated with the private lives of blues, jazz, country, and rock musicians. These links, however, became much more public in the late 1960s and early 1970s, when authorities busted members of the Rolling Stones and the Beatles. With the increasing role of drugs in youth culture and the availability of LSD (not illegal until the mid-1960s), more and more rock musicians experimented with and sang about drugs in what were frequently labeled rock's psychedelic years. Many groups and performers of the *psychedelic* era (named for the mind-altering effects of LSD and other drugs) like the Jefferson Airplane, Big Brother and the Holding Company (featuring Janis Joplin), the Jimi Hendrix Experience, the Doors, and the Grateful Dead (as well as established artists like the Beatles and the Stones) believed that artistic expression could be enhanced by mind-altering drugs. In the past, musicians had not publicized their drug and alcohol habits. The 1960s drug explorations, however, coincided with the free-speech movement, in which taking drugs was seen by many artists and followers as a form of personal expression and a response to the failure of traditional institutions to deal with social and political problems such as racism and America's involvement in the Vietnam War. Although psychedelic rock inspired many to protest the war, participate in peace rallies, and view the world with a greater openness, drug use soon undermined further progress.

After a surge of optimism that culminated in the historic Woodstock concert in August 1969, the psychedelic movement was quickly overshadowed. In 1970, a similar concert at the Altamont racetrack in California started in chaos and ended in tragedy when one of the Hell's Angels hired as a bodyguard for the show murdered a concertgoer. Around the same time, the shocking multiple murders committed by the Charles Manson "family" cast a negative light on hippies, drug use, and psychedelic culture. Then, in quick succession, a number of the psychedelic movement's greatest stars died from drug overdoses, including Janis Joplin, Jimi Hendrix, and Jim Morrison of the Doors.

Punk, Grunge, and Alternative Respond to Mainstream Rock

Considered a major part of the rebel counterculture in the 1960s, rock music in the 1970s was increasingly viewed as just another part of mainstream consumer culture. With major music acts earning huge profits, rock soon became another product line for manufacturers and retailers to promote, package, and sell. Although some rock musicians like Bruce Springsteen and Elton John; glam artists like David Bowie, Lou Reed, and Iggy Pop; and soul artists like Curtis Mayfield and Marvin Gaye continued to explore the social possibilities of rock or at least keep its legacy of outrageousness alive, the radio and sound recording businesses had returned

BOB DYLAN
Born Robert Allen Zimmerman in Minnesota, Bob Dylan took his stage name from Welsh poet Dylan Thomas. He led a folk music movement in the early 1960s with engaging, socially provocative lyrics. He also was an astute media critic, as is evident in the seminal documentary *Don't Look Back* (1967).

"The pump don't work 'cause the vandals took the handles."

BOB DYLAN, "SUBTERRANEAN HOMESICK BLUES," 1965

to marketing music primarily to middle-class white male teens. According to critic Ken Tucker, this situation gave rise to "faceless rock—crisply recorded, eminently catchy," featuring anonymous hits by bands with "no established individual personalities outside their own large but essentially discrete audiences" of young white males.[18] Challenging artists, for the most part, didn't sell records anymore. They had been replaced by "faceless" supergroups like REO Speedwagon, Styx, Boston, and Kansas that could fill up stadiums and entertain the largest number of people with the least amount of controversy. By the late 1970s, rock could only seem to define itself by saying what it wasn't; "Disco Sucks" became a standard rock slogan against the popular dance music of the era.

Punk Revives Rock's Rebelliousness

After a few years, **punk rock** rose in the late 1970s to challenge the orthodoxy and commercialism of the record business. By this time, the glory days of rock's competitive independent labels had ended, and rock music was controlled by just a half-dozen major companies. By avoiding rock's consumer popularity, punk attempted to return to the basics of rock and roll: simple chord structures, catchy melodies, and politically or socially challenging lyrics. The premise was "do it yourself": any teenager with a few weeks of guitar practice could learn the sound and make music that was both more democratic and more provocative than commercial rock.

The punk movement took root in the small dive bar CBGB in New York City around bands such as the Ramones, Blondie, and Talking Heads. (The roots of punk essentially lay in four pre-punk groups from the late 1960s and early 1970s—the Velvet Underground, the Stooges, the New York Dolls, and the MC5—none of whom experienced commercial success in their day.) Punk quickly spread to England, where a soaring unemployment rate and growing class inequality insured the success of socially critical rock. Groups like the Sex Pistols, the Clash, the Buzzcocks, and Siouxsie and the Banshees sprang up and even scored Top 40 hits on the

"Through their raw, nihilistic singles and violent performances, the [Sex Pistols] revolutionized the idea of what rock and roll could be."

STEPHEN THOMAS ERLEWINE, *ALL-MUSIC GUIDE*, 1996

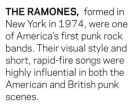

THE RAMONES, formed in New York in 1974, were one of America's first punk rock bands. Their visual style and short, rapid-fire songs were highly influential in both the American and British punk scenes.

U.K. charts. Despite their popularity, the Sex Pistols, one of the most controversial groups in rock history, was eventually banned for offending British decorum.

Punk, which condemned the mainstream music industry, was not a commercial success in the United States, where (not surprisingly) it was shunned by radio. However, punk's contributions continue to be felt. Punk broke down the "boy's club" mentality of rock, launching unapologetic and unadorned front women like Patti Smith, Joan Jett, Debbie Harry, and Chrissie Hynde; and introduced all-women bands (writing and performing their own music) like the Go Go's into the mainstream. It also reopened the door to rock experimentation at a time when the industry had turned music into a purely commercial enterprise. The influence of experimental, or post-punk, is still felt today in popular bands such as Interpol, the Yeah Yeah Yeahs, and Franz Ferdinand.

Grunge and Alternative Reinterpret Rock

Taking the spirit of punk and updating it, the **grunge** scene represented a significant development in rock in the 1990s. Getting its name from its often messy guitar sound and the anti-fashion torn jeans and flannel shirt appearance of its musicians and fans, grunge's lineage can be traced back to 1980s bands like Sonic Youth, the Minutemen, and Husker Du. In 1992, after years of limited commercial success, the younger cousin of punk finally broke into the American mainstream with the success of Nirvana's "Smells Like Teen Spirit" on the album *Nevermind*. Led by enigmatic singer Kurt Cobain–who committed suicide in 1994–Nirvana produced songs that one critic described as "stunning, concise bursts of melody and rage that occasionally spilled over into haunting, folk-styled acoustic ballad."[19] Nirvana opened up the floodgates to bands such as Green Day, Pearl Jam, Soundgarden, the Breeders, Hole, Nine Inch Nails, and many others.

In some critical circles, both punk and grunge are considered subcategories or fringe movements of **alternative rock**, even though grunge was far more commercially successful than punk. This vague label describes many types of experimental rock music that offered a departure from the theatrics and staged extravaganzas of 1970s glam rock, which showcased such performers as David Bowie and Kiss. Appealing chiefly to college students and twentysomethings, alternative rock has traditionally opposed the sounds of Top 40 and commercial FM radio. In the 1980s and 1990s, U2 and R.E.M. emerged as successful groups often associated with alternative rock. A key dilemma for successful alternative performers, however, is that their popularity results in commercial success, ironically a situation that their music often criticizes.

In more recent times, critics argue that alternative rock has fragmented. While rock music has more variety than ever, it is also not producing mega-groups like Nirvana, Pearl Jam, and Green Day. Perhaps, due to the Internet, alternative music is more alternative (that is, less commercial) than ever. With both legal and illegal downloading running rampant today, music fans often go their own ways, discovering independent or unsigned bands on regional Web sites or MySpace. Moreover, as noted earlier, some established rock acts like Radiohead and Nine Inch Nails are taking the "alternative" approach to their business model, shunning major labels and using the Internet to directly reach their fans. Still, alternative groups like Arcade Fire, The National, and Bright Eyes have launched successful recording careers the old-school way, but with a twist: starting out on independent labels, playing small concerts, and growing popular quickly with alternative music audiences through the immediate buzz of the Internet.

NIRVANA'S lead singer, Kurt Cobain, during his brief career in the early 1990s. The release of Nirvana's *Nevermind* in September 1991 bumped Michael Jackson's *Dangerous* from the top of the charts and signaled a new direction in popular music. Other grunge bands soon followed Nirvana onto the charts, including Pearl Jam, Alice in Chains, Stone Temple Pilots, and Soundgarden.

Hip-Hop Redraws Musical Lines

With the growing segregation of radio formats and the dominance of mainstream rock by white male performers, the place of black artists in the rock world diminished from the late 1970s onward. By the 1980s, few popular black successors to Chuck Berry or Jimi Hendrix had emerged in rock, though Michael Jackson and Prince were extremely popular exceptions. These trends, combined with the rise of "safe" dance disco by white bands (the Bee Gees), black artists (Donna Summer), and integrated groups (the Village People), created a space for a new sound to emerge: **hip-hop**, a term for the urban culture that includes *rapping, cutting* (or *sampling*) by deejays, breakdancing, street clothing, poetry slams, and graffiti art.

Similar to punk's opposition to commercial rock, hip-hop music stood in direct opposition to the polished, professional, and often less political world of soul. Its combination of social politics, swagger, and confrontational lyrics carried forward long-standing traditions in blues, R&B, soul, and rock and roll. Like punk, hip-hop was driven by a democratic, nonprofessional spirit—accessible to anyone who could rap or cut records on a turntable. Deejays, like the pioneering Jamaica émigré Clive Campbell (a.k.a. DJ Kool Herc), emerged first in New York, scratching and re-cueing old reggae, disco, soul, and rock albums. These deejays, or MCs (masters of ceremony), used humor, boasts, and "trash talking" to entertain and keep the peace at parties.

Not knowing about the long-standing party tradition, the music industry initially saw hip-hop as a novelty, despite the enormous success of the Sugarhill Gang's "Rapper's Delight" in 1979 (which sampled the bass beat of a disco hit from the same year, Chic's "Good Times"). Then, in 1982, Grandmaster Flash and the Furious Five released "The Message" and forever infused hip-hop with a political take on ghetto life, a tradition continued by artists like Public Enemy and Ice T. By 1985, hip-hop exploded as a popular genre with the commercial successes of groups like Run-DMC, the Fat Boys, and LL Cool J. That year, Run-DMC's album *Raising Hell* became a major crossover hit, the first No. 1 hip-hop album on the popular charts (thanks in part to a collaboration with Aerosmith on a rap version of the group's 1976 hit "Walk This Way"). Like punk and early rock and roll, hip-hop was cheap to produce, requiring only a few mikes, speakers, amps, turntables, and vinyl record albums. With CDs displacing LPs as the main recording format in the 1980s, partially obsolete hardware was "reemployed" for use by hip-hop artists, many of whom had trained in vocational colleges for industrial jobs that evaporated in the 1970s and 1980s. Because most major labels and many black radio stations rejected the rawness of hip-hop, the music spawned hundreds of new independent labels. Although initially dominated by male performers, hip-hop was open to women, and some—Salt-N-Pepa and Queen Latifah among them—quickly became major players. Soon, white groups like the Beastie Boys, Limp Bizkit, and Kid Rock were combining hip-hop and punk rock in a commercially successful way, while Eminem found enormous success emulating black rap artists.

On the one hand, the conversational style of rap makes it a forum in which performers can debate issues of gender, class, sexuality, violence, and drugs. On the other hand, hip-hop, like punk, has often drawn criticism for lyrics that degrade women, espouse homophobia, and applaud violence. In addition, a few hip-hop artists have fought extended battles over copyright infringement, since their music continues to sample rock, soul, funk, and disco. (See Chapter 16.)

Although hip-hop encompasses many different styles, including various Latin and Asian offshoots, its most controversial subgenre is probably **gangster rap**, which, in seeking to tell the truth about gang violence in American culture, has been accused of creating violence. Gangster rap drew national attention in 1996 with the shooting death of Tupac Shakur, who lived the violent life he rapped about on albums like *Thug Life*. Then, in 1997, Notorious B.I.G. (Christopher Wallace, a.k.a. Biggie Smalls), whose followers were prominent suspects in Shakur's death, was shot to death in Hollywood. The result was a change in the hip-hop

industry. Most prominently, Sean "Diddy" Combs led Bad Boy Entertainment (former home of Notorious B.I.G.) away from gangster rap to a more danceable hip-hop that combined singing and rapping with musical elements of rock and soul. Today, hip-hop's stars include artists such as 50 Cent, who emulates the gangster genre, and artists like Kanye West, Lupe Fiasco, Mos Def, and Talib Kweli, who bring an old-school social consciousness to their performances.

From its beginnings as an urban American subculture, hip-hop is now a major part of mainstream global culture. Like rock and roll, hip-hop is big business, and its successful entrepreneurs like Jay-Z, Diddy, Dr. Dre, and Russell Simmons have diversified from record labels to clothing lines, restaurants, and movie production companies. But, like rock and roll, hip-hop's appeal still remains rooted in a cultural style that questions class and racial boundaries and challenges status quo values.

The Business of Sound Recording

For many in the recording industry, the relationship between music's business and artistic elements is an uneasy one. The lyrics of hip-hop or alternative rock, for example, often question the commercial value of popular music. Both genres are built on the assumption that musical integrity requires a complete separation between business and art. But, in fact, the line between commercial success and artistic expression is hazier than simply arguing that the business side is driven by commercialism and the artistic side is free of commercial concerns. The truth, in most cases, is that the business needs artists who are provocative, original, and appealing to the public; and the artists need the expertise of the industry's marketers, promoters, and producers to hone their sound and reach the public. And both sides stand to make a lot of money from the relationship. But such factors as the enormity of the major labels and the complexities of making, selling, and profiting from music affect the business of sound recording.

Music Labels Influence the Industry

After several years of steady growth, revenues for the recording industry experienced significant losses beginning in 2000 as file-sharing began to undercut CD sales. By 2006, U.S. music sales fell to $11.5 billion, down from a peak of $14.5 billion in 1999. The U.S. market accounts for about one-third of global sales, followed by Japan, the United Kingdom, France, Germany, and Canada. Despite the losses, the U.S. and global music business still constitutes a powerful **oligopoly**: a

"The one good thing I can say about file-sharing is it affords us a chance to get our music heard without the label incurring crazy marketing expenses."

GERARD COSLEY, CO-PRESIDENT OF THE INDIE RECORD LABEL MATADOR, 2003

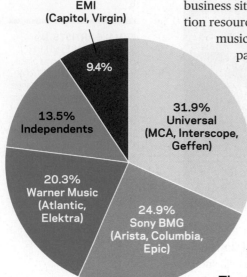

EMI
(Capitol, Virgin)

9.4%

13.5%
Independents

31.9%
Universal
(MCA, Interscope,
Geffen)

20.3%
Warner Music
(Atlantic,
Elektra)

24.9%
Sony BMG
(Arista, Columbia,
Epic)

▲

FIGURE 3.2

**U.S. MARKET SHARE
OF THE MAJOR LABELS
IN THE RECORDING
INDUSTRY, 2007**

*Source: Nielsen SoundScan.
Billboard.com, Jan. 12, 2008.*

"We're on the
threshold of a
whole new system.
The time where
accountants decide
what music people
hear is coming to
an end. Account-
ants may be good
at numbers, but
they have terrible
taste in music."

ROLLING STONES
GUITARIST
KEITH RICHARDS, 2002

business situation in which a few firms control most of an industry's production and distribution resources. This global reach gives these firms enormous influence over what types of music gain worldwide distribution and popular acceptance. (See "What Sony Owns" on page 97.)

Fewer Major Labels Control More Music

From the 1950s through the 1980s, the music industry, though powerful, consisted of a large number of competing major labels, along with numerous independent labels. Over time, the major labels began swallowing up the independents and then buying each other. By 1998, only six major labels remained—Universal, Warner, Sony, BMG, EMI, and Polygram. That year, Universal acquired Polygram, and in 2003 BMG and Sony merged. Today, only four major music corporations remain: Sony BMG Music Entertainment, Universal Music Group, EMI, and Warner Music Group. Together, the four companies control more than 85 percent of the recording industry market in the United States (see Figure 3.2).

The Indies Spot the Trends

In contrast to the four global players, some five thousand large and small independent production houses—or **indies**—record less commercially viable music, or music they hope will become commercially viable. Producing between 11 and 15 percent of America's music, indies often enter into deals with majors to gain wider distribution for their artists. The Internet has also become a low-cost distribution outlet for independent labels, who sell recordings and merchandise and list tour schedules online. (See "Alternative Voices" on page 99.)

The majors frequently rely on indies to discover and initiate distinctive musical trends that first appear on a local level. For instance, indies such as Sugarhill, Tommy Boy, and Uptown emerged in the 1980s to produce regional hip-hop. In the early 2000s, bands of the "indie-rock" movement, such as Yo La Tengo and Arcade Fire, found their home on indie labels Matador and Merge. Once indies become successful, the financial inducement to sell out to a major label is enormous. Seattle indie Sub Pop (Nirvana's initial recording label) sold 49 percent of its stock to Time Warner for $20 million in 1994. However, the punk label Epitaph rejected takeover offers as high as $50 million in the 1990s and remains independent. All four major labels look for and swallow up independent labels that have successfully developed artists with national or global appeal.

Making, Selling, and Profiting from Music

Like most mass media, the music business is divided into several areas, each working in a different capacity. In the music industry, those areas are making the music (signing, developing, and recording the artist), selling the music (selling, distributing, advertising, and promoting the music), and sharing the profits. All of these areas are essential to the industry but have always shared in the conflict between business concerns and artistic concerns.

Making the Music

Labels are driven by **A&R (artist & repertoire) agents**, the talent scouts of the music business, who discover, develop, and sometimes manage artists. A&R executives listen to demonstration tapes, or *demos*, from new artists and decide whom to sign and which songs to record. A&R executives naturally look for artists who they think will sell, and they are often forced to avoid artists with limited commercial possibilities or to tailor artists to make them viable for the recording studio.

A typical recording session is a complex process that involves the artist, the producer, the session engineer, and audio technicians. In charge of the overall recording process, the producer handles most nontechnical elements of the session, including reserving studio space, hiring session musicians (if necessary), and making final decisions about the sound of the recording. The session engineer oversees the technical aspects of the recording session, everything from choosing recording equipment to managing the audio technicians. Most popular records are recorded part by part. Using separate microphones, the vocalists, guitarists, drummers, and other musical sections are digitally recorded onto separate audio tracks, which are edited and remixed during postproduction, and ultimately mixed down to a two-track stereo master copy for reproduction to CD or online digital distribution.

Selling the Music

Selling and distributing music is a tricky part of the business. For years, the primary sales outlets for music were direct-retail record stores (independents or chains such as Sam Goody and Virgin) and general retail outlets like Wal-Mart, Best Buy, and Target. Such direct retailers could specialize in music, carefully monitoring new releases and keeping large, varied inventories. Record stores and general retail stores still account for the majority of music sales. Another 10 percent of recording sales comes from music clubs such as BMG Music Service. Like book clubs, music clubs use advertisements to offer prospective members twelve CDs for the price of one as an incentive to join. In exchange, consumers agree to buy a few CDs at the regular price (about $15 to $19, plus shipping charges). (To explore how personal taste influences music choices, see "Media Literacy and the Critical Process" on page 101.)

In the past decade, the Internet has become a major music retailer in two ways. First, online stores like Amazon.com and Barnes & Noble and independents like Insound sell recordings as part of their media product mix. On these Web sites, customers can listen to music samples as they browse through possible purchases. Second, digital downloading, initially stigmatized by the music industry as the method of copyright violators, is now the fastest-growing segment of music sales. After failed starts by other companies, Apple Computer opened the first successful online music store, iTunes, in 2003, selling songs for just ninety-nine cents each. Since then, the legal music download business (which includes other online stores like eMusic) has flourished. iTunes is now the No. 1 music retailer, and digital sales (which include mobile telephone downloads for songs and ringtones) now account for almost 30 percent of the music market in the United States.[20]

As digital sales have climbed, CD sales have fallen, hurting direct retail sales considerably. In 2006, Tower Records declared bankruptcy, closed its retail locations and became an online-only retailer. Meanwhile, other music-only outlets (especially independent record stores) either went out of business or experienced great losses, and general retail outlets began to offer considerably less variety, stocking only the top-selling CDs.

Adding to the decline in legitimate music sales are unauthorized recordings, which skirt official copyright permissions. Such recordings have been a part of the music industry for much of the twentieth century and include **counterfeiting**—illegal reissues of out-of-print recordings and the unauthorized duplication of manufacturer recordings sold on the black market at cut-rate prices; **bootlegging**—the unauthorized videotaping or audiotaping of live performances, which are then sold illegally for profit; and finally, **online piracy**—unauthorized online file-sharing, as discussed earlier.

Dividing the Profits

The upheaval in the music industry in recent years has shaken up the once predictable (and high) cost of CDs. With general retail outlets now the primary sellers of CDs, the music industry's suggested retail price of $15 to $17 is often not the actual sale price, as stores like Wal-Mart and Best Buy lure customers by selling CDs near wholesale rates, ranging from $9.49 to $12. The pricing of new CDs now varies widely depending on the music label and the retailer. But for the sake of example, we will look at the various costs and profits from a typical CD that retails at

WHAT DOES THIS MEAN?

$16.98. The wholesale price for that CD is about $10.70, leaving the remainder as retail profit. The more heavily discounted the CD, the less retail profit there is. The wholesale price represents the actual cost of producing and promoting the recording, plus the recording label's profits. The record company reaps the highest profit (close to $5.50 on a typical CD) but, along with the artist, bears the bulk of the expenses: manufacturing costs, packaging and CD design, advertising and promotion, and artists' royalties (see Figure 3.3). The physical product of the CD itself costs less than a quarter to manufacture.

New artists usually negotiate a royalty rate of between 8 and 12 percent on the retail price of a CD, while more established performers might negotiate for 15 percent or higher. An artist who has negotiated a typical 11 percent royalty rate would earn about $1.80 per CD whose suggested retail price is $16.98. So, a CD that "goes gold"—that is, sells 500,000 units—would net the artist around $900,000. But out of this amount, artists must repay the record company the money they have been advanced—from $100,000 to $500,000—for recording and music video costs, travel expenses, and promotional efforts. Another $150,000 might have to be set aside in a reserve account to cover any unsold recordings returned by record stores. After band members, managers, and attorneys are paid with the remaining money, it's quite possible that an artist will end up with almost nothing—even after a certified gold CD. (See "Case Study: In the Jungle, the Unjust Jungle, a Small Victory" on page 100.)

In addition to sales royalties, there are also performance and mechanical royalties. A *performance royalty* is paid when the song is played on the radio, television, in a film, a public space, etc. Performance royalties are collected and paid to artists and publishers by the three major music performance rights organizations: The American Society of Composers, Authors, and Publishers (ASCAP); the Society of European Stage Authors and Composers (SESAC); and Broadcast Music, Inc. (BMI). These groups keep track of recording rights, collect copyright fees, and license music for use in commercials and films; on radio, television, and the Internet; and in public places. For example, commercial radio stations pay licensing fees of between 1.5 and 2 percent of their gross annual revenues, and they generally play only licensed music. Large restaurants and offices pay from a few hundred to several thousand dollars annually to play licensed background music.

FIGURE 3.3

WHERE MONEY GOES ON A $16.98 CD

▼

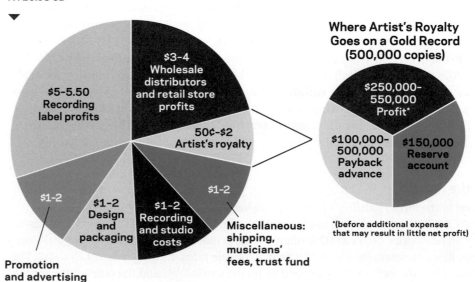

Where Artist's Royalty Goes on a Gold Record (500,000 copies)

$5-5.50 Recording label profits

$3-4 Wholesale distributors and retail store profits

50¢-$2 Artist's royalty

$1-2 Design and packaging

$1-2 Recording and studio costs

$1-2

Promotion and advertising

Miscellaneous: shipping, musicians' fees, trust fund

$250,000-550,000 Profit*

$100,000-500,000 Payback advance

$150,000 Reserve account

*(before additional expenses that may result in little net profit)

Songwriters protect their work by obtaining an exclusive copyright on each song, ensuring that it will not be copied or performed without permission. Then they receive a *mechanical royalty* each time a recording of their song is sold. The mechanical royalty is usually split between the music publisher and the songwriter. However, songwriters sometimes sell their copyrights to music publishers for a short-term profit and forgo the long-term royalties they could receive if they retained the copyright.

The profits are divided somewhat differently in digital download sales. A $0.99 iTunes download generates about $0.33 for iTunes and a standard $0.09 mechanical royalty for the song publisher and writer, leaving about $0.57 for the record company.[21] (See Figure 3.4.) With no CD printing and packaging costs, record companies can retain more of the revenue on download sales. Some record companies retain this entire amount for recordings in which artists have no provisions for digital download royalties in their contract. For more recent contracts, artists typically get royalties for downloads, but the percentage depends on how online sales are defined. Artists prefer a higher royalty rate (about 50 percent) which treats digital down-loads as licensed use of their music—like having it in a television commercial or movie soundtrack. Recording labels prefer a lower rate (about 12 percent) which treats each download as a retail sale. (In a lawsuit against Sony, the Allman Brothers and Cheap Trick argue that they are getting even less—only about $0.045 for each song sold on iTunes.) By 2008, dividing the profits for online sales was in great flux, as the recording industry moved to cut artist and mechanical royalties, publishers attempted to increase mechanical royalties, and artists worked to get a fair share.

Alternative Voices

A vast network of independent (indie) labels, distributors, stores, publications, and Internet sites devoted to music outside of the major label system has existed since the early days of rock and roll. Although not as lucrative as the major label music industry, the indie industry nonetheless continues to thrive, providing music fans access to all styles of music, including some of the world's most respected artists.

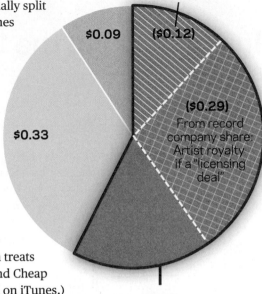

From record company share: Artist royalty if a "retail sale"

$0.09   ($0.12)

$0.33

($0.29) From record company share: Artist royalty if a "licensing deal"

$0.57 Full record company share

- $0.33 - iTunes retains
- $0.09 - Mechanical royalty to publisher/writer
- $0.57 - Net money to record company

FIGURE 3.4

WHERE MONEY GOES ON A $0.99 iTUNES DOWNLOAD

ARCADE FIRE
With their 2004 debut album, *Funeral*, the Canadian rock band Arcade Fire became an international indie rock phenomenon. Started in Montreal, the band is known for "lush, anthemic arrangements and diverse instrumenta-tion, necessitating a larger personnel than a traditional rock band"—which means the band usually has about ten members on stage during concerts. In 2007 the band released a second successful album, *Neon Bible*.

In the Jungle, the Unjust Jungle, a Small Victory

By Sharon Lafraniere

As Solomon Linda first recorded it in 1939, it was a tender melody, almost childish in its simplicity—three chords, a couple of words and some baritones chanting in the background.

But the saga of the song now known worldwide as "The Lion Sleeps Tonight" is anything but a lullaby. It is fraught with racism and exploitation and, in the end, 40-plus years after his death, brings a measure of justice. Were he still alive, Solomon Linda might turn it into one heck of a ballad. Born in 1909 in the Zulu heartland of South Africa, Mr. Linda never learned to read or write, but in song he was supremely eloquent. After moving to Johannesburg in his mid-twenties, he quickly conquered the weekend music scene at the township beer halls and squalid hostels that housed much of the city's black labor force.

He sang soprano over a four-part harmony, a vocal style that was soon widely imitated. By 1939, a talent scout had ushered Mr. Linda's group, the Original Evening Birds, into a recording studio where they produced a startling hit called "Mbube," Zulu for "The Lion." Elizabeth Nsele, Mr. Linda's youngest surviving daughter, said it had been inspired by her father's childhood as a herder protecting cattle in the untamed hinterlands.

From there, it took flight worldwide. In the early fifties, Pete Seeger recorded it with his group, the Weavers. His version differed from the original mainly in his misinterpretation of the word "mbube" (pronounced "EEM-boo-beh"). Mr. Seeger sang it as "wimoweh," and turned it into a folk music staple.

There followed a jazz version, a nightclub version, another folk version by the Kingston Trio, a pop version and finally, in 1961, a reworking of the song by an American songwriter, George Weiss. Mr. Weiss took the last 20 improvised seconds of Mr. Linda's recording and transformed it into the melody. He added lyrics beginning "In the jungle, the mighty jungle." A teen group called the Tokens sang it with a doo-wop beat— and it topped charts worldwide. Some 150 artists eventually recorded the song. It was translated into languages from Dutch to Japanese. It had a role in more than 13 movies. By all rights, Mr. Linda should have been a rich man.

Instead, he lived in Soweto with barely a stick of furniture, sleeping on a dirt floor carpeted with cow dung. Mr. Linda received 10 shillings—about 87 cents today—when he signed over the copyright of "Mbube" in 1952 to Gallo Studios, the company that produced his record. When Mr. Linda died in 1962, at 53, with the modern equivalent of $22 in his bank account, his widow had no money for a gravestone.

How much he should have collected is in dispute. Over the years, he and his family have received royalties for "Wimoweh" from the Richmond Organization, the publishing house that holds the rights to that song, though not as much as they should have, Mr. Seeger said. But where Mr. Linda's family really lost out, his lawyers claim, was in "The Lion Sleeps Tonight," a megahit. From 1991 to 2000, the years when "The Lion King" began enthralling audiences in movie theaters and on Broadway, Mr. Linda's survivors received a total of perhaps $17,000 in royalties, accord-

ing to Hanro Friedrich, the family's lawyer.

The Lindas filed suit in 2004, demanding $1.5 million in damages, but their case was no slam-dunk. Not only had Mr. Linda signed away his copyright to Gallo in 1952, Mr. Dean said, but his wife, who was also illiterate, signed them away again in 1982, followed by his daughters several years later. In their lawsuit, the Lindas invoked an obscure 1911 law under which the song's copyright reverted to Mr. Linda's estate 25 years after his death. On a separate front, they criticized the Walt Disney Company, whose 1994 hit movie "The Lion King" featured a meerkat and warthog singing "The Lion Sleeps Tonight." Disney argued that it had paid Abilene Music for permission to use the song, without knowing its origins.

In February 2006, Abilene agreed to pay Mr. Linda's family royalties from 1987 onward, ending the suit. No amount has been disclosed, but the family's lawyers say their clients should be quite comfortable. ◢

Source: Excerpted from Sharon Lafraniere, "In the Jungle, the Unjust Jungle, a Small Victory," New York Times, March 22, 2006, p. A1.

Media Literacy and the Critical Process

1 DESCRIPTION. Arrange to interview four to eight friends or relatives of different ages about their musical tastes and influences. Devise questions about what music they listen to and have listened to at different stages of their lives. What music do they buy or collect? What's the first album (or single) they acquired? What's the latest album? What stories or vivid memories do they relate to particular songs or artists? Collect demographic and consumer information: age, gender, occupation, educational background, place of birth, and current place of residence.

2 ANALYSIS. Chart and organize your results. Do you recognize any patterns emerging from the data or stories? What kinds of music did they listen to when they were younger? What kinds of music do they listen to now? What formed/ influenced their musical interests? If their musical interests changed, what happened? (If they stopped listening to music, note that and find out why.) Do they have any associations between music and their everyday lives? Are these music associations and lifetime interactions with songs and artists important to them?

Music Preferences across Generations

We make judgments about music all the time. Older generations don't like some of the music younger people prefer, and young people often dismiss some of the music of previous generations. Even among our peers, we have different tastes in music and often reject certain kinds of music that have become too popular or that don't conform to our own preferences. The following exercise aims to understand musical tastes beyond our own individual choices. Always include yourself in this project.

3 INTERPRETATION. Based on what you have discovered and the patterns you have charted, determine what the patterns mean. Does age, gender, geographic location, or education matter in musical tastes? Over time, are the changes in musical tastes and buying habits significant? Why or why not? What kind of music is most important to your subjects? Finally, and most importantly, why do you think their music preferences developed as they did?

4 EVALUATION. Determine how your interview subjects came to like particular kinds of music. What constitutes "good" and "bad" music for them? Did their ideas change over time? How? Are they open- or closed-minded about music? How do they form judgments about music? What criteria did your interview subjects offer for making judgments about music? Do you think their criteria are a valid way to judge music?

5 ENGAGEMENT. To expand on your findings and see how they match up with industry practices, contact music professionals. Track down record label representatives from a small indie label and a large mainstream label and ask them whom they are trying to target with their music. How do they find out about the musical tastes of their consumers? Share your findings with them and discuss whether it matches their practices. Speculate whether the music industry is serving the needs and tastes of you and your interview subjects. If not, what might be done to change the current system?

Independent Record Labels

The rise of rock and roll in the 1950s and early 1960s showcased a rich diversity of independent labels, all vying for a share of the new music. These labels included Sun, Stax, Chess, and Motown. As we discussed above, most of the original indies have folded or have been bought by the major labels. Often struggling enterprises, indies require only a handful of people to operate them. They identify and reissue forgotten older artists and record new innovative performers. To keep costs down, indies usually depend on wholesale distributors to promote and sell their music. Indies may also entrust their own recordings or contracts to independent distributors, who ship new recordings to retail outlets and radio stations. Indies play a major role as the music industry's risk-takers, since major labels are reluctant to invest in lost or commercially unproven artists.

SINGER-SONGWRITER
COLBIE CAILLAT launched
her career by being the most-
played unsigned act on
MySpace.

"The music busi-
ness, as a whole,
has lost its faith in
content."

"The subscription
model is the only
way to save the
music business."

DAVID GEFFEN, MUSIC
MOGUL, 2007

The Internet, MySpace, and Alternative Music

Independent labels have become even more viable by using the Internet as a low-cost distribution and promotional outlet for CD and merchandise sales, fan discussion groups, regular e-mail updates of tour schedules, promotion of new releases, and music downloads. Consequently, bands that in previous years would have signed to a major label have found another path to success in the independent music industry, with labels like Rounder Records (Alison Krauss, Girl Authority) and Matador Records (Cat Power, Mission of Burma). Unlike an artist on a major label needing to sell 500,000 copies or more in order to recoup expenses and make a profit, indie artists "can turn a profit after selling roughly 25,000 copies of an album."[22]

In addition to signing with indies, unsigned artists and bands now build online communities around their personal Web sites–a key self-promotional tool–listing shows, news, tours, photos, downloadable songs, and locations where fans can buy albums. But the biggest new players in the online music scene are social networking sites like MySpace–"the prime convergence point for bands and fans."[23] MySpace and other sites like Facebook, Friendster, MOG, and TagWorld have created spaces for unsigned and signed bands to promote their music (and themselves). Currently, more than three million bands and individual artists use MySpace "to upload songs and videos, announce shows, promote albums and interact with fans." MySpace (owned by media giant News Corp.) has even created its own small record label–MySpace Records. With more than one hundred million active users, MySpace has the power to launch new artists. For example, California singer-songwriter Colbie Caillat set up a MySpace page to feature her music in 2005. After she became the most-played unsigned performer on MySpace, *Rolling Stone* magazine and major labels took notice. In 2007 she was signed to a contract with Universal and became one of the biggest new acts of the year.

Sound Recording, Free Expression, and Democracy

From sound recording's earliest stages as a mass medium, when the music industry began stamping out flat records, to the breakthrough of MP3s and Internet-based music services, fans have been sharing music and pushing culture in unpredictable directions. Sound recordings allowed for the formation of rock and roll, a genre drawing from such a diverse range of musical styles that its impact on culture is unprecedented: Low culture challenged high-brow propriety; black culture spilled into white; southern culture infused the North; masculine and feminine stereotypes broke down; rural and urban styles came together; and artists mixed the sacred and the profane. Attempts to tame music were met by new affronts, including the British invasion, the growth of soul, and the political force of folk and psychedelic music. The gradual mainstreaming of rock led to the establishment of other culture-shaking genres, including punk, grunge, alternative, and hip-hop.

The battle over rock's controversial aspects speaks to the heart of democratic expression. Nevertheless, rock and other popular recordings–like other art forms–also have a history of reproducing old stereotypes: limiting women's access as performers, fostering racist or homophobic attitudes, and celebrating violence and misogyny.

Popular musical forms that test cultural boundaries face a dilemma: how to uphold a legacy of free expression while resisting giant companies bent on consolidating independents and maximizing profits. Since the 1950s, forms of rock music have been breaking boundaries, then becoming commercial, then reemerging as rebellious, and then repeating the pattern. The congressional payola hearings of 1959 and the Senate hearings of the mid-1980s triggered by Tipper Gore's Parents Music Resource Center (which led to music advisory labels) are a few of the many attempts to rein in popular music, whereas the infamous antics of performers from Elvis Presley onwards, the blunt lyrics of artists from rock and roll and rap, and the independent paths of the many garage bands and cult bands of the early rock and roll era through the present are among those actions that pushed popular music's boundaries.

Still, this dynamic between popular music's clever innovations and capitalism's voracious appetite is crucial to sound recording's constant innovation and mass appeal. The major labels need resourceful independents to develop new talent. So, ironically, successful commerce requires periodic infusions of the diverse sounds that come from ethnic communities, backyard garages, dance parties, and neighborhood clubs. At the same time, nearly all musicians need the major labels if they want wide distribution or national popularity. Such an interdependent pattern is common in contemporary media economics.

No matter how it is produced and distributed, popular music endures because it speaks to both individual and universal themes, from a teenager's first romantic adventure to a nation's outrage over social injustice. Music often reflects the personal or political anxieties of a society. It also breaks down artificial or hurtful barriers better than many government programs do. Despite its tribulations, music at its best continues to champion a democratic spirit. Writer and free-speech advocate Nat Hentoff addressed this issue in the 1970s when he wrote: "Popular music always speaks, among other things, of dreams–which change with the times."[24] The recording industry continues to capitalize on and spread those dreams globally, but in each generation, musicians and their fans keep imagining new ones. ▶

"For finally finding a middle ground between the foot-dragging record labels and the free-for-all digital pirates and for creating a bandwagon onto which its competitors immediately jumped, Apple's iTunes Music Store is TIME's Coolest Invention of 2003."

TIME MAGAZINE, 2003

"People seem to need their peers to validate their musical tastes, making the Internet a perfect medium for the intersection of MP3s and mob psychology."

INTERNATIONAL HERALD TRIBUNE, 2008

CHAPTER REVIEW

REVIEW QUESTIONS

The Development of Sound Recording

1. The technological configuration of a particular medium sometimes elevates it to mass market status. Why did Emile Berliner's flat disk replace the wax cylinder, and why did this reconfiguration of records matter in the history of the mass media? Can you think of other mass media examples in which the size and shape of the technology have made a difference?

2. How did sound recording survive the advent of radio?

U.S. Popular Music and the Formation of Rock

3. How did rock and roll significantly influence two mass media industries?

4. Although many rock-and-roll lyrics from the 1950s are tame by today's standards, this new musical development represented a threat to many parents and adults at that time. Why?

5. What moral and cultural boundaries were blurred by rock and roll in the 1950s?

6. Why did cover music figure so prominently in the development of rock and roll and the record industry in the 1950s?

A Changing Industry: Reformations in Popular Music

7. Explain the British invasion. What was its impact on the recording industry?

8. How did soul music manage to survive the British invasion in the 1960s?

9. What were the major influences of folk music on the recording industry?

10. Why did hip-hop and punk rock emerge as significant musical forms in the late 1970s and 1980s? What do their developments have in common, and how are they different?

The Business of Sound Recording

11. What companies control the bulk of worldwide music production and distribution?

12. Why are independent labels so important to the music industry?

13. What are the three types of unauthorized recordings that plague the recording business?

14. What accounts for the cost of a typical CD recording? Where do the profits go? Where does the revenue of an iTunes download go?

Sound Recording, Free Expression, and Democracy

15. Why is it ironic that so many forms of alternative music become commercially successful?

QUESTIONING THE MEDIA

1. Who was your first favorite group or singer? How old were you at the time? What was important to you about this music?

2. If you ran a noncommercial campus radio station, what kind of music would you play and why?

3. Think about the role of the 1960s drug culture in rock's history. How are drugs and alcohol treated in contemporary and alternative forms of rock and hip-hop today?

4. Is it healthy for, or detrimental to, the music business that so much of the recording industry is controlled by four large international companies? Explain.

5. Do you think the Internet as a technology helps or hurts musical artists? Why do so many contemporary musical performers differ in their opinions about the Internet?

6. Do you think the global popularity of rock music is mainly a positive or a negative cultural influence? What are the pros and cons of rock's influence?

For review quizzes, chapter summaries, links
to media-related Web sites, and more, go to
bedfordstmartins.com/mediaculture.

COMMON THREADS

The "Commercial Nature of Mass Media" Common Thread includes the idea of portability—being able to take your media content with you wherever you go. Media technologies have evolved to become increasingly small and portable. But what do portable media mean in terms of cultural expression?

When Apple CEO Steve Jobs introduced the very first iPod in 2001, he said that it would enable you to listen to your music "wherever you go" and that "listening to music will never be the same again." Although iPod users have more recorded music available at their fingertips than ever before, the idea of taking your music "wherever you go" is not a new one. A generation earlier, in the 1980s and 1990s, people used Sony Walkmans and Discmans on their commutes and workouts. Others toted boom box stereos (the bigger, the better) that pumped out the heavy bass lines of hip-hop or rock. In the 1950s, music was made portable with the transistor radio. You didn't have your own music per se, but you did have powerful Top 40 stations, which played the music that mattered. And since Motorola's first car radio in the 1930s, cars have had built-in music. (Car stereo systems today can communicate the deep thump of subwoofers from more than a block away.)

What does it mean to take our music with us, playing it directly to our ears with conspicuous devices, or playing it loud enough that everyone in earshot is aware of our presence and music? Why is it that we need our music with us? Are we connecting ourselves to, or disassociating ourselves from, others?

Portable media doesn't end with sound. In the 1980s, Sony gave the world the Watchman, a handheld television. Today, iPods can store and play movies and TV shows on demand. Satellite television companies offer portable satellite TV dish systems, usable almost anywhere. Cheap, portable DVD players have flooded the market, and a laptop computer connected with WiFi can connect to anything on the Internet.

Which brings us to newspapers, magazines, and the book, the original portable medium. As Chapter 10 explains, since the development of the printing press by Gutenberg in the 1450s, "people could learn for themselves . . . they could differentiate themselves as individuals; their social identities were no longer solely dependent on what their leaders told them or on the habits of their families, communities, or social class."

Is this what the iPod revolution is all about?

KEY TERMS

The definitions for the terms listed below can be found in the glossary at the end of the book. The page numbers listed with the terms indicate where the term is highlighted in the chapter.

4

Popular Radio and the Origins of Broadcasting

In the early 2000s, Clear Channel Communications was at its high point. Just a few years earlier, in 1995, it owned only 39 radio stations, near the maximum number then allowed by the Federal Communications Commission (FCC). But the Telecommunications Act of 1996 overturned most radio ownership rules, and Clear Channel went on a station-buying spree. By 2000, it owned more than 1,000 stations, and within a few more years, it surpassed 1,200, over three times the number of its nearest competitor. It was also the largest billboard company in the world, the nation's largest live music concert promoter, operator of an athlete management firm, owner of 56 television stations, and an investor in 240 radio stations in other countries.

Protestors rally against Clear Channel's consolidation of radio station ownership in 2003.

The corporate world loved the ever-growing communication behemoth, and *Fortune* magazine lauded Clear Channel's business model of domination by naming it to its list of "America's Most Admired Companies" for several consecutive years. Yet, regular radio-listening Americans in places like Atlanta, Chicago, Cincinnati, Denver, Houston, Los Angeles, Phoenix, and Washington, D.C., weren't so admiring of Clear Channel, which owned the majority of their city's major radio stations.

Clear Channel's rise ushered in a new era of homogenized corporate radio, characterized by centralized control and a greater reliance on syndicated radio programming. Citizens and community groups complained about the decline of minority ownership; the lack of musical diversity on the airwaves; the near-disappearance of local radio news; and the replacement of live, local radio deejays with imported or prerecorded announcers.[1] Concerns about Clear Channel inspired a formal grassroots media reform movement in 2002. Citizen pressure forced the FCC to begin public hearings on localism in broadcasting, and more than three million Americans contacted the FCC to oppose further relaxation of media ownership rules.

Ultimately, in its move to make itself into an extraordinary vehicle for advertisers, Clear Channel lost sight of its most precious commodity—listeners—and its duty to operate in the public interest. While Clear Channel was amassing an unprecedented number of radio stations as an advertising vehicle, listeners found homogenized local radio increasingly less relevant to their lives and began migrating to satellite and Internet radio, or their own iPods.

In 2005, just ten years after its meteoric rise began, Clear Channel failed to make *Fortune*'s "Most Admired" list and began to generate revenue by disassembling itself—selling its concert business and its television station group, and offering some of its radio stations for sale. In 2008 it was bought for $24 billion by private equity investors Bain Capital and Thomas H. Lee Partners, and 173 stations were taken off the market. Clear Channel is still the largest radio station chain in the country, with over 1,100 stations.

Still, there remains little diversity in radio station ownership these days. A study indicated that women, who comprise 51 percent of the U.S. population, own just 6 percent of full-power commercial broadcast radio stations. Racial minorities, who make up 33 percent of the country's population, own only 7.7 percent of the stations.[2] Diversity in media ownership is crucial to democracy, argues Loris Taylor, executive director of Native Public Media, an advocacy group for the country's thirty-three American Indian–owned public stations. "If you don't have access and ownership and control of a media system, you really don't exist," she says. "You don't matter in terms of being citizens in a democracy who are entitled to the ability to tell, and have a conversation about, your own stories."[3]

"Clear Channel's rise ushered in a new era of homogenized corporate radio . . ."

◢ **THE STORY OF RADIO FROM ITS INVENTION** in the late nineteenth century to its survival in the age of television is one of the most remarkable in media history. Even with the arrival of TV in the 1950s and the recent "corporatization" of broadcasting, the historical and contemporary roles played by radio have been immense. From the early days of network radio, which gave us "a national identity" and "a chance to share in a common experience,"[4] to the more customized, demographically segmented medium today, radio's influence continues to reverberate throughout our society. Though television displaced radio as our most common media experience, radio specialized and adapted. The daily music and persistent talk that resonate from radios all over the world continue to play a key role in our contemporary culture.

In this chapter, we examine the scientific, cultural, political, and economic factors surrounding radio's development and perseverance. We explore the origins of broadcasting, from the early theories about radio waves to the critical formation of RCA as a national radio monopoly. We then probe the evolution of commercial radio, including the rise of NBC as the first network, the development of CBS, and the establishment of the first federal radio legislation. Reviewing the fascinating ways in which radio reinvented itself in the 1950s, we examine television's impact on radio programming, the invention of FM radio, radio's convergence with sound recording, and the influence of various formats. Finally, we survey the economic health, increasing conglomeration, and cultural impact of commercial and noncommercial radio today, including the emergence of noncommercial low-power FM service.

Early Technology and the Development of Radio

Radio did not emerge as a full-blown mass medium until the 1920s, though it had been evolving for years. The **telegraph**—the precursor of radio technology—was invented in the 1840s. American artist and inventor Samuel Morse developed the first practical system, sending electrical impulses from a transmitter through a cable to a reception point. Using what became known as **Morse code**—a series of dots and dashes that stood for letters in the alphabet—telegraph operators transmitted news and messages simply by interrupting the electrical current along a wire cable. By 1844, Morse had set up the first telegraph line between Washington, D.C., and Baltimore, Maryland. By 1861, telegraph lines ran coast to coast. By 1866, the first transatlantic cable, capable of transmitting about six words a minute, ran between Newfoundland and Ireland along the ocean floor.

Although a revolutionary technology, the telegraph had its limitations. For instance, while it dispatched complicated language codes, it was unable to transmit the human voice. Moreover, ships at sea still had no contact with the rest of the world. As a result, navies could not find out that wars had ceased on land and often continued fighting for months. Commercial shipping interests also lacked an efficient way to coordinate and relay information from land and between ships. What was needed was a telegraph without the wires.

Maxwell and Hertz Discover Radio Waves

The key development in wireless transmissions came from James Maxwell, a Scottish physicist who in the mid-1860s theorized the existence of **electromagnetic waves**: invisible electronic impulses similar to visible light. Maxwell's equations showed that electricity, magnetism, light, and heat are part of the same electromagnetic spectrum and radiate in space at the speed of light, about 186,000 miles per second (see Figure 4.1). Maxwell further theorized that a portion

"The telegraph and the telephone were instruments for private communication between two individuals. The radio was democratic; it directed its message to the masses and allowed one person to communicate with many.

The new medium of radio was to the printing press what the telephone had been to the letter: it allowed immediacy. It enabled listeners to experience an event as it happened."

TOM LEWIS,
EMPIRE OF THE AIR,
1991

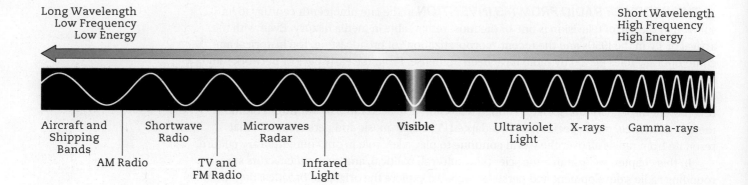

Long Wavelength
Low Frequency
Low Energy

Short Wavelength
High Frequency
High Energy

Aircraft and Shipping Bands | AM Radio | Shortwave Radio | TV and FM Radio | Microwaves Radar | Infrared Light | Visible | Ultraviolet Light | X-rays | Gamma-rays

FIGURE 4.1

THE ELECTROMAGNETIC SPECTRUM

*Source: NASA, http://imagine.gsfc
.nasa.gov/docs/science/know_l1/
emspectrum.html.*

of these phenomena, later known as **radio waves,** could be harnessed so that signals could be sent from a transmission point to a reception point.

It was German physicist Heinrich Hertz, however, who in the 1880s proved Maxwell's theories. Hertz created a crude device that permitted an electrical spark to leap across a small gap between two steel balls. As the electricity jumped the gap, it emitted electromagnetic waves; this was the first recorded transmission and reception of a radio wave. Hertz's experiments significantly advanced the development of wireless communication.

Marconi and the Inventors of Wireless Telegraphy

In 1894, Guglielmo Marconi, a twenty-year-old, self-educated Italian engineer, read Hertz's work and understood that developing a way to send high-speed messages over great distances would transform communication, the military, and commercial shipping. Although revolutionary, the telephone and the telegraph were limited by their wires, so Marconi set about trying to make wireless technology practical. First, he attached Hertz's spark-gap transmitter to a Morse

▼ **Popular Radio and the Origins of Broadcasting**

Samuel Morse
The first telegraph line is set up between Washington, D.C., and Baltimore, Maryland, in 1844. For the first time in history, communication exceeds the speed of land transportation (p. 109).

Guglielmo Marconi
The Italian inventor begins experiments on wireless telegraphy in 1894. He sees his invention as a means for point-to-point communication (p. 110).

Practical Use for Wireless Technology
Wireless operators save 705 lives during the *Titanic* tragedy in 1912, boosting interest in amateur radio across the United States (p. 114).

Commercial Radio
The first advertisements beginning in 1922 cause an uproar as people question the right to pollute the public airwaves with commercial messages (p. 117).

| 1830 | 1850 | 1870 | 1890 | 1910 |

Nikola Tesla
The Serbian-Croatian inventor creates a wireless device in America in 1892. His transmitter can make a tube thirty feet away light up (p. 112).

Lee De Forest
American inventor writes the first dissertation on wireless technology in 1899 and goes on to invent wireless telephony and a means for amplifying radio sound (p. 113).

Wireless Ship Act
In 1910, Congress passes this act requiring that all major ships be equipped with wireless radio (p. 114).

Amateur Radio Shutdown
The navy closes down all amateur radio operations in 1917 to ensure military security as the United States enters World War I (p. 115).

telegraph key, which could send out dot-dash signals. The electrical impulses traveled into a Morse inker, the machine that telegraph operators used to record the dots and dashes onto narrow strips of paper. Second, Marconi discovered that grounding–connecting the transmitter and receiver to the earth–greatly increased the distance over which he could send signals.

In 1896 Marconi traveled to England, where he received a patent on **wireless telegraphy**, a form of voiceless point-to-point communication. In London, in 1897, he formed the Marconi Wireless Telegraph Company, later known as British Marconi, and began installing wireless technology on British naval and private commercial ships. In 1899, he opened a branch in the United States, establishing a company nicknamed American Marconi. That same year, he sent the first wireless Morse code signal across the English Channel to France, and in 1901, he

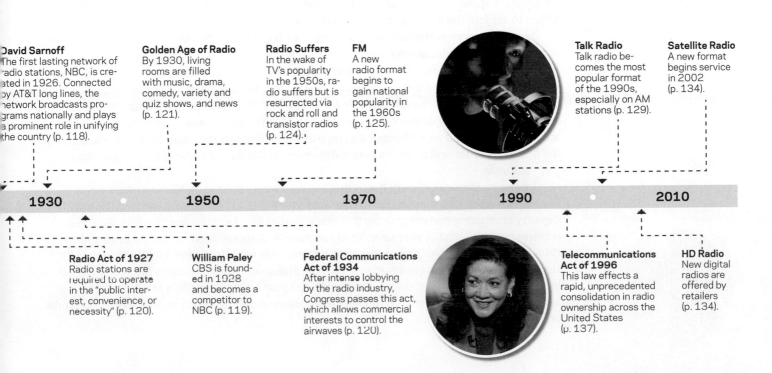

David Sarnoff
The first lasting network of radio stations, NBC, is cre-ated in 1926. Connected by AT&T long lines, the network broadcasts pro-grams nationally and plays a prominent role in unifying the country (p. 118).

Golden Age of Radio
By 1930, living rooms are filled with music, drama, comedy, variety and quiz shows, and news (p. 121).

Radio Suffers
In the wake of TV's popularity in the 1950s, ra-dio suffers but is resurrected via rock and roll and transistor radios (p. 124).

FM
A new radio format begins to gain national popularity in the 1960s (p. 125).

Talk Radio
Talk radio be-comes the most popular format of the 1990s, especially on AM stations (p. 129).

Satellite Radio
A new format begins service in 2002 (p. 134).

1930   **1950**   **1970**   **1990**   **2010**

Radio Act of 1927
Radio stations are required to operate in the "public inter-est, convenience, or necessity" (p. 120).

William Paley
CBS is found-ed in 1928 and becomes a competitor to NBC (p. 119).

Federal Communications Act of 1934
After intense lobbying by the radio industry, Congress passes this act, which allows commercial interests to control the airwaves (p. 120).

Telecommunications Act of 1996
This law effects a rapid, unprecedented consolidation in radio ownership across the United States (p. 137).

HD Radio
New digital radios are offered by retailers (p. 134).

To Prof. A. Slaby with expressions of esteem from Nikola Tesla

NIKOLA TESLA
A double-exposed photograph combines the image of inventor Nikola Tesla reading a book in his Colorado Springs, Colorado, laboratory in 1899 with the image of his Tesla coil discharging several million volts.

relayed the first wireless signal across the Atlantic Ocean. Although Marconi was a successful innovator and entrepreneur, he saw wireless telegraphy only as point-to-point communication, much like the telegraph and the telephone, not as a one-to-many mass medium. He also confined his applications to Morse code messages for military and commercial ships, leaving others to explore the wireless transmission of voice and music.

History often cites Marconi as the "father of radio," but another inventor unknown to him was making parallel discoveries about wireless telegraphy in Russia. Alexander Popov, a professor of physics in St. Petersburg, was experimenting with sending wireless messages over distances just as Marconi was undertaking similar work in Bologna, Italy. Popov announced to the Russian Physicist Society of St. Petersburg on May 7, 1895, that he had transmitted and received signals over a distance of six hundred yards.[5] Yet, Popov was more of an academic than an entrepreneur, and after Marconi accomplished a similar feat that same summer, Marconi was the first to apply for and receive a patent. However, to this day, May 7 is celebrated as "Radio Day" in Russia.

Ironically, the work of both Popov and Marconi was preceded by Nikola Tesla, a Serbian-Croatian inventor who immigrated to New York in 1884. Tesla, who also conceived the high capacity alternating-current systems that made worldwide electrification possible, invented a wireless device in 1892. A year later, Tesla successfully demonstrated his device in an auditorium in St. Louis, with his transmitter causing a receiver tube thirty feet away to light up.[6] However, Tesla is not always associated with the invention of radio because his device did not involve the transmission of sound. But in 1943, the year he died penniless in a New York apartment, the U.S. Supreme Court overturned Marconi's wireless patent and deemed Tesla the original inventor of radio.[7]

Wireless Telephony: De Forest and Fessenden

In 1899, inventor Lee De Forest (who, in defiance of other inventors, liked to call himself the "father of radio") wrote the first Ph.D. dissertation on wireless technology, building on Marconi's innovations. In 1901, De Forest challenged the Italian inventor, who was covering New York's International Yacht Races for the Associated Press, by signing up to report the races for a rival news service. The competing transmitters jammed each other's signals so badly, however, that officials ended up relaying information on the races the traditional way—with flags and hand signals. The event exemplified a problem that would persist throughout radio's early development: noise and interference from competition for the finite supply of radio waves.

In 1902, De Forest set up the Wireless Telephone Company to compete head-on with American Marconi, by then the leader in wireless communication. A major difference between Marconi and De Forest was the latter's interest in wireless voice and music transmissions, later known as **wireless telephony** and eventually radio. Although sometimes an unscrupulous competitor (inventor Reginald Fessenden won a lawsuit against De Forest for using one of his patents without permission), De Forest went on to patent more than three hundred inventions.

De Forest's biggest breakthrough was the development of the Audion, or triode, vacuum tube, which detected radio signals and then amplified them. De Forest's improvements greatly increased listeners' ability to hear dots and dashes and, later, speech and music on a receiver set. His modifications were essential to the development of voice transmission, long-distance radio, and television. In fact, the Audion vacuum tube, which powered radios until the arrival of transistors and solid state circuits in the 1950s, is considered by many historians to be the beginning of modern electronics. But again bitter competition taints De Forest's legacy; although De Forest won a twenty-year court battle for the rights to the Audion patent, most engineers at the time agreed that Edwin Armstrong (who later developed FM radio) was the true inventor and disagreed with the U.S. Supreme Court's final decision on the case in 1934.[8]

The credit for the first voice broadcast belongs to Canadian engineer Reginald Fessenden, formerly a chief chemist for Thomas Edison. Fessenden went to work for the U.S. Navy and eventually for General Electric (GE), where he played a central role in improving wireless signals. Both the navy and GE were interested in the potential for voice transmissions. On Christmas Eve in 1906, after GE built Fessenden a powerful transmitter, he gave his first public demonstration, sending a voice through the airwaves from his station at Brant Rock, Massachusetts. A radio historian describes what happened:

That night, ship operators and amateurs around Brant Rock heard the results: "someone speaking! . . . a woman's voice rose in song. . . . Next someone was heard reading a poem." Fessenden himself played "O Holy Night" on his violin. Though the fidelity was not all that it might be, listeners were captivated by the voices and notes they heard. No more would sounds be restricted to mere dots and dashes of the Morse code.[9]

Ship operators were astonished to hear voices rather than the familiar Morse code. (Some operators actually thought they were having a supernatural encounter.) This allowed wireless telephony to quickly move from a point-to-point communication tool (wireless operator to

> "I discovered an Invisible Empire of the Air, intangible, yet solid as granite."
>
> LEE DE FOREST, INVENTOR

INVENTOR LEE DE FOREST (1873–1961) continued working in his Los Angeles workshop well into the 1950s. His lengthy radio career was marked by incredible innovations, missed opportunities, and poor business practices. In the end, De Forest was upset that radio content had stooped, in his opinion, to such low standards. With a passion for opera, he had hoped radio would be a tool for elite culture. If De Forest were alive today, what might be his reaction to the state of modern radio?

wireless operator) toward a one-to-many communication tool. **Broadcasting**, once an agricultural term that referred to the process of casting seeds over a large area, would come to mean the transmission of radio waves (and, later, TV signals) to a broad public audience. Prior to radio broadcasting, wireless was considered a form of **narrowcasting**, or person-to-person communication, like the telegraph and telephone.

In 1907, De Forest broadcast, via radio, voices and music—actually, a performance by Metropolitan Opera tenor Enrico Caruso—to his friends in New York. The next year, he and his wife, Nora, played records into a microphone from atop the Eiffel Tower in Paris. The signals were picked up four hundred miles away. At this point in time, radio passed from an inventor's toy in the novelty stage to the entrepreneurial stage, where various practical uses would be tested before discovering the application that would launch radio as a mass medium.

NEWS OF THE *TITANIC*
Despite the headline in the *St. Louis Post-Dispatch,* actually 1,523 people died and only 705 were rescued when the *Titanic* hit an iceberg on April 14, 1912 (the ship technically sank at 2:20 A.M. on April 15). The crew of the *Titanic* used the Marconi wireless equipment on board to send distress signals to other ships. Of the eight ships nearby, the *Carpathia* was the first to respond with lifeboats.

Regulating a New Medium

The two most important international issues affecting radio in the 1900s were ship radio requirements and signal interference. Congress passed the Wireless Ship Act in 1910, which required that all major U.S. seagoing ships carrying more than fifty passengers and traveling more than two hundred miles off the coast be equipped with wireless equipment with a one-hundred-mile range. The importance of this act was underscored by the *Titanic* disaster two years later. A brand-new British luxury steamer, the *Titanic* sank in 1912. Although more than fifteen hundred people died in the tragedy, wireless reports played a critical role in pinpointing the *Titanic*'s location, enabling rescue ships to save over seven hundred lives.

Radio Waves as a Natural Resource

In the wake of the *Titanic* tragedy, Congress passed the **Radio Act of 1912,** which addressed the problem of amateur radio operators increasingly cramming the airwaves. Because radio waves crossed state and national borders, legislators determined that broadcasting constituted a "natural resource"—a kind of interstate commerce. This meant that radio waves could not be owned; they were the collective property of all Americans, just like national parks. Therefore, transmitting on radio waves would require licensing in the same way that driving a car requires a license.

A short policy guide, the first Radio Act required all wireless stations to obtain radio licenses from the Commerce Department. This act, which governed radio until 1927, also formally adopted the SOS Morse-code distress signal that other countries had been using for several years. Further, the "natural resource" mandate led to the idea that radio, and eventually television, should provide a benefit to society—in the form of education and public service. The eventual establishment of public radio stations was one consequence of this idea, and the Fairness Doctrine was another.

The Impact of World War I

By 1915, more than twenty American companies sold wireless point-to-point communication systems, primarily for use in ship-to-shore communication. Having established a reputation for efficiency and honesty, American Marconi (a subsidiary of British Marconi) was the biggest and best of these companies. But in 1914, with World War I beginning in Europe and with America warily watching the conflict, the U.S. Navy questioned the wisdom of allowing a foreign-controlled company to wield so much power. American corporations, especially GE and AT&T, capitalized on the navy's xenophobia and succeeded in undercutting Marconi's influence.

As wireless telegraphy played an increasingly large role in military operations, the navy sought tight controls on information. When the United States entered the war in 1917, the navy closed down all amateur radio operations and took control of key radio transmitters to ensure military security. As the war was nearing its end in 1919, British Marconi placed an order with GE for twenty-four potent new alternators, which were strong enough to power a transoceanic system of radio stations that could connect the world. But the U.S. Navy–influenced by Franklin Roosevelt, at that time the navy's assistant secretary–grew concerned and moved to ensure that such powerful new radio technology would not fall under foreign control.

Roosevelt was guided in turn by President Woodrow Wilson's goal of developing the United States as an international power, a position greatly enhanced by American military successes during the war. Wilson and the navy saw an opportunity to slow Britain's influence over communication and to promote a U.S. plan for the control of the emerging wireless operations. Thus corporate heads and government leaders conspired to make sure radio communication would serve American interests.

The Formation of RCA

Some members of Congress and the corporate community opposed federal legislation that would grant the government or the navy a radio monopoly. Consequently, GE developed a compromise plan that would create a *private sector monopoly*–that is, a private company that would have the government's approval to dominate the radio industry. First, GE broke off negotiations to sell key radio technologies to European-owned companies like British Marconi, thereby limiting those companies' global reach. Second, GE took the lead in founding a new company, **Radio Corporation of America (RCA),** which soon acquired American Marconi and radio patents of other U.S. companies. Upon its founding in 1919, RCA had pooled the necessary technology and patents to monopolize the wireless industry and expand American communication technology throughout the world.[10]

Under RCA's patents pool arrangement, wireless patents from the navy, AT&T, GE, the former American Marconi, and other companies were combined to ensure U.S. control over the manufacture of radio transmitters and receivers. Initially, AT&T, then the government-sanctioned monopoly provider of telephone services, manufactured most transmitters, while GE (and later Westinghouse) made radio receivers. RCA administered the pool, collecting patent royalties and distributing them to pool members. To protect these profits, the government did not permit RCA to manufacture equipment or to operate radio stations under its own name for several years. Instead, RCA's initial function was to ensure that radio parts were standardized by manufacturers and to control frequency interference by amateur radio operators, which increasingly became a problem after the war.

WIRELESS RADIO
A radio operator at the controls in Minnesota (left), in October 1923. In that year, only about a half million U.S. households had a radio receiver to hear the signals. Within two years, more than five million households would own radios (right).

A government restriction at the time mandated that no more than 20 percent of RCA—and eventually any U.S. broadcasting facility—could be owned by foreigners. This restriction, later raised to 25 percent, became law in 1927 and applied to all U.S. broadcasting stocks and facilities. It is because of this rule that in 1985 Rupert Murdoch, the head of Australia's giant News Corp., became a U.S. citizen so he could buy a number of TV stations and form the Fox television network.

RCA's most significant impact was that it gave the United States almost total control over the emerging mass medium of broadcasting. At the time, the United States was the only country that placed broadcasting under the care of commercial, rather than military or government, interests. By pooling more than two thousand patents and sharing research developments, RCA ensured the global dominance of the United States in mass communication, a position it maintained in electronic hardware into the 1960s and maintains in program content today.

The Evolution of Radio

> "I believe the quickest way to kill broadcasting would be to use it for direct advertising."
>
> HERBERT HOOVER, SECRETARY OF COMMERCE, 1924

When Westinghouse engineer Frank Conrad set up a crude radio studio above his Pittsburgh garage in 1916, placing a microphone in front of a phonograph to broadcast music and news to his friends (whom Conrad supplied with receivers) two evenings a week on experimental station 8XK, he unofficially became one of the medium's first disc jockeys. In 1920, a Westinghouse executive, intrigued by Conrad's curious hobby, realized the potential of radio as a mass medium. Westinghouse then established station KDKA, which is generally regarded as the first commercial broadcast station. KDKA is most noted for airing national returns from the Cox-Harding presidential election on November 2, 1920, an event most historians consider the first professional broadcast.

Other amateur broadcasters could also lay claim to being first. One of the earliest stations, operated by Charles "Doc" Herrold in San Jose, California, began in 1909 and later became KCBS. Additional experimental stations—in places like New York; Detroit; Medford, Massachusetts; and Pierre, South Dakota—broadcast voice and music prior to the establishment of KDKA. But KDKA's success, with the financial backing of Westinghouse, signaled the start of broadcast radio.

In 1921, the U.S. Commerce Department officially licensed five radio stations for operation; by early 1923, more than six hundred commercial and noncommercial stations were operating. Some stations were owned by AT&T, GE, and Westinghouse, but many were run by amateurs or were independently owned by universities or businesses. By the end of 1923, as many as 550,000 radio receivers, most manufactured by GE and Westinghouse, had been sold for about $55 each (about $664 in today's dollars). Just as the "guts" of the phonograph had been put inside a piece of furniture to create a consumer product, the vacuum tubes, electrical posts, and bulky batteries that made up the radio receiver were placed inside stylish furniture and marketed to households. By 1925, 5.5 million radio sets were in use across America, and radio was officially a mass medium.

The RCA Partnership Unravels

In 1922, in a major power grab, AT&T, which already had a government-sanctioned monopoly in the telephone business, decided to break its RCA agreements in an attempt to monopolize radio as well. Identifying the new medium as the "wireless telephone," AT&T argued that broadcasting was merely an extension of its control over the telephone. Ultimately, the corporate giant complained that RCA had gained too much monopoly power. In violation of its early agreements with RCA, AT&T began making and selling its own radio receivers.

In the same year, AT&T started WEAF (now WNBC) in New York, the first radio station to regularly sell commercial time to advertisers. AT&T claimed that under the RCA agreements, it had the exclusive right to sell ads, which AT&T called *toll broadcasting*. Most people in radio at the time recoiled at the idea of using the medium for crass advertising, viewing it instead as a public information service. In fact, stations that had earlier tried to sell ads received "cease and desist" letters from the Department of Commerce. But by August 1922, AT&T had nonetheless sold its first ad to a New York real estate developer for $50. The idea of promoting the new medium as a public service, along the lines of today's noncommercial National Public Radio (NPR), ended when executives realized that radio ads offered another opportunity for profits. Advertising would ensure profits long after radio-set sales had saturated the consumer market.

The initial strategy behind AT&T's toll broadcasting idea was an effort to conquer radio. By its agreements with RCA, AT&T retained the rights to interconnect the signals between two or more radio stations via telephone wires. In 1923, when AT&T aired a program simultaneously on its flagship WEAF station and on WNAC in Boston, the phone company created the first **network**: a cost-saving operation that links (at that time, through special phone lines and, today, through satellite relays) a group of broadcast stations that share programming produced at a central location. By the end of 1924, AT&T had interconnected twenty-two stations to air a talk by President Calvin Coolidge. Some of these stations were owned by AT&T, but most simply consented to become AT&T "affiliates," agreeing to air the phone company's programs. These network stations informally became known as the *telephone group* and later as the Broadcasting Corporation of America (BCA).

In response, GE, Westinghouse, and RCA interconnected a smaller set of competing stations, known as the *radio group*. Initially, their network linked WGY in Schenectady, New York (then GE's national headquarters), and WJZ in Manhattan. The radio group had to use inferior Western Union telegraph lines when AT&T denied them access to telephone wires. By this time, AT&T had sold its stock in RCA and refused to lease its lines to competing radio networks. The telephone monopoly was now enmeshed in a battle to defeat RCA for control of radio.

This clash, among other problems, eventually led to a government investigation and an arbitration settlement in 1925. In the agreement, the Justice Department, irritated by AT&T's power grab, redefined patent agreements. AT&T received a monopoly on providing the wires, known as *long lines*, to interconnect stations nationwide. In exchange, AT&T sold its BCA network to RCA for $1 million and agreed not to reenter broadcasting for eight years (a banishment that actually extended into the 1990s).

Sarnoff and NBC: Building the "Blue" and "Red" Networks

After Lee De Forest, David Sarnoff was among the first to envision wireless telegraphy as a modern mass medium. From the time he served as Marconi's personal messenger (at age fifteen), Sarnoff rose rapidly at American Marconi. He became a wireless operator, helping to relay information about the *Titanic* survivors in 1912. Promoted to a series of management positions, Sarnoff was closely involved in RCA's creation in 1919, when most radio executives

WESTINGHOUSE ENGINEER FRANK CONRAD
Broadcasting from his garage, Conrad turned his hobby into Pittsburgh's KDKA, one of the first radio stations. Although this early station is widely celebrated in history books as the first broadcasting outlet, one can't underestimate the influence Westinghouse had in promoting this "historical first." Westinghouse clearly saw the celebration of Conrad's garage as a way to market the company and its radio equipment. The resulting legacy of Conrad's garage has thus overshadowed other individuals who also experimented with radio broadcasting.

saw wireless merely as point-to-point communication. But with Sarnoff as RCA's first commercial manager, radio's potential as a mass medium was quickly realized. In 1921, at age thirty, Sarnoff became RCA's general manager.

After RCA bought AT&T's telephone group network (BCA), Sarnoff created a new subsidiary in September 1926 called the National Broadcasting Company (NBC). Its ownership was shared by RCA (50 percent), General Electric (30 percent), and Westinghouse (20 percent). This loose network of stations would be hooked together by AT&T long lines. Shortly thereafter, the original telephone group became known as the NBC-Red network, and the radio group (the network previously established by RCA, GE, and Westinghouse) became the NBC-Blue network.

Although NBC owned a number of stations by the late 1920s, many independent stations also began affiliating with the NBC networks to receive programming. An affiliate station, though independently owned, signs a contract to be part of a network and receives money to carry the network's programs. In exchange, the network reserves time slots, which it sells to national advertisers. By 1933, NBC-Red had twenty-eight affiliates and NBC-Blue had twenty-four.

Recall that the rationale behind a network is an economic one: A network enables stations to control program costs and avoid unnecessary duplication. As early as 1923, AT&T had realized that it would be cheaper to produce programs at one station and broadcast them simultaneously over a network of owned or affiliated stations than for each station to generate its own programs. Such a network centralized costs and programming by bringing the best musical, dramatic, and comedic talent to one place, where programs could be produced and then distributed all over the country.

Network radio may actually have helped modernize America by de-emphasizing the local and the regional in favor of national programs broadcast to nearly everyone. For example, when Charles Lindbergh returned from the first solo transatlantic flight in 1927, an estimated twenty-five to thirty million people listened to his welcome-home party on the six million radio sets then in use. At the time, it was the largest shared audience experience in the history of any mass medium.

David Sarnoff's leadership at RCA was capped by two other negotiations that solidified his stature as the driving force behind radio's development as a modern medium. In 1929, Sarnoff cut a deal with General Motors for the manufacture of car radios, which had been invented a year earlier by William Lear (later the designer of the Learjet), who sold the radios under the brand name Motorola. Sarnoff also merged RCA with the Victor Talking Machine Company. Afterward, until the mid-1960s, the company was known as RCA Victor, adopting as its corporate symbol the famous terrier sitting alertly next to a Victrola radio-phonograph. The merger gave RCA control over Victor's records and recording equipment, making the radio company a major player in the sound recording industry. In 1930, David Sarnoff became president of RCA, and he ran it for the next forty years.

Government Scrutiny Ends RCA-NBC Monopoly

As early as 1923, the Federal Trade Commission had charged RCA with violations of antitrust laws but allowed the monopoly to continue. By the late 1920s, the government, concerned about NBC's growing control over radio content, intensified its scrutiny. Then, in 1930, when RCA bought GE and Westinghouse's interests in the two NBC networks, federal marshals charged RCA/NBC with a number of violations, including exercising too much control over manufacturing and programming. Although the government had originally sanctioned a closely supervised monopoly for wireless communication, RCA products, its networks, and the growth of the new mass medium dramatically changed the radio industry by the late 1920s. After the collapse of the stock market in 1929, the public became increasingly distrustful of big business. In 1932, the government revoked RCA's monopoly status.

RCA acted quickly. To eliminate its monopolizing partnerships, Sarnoff's company bought out GE's and Westinghouse's remaining shares in RCA's manufacturing business. Now RCA would compete directly against GE, Westinghouse, and other radio manufacturers, encouraging more competition in the radio manufacturing industry. Ironically, in the mid-1980s, GE bought RCA, a shell of its former self and no longer competitive with foreign electronics firms.[11] GE was chiefly interested in RCA's brand-name status and its still-lucrative subsidiary, NBC.

CBS and Paley: Challenging NBC

Even with RCA's head start and its favored status, the two NBC networks faced competitors in the late 1920s. The competitors, however, all found it tough going. One group, United Independent Broadcasters (UIB), even lined up twelve prospective affiliates and offered them $500 a week for access to ten hours of station time in exchange for quality programs. UIB was cash-poor, however, and AT&T would not rent the new company its lines to link the affiliates.

Enter the Columbia Phonograph Company, which was looking for a way to preempt RCA's merger with the Victor Company, then the record company's major competitor. With backing from Columbia, UIB launched the new Columbia Phonograph Broadcasting System, a wobbly sixteen-affiliate network in 1927, nicknamed CPBS. But after losing $100,000 in the first month, the record company pulled out. Later, CPBS dropped the word *Phonograph* from its title, creating the Columbia Broadcasting System (CBS).

In 1928, William Paley, the twenty-seven-year-old son of Sam Paley, owner of a Philadelphia cigar company, bought a controlling interest in CBS to sponsor their cigar brand, La Palina. One of Paley's first moves was to hire the public relations pioneer (and Sigmund Freud's nephew) Edward Bernays to polish the new network's image. (Bernays played a significant role in the development of the public relations industry; see Chapter 12.) Paley and Bernays modified a concept called **option time**, in which CBS paid affiliate stations $50 per hour for an option on a portion

WILLIAM S. PALEY (left) ran CBS for more than fifty years. He first took control of the struggling radio network in 1928, saw CBS through its transition into TV, and helped earn CBS the label "Tiffany Network" for his early support of quality programming and network news. But he was also criticized for undermining his news division to sidestep controversy or to increase profits.

of their time. The network provided programs to the affiliates and sold ad space or sponsorships to various product companies. In theory, CBS could now control up to twenty-four hours a day of its affiliates' radio time. Some affiliates received thousands of dollars per week merely to serve as conduits for CBS programs and ads. Because NBC was still charging some of its affiliates as much as $96 a week to carry its network programs, the CBS offer was extremely appealing.

By 1933, Paley's efforts had netted CBS more than ninety affiliates, many of them defecting from NBC. Paley also concentrated on developing news programs and entertainment shows, particularly soap operas and comedy-variety series. In the process, CBS successfully raided NBC, not just for affiliates but for top talent as well. Throughout the 1930s and 1940s, Paley lured a number of radio stars from NBC, including Jack Benny, Frank Sinatra, George Burns, Gracie Allen, and Groucho Marx. During World War II, Edward R. Murrow's powerful firsthand news reports from bomb-riddled London established CBS as the premier radio news network, a reputation it carried forward to television. In 1949, near the end of big-time network radio, CBS finally surpassed NBC as the highest-rated network. Although William Paley had intended to run CBS only for six months to help get it off the ground, he ultimately ran it for more than fifty years.

Bringing Order to Chaos with the Radio Act of 1927

In the 1920s, as radio moved from narrowcasting to broadcasting, the battle for more frequency space and less channel interference intensified. Manufacturers, engineers, station operators, network executives, and the listening public demanded action. Many wanted more sweeping regulation than the simple licensing function granted under the Radio Act of 1912, which gave the Commerce Department little power to deny a license or to unclog the airwaves.

Beginning in 1924, Commerce Secretary Herbert Hoover ordered radio stations to share time by setting aside certain frequencies for entertainment and news and others for farm and weather reports. To challenge Hoover, a station in Chicago jammed the airwaves, intentionally moving its signal onto an unauthorized frequency. In 1926, the courts decided that based on the existing Radio Act, Hoover had the power only to grant licenses, not to restrict stations from operating. Within the year, two hundred new stations clogged the airwaves, creating a chaotic period in which nearly all radios had poor reception. By early 1927, sales of radio sets had declined sharply.

To restore order to the airwaves, Congress passed the **Radio Act of 1927**, which stated an extremely important principle–licensees did not *own* their channels but could only license them as long as they operated to serve the "public interest, convenience, or necessity." To oversee licenses and negotiate channel problems, the 1927 act created the **Federal Radio Commission (FRC)**, whose members were appointed by the president. Although the FRC was intended as a temporary committee, it grew into a powerful regulatory agency. In 1934, with passage of the **Federal Communications Act of 1934**, the FRC became the **Federal Communications Commission (FCC)**. Its jurisdiction covered not only radio but also the telephone and the telegraph (and later television, cable, and the Internet). More significantly, by this time Congress and the president had sided with the already-powerful radio networks and acceded to a system of advertising-supported commercial broadcasting as best serving "public interest, convenience or necessity," overriding the concerns of educational, labor, and citizen broadcasting advocates.[12] (See Table 4.1.)

In 1941, an activist FCC went after the networks. Declaring that NBC and CBS could no longer force affiliates to carry programs they did not want, the government outlawed the practice of option time that Paley had used to build CBS into a major network. The FCC also demanded that RCA sell one of its two NBC networks. RCA and NBC claimed that the rulings would bankrupt them. The Supreme Court sided with the FCC, however, and RCA eventually

Act	Provisions	Effects
Wireless Ship Act of 1910	Required U.S. seagoing ships carrying more than fifty passengers and traveling more than two hundred miles off the coast to be equipped with wireless equipment with a one-hundred-mile range.	Saved lives at sea, including more than seven hundred rescued by ships responding to the *Titanic*'s distress signals two years later.
Radio Act of 1912	Required radio operators to obtain a license, gave the Commerce Department the power to deny a license, and began a uniform system of assigning call letters to identify stations.	The federal government begins to assert control over radio. Penalties established for stations that interfere with other stations' signals.
Radio Act of 1927	Established the Federal Radio Commission (FRC) as a temporary agency to oversee licenses and negotiate channel assignments.	First expressed the now-fundamental principle that licensees did not *own* their channels but could only license them as long as they operated to serve the "public interest, convenience, or necessity."
Communications Act of 1934	Established the Federal Communications Commission (FCC) to replace the FRC. The FCC regulated radio, the telephone, the telegraph, and later television, cable, and the Internet.	Congress tacitly agrees to a system of advertising-supported commercial broadcasting despite concerns of the public.
Telecommunications Act of 1996	Eliminated most radio and television station ownership rules, some dating back more than fifty years.	Enormous national and regional station groups form, dramatically changing the sound and localism of radio in the United States.

sold NBC-Blue to a group of businessmen for $8 million in the mid-1940s. It became the American Broadcasting Company (ABC). These government crackdowns brought long-overdue reform to the radio industry, but they had not come soon enough to prevent considerable damage to noncommercial radio.

TABLE 4.1
MAJOR ACTS IN THE HISTORY OF U.S. RADIO

The Golden Age of Radio

Many programs on television today were initially formulated for radio. The first weather forecasts and farm reports on radio began in the 1920s. Regularly scheduled radio news analysis started in 1927, with H. V. Kaltenborn, a reporter for the *Brooklyn Eagle,* providing commentary on AT&T's WEAF. The first regular network news analysis began on CBS in 1930, featuring Lowell Thomas, who would remain on radio for forty-four years.

Early Radio Programming

Early on, only a handful of stations operated in most large radio markets, and popular stations were affiliated with CBS, NBC-Red, or NBC-Blue. Many large stations employed their own in-house orchestras and aired live music daily. Listeners had favorite evening programs, usually fifteen minutes long, to which they would tune in each night. Families gathered around the radio to hear such shows as *Amos 'n' Andy, The Shadow, The Lone Ranger, The Green Hornet,* and *Fibber McGee and Molly,* or one of President Franklin Roosevelt's fireside chats.

Among the most popular early programs on radio, the variety show was the forerunner to popular TV shows like the *Ed Sullivan Show*. The variety show, developed from stage acts and vaudeville, began with the *Eveready Hour* in 1923 on WEAF. Considered experimental, the program presented classical music, minstrel shows, comedy sketches, and dramatic readings. Stars from vaudeville, musical comedy, and New York theater and opera would occasionally make guest appearances.

By the 1930s, studio-audience quiz shows—*Professor Quiz* and the *Old Time Spelling Bee*—had emerged. Other quiz formats, used on *Information Please* and *Quiz Kids,* featured guest panelists. The quiz formats were later copied by television, particularly in the 1950s. *Truth or Consequences,* based on a nineteenth-century parlor game, first aired on radio in 1940 and featured guests performing goofy stunts. It ran for seventeen years on radio and another

"Adolf Hitler, the German fascist chief, is snorting fire. There are now two Mussolinis in the world, which seems to offer a rousing time."

LOWELL THOMAS'S FIRST REPORT FOR CBS IN 1930

"There are three
things which I shall
never forget about
America—the
Rocky Mountains,
Niagara Falls, and
Amos 'n' Andy."

GEORGE BERNARD
SHAW, IRISH
PLAYWRIGHT

twenty-seven on television, influencing TV stunt shows like CBS's *Beat the Clock* in the 1950s and NBC's *Fear Factor* in the early 2000s.

Dramatic programs, mostly radio plays that were broadcast live from theaters, developed as early as 1922. Historians mark the appearance of *Clara, Lu, and Em* on WGN in 1931 as the first soap opera. One year later, Colgate-Palmolive bought the program, put it on NBC, and began selling the soap products that gave this dramatic genre its distinctive nickname. Early "soaps" were fifteen minutes in length and ran five or six days a week. It wasn't until mid-1960s television that soaps were extended to thirty minutes, and by the late 1970s, some had expanded to sixty minutes. Still a fixture on CBS, *Guiding Light* actually began on radio in 1937 and moved to television in 1952 (the only radio soap to successfully make the transition). By 1940, sixty different soap operas occupied nearly eighty hours of network radio time each week.

Most radio programs had a single sponsor that created and produced each show. The networks distributed these programs live around the country, charging the sponsors advertising fees. Many shows—the *Palmolive Hour, General Motors Family Party,* the *Lucky Strike Orchestra,* and the *Eveready Hour* among them—were named after the sole sponsor's product.

Radio Programming as a Cultural Mirror

The situation comedy, a major staple of TV programming today, began on radio in the mid-1920s. By the early 1930s, the most popular comedy was *Amos 'n' Andy,* which started on Chicago radio in 1925 before moving to NBC-Blue in 1929. *Amos 'n' Andy* was based on the conventions of the nineteenth-century minstrel show and featured black characters stereotyped as shiftless and

▲

**RADIO BRINGS
ADVENTURE HOME**
Aviator Amelia Earhart was
one of a number of people
to speak via radio with
explorer Richard Byrd and
his expedition team as they
explored the Antarctic in
1929. These conversations
were broadcast to the
American public every two
weeks. The Byrd expedition
(1928-30) brought the
novelty of advanced radio
systems to a captivated
home audience.

stupid. Created as a blackface stage act by two white comedians, Charles Correll and Freeman Gosden, the program was criticized as racist. But NBC and the program's producers claimed that *Amos 'n' Andy* was as popular among black audiences as among white listeners.[13]

    Amos 'n' Andy also launched the idea of the serial show: a program that featured continuing story lines from one day to the next. The format was soon copied by soap operas and other radio dramas. The show aired six nights a week from 7:00 to 7:15 P.M. During the show's first year on the network, radio-set sales rose nearly 25 percent nationally. To keep people coming to restaurants and movie theaters, owners broadcast *Amos 'n' Andy* in lobbies, rest rooms, and entryways. Early radio research estimated that the program aired in more than half of all radio homes in the nation during the 1930-31 season, making it the most popular radio series in history. In 1951 it made a brief transition to television (Correll and Gosden sold the rights to CBS for $1 million), becoming the first TV series to have an entirely black cast. But, amidst a strengthening Civil Rights movement and a formal protest by the NAACP (it argued that "every character is either a clown or a crook"), CBS canceled the program in 1953.[14]

The Authority of Radio

The most famous single radio broadcast of all time was an adaptation of H. G. Wells's *War of the Worlds* on the radio series *Mercury Theater of the Air*. Orson Welles produced, hosted, and acted in this popular series, which adapted science fiction, mystery, and historical adventure dramas for radio. On Halloween eve in 1938, the twenty-three-year-old Welles aired the 1898 Martian invasion novel in the style of a radio news program. For people who missed the opening disclaimer, the program sounded like a real news report, with eyewitness accounts of battles between Martian invaders and the U.S. Army.

    The program created a panic that lasted several hours. In New Jersey, some people walked through the streets with wet towels around their heads for protection from deadly Martian heat rays. In New York, young men reported to their National Guard headquarters to prepare for battle.

EARLY RADIO'S EFFECT AS A MASS MEDIUM
On Halloween eve in 1938, Orson Welles's radio dramatization of *War of the Worlds* (*left*) created a panic up and down the East Coast, especially in Grover's Mill, New Jersey—the setting for the fictional Martian invasion that many listeners assumed was real. A seventy-six-year-old Grover's Mill resident (*right*) guards a warehouse against alien invaders.

Across the nation, calls jammed police switchboards. Afterward, Orson Welles, once the radio voice of *The Shadow*, used the notoriety of this broadcast to launch a film career. Meanwhile, the FCC called for stricter warnings both before and during programs that imitated the style of radio news.

Radio Reinvents Itself

Older media forms do not generally disappear when confronted by newer forms. Instead, they adapt. Although radio threatened sound recording in the 1920s, the recording industry adjusted to the economic and social challenges posed by radio's arrival. Remarkably, the arrival of television in the 1950s marked the only time in media history in which a new medium stole virtually every national programming and advertising strategy from an older medium. Television snatched radio's advertisers, program genres, major celebrities, and large evening audiences. The TV set even physically displaced the radio as the living room centerpiece across America. Nevertheless, radio adapted and continued to reach an audience.

The story of radio's evolution and survival is especially important today, as newspapers and magazines appear online and as publishers produce audio books and e-books for new generations of "readers." In contemporary culture, we have grown accustomed to such media convergence, but to best understand this blurring of the boundaries between media forms, it is useful to look at the 1950s and the ways in which radio responded to the advent of television.

Transistors Make Radio Portable

A key development in radio's adaptation to television occurred with the invention of the transistor by Bell Laboratories in 1947. **Transistors** were small electrical devices that, like vacuum tubes, could receive and amplify radio signals. However, they used less power and heat than vacuum tubes, and they were more durable and less expensive. Best of all, they were tiny.

Transistors, which also revolutionized hearing aids, constituted the first step in replacing bulky and delicate tubes, leading eventually to today's integrated circuits.

Texas Instruments marketed the first transistor radio in 1953 for about $40. Using even smaller transistors, Sony introduced the pocket radio in 1957. But it wasn't until the 1960s that transistor radios became cheaper than conventional tube and battery radios. For a while, the term *transistor* became a synonym for a small, portable radio.

The development of transistors let radio go where television could not—to the beach, to the office, into bedrooms and bathrooms, and into nearly all new cars. (Before the transistor, car radios were a luxury item.) By the 1960s, most radio listening took place outside the home. For economic reasons, radio turned to the recording industry for content to replace the shows it had lost to television.

POCKET TRANSISTOR RADIOS like this early model became popular in the late 1950s.

The FM Revolution and Edwin Armstrong

By the time the broadcast industry launched commercial television in the 1950s, many people, including David Sarnoff of RCA, were predicting radio's demise. To fund television's development and protect his radio holdings, Sarnoff had even delayed a dramatic breakthrough in broadcast sound, what he himself called a "revolution"—FM radio.

Edwin Armstrong, who first discovered and developed FM radio in the 1920s and early 1930s, is often considered the most prolific and influential inventor in radio history. He understood the impact of De Forest's vacuum tube, and he used it to invent an amplifying system that enabled radio receivers to pick up distant signals. Armstrong's innovations rendered obsolete the enormous alternators used for generating power in early radio transmitters. In 1922, he sold a "super" version of his circuit to RCA for $200,000 and sixty thousand shares of RCA stock, which made him a millionaire as well as RCA's largest private stockholder.

Armstrong also worked on the major problem of radio reception—electrical interference. Between 1930 and 1933, the inventor filed five patents on **FM**, or frequency modulation. Offering static-free radio reception, FM supplied greater fidelity and clarity than AM, making FM ideal for music. **AM**, or amplitude modulation, stressed the volume, or height, of radio waves; FM accentuated the pitch, or distance, between radio waves (see Figure 4.2 on page 126).

Although David Sarnoff, the president of RCA, thought that television would replace radio, he helped Armstrong set up the first experimental FM station atop the Empire State Building in New York City. Eventually, though, Sarnoff thwarted FM's development (which he was able to do because RCA had an option on Armstrong's new patents). Instead, in 1935 Sarnoff threw RCA's considerable weight behind the development of television. With the FCC allocating and reassigning scarce frequency spaces, RCA wanted to ensure that channels went to television before they went to FM. But most of all, Sarnoff wanted to protect RCA's existing AM empire. Given the high costs of converting to FM and the revenue needed for TV experiments, Sarnoff decided to close down Armstrong's station.

Armstrong forged ahead without RCA. He founded a new FM station and advised other engineers, who started more than twenty experimental stations between 1935 and the early 1940s. In 1941, the FCC approved limited space allocations for commercial FM licenses. During the next few years, FM grew in fits and starts. Between 1946 and early 1949, the number of commercial FM stations expanded from 48 to 700. But then the FCC moved FM's frequency space to a new band on the electromagnetic spectrum, rendering some 400,000 prewar FM receiver sets useless. FM's future became uncertain, and by 1954, the number of FM stations had fallen to 560.

"Armstrong was a lone experimenter, Sarnoff a company man."

ERIK BARNOUW, MEDIA HISTORIAN

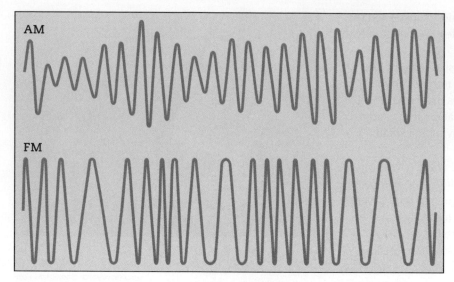

FIGURE 4.2

AM AND FM WAVES

Source: Adapted from David Cheshire, The Video Manual, 1982.

On January 31, 1954, Edwin Armstrong, weary from years of legal skirmishes over patents with RCA, Lee De Forest, and others, wrote a note apologizing to his wife, removed the air conditioner from his thirteenth-story New York apartment, and jumped to his death. A month later, David Sarnoff announced record profits of $850 million for RCA, with TV sales accounting for 54 percent of the company's earnings. In the early 1960s, the FCC opened up more spectrum space for the superior sound of FM, infusing new life into radio.

Although AM stations had greater reach, they could not match the crisp fidelity of FM, which made FM preferable for music. In the early 1970s, about 70 percent of listeners tuned almost exclusively to AM radio. By the 1980s, however, FM had surpassed AM in profitability. By the 2000s, more than 75 percent of all listeners preferred FM, and about 3,600 commercial and almost 2,900 educational FM stations were in operation. The expansion of FM represented one of the chief ways radio survived television and Sarnoff's gloomy predictions.

The Rise of Format and Top 40 Radio

Live and recorded music had long been radio's single biggest staple, accounting for 48 percent of all programming in 1938. Although live music on radio was generally considered superior to recorded music, early disc jockeys made a significant contribution to the latter. They demonstrated that music alone could drive radio. In fact, when television snatched radio's program ideas and national sponsors, radio's dependence on recorded music became a necessity and helped the medium survive the 1950s.

As early as 1949, station owner Todd Storz in Omaha, Nebraska, experimented with formula-driven radio, or **format radio**. Under this system, management rather than deejays controlled programming each hour. When Storz and his program manager noticed that bar patrons and waitresses repeatedly played certain favorite songs from the forty records available in a jukebox, they began researching record sales to identify the most popular tunes. From observing jukebox culture, Storz hit on the idea of **rotation**: playing the top songs many times during the day. By the mid-1950s, the management-control idea combined with the rock-and-roll explosion, and the **Top 40 format** was born. Although the term *Top 40* derived from the number of records stored in a jukebox, this format came to refer to the forty most popular hits in a given week as measured by record sales.

As format radio grew, program managers combined rapid deejay chatter with the best-selling songs of the day and occasional oldies—popular songs from a few months earlier. By the early 1960s, to avoid "dead air," managers asked deejays to talk over the beginning and the end of a song so that listeners would feel less compelled to switch stations. Ads, news, weather forecasts, and station identifications were all designed to fit a consistent station environment. Listeners, tuning in at any moment, would recognize the station by its distinctive sound.

In format radio, management carefully coordinates, or programs, each hour, dictating what the deejay will do at various intervals throughout each hour of the day (see Figure 4.3). Management creates a program log—once called a *hot clock* in radio jargon—that dee-jays must follow. By the mid-1960s, one study had determined that in a typical hour on Top 40, listeners could expect to hear about twenty ads; numerous weather, time, and contest announcements;

"Radio affects most people intimately, person-to-person, offering a world of unspoken communication between writer-speaker and listener. That is the immediate aspect of radio. A private experience."

MARSHALL McLUHAN, *UNDERSTANDING MEDIA*, 1964

multiple recitations of the station's call letters; about three minutes of news; and approximately twelve songs.

Radio managers further sectioned off programming into *day parts*, which typically consisted of time blocks covering 6 to 10 A.M., 10 A.M. to 3 P.M., 3 to 7 P.M., and 7 P.M. to midnight. Each day part, or block, was programmed through ratings research according to who was listening. For instance, a Top 40 station would feature its top deejays in the morning and afternoon periods when audiences, many riding in cars, were largest. From 10 A.M. to 3 P.M., research determined that women at home and secretaries at work usually controlled the dial, so program managers, capitalizing on the gender stereotypes of the day, played more romantic ballads and less hard rock. Teenagers tended to be heavy evening listeners, so program managers often discarded news breaks at this time, since research showed that teens turned the dial when news came on.

Critics of format radio argued that only the top songs received play and that lesser-known songs deserving air time received meager attention. Although a few popular star deejays continued to play a role in programming, many others quit when managers introduced formats. Owners approached programming as a science, but deejays considered it an art form. Program managers argued that deejays had different tastes than the average listener and therefore could not be fully trusted to know popular audience tastes. The owners' position, which generated more revenue, triumphed.

MIX96		5PM–6PM	Thursday July 5, 2007
Teri Lynn			
0:00	02056	Donna Summer BAD GIRLS	:12/3:55/FADE
3:55	02370	THE FRAY HOW TO SAVE A LIFE	07/4:20/COLD
8:15	00011	PHIL COLLINS TAKE ME HOME	:24/5:38/FADE
13:53	01843	CHRISTINA AGUILERA FIGHTER	:10/4:05/COLD
17:58	02261	BOB SEGER WAIT FOR ME	18/3:35/FADE
21:33	02080	MAROON 5 SHE WILL BE LOVED	:10/4:14/FADE
25:47	00779	ROD STEWART SO FAR AWAY	:13/4:11/FADE
29:58	01451	PINK MOST GIRLS	:09/4:00/FADE
33:58	02378	SNOW PATROL CHASING CARS	06/4:23/COLD
38:21		STOP SET	1:00 (Sweep: 38:21)
39:21	00871	LOU BEGA MAMBO #5	COLD/3:37/COLD
42:58	02235	NICK LACHEY WHAT'S LEFT OF ME	13/4:00/COLD
46:58	01903	FLEETWOOD MAC DON'T STOP	:17/3:06/FADE
50:04	02229	NATASHA BEDDINGFILELD UNWRITTEN	12/3:43/FADE
53:47		STOP SET	4:00 (Sweep: 14:26)
57:47	01605	MODERN ENGLISH I MELT WITH YOU	:13/3:52/FADE

FIGURE 4.3

RADIO PROGRAM LOG FOR AN ADULT CONTEMPORARY (AC) STATION

Source: KCVM, Cedar Falls, IA, 2007.

Resisting the Top 40

The expansion of FM in the mid-1960s created room for experimenting, particularly with classical music, jazz, blues, and non-Top 40 rock songs. **Progressive rock** emerged as an alternative to conventional formats. Many noncommercial stations broadcast from college campuses, where student deejays and managers rejected the commercialism associated with Top 40 tunes and began playing lesser-known alternative music and longer album cuts (such as Bob Dylan's "Desolation Row" and The Doors' "Light My Fire"). Until that time, most rock on radio had been consigned almost exclusively to Top 40 AM formats, with song length averaging about three minutes.

Experimental FM stations, both commercial and noncommercial, offered a cultural space for hard-edged political folk music and for rock music that commented on the Civil Rights movement and protested America's involvement in the Vietnam War. By the 1970s, however, progressive rock had been copied, tamed, and absorbed by mainstream radio under the format labeled **album-oriented rock (AOR)**. By 1972, AOR-driven album sales accounted for more than 85 percent of the retail record business. By the 1980s, as first-generation rock and rollers aged and became more affluent, AOR stations became less political and played mostly white, post-Beatles music featuring such groups as Pink Floyd, Led Zeppelin, Cream, and Queen.[15] Today, AOR has been subsumed under the more general classic rock format.

Host: The Origins of Talk Radio

By David Foster Wallace

The origins of contemporary political talk radio can be traced to three phenomena of the 1980s. The first of these involved AM music stations' getting absolutely murdered by FM, which could broadcast music in stereo and allowed for much better fidelity on high and low notes. The human voice, on the other hand, is midrange and doesn't require high fidelity. The eighties' proliferation of talk formats on the AM band also provided new careers for some music deejays—e.g., Don Imus, Morton Downey Jr.—whose chatty personas didn't fit well with FM's all-about-the-music ethos.

The second big factor was the repeal, late in Ronald Reagan's second term, of what was known as the Fairness Doctrine. This was a 1949 FCC rule designed to minimize any possible restrictions on free speech caused by limited access to broadcasting outlets. The idea was that, as one of the conditions for receiving an FCC broadcast license, a station had to "devote reasonable attention to the coverage of controversial issues of public importance," and consequently had to provide "reasonable, although not necessarily equal" opportunities for opposing sides to express their views. Because of the Fairness Doctrine, talk stations had to hire and program symmetrically: if you had a three-hour program whose host's

politics were on one side of the ideological spectrum, you had to have another long-form program whose host more or less spoke for the other side. Weirdly enough, up through the mid-eighties it was usually the U.S. right that benefited most from the Doctrine. Pioneer talk syndicator Ed McLaughlin, who managed San Francisco's KGO in the 1960s, recalls that "I had more liberals on the air than I had conservatives or even moderates for that matter, and I had a hell of a time finding the other voice."

The Fairness Doctrine's repeal was part of the sweeping deregulations of the Reagan era, which aimed to liberate all sorts of industries from government interference and allow them to compete freely in the marketplace. The old, Rooseveltian logic of the Doctrine had been that since the airwaves belonged to everyone, a license to profit from those airwaves conferred on the broadcast industry some special obligation to serve the public interest. Commercial radio broadcasting was not, in other words, originally conceived as just another for-profit industry; it was supposed to meet a higher standard of social responsibility. After 1987, though, just another industry is pretty much what radio became, and its only real responsibility now is to attract and retain listeners in order to generate revenue. In other

words, the sort of distinction explicitly drawn by FCC Chairman Newton Minow in the 1960s—namely, that between "the public interest" and "merely what interests the public"—no longer exists.

More or less on the heels of the Fairness Doctrine's repeal came the West Coast and then national syndication of *The Rush Limbaugh Show* through Mr. McLaughlin's EFM Media. Limbaugh is the third great progenitor of today's political talk radio partly because he's a host of extraordinary, once-in-a-generation talent and charisma—bright, loquacious, witty, complexly authoritative—whose show's blend of news, entertainment, and partisan analysis became the model for legions of imitators. But he was also the first great promulgator of the Mainstream Media's Liberal Bias idea. This turned out to be a brilliantly effective rhetorical move, since the MMLB concept functioned simultaneously as a standard around which Rush's audience could rally, as an articulation of the need for right-wing (i.e., unbiased) media, and as a mechanism by which any criticism or refutation of conservative ideas could be dismissed (either as biased or as the product of indoctrination by biased media). Boiled way down, the MMLB thesis is able both to exploit and to perpetuate many conservatives' dissatisfaction with extant media sources—and it's this dissatisfaction that cements political talk radio's large and loyal audience. ◢

Source: Excerpted from David Foster Wallace, "Host: The Origins of Talk Radio," Atlantic, *April 2005, 66–68.*

The Sounds of Commercial Radio

Contemporary radio sounds very different from its predecessor. In contrast to the few stations per market in the 1930s, most large markets today include more than forty stations that vie for listener loyalty. With the exception of national network-sponsored news segments and nationally syndicated programs, most programming is locally produced and heavily dependent on the music industry for content. Although a few radio personalities, such as Howard Stern, Adam Corolla, Rush Limbaugh, Tom Joyner, Dr. Laura Schlessinger, Tavis Smiley, and Jim Rome, are nationally prominent, local deejays and their music are the stars at most radio stations.

However, listeners today are unlike radio's first audiences in several ways. First, listeners in the 1930s tuned in their favorite shows at set times. Listeners today do not say, "Gee, my favorite song is coming on at 8 P.M., so I'd better be home to listen." Instead, radio has become a secondary, or background, medium that follows the rhythms of daily life. Radio programmers today worry about channel cruising–listeners' tendency to search the dial until they find a song they like.

Second, in the 1930s, peak listening time occurred during evening hours–dubbed *prime time* in the TV era–when people were home from work and school. Now, the heaviest radio listening occurs during **drive time,** between 6 and 9 A.M. and 4 and 7 P.M., when people are commuting to and from work or school.

Third, stations today are more specialized. Listeners are loyal to favorite stations, music formats, and even radio personalities, rather than to specific shows. People generally listen to only four or five stations that target them. Nearly fourteen thousand radio stations now operate in the United States, customizing their sounds to reach niche audiences through format specialization and alternative programming.

Format Specialization

Stations today use a variety of formats based on managed program logs and day parts. All told, more than forty different radio formats, plus variations, serve diverse groups of listeners. (See Figure 4.4 on page 130.) To please advertisers, who want to know exactly who is listening, formats usually target audiences according to their age, income, gender, or race/ethnicity. Radio's specialization enables advertisers to reach smaller target audiences at costs that are much lower than those for television.

Targeting listeners has become extremely competitive, however, because forty or fifty stations may be available in a large radio market. In the last decade, according to the Center for Radio Information, more than one thousand stations a year (roughly 10 percent of all stations) switched formats in an effort to find the formula that would generate more advertising money. Some stations, particularly those in large cities, even rent blocks of time to various local ethnic or civic groups; this enables the groups to dictate their own formats and sell ads.

News and Talk Radio

The nation's fastest-growing format throughout much of the 1990s was the **news/talk format** (see "Case Study–Host: The Origins of Talk Radio" on page 128). In 1987, only 170 radio stations operated formats dominated by either news programs or talk shows, which tend to appeal to adults over age thirty-five (except for sports talk programs, which draw mostly male sports fans of all ages). Buoyed by the notoriety and popularity of personalities like Tavis Smiley and Rush

TOM JOYNER has the nation's No. 1 urban radio show, targeting African Americans between the ages of twenty-five and fifty-four with a mix of political discussion, comedy, sketches, social activism, and old-school R&B music. The syndicated program can be heard in more than a hundred broadcast markets, including Chicago; Dallas; Detroit; Miami; Washington, D.C.; and Los Angeles.

**Among Persons
Age 12 and Older**

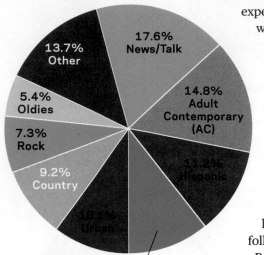

FIGURE 4.4

**MOST POPULAR RADIO
FORMATS IN THE
UNITED STATES**

Source: Radio Marketing Guide
and Fact Book, 2007–08.

Limbaugh, more than 1,300 stations used some combination of news and talk by 2008, making it the most popular format in the nation. (See Table 4.2.) A news/talk format, though more expensive to produce than a music format, appeals to advertisers looking to target working- and middle-class adult consumers. Nevertheless, most radio stations continue to be driven by a variety of less expensive music formats.

Music Formats

The **adult contemporary (AC)** format, also known as middle-of-the-road or MOR, is among radio's oldest and most popular formats, reaching almost 15 percent of all listeners, most of them older than forty, with an eclectic mix of news, talk, oldies, and soft rock music—what *Broadcasting* magazine describes as "not too soft, not too loud, not too fast, not too slow, not too hard, not too lush, not too old, not too new." Now encompassing everything from rap to pop punk songs, Top 40 radio—also called **contemporary hit radio (CHR)**—still appeals to many teens and young adults. Since the mid-1980s, however, these stations have lost ground steadily as younger generations have followed music first on MTV and now online rather than on radio.

By far, **country** claims the most stations—more than two thousand, nearly twice as many stations as those with the news/talk format. Many stations are in tiny markets where country is traditionally the default format for communities with only one radio station. Country music has old roots in radio, starting in 1925 with the influential Grand Ole Opry program on WSM in Nashville. Although Top 40 drove country music out of many radio markets in the 1950s, the growth of FM in the 1960s brought it back, as station managers looked for market niches not served by rock music. As diverse as rock music, country today includes such subdivisions as old-time, progressive country, country-rock, western swing, and country-gospel.

Many formats appeal to particular ethnic or racial groups. In 1947, WDIA in Memphis was the first station to program exclusively for black listeners. Now called **urban,** this format

TABLE 4.2

**TALK RADIO WEEKLY
AUDIENCE (IN MILLIONS)**

Source: Talkers *magazine,* "Top
Talk Personalities," *Spring 2007.*

Note: * = Information
unavailable; N/A = Talk host not
nationally broadcast.

Talk Show Host	2003	2006	2007
Rush Limbaugh (Conservative)	14.5	13.5	13.5
Sean Hannity (Conservative)	11.75	12.5	12.5
Michael Savage (Conservative)	7	8.25	8
Dr. Laura Schlessinger (General Advice)	8.5	8	8
Laura Ingraham (Conservative)	1.25	5	5
Glenn Beck (Conservative)	*	3	5
Neal Boortz (Conservative)	2.5	3.75	4
Mark Levin (Conservative)	N/A	1	4
Dave Ramsey (Financial Advice)	*	2.75	4
Mike Gallagher (Conservative)	2.5	3.75	3.75
Michael Medved (Conservative)	*	2.25	3.75
Jim Bohannon (Ind. / Moderate)	4	3.25	3.25
Clark Howard (Consumer Advocacy)	2.5	3.25	3.25
Bill O'Reilly (Conservative)	1.75	3.25	3.25
Doug Stephen (Ind. / Moderate)	2	3.25	3.25
Ed Schultz (Liberal / Progressive)	N/A	2.25	3.25

targets a wide variety of African American listeners, primarily in large cities. Urban, which typically plays popular dance, rap, R&B, and hip-hop music (featuring performers like Rihanna and Kanye West), also subdivides by age, featuring an Urban AC category with performers like Mario, Fantasia, and Mary J. Blige.

Spanish-language radio, one of radio's fastest-growing formats, is concentrated mostly in large Hispanic markets such as Miami, New York, Chicago, Las Vegas, California, Arizona, New Mexico, and Texas (where KCOR, the first all-Spanish-language station, originated in San Antonio in 1947). Besides talk shows and news segments in Spanish, this format features a variety of Spanish, Caribbean, and Latin American musical styles, including calypso, flamenco, mariachi, merengue, reggae, samba, salsa, and Tejano.

In addition, today there are other formats that are spin-offs from AOR. Classic rock serves up rock favorites from the mid-1960s through the 1980s to the baby-boom generation and other listeners who have outgrown the Top 40. The oldies format originally served adults who grew up on 1950s and early 1960s rock and roll. As that audience has aged, oldies formats now target younger audiences by featuring hits from the 1970s and 1980s. The alternative music format recaptures some of the experimental approach of the FM stations of the 1960s, although with much more controlled playlists, and has helped to introduce artists such as the White Stripes and Modest Mouse.

Research indicates that most people identify closely with the music they listened to as adolescents and young adults. This tendency partially explains why oldies and classic rock stations combined have surpassed Top 40 stations today. It also helps to explain the recent nostalgia for music from the 1980s and early 1990s.

Nonprofit Radio and NPR

Although commercial radio (particularly those stations owned by huge radio conglomerates) dominates the radio spectrum, nonprofit radio maintains a voice. But the road to viability for nonprofit radio in the United States has not been easy. In the 1930s, the Wagner-Hatfield Amendment to the 1934 Communications Act intended to set aside 25 percent of radio for a

"NPR has transformed itself from rag-tag alternative radio into a mainstream news powerhouse with more bureaus worldwide than the *Washington Post* and 26 million listeners a week—twice as many as a decade ago."

WASHINGTONIAN,
2007

> "We have a huge responsibility to keep the airwaves open for what I think is the majority—representing the voices that are locked out of the mainstream media."
>
> AMY GOODMAN,
> CO-HOST OF RADIO'S
> *DEMOCRACY NOW!*
> 2001

MICHELLE NORRIS is one of the hosts on NPR's *All Things Considered,* a daily news show that features a "trademark mix of news, interviews, commentaries, reviews and offbeat features." *All Things Considered* has been on the air since 1971 and is one of NPR's most popular programs.

wide variety of nonprofit stations. When the amendment was defeated in 1935, the future of educational and noncommercial radio looked bleak. Many nonprofits had sold out to for-profit owners during the Great Depression of the 1930s. The stations that remained were often banished from the air during the evening hours or assigned weak signals by federal regulators who favored commercial owners and their lobbying agents. Still, nonprofit public radio survived. Today, almost twenty-nine hundred nonprofit stations operate, most of them on the FM band.

The Early Years of Nonprofit Radio

Two government rulings, both in 1948, aided nonprofit radio. First, the government began authorizing noncommercial licenses to stations not affiliated with labor, religion, education, or a civic group. The first license went to Lewis Kimball Hill, a radio reporter and pacifist during World War II who started the **Pacifica Foundation** to run experimental public stations. Pacifica stations, like Hill, have often challenged the status quo in radio as well as in government. Most notably, in the 1950s they aired the poetry, prose, and music of performers considered radical, left-wing, or communist who were blacklisted by television and seldom acknowledged by AM stations. Over the years, Pacifica has also been fined and reprimanded by the FCC and Congress for airing programs that critics considered inappropriate for public airwaves. Today, Pacifica has about ninety affiliate stations.

Second, the FCC approved 10-watt FM stations. Prior to this time, radio stations had to have at least 250 watts to get licensed. A 10-watt station with a broadcast range of only about seven miles took very little capital to operate, so more people could participate, and they became training sites for students interested in broadcasting. Although the FCC stopped licensing new 10-watt stations in 1978, about one hundred longtime 10-watters are still in operation.

Creation of the First Noncommercial Networks

During the 1960s, nonprofit broadcasting found a Congress sympathetic to an old idea: using radio and television as educational tools. As a result, **National Public Radio (NPR)** and the **Public Broadcasting Service (PBS)** were created as the first noncommercial networks. Under the provisions of the **Public Broadcasting Act of 1967** and the **Corporation for Public Broadcasting (CPB)**, NPR and PBS were mandated to provide alternatives to commercial broadcasting. Now, NPR's popular news and interview programs, *Morning Edition* and *All Things Considered*, draw three to four million listeners per day. Over the years, however, more time and attention have been devoted to public television than to public radio. When government funding tightened in the late 1980s and 1990s, television received the lion's share. In 1994, a conservative majority in Congress cut financial support and threatened to scrap the CPB, the funding authority for public broadcasting. Consequently, stations became more reliant than ever on private donations and corporate sponsorship. While depending on handouts, especially from big business, public broadcasters steered clear of some controversial subjects, especially those that critically examined corporations. (See "Media Literacy and the Critical Process: Comparing Commercial and Noncommercial Radio" on page 133.)

Like commercial stations, nonprofit radio has adopted the format style. Unlike commercial radio, however, the dominant style in public radio is a loose variety format whereby a station may actually switch from jazz, classical music, and alternative rock to news and talk during different parts of the day. Noncommercial radio remains the place for both tradition and experimentation, as well as for programs that do not draw enough listeners for commercial success.

Media Literacy and the Critical Process

1 DESCRIPTION. Listen to a typical morning or late afternoon hour of a popular local commercial talk-news radio station and a typical hour of your local NPR station, from the same time period over a two- to three-day period. Keep a log of what topics are covered and what news stories are reported. For the commercial station, log what commercials are carried and how much time in an hour is devoted to ads. For the noncommercial station, note how much time is devoted to recognizing the station's sources of funding support and who the supporters are.

2 ANALYSIS. Look for patterns. What kinds of stories are covered? What kinds of topics are discussed? Create a chart to categorize the stories. To cover events and issues, do the stations use actual reporters at the scene? How much time is given to reporting compared to time devoted to opinion? How many sources are cited in each story? What kinds of interview sources are used? Are they expert sources or regular person-on-the-street interviews? How many sources are men and how many are women?

Comparing Commercial and Noncommercial Radio

After the arrival and growth of commercial TV, the Corporation for Public Broadcasting (CPB) was created in 1967 as the funding agent for public broadcasting—an alternative to commercial TV and radio for educational and cultural programming that could not be easily sustained by commercial broadcasters in search of large general audiences. As a result, NPR (National Public Radio) developed to provide national programming to public stations to supplement local programming efforts. Today, NPR affiliates get as little as 2 percent of their funding from the government. Most money for public radio comes instead from corporate sponsorships, individual grants, and private donations.

3 INTERPRETATION. What do these patterns mean? Is there a balance between reporting and opinion? Do you detect any bias, and if so, how did you determine this? Are the stations serving as watchdogs to ensure that democracy's best interests are being served? What effect, if any, do you think the advertisers/supporters have on the programming? What arguments might you make about commercial and noncommercial radio based on your findings?

4 EVALUATION. Which station seems to be doing a better job serving its local audience? Why? Do you buy the 1930s argument that noncommercial stations serve narrow, special interests while commercial stations serve capitalism and the public interest? Why or why not? From which station did you learn the most, and which station did you find most entertaining? Explain. What did you like and dislike about each station?

5 ENGAGEMENT. Contact the local general manager, program director, or news director at the stations you analyzed. Ask them what their goals are for a typical hour of programming and what audience they are trying to reach. Incorporate their comments into a report on your findings. Finally, offer suggestions on how to make the programming at each station better.

Radio Goes Digital

Over the past decade or so, four alternative radio technologies have helped bring more diverse sounds to listeners: the Internet, satellite, podcasts, and HD (digital) radio.

Internet Radio

Internet radio emerged in the 1990s with the popularity of the Web. Internet radio stations come in two types: An existing station may "stream" a simulcast version of its on-air signal over the Web, or a station may be created exclusively for the Internet. Some of the most popular Internet radio stations are those that carry music formats unavailable on local radio, such as jazz, blues, and New Age music. Beginning in 2002, a Copyright Royalty Board established by the Library of Congress began to assess royalty fees based on a percentage of each station's revenue for the right to stream copyrighted songs over the Internet. In 2007, the board proposed to change the royalty fees to a per-song basis, which would increase station payments to

"We are skirting dangerously close to taking the public interest out of the public airwaves."

MICHAEL COPPS,
FCC COMMISSIONER,
2004

the recording industry anywhere from 300 to 1,200 percent. Although the recording industry was pleased with the plan, Webcasters–who have more than 55 million online listeners each week–claimed the higher rates threatened their financial viability.[16] After Internet stations and their listeners protested online, the recording industry (through SoundExchange, its Web performance rights organization) responded by offering to let small commercial Webcasters continue to operate under the older, lower royalty rates, and capping maximum royalty payments for larger Webcasters.

Satellite Radio

Another alternative radio technology added a third band–**satellite radio**–to AM and FM. Two services, XM and Sirius, completed their national introduction by 2002 and now offer more than one hundred digital music, news, and talk channels to the continental United States via satellite, at monthly prices starting at $12.95 and satellite radio receivers costing from $15 to $350. Programming includes a range of music channels, from rock to reggae, to Spanish Top 40 and opera, as well as channels dedicated to NASCAR, NPR, cooking, and comedy. Another feature of satellite radio's programming is popular personalities who host their own shows or have their own channels, including Howard Stern, Martha Stewart, Oprah Winfrey, and Bob Dylan. In 2002, U.S. automakers (investors in the satellite radio companies) began equipping most new cars with a satellite band, in addition to AM and FM, helping to ensure the adoption of satellite radio.

In 2007, XM and Sirius, which struggled to make a profit as they built competing satellite systems and battled for listeners, proposed a merger. The traditional terrestrial radio industry complained that a merger would create an illegal noncompetitive monopoly in satellite radio. But the satellite radio companies argued that because they compete with all kinds of audio entertainment–including radio, Webcasters, and podcasts–there was still plenty of competition in the market. The FCC approved the merger in 2008.

Podcasting

Developed in 2004, **podcasting** (the term marries "iPod" and "broadcasting") refers to the practice of making audio files available on the Internet so listeners can download them onto their computers and transfer them to portable MP3 players or listen to the files on the computer. This popular distribution method quickly became mainstream, as mass media companies created commercial podcasts to promote and extend existing content, such as news and reality TV, while independent producers kept pace with their own podcasts on niche topics like knitting, fly fishing, and learning Russian.

HD Radio

Approved by the FCC in 2002, **HD radio** is a digital technology that enables AM and FM radio broadcasters to multicast two to three additional compressed digital signals within their traditional analog frequency. For example, KNOW, a public radio station at 91.1 FM in Minneapolis-St. Paul, runs its National Public Radio news format on 91.1 HD1, BBC News on 91.1 HD2, and the BBC Mundo Spanish language news service on 91.1 HD3. More than fifteen hundred radio stations now broadcast in digital HD. To tune in, listeners need a radio with the HD band, devices available by 2007. (See "Tracking Technology: HD Radio.")

TRACKING TECHNOLOGY

HD Radio

By Marc Fisher

Chasing an audience that has migrated to iPods, Internet radio, pay satellite services and the burgeoning world of cellphone music, the AM and FM radio industry has spent the past couple of years beckoning listeners to discover the "secret stations" of HD radio.

HD radio—the abbreviation summons the TV term "high-definition" but actually stands for "hybrid digital"—is a technology designed to offer clearer sound and a way to add extra signals onto existing broadcast frequencies. (On an HD radio, you turn the tuning dial one notch up from the regular FM frequency and the second channel appears.)

Along with providing a free alternative to the broader array of music available on the pay XM and Sirius satellite services, HD's promise is to push the pendulum back from the extreme narrowing of choice that swept through radio in the 1990s. And so [a station] can supplement its regular light-rock format with an HD channel of nothing but love songs. Or, on [a station] that plays current country hits, its HD channel is devoted to classic country numbers.

But for all the hype about HD, are people listening? Even after the biggest ad campaign anywhere on radio—with more ad spots than Geico, Budweiser or General Motors last year—the answer is not many, according to the latest estimates.

When Bridge Ratings, a radio consulting company, conducted a survey about HD, it found that 75 percent of respondents have heard of the new technology, thanks to radio's aggressive ad campaign. But only 13 percent of the sample could say what HD radio is, and only 7 percent expressed interest in owning an HD set.

Bridge projects slow, poor growth for HD, especially compared with the galloping interest in Web and cellphone radio. "New cell phone capabilities which will turn the mobile phone into a more dynamic part of daily life will potentially surpass Internet radio as the most significant challenger to traditional radio," Bridge concluded.

Bob Struble, president of iBiquity, the Columbia-based company that developed the HD technology, disagrees. With Circuit City and Best Buy adding HD radios to their product line, and Ford and Volvo installing HD radios in their cars, he sees a brighter future. "We're still early in the game," Struble says. The company won't say how many

HD radios have been sold, but industry observers put the figure at fewer than 500,000.

The slow adoption is the main reason some stations have not added HD-only programming. "It's still an evolving technology," says Dan DeVany, general manager of WETA (90.9 FM) [Washington, D.C.], a public classical music station, which has no extra HD channel. "I'd like to see more of those units sold before we'd plan anything."

The chicken-egg question for HD radio is whether stations should invest in new programming now to lure new listeners or after an audience develops. And if stations wait, why would anyone invest in a new radio?

"You're onto something there," Struble says. "The initial push was around the basic concept—there's a lot more out there. But there's a very important role to be played by individual stations." He hopes more stations will do as Baltimore's 98 Rock does, giving listeners of the indie-rock station a taste of its classic-rock HD station for four hours every Sunday morning.

But far from pushing their HD offerings, most stations seem only halfheartedly invested in the technology. HD remains a promising technology, but so far, many more people listen to the new programming via online streaming than on an HD radio. Listeners are voting with their ears, and they're choosing Web-based and mobile audio, in part because most HD radio programming just isn't compelling enough to lure people to a different gadget. ◢

Excerpted from: Marc Fisher, "HD: If a Tree Falls & No One Hears It . . .," Washington Post, February 10, 2008, p. M05.

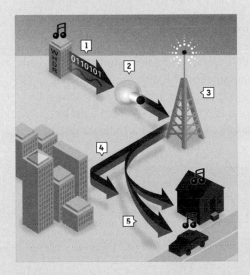

HOW HD RADIO WORKS
(1) The radio station sends the analog and digital AM or FM signals out simultaneously. (2) The digital signal is compressed, so it takes up less bandwidth. (3) The radio tower transmits the combined analog and digital signals. (4) HD signals are designed to filter through reflected signals and reduce fading, static, hisses, and pops. (5) Older radios receive only the analog signal. New HD Radio receivers pick up the CD-quality digital AM or FM signals.

The Economics of Broadcast Radio

Radio continues to be one of the most-used mass media, reaching 72 percent of American teenagers and adults every day.[17] Because of radio's broad reach, the airwaves are very desirable real estate for advertisers, who want to reach people in and out of their homes; for record labels, who want their songs played; and for radio station owners, who want to create large radio groups to dominate multiple markets.

Local and National Advertising

About 8 percent of all U.S. spending on media advertising goes to radio stations. Like newspapers, radio generates its largest profits by selling local and regional ads. Thirty-second radio spot ads range from $1,500 in large markets to just a few dollars in the smallest markets. Today, gross advertising receipts for radio are more than $20 billion (about three-quarters of the revenues from local ad sales, with the remainder in national spot and network sales), up from about $12.4 billion in 1996. The industry is economically healthy, with approximately 13,800 stations (almost 4,800 AM stations, about 6,200 FM commercial stations, and about 2,800 FM educational stations). Unlike television, where nearly 40 percent of a station's expenses goes to buy syndicated programs, local radio stations get much of their content free from the recording industry. Therefore, only about 20 percent of a typical radio station's budget goes to cover programming costs.

When radio stations want to purchase programming, they often turn to national network radio, which generates more than $1.1 billion in ad sales annually by offering dozens of specialized services. For example, Westwood One, the nation's largest radio network service, managed by CBS Radio, syndicates more than 150 programs, including regular news features (e.g., CBS Radio News, CNN Radio News), entertainment programs (e.g., *Country Countdown USA, Saturday Night All Request 80*s), talk shows (e.g., the *Dennis Miller Show, Loveline*), and complete twenty-four-hour formats (e.g., adult rock and roll, bright adult contemporary, hot country, mainstream country, and CNN Headline News). More than sixty companies offer national program and format services, typically providing local stations with programming in exchange for time slots for national ads. The most successful radio network programs are the shows broadcast by affiliates in the Top 20 markets, which offer advertisers half of the country's radio audience.

TABLE 4.3
TOP RADIO INDUSTRY COMPANIES, 2007

*Dollars in millions.

Source: "100 Leading Media Companies," Advertising Age, http://adage.com/datacenter/article.php?article_id=106352 (accessed November 8, 2007).

Rank	Company	Radio Net Revenue*
1	Clear Channel Communications (Top Property: WLTW-FM, New York)	$3,697
2	CBS Corp. (KROQ-FM, Los Angeles)	1,948
3	Citadel Broadcasting Corp. (WPLJ-FM, New York)	986
4	XM Satellite Radio Holdings (XM Satellite Radio)	877
5	Sirius Satellite Radio (Sirius Satellite Radio)	606
6	Cumulus Media (KNBR-AM, San Francisco)	575
7	Westwood One (supplies programming to stations)	494
8	Entercom Communications Corp. (WEEI-AM, Boston)	441
9	Cox Enterprises (WSB-AM, Atlanta)	440
10	Univision Communications (KLVE-FM, Los Angeles)	382

Manipulating Playlists with Payola

Radio's impact on music industry profits—radio airplay can help to popularize recordings—has required ongoing government oversight to expose illegal playlist manipulation. **Payola**, the practice by which record promoters pay deejays to play particular records, was rampant during the 1950s as record companies sought to guarantee record sales (see Chapter 3). In response, management took control of programming, arguing that if individual deejays had less impact on which records would be played, the deejays would be less susceptible to bribery.

Despite congressional hearings and new regulations, payola persisted. Record promoters showered their favors on a few influential, high-profile deejays, whose backing could make or break a record nationally, or on key program managers in charge of Top 40 formats in large urban markets. Although a 1984 congressional hearing determined that there was "no credible evidence" of payola, NBC News broke a story in 1986 about independent promoters who had alleged ties to organized crime. A subsequent investigation led major recording companies to break most of their ties with independent promoters. Prominent record labels had been paying such promoters up to $80 million per year to help records become hits.

Recently, there has been increased enforcement of payola laws. In 2005, two major labels—Sony-BMG and Warner Music—paid $10 million and $5 million, respectively, to settle payola cases in New York State, where label executives were discovered bribing radio station programmers to play particular songs. A year later, New York went after radio chain Entercom Communications "for soliciting money and gifts from record companies in exchange for playing songs." Evidence revealed a 2003 e-mail from a Buffalo, New York, pop music station owned by Entercom to an executive at Columbia Records: "Do you need help on Jessica [Simpson] this week? 1250? If you don't need help, I certainly don't need to play it."[18] And in 2007, four of the largest broadcasting companies—CBS Radio, Clear Channel, Citadel, and Entercom—agreed to pay $12.5 million to settle an FCC payola investigation. The companies also agreed to an unprecedented "independent music content commitment," which requires them to provide eighty-four hundred half-hour blocks of airtime to play music from independent record labels.

A controversial and "legal" alternative to payola emerged in 1998. **Pay-for-play** is a promotional strategy that typically involves up-front payments from record companies to radio stations to play a song a specific number of times.[19] Stations that use pay-for-play sidestep FCC regulations by broadcasting disclosures that state that the song has been paid for by the record company. In effect, the time to play the song is being purchased, not unlike the paid programming of television infomercials. If the station's listeners ultimately like the pay-for-play song, the song can become part of the station's regular, unsponsored lineup. Another form of pay-for-play involves a weekly, infomercial-like music program sponsored by a music label or department store that airs in several markets of a national radio chain. Although some see pay-for-play as a direct, honest way to introduce new music on radio stations, others object to having commercial interests blatantly tamper with playlists and the weekly Billboard music charts.

Radio Ownership: From Diversity to Consolidation

The **Telecommunications Act of 1996** substantially changed the rules concerning ownership of the public airwaves because the FCC eliminated most ownership restrictions on radio. As a result, some twenty-one hundred stations and $15 billion changed hands that year alone. From 1995 to 2005, the number of radio station owners declined by one-third, from sixty-six hundred to about forty-four hundred.[20]

Once upon a time, the FCC tried to encourage diversity in broadcast ownership. From the 1950s through the 1980s, a media company could not own more than seven AM, seven FM, and seven TV stations nationally, and only one radio station per market. Just prior to the 1996 act, the ownership rules were relaxed to allow any single person or company to own up to twenty AM, twenty FM, and twelve TV stations nationwide, but only two in the same market.

KFI-AM One of Clear Channel's major assets is KFI-AM, the dominant talk radio station in Los Angeles.

The 1996 act allows individuals and companies to acquire as many radio stations as they want, with relaxed restrictions on the number of stations a single broadcaster may own in the same city: The larger the market or area, the more stations a company may own within that market. For example, in areas where forty-five or more stations are available to listeners, a broadcaster may own up to eight stations, but not more than five of one type (AM or FM). In areas with fourteen or fewer stations, a broadcaster may own up to five stations (three of any one type). In very small markets with a handful of stations, a broadcast company may not own more than half the stations.

With few exceptions, for the past two decades the FCC has embraced the consolidation schemes pushed by the powerful National Association of Broadcasters (NAB) lobbyists in Washington, D.C., under which fewer and fewer owners control more and more of the airwaves.

The consequences of the 1996 Telecommunications Act and other deregulation have been significant. Consider the cases of Clear Channel Communications and CBS Radio, which are the two largest radio chain owners in terms of total revenue (see Table 4.3 on page 136). Clear Channel Communications was formed in 1972 with one San Antonio station. In 1998, it swallowed up Jacor Communications, the fifth-largest radio chain, and became the nation's second-largest group, with 454 stations in 101 cities. In 1999, Clear Channel gobbled up another growing conglomerate, AMFM (formerly Chancellor Media Corporation), which had 463 stations and an estimated $1.6 billion in revenue. The deal broadened Clear Channel's operation to 874 stations in 187 U.S. markets, providing access to more than 110 million listeners. By 2008, Clear Channel had shed some of the 1,205 stations it owned at its peak in 2005. Still, it owned over 1,100 radio stations and about 900,000 billboard and outdoor displays in the United States and around the world, and an interest in more than 240 stations internationally. Clear Channel also distributes many of the leading syndicated programs, including Dr. Laura, Rush Limbaugh, The Jim Rome Show, Ryan Seacrest, Delilah, and The Bob & Tom Show. (See "What Clear Channel Owns" on page 137.)

CBS Radio, formerly Infinity Broadcasting, was created when media giant Viacom split into two companies in late 2005. CBS Radio is the second leading radio conglomerate in terms of revenue, with 140 stations. It is also one of the leading outdoor advertising companies in the nation. Clear Channel and CBS Radio dominate the nation's top markets, with the majority of their stations located in the fifty largest markets.

CBS Radio also operates the Westwood One radio network, the nation's leading programming and radio news syndicator. Combined, Clear Channel and CBS own roughly 1,250 radio stations—about 9 percent of all commercial U.S. stations—and control about 26 percent of the entire radio industry's $19.6 billion revenue. Competing major radio groups that have grown in the recent radio industry consolidations include Cox, Entercom, Cumulus, Citadel, and Radio One. As a result of the consolidations permitted by deregulation, in most American cities, just two corporations dominate the radio market.

A smaller but perhaps the most dominant radio conglomerate in a single format area is Univision. With a $3 billion takeover of Hispanic Broadcasting in 2003, Univision is the top Spanish-language radio broadcaster in the United States. The company is also the largest Spanish-language television broadcaster in the United States (see Chapter 5), as well as being the owner of the top two Spanish-language cable networks (Galavisión and Telefutura) and Univision Online, the most popular Spanish-language Web site in the United States.

Alternative Voices

As large corporations gained control of America's radio airwaves, activists in hundreds of communities across the United States in the 1990s protested by starting up their own noncommercial "pirate" radio stations capable of broadcasting over a few miles with low-power FM signals of 1 to 10 watts. The NAB and other industry groups pressed to have the pirate broadcasters closed down, citing their illegality and their potential to create interference with existing stations. Between 1995 and 2000, more than five hundred illegal micropower radio stations were shut down. Still, an estimated one hundred to one thousand pirate stations are in operation in the United States, in both large urban areas and small rural towns.

The major complaint of pirate radio station operators was that the FCC had long ago ceased licensing low-power community radio stations. In 2000 the FCC, responding to tens of thousands of inquiries about the development of a new local radio broadcasting service, approved a new noncommercial **low-power FM (LPFM)** class of 10- and 100-watt stations in order to give voice to local groups lacking access to the public airwaves. LPFM station licensees included mostly religious groups but also high schools, colleges and universities, Native American tribes, labor groups, and museums.

The technical plans for LPFM located the stations in unused frequencies on the FM dial. Still, the NAB and National Public Radio fought to delay and limit the number of LPFM stations, arguing that such stations would cause interference with existing full-power FM stations. Then FCC chairman William E. Kennard, who fostered the LPFM initiative, responded: "This is about the haves–the broadcast industry–trying to prevent many have-nots–small community and educational organizations–from having just a little piece of the pie. Just a little piece of the airwaves which belong to all of the people."[21] By 2008, more than 860 LPFM stations were broadcasting, and another 92 organizations had gained permission to build LPFM stations.

LOW-POWER FM RADIO
The Coalition of Immokalee Workers (CIW) launched its 100-watt low-power FM station, WCTI, 107.9 FM, in December 2003. The CIW is a community-based organization, composed mostly of immigrant farm workers in Florida. The station covers a 15-mile radius, is run by farm workers, and broadcasts news, educational programs, and music in Spanish, Haitian Creole, and indigenous languages of Mexico and Guatemala. The CIW has been successful in its "Campaign for Fair Food" to get Taco Bell, McDonald's, and Burger King to pay a penny more per pound for tomatoes they buy so that farm workers can make a decent wage.

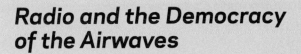

Radio and the Democracy of the Airwaves

As the first national electronic mass medium, radio's influence in the formation of American culture cannot be overestimated. Radio has given us soap operas, situation comedies, and broadcast news; it helped to popularize rock and roll, car culture, and the politics of talk radio. Yet, for all of its national influence, broadcast radio is still a supremely local medium. For decades, listeners have tuned in to hear the familiar voices of their community's deejays and talk show hosts and hear the regional flavor of popular music over airwaves that the public owns.

The early debates over radio gave us one of the most important and enduring ideas in communication policy: a requirement to operate in the "public interest, convenience, or necessity." But the broadcasting industry has long been at odds with this policy, arguing that radio corporations invest heavily in technology and should be able to have more control over the radio frequencies on which they operate, and moreover own as many stations as they want. Deregulation in the past few decades has moved closer to that corporate vision, as nearly every radio market in the nation is dominated by a few owners, and those owners are required to renew their broadcasting licenses only every eight years.

This trend in ownership has moved radio away from its localism, as radio groups often manage hundreds of stations from afar. Given broadcasters' reluctance to publicly raise questions about their own economic arrangements, public debate regarding radio as a natural resource has remained minuscule. Looking to the future, a big question remains to be answered: With a few large broadcast companies now permitted to dominate radio ownership nationwide, how much is consolidation of power restricting the number and kinds of voices permitted to speak over public airwaves? To ensure that mass media industries continue to serve democracy and local communities, the public needs to play a role in developing the answer to this question. ▶

CHAPTER REVIEW

REVIEW QUESTIONS

Early Technology and the Development of Radio

1. Why was the development of the telegraph important in media history? What were some of the disadvantages of telegraph technology?
2. How is the concept of the wireless different from that of radio?
3. What was Guglielmo Marconi's role in the development of the wireless?
4. What were Lee De Forest's contributions to radio?
5. Why were there so many patent disputes in the development of radio?
6. Why was the RCA monopoly formed?
7. How did broadcasting, unlike print media, come to be federally regulated?

The Evolution of Radio

8. What was AT&T's role in the early days of radio?
9. How did the radio networks develop? What were the contributions of David Sarnoff and William Paley to network radio?
10. Why did the government-sanctioned RCA monopoly end?
11. What is the significance of the Radio Act of 1927 and the Federal Communications Act of 1934?

Radio Reinvents Itself

12. How did radio adapt to the arrival of television?
13. What was Edwin Armstrong's role in the advancement of radio technology? Why did RCA hamper Armstrong's work?

14. How did music on radio change in the 1950s?
15. What is format radio, and why was it important to the survival of radio?

The Sounds of Commercial Radio

16. Why are there so many radio formats today?
17. Why did Top 40 radio diminish as a format in the 1980s and 1990s?
18. What is the state of nonprofit radio today?
19. How do Internet radio, satellite radio, podcasts, and HD radio present an alternative to standard broadcast radio?

The Economics of Broadcast Radio

20. What are the current ownership rules governing American radio?
21. What has been the main effect of the Telecommunications Act of 1996 on radio station ownership?
22. Why did the FCC create a new class of low-power FM stations?
23. Why did existing full-power radio broadcasters seek to delay and limit the emergence of low-power FM stations?

Radio and the Democracy of the Airwaves

24. Throughout the history of radio, why did the government encourage monopoly or oligopoly ownership of radio broadcasting?
25. What is the relevance of localism to debates about ownership in radio?

QUESTIONING THE MEDIA

1. Describe your earliest memories of listening to radio. Do you remember a favorite song? How old were you? Do you remember the station's call letters? Why did you listen?
2. Count the number and types of radio stations in your area today. What formats do they use? Do a little research and compare today's situation with the number and types of stations available in the 1930s and the 1950s. Describe the changes that have occurred.
3. If you could own and manage a commercial radio station, what format would you choose, and why?

4. If you ran a noncommercial radio station in your area, what services would you provide that are not being met by commercial format radio?
5. How might radio be used to improve social and political discussions in the United States?
6. If you were the head of a large radio group, what arguments would you make in response to charges that your company limited the number of voices in the local media?

For review quizzes, chapter summaries, links to media-related Web sites, and more, go to bedfordstmartins.com/mediaculture.

COMMON THREADS

One of the Common Threads discusses the development of the mass media. Like other mass media, radio evolved in three stages. But it also influenced an important dichotomy in mass media technology: wired versus wireless.

In radio's novelty stage, several inventors transcended the wires of the telegraph and telephone to solve the problem of wireless communication. In the entrepreneurial stage, inventors tested ship-to-shore radio, while others developed person-to-person toll radio transmissions and other schemes to make money from wireless communication. Finally, when radio stations began broadcasting to the general public (who bought radio receivers for their homes), radio became a mass medium.

As the first electronic mass medium, radio set the pattern for an ongoing battle between wired and wireless technologies. For example, television brought images to wireless broadcasting. Then cable television's wires brought television signals to places where receiving antennas didn't work. Satellite television (wireless from outer space) followed as an innovation to bring TV where cable didn't exist. Now, broadcast, cable, and satellite all compete against each other.

Similarly, think of how cell phones have eliminated millions of traditional phone, or land, lines. The Internet, like the telephone, also began with wires, but WiFi and home wireless systems are eliminating those wires, too. And radio? Most listeners get traditional local (wireless) radio broadcast signals, but now listeners may use a wired Internet connection to receive Webcasts or podcasts.

Both wired and wireless technology have advantages and disadvantages. Do we want the stability but tethers of a wired connection? Or do we want the freedom and occasional instability ("Can you hear me now?") of wireless media? Can radio's development help us understand wired versus wireless battles in other media?

KEY TERMS

The definitions for the terms listed below can be found in the Glossary at the end of the book. The page numbers listed with the terms indicate where the term is highlighted in the chapter.

telegraph, 109
Morse code, 109
electromagnetic waves, 109
radio waves, 110
wireless telegraphy, 111
wireless telephony, 113
broadcasting, 114
narrowcasting, 114
Radio Act of 1912, 114
Radio Corporation of America (RCA), 115
network, 117
option time, 119
Radio Act of 1927, 120
Federal Radio Commission (FRC), 120
Federal Communications Act of 1934, 120
Federal Communications Commission (FCC), 120
transistors, 124
FM, 125
AM, 125
format radio, 126
rotation, 126
Top 40 format, 126

progressive rock, 127
album-oriented rock (AOR), 127
drive time, 129
news/talk format, 129
adult contemporary (AC), 130
contemporary hit radio (CHR), 130
country, 130
urban, 130
Pacifica Foundation, 132
National Public Radio (NPR), 132
Public Broadcasting Service (PBS), 132
Public Broadcasting Act of 1967, 132
Corporation for Public Broadcasting (CPB), 132
Internet radio, 133
satellite radio, 134
podcasting, 134
HD radio, 134
payola, 137
pay-for-play, 137
Telecommunications Act of 1996, 137
low-power FM (LPFM), 139

5

Television and the Power of Visual Culture

The *sitcom*—short for "situation comedy"—is the only story genre ranked among the Top 10 most-watched programs in *every* TV season between 1949 and 2005. Every decade since the 1950s has produced No. 1 hit sitcoms, including *I Love Lucy* (1952-55; 1956-57); the *Beverly Hillbillies* (1962-64); *The Andy Griffith Show* (1967-68); *All in the Family* (1971-76); *Laverne & Shirley* (1977-79); the *Cosby Show* (1985-89); *Seinfeld* (1994-95; 1997-98); and *Friends* (2001-02). Since 2002, the franchise drama *CSI* (No. 1 from 2002-04) and hit reality show *American Idol* (2004-08) have taken over as the nation's most popular programs and helped drive sitcoms from the Top 10. What happened to the sitcom, and what does its decline tell us about American television and storytelling?

On the surface, it's hard to understand why the sitcom is in trouble. After all, TV executives highly value the strength of the sitcom in reruns, where its narrative structure allows regional TV stations or cable services to lease a hit show and show it, out of order, as a valuable lead-in program for local news and other programs (thereby boosting ratings). Long-running sitcoms like the *Cosby Show, Seinfeld,* and *Friends* earn billions of dollars in syndication. By contrast, TV station and cable channel managers have shown very little interest in leasing older episodes of reality series like *American Idol, Survivor,* and *Extreme Makeover,* which are generally found to be less compelling when watched more than once. Sitcoms also surpass reality programs in DVD sales. Network television executives continue to commission sitcoms, but in 2007–08 "as few as five new half-hour comedies . . . help fill almost 100 hours of prime time each week."[1]

To understand the sitcom's decline, then, we may need to look at cultural rather than economic explanations. We seem to be in the midst of a cultural shift in our taste and interest in storytelling. Defenders of the sitcom, like TV critic David Blum, suggest that sitcoms "fill our need for group experience—all of us laughing along with a studio audience at the comforting cadence of sitcom humor."[2] TV writers and other sitcom aficionados argue that the quality of the writing in the best sitcoms trumps the meandering, unscripted story lines of reality programs.

On the other hand, the way the Internet and video game generation views television and tells stories is changing. In popular video games like *The Sims* or *The World of Warcraft,* players have some control over story lines and character development. This is obviously a different narrative experience from simply watching a scripted TV story. In addition, watching less predictable reality programs—about "real" people instead of trained actors—provides a level of appeal and personal identification that is hard for traditional genre television to match.

In response, the creators of a current network sitcom, *The Office,* have broken new ground by revamping the show's look and structure, shooting the program documentary style (like the original British version). *The Office* feels like a hybrid program, located somewhere between the more traditional comedy and a reality program. As a faux documentary, the program lacks the familiar "laugh track" provided by an audience and features characters looking uncomfortably at the camera. While the show's ratings aren't high enough to crack the Top 10, advertisers support the show to reach its young, affluent fan base.

In the end, viewers have usually rewarded quality storytelling. That's the edge the sitcom has as it adapts to new genre challengers and attempts to extend its historical claim as the most popular narrative form in TV's relatively brief history. While the sitcom may have hit a rough patch up against the reality show trend, *The Office* is one example of how the sitcom will adapt and endure.

"We seem to be in the midst of a cultural shift in our taste and interest in storytelling."

◢ **WITH THE TRADITIONAL SITCOM DECLINING IN POPULARITY,** television networks today are surviving and prospering by developing cheaper reality series like *Dancing with the Stars,* by recycling old program ideas like the quiz show, by swiping concepts from European programmers (*American Idol*'s predecessor was Britain's *Pop Idol*), or just by stealing shows from each other. There is a long history behind all these strategies. After all, in its beginning, television borrowed extensively from radio, snatching radio's national sponsors, program ideas, and even its prime-time evening audience. Old radio scripts began reappearing in TV form. In 1949, for instance, *The Lone Ranger* rode over to television from radio, where the program had originated in 1933. *Amos 'n' Andy*, a fixture on network radio since 1928, became the first TV series to have an entirely black cast in 1951. Jack Benny, Red Skelton, George Burns, and Gracie Allen, among the most prominent comedians of their day, all left radio for television. Similarly, the radio news program *Hear It Now* turned into TV's *See It Now*, and *Candid Microphone* became *Candid Camera.*

Since replacing radio in the 1950s as our most popular mass medium, television has sparked repeated arguments about its social and cultural impact. Television has been accused of having a negative impact on children and young people, influencing their intake of sugary cereals and contributing to increases in teenage sex and violence. Television has also faced calls for reform during political campaigns. Some critics argue that the TV industry sustains a sharply partisan, outmoded two-party political system because of all the money television earns from serious candidates who need to buy TV advertising time to get elected.

But there is another side to this story. In times of crisis, our fragmented and pluralistic society has embraced television as common ground. It is the one mass medium that delivers content millions share simultaneously. It was TV that exposed us to Civil Rights violations in the South, to the shared pain and healing rituals after the Kennedy and King assassinations in the 1960s, and to the political turmoil of Watergate in the 1970s. In September 2001–in shock and horror–we all tuned in to television to learn that nearly three thousand people had been killed in terrorist attacks on the World Trade Center and the Pentagon and in a plane crash in Pennsylvania. In late summer 2005, we watched the coverage of Hurricane Katrina and saw haunting images of people drowned in the floods or displaced forever from their homes. And

> "Television is the medium from which most of us receive our news, sports, entertainment, cues for civic discourse, and, most of all, our marching orders as consumers."
>
> FRANK RICH, *NEW YORK TIMES*, 1998

◀

BORROWING PROGRAM IDEAS
America's most popular TV program over the past several years, *American Idol*, is actually a spin-off from creator Simon Cowell's original British program, *Pop Idol*, which has been replaced in the UK by Cowell's *X Factor*.

through 2008, we view the ongoing wars in Afghanistan and Iraq. For better or worse, television has woven itself into the cultural fabric of our daily lives.

In this chapter, we examine television's impact: the cultural, social, and economic factors surrounding the most influential media innovation since the printing press. We begin by reviewing the medium's early technological development. We then focus on the TV boom in the 1950s, including the end of sponsor-controlled content, the impact of the quiz-show scandals, and the development of TV's historical programming genres: news, comedy, and drama. We trace the traditional audience decline that has affected the major networks—especially people watching television on their cell phones or iPods. We also explore television as a prime-time money factory, examining various developments and costs in the production, distribution, and syndication of programs. Finally, we look at television's impact on democracy and culture.

The Origins and Early Development of Television

In 1948, only 1 percent of America's households had a television set; by 1953, more than 50 percent had one; and by the early 1960s, more than 90 percent of all homes had a TV set. With television on the rise throughout the 1950s, many feared that radio—as well as books, magazines, and movies—would become irrelevant and unnecessary; but both radio and print media adapted to this new technology. In fact, today more radio stations are operating and more books and magazines are published than ever before; only ticket sales for movies have flattened and declined slightly since the 1960s.

Three major historical developments in television's early years helped shape the new medium: technological innovations and patent wars, economic developments that wrested control of content away from advertisers and put contemporary business practices in place, and the sociocultural impact of the infamous quiz show scandals that took much of the shine off television's early promise.

▼ **Television and the Power of Visual Culture**

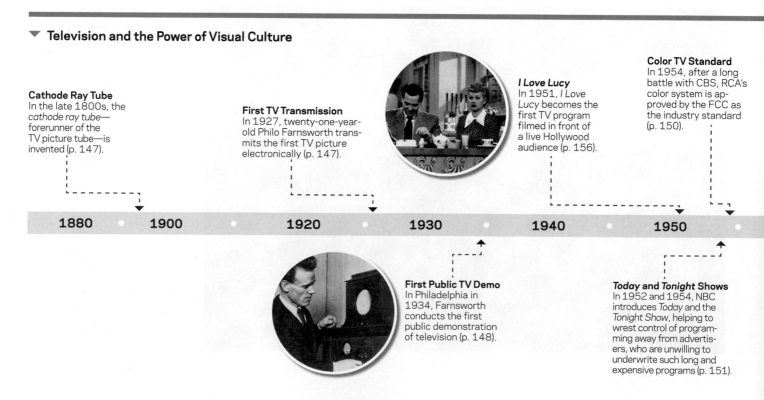

Cathode Ray Tube
In the late 1800s, the *cathode ray tube*—forerunner of the TV picture tube—is invented (p. 147).

First TV Transmission
In 1927, twenty-one-year-old Philo Farnsworth transmits the first TV picture electronically (p. 147).

I Love Lucy
In 1951, *I Love Lucy* becomes the first TV program filmed in front of a live Hollywood audience (p. 156).

Color TV Standard
In 1954, after a long battle with CBS, RCA's color system is approved by the FCC as the industry standard (p. 150).

1880   1900   1920   1930   1940   1950

First Public TV Demo
In Philadelphia in 1934, Farnsworth conducts the first public demonstration of television (p. 148).

Today and ***Tonight*** **Shows**
In 1952 and 1954, NBC introduces *Today* and the *Tonight Show*, helping to wrest control of programming away from advertisers, who are unwilling to underwrite such long and expensive programs (p. 151).

Early Innovations in TV Technology

In its novelty stage, TV's earliest pioneers were trying to isolate TV waves from the electromagnetic spectrum (as radio's pioneers had done with radio waves). The big question was: If a person could transmit audio signals from one place to another, why not visual images as well? Inventors from a number of nations toyed with the idea of sending "tele-visual" images for nearly a hundred years before what we know as TV developed.

In the late 1800s, the invention of the *cathode ray tube*, the forerunner of the TV picture tube, combined principles of the camera and electricity. Because television images could not physically float through the air, technicians and inventors developed a method of encoding them at a transmission point (TV station) and decoding them at a reception point (TV set). In the 1880s, German inventor Paul Nipkow developed the *scanning disk*, a large flat metal disk with a series of small perforations organized in a spiral pattern. As the disk rotated, it separated pictures into pinpoints of light that could be transmitted as a series of electronic lines. As the disk spun, each small hole scanned one line of a scene to be televised. For years, Nipkow's mechanical disk served as the foundation for experiments on the transmission of visual images.

Electronic Technology: Zworykin and Farnsworth

The story of television's invention included a complex patents battle between two independent inventors: Vladimir Zworykin and Philo Farnsworth. It began in Russia in 1907, when physicist Boris Rosing improved Nipkow's mechanical scanning device. Rosing's lab assistant, Vladimir Zworykin, left Russia for America in 1919 and went to work for Westinghouse and then RCA. In 1923 Zworykin invented the *iconoscope*, the first TV camera tube to convert light rays into electrical signals, and received a patent for it in 1928.

Around the same time, Idaho teenager Philo Farnsworth also figured out that a mechanical scanning system would not send pictures through the air over long distances. On September 7, 1927, the twenty-one-year-old Farnsworth transmitted the first electronic TV picture; he rotated a straight line scratched on a square of painted glass by 90 degrees. RCA, then the world leader in broadcasting technology, challenged Farnsworth in a major patents battle, in part over

> "There's nothing on it worthwhile, and we're not going to watch it in this household, and I don't want it in your intellectual diet."
>
> KENT FARNSWORTH, RECALLING THE ATTITUDE OF HIS FATHER (PHILO) TOWARD TV WHEN KENT WAS GROWING UP

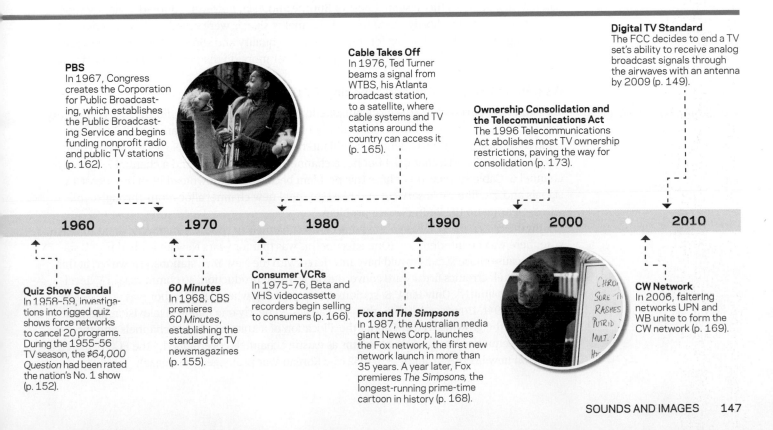

PBS
In 1967, Congress creates the Corporation for Public Broadcasting, which establishes the Public Broadcasting Service and begins funding nonprofit radio and public TV stations (p. 162).

Cable Takes Off
In 1976, Ted Turner beams a signal from WTBS, his Atlanta broadcast station, to a satellite, where cable systems and TV stations around the country can access it (p. 165).

Ownership Consolidation and the Telecommunications Act
The 1996 Telecommunications Act abolishes most TV ownership restrictions, paving the way for consolidation (p. 173).

Digital TV Standard
The FCC decides to end a TV set's ability to receive analog broadcast signals through the airwaves with an antenna by 2009 (p. 149).

1960   1970   1980   1990   2000   2010

Quiz Show Scandal
In 1958–59, investigations into rigged quiz shows force networks to cancel 20 programs. During the 1955–56 TV season, the *$64,000 Question* had been rated the nation's No. 1 show (p. 152).

60 Minutes
In 1968, CBS premieres *60 Minutes*, establishing the standard for TV newsmagazines (p. 155).

Consumer VCRs
In 1975–76, Beta and VHS videocassette recorders begin selling to consumers (p. 166).

Fox and *The Simpsons*
In 1987, the Australian media giant News Corp. launches the Fox network, the first new network launch in more than 35 years. A year later, Fox premieres *The Simpsons*, the longest-running prime-time cartoon in history (p. 168).

CW Network
In 2006, faltering networks UPN and WB unite to form the CW network (p. 169).

Zworykin's innovations for Westing-house and RCA. Farnsworth had to rely on his high-school science teacher to produce his original drawings from 1922. Finally, in 1930, Farnsworth received a patent for the first electronic television.

After the company's court defeat, RCA's president, David Sarnoff, had to negotiate to use Farnsworth's patents. Farnsworth later licensed these patents to RCA and AT&T for use in the commercial development of television. At the end of this development or novelty stage, Farnsworth conducted the first public demonstration of television at the Franklin Institute in Philadelphia in 1934—five years *before* RCA's famous public demonstration at the 1939 World's Fair.

PHILO FARNSWORTH, one of the inventors of television, experiments with an early version of an electronic TV set.

Setting Technical Standards

Figuring out how to push TV as a business and elevate it to a mass medium meant creating a coherent set of technical standards for product manufacturers. In the late 1930s, then, amid the competing technical standards and dueling patents war, the National Television Systems Committee (NTSC), a group representing major electronics firms, began outlining industry-wide manufacturing practices and compromising on technical standards. As a result, in 1941 the Federal Communications Commission (FCC) adopted an **analog** standard for all U.S. TV sets. About thirty countries, including Japan, Canada, Mexico, Saudi Arabia, and most Latin American nations, adopted this system. (Most of Europe and Asia, however, adopted a slightly superior technical system shortly after.) In the U.S., analog signals were scheduled to be replaced by **digital** signals in 2009, allowing for improved image quality and sound. (See "Tracking Technology: Digital Television Takes Over" on page 149 for more on the switch to digital television.)

Assigning Frequencies and Freezing TV Licenses

TV signals are part of the same electromagnetic spectrum that carries radio signals. This means that in the early days of television the number of TV stations a city or market could support was limited because airwave frequencies would interfere with one another. So a TV market could have a channel 2 and a channel 4 but not a channel 3; or a channel 5 and a channel 7 but not a channel 6. Cable systems don't have this problem because they download both broadcast TV signals and satellite cable services and reassign them new channel allocations through cable wires, clearing up the limited space problem.

In the 1940s, the FCC began assigning certain channels in specific geographic areas to make sure there was no interference. (One effect of this was that for years New Jersey had no TV stations because those signals would have interfered with the New York stations.) However, at this time, most electronics firms were converting to wartime production, so commercial TV development was limited: Only ten U.S. stations were operating when Pearl Harbor was attacked in December 1941. However, by 1948, the FCC had issued nearly one hundred television licenses. Because of the growing concern about the allocation of a finite number of channels and the growing frequency-interference problems as existing channels "overlapped," the FCC declared a freeze on new licenses from 1948 to 1952 (the Korean War prolonged the freeze).

TRACKING TECHNOLOGY

Digital Television Takes Over

Starting in the late 1940s, television sets received their programming from analog signals made of radio waves—frequencies that TV sets translate into pictures and sounds. An analog signal reaches a TV set over the airwaves, through a cable wire, or by satellite transmission. This analog system, which was in place for over sixty years, had some disadvantages: limited resolution (the bigger the TV set, the lousier the image) and a picture quality that never really compared with the rich texture of film at the movies. To help remedy the situation, the U.S. and other nations, particularly Japan, gradually began making technological advances to improve image quality. Eventually the FCC decided to change from the old analog standard to a variety of approved digital television standards (DTV) among which HDTV, or *high-definition television*, offers the highest resolution and best image (and also requires more bandwidth or space to transmit the image and sound). The official switch to DTV was scheduled to occur in February 2009, and afterwards all broadcast TV signals will be sent digitally. (Before the analog shut-off date, broadcasters could send their signal on an analog channel and a digital channel, but you had to be tuned in to the broadcaster's digital channel and have a digital set to access it.)

DTV signals have several advantages over analog, including better picture quality (for comparison, think of the difference between an analog recording on a vinyl record and a digital CD) and better resolution, allowing an improved picture on a larger TV screen. Also, a digital signal translates TV images and sounds into binary code—ones and zeroes—meaning that DTV signals require much less frequency space. The big disadvantage of DTV is that older analog sets can't decode and display digital signals. So when analog broadcasting ended, many older analog TVs (with the bulky picture tubes—unlike trim digital flat-screen TVs) were not usable without a cable or satellite service and/or a set-top digital converter. To ensure that uninterrupted access to free, over-the-air television did not pose a financial hardship for viewers, in January 2008 the government began issuing $40 gift cards (up to two per household) to consumers who needed to purchase digital converters. The government will regain some of that expense by auctioning off the old analog broadcast spectrum to mobile cell phone companies.[1] (See Chapter 2.)

Of course, there are other pluses to going digital. Because digital signals require less frequency space than analog signals, TV stations can compress a digital signal and carry several different signals using the same frequency or bandwidth. This means that networks, cable channels, and local TV stations can assign more digital channels to the same frequency that used to handle just one analog channel, or use that frequency space to carry an HDTV signal, which requires more bandwidth. While all digital standards are better in quality than the old analog signals, HDTV standards are the best of the digital signals. So even though a digital signal is better quality than an analog signal, it isn't necessarily high definition. HDTV is the top tier of all the DTV standards. Whether you see an HD picture depends on two things: the network, TV station, cable company, or DBS service must use a high-definition signal, and you need HDTV equipment to receive and view it.

As Richard Wiley, a former chairman of the FCC, said about the switch to digital television in 2009, "The moment coming is the end of something that has been around for 60 years—conventional television—and it has been a wonderful era. With that ending will come this new digital world, this much greater world."[2]

DIGITAL TELEVISION: Experience the Benefits

1-888-DTV-2009   www.DTV2009.gov

THE SWITCH TO DTV
In the final transition from analog to digital television, the FCC financed a campaign to make consumers aware of the switch to DTV. The consumer outreach program included television commercials, print ads, a Web site, press releases, and posters.

During this time, cities such as New York, Chicago, and Los Angeles had several TV stations, while other areas—including Little Rock, Arkansas, and Portland, Oregon—had none. In non-TV cities, movie audiences increased. But cities with TV stations saw a 20 to 40 percent drop in movie attendance during this period; more than sixty movie theaters closed in the Chicago area alone. Taxi receipts and nightclub attendance also fell in TV cities, as did library book circulation. Radio listening also declined; for example, Bob Hope's network radio show lost half its national audience between 1949 and 1951. By 1951, sales of television sets had surpassed sales of radio receivers.

After a second NTSC conference in 1952 sorted out technical problems, the FCC ended the licensing freeze, and almost thirteen hundred communities received TV channel allocations. In order for broadcast signals not to interfere with one another, the FCC created a national map and tried to distribute all available channels evenly throughout the country. By the mid-1950s, there were more than four hundred television stations in operation—a 400 percent surge since the pre-freeze era—and television became a mass medium. Today, about seventeen hundred TV stations are in operation, including more than three hundred nonprofit stations.

FIRST COLOR TV
On the assembly line, this 1954 color television set— the RCA CT-100—was the first mass-produced electronic color TV set. Only affluent consumers could afford these early sets, priced at $1,000 or more.

"[Digital] TV doesn't sink in until you see it. It's like TV in the 1940s and color TV in the 1960s—once the rich guy down the block gets it, so will you."

DAVID ARLAND,
THOMSON
ELECTRONICS, 2002

The Introduction of Color Television

The 1952 NTSC conference also finalized technical standards for TV sets (many of which would still be in use until the U.S. converted to digital standards in 2009). Then, deliberations about the standards for a color TV system began. In 1952, the FCC tentatively approved an experimental CBS color system. Because its signal could not be received by black-and-white sets, however, the system was incompatible with the sets most Americans owned. In 1954, RCA's color system, which sent TV images in color but allowed older sets to receive the color images as black-and-white, usurped CBS's system to become the color standard. Although NBC began broadcasting a few shows in color in the mid-1950s, it wasn't until 1966, when the consumer market for color sets had taken off, that all three networks (CBS, NBC, and ABC) broadcast their entire evening lineups in color.

Controlling Content—TV Grows Up

By the end of the 1950s, television had become a dominant mass medium and cultural force, with more than 90 percent of U.S. households owning at least one set. Television's new standing came as it moved away from the influence of radio and established a separate identity. Two important contributors to this identity were a major change in the advertising and sponsorship structure of television and, more significant, a major scandal.

Program Format Changes Affect Sponsorship

Like radio in the 1930s and 1940s, early television programs were often developed, produced, and supported by a single sponsor. Many of the top-rated programs in the 1950s even included the sponsor's name in the title: *Buick Circus Hour, Camel News Caravan, Colgate Comedy Hour,* and *Goodyear TV Playhouse.* Today no regular program on network television is named after and controlled by a single sponsor.

Throughout the early 1950s, the broadcast networks became increasingly unhappy with the control sponsors exerted over program content. The growing popularity of television, though, offered opportunities to alter prior financial arrangements, especially given the high cost of producing programs on a weekly basis. In 1952, for example, a single one-hour TV show cost a sponsor about $35,000, a figure that rose to $90,000 by the end of the decade. These weekly costs, especially when added to the network expenses in the development of color technology, became more difficult for sponsors to bear.

David Sarnoff, then head of RCA/NBC, and William Paley, head of CBS, saw the opportunity to diminish the role of sponsors. In 1953 Sarnoff appointed Sylvester "Pat" Weaver (father of actress Sigourney Weaver) as the president of NBC. A former advertising executive, Weaver had controlled radio content for his clients, meaning he helped decide which shows got on the air and best served his clients' interests. In his move to television, Weaver undermined his former profession, diminishing the role of advertisers in deciding TV content. By increasing program length from fifteen minutes (then standard for radio programs) to thirty minutes and longer, Weaver substantially raised program costs for advertisers.

The Magazine Format and the TV Spectacular

In addition, the introduction of two new types of programs—the magazine format and the TV spectacular—greatly helped the networks gain control over content. The television magazine program featured multiple segments—news, talk, comedy, and music—similar to the content variety found in a general interest or newsmagazine of the day, such as *Life* or *Time.* In January 1952, NBC introduced the *Today* show as a three-hour morning talk-news program. Then in September 1954, NBC premiered the ninety-minute *Tonight Show.*

Because both shows ran daily rather than weekly, studio production costs were prohibitive for a single sponsor. Consequently, NBC offered spot ads within the shows: Advertisers paid the network for thirty- or sixty-second time slots. The network, not the sponsor, now produced and owned the programs or bought them from independent producers. More than fifty years later, *Today* and the *Tonight Show* remain fixtures on NBC.

MAGAZINE FORMAT TV SHOWS
In 2009, Conan O'Brien—the Harvard-educated former Emmy-winning writer on *Saturday Night Live* and *The Simpsons*—took over the *Tonight Show* from Jay Leno. O'Brien's former show *Late Night* (above) found a new host in Jimmy Fallon.

The television spectacular is today recognized by a more modest term, the *television special*. At NBC, Weaver bought special programs, like Sir Laurence Olivier's filmed version of *Richard III* and the Broadway production of *Peter Pan*, and sold spot ads to multiple sponsors. The 1955 TV version of *Peter Pan* was a particular success, watched by some sixty-five million viewers (in comparison, the final episode of NBC's *Friends* was watched by about fifty million viewers in spring 2004). More typical specials featured music-variety shows hosted by top singers such as Judy Garland and Frank Sinatra.

The Quiz-Show Scandals Diminish the Promise of TV

In the mid-1950s, the networks revived the radio quiz-show genre. CBS aired the *$64,000 Question*, originally radio's more modest *$64 Question*, signaling how much television had raised the economic stakes. Sponsored by Revlon, who in 1955 bought a half-hour block of evening **prime time**, the program ranked as the most popular TV show in America during its first year. As one historian suggested, "It is impossible to explain fully the popular appeal of the *$64,000 Question*. Be it the lure of sudden wealth, the challenge to answer esoteric questions, happiness at seeing other people achieving financial success, whatever the program touched in the American psyche at mid-century, this was stunning TV."[3] Revlon followed its success with the *$64,000 Challenge* in 1956; by the end of the 1957-58 season, twenty-two quiz shows aired on network television. At one point, Revlon's shows were running first and second in the ratings, and the cosmetic company's name recognition was so enhanced that drugstores often ran out of Revlon lipstick and mascara. In fact, the company's cosmetic sales skyrocketed from $1.2 million before its sponsorship of the quiz shows to nearly $10 million by 1959.

Rigging of the Quiz Shows

Compared with dramas and sitcoms, quiz shows were (and are today) cheap to produce, with inexpensive sets and mostly nonactors as guests. In addition, these programs offered the corporate sponsor the opportunity to have its name displayed on the set throughout the program. The problem was that most of these shows were rigged. To heighten the drama and

TWENTY-ONE
In 1957, the most popular contestant on the quiz show *Twenty-One* was college professor Charles Van Doren (left). Congressional hearings on rigged quiz shows revealed that Van Doren had been given some answers. Host Jack Barry, pictured here above the sponsor's logo, nearly had his career ruined, but made a comeback in the late 1960s with the syndicated game show *The Joker's Wild*.

get rid of guests whom the sponsors or producers did not find appealing, key contestants were rehearsed and given the answers.

The most notorious rigging occurred on *Twenty-One*, a quiz show owned by Geritol (whose profits climbed by $4 million one year after it began to sponsor the program in 1956). The show and its most infamous contestant, Charles Van Doren, became the subject of Robert Redford's 1994 film *Quiz Show*. A Columbia University English professor from a famous literary family, Van Doren won $129,000 in 1957 during his fifteen-week run on the program; his fame then landed him a job on NBC's *Today* show. In 1958, after a series of contestants accused the show *Dotto* of being fixed, the networks quickly dropped twenty quiz shows. Following further rumors, a *TV Guide* story, a New York grand jury probe, and a 1959 congressional investigation during which Van Doren admitted to cheating, big-money prime-time quiz shows ended—until ABC revived the format forty years later with *Who Wants to Be a Millionaire*.

A Change in Cultural Attitudes

The impact of the quiz-show scandals was enormous. First, the sponsors' pressure on TV executives to rig the programs and the subsequent fraud effectively put an end to any role sponsors might have in creating television content. Second, and more important, the fraud tended to undermine Americans' expectation of the democratic promise of television—to bring inexpensive information and entertainment into every household. Many people had trusted their own eyes—what they saw on TV—more than *words* they heard on radio on read in print. But the scandals provided the first dramatic indication that TV images could be manipulated. Our contemporary cynicism about electronic culture began in this time, and by the end of the decade, some middle-class parents were not allowing their children to watch television.

The third, and most important, impact of the quiz-show scandals was that they magnified the separation between the privileged few and the general public, a division between the "high" and "low" cultures that would keep quiz shows out of prime time for forty years. That Charles Van Doren had come from a family of Ivy League intellectuals and cheated for fame and money drove a wedge between intellectuals and the popular new medium. At the time, many well-educated people aimed a wary skepticism toward television. This was best captured in the famous 1961 speech by FCC commissioner Newton Minow, who labeled game shows, westerns, cartoons, and other popular genres part of commercial television's "vast wasteland." Critics have used the wasteland metaphor ever since to admonish the TV industry for failing to live up to its potential.

After the quiz-show scandal, non-network, non-prime-time, independently produced programs like *Jeopardy!* and *Wheel of Fortune*, then renamed *game shows*, eventually made a comeback in syndicated late-afternoon time slots and later on cable channels like ESPN and Comedy Central. The major broadcast networks, however, remained reluctant to put game shows on again in prime time. Finally, in 1999, ABC gambled that the nation was ready once again for a quiz show in prime time. The network, at least for a couple of years, had great success with *Who Wants to Be a Millionaire*.

> "I was fascinated by the seduction of [Charles] Van Doren, by the Faustian bargain that lured entirely good and honest people into careers of deception."
>
> ROBERT REDFORD, DIRECTOR, *QUIZ SHOW*, 1995

Major Programming Trends

The disappearance of quiz shows marked the end of most prime-time network programs that originated from New York. From 1955 through 1957, the three major networks gradually moved their entertainment divisions to Los Angeles because of its proximity to Hollywood production studios. Network news operations, however, remained in New York. Symbolically, New York and Los Angeles came to represent the two major branches of TV programming: *information* and entitlement, *entertainment*, respectively. Although there is considerable blurring between these categories today, at one time the two were more distinct. In the sections that follow, we examine significant network program developments, focusing primarily on historical and enduring trends.

TV Information: Our Daily News Culture

Since the 1960s, broadcast journalism has consistently topped print news in national research polls that ask which news medium is most trustworthy. Most studies suggest this has to do with television's intimacy as a medium—its ability to create loyalty with viewers who connect personally with the news anchors we "invite" into our living rooms each evening. Print reporters and editors, by comparison, seem anonymous and detached. In this section, we focus on the traditional network evening news, its history, and the changes in TV news ushered in by cable.

NBC News

Originally featuring a panel of reporters interrogating political figures, NBC's weekly *Meet the Press* (1947–) is the oldest show on television. Daily evening newscasts, though, began on NBC in February 1948 with the *Camel Newsreel Theater*, sponsored by the cigarette company. Originally a ten-minute Fox Movietone newsreel that was also shown in theaters, this filmed news service was converted to a live, fifteen-minute broadcast, renamed *Camel News Caravan*, and anchored by John Cameron Swayze in 1949.

In 1956, the *Huntley Brinkley Report* debuted with Chet Huntley in New York and David Brinkley in Washington. This coanchored NBC program became the most popular TV evening news show. To provide a touch of intimacy, the coanchors would sign off their broadcasts each day with, "Good night, Chet"/"Good night, David." Huntley and Brinkley served as the dual-anchor model for hundreds of local news broadcasts. After Huntley retired in 1970, the program was renamed *NBC Nightly News* and struggled to compete for viewers with CBS's emerging star anchor, Walter Cronkite. A series of anchors and coanchors followed before Tom Brokaw settled in as sole anchor in September 1983, passing the chair to Brian Williams following the 2004 presidential election. Away from the news set, Williams has tried to shake up the conventional image of the detached, unemotional anchor. He has hosted NBC's *Saturday Night Live*, making fun of his own anchorman persona, and has been an occasional guest on *The Daily Show with Jon Stewart*.

CBS News

The CBS-TV News with Douglas Edwards premiered on CBS in May 1948. In 1956, the program became the first news show videotaped for rebroadcast on **affiliate stations** (stations that contract with a network to carry its programs) in central and western time zones. Walter Cronkite succeeded Edwards in 1962, starting a nineteen-year run as anchor of the renamed *CBS Evening News*. Formerly a World War II correspondent for a print wire service, Cronkite in 1963 anchored the first thirty-minute network newscast, on which President John Kennedy appeared in a live interview—twelve weeks before his assassination.

In 1968, Cronkite went to Vietnam to cover the war there firsthand. Putting aside his journalistic neutrality, he concluded that the American public had been misled and that U.S. participation in the war was a mistake, declaring on air after he returned, "It seems now more certain than ever that the bloody experience of Vietnam is to end in a stalemate." With such a centrist news personality now echoing the protest movement, public opinion against U.S. intervention mounted. In fact, President

WALTER CRONKITE
In 1968, after popular CBS news anchor Walter Cronkite visited Vietnam, CBS produced the documentary "Report from Vietnam by Walter Cronkite." At the end of the program, Cronkite offered this terse observation: "It is increasingly clear to this reporter that the only rational way out then will be to negotiate, not as victors but as an honorable people who lived up to their pledge to defend democracy, and did the best they could." Most political observers said that Cronkite's opposition to the war influenced President Johnson's decision not to seek reelection.

Lyndon Johnson reportedly said to one of his advisors at the time, "If I've lost Cronkite, I've lost America."

Retiring in 1981, Cronkite gave way to Dan Rather, a former White House correspondent who had starred on CBS's news program *60 Minutes* since 1975. Despite a $22 million, ten-year contract, Rather could not sustain the program as the highest-rated evening newscast. In 1993, the network paired Rather with former *Today* host Connie Chung. Unlike CNN and many local news stations, which routinely used male-female news teams, the networks had used women anchors only as substitutes or on weekends. Ratings continued to sag, however, and CBS fired Chung after a few months. Rather resigned in 2005, and in 2006, CBS hired Katie Couric, also from the *Today* show, as the first woman to serve as the featured solo anchor on a network evening news program. With Couric anchoring, ratings dropped or remained flat, suggesting that some viewers seemed reluctant to accept their network evening news from a woman.

ABC News

After premiering an unsuccessful daily program in 1948, ABC launched a daily news show in 1953, anchored by John Daly—the head of ABC News and the host of CBS's evening game show *What's My Line?* After Daly left in 1960, a series of personalities anchored the show, including John Cameron Swayze and, in 1965, a twenty-six-year-old Canadian, Peter Jennings. Another series of rotating anchors ensued, including Harry Reasoner and Howard K. Smith. In 1976, ABC hired Barbara Walters away from NBC's *Today* show, gave her a $1 million annual contract, and made her the first woman to coanchor a network newscast. With Walters and Reasoner together, viewer ratings rose slightly, but the network was still behind CBS and NBC.

In 1978, the head of the ABC News and Sports division, Roone Arledge, started *ABC World News Tonight*, featuring four anchors: Frank Reynolds in Washington, Jennings in London, Walters in New York, and Max Robinson in Chicago. Robinson was the first black reporter to coanchor a network news program. In 1983, Jennings became the sole anchor of the broadcast. By the late 1980s, the ABC evening news had become the most-watched newscast until, in 1996, it was dethroned by Brokaw's *NBC Nightly News*. After Jennings's death in 2005, his spot was shared by coanchors Elizabeth Vargas and Bob Woodruff, who was seriously wounded covering the Iraq war that same year. In 2006 Charles Gibson—from ABC's *Good Morning America*—took over.

By early 2008, in the all-important TV ratings battle (which resets advertising rates every two to three months), Gibson and Williams were vying for first place, drawing between nine and ten million viewers each evening. Couric, in third, drew about seven million viewers each broadcast. (In comparison to the audiences for network anchors, Bill O'Reilly on cable's Fox News, who typically has the largest cable audience, draws roughly two million viewers each night.)

Contemporary Trends in News

Audiences watching the network news contributed to the eventual demise of almost all large afternoon daily newspapers. By the 1980s, though, network audiences also began to decline. Facing competition for viewers from VCRs and cable, especially CNN, the networks saw advertising revenues flatten. In response, they laid off staff, eliminating many national and foreign reporter posts. The cutbacks represented a change in thinking; news delivery came to be seen less as a public service and more as a for-profit enterprise. Unfortunately, these cutbacks would hamper the networks' ability to cover global stories and international terrorism adequately before and after 9/11.

In 1968, *60 Minutes* premiered and pioneered the **TV newsmagazine**. This format usually featured three stories per episode (rather than one topic per hour—as had been the custom on Edward R. Murrow's *See It Now* [CBS 1951-59]), alternating hard-hitting investigations of corruption or political intrigue with "softer" features on Hollywood celebrities, cultural trends, and assorted dignitaries. In an effort to duplicate the financial success of *60 Minutes*, the most

"If NBC found five more *Seinfelds*, there would be two or three fewer *Datelines* on the air. That's not news. That's filler."

DON HEWITT,
60 MINUTES FOUNDER
AND EXECUTIVE
PRODUCER, 1998

profitable show in TV history, the Big Three networks began developing their own versions: ABC's *20/20* (1978-) and *Primetime Live* (1989-) became moneymakers, and at one time, *20/20* aired three or four evenings a week. NBC's *Dateline* (1992-) appeared up to five nights a week by 2000–so often that critics accused NBC of trivializing the formula. After 2002, the program aired only two to three nights per week. In addition, independent producers developed a number of syndicated non-network newsmagazines for the local late-afternoon and late-night markets. These featured more than twenty breezy-sometimes-sleazy syndicated tabloids, including *Entertainment Tonight* and *A Current Affair*.

Cable news has certainly cut into the once large network news audiences, but more significantly it has changed the TV news game by offering viewers information and stories on demand in a 24/7 cycle. Viewers no longer have to wait until 5:30 or 6:30 P.M. to watch the national network news stories. Cable channels offer viewers news updates and breaking stories at any time of the day or night as well as constant online news updates. Cable news also challenged the old network program formulas. Daily opinion programs such as MSNBC's *Countdown*, starring Keith Olbermann, and Fox News' *The O'Reilly Factor*, starring Bill O'Reilly, have proliferated on cable. Sometimes celebrating argument, opinion, and speculation over traditional reporting based on verified facts, these programs emerged primarily because of their low cost compared with traditional news. It is much cheaper to anchor a program around one "star" anchor and a few guests than to dispatch expensive equipment and several field reporters to cover stories from multiple locations (see Chapter 6). In addition, the rise of Internet news blogs and satirical fake news programs has presented a challenge to traditional news outlets (see Chapter 14).

TV Entertainment: Our Comic Culture

The networks began to move their entertainment divisions to Los Angeles in the mid 1950s. This was partly because of the success of the pioneering comedy series *I Love Lucy* (1951-57). *Lucy*'s owners and costars, Lucille Ball and Desi Arnaz, began filming the top-rated sitcom in California near their home, although CBS originally wanted them to shoot live in New York. In 1951, *Lucy* became the first TV program filmed before a live Hollywood audience.

Before the days of videotape (invented in 1956), the only way to preserve a live broadcast, other than filming it like a movie, was through a technique called **kinescope**. In this process, an inexpensive camera recorded a live TV show off a studio monitor. The quality of the kinescope was poor, and most series that were saved in this way have not survived. *I Love Lucy*, *Alfred Hitchcock Presents*, and the original *Dragnet* are among a handful of series from the 1950s that endured because they were originally shot and preserved on film, like movies. Even during the quiz-show boom, the primary staples of television entertainment were comedy and drama programs, both heavily influenced by New York radio, vaudeville, and theater. In television history, comedy has usually come in three varieties: sketch comedy, situation comedy (or sitcom), and domestic comedy.

Sketch Comedy

Sketch comedy, or comedy skits, was a key element in early TV variety shows, which also included singers, dancers, acrobats, animal acts, stand-up comics, and ventriloquists. The shows "resurrected the essentials of stage variety entertainment" and played to noisy studio

TV COMEDY
Your Show of Shows (NBC, 1950–54), starring Sid Caesar and Imogene Coca, was one of the most ambitious and influential comedy programs in TV history. Each week it featured ninety minutes of original, high-quality, live sketch comedy. A major influence on programs like *Saturday Night Live* (NBC, 1975-), *Your Show of Shows* also jump-started the careers of a number of comedy writers, including Neil Simon, Mel Brooks, and Woody Allen.

audiences.[4] Vaudeville performers were television's first stars of sketch comedy and included Milton Berle, TV's first major celebrity, in *Texaco Star Theater* (1948-67); Red Skelton in the *Red Skelton Show* (1951-71); and Sid Caesar, Imogene Coca, and Carl Reiner in *Your Show of Shows* (1950-54), for which playwright Neil Simon, filmmakers Mel Brooks and Woody Allen, and writer Larry Gelbart (*M*A*S*H*) all served for a time as writers.

Sketch comedy, though, had some major drawbacks. The hour-long variety series in which these skits appeared were more expensive to produce than half-hour sitcoms. Also, skits on weekly variety shows, such as the *Perry Como Show* (1948-63) and the *Carol Burnett Show* (1967-79), used up new routines very quickly. The ventriloquist Edgar Bergen (father of actress Candice Bergen) once commented that "no comedian should be on TV once a week; he shouldn't be on more than once a month."[5] With original skits and new sets required each week, production costs mounted, and the vaudeville-influenced variety series faded. Since the early 1980s, network variety shows have appeared only as yearly specials.

Situation Comedy

Until recently, the most dependable entertainment program on television has been the half-hour comedy series. (See Table 5.1.) The **situation comedy**, or *sitcom*, features a recurring cast, and each episode establishes a situation, complicates it, develops increasing confusion among

TABLE 5.1

SELECTED SITUATION AND DOMESTIC COMEDIES RATED IN THE TOP 10 SHOWS

Source: Variety.com, "Top 100 TV Shows of all Time," http://www.variety.com/index.asp?layout=chart_pass&charttype=chart_topshowsalltime&dept=TV#ev_top, accessed October 16, 2008.

The most durable genre in the history of television has been the half-hour comedy. Until 2005–06, it was the only genre that had been represented in the Nielsen rating Top 10 lists every year since 1949. Below is a selection of top-rated comedies at five-year intervals, spanning fifty years.

1955-56	1975-76	1990-91 (cont.)
I Love Lucy (#2)	All in the Family (#1)	A Different World (#4)
Jack Benny Show (#5)	Laverne & Shirley (#3)	Cosby Show (#5)
December Bride (#6)	Maude (#4)	Murphy Brown (#6)
	Phyllis (#6)	Empty Nest (#7)
	Sanford and Son, Rhoda (tie #7)	Golden Girls, Designing Women (tie #10)
1960-61	**1980-81**	**1995-96**
Andy Griffith Show (#4)	M*A*S*H (#4)	Seinfeld (#2)
The Real McCoys (#8)	The Jeffersons (#6)	Friends (#3)
Jack Benny Show (#10)	Alice (#7)	Caroline in the City (#4)
	House Calls, Three's Company (tie # 8)	The Single Guy (#6)
		Home Improvement (#7)
		Boston Common (#8)
1965-66	**1985-86**	**2000-01**
Gomer Pyle, U.S.M.C. (#2)	Cosby Show (#1)	Friends (#3)
The Lucy Show (#3)	Family Ties (#2)	Everybody Loves Raymond (#4)
Andy Griffith Show,	Cheers (#5)	Will & Grace (#10)
Bewitched, Beverly Hillbillies (tie #7)	Golden Girls (#7)	
Hogan's Heroes (#9)	Who's the Boss? (#10)	
1970-71	**1990-91**	**Since 2005**
Here's Lucy (#3)	Cheers (#1)	For the first time in TV history,
	Roseanne (#3)	a half-hour comedy series did not rate
		among the season's Top 10 programs.

its characters, and then usually resolves the complications.[6] *I Love Lucy*, the *Beverly Hillbillies*, *Sanford and Son*, *Night Court*, *Seinfeld*, *Will & Grace*, *30 Rock*, and HBO's *Curb Your Enthusiasm* are all part of this once indispensable genre.

In most sitcoms, character development is downplayed in favor of zany plots. Characters are usually static and predictable, and they generally do not develop much during the course of a series. Such characters "are never troubled in profound ways." Stress, more often the result of external confusion rather than emotional anxiety, "is always funny."[7] Viewers of situation comedies usually think of themselves as slightly superior to the characters. Much like viewers of soap operas, sitcom fans feel just a little bit smarter than the characters, whose lives seem wacky and out of control.

Domestic Comedy

In a **domestic comedy**, characters and settings are usually more important than complicated predicaments. Although an episode might offer a goofy situation as a subplot, more typically the main narrative features a personal problem or family crisis that characters have to solve. Greater emphasis is placed on character development than on reestablishing the order that has been disrupted by confusion. Domestic comedies take place primarily at home (*Two and a Half Men*), at the workplace (*The Office*), or at both (*Will & Grace*).

The main emphasis in a domestic comedy is how the characters react to one another. Family and workplace bonds are tested and strengthened by the end of the show. Generally, viewers identify more closely with the major characters in domestic comedies than with those in a sitcom. For example, in an episode of the sitcom *Happy Days* (1974-84), the main characters are accidentally locked in a vault over a weekend. The plot focuses on how they are going to free themselves, which they do after assorted crazy adventures. Contrast this with an episode from the domestic comedy *All in the Family* (1971-83), in which archconservative Archie and his ultraliberal son-in-law Mike are accidentally locked in the basement. The physical predicament

COMEDIES are often among the most popular shows on television. *I Love Lucy* (below) was the top-ranked show from 1952 to 1955 and was a model for other shows such as *Dick Van Dyke*, *Laverne & Shirley*, *Roseanne*, and *Will & Grace*. *All in the Family* (below, right) was the No. 1 rated sitcom five years running—between 1971 and 1976—and explored issues of class, race, gender, and ethnicity, which previously had been considered taboo topics for U.S. comedy programs.

becomes a subplot as the main "action" shifts to the characters themselves, who reflect on their generational and political differences.

Today, many programs are a mix of both situation and domestic comedy. For example, an episode of *Friends* (1994-2004) might offer a character-driven plot about the generation gap and a minor subplot about a pet monkey gone berserk. Domestic comedies may also mix dramatic and comedic elements. An episode of *Roseanne* (1988-97) might juxtapose a dramatic scene in which a main character has a heart attack with another in which Roseanne's family intentionally offends their neighbors by decorating their home in a cheap and "trashy" holiday motif. This blurring of serious and comic themes marks a contemporary hybrid, sometimes labeled *dramedy*, which includes such series as the *Wonder Years* (1988-93), *Northern Exposure* (1990-95), *Ally McBeal* (1997-2002), HBO's *Sex and the City* (1999-2004), and *Desperate Housewives* (2005-).

TV Entertainment: Our Dramatic Culture

Because the production of TV entertainment was centered in New York in its early days, many of its ideas, sets, technicians, actors, and directors came from New York theater. Young stage actors—including Anne Bancroft, Ossie Davis, James Dean, Grace Kelly, Paul Newman, Sidney Poitier, Robert Redford, and Joanne Woodward—often worked in television if they could not find stage work. The TV dramas that grew from these early influences fit roughly into two categories: the anthology drama and the episodic series.

Anthology Drama

In the early 1950s, television—like cable in the early 1980s—served a more elite and wealthier audience. **Anthology dramas** brought live dramatic theater to that television audience. Influenced by stage plays, anthologies offered new, artistically significant *teleplays* (scripts written for television), casts, directors, writers, and sets from one week to the next. This genre launched the careers of such writers as William Gibson (*The Miracle Worker*), Reginald Rose (*Twelve Angry Men*), and Paddy Chayefsky (*Marty*) whose teleplays were often later made into movies. (Chayefsky, in fact, wrote the screenplay for the 1976 film *Network*, a biting condemnation of television.) In the 1952-53 season alone, there were eighteen anthology dramas competing on the networks, offering original plays each week. These included *Studio One* (1948-58), *Alfred Hitchcock Presents* (1955-65), the *Twilight Zone* (1959-64), and *Kraft Television Theater* (1947-58), which was actually created to introduce Kraft's Cheez Whiz.

The anthology's brief run as a dramatic staple on television ended for both economic and political reasons. First, advertisers disliked anthologies because they often presented stories that confronted complex human problems that were not easily resolved. The commercials that interrupted the drama, however, told upbeat stories in which problems were easily solved by purchasing a product; so anthologies made the simplicity of the commercial pitch ring false. These dramas also often cast "non-beautiful heroes and heroines,"[8] unlike the stars of the commercials. Chayefsky once referred to the narrative plots of anthologies as the "marvelous world of the ordinary."[9]

"Aristotle once said that a play should have a beginning, a middle, and an end. But what did he know? Today, a play must have a first half, a second half, and a station break."

ALFRED HITCHCOCK, DIRECTOR

THE BRITISH DIRECTOR ALFRED HITCHCOCK, known for his classic suspense movies *Psycho, North By Northwest,* and *Vertigo,* was one of just a few Hollywood directors who also enjoyed a successful TV career, hosting the anthology drama *Alfred Hitchcock Presents* on CBS and NBC from 1955 to 1965.

In 1954, these concerns led sponsors and ad agencies to seek control over content by demanding more input into scripts. For instance, Reginald Rose's teleplay *Thunder on Sycamore Street* was based on a real incident in which a black family moved into an all-white neighborhood and felt pressured to leave. CBS, at the behest of advertisers who wanted to avoid public controversy, asked that the black family be changed to "something else." Rose rewrote the script, abandoning the black family in favor of a white ex-convict. Faced with ever-increasing creative disagreements between writers and producers, sponsors began to move from anthologies to quiz shows and sitcoms.

A second reason for the demise of anthology dramas was a change in audience. The people who could afford TV sets in the early 1950s could also afford tickets to a play. For these viewers, the anthology drama was a welcome addition given their cultural tastes. By 1956, however, 71 percent of all U.S. households had sets, as working- and middle-class families were increasingly able to afford television and the prices of sets dropped. Anthology dramas, however, were not as popular in this expanded market as they were with upscale theatergoers. In addition, the networks' relocation to Hollywood reduced the influence of New York theater on television. As a result, by the end of the decade, westerns, which were inexpensively produced by film studios on location near Los Angeles, had become the dominant TV genre.

Third, anthology dramas were expensive to produce—double the price of most other TV genres in the 1950s. Each week meant a completely new story line, as well as new writers, casts, and expensive sets. (Many anthology dramas also took more than a week to produce and had to alternate biweekly with other programs.) Sponsors and networks came to realize that it would be cheaper to use the same cast and set each week, and it would also be easier to build audience allegiance with an ongoing program. In an anthology series of individual plays, there were no continuing characters with whom viewers could identify over time.

Finally, anthologies that dealt seriously with the changing social landscape were sometimes labeled "politically controversial." This was especially true during the attempts by Senator Joseph McCarthy and his followers to rid media industries and government agencies of left-leaning political influences. (See Chapter 16 on blacklisting.) Eventually, both sponsors and networks came to prefer less controversial programming. By the early 1960s, this dramatic form had virtually disappeared from network television, although its legacy continues on American public television, especially with the imported British program *Masterpiece Theatre* (1971-), now known simply as *Masterpiece*—the longest running prime-time drama series on U.S. television.

Episodic Series

Abandoning anthologies, producers and writers increasingly developed **episodic series**, first used on radio in 1929. In this format, main characters continue from week to week, sets and locales remain the same, and technical crews stay with the program. Story concepts are broad enough to accommodate new adventures each week, establishing ongoing characters with whom viewers can regularly identify. The episodic series comes in two general types: chapter shows and serial programs.

Chapter Shows.   **Chapter shows** are self-contained stories that feature a problem, a series of conflicts, and a resolution. This structure can be used in a wide range of dramatic genres, including adult westerns like *Gunsmoke* (1955-75); medical dramas like *Grey's Anatomy* (2005-); police/detective shows like *CSI: Crime Scene Investigation* (2000-); family dramas like *Little House on the Prairie* (1974-82); and fantasy/science fiction like *Star Trek* (1966-69) and some episodes of *The X-Files* (1993-2002).

Culturally, television dramas often function as a window into the hopes and fears of the American psyche. For example, the western, which was one of the most popular chapter genres in television's early history, marked a period of change in the U.S. Its theme of civilization confronting the frontier provided a symbol for many Americans relocating to the suburbs—between the country and the city. When movie studios such as Warner Brothers began dabbling in television in the 1950s, they produced a number of well-received series for ABC, such as *Cheyenne* (1955-63) and *Maverick* (1957-63). By the 1958-59 season, thirty prime-time westerns aired. Until 1961, *Gunsmoke* (1955-75; TV's longest-running chapter series), *Wagon Train* (1957-65), and *Have Gun-Will Travel* (1957-63) were the three most popular programs in America.

In the 1970s, police/detective dramas became a staple, mirroring anxieties about the urban unrest of the late 1960s. The 1970s brought more urban problems, which were precipitated by the loss of factory jobs and the decline of manufacturing. Americans' popular entertainment reflected the idea of heroic police and tenacious detectives protecting a nation from menacing forces that were undermining the economy and the cities. Such shows as *Ironside* (1967-75), *Mannix* (1967-75), *Hawaii Five-O* (1968-80), *The Mod Squad* (1968-73), *Kojak* (1973-78; 1989-90), and *The Rockford Files* (1974-80) all ranked among the nation's top-rated programs.

A spin-off of the police drama is the law-enforcement documentary-like program, sometimes called the *cop doc*. Series like Fox's *Cops* (1989-) are cheap to produce, with low overhead and a big return on a minimal investment. In fact, *Cops* got its start because of the 1988 Writers Guild of America strike: Fox needed an unscripted show that did not require union writers to help supply programming to the relatively new network. Cop docs, like many contemporary daytime talk shows, generally focus their stories on emotional situations and individual pathology rather than on a critical examination of the underlying larger social conditions that make crime and its related problems more likely.

Serial Programs. In contrast to chapter shows, **serial programs** are open-ended episodic shows; that is, most story lines continue from episode to episode. Cheaper to produce than chapter shows, employing just a few indoor sets, and running five days a week, daytime *soap operas* are among the longest-running serial programs in the history of television. Acquiring their name from soap product ads that sponsored these programs in the days of fifteen-minute radio dramas, soaps feature cliff-hanging story lines and intimate close-up shots that tend to create strong audience allegiance. Soaps also probably do the best job of any genre at imitating the actual open-ended rhythms of daily life. Popular soaps include *Guiding Light* (1952-), *As the World Turns* (1956-), *General Hospital* (1963-), *Days of Our Lives* (1965-), and *One Life to Live* (1968-).

The success of the daytime soap formula opened a door to prime time. Although the first popular prime-time serial, *Peyton Place* (1964-69), ran two or three nights a week, producers later shied away from such programs because they had less value as syndicated reruns. Most reruns of old network shows are **stripped**—that is, shown five days a week in almost any order, not requiring viewers to watch them on a daily basis. Serials, however, require that audiences watch every day so that they don't lose track of the multiple story lines.

In the 1970s, however, with the popularity of the network *miniseries*—a serial that runs over a two-day to two-week period, usually on consecutive nights—producers and the networks began to look at the evening serial differently. The twelve-part *Rich Man, Poor Man*, adapted from an Irwin Shaw novel, ranked No. 3 in national ratings in 1976. The next year, the eight-part *Roots* mini-series, based on writer Alex Haley's search for his African heritage, became the most-watched miniseries in TV history.

These miniseries demonstrated that viewers would watch a compelling, ongoing story in prime time. Their success spawned such soap opera-style series as *Dallas* (1978-91), *Dynasty* (1981-89), *Knots Landing* (1979-92), and *Falcon Crest* (1981-90). All these shows ranked among America's Top 10 most-viewed programs in the 1984-85 season. In fact, as the top-rated shows in America in the early 1980s, *Dallas* and *Dynasty* both celebrated and criticized the excesses of the rich and spoiled. These shows reached their popular peak during the early years of the

ABC'S GREY'S ANATOMY, consistently the most popular program for adult women over the last several years, earned about $400,000 per thirty-second commercial in 2007-08 (*American Idol*—TV's top-rated show from 2004 to 2008—earned almost $1 million for a thirty-second ad in spring 2008).

"The show's original spirit has become kind of the spirit of the country—if not the world.... With the Berlin Wall down, with the global nuclear threat gone, with Russia trying to be a market economy, there is a growing paranoia because ... there are no easy villains anymore."

CHRIS CARTER, *THE X-FILES* CREATOR, 1998

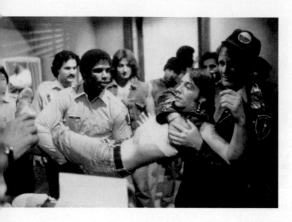

HILL STREET BLUES
(1981–87) began the hybrid
form of dramas with its mix
of comic and serious plot
lines.

administration of President Ronald Reagan, a time when the economic disparity between rich and poor Americans began to widen dramatically.

Another type of serial is the *hybrid,* which developed in the early 1980s with the appearance of *Hill Street Blues* (1981–87). Mixing comic situations and grim plots, this multiple-cast show looked like an open-ended soap opera. On occasion, as in real life, crimes were not solved and recurring characters died. As a hybrid form, *Hill Street Blues* combined elements of both chapter and serial television. Juggling multiple story lines, *Hill Street* featured some self-contained plots that were brought to resolution in a single episode as well as other plot lines that continued from week to week. This technique was copied by several successful dramatic hybrids, including *The X-Files* (1993–2002), *Law & Order* (1990–), *NYPD Blue* (1993–2005), *ER* (1994–2009), *Buffy the Vampire Slayer* (1997–2003), *The West Wing* (1999–2006), and *Lost* (2004–).

Other Enduring Trends and Reality TV

Up to this point, we have focused on the long-standing major network TV program trends, but many other genres have played major roles in TV's history, both inside and outside prime time. Talk shows like the *Tonight Show* (1954–) have fed our curiosity about celebrities and politicians, and offered satire on politics and business. Game shows like *Jeopardy!* (which has been around in some version since 1964) have provided families with easy-to-digest current events fare and history quizzes around the dinner table. Variety programs like the *Ed Sullivan Show* (1948–71) took center stage in Americans' cultural lives by introducing new comics, opera divas, classical pianists, and popular musical phenomena like Elvis Presley and the Beatles. Newsmagazines like *60 Minutes* (1968–) shed light on major events from the Watergate scandal in the 1970s to the 2008 presidential race. And all kinds of sporting events—from boxing and wrestling to the World Series and Superbowl—have allowed us to follow our favorite teams.

Now, reality-based programs, the newest significant trend, have introduced us to characters and people who seem more like us and less like celebrities. These programs have also helped the networks (and cable) deal with the high cost of programming. Featuring non-actors, cheap sets, and no extensive scripts, reality shows are much less expensive to produce than sitcoms and dramas. While reality-based programs have played a major role in network prime time since the late 1990s, the genre was actually inspired by a cable TV program: *The Real World* (1992–), the longest-running program on MTV (see Chapter 6). Changing locations and casts from season to season, *The Real World* brings together seven strangers who live and work together for a few months. In documentary style, cameras record their interpersonal entanglements and up-and-down relationships. *The Real World* and subsequent cable shows like *Project Runway* and *Top Chef* have significantly influenced the structure of reality TV programs that populate today's network prime-time schedule, including *Survivor, American Idol, The Amazing Race, Dancing with the Stars,* and *Extreme Makeover.* Unscripted reality shows also got a boost during the writers' strike in 2007-08, filling in for scripted sitcoms and dramas. (See "Media Literacy and the Critical Process: TV and the State of Storytelling" on page 163.)

The Rise and Fall of Public Television

Another key programmer in TV history has been public television. Under President Lyndon Johnson, Congress passed the Public Broadcasting Act of 1967, establishing the Corporation for Public Broadcasting (CPB) and later, in 1969, Public Broadcasting Service (PBS). The act grew out of a report from the Carnegie Commission on Educational Television, a group representing higher education, the arts, major media, business, and government. The report recommended that the government finance public television in order to serve the interests of the American people not being served by the commercial sector. The commission chose the word *public* rather than *educational* to distinguish the intended new programming from the "somber and

Media Literacy and the Critical Process

1 DESCRIPTION. Pick a current reality program and a current sitcom or drama. Choose programs that either started in the last year or two or that have been on television for roughly the same period of time. Now develop a "viewing sheet" that allows you to take notes as you watch the two programs over a three- to four-week period. Keep track of main characters, plot lines, settings, conflicts, and resolutions. Also track the main problems that are posed in the programs and how they are worked out in each episode. Find out and compare the basic production costs of each program.

2 ANALYSIS. Look for patterns and differences in the ways stories are told in the two programs. At a general level, what are the conflicts about (for example, men versus women, managers versus employees, tradition versus change, individuals versus institutions, honesty versus dishonesty, authenticity versus artificiality)? How complicated or simple are the tensions in the two programs, and how are problems resolved? Are there some conflicts that should not be permitted–like pitting white against black contestants? Are there noticeable differences between "the look" of each program?

TV and the State of Storytelling

The rise of the reality program over the past decade has more to do with the cheaper costs of this genre than with the wild popularity of these programs. In fact, in the history of television and viewer numbers, traditional sitcoms and dramas—and even prime-time news programs like *60 Minutes* and *20/20*—have been far more popular than even successful reality programs like *American Idol*. But, when national broadcast television cuts costs by reducing writing and production staffs and hiring "regular people" instead of trained actors, does the craft of storytelling suffer for the short-term gratification of commercial savings? In this exercise, let's compare the storytelling competence of a reality program with a more traditional comedy or dramatic genre.

3 INTERPRETATION. What do some of the patterns mean? What seems to be the point of each program? What are they each trying to say about relationships, values, masculinity or femininity, power, social class, and so on?

4 EVALUATION. What are the strengths and weaknesses of each program? Which program would you judge as better at telling a compelling story that you want to watch each week? How could each program improve its storytelling?

5 ENGAGEMENT. Either through online forums or personal contacts, find other viewers of these programs. Ask them follow-up questions about these programs–about what they like or don't like about them, about what they might change, about what the programs' creators might do differently. Then report your findings to the programs' producers through a letter, a phone call, or an e-mail. Try to elicit responses from the producers about the status of their programs. How did they respond to your findings?

---

static image" of early educational and instructional television, which often merely filmed teachers lecturing in classrooms. PBS was created as "a nongovernmental entity" and charged with creating programs of "high quality."[10]

In part, Congress intended public television to target viewers who were "less attractive" to commercial networks and advertisers. Besides providing programs for the over-fifty viewer, public television has figured prominently in programming for audiences under age twelve–another demographic not valued by many prime-time advertisers and often neglected by the networks–with children's series like *Mister Rogers' Neighborhood* (1968-2001), *Sesame Street* (1969-), and *Barney* (1991-). With the exception of CBS's long-running *Captain Kangaroo* (1955-84), the major networks have pretty much abdicated the responsibility of developing educational series aimed at children under age twelve. When, in 1996, Congress passed a law ordering the networks to offer three hours of children's educational programming per week, the networks sidestepped this mandate by taking advantage of the law's vagueness on what constituted "educational" to claim that many of their routine sitcoms, cartoons, and dramatic shows satisfied the legislation.

> "The average PBS show on prime time now scores about a 1.4 Nielsen rating, or roughly what the wrestling show *Friday Night Smackdown* gets."
>
> CHARLES MCGRATH, *NEW YORK TIMES*, FEBRUARY 2008

PUBLIC TELEVISION

The most influential children's show in TV history, *Sesame Street* (left, 1969–) has been teaching children their letters and numbers for more than thirty years. The program has also helped break down ethnic, racial, and class barriers by introducing TV audiences to a rich and diverse cast of puppets and people.

Mr. Rogers' Neighborhood (right, 1968–2001) aired more than seventeen hundred episodes, three hundred of which are still syndicated by PBS. In the show, known for its welcoming song, "It's a beautiful day in the neighborhood," Mr. Rogers talked easily to children—even about difficult subjects like death and divorce. Perhaps *Mr. Rogers' Neighborhood*'s greatest achievement was its enduring success and popularity as a low-tech production—primitive puppet shows and cardboard cutout sets—in the high-tech world of television.

The original Carnegie Commission report also recommended that Congress create a financial plan to provide long-term support for public television, in part to protect it from political interference. However, Congress did not do this, leading to PBS's treatment as a political football over the years, particularly when more fiscally conservative administrations want to trim the federal budget and, on occasion, to punish PBS for controversial programming. Because the government never required wealthy commercial broadcasters to subsidize public television (as many other countries do), politics played an increasing role in the fate of PBS. As federal funding levels dropped in the 1980s, PBS depended more and more on corporate underwriting.

In the early 2000s, the future of PBS and noncommercial television remained cloudy. By 2006, corporate sponsors funded more than 25 percent of all public television. While this development has supported many PBS programs, it has had a chilling effect on PBS's traditional independence from corporate America. As a result, PBS has sometimes rejected controversial programming or found ways to soften its impact. For example, in January 1998 PBS decided to "bury" *Surviving the Bottom Line*, a probing documentary produced by the journalist Hedrick Smith, by airing it on successive Friday evenings, which typically draw a smaller TV audience. This pre-2008 financial crisis film offered "a provocative attack on the kind of Wall Street thinking that places short-term shareholder interests above the welfare of communities." Bill Moyers, a longtime PBS journalist (and former press secretary to President Johnson), sharply criticized PBS's scheduling decision, which, he argued, placed the "life of business" before the "business of life."[11]

By 2008, many critics, along with fiscally conservative politicians, were arguing that PBS had run its course. With the rise of cable, audiences that had long been served by PBS could find alternative programming on cable or DBS. In fact, the BBC—historically a major provider of British programs to PBS—was selling its shows to cable. The expensive nature series *Planet Earth*, once a natural fit for PBS, appeared instead on the Discovery Channel, which could better afford the cost of the series. Nickelodeon, unlike the traditional networks, carried plenty of educational programming for children. Lavish historical drama series—once a staple on PBS—

are also more likely today to appear on cable. For example, Showtime produced *The Tudors*, while HBO made *John Adams*. Plus, in contrast to public radio, which has increased its audience from two million in 1980 to more than thirty million listeners per week today, the audience for PBS has declined at a faster rate than that of commercial television.[12]

The Decline of the Networks

Most historians mark the period from the late 1950s, when the networks gained control over TV's content, to the end of the 1970s as the **network era**. Except for British and American anthology dramas on PBS, this was a time when CBS, NBC, and ABC dictated virtually every trend in prime-time programming. This network dominance was significant because it offered America's rich and ethnically diverse population a cultural center and common topics for daily conversation. Television is often credited, for example, with helping to heal the nation after the assassination of President Kennedy in 1963 by creating a shared experience of mourning.

During this period, the networks collectively accounted for more than 95 percent of all prime-time TV viewing. By 2005, however, this figure had dropped to below 45 percent. To understand the decline of the network era, we will look at several factors: technological changes, government regulations, and the development of new networks. Finally, we will look at another factor that affects not only networks, but our entire television experience–digital transmission technology.

New Technologies Reduce Network Control

Two major technological developments contributed significantly to the erosion of network dominance: the arrival of communication satellite services for cable television and the home video market.

Satellite Transmission of Cable

Prior to the early 1970s, broadcast lobbyists and local stations, fearing that competition would lead to the loss of advertising revenue, effectively limited the growth of cable television, which had been around since the late 1940s. But a series of moves by the FCC sprang cable loose in 1972. That year, Time Inc. founded HBO, sending movies to hotels and motels, and making the first crack in the network dam. In 1975, HBO became available to individual cable markets throughout the country, offering the "Thrilla from Manila"–the historic heavyweight boxing match between Muhammad Ali and Joe Frazier–via satellite from the Philippines.

Then, in December 1976, Ted Turner beamed, or *uplinked*, the signal from WTBS, his Atlanta-based **independent station** (not affiliated with a network) to a satellite, from which cable systems and broadcast stations around the country could access, or *downlink*, the Atlanta station. To encourage interest, the signal was initially provided free, supported only by the ads Turner sold during WTBS programs. But as Turner expanded services by creating new channels like CNN, he began charging monthly subscription fees for his cable services.

In its early days, WTBS delivered a steady stream of old TV reruns, wrestling, and live sports from the Atlanta Hawks and the Atlanta Braves (both owned by Turner). Turner and a number of investors would eventually buy the MGM film library to provide additional movie programming. As more Americans received cable, the TV networks, for the first time, began to face serious competition.

Home Video

Early in the 1970s, Japan's Sony Corporation introduced the TV industry to a professional grade videocassette that quickly revolutionized TV news; until that time, TV news crews had relied solely on shooting expensive film footage, which often took hours to develop and edit. In 1975-76, the consumer introduction of videocassettes and **videocassette recorders (VCRs)** enabled viewers, for the first time, to tape-record TV programs and play them back later. Sony introduced a consumer videocassette–Betamax ("Beta")–in 1975, and JVC in Japan introduced a slightly larger format, VHS (Video Home System) in 1976, which was incompatible with Beta. This triggered a marketing war, which helped drive costs down and put VCRs in more homes. Beta ultimately lost the consumer marketplace battle to VHS, whose larger tapes held more programming space.

VCRs also got a big boost from a failed suit brought against Sony by Disney and MCA (now GE-owned NBC Universal) in 1976: The two film studios alleged that home taping violated their movie copyrights. In 1979, a federal court ruled in favor of Sony and permitted home taping for personal use. In response, the movie studios quickly set up videotaping facilities so that they could rent and sell movies in video stores, which popped up everywhere in the early 1980s. Recently, of course, just as Beta gave way to VHS, the VHS format surrendered to the DVD.

Today, the standard DVD is threatened by both Internet downloading and a consumer market move toward **high-definition** DVD pictures and players. In fact, in 2007 another format war pitted high-definition Blu-ray DVDs (developed by Sony, used in Playstation 3, and backed by several film studios) against the HD DVD format (developed by Toshiba and backed by Microsoft and other film studios). Blu-ray was declared the victor when, in February 2008, Best Buy and Wal-mart, the nation's leading sellers of DVDs, decided to stop carrying HD DVDs players and discs (see Chapter 7).

The impact of home video on television networks is enormous. Nearly 90 percent of American homes today are equipped with VCRs and/or DVD players, which are used for two major purposes: movie rentals and time shifting. **Time shifting** occurs when viewers record shows and watch them at a later, more convenient time. This produces complex audience measurement problems; and along with the remote control's mute button, time shifting has made it possible to avoid ads altogether. Time shifting and movie rentals shook the TV industry; when viewers watch videotapes or DVDs, they often aren't watching network shows and certainly aren't viewing network ads.

Today, more than 20 percent of U.S. homes have **DVRs (digital video recorders)**, which enable users to download specific shows onto the DVR's computer memory. DVRs can seek out specific shows or even types of shows that appear on any channel; for example, with one command a user can store all prime-time and syndicated versions of *Seinfeld* or *CSI* the household receives. The newest versions of DVRs are also recordable–like VCRs–and allow users to make DVD collections of their favorite shows. Some critics argue that DVRs have shattered our notion of prime-time television because viewers can now watch whatever show they like at any time.

While offering greater flexibility for viewers, DVRs also provide a means to watch the watchers. DVRs give advertisers information about what is viewed in each household, thereby altering the ways in which TV ratings are compiled and advertising dollars are divided. DVR technology is even capable of allowing advertisers to target viewers with specific ads when they play back their saved programs. By 2008, local TV stations, cable companies, lawmakers, and consumer groups were battling over how to protect audience members who did not want to have their personal viewing and buying habits tracked by advertisers and market researchers. For example, the Nielsen Company, which provides the main audience ratings service for television, is trying to figure out how to coordinate tracking TV habits, buying patterns, cell phone use, and Web preferences. Nielsen ran tests in 2007 "to determine the willingness of its television-monitoring households to allow tracking of a second behavior, Web usage."

However, so many people refused because of privacy concerns that Nielsen said "it would scale back the plan—for now, at least—making Web tracking optional."[13]

Government Regulations Temporarily Restrict Network Control

By the late 1960s, a progressive and active FCC, increasingly concerned about the monopoly-like impact of the three networks, passed a series of regulations that began undercutting their power. The first, the Prime Time Access Rule (PTAR), passed in April 1970, reduced network control over prime time (7-11 P.M. EST) programming from four to three hours. Under this scenario, local TV stations often ran their own news programs from 7-7:30 P.M., and the networks "agreed to give up the 7:30-8 P.M. time slot. This one-hour block became known as *access time*."[14] Affecting the nation's fifty largest TV markets, the FCC hoped that this new access rule might encourage more local news and public-affairs programs. However, most stations simply acquired syndicated quiz shows (*Wheel of Fortune*) or **infotainment** programs (*Entertainment Tonight*). These infotainment shows, during which local affiliates sold lucrative regional ads, packaged human-interest and celebrity stories in TV news style.

In a second move, in 1970 the FCC created the Financial Interest and Syndication Rules—called **fin-syn**—which "constituted the most damaging attack against the network TV monopoly in FCC history."[15] Throughout the 1960s, the networks had run their own syndication companies. They sometimes demanded as much as 50 percent of the profits that producers earned from airing older shows as reruns in local TV markets. This was the case even though those shows were no longer on the networks and most of them had been developed not by the networks but by independent companies. The networks claimed that since popular TV series had gained a national audience because of the networks' reach, production companies owed them compensation even after shows completed their prime-time runs. The FCC banned the networks from reaping such profits from program syndication.

The Department of Justice instituted a third and separate action in 1975. Reacting to a number of legal claims against monopolistic practices, the Justice Department limited the networks' production of non-news shows, requiring them to seek most of their programming from independent production companies and film studios. Initially, the limit was three hours of network-created prime-time entertainment programs per week, but this was raised to five hours by the late 1980s. In addition, ABC, CBS, and NBC were limited to producing eight hours per week of in-house entertainment or non-news programs outside prime time, most of which was devoted to soap operas (inexpensive to produce and popular with advertisers). Given that the networks could produce their own TV newsmagazines and select which programs to license, however, they retained a great deal of power over the content of prime-time television.

With the growth of cable and home video in the 1990s, the FCC gradually phased out the ban limiting network production, arguing that now the TV market was more competitive. Beginning in 1995, the networks also were again allowed to syndicate and profit from rerun programs, but only those they had produced in-house. The elimination of fin-syn and other rules opened the door for megamerger deals. For example, Disney, which bought ABC in 1995, can use its vast movie production resources to develop more entertainment programming for its ABC network. This has reduced the opportunities for independent producers to create new shows and compete for prime-time slots on ABC. In fact, in fall 2000, ABC introduced only four new TV shows in prime time—the lowest number of new shows ever by a major network. Relying on multiple nights of its own *Who Wants to Be a Millionaire*, *20/20*, and cheap reality shows like *The Bachelor*, ABC ignored many new series possibilities from independent sources.

Just as networks may now favor running programs that they own, shows developed by non-network companies now have a much shorter time to prove themselves. To cite an extreme example, after only two episodes, in May 2000 ABC canceled the critically acclaimed

WHAT DOES THIS MEAN?

- News Corp. employs more than forty-seven thousand people worldwide.[1]
- News Corp.'s 2007 revenues were $28 billion, $15 billion in the U.S. and Canada.
- Rupert Murdoch, Chairman and CEO of News Corp., began his rise as an international media mogul after inheriting two Australian newspapers from his father in 1952.
- In 1986, Murdoch launched Fox Broadcasting, the first new and successful U.S. TV network since the 1940s.
- In 2005, News Corp. bought MySpace.com for $580 million.
- In 2007, News Corp. acquired publishing giant Dow Jones and its flagship newspaper, the *Wall Street Journal*, the nation's No. 2-ranked newspaper in daily circulation, for $5.6 billion.
- In 2008, the company exchanged its 40 percent stake in DirecTV for Liberty Media's 19 percent stake in News Corp.
- In 2007, Fox Interactive's revenues increased by 57 percent.
- Fox's most profitable division is film.
- Fox's *American Idol* was the No. 1-rated show on TV from 2005 to 2008.

Fox's *House* has earned Emmys for British actor Hugh Laurie as Dr. Greg House, who one critic said makes "the Grinch look like the Easter Bunny." This popular drama is really a hybrid narrative, combining medical drama with detective mystery. Laurie's character is, in fact, modeled on the nineteenth-century detective Sherlock Holmes.

TABLE 5.2

NUMBER OF TV STATIONS HELD BY TOP COMPANIES, 1995-2008

Year	Fox (News Corp.)	Viacom/ CBS TV*	GE/ NBC	ABC	Tribune	Gannett	Hearst	Sinclair	Belo	Cox
1995	13	12	9	11	10	15	7	14	7	6
1996	24	11	11	10	16	18	7	22	19	8
1998	24	19	13	10	18	21	29	50	20	9
2001	42	41	35	10	23	22	32	54	20	14
2006	35	31	32	10	27	23	26	58	23	15
2008	35	29	26	10	23	23	26	58	20	15

*2006 split of Viacom saw the emergence of CBS Corporation.

Sources: "Number of Stations Held by Top Companies, 1995-2006," State of the News Media 2008, Local TV, Project for Excellence in Journalism, http://www.stateofthenewsmedia.org/2008 (accessed August 20, 2008). 2008 data from individual company Web sites.

show *Wonderland*, a drama set in a mental hospital, because of its controversial subject matter and low ratings. Indeed, many independent companies and TV critics fear that the few corporations that now own the networks—Disney, CBS, News Corp., and GE—dictate the terms for broadcast television (see Table 5.2 above).

Emerging Networks Target Youth and Minority Markets

In addition to the number of cable services now available to consumers, the three major networks, which have lost about half of their audience since the 1980s, faced further challenges from the emergence of new networks. Rupert Murdoch, who heads the multinational company News Corp., launched the Fox network in 1986 after purchasing several TV stations and buying a major Hollywood film studio, Twentieth Century Fox (see "What News Corp. Owns" on page 167). Not since the mid-1950s, when the short-lived Dumont network collapsed, had another network challenged the Big Three.

At first, Fox lost money because it had fewer than a hundred affiliated stations—less than half the two-hundred-plus affiliates each that were contracted to ABC, CBS, and NBC. Presenting programs just two nights a week, the Fox network began by targeting both young and black audiences with shows like *The Simpsons*, *Beverly Hills 90210*, *In Living Color*, *Martin*, *Roc*, and *Melrose Place*. By 1994, after outbidding CBS for a portion of pro-football broadcasts, Fox was competing every night of the week. It had managed to lure more than sixty affiliates away from the other networks or from independent status. Some of these stations were in major markets, where traditional networks suddenly found themselves without affiliates. By the early 1990s, Fox was making money. By the mid-1990s, the new network's total number of affiliates rivaled each of the Big Three's.

Fox's success continued the erosion of network power and spurred other new networks. Paramount, which had recently been acquired by Viacom, and Time Warner, the world's largest media company, both debuted networks in January 1995: UPN and the WB, respectively. Using Fox's strategy, the new networks offered original programs two nights a week in 1995, added a third night in 1996, and were programming every night except Saturday by 2000. Backed by multinational financing, these companies slowly began going after independent outlets and luring other stations away from their old network affiliations. Their main strategy, like Fox's,

targeted minority and young viewers with such programs as *Moesha,*
Buffy the Vampire Slayer, Felicity, Dawson's Creek, Charmed, Small-
ville, Girlfriends, and *Gilmore Girls.* But after some success in the
late 1990s, by 2005 not one WB or UPN show ranked among the
Top 100 programs according to audience ratings. After losing
$1 billion each, CBS (now split off from Viacom) and Time Warner
decided in 2006 to merge the most popular shows into one
network—the CW. By 2008, the CW performed better than either
the old WB or UPN, but its top programs—*Friday Night Smackdown!*
and *America's Next Top Model*—drew less than 5 million viewers,
compared with the 28 million reached by the most highly rated
network program, Fox's *American Idol.*

Despite these improvements, the CW is not the fifth-ranked
network behind Fox, CBS, ABC, and NBC. That spot belongs to Univision, the Spanish-language television network. In 2008 Univision
reached about 3.5 million viewers on average in prime time each
day (compared with 2.6 million for the CW, or for Fox, No. 1
in early 2008 with 11.5 million on average). The first foreign-
language U.S. network began in 1961 when the owners of the
nation's first Spanish-language TV station in San Antonio acquired
a TV station in Los Angeles, setting up what was then called the
Spanish International Network. It officially became Univision in
1986 and has built audiences in major urban areas with large
Hispanic populations through its popular talk-variety programs
and *telenovelas*—Spanish-language soap operas, mostly produced
in Mexico—which air each weekday evening. A popular program
in 2008, *Al Diablo con los Guapos* (*To Hell with Handsome Men*),
attracts about 5 million viewers for each episode. Today Univision Communications owns and
operates more than sixty TV stations in the United States and Puerto Rico, offering local news,
sports, and entertainment programs. Its Univision Network, carried by seventeen hundred
cable affiliates, reaches about 99 percent of U.S. Hispanic households. Univision was acquired
in 2006 for more than $12 billion by a consortium of private investment firms.

UGLY BETTY Inspired by the
Colombian *telenovela Betty
La Fea, Ugly Betty* chronicles
the life of an unglamorous
assistant at the fictional
fashion magazine *Mode.* The
U.S. incarnation has won
Peabody, Golden Globe, and
Emmy awards and has been
praised for its positive profile
of Latin and Hispanic
communities.

Digital Technology Changes Our Experience of Television

Among the biggest technical innovations in TV are non-television delivery systems. On the
Internet, for example, we can download traditional TV shows, including *CSI, Lost, House, 24,*
Grey's Anatomy, and *Desperate Housewives.* These programs are available through iPods and
cell phones—for fees ranging from 99 cents to $1.99 per episode. Or, on some sites like NBC and
Fox's hulu.com, you can watch full episodes for free (with advertisements). In addition, cable
TV giants like Comcast and Time Warner are making traditional network programs available
as part of their *video-on-demand* (VOD) services, which allow customers to buy TV shows and
watch them when they want—minus commercials. As Paul Saffo, director of the Institute for the
Future, argued in 2005: "No old media form ever disappears. They just get reinvented into a
new purpose. TV is about to go through a profound reinvention."[16] (See "Case Study: Golden
Years of Television Find New Life on the Web" on page 170.)

Not only is TV being reinvented but its audience—although fragmented—is also growing,
given all the new ways there are to watch television. Just a few years ago, televisions glimmered
in the average U.S. household just over seven hours a day, but by late 2006, when you add in
downloading or streaming and iPod viewing, that figure had expanded to eight hours a day.

CASE STUDY

Golden Years of Television Find New Life on the Web

By Brian Stelter

Is there still money to be made from *Matlock*? Recently, television distributors have opened up their libraries of classic content online, making thousands of episodes of programs like *The Twilight Zone* and *The Mary Tyler Moore Show* available free. [In 2008], Warner Brothers add[ed] a new twist, announcing the rebirth of the WB broadcast network as an Internet destination and offering programs like *Everwood* online.

In putting old episodes online, broadcasters are tapping into the "long tail" of niche content that the Internet has monetized. While executives are reticent about the costs involved, and while syndicated and DVD sales remain dominant sources of revenue, the repurposing of long-dead shows is creating another new revenue stream for distributors.

The online re-creation of the WB represents another step in that direction. Bruce Rosenblum, the president of Warner Brothers' television group, says that "premium ad-supported digital destinations that are demographic-specific" are a key part of its strategy going forward.

"We have all this library content, and we've been surprised at how much interest there is in it," Jeff Zucker, the chief executive of NBC Universal, said recently. "Frankly, if there is one person interested in it—and there are streaming costs so you have to make sure you're covering that—we've found it's a new opportunity for our content."

The online shows also create new payment opportunities for the writers, producers and actors of TV's golden years. Royalties for Internet streaming were a pivotal issue in the writers' strike that halted television production

[in 2007–08]. The Hollywood studios agreed to pay writers a 2 percent cut of the receipts for ad-supported streaming of all shows produced after 1977.

But online streaming isn't making anyone rich, at least not yet. As Mitchell Hurwitz, the co-creator of *Arrested Development*, put it, the online popularity of his former program is "enormously rewarding in every way except for financially."

Arrested Development, a comedy that never attracted a sufficient audience on Fox from 2003 to 2006, consistently ranks among the top three series on Hulu, an online video site founded as a joint venture between NBC Universal and the News Corporation. Mr. Hurwitz wasn't aware of his show's top-ranked status until Jason Kilar, the chief executive of Hulu, mentioned it at a broadcasting conference in Las Vegas.

"Isn't that crazy?" Mr. Hurwitz remarked. "This was a largely unwatched show when it was on network television." *Arrested Development* has had a cult

ARRESTED DEVELOPMENT

fan base for years, as indicated by its strong sales on DVD. Mr. Hurwitz called it the "perfect show" for on-demand viewing because of hidden gems—jokes that make sense only after the viewer has seen a full season.

If Web streaming had been widespread a few years ago, Mr. Hurwitz said, perhaps *Arrested Development* could have stayed on the air. He also suggested that the show's streaming success could enhance prospects for a film based on the series (which was in production in 2008).

Hulu now offers 3,000 full-length episodes of archived television shows, including ones as old as *Alfred Hitchcock Presents* from 1955. "So you could definitely spend some time consuming the content," Mr. Kilar said modestly. Perhaps surprisingly, four out of five titles in the Hulu library are viewed each day. Clearly, an audience is pursuing the archives.

"Very talented people spend their lives telling these stories. It's a bit unusual that they're only given the stage for a very discrete period of time," he said.

The broadcast networks present many of the same shows on their own Web sites: for example, NBC.com offers episodes of *The A-Team*, *Miami Vice*, and *Buck Rogers*, and CBS.com shows *Star Trek*, *The Twilight Zone*, and *MacGyver*.

Even TV Land, the cable channel devoted to classic TV, is starting to stream. Episodes of *Gunsmoke* and the *Andy Griffith Show* are now available on TVLand.com. "The goal is to whet viewers' appetites, and drive people back to the linear channel," said Larry W. Jones, the president of TV Land. ◢

Source: Brian Stelter, "Golden Years of Television Find New Life on the Web," New York Times, April 28, 2008, Section C, p. 3.

MONDAY 8 p.m. (ET)   9 p.m.   10 p.m.

	8 p.m.			9 p.m.	10 p.m.
ABC	Dancing With the Stars $196,000			Samantha Who? $113,000	The Bachelor $128,000
CBS	How I Met Your Mother $138,000	Big Bang $133,000	Two and a Half Men $231,000	Rules of Engagement $177,000	CSI: Miami $180,000
NBC	Chuck $108,000		Heroes $296,000		Journeyman $137,000
FOX	Prison Break $200,000		K-Ville $184,000		No Fox programming

THURSDAY 8 p.m. (ET)   9 p.m.   10 p.m.

	8 p.m.		9 p.m.		10 p.m.
ABC	Ugly Betty $149,000		Grey's Anatomy $419,000		Big Shots $151,000
CBS	Survivor: China $208,000		CSI: Crime Scene Investigation $248,000		Without a Trace $190,000
NBC	Earl $151,000	30 Rock $129,000	The Office $186,000	Scrubs $145,000	ER $140,000
FOX	Smarter Than a Fifth-Grader $105,000		Don't Forget the Lyrics $100,000		No Fox programming

FIGURE 5.1

PRIME-TIME NETWORK TV PRICING

The average costs in 2007 for a thirty-second commercial during popular prime-time programs on network television for a Monday and Thursday night.

Source: "2007 FactPack," Advertising Age, *www.adage.com, p. 41.*

And with the growth of DVR systems like TiVo, TV viewing was up 5 percent in DVR-equipped homes. Forecasters predict that more than 25 percent of homes will have DVR technology by 2010. All these options mean that we are still watching TV, just at different times, places and on different screens.

The Economics of Television

Despite their declining reach, the traditional networks have remained attractive business investments. In 1985, General Electric, which once helped start RCA/NBC, bought back NBC. In 1995, Disney bought ABC for $19 billion; in 1999, Viacom acquired CBS for $37 billion (Viacom and CBS split in 2005, but Viacom's CEO remains CBS's main stockholder).

Even though their audiences and profits may have declined, the networks continue to attract larger audiences than their cable or online competitors. But the business of television is not just about larger audiences. To understand the TV business today, we need to examine the production, distribution, and syndication of programming. In fact, it would not be much of a stretch to define TV programming as a system that delivers viewers to merchandise displayed in blocks of ads–and at stake is $60 billion in advertising revenues each year. (See Figure 5.1 above.)

Prime-Time Production

The key to the TV industry's appeal is its ability to offer programs and stories that American households will habitually watch each week. The networks, producers, and film studios spend fortunes creating programs that they hope will keep us coming back. In 1988, while film studios produced a large chunk of network television, more than half of the prime-time schedule was created by independent producers. These companies, such as Carsey-Werner (the *Cosby Show, Roseanne, Third Rock from the Sun, That '70s Show*), license, or "rent," each episode to a network

"When you have an event that transcends popular culture, the only place you can aggregate these audiences is network television."

JEFF ZUCKER, CEO OF NBC UNIVERSAL ON THE 2008 BEIJING OLYMPICS

for two broadcasts, one in the fall or winter and one in the spring or summer. (For each series, about twenty-two new episodes are produced each TV season.) Today, with the relaxation of regulations, networks and their film studio allies generally produce more than 85 percent of prime-time fare.

Production costs in television generally fall into two categories: below-the-line and above-the-line. *Below-the-line costs*, which account for roughly 40 percent of a new program's production budget, include the technical, or "hardware," side of production: equipment, special effects, cameras and crews, sets and designers, carpenters, electricians, art directors, wardrobe, lighting, and transportation. More demanding are the *above-the-line*, or "software," costs, which include the creative talent: actors, writers, producers, editors, and directors. These costs account for about 60 percent of a program's budget, except in the case of successful long-running series (like *Friends* or *ER*), in which salary demands by actors can drive up above-the-line costs to more than 90 percent.

Risky Business: Deficit Financing and the Independents

Many prime-time programs today are developed by independent production companies that are owned or backed by a major film studio such as Sony or Disney. In addition to providing and renting production facilities, these film studios serve as a bank, offering enough capital to carry producers through one or more seasons. In television, after a network agrees to carry a program, keeping it on the air is done through **deficit financing**. This means that the production company leases the show to a network for a license fee that is actually less than the cost of production. (The company hopes to recoup this loss later in lucrative rerun syndication.) Typically, the networks might lease an episode of a new half-hour sitcom for about $600,000 for two airings. Each episode, however, costs the producers about $800,000 to make, in which case they lose about $200,000 per episode. After two years of production (forty-four episodes), an average show builds up a deficit in the millions. This is where film studios have been playing an increasingly crucial role: They finance the deficit and hope to profit on lucrative deals when the show, like *Friends, Seinfeld, The Simpsons,* or *Everybody Loves Raymond,* goes into syndication.

The key to erasing the losses generated by deficit financing is **rerun syndication**. In this process, programs that stay in a network's lineup long enough to build up sufficient episodes (usually four seasons' worth) are leased, or *syndicated*, to hundreds of TV stations in the United States and overseas. With a successful program, the profits can be enormous. For instance, the early rerun cycle of *Friends* earned nearly $4 million an episode from syndication in 250-plus markets, totaling $944 million. Because the show had already been produced and the original production costs were covered when the show first aired, the syndication market became almost pure profit for the producers and their backers. This is why deficit financing endures: Although investors rarely hit the jackpot, when they do, the revenues can more than cover a lot of losses.

Network Cost-Saving Strategies

Although the networks still purchase or license many prime-time TV programs, they create more of their own prime-time fare thanks to the relaxation of fin-syn rules in the mid-1990s. Producing TV newsmagazines and reality programs, for instance, became a major way for networks to save money and control content. Programs such as Fox's *American Idol* or NBC's *Dateline* require only about half the outlay (between $600,000 and $800,000 per episode) demanded by an hour's worth of drama. In addition, the networks, by producing projects in-house, avoid paying license fees to independent producers.

Over the years, CBS's highly rated program *60 Minutes* has been a money machine. By 1980, a commercial minute on *60 Minutes*, the nation's highest-rated program that year, sold for a then-record $230,000. By the late 1990s, *60 Minutes* commanded more than $400,000 per minute while a low-rated program brought in only $100,000. This meant that the network generally earned back its production costs and fees paid to local affiliates after selling just a couple of minutes of ad time on *60 Minutes*. Don Hewitt, the creator of *60 Minutes*, estimates that in its first twenty-five years on the air, the program grossed well over $1 billion for CBS.[17] In 2007, *60 Minutes* was ranked twenty-ninth in the ratings, earning about $200,000 for a commercial minute.

Prime-Time Distribution

The networks have always been the main distributors of prime-time TV programs to their affiliate stations around the country. In 2008, ABC, CBS, NBC, Fox, and the CW were each allied with 200 to 250 stations. The networks pay a fee to affiliate stations to carry network programs; in return, networks sell the bulk of advertising time and recoup their investments in these programs. In this arrangement, local stations receive national programs that attract large local audiences. In addition, some local ad spaces are allocated during prime time so that stations can sell their own time during these slots.

A common misconception is that TV networks own their affiliated stations. This is not usually true. Although networks own stations in major markets like New York, Los Angeles, and Chicago, throughout most of the country, networks sign short-term contracts to rent time on local stations. For example, WDIV (Channel 4) in Detroit has a contract to carry NBC programs but is owned by the Washington Post/Newsweek Company, based in Washington, D.C. Years ago, the FCC placed restrictions on network-owned-and-operated stations (called **O & Os**). In the 1960s, networks and other companies were limited to owning five VHF (Very High Frequency) and two UHF (Ultra High Frequency) stations, but the limit was raised to twelve total stations during the 1980s. Hoping to ensure more diversity in ownership, the FCC also mandated that an owner's combined TV stations could reach no more than 25 percent of the nation's then 90-million-plus TV households. But the sweeping Telecommunications Act of 1996, as we have seen, abolished most ownership restrictions. By 2007, one owner was permitted to reach up to 39 percent of the nation's 120-million-plus TV households.

Although a local affiliate typically carries network programs, the station may preempt a network's offering by substituting other programs. According to *clearance rules*, established in the 1940s by the Justice Department and the FCC, all local affiliates are ultimately responsible for the content of their channels and must clear, or approve, all network programming. Over the years, some of the circumstances in which local affiliates have rejected the network's programming have been controversial. For example, in 1956, Nat King Cole (singer Natalie Cole's father) was one of the first African American performers to host a network variety program. As a result of pressure applied by several white southern organizations, though, the program had trouble attracting a national sponsor. When some affiliates, both southern and northern, refused to carry the program, NBC canceled it in 1957.

More recently, in May 2004, the Maryland-based Sinclair Broadcast Group, which at the time owned sixty-two stations in thirty-nine TV markets, barred its seven ABC-affiliated stations from airing a special episode of ABC's *Nightline*. In a tribute to the more than seven hundred U.S. men and women who had died in the Iraq war at the time, the program's anchor Ted Koppel read the names and displayed an image of every soldier. Sinclair's management, however, in refusing to clear the program, argued that broadcasting the obituaries constituted an antiwar position, offering "political statements . . . disguised as news content." At the time, 98 percent of all Sinclair's presidential campaign contributions had gone to the Republican Party and then-President George W. Bush. Bush had supported the further deregulation of the TV industry that allowed Sinclair to acquire so many stations.

Syndication Keeps Shows Going and Going . . .

Syndication—leasing TV stations the exclusive right to air TV shows—is a critical component of the distribution process. Early each year, executives from thousands of local TV stations and cable firms gather at the world's main "TV supermarket," the National Association of Television Program Executives (NATPE) convention, to buy or barter for programs that are up for syndication. In so doing, they acquire the exclusive local market rights, usually for two- or three-year periods, to game shows, talk shows, and **evergreens**—popular old network reruns such as the *Andy Griffith Show* or *I Love Lucy*.

Syndication plays a large role in programming for the hours outside prime time. The distribution/syndication company King World, for example, began in 1972 after the fin-syn rules

> "For the networks, the hit show is the hub in a growing wheel of interests: promotion platforms for related businesses; sales of replays on cable television or even Internet sites; and the creation of direct links between advertisers and viewers."
>
> BILL CARTER, *NEW YORK TIMES*, 1999

prevented the networks from participating in syndication. It started out by distributing 1930s *Little Rascals* film shorts, and by the end of the 1980s it had become the distributor of the top three shows in syndication—*Wheel of Fortune*, *Jeopardy!*, and the *Oprah Winfrey Show*—earning a gross profit of nearly $400 million per year. (For 2006-07, these three programs remained the top-rated syndicated shows.) With the suspension of fin-syn (the networks could syndicate programming again), CBS (then Viacom) bought King World for $5 billion in 1999.

Other major syndicators of TV programming include film studios such as Twentieth Century Fox, Disney, and Time Warner, all of which are also involved in the production of TV shows. Networks usually select and distribute three hours of programming each night (four on Sunday) during prime time and another three to four hours of daytime programming, leaving many hours for local affiliates to schedule. Because it is often cheaper to buy syndicated programs than to produce local programs (other than news), many station managers take the most profitable path rather than create topical shows that focus on issues in their own communities.

Off-Network and First-Run Syndication

For local affiliate stations, syndicated programs are often used during **fringe time**—programming immediately before the evening's prime-time schedule (*early fringe*) and following the local evening news or the network's main late-night talk show (*late fringe*). Syndicated shows that fill these slots are either "off-network" or "first-run."

In **off-network syndication**, older programs that no longer run during network prime time are made available for reruns to local stations, cable operators, online services, and foreign markets. A local station may purchase old *Cosby Show* or *The Simpsons* episodes as a lead-in to boost the ratings for its late-afternoon news, or it may purchase *Friends* or *Everybody Loves Raymond* to boost its ratings after the late-evening news.

First-run syndication is any program specifically produced for sale into syndication markets. Quiz programs such as *Wheel of Fortune* and daytime talk or advice shows like the *Oprah Winfrey Show* are made for first-run syndication. The producers of these programs sell them directly to local markets around the country and the world. When the FCC established the Prime Time Access Rule in 1970 (to turn more prime time over to local stations), it created an immediate market for new non-network programs.

Barter vs. Cash Deals

Most financing of television syndication is either a cash or a barter deal. In a *cash deal*, the distributor offers a series for syndication to the highest bidder in a market—typically a station trying to fill a particular time slot. Because of exclusive contractual arrangements, programs air on only one broadcast outlet per city in a major TV market. For example, CBS and its syndicator King World offer early episodes of *CSI* in hundreds of television markets around the country. Whichever local station bids the most in a particular market gets the rights to that program, usually for a contract period of two or three years. A small-market station in Fargo, North Dakota, might pay a few thousand dollars to air a week's worth of episodes while some Top 10 markets and cable channels pay well over $250,000 a week for *CSI* reruns that are aired daily.

In a variation of a cash deal called *cash-plus*, distributors retain some time to sell national commercial spots for successful syndicated shows. Since *CSI* went into syndication, for example,

OPRAH WINFREY
The highest-rated talk show in American history, the *Oprah Winfrey Show* is made for first-run syndication and independently produced by Oprah's Harpo company. Approximately 48 million people a week watch *Oprah*, which first aired in 1986.

CBS–which produces and distributes *CSI*–receives cash for the show from various local outlets and cable's Spike TV network, but also sells two to three minutes of ad time to national advertisers. When local stations receive the programs, they already contain the national ads. Some syndicators use cash-plus deals to keep down the cost per episode; in other words, stations pay less per episode in exchange for giving up ad slots to a syndicator's national advertisers.

Although syndicators prefer cash deals, *barter deals* are usually arranged for new, untested, or older programs. In a straight barter deal, no money changes hands. Instead, a syndicator offers a program to a local TV station in exchange for a split of the advertising revenue. The program's syndicator will try to make an arrangement with the station that attracts the largest number of local viewers, though this is not always possible. The syndicator then sells some ads at the national level, charging advertisers more money if the program has been sold into a large number of markets. Many TV talk shows begin as barter deals. For example, in a 7/5 barter deal, during each airing, the show's producers and syndicator retain seven minutes of ad time for national spots and leave stations with five minutes of ad time for local spots. As programs become more profitable, syndicators repackage and lease the shows as cash-plus deals.

Measuring Television Viewing

Primarily, TV shows live or die based on how satisfied advertisers are with the quantity and quality of the viewing audience. Since 1950, the major organization tracking and rating prime-time viewing has been the A.C. Nielsen Market Research Company, which estimates what viewers are watching in the nation's major markets. Ratings services like Nielsen provide advertisers, networks, and local stations with considerable detail about viewers–from race and gender to age, occupation, and educational background.

Calculating Ratings and Shares

In TV measurement, a **rating** is a statistical estimate expressed as the percent of households tuned to a program in the market being sampled (see Table 5.3 on page 176). In 2008, one

CSI: CRIME SCENE INVESTIGATION premiered on CBS in 2000. This popular, episodic cop-and-crime drama carries forward a tradition of "realistic" police shows. Its success led to two spin-offs, *CSI: Miami* and *CSI: New York*, and to syndication deals for the original and Miami versions.

TABLE 5.3

THE TOP 10 HIGHEST-RATED TV SERIES; INDIVIDUAL PROGRAMS (SINCE 1960)

Note: The *Seinfeld* finale, which aired in May 1998, drew a rating of 41-plus and a total viewership of 76 million; in contrast, the final episode of *Friends* in May 2004 had a 25 rating and drew about 52 million viewers. (The *M*A*S*H* finale in 1983 had more than 100 million viewers.)

Source: The World Almanac and Book of Facts 1997 *(Mahwah, N.J.: World Almanac Books, 1996), 296; Corbett Steinberg,* TV Facts *(New York: Facts on File Publications, 1985); A.C. Nielsen Media Research.*

	Program	Network	Date	Rating
1	*M*A*S*H* (final episode)	CBS	2/28/83	60.2
2	*Dallas* ("Who Shot J. R.?" episode)	CBS	11/21/80	53.3
3	*The Fugitive* (final episode)	ABC	8/29/67	45.9
4	*Cheers* (final episode)	NBC	5/20/93	45.5
5	*Ed Sullivan Show* (Beatles' first U.S. TV appearance)	CBS	2/9/64	45.3
6	*Beverly Hillbillies*	CBS	1/8/64	44.0
7	*Ed Sullivan Show* (Beatles' second U.S. TV appearance)	CBS	2/16/64	43.8
8	*Beverly Hillbillies*	CBS	1/15/64	42.8
9	*Beverly Hillbillies*	CBS	2/26/64	42.4
10	*Beverly Hillbillies*	CBS	3/25/64	42.2

Nielsen national ratings point represented about 1.2 million television households. Another audience measure is the **share**, a statistical estimate of the percent of homes tuned to a specific program compared with those using their sets at the time of the sample. For instance, let's say on a typical night 5,000 metered homes are sampled by Nielsen in 210 large U.S. cities, and 4,000 of those households have their TV sets turned on. Of those 4,000, about 1,000 are tuned to *Lost* on ABC. The rating for that show is 20 percent–that is, 1,000 households watching *Lost* out of 5,000 TV sets monitored. The share is 25 percent–1,000 homes watching *Lost* out of a total of 4,000 sets turned on.

Impact of Ratings and Shares on Programming

Over the years, share measurements became increasingly important, especially for competitive markets. Shares are also good measures during fringe time, when most sets may be turned off. For example, on a given night, only 1,000 of the 5,000 sets may still be on for late-night viewing. If 500 of that 1,000 are tuned to the *Late Show*, its rating would be only 10 percent (500 out of 5,000), but its share of the audience actually watching TV would be 50 percent (500 out of 1,000).

The historical importance of ratings and shares to the survival of specific TV programs cannot be overestimated. In practice, television is an industry in which networks, producers, and distributors target, guarantee, and "sell" viewers in blocks to advertisers. Audience measurement tells advertisers not only how many people are watching but, more importantly, what kind of people are watching. Prime-time advertisers are mainly interested in reaching relatively affluent eighteen- to forty-nine-year-old viewers, who account for most consumer spending. If a show is attracting those viewers, advertisers will compete to buy time during that program. Typically, as many as nine out of ten new shows introduced each fall either do not attain the required ratings or fail to reach enough of the "right" viewers. The result is cancellation.

Assessing Today's Markets

During the height of the network era, a prime-time series with a rating of 17 or 18 and a share of between 28 and 30 was generally a success. By the early 2000s, though, with increasing competition from cable, DVDs, and the Internet, the threshold for success had dropped to a rating of 8 or 9 and a share of under 14. Unfortunately, many popular programs have been canceled over the years because advertisers considered their audiences too young, too old, or too poor. To account for the rise of DVRs, Nielsen in 2006 began offering three versions of its

"The ultimate research dream is to be able to measure everything in the universe. It's not realistic, obviously."

SCOTT SPRINGER, SENIOR VICE PRESIDENT FOR MEDIA PRODUCT LEADERSHIP AT NIELSEN, 2008

ratings: "live . . . ; live plus 24 hours, counting how many people who own DVRs played back shows within a day of recording them; and live plus seven days."[18] Today, however, with the fragmentation of media audiences and the decline in viewership, targeting smaller niche markets and consumers has become advertisers' main game.

Alternative Voices

Moving beyond mainstream programming, the Internet has provided an opening for alternative forms of TV programming. In 2007 NBC signed a "first-of-its-kind deal" to buy the rights to the series *Quarterlife*, which originally debuted on MySpace.[19] The online version was considered a hit, with seven million viewers in its first four months. In March 2008, it aired as a sixty-minute dramatic series on NBC while also running on multiple Web sites in eight-minute segments. *Quarterlife*, about "a group of creative 25-year-olds and how their personal lives are described in the [blog] of the lead character," had a connection to network TV because its producers, Marshall Herskovitz and Ed Zwick, developed the TV series *Thirtysomething* and *My So-Called Life*.[20]

NBC's interest in *Quarterlife* sprang from the network's search for innovative ways to reach younger audiences with new story forms. In its broadcast debut, however, the program drew just 3.1 million viewers, making it No. 96 for the week (one spot ahead of ABC's *An All-Star Salute to Jimmy Kimmel*, the lowest-ranked program on any major network that week). NBC decided to move the program to its Bravo cable channel before canceling it outright.

The show is still available online, including at hulu.com, a joint venture of Fox and NBC that also works with other content partners from MGM, Sony Pictures Television, Warner Brothers, and Lionsgate. Hulu.com airs full episodes of current TV shows the day after they air on the networks, favorites from past TV series, and some full-length feature films—all with ads, of course. This site is a more direct attempt to go after audiences who have left network television for the Internet. Despite its failure, *Quarterlife* showed that the networks were open to scouring the Internet as a source for new program ideas, and hulu.com may prove to be another avenue for bringing broadcast shows online.

▶

HULU
A screenshot from the NBC/ Fox venture hulu.com. The site allows viewers to watch TV shows, both current and old favorites, for free. The site is supported by the ads that are shown with the shows, although there are fewer ads than on regular TV.

Television, Culture, and Democracy

"Those who complain about a lack of community among television viewers might pay attention to the vitality and interaction of TV sports watchers wherever they assemble."

BARBRA MORRIS, UNIVERSITY OF MICHIGAN, 1997

In the 1950s, television's appearance significantly changed the media landscape—particularly the radio and magazine industries, both of which had to cultivate specialized audiences and markets to survive. In its heyday, television carried the egalitarian promise that it could bypass traditional print literacy and reach all segments of society. In such a heterogeneous and diverse nation, the concept of a visual, affordable mass medium, giving citizens entertainment and information that they could all talk about the next day, held great appeal. However, since its creation, commercial television has tended to serve the interests of profit more often than those of society. With the arrival of DTV and the disappearance of "free" over-the-air broadcasts in 2009, most households found themselves paying for tiers of cable or direct satellite programming, with the more affluent able to afford more services and shows.

Television is the main storytelling medium of our time. However, the news, comedy, and drama of television are increasingly controlled by larger and larger companies—like Disney (ABC), Viacom-Paramount (and its partner CBS), GE (NBC), and News Corp. (Fox)—who have seized control of programming. The TV executives wielding this storytelling power, however, have not yet figured out how to bring back viewers increasingly drawn to the more interactive and specialized terrain of cable, direct broadcast satellites (DBS), the Internet, and other digital technologies. Since the 1980s, the original Big Three networks have lost more than half their audience. And their main "new" idea is to recycle reality programs that lack the storytelling power of a well-crafted drama or a smart comedy.

The development of cable, VCRs and DVD players, new networks, DVRs, MP3 players, and Internet and cell phone services has fragmented television's audience by appealing to viewers' individual and special needs. These changes and services, by providing more

TV AND DEMOCRACY
The first televised presidential debates took place in 1960, pitting Massachusetts senator John F. Kennedy against Vice President Richard Nixon. Don Hewitt, who later created the long-running TV newsmagazine *60 Minutes*, directed the first debate and has argued that the TV makeup that Nixon turned down would have helped create a better appearance alongside that of his tanned opponent. In fact, one study at the time reported that a majority of radio listeners thought Nixon won the first debate while the majority of TV viewers believed Kennedy won.

specialized and individual choices, also alter television's role as a national unifying force, potentially de-emphasizing the idea that we are all citizens who are part of a larger nation and world. In addition, the MP3 players, cell phones, and Internet services that now offer our favorite TV shows and news programs are breaking down the distinctions between our computer and TV screens.

However, the ideal of television as a prevailing cultural center is not lost. Certainly the coverage of the aftermath of 9/11, the war in Iraq, Hurricane Katrina, and the Iowa floods and Hurricane Ike of 2008 demonstrated television's continuing ability to serve as a touchstone for important national events. Perhaps most important, though, is the increasingly influential role of television in our national political lives. In the run-up to the presidential nominations in 2008, senators Hillary Clinton, John McCain, and Barack Obama had to raise millions of dollars each month just to pay for the expensive political ads shown on television during each state's primary campaign. Such political ads are considered crucial both to securing a party's nomination and to eventually winning the national election. Any candidate misstep or error in the primary and election that comes within the view of a cell phone or digital camera can easily end up circulating on cable and network news and on YouTube. Easily reaching tens of millions of viewers and influencing opinions about political leaders, this new online reality demonstrates the lasting power of television in our culture. ▸

CHAPTER REVIEW

REVIEW QUESTIONS

The Origins and Early Development of Television

1. What were the major technical standards established for television in the 1940s?

2. Why did the FCC freeze the allocation of TV licenses between 1948 and 1952?

3. How did the sponsorship of network programs change during the 1950s?

4. Why did it take forty years for the networks to put a quiz show—*Who Wants to Be a Millionaire*—back on the air in prime time?

Major Programming Trends

5. How did visual news develop at the networks in the late 1940s and 1950s?

6. What are the differences among sketch, situation, and domestic comedies on television?

7. Why did the anthology drama fade as a network programming staple?

8. What are the types of episodic TV series? Why did they survive as a TV staple?

The Decline of the Networks

9. What were the technological changes that contributed to the decline of network control over television?

10. What rules and regulations did the government impose to restrict the networks' power?

11. How have new networks managed to grow during the last decade?

The Economics of Television

12. Why has it become more difficult for independent producers to create programs for television?

13. What are the differences between off-network and first-run syndication?

14. Why do syndicated American television shows have advantages in the global marketplace?

15. What is the difference between a rating and a share in audience measurement?

Television, Culture, and Democracy

16. How has television served as a national cultural center or reference point over the years?

17. What problems does traditional network television face in the early twenty-first century?

QUESTIONING THE MEDIA

1. Describe your earliest memories of watching television. What was your favorite show? Which, if any, shows did your family watch together? Were there shows that you were not allowed to watch? Which ones and why?

2. How much television do you watch today? Which programs do you try to watch regularly? What attracts you to your favorite program(s)?

3. If you were a network television executive, what changes would you try to make in the programs that America watches?

4. If you ran a public television station, what programming would you provide that isn't currently being supplied by commercial television? How would you finance such programming?

5. How could television be used to improve social and political life in the United States?

For review quizzes, chapter summaries, links to media-related Web sites, and more, go to bedfordstmartins.com/mediaculture.

COMMON THREADS

As television changes its shapes and sizes, does it remain the dominant way our culture tells stories?

By the end of the 1950s, television had become an "electronic hearth" where families gathered in living rooms to share cultural experiences. By 2008, though, the television experience had splintered. Now we watch TV on our laptops, cell phones, and iPods, making it increasingly an individual rather than communal experience. Still, television remains the mass medium that can reach most of us at a single moment in time, whether it's during a popular sitcom or a presidential debate.

In this shift, what has been lost and what has been gained? As an electronic hearth, television has offered coverage of special moments—inaugurations, assassinations, moon walks, space disasters, Super Bowls, *Roots*, the Olympics, 9/11, hurricanes, presidential campaigns—that brought large heterogeneous groups together for the common experiences of sharing information, celebrating triumphs, mourning loss, and electing presidents.

Accessible now in multiple digitized versions, the TV image has become portable, the way radio became portable in the 1950s. Today, we can watch TV in cars, in the park, even in class (when we're not supposed to).

The bottom line is that today television is both electronic hearth and digital encounter. It still provides a gathering place for friends and family, while at the same time we can watch a favorite show almost whenever or wherever we want. Like all media forms before it, television is adapting to changing technology and shifting economics. As technology becomes more portable and personal, the TV industry searches for less expensive ways to produce and deliver television. But what remains solid ground on this shifting terrain is that television continues as our nation's chief storyteller, whether those stories are told in the form of news bulletins, sporting events, or network sitcoms. In what ways do you think this will remain the case in the future?

KEY TERMS

The definitions for the terms listed below can be found in the Glossary at the end of the book. The page numbers listed with the terms indicate where the term is highlighted in the chapter.

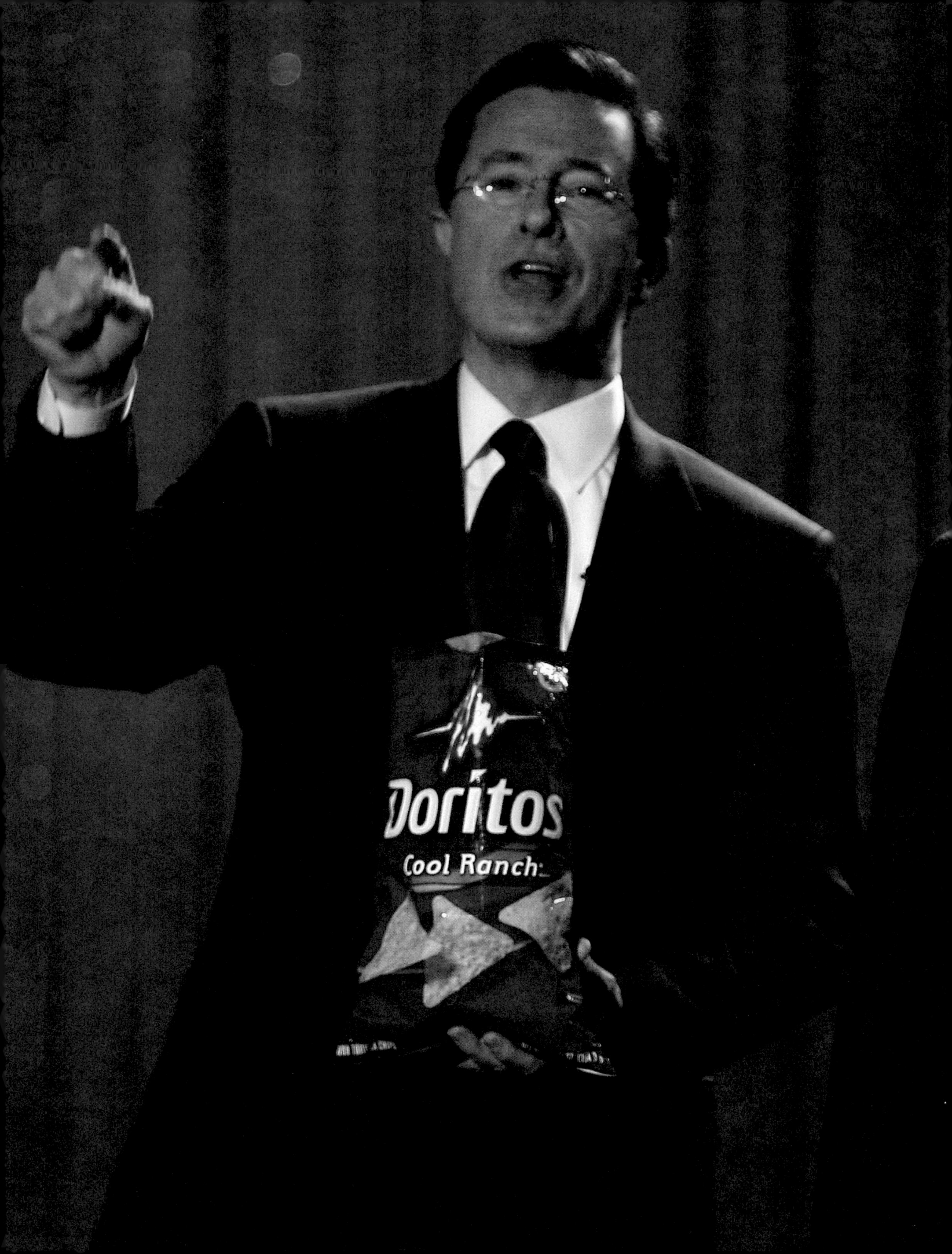
Doritos
Cool Ranch

6

Cable:

A Wired versus Wireless World

The Daily Show began on Comedy Central in 1996 with Craig Kilborn as anchor and the motto "When the news breaks, we fix it." A good satire of the nightly news programs, the show got even better when Jon Stewart—formerly on MTV—took over in 1999 as news anchor. In each program, Stewart and a team of correspondents—including Samantha Bee, Jason Jones, Aasif Mandvi, John Oliver, and Rob Riggle (a major in the U.S. Marine Corps Reserves who served in Kosovo and Afghanistan)—comment on the day's major stories, employing actual news footage, taped field pieces, and in-studio guests. A continuing gag features team members as expert "senior correspondents," pretending to report live from news events around the world, when they are clearly in-studio in front of a blue screen.

Through satire and sharp-witted lampoon of politics, the "fake news" on *The Daily Show* has become an effective critic of television and cable news, and the program has won Emmy and Peabody awards. The program's coverage is often just as substantive as that of major network news programs; it mixes news with a constant stream of major politicians, celebrities, and authors—both liberal and conservative—who go on to appear with Stewart. In addition, one of the show's regular features is to show clips of politicians contradicting themselves. This strategy, though humorous, is another way to critique both the media—for often not exposing these incidents—and the subjects of media coverage.

The Daily Show proved so successful that in fall 2005, former *Daily Show* correspondent Stephen Colbert began a spin-off program, *The Colbert Report*. In this half-hour comedy following *The Daily Show*, Colbert plays a narcissistic opinion program host, satirizing pundits like Fox News Channel's Bill O'Reilly and MSNBC's Chris Matthews. Colbert has also become a figure with large impact. In April 2006, Colbert was the main speaker at the White House Correspondents Association dinner. Just steps away from then-President George W. Bush, Colbert delivered a sharp, heavily ironic address that skewered both the president and the White House press. Colbert's address was watched by relatively few on C-Span but became a viral video on the Internet and generated a debate over whether Colbert was funny (the president and his wife weren't laughing by the end) and whether his satire was too painfully on-target for this Washington occasion.

The Daily Show and *The Colbert Report* are two top programs on the Comedy Central cable network, which is available in more than ninety-one million homes nationwide. And, although the programs' audiences average only 1.3 to 1.5 million viewers per night, their influence on young people and politics is significant. Recent studies have shown that *The Daily Show* serves as the main source of political news for many eighteen- to twenty-nine-year-olds.[1] And a 2007 study by the Pew Research Center demonstrated that viewers of *The Daily Show* and *The Colbert Report* had better knowledge of national and international current affairs than any other news audience.[2] These ratings and influences secure the lock that Comedy Central's parent company Viacom has on the young adult cable television market; its other holdings include MTV, VH1, BET, TV Land, Spike TV, CMT, and Logo.

"**Through satire and sharp-witted lampoon of politics, the 'fake news' on *The Daily Show* has become an effective critic of television and cable news . . .**"

▲ ALTHOUGH CABLE TELEVISION IS ALMOST AS OLD AS BROADCAST TELEVISION, broadcasters worked hard to stunt its growth throughout its first twenty-five years. Since the mid-1970s, however, when both HBO (Time Warner's premium movie service) and WTBS (Ted Turner's Atlanta TV station) became available to cable companies across the nation, cable television's growth has been rapid. In 1977, only 14 percent of all American homes received cable (which usually carried just twelve channels). By 1985, that percentage had climbed to 46. In 1999, cable penetration hit about 70 percent, but it fell to 58 percent by 2008, as direct broadcast satellite (DBS) services like DirecTV and Dish TV captured bigger pieces of the market.

The cable industry's rapid rise to prominence was due partly to the shortcomings of broadcast television. For example, cable improved signal reception in most communities. In addition, while prime-time broadcast television has traditionally tried to reach the largest possible audiences, cable channels–like magazines and radio–focused on providing specialized services for smaller audiences that broadcasters often ignored. Furthermore, through its greater channel capacity, cable has provided more access. In many communities, various public, government, and educational channels have made it possible for anyone to air a point of view or produce a TV program. When it has lived up to its potential, cable has offered the public greater opportunities to participate more fully in the democratic promises of television.

In this chapter, we examine cable's technological development and traditional broadcasters' attempts to restrict its growth. We discuss the impact of key rules and regulations aimed at the cable industry, including the Telecommunications Act of 1996. We explore various programming strategies, including basic service, premium cable, pay-per-view, and video-on-demand, as well as the innovative contributions of CNN, MTV, and HBO. We discuss the impact of direct broadcast satellite and cell phone services on cable. Finally, we look at business and ownership patterns and investigate cable's role in a democratic society.

Technology and the Development of Cable

Cable television's earliest technical breakthroughs came from a fairly anonymous and practical group of people. In rural and small-town communities in the late 1940s, appliance store owners faced a major obstacle in selling TV sets to people who lived in remote areas: Hills and mountains blocked broadcast signals. In response, TV dealers and electronics firms built antenna relay towers on the outskirts of communities to pick up blocked signals. They strung wire from utility poles and then ran cables from the towers into individual homes. The cables created a market for TV sets by ensuring clear TV reception.

Cable TV continues to operate in pretty much the same way today. The key technical distinction between cable and broadcasting is that in cable, programs reach TV sets through signals transmitted via wire; in broadcasting, signals are transmitted over the air. The advantage of cable is that the airwaves in any given community can accommodate only about fifteen channels without electrical interference, but cable wires can transmit hundreds of channels with no interference.

CATV—Community Antenna Television

The first small cable systems–called **CATV**, or community antenna television–originated in Oregon, Pennsylvania, and New York City, where mountains or tall buildings blocked TV signals. These systems served roughly 10 percent of the country and, because of early technical and regulatory limits, contained only twelve channels. Even at this early stage, though, TV sales personnel,

"New viewers are not coming to network television. How do you build for the future? If I was a young executive, I don't know if I would come into the network business. I'd probably rather program Comedy Central."

LESLIE MOONVES, PRESIDENT OF CBS TELEVISION, 1998

"If Mark Twain were back today, he'd be on Comedy Central."

BILL MOYERS, TALKING TO JON STEWART ON *THE DAILY SHOW*

broadcasters, and electronics firms recognized the two big advantages of cable. First, by routing and reamplifying each channel in a separate wire, cable eliminated over-the-air interference. Second, running signals through coaxial cable increased channel capacity.

In the beginning, small communities with CATV often received twice as many channels as were available over the air in much larger cities. That technological advantage, combined with cable's ability to deliver clear reception, would soon propel the new cable industry into competition with conventional broadcast television. But unlike radio, which inventors intended to free mass communication from unwieldy wire, early cable technology relied on wire to improve the potential of television.

The Wires and Satellites behind Cable Television

The idea of using space satellites to receive and transmit communication signals was literally right out of science fiction: In 1945, Arthur C. Clarke (who studied physics and mathematics and would later write dozens of sci-fi books, including *2001: A Space Odyssey*) published the original theories for a global communications system based on three satellites equally spaced from one another, rotating with the earth's orbit. In the mid-1950s, these theories became reality, as the Soviet Union and then the United States successfully sent satellites into orbit around the earth.

In 1960, AT&T launched Telstar, the first communication satellite capable of receiving, amplifying, and returning signals. Telstar received transmissions from the ground, beamed from an uplink facility, and retransmitted the signals to a receiving dish called a downlink. An active satellite, Telstar was able to process and relay telephone and occasional television signals between the United States and Europe. By the mid-1960s, scientists figured out how to lock a communication satellite into **geosynchronous orbit**. Hovering 22,300 miles from the equator, satellites could travel at more than 6,800 mph and circle the earth at the same speed at which the earth revolves on its axis. For cable television, the breakthrough was the launch of domestic communication satellites, first with Canada's *Anik* satellite in 1972, followed by the United States' *Westar* in 1974.

The first satellites were capable of operating for seven or eight years and had twelve or twenty-four **transponders**, the relay points on a satellite that perform the receive-and-transmit functions.

▼ **Cable: A Wired versus Wireless World**

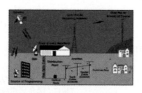

Cable TV
Community antenna television systems originate in the late 1940s in Oregon, Pennsylvania, New York City, and elsewhere to bring in TV signals blocked by mountains and tall buildings (p. 185).

HBO Uplinks to Satellite
The first premium channel is launched in the U.S. in 1975 (p. 188).

1940   **1950**   **1960**   **1970**

Satellites
In 1945, writer Arthur C. Clarke envisions a network of communication satellites (p. 186).

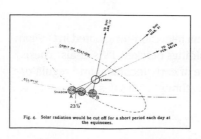

Fig. 4. Solar radiation would be cut off for a short period each day at the equinoxes.

Telstar
The first communication satellite relays telephone and television signals in 1960 (p. 186).

Franchising Frenzy
By the late 1970s, cable companies rush to win local cable franchises across the United States (p. 190).

By the mid-1990s, the newest satellites had forty-eight transponders and lifetimes of more than fifteen years. Cable program services such as MSNBC or the Discovery Network rent these transponders from satellite companies for million-dollar monthly fees. At first, a transponder could only process one TV signal or about three thousand simultaneous long-distance phone calls. Now, as companies have begun using digital compression as a way of increasing the number of signals transmitted, one transponder can handle four to six TV signals.

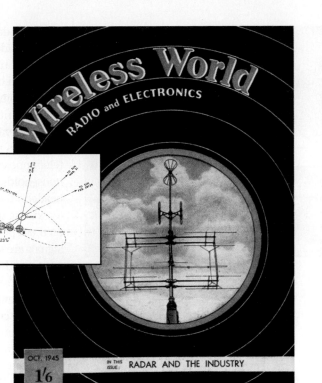

With cable, TV signals are processed at a computerized nerve center, or **headend**, which operates various large satellite dishes that receive and process long-distance signals from, say, CNN in Atlanta or MTV in New York. In addition, the headend's receiving equipment can pick up an area's local broadcast signals or a nearby city's PBS station. The headend relays each channel, local network affiliate, independent station, or public TV signal along its own separate line. Until the 1980s, when scientists developed *fiber-optic* technology–sending coded information along beams of laser light–most cable systems transmitted electronic TV signals via *coaxial cable,* a solid core of copper-clad aluminum wire encircled by an outer layer of braided wires. These bundles of thin wire could

SATELLITE TECHNOLOGY
Writer Arthur C. Clarke published a paper, "Extra-Terrestrial Relays: Can Rocket Stations Give World-wide Radio Coverage?" in the October 1945 issue of *Wireless World Magazine,* envisioning a global communications network based on three satellites in geosynchronous orbit. He wrote, "A true broadcast service . . . over the whole globe would be invaluable, not to say indispensable, in a world society."

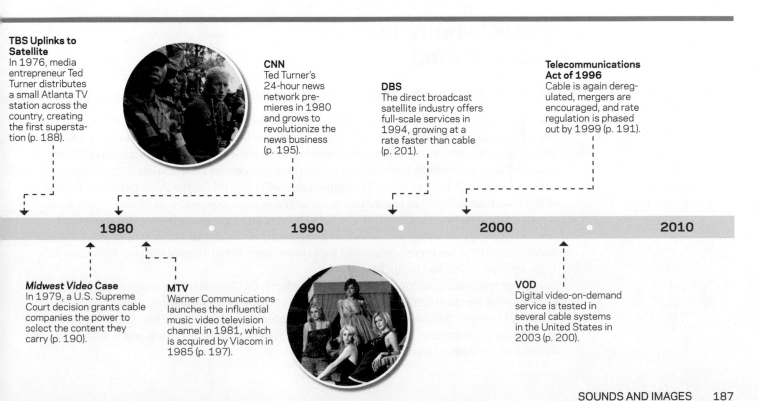

TBS Uplinks to Satellite
In 1976, media entrepreneur Ted Turner distributes a small Atlanta TV station across the country, creating the first superstation (p. 188).

CNN
Ted Turner's 24-hour news network premieres in 1980 and grows to revolutionize the news business (p. 195).

DBS
The direct broadcast satellite industry offers full-scale services in 1994, growing at a rate faster than cable (p. 201).

Telecommunications Act of 1996
Cable is again deregulated, mergers are encouraged, and rate regulation is phased out by 1999 (p. 191).

1980 **1990** **2000** **2010**

Midwest Video Case
In 1979, a U.S. Supreme Court decision grants cable companies the power to select the content they carry (p. 190).

MTV
Warner Communications launches the influential music video television channel in 1981, which is acquired by Viacom in 1985 (p. 197).

VOD
Digital video-on-demand service is tested in several cable systems in the United States in 2003 (p. 200).

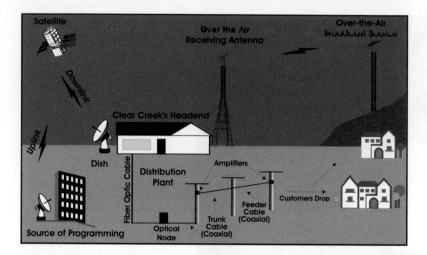

FIGURE 6.1

A BASIC CABLE TELEVISION SYSTEM

Source: Clear Creek Telephone & TeleVision, www.ccmtc.com.

accommodate many separate channels, or lines, running side by side with virtually no interference.

What travels on these lines mostly combines traditional broadcast signals and cable services accessed from communication satellites. After downlinking various channels from satellites and pulling in nearby broadcast stations from the airwaves, headend computers relay the channels in the same way that telephone calls and electric power reach individual households. Most TV channels are relayed from the headend through *trunk* and *feeder cables* attached to existing utility poles. Cable companies rent space on these poles from phone and electric companies. Signals are then transmitted to *drop* or *tap lines* that run from the utility poles into subscribers' homes. TV signals either move from drop lines to cable-ready TV sets or pass through a cable converter box, enabling older TV sets to receive each channel. The newest set-top cable converter boxes can also bring digital channels and on-demand services to subscribers. (See Figure 6.1.)

Advances in satellite technology in the 1970s dramatically changed the fortunes of cable by creating a reliable system for the distribution of programming to cable companies across the nation. Throughout the late 1970s and 1980s, cable television became popular, with dozens of new cable channel start-ups. The first cable network to use satellites for regular transmission of TV programming was Home Box Office (HBO), which began delivering programming such as uncut, commercial-free movies and exclusive live coverage of major boxing matches for a monthly fee in 1975. The second cable network began in 1976, when media owner Ted Turner distributed his small Atlanta broadcast TV station, WTBS, to cable systems across the country. Eventually naming his cable operation the Turner Broadcasting Service, Turner also inaugurated the Cable News Network (CNN) in 1980 and followed it with a number of other cable channels.

Cable Threatens Broadcasting

Though the technology for cable has existed since the late 1940s, cable's growth was effectively short-circuited by conventional broadcasters. For nearly thirty years, local broadcasters, the major networks, and television's professional organization—the National Association of Broadcasters (NAB)—successfully lobbied the Federal Communications Commission (FCC) to curb cable development in most cities. Throughout the 1950s and 1960s, the FCC operated on behalf of the broadcast industry to ensure that cable would not compete with conventional television. Local broadcasters worried that if towns could receive faraway signals from more glamorous cities like Chicago or New York, viewers would reject their local stations—and their local advertisers. Early FCC rules therefore blocked cable companies from bringing distant TV stations into cities and towns that had local channels.

There was one exception to these lobbying efforts: CATV services for sparsely populated communities. Because CATV generally served towns that had no TV stations of their own, the broadcast industry welcomed the distribution of distant signals to these areas via cable. After all, relaying a commercial signal to rural areas increased the audience reach and potential ad revenue of a broadcast station.

Balancing Cable's Growth against Broadcasters' Interests

By the early 1970s, particularly with the advent of communication satellites, it was clear that cable's growth could no longer be limited to small, isolated communities. With cable's capacity for more channels and better reception, the FCC began to seriously examine industry issues. In 1972, the commission updated or enacted two regulations with long-term effects on cable's expansion–must-carry rules and access-channel mandates.

Must-Carry Rules

First established by the FCC in 1965 and reaffirmed in 1972, the **must-carry rules** required all cable operators to assign channels to and carry all local TV broadcasts on their systems. This rule ensured that local network affiliates, independent stations (those not carrying network programs), and public television channels would benefit from cable's clearer reception. The FCC guidelines also allowed additional noncommercial channels to be introduced into bigger TV markets. However, to protect regional TV stations and their local advertising, the guidelines limited the number of distant commercial TV signals to two or three independent stations per cable system. The guidelines also prohibited cable companies from bringing in a network affiliate from another city when a local station already carried that network's programming. For example, a local broadcaster carrying NBC programs did not want its audience to be able to watch NBC programs on an imported station from another city. This would siphon off viewers and threaten local ad rates.

Access-Channel Mandates

In 1972 the FCC mandated **access channels** in the nation's top one hundred TV markets, requiring cable systems to carry their own original programming. In other words, operators of cable systems were forced to provide and fund a tier of nonbroadcast channels dedicated to local education, government, and the public. The FCC required large-market cable operators to assign separate channels for each access service, while cable operators in smaller markets (and with fewer channels) could require education, government, and the public to share one channel. In addition to free public-access channels, the FCC called for **leased channels**. Citizens could buy time on these channels and produce their own programs or present controversial views.

Cable's Role: Electronic Publisher or Common Carrier?

Despite the 1972 ruling requiring cable firms to provide local-access channels and a selection of leased channels to local bidders, the cable industry preferred to view its content (the programming provided on its cable systems) as similar to that provided by **electronic publishers**. Cable companies wanted the same "publishing" freedoms and legal protections that broadcast and print media enjoy in selecting content: the ability to pick and choose content (which channels to carry). Just as local broadcasters could choose to carry local news or *Jeopardy!* at 6 P.M., cable companies wanted to choose to carry a comedy or history channel as part of their service.

The FCC argued the opposite: that cable systems were **common carriers**–services that do not get involved in channel content. Like telephone operators, who do not question the topics of personal conversations ("Hi, I'm the phone company, and what are you going to be talking about today?"), cable companies, the FCC argued, should offer at least part of their services on a first-come, first-served basis to whoever could pay the rate. For these access services, then, cable companies could not control the content. That would be determined by whoever paid the money to lease the channel.

PROJECT RUNWAY, a runaway cable hit about fashion designers, averaged nearly four million viewers an episode in 2007–08, making it cable's top-rated reality series. Season four's big winner, 21-year-old Christian Siriano (here with host and supermodel Heidi Klum), won $100,000, a new car, and a spread highlighting his clothing in *Elle* magazine.

In 1979, the debate over this issue ended in the landmark *Midwest Video* case, when the U.S. Supreme Court upheld the rights of cable companies to determine their content and defined the industry as a form of "electronic publishing."[3] Although the FCC could no longer mandate channels' content, the Court said that it was proper for communities to "request" access channels as part of contract negotiations in the franchising process. Access channels are no longer a requirement, but most cable companies continue to offer them to remain on good terms with their communities.

Franchising Frenzy

By the end of the 1970s, particularly after the *Midwest Video* decision, the future of cable programming was secure, and competition to obtain franchises to supply local cable service had become intense. Essentially, a cable franchise was a mini-monopoly awarded by a local community to the most attractive bidder, usually for a fifteen-year period. Although a few large cities permitted two companies to build different parts of their cable systems, in most cases communities granted franchises to only one company. Cities and states employed the same logic that had been used in granting monopoly status to AT&T for more than a hundred years: They did not want more than one operator trampling over private property to string wire from utility poles or to bury cables underground. The period from the late 1970s through the early 1990s constituted a unique, if turbulent, era in media history, for it was during this time that most of the nation's cable systems were built (see Figure 6.2).

During the franchising process, a city (or state) would outline its cable system needs and request bids from cable companies. Then a number of companies would compete for the right to install and manage the cable system. (Potential cable companies were prohibited from also owning broadcast stations or newspapers in the community.)

In its bid, a company would make a list of promises to the city about construction schedules, system design, subscription rates, channel capacity, types of programming, financial backing, deadlines, and a *franchise fee*: the money the cable company would pay the city annually for the right to operate the local cable system. In the early 1980s, for example, Sammon Communication bid for the Fort Worth, Texas, franchise by offering that city a multimillion-dollar community-access package that included three mobile television vans (for producing community programs), $50,000 for student internship training programs, an annual budget of $175,000 for access channels, and $100,000 to modernize educational buildings and studios. Such offers were typical in large cable markets.

From the late 1970s through the 1980s, lots of wheeling and dealing transpired, along with occasional corruption as few laws existed to regulate franchise negotiations. Cable companies sometimes offered far more than they could deliver, and some cities and suburbs occasionally made unfair demands on the franchise awardees. Often, battles over broken promises, unreasonable contracts, or escalating rates ended up in court.

FIGURE 6.2

U.S. CABLE SYSTEMS, 1970–2010

Source: National Cable & Telecommunications Association, www.ncta.com.

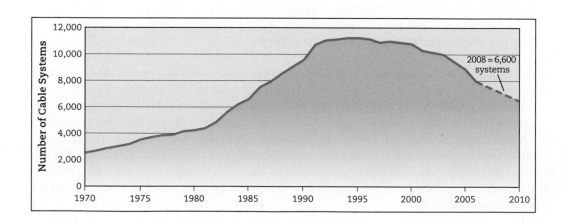

Today, a federal cable policy act from 1984 dictates the franchise fees for most U.S. municipalities that have agreements with cable companies. This act calls for cable providers to establish and fund access channels for local government, educational, and community programming as part of their license agreement. For example, Groton, Massachusetts (population around 10,000), has a cable contract with Charter Communications. According to the terms of the contract with Groton, Charter returns 4.25 percent of its revenue to the town (5 percent is the maximum a city can charge a cable operator). This money, which amounts to about $100,000 a year, helps underwrite the city's cable access programs. There are other communities, though, like nearby Hooksett, New Hampshire (population 3,700), that have chosen not to use their franchise fee money for access programming. Instead, Hooksett puts the fee revenue from its cable company, Comcast, toward a general fund that helps keep taxes lower. In 2008, although Hooksett still had no access channel, a move was afoot in town to redirect the franchise fee toward the creation of such a channel.

The Telecommunications Act of 1996

From the very beginning of cable, no one seemed to know who held legal jurisdiction over it. Because the Communications Act of 1934 had not anticipated cable, its regulatory status was problematic at first. However, once cable began importing distant signals into bigger television markets, the FCC's interest perked up. By the mid-1980s, Congress, the FCC, and the courts had repealed most early cable regulations, stimulating growth in the medium with new program forms like music videos on MTV and the 24/7 news service provided by CNN. But this also triggered regular rate increases for cable customers. Between 1984 and 1996 lawmakers went back and forth on rates and rules, creating a number of cable acts. One Congress would end must-carry rules and/or rate regulation, and then a later one would restore the rules.

Congress finally rewrote the nation's communications laws in the **Telecommunications Act of 1996**, bringing cable fully under the federal rules that had long governed the telephone, radio, and TV industries. In its most significant move, Congress used the Telecommunications Act to knock down regulatory barriers, allowing regional phone companies, long-distance carriers, and cable companies to enter one another's markets. The act allows cable companies to offer telephone services, and permits phone companies to offer Internet services and buy or construct cable systems in communities where there are fewer than fifty thousand residents. For the first time, owners could operate TV or radio stations in the same market where they owned a cable system. Congress hoped that the new rules would spur competition and lower both phone and cable rates, although this has not usually happened. Instead, cable and phone companies have merged operations in many markets, keeping prices at a premium and competition to a minimum.

The Telecommunications Act also reaffirmed broadcasters' need for must-carry rules. However, cable companies with limited channel capacity still objected to having to carry low-rated stations; cable operators could make more money carrying satellite-delivered movie services and specialty channels that focused on history or health. The nation's cable companies continued to ask the courts to repeal must-carry rules and free the cable companies to carry whatever channels best served their commercial interests. Ultimately, in 1997, the U.S. Supreme Court upheld the constitutionality of must-carry rules, ensuring that in most cases broadcasters would be carried by their local cable companies.

The 1996 act has had a mixed impact on cable customers. Cable companies argued that it would lead to more competition and innovations in programming, services, and technology. But, in fact, there is not extensive competition in cable. About 92 percent of U.S. cable subscribers live in communities that still have no viable competition to the local cable company. In these areas, cable rates have risen faster than the rate of inflation. In the few communities with multiple cable providers, the competition makes a difference—monthly rates are as much as 16 percent lower, according to an FCC study.[4] But where there is no competition, cable rates are determined by local cable companies, and the FCC has no authority to enforce rate freezes or cuts because the 1996 act required the FCC to end rate regulation in 1999.

"If this [telecommunications] bill is a blueprint, it's written in washable ink. Congress is putting out a picture of how things will evolve. But technology is transforming the industry in ways that we don't yet understand."

MARK ROTENBERG, ELECTRONIC PRIVACY INFORMATION CENTER, 1996

However, the cable industry has delivered on the technology, investing more than $110 billion in technological infrastructure between 1996 and 2007. This has enabled cable companies to offer what they call the "triple play"—digital cable television, broadband Internet, and telephone service, all bundled through the same household cable connection. By early 2008, U.S. cable companies had signed more than thirty-seven million households to digital programming packages; thirty-five million households had cable Internet service; and nearly eleven million households received their telephone service via cable.[5]

Cable Comes of Age

During the old network era in television, ABC, CBS, and NBC accounted for more than 95 percent of prime-time viewing; independent stations and public television accounted for the rest. By the summer of 1997, however, basic cable channels had captured a larger prime-time audience than the broadcast networks by offering original series. The networks responded by increasing the profile of their summer offerings (summer traditionally being a "lull" or "down" time for programming). This strategy was partially successful. The cable channels, in the end, had capitalized on the networks' taking the summer off and increased the number of new cable services.

Although its audience and advertising revenues remain smaller than those of traditional broadcast networks, cable emerged as a serious partner to broadcasting. As the broadcast audience eroded throughout the 1990s and 2000s, the major networks began acquiring or developing cable channels in order to capture some of the migrating viewers. Recent consolidations in media ownership mean that the broadcast networks may control many of the leading cable channels. Thus, what appears to be competition is sometimes just an illusion.

NBC, for example, operates cable news services MSNBC (with Microsoft), CNBC, and the entertainment channel Bravo. ABC, a subsidiary of Disney since 1995, owns the successful ESPN sports franchise, along with portions of Lifetime, A&E, E!, and History. CBS, on the other hand, was the slowest to develop cable holdings; its once successful TNN (now Spike TV) and CMT (Country Music TV) channels are controlled by its former parent company Viacom (although CBS's largest shareholder is Sumner Redstone, the chairman of Viacom).

Cable Targets Niche Audiences

In the new cable era, **narrowcasting**—providing specialized programming for diverse and fragmented groups—helped cable cut into broadcasting's large mass audience. Cable programs provide access to specific target audiences that cannot be guaranteed in broadcasting, something that attracts both advertisers and audiences (see "Case Study: The United Segments of America" on page 193). For example, a golf-equipment manufacturer can buy ads on the Golf Channel and reach only golf enthusiasts. Because audiences are small and specialized, cable ads are a fraction of the cost of network ads. As cable channels have become more and more like specialized magazines or radio formats (see Table 6.1 on page 194.), they have siphoned off network viewers, and the networks' role as the chief programmer of our shared culture has eroded.

▲

BATTLESTAR GALACTICA, a critically acclaimed but low-rated cable program on the Sci Fi channel, has been described by one critic as "a postapocalyptic battle between man and machines in deep space." There was an earlier show with the same name—considered a rip-off of the original *Star Wars* film—that aired for two years on CBS in the late 1970s. That show starred Lorne Greene, who had also played the ranching patriarch on the popular 1960s family western series *Bonanza.*

The United Segments of America: Niche Marketing in Cable

Individually, most cable television programs don't generate large audiences. A top network television program like *Grey's Anatomy* on ABC delivers more than twenty million television viewers an episode. A top cable television program like *SpongeBob SquarePants* on Nickelodeon delivers about four million viewers.

Yet taken together, cable television now attracts a larger total audience than the traditional television networks (ABC, CBS, NBC, Fox, and CW). Moreover, a number of top advertisers such as General Motors are putting the majority of their television advertising budget into cable, not broadcast network television. The key to cable's success is its ability to attract highly specific audiences. The profiles of cable viewers provided by the Cable Television Advertising Bureau read much like profiles of magazine audiences; cable channels target precise audience segments.

For example, Bravo, home of *Top Chef*, bills itself as the best cable network to reach adult viewers, ages twenty-five to fifty-four, who have household incomes greater than $150,000, hold top management positions, and have graduate degrees. The Food Network is a top choice for reaching what it calls "upscale" women in this age bracket. These viewers are likely to be working women who have a household income of $75,000 or more and a Visa or MasterCard Gold card. Even news channels have niche audiences—Fox News Channel is known for being politically to the right of CNN and draws more male viewers, while CNN draws slightly more female viewers.

MTV offers itself to advertisers as the one channel that "owns the young adult demographic." MTV says that it is the "best way to connect" with the twelve to thirty-four age group, which at ninety-one million strong and growing rep-

resents 33 percent of the population and more than $250 billion in spending power. The median age of MTV's viewers is twenty. Similarly, Black Entertainment Television (BET) markets itself as the best way to reach African Americans, who spend more than $500 billion on consumer products annually. BET's main focus, especially in prime time, is the demographic of African Americans ages eighteen to thirty-four.

Where do you find the older demographics? Flip between the History Channel and the Weather Channel (median age forty-six) and A&E (median age forty-seven). To reach children, advertisers can look to Nickelodeon, which delivers more children under twelve than any other basic cable network. Its shows *SpongeBob SquarePants* and *Fairly Odd Parents* are the two leading children's programs on cable. Overall, 62 percent of Nickelodeon's audience is ages two to eleven, 12 percent ages twelve to seventeen, and 26 percent adults eighteen and above. Nickelodeon claims to deliver more women ages eighteen to forty-nine who have children under twelve years of age than any other basic cable network (apparently, moms are watching with their children).

For women, Lifetime (with an audience of 76 percent women) is the top cable network, followed by Oxygen, SoapNet, and HGTV. For men, ESPN (with an audience of 75 percent men) is the leader, and it claims more high-income male viewers than any other ad-supported network. Other cable networks that skew heavily male include the Speed Channel (85 percent men) and Comedy Central (its hit series *South Park* "out-delivers all cable programs among [boys and] men [ages] 12–34"). ◢

TABLE 6.1

THE TOP CABLE NETWORKS, 2008 (RANKED BY NUMBER OF SUBSCRIBERS)

Source: National Cable & Telecommunications Association, www.ncta.com.

© 2008 SNL Kagan, a division of SNL Financial LC.

Rank	Network	Subscribers
1	TBS	97,200,000
2	CNN/HN	96,800,000
3	Discovery Channel	96,700,000
4	ESPN	96,400,000
4	Lifetime Television	96,400,000
6	TNT (Turner Network Television)	96,300,000
6	Nickelodeon/Nick At Nite	96,300,000
8	USA Network	96,200,000
9	A&E	96,100,000
10	The Learning Channel	96,000,000
10	ESPN2	96,000,000
12	Spike TV	95,900,000
13	HGTV	95,800,000
14	Food Network	95,500,000
14	Cartoon Network	95,500,000
16	ABC Family	95,400,000
17	Comedy Central	95,100,000
17	VH1	95,100,000
19	CNBC	94,800,000
19	Disney Channel	94,800,000

Cable consumers usually choose programming from a two-tiered structure: Basic cable services are part of a monthly fee, and premium cable services are available individually to customers at an extra monthly or per-use fee. These services are the production arm of the cable industry, supplying programming to the nation's six-thousand-plus cable operations, which function as program distributors to cable households.

Basic Cable Services

A typical **basic cable** system today includes a hundred-plus channel lineup composed of local broadcast signals, access channels (for local government, education, and general public use), regional PBS stations, and a variety of services downlinked from national communication satellites. Basic cable channels may include ESPN, CNN, MTV, VH1, USA, Bravo, Nickelodeon, Lifetime, ABC Family, Comedy Central, CNBC, C-Span and C-Span2, Black Entertainment Television, Telemundo, the Weather Channel, a home-shopping channel, **superstations** (independent TV stations uplinked to a satellite) such as WGN (Chicago) or WPIX (New York), and additional channels, depending on a cable system's capacity and regional interests.

Typically, local cable companies pay each of these satellite-delivered services between a few cents per month per subscriber for low-cost, low-demand channels like C-Span to as much as $3.50 per month per subscriber for high-cost, high-demand channels like ESPN. A standard basic cable channel like CNN, MTV, or TNT may negotiate a fee somewhere between 25 cents and $1 per subscriber per month, usually demanding more in areas that serve larger populations. That fee is passed along to consumers as part of their basic monthly cable rate.

Unlike local broadcasting stations, which make money almost exclusively through advertising, cable companies earn revenue in a variety of ways: through monthly subscriptions for basic service, local ad sales, pay-per-view programming, and premium movie channels. Most basic cable channels, such as ESPN or A&E, block out time for inexpensive local and regional ads. These local ads are cheaply produced compared with national network ads and reach a smaller audience. Cable, in fact, has permitted many small local companies—from restaurants to clothing stores—that might not otherwise be able to afford TV spots to use television as a means of advertising.

The 1990s witnessed a proliferation of new basic cable channels, increasingly specialized for smaller but more definable audiences. These include the popular SciFi Channel (owned by NBC Universal), the Cartoon Network (owned by Time Warner), Comedy Central (owned by Viacom), and FX (owned by News Corp.). Other services today feature channels devoted to food, decorating, history, health and fitness, self-help, games, parenting, and pets.

Regional cable providers, who target audiences geographically, often battle with the national cable channels. More than ninety regional channels exist in the United States, and nearly all of them are located in large metropolitan areas that can support their specialized programming. Many of the regional channels are news/talk formats modeled on CNN, but with coverage limited to a single media market. New York, for example, has NY1 News, a twenty-four-hour service that began in 1992. The New York region also has News 12 Interactive cable, which covers the Bronx, Brooklyn, Connecticut, New Jersey, Westchester, and the Hudson Valley. Similar services include NorthWest Cable News (Seattle), News Channel 8 (Washington, D.C.), and ChicagoLand Television News. Regional sports channels—many of them affiliates of the national Fox Sports Network—also thrive in large TV markets and regions that are home to multiple professional sports teams.

In 1992, 87 cable networks were in business. By 2008, that number had grown to more than 560, including cable and satellite television services.[6] Cable system capacities continue to increase as a result of the rebuilding of cable systems with high-bandwidth fiber-optic cable and the advent of *digital cable* in the late 1990s, which enabled cable systems to expand their offerings beyond the basic analog cable channels. Digital cable typically uses set-top cable boxes to offer interactive on-screen program guides and dozens of additional premium, pay-per-view, and audio music channels, increasing total cable capacities to between 150 and 200 channels.

The general success rate of new cable channels has been about 10 to 15 percent, which means that about 85 to 90 percent fail or are bought out. The most difficult challenge new channels face is getting onto enough cable systems—with limited channel capacity—to become profitable. While several basic cable channels, such as the Discovery Channel and ESPN (each with around ninety-six million cable subscribers), have been extremely successful, two early basic channels—CNN and MTV—made important marks both on American society and global culture. (For more on ESPN, see "Case Study—ESPN: Sports and Stories" on page 196.)

CNN's Window to the World

When it premiered in 1980, many people viewed Cable News Network (CNN), the first 24/7 cable TV news channel, as a joke—the "Chicken Noodle Network." CNN was the brainchild of Ted Turner, who had already revolutionized cable by uplinking his small independent Atlanta station WTBS (Turner Broadcast Service) to a satellite, creating the first superstation. It wasn't until Turner launched the Headline News channel in 1982, and turned a profit with both it and

THE DEADLIEST CATCH is a popular cable reality program on the Discovery Channel. "Full of crashing waves and heaving ships and skittering crabs," according to one TV critic, the show tracks the adventures of a crab ship crew off the Alaskan coast.

"Watching TV right now is exponentially more complicated than it was even five or ten years ago."

JEFF SHELL, CHIEF EXECUTIVE OF GEMSTAR-TV GUIDE INTERNATIONAL, 2004

CASE STUDY

ESPN:
Sports and Stories

A common way many of us satisfy our cultural and personal need for storytelling is through sports: We form loyalties to local and national teams. We follow the exploits of favorite players. We boo our team's rivals. We suffer with our team when the players have a bad game or an awful season. We celebrate the victories.

The appeal of following sports is similar to the appeal of our favorite books, TV shows, and movies—we are interested in characters, in plot development, in conflict and drama. Sporting events have all of this. It's no coincidence, then, that the Superbowl is annually the most watched single TV show around the world.

One of the best sports stories on television over the past thirty years, though, may not be a single sporting event but the tale of an upstart cable network based in Bristol, Connecticut. ESPN (Entertainment Sports Programming Network) began in 1979 and has now surpassed all the major broadcast networks as the "brand" that shows sports on TV. In fact, cable operators around the county regard ESPN as the top service when it comes to helping them "gain and retain customers."[1]

Today the ESPN flagship channel reaches into more than ninety-six million U.S. homes. And ESPN, Inc., now provides a sports smorgasbord—a menu of media offerings that includes ESPN2 (sporting events, news, and original programs), ESPN Classic (historical sporting events), ESPN Deportes (Spanish-language sports network), ESPN HD (a high-definition

channel), ESPN Radio, *ESPN The Magazine*, ESPNEWS (24-hour sports news channel), ESPN Outdoors, and ESPNU (college games). ESPN also creates original programming for TV and radio and operates ESPN.com, among the most popular sites on the Internet. Like CNN and MTV, ESPN makes its various channels available in more than 190 countries.

Each year ESPN's channels air more than five thousand live and original hours of sports programming, covering more than sixty-five different sports. In 2002, ESPN even outbid NBC for six years of NBA games—offering $2.4 billion, which at the time was just over a year's worth of ESPN revenues. But the major triumph of ESPN over the broadcast networks was probably wrestling the *Monday Night Football* contract from its sports partner ABC (both ESPN and ABC are owned by Disney). For eight years, starting in 2006, ESPN agreed to pay the NFL $1.1 billion a year for the broadcasting rights to *MNF*, the most highly rated sports series in prime-time TV history. In 2006, ABC turned over control of its sports programming division, ABC Sports, to ESPN, which now carries games on ABC under the ESPN logo.

The story of ESPN's "birth" also has its share of drama. The creator of ESPN was Bill Rasmussen, an out-of-work sports announcer who

had been fired in 1978 by professional hockey's New England Whalers (now the Carolina Hurricanes). Rasmussen wanted to bring sports programs to cable TV, which was just emerging from the shadow of broadcast television. But few backers thought this would be a good idea. Eventually, Rasmussen managed to land a contract with the NCAA to cover college games. He also lured Anheuser-Busch to become cable's first million-dollar advertiser. Getty Oil then agreed to put up $10 million to finance this sports adventure, and ESPN took off.

Today ESPN is 80 percent owned by the Disney Company while the Hearst Corporation holds the other 20 percent interest. ESPN earned more than $4 billion in revenue in 2007 and has more than thirty-four hundred employees worldwide; it is one of the success stories of narrowcasting on cable television. ◢

CNN in 1985, that the traditional networks began to take notice of cable news.

During the Gulf War in 1991, CNN emerged as a serious news competitor to ABC, CBS, and NBC, when two of its reporters were able to maintain a live phone link from a downtown Baghdad hotel during the initial U.S. bombing of the Iraqi capital. Even Iraq's military leaders watched the channel. CNN's ratings soared–from an audience of fewer than one million households before the crisis to about ten million after the war began.

CNN changed the way people watch news by offering viewers an ever-present window into news happenings around the world. Early on, CNN mastered continuous coverage of breaking news events, such as natural disasters and wars, and aimed to put news first, refusing to transform news anchors into celebrities. And because it wasn't forced to compress the news into a half-hour show, it was able to deliver more timely news in greater detail and feature live, unedited coverage of news conferences, press briefings, and special events. Moreover, with a commitment to maintaining international bureaus (while other networks were shutting them down), CNN made a big impact on international news coverage. Today, CNN appears in more than two hundred countries and territories around the globe, and more than two billion people have access to a CNN service.

The success of CNN proved that there is both a need and a lucrative market for twenty-four-hour news. Spawning a host of competitors in the United States and worldwide, CNN now battles for viewers with other twenty-four-hour news providers, including Fox News Channel, MSNBC, CNBC, EuroNews, Britain's Sky Broadcasting, and millions of Web and blog sites, like Politico.com and Salon.com. Ironically, in the same manner that CNN rose to prominence during the Gulf War, its main rival, Fox News, surpassed CNN's ratings in 2002, as international terrorism and the buildup to a second U.S.-Iraq war were main news events. Despite being beaten often in the prime-time ratings by Fox News opinion shows, particularly *The O'Reilly Factor*, CNN still commands higher advertising rates on the strength of its worldwide news reputation.

CNN NEWS COVERAGE
After an early career that included stints with the school news service Channel One and the ABC reality show *The Mole,* Anderson Cooper joined CNN in 2001. He became one of its top newscasters in 2003, anchoring the news program *Anderson Cooper 360°.* Cooper is best known for his live reports from news locations around the world.

"I Want My MTV"

Created in 1981 by Warner Communications and purchased by Viacom in 1985, MTV (the Music Television Network) and its global offspring–including MTV Europe, MTV Brasil, MTV Latin America, MTV Russia, MTV Australia, MTV Africa, and MTV Asia–reach more than four hundred million homes worldwide. Its international brand appeal is so great that when Poland became free of Soviet control in the late 1980s, its national television operation immediately began broadcasting MTV.

Throughout the 1980s, MTV sought control over music video distribution and exhibition, employing two monopoly tactics to ensure dominance. First, MTV paid record companies for exclusive rights to the most popular music videos (for periods ranging from thirty days to one year). Although this was a form of payola (see Chapters 3 and 4), federal laws prohibiting this practice applied only to broadcasting, not to cable.

Second, MTV signed agreements with the major cable companies to ensure that it would become the music video network in the main U.S. cable markets. Other music video services were quickly countered. MTV's launch of VH1 (geared toward baby-boomers, the parents of the MTV generation) became part of a bundled MTV-VH1 package sold to cable operators.

MTV exerts a powerful influence on culture nationally and globally, but one early flaw was how little airtime it gave to African American artists. This echoed the 1950s and the problems black musicians and singers faced in getting mainstream radio play. In the early 1980s, however,

MTV CULTURE
Fans in the studio of MTV's once-popular afternoon request show *Total Request Live* (left) applaud singer Beyoncé. *TRL*, one of the last music video-based programs on MTV, ended its 10-year run in 2008. While another music-based show, FNMTV, replaced it, MTV now concentrates more on its reality series, like *The Hills* (right).

> "I may have destroyed world culture, but MTV wouldn't exist today if it wasn't for me."
>
> ADVERTISING ART DIRECTOR GEORGE LOIS, WHO COINED THE PHRASE "I WANT MY MTV," 2003

MTV's reluctance to play music videos by black artists was related to cable economics as much as it was to racial divisions. At that time, most cable companies were primarily operating in affluent white communities in U.S. suburbs—the areas that could most easily afford cable. Because rock, especially on mainstream radio, had been taken over by white male groups throughout the 1970s, MTV thought affluent white suburban teens probably wanted to see similar groups in their music videos.

It took Michael Jackson's *Thriller* album in 1982 to break down music video's color barrier. The album's large crossover appeal, coupled with the expansion of cable into more urban areas, opened the door to far more diverse videos. With hip-hop's rise in popularity throughout the 1980s and 1990s among all American audiences, MTV began to add more diverse offerings, including hip-hop and R&B videos, as well as programs like *Yo! MTV Raps*. Through its programming, MTV helped sell African American hip-hop culture—its beats, baggy clothes, urban sensibility, and street language—to suburban America and the world at large.

In the early 1990s MTV began to shift from music video programming to creating original programming, including the first U.S. reality-based soap opera, *The Real World*, the cartoon *Beavis and Butt-head*, as well as more recent hits like *The Hills* and *MADE*. The shift was an effort to provide advertisers with more regular audiences during specific viewing times, but it ended up infuriating record labels and many MTV viewers by narrowing the channel's video playlists. MTV responded in 1996 by launching MTV2, to present music videos the way MTV first did, and in 1998 *Total Request Live* (*TRL*) to regularly show popular music videos.

A subsidiary of Viacom—one of the world's largest media conglomerates—MTV has drawn a great deal of criticism for its cultural impact. Many critics worry that its influence has eroded local culture-specific traits among the world's young people and has substituted an overabundance of U.S. culture in their place. Others argue that MTV has contributed to the decline of civility through its often vulgar programming, which at times glorifies violence and drug use. Most of all, critics condemn the network for its overt sexism—particularly the use of women in roles clearly exploitative and subordinate to men. Defenders of the network, however, point out that MTV and cable in general have created a global village, giving the world a common language. They also applaud a variety of MTV's special programs on issues ranging from drug addiction to racism and social activism. The visual style of MTV—shaky camera footage, quick cuts, bright colors, and other dazzling visual innovations—has also greatly influenced the media landscape.

In recent years the music video channel Fuse, owned by Cablevision Systems (which also owns channels such as AMC and the Independent Film Channel), has presented MTV with its most spirited challenge. Fuse targets the teen to twenty-four-year-old audience with music videos, live music performances, and an underdog image that tries to out-cool MTV. Cablevision's channel was available to more than fifty million households by 2008.

Beyond the world of music, another major programming innovation aimed at younger audiences is Nickelodeon (also owned by Viacom).[7] Since the major networks largely abandoned children's programming because it wasn't lucrative enough, competitors such as PBS and Nickelodeon have tried to fill the gap. Because Nickelodeon and MTV kids grew up watching cable networks, when they reach adulthood, they do not view the traditional networks as superior to cable. Ironically, Nickelodeon, especially its "Nick at Nite" programming, often shows network reruns like *Alfred Hitchcock Presents*, *I Love Lucy*, the *Mary Tyler Moore Show*, *Home Improvement*, *The Fresh Prince of Bel Air*, and *Roseanne*–all once popular on traditional broadcast channels, although younger generations now associate these programs with cable. Some TV critics and academics argue that one contribution of Nickelodeon, besides some original children's programming, is the creation of an informal repository for old network shows–shows that, without cable's appetite for 24/7 programming, younger generations might never have seen.

Premium Cable Services

Besides basic programming, cable offers a wide range of special channels, known as **premium channels**, which lure customers with the promise of no advertising, both recent and classic Hollywood movies, and original movies or series like HBO's *Entourage* and Showtime's *Big Love*. These channels are a major source of revenue for cable companies: The cost to them is four to six dollars per month per subscriber to carry a premium channel, but the cable company can charge customers ten dollars or more per month and reap a nice profit. In addition to movie channels like HBO and Showtime, premium services also include pay-per-view (PPV) programs; video-on-demand (VOD); and interactive services that enable consumers to use their televisions to bank, shop, play games, and access the Internet. Subscribers to such services pay extra fees in addition to the charges for their standard cable service.

The HBO Alternative

By far the oldest and most influential premium channel is HBO (Home Box Office)–a subsidiary of Time Warner, one of the nation's largest owners of cable companies. Although HBO reaches less than one-third the audience of a popular basic channel, it has remained the dominant premium channel, selling monthly subscriptions to more than twenty-nine million homes by 2008. HBO and Cinemax (the second-highest-rated premium channel) bring more than forty million premium subscribers to parent corporation Time Warner. Competing premium channels include Liberty Media's Encore and STARZ! channels, CBS's Showtime (which has about fourteen million subscribers), the Movie Channel, and Flix. The Sundance Channel (owned jointly by actor Robert Redford, Universal Studios, and Showtime) and the Independent Film Channel (owned by Cablevision) emerged with the growing market of independent films in the mid-1990s.

The movie business initially feared that HBO would be a detriment to film attendance in theaters. Eventually, though, HBO and the other premium channels brought a lucrative source of income to the movie studios, which earn roughly 15 percent of premium cable's profits. Film companies recognized that they could recoup losses from a weak theater run by extending a film's life through

ENTOURAGE, an HBO series nominated for an Emmy for best comedy in 2007–08, is loosely based on the Hollywood adventures of actor Mark Wahlberg and his friends. The show frequently casts actual Hollywood actors who play themselves.

SHOWTIME'S *WEEDS* was the premium cable channel's top-rated series in 2008. This dark comedy features actress Mary Louise Parker playing a pot-dealing single mom struggling to make ends meet. As one critic put it, she's just trying to get in touch "with her inner gangsta amid the manicured lawns and granite-countered hypocrisy of a Southern California planned community."

lucrative arrangements with premium cable channels. Today, HBO runs more than ninety theatrical motion pictures a month.

In the early 1980s, when there was little competition, HBO dictated to movie studios which films it wanted and how much it was willing to pay. HBO and other premium channels ran into trouble, however, as videotapes became the preferred method of viewing movies after their theater runs. Both VCRs and PPV (pay-per-view) options brought competition to the movie channels. In the mid-1980s, film studios started releasing movies to PPV channels and to video stores before offering them to movie channels.

The new competition forced the movie channels to expand their services. HBO, for example, began developing its own programming—from children's shows like *Fraggle Rock* to comedies like the *Larry Sanders Show*, an Emmy award-winning satire of late-night talk shows. HBO's successes in original programming continue today, with critical praise for programs like *Curb Your Enthusiasm*, *Entourage*, *The Wire*, and *Big Love*.

Threatened by another industry making movies, film studios felt threatened when HBO made its own feature-length films. In 1982, HBO arranged with CBS and Columbia Pictures (later bought by Sony) to form a new production house, TriStar Pictures. Many in the movie industry charged that HBO's movie productions constituted **vertical integration**, an economic structure in which a mass media industry controls three essential levels of a media business—usually production, distribution, and exhibition. The studios argued that when Time Inc. (before its merger with Warner Brothers) began making movies through HBO and TriStar, the media conglomerate was permitted to do something that film studios could not do. A Supreme Court decision in 1948 had broken up the film industry's vertical structure by forcing the major studios to sell their theaters—the exhibition part of their operations (see Chapter 7). In the 1980s, Time Inc. was the second-largest owner of cable systems—the movie studio equivalent of owning theaters. The movie studios argued that allowing Time to vertically integrate constituted a prohibited monopolistic practice. But because so many cable companies and services existed by the 1980s, the more conservative, business-friendly, and antiregulation administration of President Ronald Reagan did not seriously challenge HBO's role in movie production.

Pay-per-View and Video-on-Demand

Beginning in 1985, cable companies began introducing new viewing options for their customers. **Pay-per-view (PPV)** channels came first, offering recently released movies or special one-time sporting events to subscribers who paid a designated charge to their cable company, allowing them to view the program. Despite this "convenience," many consumers preferred the greater variety and flexibility offered by rented videos and DVDs, even if they had to drive to the store to get them and pay late fees.

U.S. cable companies introduced a new and improved pay-per-view option to their digital customers in the early 2000s—**video-on-demand (VOD)**. This digital cable service enabled customers to choose among hundreds of titles, then download a selection from the cable operator's server onto their cable TV box hard drive for one to four dollars and watch the movie the same way they would watch a video, pausing and fast-forwarding when desired. Now, the largest cable companies and DBS (direct broadcast satellite) services also offer digital video recorders (DVRs) to their customers. Along with ordering or streaming DVDs through online services like Netflix and downloading movies to iPods, digital VOD services today threaten to end the era of the local video store (see Chapter 7).

Challenges to Cable: DBS and Cell Phones

Of all the emerging technologies, including the Internet, the distribution of television by **direct broadcast satellite (DBS)** and by cell phones presents the biggest challenge to the existing cable and television industries. DBS transmission is especially competitive with cable in regions with rugged terrain and isolated homes, where the installation of cable wiring hasn't always been possible or profitable.

DBS: Cable without Wires

The earliest industrial earth-station antennas, or satellite dishes, were set up in the mid-1970s to receive cable programming. They were large, measuring twenty to forty feet in diameter, and expensive (with FCC license fees adding to their high cost). From the beginning, however, engineers worked to reduce the size and cost of the receiving dishes in order to develop an affordable consumer model (the larger industrial models that cable systems and TV stations use for satellite downlinks cost thousands of dollars). To protect the fledgling cable business throughout the 1970s and 1980s, the FCC restricted the development of DBS companies, which get their programming from the same satellite channels (such as CNN, MTV, ESPN, and HBO) that supply the regular cable industry.

From Free Transmission to Big Business

In the United States, beginning in the 1970s, small-town and rural residents bypassed FCC restrictions by buying seven- to ten-foot receiving dishes and downlinking, for free, the same channels that cable companies were supplying to wired communities. These early home satellite dishes, like early cable systems, appeared mostly in sparsely populated areas that were too costly for cable companies to wire.

Initially, households could pick up channels once they had invested $2,000 to $3,000 in a large receiving dish. Not surprisingly, satellite programmers filed a flurry of legal challenges against farmers and small-town residents who were receiving their signals for free. Rural communities countered that they had the rights to the airspace above their own property; the satellite firms contended that their signals were being stolen. Because the law was unclear, a number of cable channels began scrambling their signals. As a result, most satellite users had to buy or rent descramblers and subscribe to services, as cable customers did.

Signal scrambling spawned companies that provided both receiving dishes and satellite program services for a monthly fee. In 1978, Japanese companies, which had been experimenting with "wireless cable" alternatives for years, started the first DBS system in Florida. With gradual improvements in satellite technology, the diameters of satellite-receiving dishes decreased from more than twenty feet to three feet in a few years. By 1994, full-scale DBS service was available, and consumers could buy satellite dishes the size of an extra large pizza.

Today, there are two U.S.-based DBS companies: DirecTV and the DISH Network (formerly known as EchoStar Communication). By 2008 DirecTV had seventeen million U.S. customers and another five million in Latin America while the DISH Network served fourteen million subscribers. These companies offer consumers most of the channels and tiers of service that cable companies carry, sometimes at a slightly lower monthly cost. In addition, DBS systems can carry between 350 and 500 basic, premium, and pay-per-view channels, which can be purchased by customers in various packages. Thus DBS presents many more options than those available on most conventional cable systems, which are limited by channel capacity.

Pros and Cons of DBS Systems

Buoyed by high consumer interest and competing in large cities as well as rural areas, DBS firms are challenging the long-standing monopoly status of most cable systems, offering distinct advantages—and disadvantages—compared with cable.

One advantage is that DBS's digital technology has generally been superior to standard cable and broadcast signals. For example, the quality of a DBS high-definition image is better than that of a cable HDTV picture. Another big drawing card for DBS is the ability to give subscribers nationwide access (in packages that cost between $10 and $40 per month) to more professional sports leagues—including hockey, football, baseball, soccer, and men's and women's basketball—that aren't carried locally on broadcast networks or on basic cable channels.

An early disadvantage of DBS systems was remedied in 1999, when Congress passed legislation allowing them to carry local broadcast channels. Until that time, DBS did not pick up an area's local broadcast signals, which were not uplinked to satellites. This meant that most subscribers had to use a local cable company or TV antennas to get the local PBS, independent, and broadcast network programming. The addition of local broadcast signals to DBS was a major catalyst for DBS to compete directly with cable.

Initially, DBS systems did not have the same ability as cable to bundle high-speed Internet and telephone service with their video programming. By 2007, this situation also changed. Even though cable companies had a head start in packaging their Internet, television, and phone services into one monthly bill, by 2008 both cable and DBS were offering bundled services at about $100 per month. (Depending on whether customers added more premium channels or the new HD tier of channels, packages could go up to $200 per month.) In the end, these packages helped the DBS share of the multichannel video market grow from 14 percent in 2000 to more than 33 percent in 2008.

> **"Prices rapidly dropped from $75,000 to $25,000 for a dish antenna, a low noise amplifier, and two receivers."**
>
> FRANK BAYLIN, MEDIA HISTORIAN, ON THE APPROVAL OF "SMALLER" (FIFTEEN FEET IN DIAMETER) SATELLITE DISHES IN 1976

Cell Phones, Mobile Video, and WiMax

Telephones were originally not considered a mass medium but rather a point-to-point, or one-to-one, communication technology. In "qualifying" as mass communication media, books, newspapers, and magazines reach millions of readers; and radio, television, and the Internet connect millions of listeners and viewers. But in our digital and wireless age, we can now download music, TV programs, and movies onto our cell phones as well as our laptops.

The latest wireless development involves **WiMax** (short for Worldwide Interoperability for Microwave Access)—a communication technology that provides data over long distances in multiple ways, from traditional cell phone connections to services that link mobile phones to traditional mass media. WiMax differs from Wi-Fi (see Chapter 2), which is a wireless system that uses spectrum space to provide short-range access to a network, typically covering only the network operator's own space or property, as in those systems used at a university, in an office building, or in a city. There is also less interference with a WiMax signal. Here is a useful way to think about the difference in range between Wi-Fi and WiMax: Wi-Fi is to the cordless phone what WiMax is to the cell phone.

WIMAX
Creating mobile video for cell phones is one of the goals of emerging technology like WiMax.

In 2008, major cable, phone, and Internet companies all began talks to create a U.S. wireless network to link computers, televisions, and cell phones using WiMax technology. In addition to Comcast and Time Warner—the nation's two biggest cable providers—Google, Intel, and Sprint Nextel also were considering investing billions of dollars in WiMax business ventures and partnerships. One

Media Literacy and the Critical Process

A Democracy of Channels?

For a new basic cable programming service to have a chance of financial viability, it needs to reach at least 50 percent of the cable audience. But what companies have the opportunity to create a successful cable channel?

1 DESCRIPTION. Take note of the Top 20 cable networks, ranked by number of subscribers (see Table 6.1 on page 194 and also the Web site for the National Cable & Telecommunications Association, http://www.ncta.com).

2 ANALYSIS. Compare ownership among the top networks. There should be clear patterns. For example, Time Warner owns TBS, TNT, and CNN, among several other cable networks.

3 INTERPRETATION. What do the patterns mean? For example, cable television programming companies have negotiated with or forced cable systems to adopt their new channel offerings. Thus, Disney owns not only ESPN but also highly rated ESPN2, ESPN News, and ESPN Classic. Other media corporations have been able to purchase larger shares of the cable audience. For example, Viacom owns MTV Networks (which operates MTV, Nickelodeon/Nick at Nite, VH1, Logo, and other channels) as well as CMT and Spike TV.

4 EVALUATION. Does the fact that a handful of large media corporations control many of cable's most popular networks reduce cable's promise of a multiplicity of networks representing a wide range of voices? Are networks such as CNBC and MSNBC just an extension of NBC Universal; or does ownership not matter? Does each of the top cable networks serve as an independent, unique voice? How is the quality of programming affected?

5 ENGAGEMENT. Talk to your local cable operator(s) and find out when channel capacity will increase, or when there will be a review of the cable channel lineup. Find out what it takes to add a cable network to the system. Few people ever bother to write their cable operator requesting a network, so if there is a network that would bring a valuable perspective to your community, consider developing a petition or letter-writing campaign to argue persuasively for it.

of the chief interests in this technology is how fast WiMax can deliver the Internet to laptops and cell phones. Cable companies are particularly interested because WiMax technology allows them to take part in the wireless business without owning mobile phone companies. For some in the wired cable industry, entering into WiMax would provide a wireless strategy for competing against DBS systems.

Ownership and Business Issues in Cable and DBS

Today there are about 6,600 U.S. cable systems, down from 7,900 in 2005 and 11,200 in 1994. Increasingly, these systems are being bought by **multiple-system operators (MSOs)**, a small number of large corporations, like Comcast and Time Warner, that own many cable systems. This consolidation has happened quickly: In 1998, the Top 12 MSOs controlled the lines into 70 percent of all households wired for cable. By 2008, the Top 5 MSOs served more than 80 percent of all U.S. cable subscribers (see Figure 6.3 on page 204). As with other media, this economic trend points to an industry moving toward an **oligopoly**, where just a handful of media megafirms control cable and DBS programming. Like the Internet, however, cable and DBS hold the promise of offering more specialized services through which the diverse needs and tastes of individuals and communities might be met. But unlike the Internet–so far–cable programming and DBS services are in the hands of fewer and fewer large companies and MSOs.

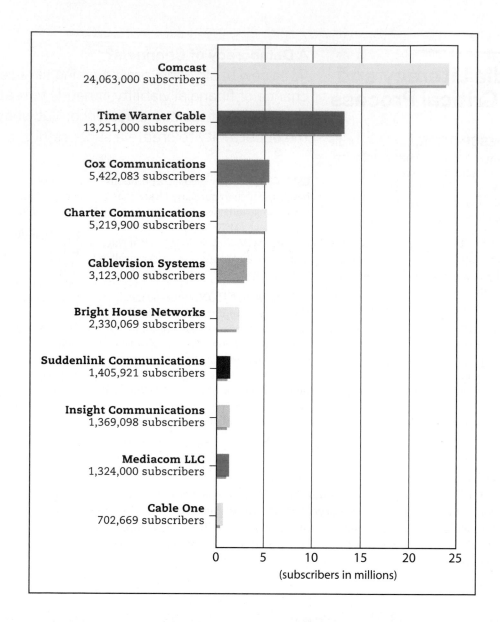

FIGURE 6.3

TOP 10 U.S. CABLE OPERATORS (RANKED BY NUMBER OF SUBSCRIBERS), 2008

Note: Unless otherwise noted, counts include owned and managed subscribers.

Source: National Cable & Telecommunications Association; April 2008, www.ncta.com.

©2008 SNL Kagan, a division of SNL Financial LC.

Comcast
24,063,000 subscribers

Time Warner Cable
13,251,000 subscribers

Cox Communications
5,422,083 subscribers

Charter Communications
5,219,900 subscribers

Cablevision Systems
3,123,000 subscribers

Bright House Networks
2,330,069 subscribers

Suddenlink Communications
1,405,921 subscribers

Insight Communications
1,369,098 subscribers

Mediacom LLC
1,324,000 subscribers

Cable One
702,669 subscribers

0   5   10   15   20   25

(subscribers in millions)

The Major Cable and DBS Corporations

For much of the 1980s and 1990s, TCI (Tele-Communications, Inc.) and Time Warner Cable dominated the acquisition of smaller cable companies and the accumulation of cable subscribers. But by the late 1990s, cable became a coveted investment, not so much for its ability to carry television programming as for its access to households connected with high-bandwidth wires.

AT&T, TCI, and Comcast

With increasing competition and declining long-distance revenues, AT&T, the nation's leading long-distance phone company, developed a new business plan in the 1990s to buy its way into the lucrative emerging broadband cable and Internet business. In 1998, AT&T purchased TCI, then the leading cable MSO with thirteen million households, and renamed the cable division AT&T Broadband & Internet Services. In 2000, AT&T struck again, acquiring MediaOne, the third-largest cable firm, and boosting its direct subscriber base to sixteen million.

Ultimately, AT&T's appetite for acquisitions gave it a bad case of debt, and its stock lost half of its value in 2000. In late 2000, AT&T made a surprise announcement of a decision to voluntarily break the company into four components—consumer long distance, business, wireless, and broadband services. AT&T also spun off its cable programming subsidiary, Liberty Media. In late 2001, only three years after it had ventured into the cable and broadband industry, AT&T got out of the business by merging its cable division in a $72 billion deal with Comcast, then the third-largest MSO. The new Comcast instantly became the cable industry behemoth and now serves more than twenty-four million households—nearly twice as many as the next largest MSO, Time Warner. Comcast's cable properties also include interests in VERSUS (formerly the Outdoor Life Network), E! Entertainment, and the Golf Channel.

Time Warner, Turner, and AOL

Time Warner Cable is a division of the world's largest media company, Time Warner. In 1995, Time Warner Cable bought Cablevision Industries—the eighth-largest MSO—and by 2008, Time Warner had more than thirteen million cable subscribers.

Beyond its cable-subscriber base, Time Warner is also a major provider of programming services. In 1995, Time Warner buoyed its position as the world's largest media corporation by offering $6.5 billion to acquire Turner Broadcasting, which included superstation WTBS, CNN, Headline News, TNT, and CNN Radio. Although some FCC lawyers raised concerns about extending Time Warner's economic power, the commission formally signed off on the deal in the fall of 1996. Time Warner—with its magazine, movie, publishing, television, and Internet divisions—produces content for its cable services. In addition to acquiring Turner and co-owning the CW television network, Time Warner is the parent company of Cinemax and HBO and owns truTV (formerly Court TV) and the Cartoon Network. In 2008, Time Warner's AOL division also had about seventeen million Internet subscribers.

DirecTV and DISH Network

In the 2000s, the two rival DBS companies DirecTV and DISH Network vaulted onto the list of major players in the industry-defined *multichannel video programming distributor (MVPD)* market. DirecTV was established in 1977, and its DBS system debuted in 1994. News Corp., owner of several media properties including the Fox television network and Twentieth Century Fox movie studios, acquired DirecTV in 2003. In 2008, the FCC approved a deal to transfer the controlling interest in DirecTV from News Corp. to cable service provider Liberty Media, which also owns the STARZ! movie channel.

The independently owned DISH Network was founded as EchoStar Communications in 1980. Originally a distributor of big-dish television systems, the company later refocused on the emerging DBS market and launched its DISH Network service in 1995. Each of the two DBS companies operates between eight and ten satellites to deliver its service to customers in the continental United States.

The Effects of Consolidation

A number of cable and DBS critics worry that the trend toward fewer owners will limit political viewpoints, programming options, and technical innovation. (See "Media Literacy and the Critical Process: A Democracy of Channels?" on page 203.) The response from the wired and wireless cable and DBS industries is that, given the tremendous capital investment it takes to run cable, DBS, and other media enterprises, business conglomerates are necessary to buy up struggling companies and keep them afloat. This argument suggests that without today's MSOs many smaller cable ventures in programming would not be possible.

Concerns have surfaced, though, that cable, DBS, computer, and phone services will merge into giant communication overlords, fixing prices without the benefit of competition. These concerns raise an important question: In an economic climate in which fewer owners control the circulation of communication, what happens to new ideas or controversial views that may not always be profitable to circulate? Will debt or declining stocks and limited competition among a few firms be enough to check or restrain these companies and keep them competing with one another?

There is already evidence that large MSOs can wield their monopoly power unfairly. In May 2000, a business dispute between Disney and Time Warner erupted into a public spectacle as Time Warner dropped the ABC television network from 3.4 million of its cable customers in New York, Houston, Raleigh, and elsewhere for more than thirty hours. At the heart of the conflict, Disney had proposed that Time Warner expand its service by introducing Disney's new SoapNet and Toon channels, among other requirements, in return for allowing Time Warner to carry ABC on its cable systems. Talks broke down, Time Warner refused to grant Disney a contract extension, and Time Warner customers in affected areas saw nothing on their screens except messages like, "Disney has taken ABC away from you."

A similar dispute occurred in 2004, when DISH Network and Viacom deadlocked in rate negotiations for putting CBS and Viacom's cable channels on the service. Nine million DISH customers lost CBS, MTV, Nickelodeon, and other Viacom-owned channels for thirty-six hours before an agreement was reached. (See "What Viacom Owns" on page 205.) In 2006, DISH Network's dispute with Lifetime Entertainment over carriage fees resulted in the removal of Lifetime from DISH. After protests by women's consumer groups in several cities, the parties reached an agreement, restoring the channel after a month's absence.

The examples above suggest what can happen when a few large corporations engage in relatively minor arguments over prices and programs. Consumers are often left with little recourse or choice in markets where one cable system competes with two DBS systems—often with all parties dependent on programming from the same larger media companies.

Alternative Voices

After suffering through years of rising rates and limited expansion of services, some small U.S. cities have decided to challenge the private monopolies of cable giants by building competing, publicly owned cable systems. So far, the municipally owned cable systems number in the hundreds and can be found in places like Glasgow, Kentucky; Kutztown, Pennsylvania; Cedar Falls, Iowa; and Provo, Utah. In most cases, they're operated by the community-owned, nonprofit electric utilities. There are more than two thousand such municipal utilities across the United States, serving about 14 percent of the population and creating the potential for more municipal utilities to expand into communications services. As nonprofit entities, the municipal operations are less expensive for cable subscribers, too.

Cities with public cable systems argue that with no competition, the private cable corporations have been slow to replace older coaxial cables with high-speed fiber-optic networks. Moreover, the lower population densities of small towns and rural areas mean that these towns are often the last places to get innovative cable services. The first town to take on an existing private cable provider was Glasgow, Kentucky, which built its own municipal cable system in 1989. The town of fourteen thousand now has seven thousand municipal cable customers. William J. Ray, the town's Electric Plant Board superintendent and the visionary behind the municipal communications service, argues that this is not a new idea:

Cities have long been turning a limited number of formerly private businesses into public-works projects. This happens only when the people making up a local government believe that the service has become so essential to the citizens that it is better if it is operated by the government. In colonial America, it was all about drinking water. . . . In the twentieth century, the issue was electric power and natural gas service. Now, we are facing the same transformation in broadband networks. [8]

For the customer, competition in the local cable market is beneficial. For example, in 1994 in Cedar Falls, Iowa, voters approved the creation of a new municipal broadband fiber-optic cable network, capable of carrying cable and Internet service. With the new challenges of competition, commercial provider TCI then decided to upgrade its own cable system in the city. The benefits of competition in Cedar Falls did not go unnoticed by the nearby residents of Waterloo, Iowa, who were served only by TCI. In Waterloo, TCI offered only thirty-six channels for the same monthly fee that brought seventy-six channels to TCI customers in Cedar Falls. Only by threatening to build their own municipal cable system did Waterloo city officials get TCI to rebuild the Waterloo cable system and add more channels.

More than a quarter of the country's two thousand municipal utilities offer broadband services, including cable, high-speed Internet, and telephone. How will commercial cable operators fend off this unprecedented competition? Ray of Glasgow, Kentucky, has an answer: "If cable operators are afraid of cities competing with them, there is a defense that is impregnable—they can charge reasonable rates, offer consummate customer service, improve their product, and conduct their business as if they were a guest that owes their existence to the benevolence of the city that has invited them in."[9]

| Disney-owned ABC (Channel 7) has pulled its programming off of Time Warner Cable. Time Warner Cable will provide E! in its place. Please stay tuned for more information.

Democracy and Cable in a Wired / Wireless World

When cable emerged to challenge traditional broadcasting in the 1970s, expectations were high, not unlike today's expectations for the Internet. When cable service mushroomed in the 1980s, network supremacy over television ended. Offering more than new competition, cable's increased channel capacity provided the promise of access. With more channels, cable access should have created vibrant debates, allowing ordinary people a voice on television. Cable access channels have, in fact, provided some opportunities for viewers to participate in democracy and even create their own programs. But by the late 1990s, major cities like Kansas City decided that public-access channels were no longer a requirement for cable franchises. For the most part, cable and DBS have come to follow the one-way broadcast model: Their operators choose the programming from a few service providers, with little input from consumers. Most cable channels have become heavily dependent on recycling old television shows and movies to fill up their program schedules. In some ways, this has been beneficial. Cable, particularly through programming like Nickelodeon's Nick at Nite and TV Land, has become a video "library" for TV shows that are passed along from generation to generation. Ultimately, however, except for C-Span, local-access channels, and some interactive services, cable still has not developed its potential to become a clear alternative to traditional broadcasting services. In fact, with TV networks and many leading cable channels now owned by the same media conglomerates, cable has evolved into something of an ancillary service to the networks.

In the broadest sense, the development of cable has always posed a contradiction. On one hand, cable has dramatically increased the number of channels and offered previously underserved groups the opportunity to see their particular issues addressed. On the other hand, cable undermined the network era during which television worked as a kind of social adhesive, helping to give most of the population a common bond, a set of shared programs.

In discussions about video programming technologies and policies, it's important to remember that not everyone has access to cable or satellite television. In 2008, nearly 20 percent of U.S. households still relied on over-the-air broadcasts for their television programming. Although some people choose to limit their television options, others simply cannot afford the monthly cost of cable or DBS, particularly during times of economic downturn and recession. So, as we ask ourselves how we can employ cable, DBS, and related technologies to serve society while continuing to meet business and consumer needs, we need to remember to include in the discussion those who are not connected to these communication systems. ▶

CHAPTER REVIEW

REVIEW QUESTIONS

Technology and the Development of Cable

1. What is CATV, and what were its advantages over broadcast television?

2. How did satellite distribution change the cable industry?

Cable Threatens Broadcasting

3. How did cable pose a challenge to broadcasting, and how did the FCC respond to cable's early development?

4. What is the cable franchising process, and how did it work in the 1980s?

5. Why are cable companies treated more like a utility company than a common carrier?

6. How did the Telecommunications Act of 1996 change the economic shape and future of the cable industry?

Cable Comes of Age

7. What are the differences between basic cable service and premium services?

8. How have CNN and MTV influenced culture worldwide?

9. How and why did HBO develop? How has HBO threatened the film industry?

10. What is video-on-demand, and how does it differ from pay-per-view services?

Challenges to Cable: DBS and Cell Phones

11. What is DBS? How well does it compete with the cable industry?

Ownership and Business Issues in Cable and DBS

12. Who are the biggest players in the cable and DBS business, and what has driven their recently acquired cable empires?

13. What are the three basic divisions in the organization of the cable business?

14. What are the main reasons some municipalities are building their own cable systems?

Democracy and Cable in a Wired / Wireless World

15. In terms of fostering democracy, what are the main advantages of cable and DBS over traditional broadcasting?

QUESTIONING THE MEDIA

1. How many cable channels do you watch regularly? What programs do you watch? What attracts you to a certain channel?

2. If you controlled a cable public-access channel in your community, what would be your channel's goal? What could we do to make public-, government-, or educational-access programming more appealing? Should we?

3. Do you think the must-carry rules violate a cable company's First Amendment rights? Why or why not?

4. CNN and MTV have changed our society as well as the global culture. Have these changes been positive or negative? Explain.

5. Do you think DBS is an equal competitor to cable? Why or why not?

6. Some critics argue that citizens no longer participate in traditional neighborhood activities and that cable has played a role in fragmenting society, keeping us in our homes. Do you agree or disagree? What has cable done well, and in what ways has it adversely affected society?

COMMON THREADS

Cable's development was not only about reaching rural places but also about making TV more accessible to the people. How well has cable delivered on that promise?

Perhaps the most interesting technology twist in the story of cable has been the restoration of wires in a world that had been becoming increasingly wireless. After all, in using the electromagnetic spectrum to transmit sound and images through space, radio and television had freed communication technology from dependency on the wired telegraphy of the nineteenth century. Cable is partly the story of "putting the wires back" as a way to increase channel capacity and lessen frequency interference. Now cable has run up against a new wireless movement as the digital age brings us tools such as DBS, cell phones, iPods, Wi-Fi, and WiMax.

As the new wireless technologies complicate cable, we are reminded of changes in the television age. During the old network era, television operated as an "electronic hearth," providing a place where we could gather and share our nation's main stories. But for many people, television became too homogeneous—taking few risks, depending on simple formulas, and failing to provide a democratic platform for the diverse array of voices that reflect our changing nation. Cable's promise, when it erupted in the 1970s, was to be a "voice for the voiceless," to create access channels that would allow ordinary people to make their own programs, share their opinions and viewpoints, challenge the status quo, and tell their own stories. In some ways, cable's early promise has been usurped by Internet bloggers and reality television. Today we have plenty of media outlets where people can give an opinion or tell a story.

So where does this leave cable? As cable and DBS services become more expensive, cable may be able to survive if it can deliver on its original promises of providing access programming and allowing for new and diverse ownership. We have already seen this in small cities that got fed up with the cable industry not delivering on promises and instead created their own public systems that allow individuals and communities to make their own programs and tell their own stories. What can you imagine for the future of cable to help it fulfill its original promise?

KEY TERMS

The definitions for the terms listed below can be found in the Glossary at the end of the book. The page numbers listed with the terms indicate where the term is highlighted in the chapter.

CATV, 185
geosynchronous orbit, 186
transponders, 186
headend, 187
must-carry rules, 189
access channels, 189
leased channels, 189
electronic publishers, 189
common carriers, 189
Telecommunications Act of 1996, 191
narrowcasting, 192

basic cable, 194
superstations, 194
premium channels, 199
vertical integration, 200
pay-per-view (PPV), 200
video-on-demand (VOD), 200
direct broadcast satellite (DBS), 201
WiMax, 202
multiple-system operators (MSOs), 203
oligopoly, 203

7

Movies and the Impact of Images

In a pivotal scene in *Star Wars: Episode III—Revenge of the Sith* (2005), Senator Padmé Amidala (Natalie Portman) witnesses the power-hungry Supreme Chancellor's decree of the first Galactic Empire, to the cheers of the Senate. She responds, "This is how liberty dies. With thunderous applause." This is how *Star Wars* ends as well, to the thunderous applause of millions of fans. Or, rather, how *Star Wars* begins, since episode 3 sets up the story line of the original *Star Wars* from 1977 (the original three films were actually episodes 4, 5, and 6).

The enormous success of the 1977 *Star Wars*, produced, written, and directed by George Lucas, changed the culture of the movie industry. As film critic Roger Ebert explained: "*Star Wars* effectively brought to an end the golden era of early-1970s personal filmmaking and focused the industry on big-budget special-effects blockbusters, blasting off a trend we are still living through. . . . In one way or another all the big studios have been trying to make another *Star Wars* ever since."

The release of *Revenge of the Sith* had all of the now-typical blockbuster characteristics: a targeted youth audience, massive promotion, and lucrative merchandising tie-ins.

The blockbuster mentality spawned by *Star Wars* formed a new primary audience for Hollywood—teenagers. Repeat attendance and positive buzz among young people made the first *Star Wars* the most successful movie of its generation and started the initial trilogy that included *The Empire Strikes Back* (1980) and *Return of the Jedi* (1983). The youth-oriented focus begun by *Star Wars* is still evident in Hollywood today, with the largest segment of the U.S. movie audience—the twelve- to twenty-four-year-old age group—accounting for 38 percent of theater attendance.

Another part of the blockbuster mentality created by *Star Wars* and mimicked by other films is the way in which movies are made into big-budget summer releases with merchandising tie-ins and high potential for international distribution. Lucas, who also created the popular *Indiana Jones* film series, argues that selling licensing rights is one of the ways he supports his independent filmmaking. By 2008, the six *Star Wars* films had generated an estimated $12 billion in merchandising—far more than the record-breaking $4 billion worldwide box-office revenue—as *Star Wars* images appeared on an astonishing array of products, from Lego's X-Wing fighter kits to Darth Vader toothbrushes. And in 2008, a new marketing tie-in appeared in the theater release of the animated *Star Wars: The Clone Wars* and a weekly series on Cartoon Network with the same name.

Star Wars has impacted not only the cultural side of moviemaking but also the technical form. In the first *Star Wars* trilogy, produced in the 1970s and 1980s, Lucas developed technologies now commonplace in moviemaking—digital animation, special effects, and computer-based film editing. With the second trilogy, Lucas again broke new ground in the film industry—this time becoming a force in the emerging area of digital filmmaking. Several scenes of *Star Wars: Episode I—The Phantom Menace* (1999) were shot on digital video, easing integration with digital special effects. The two subsequent movies, *Star Wars: Episode II—Attack of the Clones* (2002) and *Revenge of the Sith*, were shot entirely in the digital format.

The Phantom Menace also used digital exhibition—becoming the first full-length motion picture from a major studio to use digital projectors, replacing standard film projectors. Changing exhibition technology will eventually move motion pictures away from bulky and expensive film reels toward a digital distribution system via satellite or optical disks. Digital film distribution also threatens to bypass theaters, as films could be delivered directly to a viewer's computer or digital television set-top box.

◢ DATING BACK TO THE LATE 1800s, films have had a substantial social and cultural impact on society. Blockbuster movies such as *Star Wars*, *E.T.*, *Jurassic Park*, *Titanic*, *Lord of the Rings*, *Shrek*, and *Spider-Man* represent what Hollywood has become—America's storyteller. Cinematic tales that drew us to a nickelodeon theater over a century ago and to our local video store or multiplex last weekend have long acted as contemporary myth-makers. At their best, movies tell communal stories that evoke and symbolize our most enduring values and our secret desires (from *The Wizard of Oz* to *The Godfather* and the Batman series). The most popular films often make the world seem clearer, more manage-able, and more understandable.

Throughout the twentieth century and into the twenty-first century, films have also helped moviegoers sort through experiences that either affirmed or deviated from their own values. Some movies—for instance, *Scarface*, *Last Tango in Paris*, *The Last Temptation of Christ*, *Basic Instinct*, and *Fahrenheit 9/11*—have allowed audiences to survey "the boundary between the per-mitted and the forbidden" and to experience, in a controlled way, "the possibility of stepping across this boundary."[1] Such films, appearing to some to glorify crime and violence, verge on pornography, trample on sacred beliefs, or promote unpatriotic viewpoints, have been criti-cized by religious leaders, politicians, teachers, parents, and the mass media, and are some-times banned from public viewing.

Lastly, movies have acted to bring people together. Movies distract us from our daily struggles: they evoke and symbolize universal themes of human experience (the experience of childhood, coming of age, family relations, growing older, and coping with death); they can help us understand and respond to major historical events and tragedies—for instance, the Holocaust and 9/11; and they encourage us to rethink contemporary ideas as the world evolves, particu-larly in terms of how we think about race, class, spirituality, gender, and sexuality.

In this chapter, we examine the rich legacy and current standing of movies. We begin by considering film's early technology and the evolution of film as a mass medium. We look at the arrival of silent feature films, the emergence of Hollywood, and the development of the studio system with regard to production, distribution, and exhibition. We explore the coming of sound and the power of movie storytelling. In the context of Hollywood moviemaking, we consider major film genres, directors, and alternatives to Hollywood's style, including independent films, foreign films, and documentaries. Finally, we look at the movie business today—its major play-ers, economic clout, technological advances, and implications for democracy.

> "The movie is not only a supreme expression of mechanism, but paradoxically it offers as product the most magical of consumer commodities, namely dreams."
>
> MARSHALL McLUHAN, *UNDERSTANDING MEDIA*, 1964

Early Technology and the Evolution of Movies

History often credits a handful of enterprising individuals with developing the new technologies that lead to new categories of mass media. Such innovations, however, are usually the result of simultaneous investigations by numerous people. In addition, the innovations of both known and unknown inventors are propelled by economic and social forces as well as by individual abilities.[2]

The Development of Film

The concept of film goes back as early as Leonardo DaVinci, who theorized in the late 1400s about creating a device that would reproduce reality. Other early precursors to film include the Magic Lantern in the seventeenth century, which projected images painted on glass plates using an oil lamp as a light source; the invention of the *thaumatrope* in 1824, a two-sided card with different images on each side that appeared to combine the images when twirled; and finally, the introduction in 1834 of the *zoetrope*, a cylindrical device that rapidly twirled images inside of a cylinder which appeared to make the images move.

Muybridge and Goodwin Make Pictures Move

The development stage of movies began when inventors began manipulating photographs to make them appear to move while simultaneously projecting them on a screen. Eadweard Muybridge, an English photographer living in America, is credited with being the first to do both. He studied motion by using multiple cameras to take successive photographs of humans and animals in motion. One of Muybridge's first projects was to use photography to determine if a racehorse actually lifts all four feet from the ground at full gallop (it does). By 1880, Muybridge had developed a method for projecting the photographic images on a wall for public viewing. These early image sequences were extremely brief, showing only a horse jumping over a fence or a man running a few feet, because only so many photographs could be mounted inside the spinning cylinder that projected the images.

Meanwhile, other inventors were also working on capturing moving images and projecting them. In 1884, George Eastman (founder of Eastman Kodak) developed the first roll film—a huge improvement over the heavy metal and glass plates used to make individual photos. The first roll film had a paper backing that had to be stripped off during the film developing stage. Louis Aimé Augustin Le Prince, a Frenchman living in England, invented the first motion picture camera using roll film. Le Prince, who disappeared mysteriously on a train ride to Paris in 1890, is credited with filming the first motion picture, *Roundhay Garden Scene*, in 1888. About two seconds' worth of the film survive today.

In 1889, a New Jersey minister, Hannibal Goodwin, improved Eastman's roll film by using thin strips of transparent, pliable material called **celluloid** that could hold a coating of chemicals sensitive to light. Goodwin's breakthrough solved a major problem: It enabled a strip

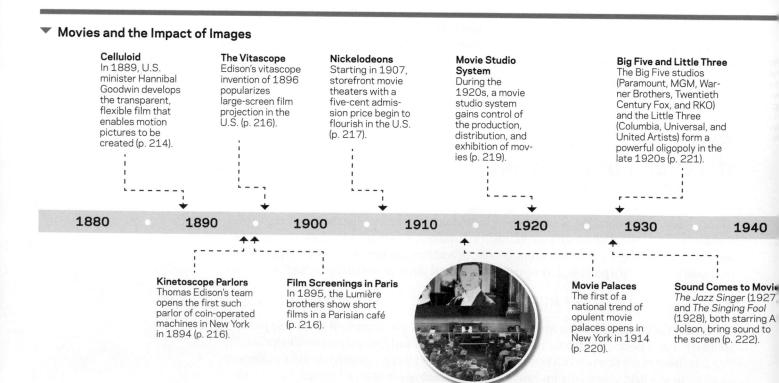

▼ **Movies and the Impact of Images**

Celluloid
In 1889, U.S. minister Hannibal Goodwin develops the transparent, flexible film that enables motion pictures to be created (p. 214).

The Vitascope
Edison's vitascope invention of 1896 popularizes large-screen film projection in the U.S. (p. 216).

Nickelodeons
Starting in 1907, storefront movie theaters with a five-cent admission price begin to flourish in the U.S. (p. 217).

Movie Studio System
During the 1920s, a movie studio system gains control of the production, distribution, and exhibition of movies (p. 219).

Big Five and Little Three
The Big Five studios (Paramount, MGM, Warner Brothers, Twentieth Century Fox, and RKO) and the Little Three (Columbia, Universal, and United Artists) form a powerful oligopoly in the late 1920s (p. 221).

1880   1890   1900   1910   1920   1930   1940

Kinetoscope Parlors
Thomas Edison's team opens the first such parlor of coin-operated machines in New York in 1894 (p. 216).

Film Screenings in Paris
In 1895, the Lumière brothers show short films in a Parisian café (p. 216).

Movie Palaces
The first of a national trend of opulent movie palaces opens in New York in 1914 (p. 220).

Sound Comes to Movie
The Jazz Singer (1927) and *The Singing Fool* (1928), both starring A Jolson, bring sound to the screen (p. 222).

EADWEARD MUYBRIDGE'S study of horses in motion, like the one shown, proved that a racehorse gets all four feet off the ground during a gallop. In his various studies of motion, Muybridge could use 12 cameras at a time.

of film to move through a camera and be photographed in rapid succession, producing a series of pictures. Because celluloid was transparent (except for the images made on it during filming), it was ideal for projection, as light could easily shine through it. George Eastman, who also announced the development of celluloid film, legally battled Goodwin for years over the patent

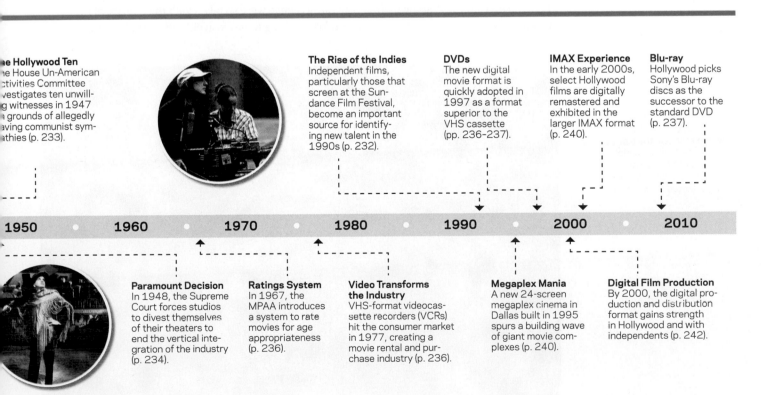

[e] Hollywood Ten
[t]he House Un-American [A]ctivities Committee [in]vestigates ten unwill[in]g witnesses in 1947 [on] grounds of allegedly [h]aving communist sym[p]athies (p. 233).

The Rise of the Indies
Independent films, particularly those that screen at the Sundance Film Festival, become an important source for identifying new talent in the 1990s (p. 232).

DVDs
The new digital movie format is quickly adopted in 1997 as a format superior to the VHS cassette (pp. 236–237).

IMAX Experience
In the early 2000s, select Hollywood films are digitally remastered and exhibited in the larger IMAX format (p. 240).

Blu-ray
Hollywood picks Sony's Blu-ray discs as the successor to the standard DVD (p. 237).

1950   **1960**   **1970**   **1980**   **1990**   **2000**   **2010**

Paramount Decision
In 1948, the Supreme Court forces studios to divest themselves of their theaters to end the vertical integration of the industry (p. 234).

Ratings System
In 1967, the MPAA introduces a system to rate movies for age appropriateness (p. 236).

Video Transforms the Industry
VHS-format videocassette recorders (VCRs) hit the consumer market in 1977, creating a movie rental and purchase industry (p. 236).

Megaplex Mania
A new 24-screen megaplex cinema in Dallas built in 1995 spurs a building wave of giant movie complexes (p. 240).

Digital Film Production
By 2000, the digital production and distribution format gains strength in Hollywood and with independents (p. 242).

rights. The courts eventually awarded Goodwin the invention, but Eastman's company still became the major manufacturer of film stock for motion pictures by buying Goodwin's patents.

Edison and the Lumières Create Motion Pictures

As with the development of sound recording, Thomas Edison takes center stage in most accounts of the invention of motion pictures. In the late 1800s, Edison initially planned to merge phonograph technology and moving images to create talking pictures (which would not happen in feature films until 1927). Because there was no breakthrough, however, Edison lost interest. He directed an assistant, William Kennedy Dickson, to combine Edison's incandescent light bulb, Goodwin's celluloid, and Le Prince's camera to create another early movie camera, the **kinetograph**, and a single-person viewing system, the **kinetoscope**. This small projection system housed fifty feet of film that revolved on spools (similar to a library microfilm reader). Viewers looked through a hole and saw images moving on a tiny plate. In 1894, the first kinetoscope parlor, featuring two rows of coin-operated machines, opened on Broadway in New York.

Meanwhile, in France, brothers Louis and Auguste Lumière developed the *cinematograph*, a combined camera, film development, and projection system. The projection system was particularly important, as it allowed more than one person at a time to see the moving images on a large screen. In a Paris café on December 28, 1895, the Lumières projected ten short movies for viewers who paid one franc each, on such subjects as a man falling off a horse and a child trying to grab a fish from a bowl. Within three weeks, twenty-five hundred people were coming each night to see how, according to one Paris paper, film "perpetuates the image of movement."

With innovators around the world now dabbling in moving pictures, Edison's lab renewed its interest in film. Edison patented several inventions and manufactured a new large-screen system called the **vitascope**, which enabled filmstrips of longer lengths to be projected without interruption and hinted at the potential of movies as a future mass medium. Staged at a music hall in New York in April 1896, Edison's first public showing of the vitascope featured shots from a boxing match and waves rolling onto a beach. The *New York Times* described the exhibition as "wonderfully real and singularly exhilarating." Some members of the audience were so taken with the realism of the film images that they stepped back from the screen's crashing waves to avoid getting their feet wet.

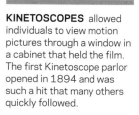

KINETOSCOPES allowed individuals to view motion pictures through a window in a cabinet that held the film. The first Kinetoscope parlor opened in 1894 and was such a hit that many others quickly followed.

Early movie demonstrations such as these marked the beginning of the film industry's entrepreneurial stage. At this point, movies consisted of movement recorded by a single continuous camera shot. Early filmmakers had not yet figured out how to move the camera around or how to edit film shots together. Nonetheless, various innovators were beginning to see the commercial possibilities of film. By 1900, short movies had become a part of the entertainment industry, utilized in amusement arcades, traveling carnivals, wax museums, and vaudeville theater.

The Introduction of Narrative

The shift to the mass medium stage for movies occurred with the introduction of **narrative films**: movies that tell stories. Audiences quickly tired of static films of waves breaking on beaches or vaudeville acts recorded by immobile cameras. To become a mass medium, the early silent films had to offer what books achieved: the suspension of disbelief. They had to create narrative worlds that engaged an audience's imagination.

Some of the earliest narrative films were produced and directed by French magician and inventor Georges Méliès, who opened the first public movie theater in France in 1896. Méliès may have been the first director to realize that a movie was not simply a means of recording reality. He understood that a movie could be artificially planned and controlled like a staged play. Méliès began producing short fantasy and fairy tale films—including *The Vanishing Lady* (1896), *Cinderella* (1899), and *A Trip to the Moon* (1902), increasingly using editing and existing camera tricks and techniques, such as slow motion and cartoon animation, that became key ingredients in future narrative filmmaking.

The first American filmmaker to adapt Méliès's innovations to narrative film was Edwin S. Porter. A cameraman who had studied Méliès's work in an Edison lab, Porter mastered the technique of editing diverse shots together to tell a coherent story. Porter shot narrative scenes out of order (for instance, some in a studio and some outdoors) and reassembled, or edited, them to make a story. In 1902, he made what is regarded as America's first narrative film, *The Life of an American Fireman*. It also contained the first close-up shot in U.S. narrative film history—a ringing fire alarm. Until then, moviemakers thought close-ups cheated the audience of the opportunity to see an entire scene. Porter's most important film, *The Great Train Robbery* (1903), introduced the western genre as well as chase scenes. In this popular eleven-minute movie that inspired many copycat movies, Porter demonstrated the art of film suspense by alternating shots of the robbers with those of a posse in hot pursuit.

The Arrival of Nickelodeons

Another major development in the evolution of film as a mass medium was the arrival of **nickelodeons**—a form of movie theater whose name combines the admission price with the Greek word for "theater." According to media historian Douglas Gomery, these small and uncomfortable makeshift theaters were often converted storefronts redecorated to mimic vaudeville theaters: "In front, large, hand-painted posters announced the movies for the day. Inside, the screening of news, documentary, comedy, fantasy, and dramatic shorts lasted about one hour."[3] Usually a piano player added live music, and sometimes theater operators used sound effects to simulate gunshots or loud crashes. Because they showed silent films that usually transcended language barriers, nickelodeons flourished during the great European immigration at the turn of the twentieth century. These theaters filled a need for many newly arrived people struggling to learn English and seeking an inexpensive escape from the hard life of the city. Often managed by immigrants, nickelodeons required a minimal investment: just a secondhand projector and a large white sheet. Between 1907 and 1909, the number of nickelodeons grew from five thousand to ten thousand. The craze peaked by 1910, when entrepreneurs began to seek more affluent spectators, attracting them with larger and more lavish movie theaters.

THE GREAT TRAIN ROBBERY (1903) may have introduced the western genre but it was actually filmed in New Jersey. The still below shows a famous scene in which a bandit shoots his gun at the audience.

The Rise of the Hollywood Studio System

By the 1910s, movies had become a major industry. Among the first to try his hand at dominating the movie business and reaping its profits, Thomas Edison formed the Motion Picture Patents Company, known as the *Trust*, in 1908. A cartel of major U.S. and French film producers, the company pooled patents in an effort to control film's major technology, acquired most major film distributorships, and signed an exclusive deal with George Eastman, who agreed to supply movie film only to Trust-approved companies.

However, some independent producers refused to bow to the Trust's terms. There was too much demand for films, too much money to be made, and too many ways to avoid the Trust's scrutiny. Some producers began to relocate from the centers of film production in New York and New Jersey to Cuba and Florida. Ultimately, though, Hollywood became the film capital of the world. Southern California offered cheap labor, diverse scenery for outdoor shooting, and a mild climate suitable for year-round production. Geographically far from the Trust's headquarters in New Jersey, independent producers in Hollywood could also easily slip over the border into Mexico to escape legal prosecution brought by the Trust for patent violations.

Wanting to free their movie operations from the Trust's tyrannical grasp, two Hungarian immigrants—Adolph Zukor, who would eventually run Paramount Pictures, and William Fox, who would found the Fox Film Corporation (which later became Twentieth Century Fox)—played a role in the collapse of Edison's Trust. Zukor's early companies figured out ways to bypass the Trust, and a suit by Fox, a nickelodeon operator turned film distributor, resulted in the Trust's breakup for restraint of trade violations in 1917.

Ironically, entrepreneurs like Zukor developed other tactics for controlling the industry. The strategies, many of which are still used today, were more ambitious than just monopolizing patents and technology. They aimed at dominating the movie business at all three essential levels—*production*, everything involved in making a movie from a script and actors to raising money and filming; *distribution*, getting the films into theaters; and *exhibition*, playing films in theaters. This control—or **vertical integration**—of all levels of the movie business gave certain studios great power and eventually spawned a film industry that turned into an **oligopoly**, a situation in which a few firms control the bulk of the business.

Production

In the early days of film, producers and distributors had not yet recognized that fans would not only seek particular film stories—like dramas, westerns, and romances—but also particular film actors. This was not unlike what happened in the 1950s, when radio station managers noticed that teenagers listened to their favorite performers again and again. Initially, film companies were reluctant to identify their anonymous actors for fear that their popularity would raise the typical $5 to $15 actor salary. Eventually, though, the industry understood how important the actors' identity would be to a film's success.

Responding to discerning audiences and competing against Edison's Trust, Adolph Zukor hired a number of popular actors and formed the Famous Players Company in 1912. His idea was to control movie production not through patents but through exclusive contracts with actors. One Famous Players performer was Mary Pickford. Known as "America's Sweetheart" for her portrayal of spunky and innocent heroines, Pickford was "unspoiled" by a theater background and better suited to the more subtle and intimate new medium. She became so

"The American cinema is a classical art, but why not then admire in it what is most admirable, i.e., not only the talent of this or that filmmaker, but the genius of the system."

ANDRÉ BAZIN, FILM THEORIST, 1957

"No, I really cannot afford to work for only $10,000 a week."

MARY PICKFORD TO ADOLPH ZUKOR, 1915

popular that audiences waited in line to see her movies, and producers were forced to pay her increasingly larger salaries.

An astute businesswoman, Mary Pickford was the key figure in elevating the financial status and professional role of film actors. In 1910 Pickford made about $100 a week, but by 1914 she earned $1,000 a week, and by 1917, she received a weekly salary of $15,000. Having appeared in nearly two hundred films, Pickford was so influential that in 1919 she broke from Zukor to form her own company, United Artists. Joining her were actor Douglas Fairbanks (her future husband), comedian-director Charlie Chaplin, and director D. W. Griffith.

Although United Artists represented a brief triumph of autonomy for a few powerful actors, by the 1920s the **studio system** firmly controlled creative talent in the industry. Pioneered by director Thomas Ince and his company, Triangle, the studio system constituted a sort of assembly-line process for moviemaking: actors, directors, editors, writers, and others all worked under exclusive contracts for the major studios. Those who weren't under contract probably weren't working at all. Ince also developed the notion of the studio head; he appointed producers to handle hiring, logistics, and finances so that he could more easily supervise many pictures at one time. The system was so efficient that each major studio was producing a feature film every week. Pooling talent, rather than patents, was a more ingenious approach for movie studios aiming to dominate film production.

Distribution

An early effort to control movie distribution occurred around 1904, when movie companies provided vaudeville theaters with films and projectors on a *film exchange* system. In exchange for their short films, shown between live acts, movie producers received a small percentage of the vaudeville ticket-gate receipts. Gradually, as the number of production companies and the popularity of narrative films grew, demand for a distribution system serving national and international markets increased as well. One way Edison's Trust sought to control distribution was by withholding equipment from companies not willing to pay the Trust's patent-use fees.

However, as with the production of film, independent film companies looked for other distribution strategies outside of the Trust. Again, Adolph Zukor led the fight, developing **block booking** distribution. Under this system, to gain access to popular films with big stars like Mary Pickford, exhibitors had to agree to rent new or marginal films with no stars. Zukor would pressure theater operators into taking a hundred movies at a time to get the few Pickford titles they wanted. Such contracts enabled the new studios to test-market new stars without taking much financial risk. Although this practice was eventually outlawed as monopolistic, rising film studios used the tactic effectively to guarantee the success of their films in a competitive marketplace.

Another distribution strategy involved the marketing of American films in Europe. When World War I disrupted the once-powerful European film production industry, only U.S. studios were able to meet the demand for films in Europe. The war marked a turning point, and made the United States the leader in the commercial movie business worldwide. After the war, no other nation's film industry could compete economically with Hollywood. By the mid-1920s, foreign revenue from U.S. films totaled $100 million. Today, Hollywood continues to dominate the world market.

Exhibition

Edison's Trust attempted to control exhibition by controlling the flow of films to theater owners. If theaters wanted to ensure they had films to show their patrons, they had to purchase a license from the Trust and pay whatever price it asked. Otherwise, they were locked out of the Trust and had to try to find enough films from independent producers to show. Eventually, the flow of films from independents in Hollywood and foreign films enabled theater owners to resist the Trust's scheme.

After the collapse of the Trust, emerging studios in Hollywood had their own ideas on how to control exhibition. When industrious theater owners began forming film cooperatives to compete with block-booking tactics, producers like Zukor conspired to dominate exhibition by buying up theaters. By 1921, Zukor's Paramount owned three hundred theaters, solidifying its ability to show the movies it produced. In 1925, a business merger between Paramount and Publix (then the country's largest theater chain with more than five hundred screens) gave Zukor enormous influence over movie exhibition.

Zukor and the heads of several major studios understood that they did not have to own all the theaters to ensure that their movies were shown. Instead, the major studios (which would eventually include MGM, RKO, Warner Brothers, Twentieth Century Fox, and Paramount) only needed to own the first-run theaters (about 15 percent of the nation's theaters), which premiered new films in major downtown areas in front of the largest audiences, and which generated 85 to 95 percent of all film revenue.

The studios quickly realized that to earn revenue from these first-run theaters they would have to draw the middle and upper-middle classes to the movies. To do so, they built **movie palaces**, full-time single-screen movie theaters that provided a more hospitable moviegoing environment. In 1914, the three-thousand-seat Strand Theatre, the first movie palace, opened in New York. With elaborate architecture, movie palaces lured spectators with an elegant décor usually reserved for high-society opera, ballet, symphony, and live theater. Taking advantage of new air-cooling systems developed by Chicago's meatpacking industry, movie palaces also

> "It's still a business where the hits make up for all the losses along the way. *Star Wars* accentuated that. Everyone wants to reproduce that success, even just once. This tells you about the strength of this kind of franchise."
>
> JILL KRUTICK,
> ANALYST, SMITH
> BARNEY, 1997

MOVIE PALACES
This movie theater in 1920s New York City had a live band to provide music and sound effects for the movie.

featured the first mechanically air-cooled theaters. Doctors even advised pregnant women to escape the summer heat by spending their afternoons at the movies.

Another major innovation in exhibition was the development of *mid-city movie theaters*. These movie theaters were built in convenient locations near urban mass transit stations to attract the business of the urban and suburban middle class (the first wave of middle-class people moved from urban centers to city outskirts in the 1920s). This idea continues today, as **multiplexes** featuring multiple screens lure middle-class crowds to interstate highway crossroads.

By the late 1920s, the major studios had clearly established vertical integration in the industry. What had once been a fairly easy and cheap business to enter was now complex and expensive. What had been many small competitive firms in the early 1900s now became a few powerful studios, including the **Big Five**—Paramount, MGM, Warner Brothers, Twentieth Century Fox, and RKO—and the **Little Three** (which did not own theaters)—Columbia, Universal, and United Artists. Together these eight companies formed a powerful oligopoly, which made it increasingly difficult for independent companies to make, distribute, and exhibit commercial films.

The Studio System's Golden Age

Many consider Hollywood's Golden Age as beginning in 1915 with innovations in feature-length narrative film in the silent era, peaking with the introduction of sound and the development of the classic Hollywood style, and ending with the transformation of the Hollywood studio system post-World War II.

Hollywood Narrative and the Silent Era

D. W. Griffith, among the first "star" directors, was the single most important director in Hollywood's early days. Griffith paved the way for all future narrative filmmakers by refining many of the narrative techniques introduced by Méliès and Porter and using nearly all of them in one

SILENT FILMS
Italian-born Rudolph Valentino came to the United States in 1913, when he was eighteen. After finding his way to California, he quickly emerged as a star in the 1920s, appearing in fourteen major films in only seven years. His sexy and passionate portrayal of Sheik Ahmed (opposite Agnes Ayres in *The Sheik*, 1921) earned him the nickname "Great Lover." Famous for his good looks and comic timing in silent films, he was also partially responsible for the popularity of the tango in the 1920s. Valentino died in 1926 at the age of thirty-one.

391-107

film for the first time, including varied camera distances, close-up shots, multiple story lines, fast-paced editing, and symbolic imagery. Despite the cringe-inducing racism of this pioneering and controversial film, *The Birth of a Nation* (1915) was the first *feature-length film* (more than an hour long) produced in America. The three-hour epic was also the first **blockbuster** and cost moviegoers a record $2 admission. Although considered a technical masterpiece, the film glorified the Ku Klux Klan and stereotyped southern blacks, leading to a campaign against the film by the NAACP and protests and riots at many screenings. Nevertheless, the movie triggered Hollywood's fascination with narrative films.

Feature films became the standard throughout the 1920s and introduced many of the film genres we continue to see produced today. The most popular films during the silent era were historical and religious epics, including *Napoleon*, *Ben-Hur*, and *The Ten Commandments*, but the silent era also produced pioneering social dramas, mysteries, comedies, horror films, science fiction films, war films, crime dramas, westerns, and even spy films. The silent era also introduced numerous technical innovations, established the Hollywood star system, and cemented the reputation of movies as a viable art form, when previously they had been seen as novelty entertainment.

The Introduction of Sound

With the studio system and Hollywood's worldwide dominance firmly in place, the next big challenge was to bring sound to moving pictures. Various attempts at **talkies** had failed since Edison first tried to link phonograph and moving picture technologies in the 1890s. During the 1910s, however, technical breakthroughs at AT&T's research arm, Bell Labs, produced prototypes of loudspeakers and sound amplifiers. Experiments with sound continued during the 1920s, particularly at Warner Brothers studios, which released numerous short sound films of vaudeville acts, featuring singers and comedians. The studio packaged them as a novelty along with silent feature films.

In 1927, Warner Brothers produced a feature-length film, *The Jazz Singer*, starring Al Jolson, a charismatic and popular vaudeville singer who wore blackface makeup as part of his act, further demonstrating, as did *The Birth of a Nation*, that American racism carried into the film industry. An experiment, *The Jazz Singer* was basically a silent film interspersed with musical numbers and brief dialogue. At first, there was only modest interest in the movie, which featured just 354 spoken words. But the film grew in popularity as it toured the Midwest, where audiences stood and cheered the short bursts of dialogue. The breakthrough film, however, was Warner Brothers' 1928 release *The Singing Fool*, which also starred Jolson. Costing $200,000 to make, the film took in $5 million and "proved to all doubters that talkies were here to stay."[4]

Warner Brothers, however, was not the only studio exploring sound technology. Five months before *The Jazz Singer*

EARLY SOUND PICTURES
Al Jolson in *The Singing Fool* (1928). The film was the box-office champ for more than ten years until 1939, when it was dethroned by *Gone with the Wind*.

opened, Fox studio premiered sound-film **newsreels**. Fox's newsreel company, Movietone, captured the first film footage with sound of the takeoff and return of Charles Lindbergh, who piloted the first solo, nonstop flight across the Atlantic Ocean in May 1927. Fox's Movietone system photographed sound directly onto the film, running it on a narrow filmstrip that ran alongside the larger, image portion of the film. Superior to the sound-on-record system, the Movietone method eventually became film's standard sound system.

Boosted by the innovation of sound, annual movie attendance in the United States rose from sixty million a week in 1927 to ninety million a week in 1929. By 1931, nearly 85 percent of America's twenty thousand theaters accommodated sound pictures, and by 1935, the world had adopted talking films as the commercial standard.

The Development of the Hollywood Style

By the time sound came to movies, Hollywood dictated not only the business, but also the style of most moviemaking worldwide. That style, or model, for storytelling developed with the rise of the studio system in the 1920s, solidified during the first two decades of the sound era, and continues to dominate American filmmaking today. The model serves up three ingredients that give Hollywood movies their distinctive flavor: the narrative, the genre, and the author (or director). The right blend of these ingredients–combined with timing, marketing, and luck–have led to many movie hits, from 1930s and 1940s classics like *It Happened One Night*, *Gone with the Wind*, *The Philadelphia Story*, *Rebecca*, and *Casablanca* to recent successes like *The Devil Wears Prada*, *Dreamgirls*, *I Am Legend*, and *No Country for Old Men*.

Hollywood Narratives

American filmmakers from D. W. Griffith to Steven Spielberg have understood the allure of *narrative*, which always includes two basic components: the story (what happens to whom) and the discourse (how the story is told). Further, Hollywood codified a familiar narrative structure across all genres. Most movies, like most TV shows and novels, feature a number of stories that play out within the larger narrative of the entire film; recognizable character types (protagonist, antagonist, romantic interest, sidekick); a clear beginning, middle, and end (even with flashbacks and flash forwards, the sequence of events is usually clear to the viewer); and a plot propelled by the main character experiencing and resolving a conflict by the end of the movie.

Within Hollywood's classic narratives, filmgoers find an amazing array of intriguing cultural variations. For example, familiar narrative conventions of heroes, villains, conflicts, and resolutions may be made more unique with inventions like computer-generated imagery (CGI) or digital remastering for an IMAX 3D Experience release. This combination of convention and invention–standardized Hollywood stories and differentiated special effects–provides a powerful economic package that satisfies most audiences' appetites for both the familiar and the distinctive.

Hollywood Genres

In general, Hollywood narratives fit a **genre**, or category, in which conventions regarding similar characters, scenes, structures, and themes recur in combination. Grouping films by category is another way for the industry to achieve the two related economic goals of *product standardization* and *product differentiation*. By making films that fall into popular genres, the movie industry provides familiar models that can be imitated. It is much easier for a studio to promote a film that already fits into a preexisting category with which viewers are familiar. Among the most familiar genres are comedy, drama, romance, action/adventure, mystery/ suspense, western, gangster, horror, fantasy/science fiction, musical, and film noir. (See Table 7.1 on pages 224–225.)

> "I think that American movies, to be honest, are just simple. You blow things up, you shoot people, you have sex and you have a movie. And I think it appeals to just the more base emotions of people anywhere."
>
> ANTHONY KAUFMANN, FILM JOURNALIST, 2004

> "The thing of a musical is that you take a simple story, and tell it in a complicated way."
>
> BAZ LUHRMANN, AT THE 2002 ACADEMY AWARDS, ON *MOULIN ROUGE!*

▶

TABLE 7.1 ·

HOLLYWOOD GENRES

Movies, especially contemporary films, are difficult to categorize because they often combine characteristics from different genres. For example, in 2007, the film *Pirates of the Caribbean: At World's End* combined aspects of action/adventure, comedy, and romance. Shown here are the categories that are generally used by video stores to sort movies. Films from different decades represent the most familiar major genres.

*Won the Academy Award for that year's best picture.

CITIZEN KANE

INDIANA JONES AND THE KINGDOM OF THE CRYSTAL SKULL

Comedy

The Gold Rush (1925)	A Fish Called Wanda (1988)
Horse Feathers (1932)	The Birdcage (1995)
Arsenic and Old Lace (1944)	American Beauty (1999)*
Some Like It Hot (1959)	Shrek 2 (2004)
Dr. Strangelove (1964)	Knocked Up (2006)
Annie Hall (1977)*	Baby Mama (2008)

Drama

Gone with the Wind (1939)	Good Will Hunting (1997)
Citizen Kane (1941)	Saving Private Ryan (1998)
On the Waterfront (1954)*	Mystic River (2003)
A Man for All Seasons (1966)*	Million Dollar Baby (2004)*
One Flew over the Cuckoo's Nest (1975)*	Crash (2005)*
Raging Bull (1980)	No Country for Old Men (2008)*
Do the Right Thing (1989)	

Romance

It Happened One Night (1934)*	Titanic (1997)*
Casablanca (1943)*	Shakespeare in Love (1998)*
Sabrina (1954)	My Big Fat Greek Wedding (2002)
The Graduate (1967)	Brokeback Mountain (2005)
The Goodbye Girl (1977)	Waitress (2007)
Tootsie (1984)	

Action/Adventure

The Adventures of Robin Hood (1938)	Die Hard (1988)
Sands of Iwo Jima (1949)	Thelma & Louise (1991)
Ben Hur (1959)*	Kill Bill-Vol. I (2003)
The Great Escape (1963)	Indiana Jones and the Kingdom of the Crystal Skull (2008)
The Sting (1973)*	

Mystery/Suspense

The Lady Vanishes (1938)	Witness (1985)
Rebecca (1940)*	Silence of the Lambs (1991)*
North by Northwest (1959)	The Sixth Sense (1999)
Psycho (1960)	Disturbia (2007)
Chinatown (1974)	The Bourne Ultimatum (2007)

Westerns

Cimarron (1931)*	The Outlaw Josey Wales (1976)
Stagecoach (1939)	Silverado (1985)
The Searchers (1956)	Unforgiven (1992)*
Butch Cassidy and the Sundance Kid (1969)	Maverick (1994)
Little Big Man (1970)	3:10 to Yuma (2007)

(continued on next page)

Gangster

Public Enemy (1931)	*Goodfellas* (1990)
Scarface (1932)	*Boyz N the Hood* (1991)
Bonnie and Clyde (1967)	*Menace II Society* (1993)
The Godfather (1972)*	*Ocean's Twelve* (2004)
The Godfather, Part II (1974)*	*The Departed* (2006)*
Scarface (1983)	*American Gangster* (2007)

Horror

Phantom of the Opera (1925)	*Nightmare on Elm Street* (1985)
Dracula (1931)	*Mary Shelley's Frankenstein* (1994)
The Wolf Man (1941)	*Scream* (1996)
The Blob (1958)	*The Blair Witch Project* (1999)
The Birds (1963)	*The Ring* (2002)
The Exorcist (1973)	*Cloverfield* (2008)

Fantasy/Science Fiction

Metropolis (1926)	*Independence Day* (1996)
The Wizard of Oz (1939)	*The Matrix* (1999)
Invasion of the Body Snatchers (1956)	*The Lord of the Rings: The Return of the King* (2003)*
2001: A Space Odyssey (1968)	*Star Wars: Episode III—Revenge of the Sith* (2005)
Star Wars (1977)	*The Chronicles of Narnia: Prince Caspian* (2008)
Blade Runner (1982)	

Musicals

Broadway Melody (1929)*	*Jesus Christ Superstar* (1973)
Top Hat (1935)	*Annie* (1982)
Meet Me in St. Louis (1944)	*Evita* (1997)
An American in Paris (1951)*	*Moulin Rouge!* (2001)
West Side Story (1961)*	*Chicago* (2002)*
The Sound of Music (1965)*	*Hairspray* (2007)

Film Noir

Double Indemnity (1944)	*Border Incident* (1949)
Detour (1945)	*Sunset Boulevard* (1950)
The Postman Always Rings Twice (1946)	*Se7en* (1995)
The Strange Love of Martha Ivers (1946)	*L.A. Confidential* (1997)
The Big Sleep (1946)	*The Man Who Wasn't There* (2001)
They Live by Night (1948)	*Mr. Brooks* (2007)

THE GODFATHER

THE CHRONICLES OF NARNIA: PRINCE CASPIAN

Variations of dramas and comedies have long dominated film's narrative history. A western typically features "good" cowboys battling "evil" bad guys or resolves tension between the natural forces of the wilderness and the civilizing influence of a town. Romances present conflicts that are mediated by the ideal of love. Another popular genre, mystery/suspense, usually casts "the city" as a corrupting place that needs to be overcome by the moral courage of a heroic detective.[5]

Because most Hollywood narratives try to create believable worlds, the artificial style of musicals is sometimes a disruption of what many viewers expect. Musicals' popularity peaked

11454-81

FILM GENRES
A classic film noir, *Sunset Boulevard* (1950) explores the dark forces behind the Hollywood dream factory. Here, Norma Desmond is a faded silent-film star (played by Gloria Swanson, a real-life faded silent-film star) who takes in struggling Hollywood writer Joe Gillis (played by William Holden). The limousine driver is Max Von Mayerling, Desmond's former husband (played by Eric Von Stroheim, himself a silent-film director who found little directorial work after the advent of talkies). In film noir style, the movie ends in madness and death.

in the 1940s and 1950s, but they showed a brief resurgence in the early 2000s, with *Moulin Rouge!* (2001) and *Chicago* (2002), the latter an Academy Award Best Picture winner. Still, no live-action musicals rank among the top fifty highest-grossing films of all time.

Another fascinating genre is the horror film, which also claims none of the top fifty highest-grossing films of all time. In fact, from *Psycho* (1960) to *Grindhouse* (2007), this lightly re-garded genre has earned only one Oscar for best picture: *Silence of the Lambs* (1991). Yet these movies are extremely popular with teenagers, among the largest theatergoing audience, who are in search of cultural choices distinct from those of their parents. Critics suggest that the teen appeal of horror movies is similar to the allure of gangster rap or heavy-metal music: that is, the horror genre is a cultural form that often carries anti-adult messages or does not appeal to most adults.

The *film noir* genre (French for "black film") developed in the United States after World War II and continues to influence movies today. Using low-lighting techniques, few daytime scenes, and bleak urban settings, films in this genre (such as *The Big Sleep*, 1946, and *Sunset Boulevard*, 1950) explore unstable characters and the sinister side of human nature. Although the French critics who first identified noir as a genre place these films in the 1940s, their influence resonates in contemporary films—sometimes called *neo-noir*—including *Raging Bull*, *Se7en*, and *Memento*.

Hollywood "Authors"

In commercial filmmaking, the director serves as the main "author" of a film. Sometimes called "auteurs," successful directors develop a particular cinematic style or an interest in particular topics that differentiates their narratives from those of other directors. Alfred Hitchcock, for in-stance, redefined the suspense drama through editing techniques that heightened tension (*Rear Window*, *Vertigo*, *North by Northwest*, *Psycho*).

The contemporary status of directors stems from two breakthrough films: Dennis Hopper's *Easy Rider* (1969) and George Lucas's *American Graffiti* (1973), which became surprise box-office hits. Their inexpensive budgets, rock-and-roll soundtracks, and big payoffs created opportunities for a new generation of directors. The success of these films exposed cracks in the Hollywood system, which was losing money in the late 1960s and early 1970s. Studio executives seemed at a loss to explain and predict the tastes of a new generation of moviegoers. Yet Hopper and Lucas had tapped into the anxieties of the postwar baby-boom generation in its search for self-realization, its longing for an innocent past, and its efforts to cope with the turbu-lence of the 1960s.

This opened the door for a new wave of directors who were trained in California or New York film schools and were also products of the 1960s, such as Francis Ford Coppola (*The Godfather*), Brian De Palma (*Carrie*), William Friedkin (*The Exorcist*), George Lucas (*Star Wars*), Martin Scorsese (*Taxi Driver*), and Steven Spielberg (*Jaws*). Combining news or documentary techniques and Hollywood narratives, these films demonstrated how mass media borders had become blurred and how movies had become dependent on audiences who were used to television and rock and roll. These films signaled the start of a period that Scorsese has called "the deification of the director." A handful of successful directors gained the kind of economic clout and celebrity standing that had belonged almost exclusively to top movie stars.

Although the status of directors grew in the 1960s and 1970s, recognition for female directors of Hollywood features remained rare.[6] In the history of the Academy Awards, only three women have received an Academy Award nomination for directing a feature film: Lina Wertmuller in 1976 for *Seven Beauties*, Jane Campion in 1993 for *The Piano*, and Sofia Coppola in 2004 for *Lost in Translation*. Both Wertmuller and Campion are from outside the United States, where women directors often receive more opportunities for film development. Women in the United States often get an opportunity because of their prominent standing as popular actors; Barbra Streisand, Jodie Foster, Penny Marshall, and Sally Field all fall into this category. Other women have come to direct films via their scriptwriting successes. Respected essayist Nora Ephron, for example, wrote *Silkwood* in 1983, wrote and produced *When Harry Met Sally* in 1989, and then went on to direct *Sleepless in Seattle* (1993) and *You've Got Mail* (1998)—each grossing more than $100 million. More recently, some women directors like Beeban Kidron (*Bridget Jones: The Edge of Reason*, 2004), Niki Caro (*North Country*, 2005), Catherine Hardwicke (*The Nativity Story*, 2006), and Nancy Meyers (*The Holiday*, 2006) have gotten past the barrier of their second and third films, proving themselves as trusted studio auteurs.

Minority groups, including African Americans, Asian Americans, and Native Americans, have also struggled for recognition in Hollywood. Still, some have succeeded as directors, crossing over from careers as actors, or gaining notoriety through independent filmmaking. Among the most successful contemporary African American directors are Kasi Lemmons (*Talk to Me*, 2007), Carl Franklin (*High Crimes*, 2002), John Singleton (*Four Brothers*, 2005), Tyler Perry (*Daddy's Little Girls*, 2007), and Spike Lee (*Do the Right Thing*, 1989, and *When the Levees Broke*, 2006). (See "Case Study: Breaking through Hollywood's Race Barrier" on p. 228.) Asian Americans M. Night Shyamalan (*The Happening*, 2008), Ang Lee (*Brokeback Mountain*, 2005), Wayne Wang (*Because of Winn-Dixie*, 2005), and documentarian Arthur Dong (*Hollywood Chinese*, 2007) have built immensely accomplished directing careers. Chris Eyre (*Smoke Signals*, 1998) remains the most noted Native American director, but works mainly as an independent.

Outside the Hollywood System

Since the rise of the studio system, the Hollywood film industry has focused on feature-length movies that command popular attention and earn the most money. However, the movie industry also has a long tradition of films made outside of the Hollywood studio system. In the following sections, we will look at three alternatives to Hollywood: foreign films, documentaries, and independent films.

"There may be more women working in the industry now . . . but you wouldn't know it from what's on the screen. . . . Some point to the lack of female directors, whose numbers in both the mainstream and independent realms hover at around 6 percent."

MANOHLA DARGIS, *NEW YORK TIMES*, 2008

Breaking through Hollywood's Race Barrier

Despite inequities and discrimination, a thriving black cinema existed in New York's Harlem district during the 1930s and 1940s. Usually bankrolled by white business executives who were capitalizing on the black-only theaters fostered by segregation, independent films featuring black casts were supported by African American moviegoers, even during the Depression. But it was a popular Hollywood film, *Imitation of Life* (1934), that emerged as the highest grossing film in black theaters during the mid-1930s. The film told the story of a friendship between a white woman and a black woman whose young daughter denied her heritage and passed for white, breaking her mother's heart.

Despite African Americans' long support of the film industry, their moviegoing experience has not been the same as that of whites. From the late 1800s until the passage of Civil Rights legislation in the mid-1960s, many theater owners discriminated against black patrons. In large cities, blacks often had to attend separate theaters where new movies might not appear until a year or two after white theaters had shown them. In smaller towns and in the South, blacks were often only allowed to patronize local theaters after midnight. In addition, some theater managers required black patrons to sit in less desirable areas of the theater.[1]

Changes took place during and after World War II, however. When the "white flight" from central cities began during the suburbanization of the 1950s, many downtown and neighborhood theaters began catering to black customers in order to keep from going out of business. By the late 1960s and early 1970s, these theaters had become major venues for popular commercial films, even featuring a few movies about African Americans, including *Guess Who's Coming to Dinner?* (1967), *In the Heat of the Night* (1967), *The Learning Tree* (1969), and *Sounder* (1972).

Based on the popularity of these films, black photographer-turned-filmmaker Gordon Parks, who directed *The Learning Tree* (adapted from his own novel), went on to make commercial action/adventure films, including *Shaft* (1971,

remade by John Singleton in 2000). Popular in urban theaters, especially among black teenagers, the movies produced by Parks and his son—Gordon Parks Jr. (*Super Fly*, 1972)—spawned a number of commercial imitators, labeled blaxploitation movies. These films were the subject of heated cultural debates in the 1970s; like some rap songs today, they were both praised for their realistic depictions of black urban life and criticized for glorifying violence. Nevertheless, these films reinvigorated urban movie attendance, reaching an audience that had not been well served by the film industry until the 1960s.

Although opportunities for black film directors expanded in the 1980s and 1990s, mainstream Hollywood is still a formidable place for outsiders to crack. Even acclaimed director Spike Lee has had difficulty in getting large budgets from the studios. For example, in making *Get on the Bus* (1996), Lee asked a number of wealthy black men to bankroll $2 million for the film, which depicted the October 1995 Million Man March on Washington, D.C., celebrating the kind of black self-reliance that Lee's own moviemaking has long illustrated. And in 2004, director and playwright Tyler Perry split the $5.5 million budget with Lions Gate Films for *Diary of a Mad Black Woman*, which went on to gross more than $50 million and spawned a series of similar films. ◢

SPIKE LEE

GORDON PARKS

Foreign Films

For generations, Hollywood has dominated the international movie scene. In many countries, American films capture up to 90 percent of the market. In striking contrast, foreign films constitute only a tiny fraction—less than 2 percent—of motion pictures seen in the United States today. Despite Hollywood's domination of global film distribution, other countries have a rich history in producing both successful and provocative short-subject and feature films. For example, cinematic movements of the twentieth century such as German expressionism (capturing psychological moods on film), Soviet social realism (presenting a positive view of Soviet life), Italian neorealism (focusing on the everyday lives of Italians), European new-wave cinema (experimenting with the language of film), and post-World War II Japanese, Hong Kong, Australian, Canadian, and British cinema have all been extremely influential, demonstrating alternatives to the Hollywood approach.

Early on, Americans showed interest in British and French short films and in experimental films such as Germany's *The Cabinet of Dr. Caligari* (1919). Foreign-language movies did reasonably well throughout the 1920s, especially in ethnic neighborhood theaters in large American cities. For a time, Hollywood studios even dubbed some popular American movies into Spanish, Italian, French, and German for these theaters. But the Depression brought cutbacks, and by the 1930s, the daughters and sons of turn-of-the-century immigrants—many of whom were trying to assimilate into mainstream American culture—preferred their Hollywood movies in English.[7]

Postwar prosperity, rising globalism, and the gradual decline of the studios' hold over theater exhibition in the 1950s and 1960s stimulated the rise of art-house theaters and saw a rebirth of interest in foreign-language films by such prominent directors as Sweden's Ingmar Bergman (*Wild Strawberries*, 1957), Italy's Federico Fellini (*La Dolce Vita*, 1960), France's François Truffaut (*Jules and Jim*, 1961), Japan's Akira Kurosawa (*Seven Samurai*, 1954), and India's Satyajit Ray (*Apu Trilogy*, 1955-59). Catering to academic audiences, art houses made a statement against Hollywood commercialism as they sought to show alternative movies.

By the late 1970s, though, the home-video market had emerged, and audiences began staying home to watch both foreign and domestic films. New multiplex theater owners rejected the smaller profit margins of most foreign titles, which lacked the promotional hype of U.S. films. As a result, between 1966 and 1990, the number of foreign films released annually in the United States dropped by two-thirds, from nearly three hundred to about one hundred titles per year.

With the growth of superstore video chains like Blockbuster and Web-based stores like Netflix in the 1990s and 2000s, viewers gained access to a larger selection of foreign-language titles. The successes of *Life Is Beautiful* (Italy, 1997), *Amélie* (France, 2001), and *The Lives of Others* (Germany, 2006) illustrate that U.S. audiences are willing to watch subtitled films with non-Hollywood perspectives. However, foreign films are losing ground as they compete with the expanding independent American film market for screen space.

FOREIGN FILMS like Brazil's *The Year My Parents Went on Vacation*—about a young boy who lives with his recently deceased grandfather's friend when his militant parents go underground in 1970 Sao Paulo—are becoming more available in the United States through home video. The film won many awards, including Best Picture at the Cinema Brazil Grand Prize.

"Growing up in this country, the rich culture I saw in my neighborhood, in my family—I didn't see that on television or on the movie screen. It was always my ambition that if I was successful I would try to portray a truthful portrait of African Americans in this country, negative and positive."

SPIKE LEE,
FILMMAKER, 1996

"Bollywood has an estimated annual worldwide audience of 3.6 billion."

ANUPAMA CHOPRA,
NEW YORK TIMES,
2008

Today, the largest film industry is in India, out of "Bollywood" (a play on words combining Bombay, now Mumbai, and Hollywood), where a thousand films a year are produced—mostly romance or adventure musicals in a distinct style.[8] In comparison, Hollywood moviemakers release five hundred to six hundred films a year. (For a broader perspective, see "Global Village—Beyond Hollywood: Asian Cinema" on page 231.)

The Documentary Tradition

Both TV news and nonfiction films trace their roots to the movie industry's *interest films* and *newsreels* of the late 1890s. In Britain, interest films compiled footage of regional wars, political leaders, industrial workers, and agricultural scenes and were screened with fiction shorts. Pioneered in France and England, newsreels consisted of weekly ten-minute magazine-style compilations of filmed news events from around the world. International news services began supplying theaters and movie studios with newsreels, and by 1911 they had become a regular part of the moviegoing menu.

Early filmmakers also produced *travelogues*, which recorded daily life in various communities around the world. Travel films reached a new status in Robert Flaherty's classic *Nanook of the North* (1922), which tracked an Inuit family in the harsh Hudson Bay region of Canada. Flaherty edited his fifty-five-minute film to both tell and interpret the story of his subject. Flaherty's second film, *Moana* (1925), a study of the lush South Pacific islands, inspired the term **documentary** in a 1926 film review by John Grierson, a Scottish film producer. Grierson defined Flaherty's work and the documentary form as "the creative treatment of actuality," or a genre that interprets reality by recording real people and settings.

Over time, the documentary developed an identity apart from its commercial presentation. As an educational, noncommercial form, the documentary usually required the backing of industry, government, or philanthropy to cover costs. In support of a clear alternative to Hollywood cinema, some nations began creating special units, such as Canada's National Film Board, to sponsor documentaries. In the United States, art and film received considerable support from the Roosevelt administration during the Depression.

By the late 1950s and early 1960s, the development of portable cameras had led to **cinema verité** (a French term for "truth film"). This documentary style allowed filmmakers to go where cameras could not go before and record fragments of everyday life more unobtrusively. Directly opposed to packaged, high-gloss Hollywood features, verité aimed to track reality, employing a rough, grainy look and shaky, handheld camera work. Among the key innovators in cinema verité were Drew and Associates, led by Robert Drew, a former *Life* magazine photographer. Through his connection to Time Inc. (which owned *Life*) and its chain of TV stations, Drew shot the groundbreaking documentary *Primary*, which followed the 1960 Democratic presidential primary race between Hubert Humphrey and John F. Kennedy.

Perhaps the major contribution of documentaries has been their willingness to tackle controversial or unpopular subject matter. For example, American documentary filmmaker Michael Moore often addresses complex topics that target corporations or the government. His films include *Roger and Me* (1989), a comic and controversial look

> "My stuff always starts with interviews. I start interviewing people, and then slowly but surely, a movie insinuates itself."
>
> ERROL MORRIS, DOCUMENTARY FILMMAKER, 2008

DOCUMENTARY FILMS, like Errol Morris's *Standard Operating Procedure* about Iraq's Abu Ghraib prison, often tackle tough or controversial issues. Though they are usually not commercially successful, critics often feel they have strong social importance and value.

Beyond Hollywood: Asian Cinema

Asian nations easily outstrip Hollywood in quantity of films produced. India alone produces about a thousand movies a year. But from India to South Korea, Asian films are increasingly challenging Hollywood in terms of quality, and these films have become more influential as Asian directors, actors, and film styles are exported to Hollywood and the rest of the world.

India

Part musical, part action, part romance, and part suspense, the epic films of Bollywood typically have fantastic sets, hordes of extras, plenty of wet saris, and symbolic fountain bursts (as a substitute for kissing and sex, which are prohibited from being shown). Indian movie fans pay from 75 cents to $5 to see these films, and they feel short-changed if they are shorter than three hours. With many films produced in less than a week, however, most of the Bollywood fare is cheaply produced and badly acted. But these production aesthetics are changing, as bigger-budget releases target middle and upper classes in India, the twenty-five million Indians living abroad, and Western audiences. Hollywood has also taken notice as Bollywood directors, producers, and actors have come to town. Indian

BOLLYWOOD STAR Aishwarya Rai stars in 2008's *Jodhaa Akbar.*

director Shekhar Kapur, for example, directed *Elizabeth* (1998), a stunning epic nominated for seven Oscars, and its sequel *The Golden Age* (2007). British director Gurinder Chadha (*Bend It Like Beckham*, 2002) brought the Bollywood musical style to *Bride and Prejudice* (2004), an adaptation of Jane Austen's classic novel.

China

Since the late 1980s, Chinese cinema has developed an international reputation. Leading this generation of directors are Zhang Yimou (*Raise the Red Lantern*, 1991; *House of Flying Daggers*, 2004; *Curse of the Golden Flower*, 2006) and Kaige Chen (*Farewell My Concubine*, 1993; *The Emperor and the Assassin*, 1999; *The Promise*, 2005), whose work has spanned genres such as historical epics, love stories, contemporary tales of city life, and action fantasy. They have also helped to make international stars out of Gong Li (*Memoirs of a Geisha*, 2005; *Hannibal Rising*, 2007) and Ziyi Zhang (*Crouching Tiger, Hidden Dragon*, 2000; *Memoirs of a Geisha*, 2005).

Hong Kong

Hong Kong films were the most talked about—and the most influential—film genre in cinema throughout the late 1980s and 1990s (Hong Kong was returned to mainland China in 1997). The style of highly choreographed action with often breathtaking, ballet-like violence became hugely popular around the world, reaching American audiences and in some cases even outselling Hollywood blockbusters. Hong Kong directors like John Woo, Ringo Lam, and Jackie Chan (who also acts in his movies) have directed Hollywood action films; and Hong Kong stars like Jet Li (*Lethal Weapon 4*, 1998; *The Forbidden Kingdom*, 2008), Chow Yun-Fat (*The Replacement Killers*, 1998; *Pirates of the Caribbean: At World's End*, 2007),

and Malaysia's Michelle Yeoh (*Memoirs of a Geisha*, 2005; *Babylon A.D.*, 2008) are landing leading roles in American movies.

Japan

Americans may be most familiar with low-budget monster movies like *Godzilla*, but the widely heralded films of the late director Akira Kurosawa have had an even greater impact: His *Seven Samurai* (1954) was remade by Hollywood as *The Magnificent Seven* (1960), and *The Hidden Fortress* (1958) was George Lucas's inspiration for *Star Wars*. New forces in Japanese cinema include Hayao Miyazaki (*Spirited Away*, 2001; *Howl's Moving Castle*, 2005), the country's top director of anime movies. Japanese thrillers like *Ringu* (1998) and *Ju-on: The Grudge* (2003) were remade into successful American horror films, *The Ring* (2002) and *The Grudge* (2004). The Hollywood sequels, *The Ring Two* (2005) and the upcoming *The Ring Three*, were directed by Hideo Nakata, director of the original *Ringu*.

South Korea

The end of military regimes in the late 1980s and corporate investment in the film business in the 1990s created a new era in Korean moviemaking. Since 2001, Korean films have overtaken Hollywood offerings in popularity at Korean theaters. Leading directors include Kim Jee-woon (*A Tale of Two Sisters*, 2003); Lee Chang-dong (winner of the Best Director award at Venice for *Oasis*, 2002); and Chan-wook Park, whose Revenge Trilogy films (*Sympathy for Mr. Vengeance*, 2002; *Old Boy*, 2003; and *Lady Vengeance*, 2005) have won international acclaim, including the Grand Prix at Cannes in 2004 for *Old Boy*. Korean films are hot properties in Hollywood, as major U.S. studios have bought the rights to a number of hits, including Kim's *A Tale of Two Sisters* and Park's *Old Boy*.

at the relationship between the city of Flint, Michigan, and General Motors; the Oscar-winning *Bowling for Columbine* (2002), which explored gun violence in the United States; *Fahrenheit 9/11* (2004), a critique of the Bush administration's Middle East policies and the Iraq war; and *Sicko* (2007), an investigation of the U.S. health-care system. Moore's recent films were part of a resurgence in high-profile documentary filmmaking, which included *Spellbound* (2002), *Super Size Me* (2004), *March of the Penguins* (2005), *An Inconvenient Truth* (2006), and Errol Morris's *The Fog of War* (2003) and *Standard Operating Procedure* (2008).

The Rise of Independent Films

The success of documentary films like *Super Size Me* and *Fahrenheit 9/11* dovetails with the rise of **indies**, or independently produced films. As opposed to directors working in the Hollywood system, independent filmmakers typically operate on a shoestring budget and show their movies in thousands of campus auditoriums and at hundreds of small film festivals. The decreasing costs of portable technology, including smaller digital cameras and computer editing, have kept many documentary and independent filmmakers in business. They make movies inexpensively, relying on real-life situations, stage actors and non-actors, crews made up of friends and students, and local nonstudio settings. Successful independents like Kevin Smith (*Clerks, Dogma*), Todd Haynes (*Far from Heaven, I'm Not There*), and Mira Nair (*Monsoon Wedding, The Name Sake*) continue to find substantial audiences in college and art-house theaters and through online DVD services like Netflix, which promote work produced outside the studio system.

The rise of independent film festivals in the 1990s—especially the Sundance Film Festival held every January in Park City, Utah—has helped Hollywood rediscover low-cost independent films as an alternative to traditional movies with *Titanic*-size budgets. Films such as *The Full Monty* (1997), *The Blair Witch Project* (1999), *Napoleon Dynamite* (2004), and *Little Miss Sunshine* (2006) were all able to generate industry buzz and major studio distribution deals through

INDEPENDENT FILMS
The Passion of the Christ (2004) remains the most successful independent film in history. Controversial because of its graphic violence and depiction of the role of Jews in Jesus' crucifixion and death, the film was rejected by Hollywood but became a blockbuster with the vigorous support of Christian groups. A tamer version of the film, *The Passion Recut*, was released a year later.

Sundance screenings, and became star vehicles for several directors and actors. As with the recording industry, the major studios have recognized that indies are a strong venue for discovering new talent. The studios have responded either by purchasing successful independent film companies (Disney's purchase of Miramax) or by developing in-house indie divisions (Sony's Sony Pictures Classics).

The Transformation of the Studio System

After years of thriving, the Hollywood movie industry began to falter after 1946. Weekly movie attendance in the United States peaked at ninety million a week in 1946, then fell to less than twenty-five million by 1963. Critics and observers began talking about the death of Hollywood, claiming that the golden age was over. However, the movie industry adapted and survived, just as it continues to do today. Among the changing conditions facing the film industry were the communist witch-hunts in Hollywood, the end of the industry's vertical integration, suburbanization, the arrival of television, and the appearance of home entertainment.

The Hollywood Ten

In 1947, in the wake of the unfolding Cold War with the Soviet Union, conservative members of Congress began investigating Hollywood for alleged subversive and communist ties. That year, aggressive witch-hunts for political radicals in the film industry by the House Un-American Activities Committee (HUAC) led to the famous **Hollywood Ten** hearings and subsequent trial. (HUAC included future president Richard M. Nixon, then a congressman from California.)

During the investigations, HUAC coerced prominent people from the film industry to declare their patriotism and to give up the names of colleagues suspected of politically unfriendly tendencies. Upset over labor union strikes and outspoken writers, many film executives were eager to testify and provide names. For instance, Jack L. Warner of Warner Brothers suggested that whenever film writers made fun of the wealthy or America's political system in their work, or if their movies were sympathetic to "Indians and the colored folks,"[9] they were engaging in communist propaganda. In addition, film producer Sam Wood, who had directed Marx Brothers comedies in the mid-1930s, testified that communist writers could be spotted because they portrayed bankers and senators as villainous characters. Other "friendly" HUAC witnesses included actors Gary Cooper and Ronald Reagan, director Elia Kazan, and producer Walt Disney. Whether they believed it was their patriotic duty or they were afraid of losing their jobs, many prominent actors, directors, and other film executives also "named names."

THE HOLLYWOOD 10
While many studio heads, producers, and actors "named names" to HUAC, others, such as the group shown above, held protests to demand the release of the Hollywood 10.

Eventually, HUAC subpoenaed ten unwilling witnesses who were questioned about their memberships in various organizations. The so-called Hollywood Ten–nine screenwriters and one director–refused to discuss their memberships or to identify communist sympathizers. Charged with contempt of Congress in November 1947, they were eventually sent to prison. Although jailing the Hollywood Ten clearly violated their free-speech rights, in the atmosphere of the Cold War, many people worried that "the American way" could be sabotaged via unpatriotic messages planted in films. Upon release from jail, the Hollywood Ten found themselves blacklisted, or boycotted, by the major studios, and their careers in the film industry were all but ruined. The national fervor over communism continued to plague Hollywood well into the 1950s.

The Paramount Decision

Coinciding with the HUAC investigations, the government also increased its scrutiny of the movie industry's aggressive business practices. By the mid-1940s, the Justice Department demanded that the five major film companies–Paramount, Warner Brothers, Twentieth Century Fox, MGM, and RKO–end vertical integration, the simultaneous control over production, distribution, and exhibition. In 1948, after a series of court appeals, the Supreme Court ruled against the film industry in what is commonly known as the **Paramount decision**, forcing the studios to gradually divest themselves of their theaters.

Although the government had hoped to increase competition, the Paramount case never really changed the oligopoly structure of the Hollywood film industry, because it failed to challenge the industry's control over distribution. However, the 1948 decision did create opportunities in the exhibition part of the industry for those outside of Hollywood. In addition to art houses showing documentaries or foreign films, thousands of drive-in theaters sprang up in farmers' fields, welcoming new suburbanites who embraced the automobile. Although drive-ins had been around since the 1930s, by the end of the 1950s, more than four thousand existed. The Paramount decision encouraged new indoor theater openings as well, but the major studios continued to dominate distribution. By producing the most polished and popular films, they still influenced consumer demand and orchestrated where the movies would play.

MOVIES TAKE ON SOCIAL ISSUES
Rebel without a Cause (1955), starring James Dean and Natalie Wood, was marketed in movie posters as "Warner Bros. Challenging Drama of Today's Teenage Violence!" James Dean's memorable portrayal of a troubled youth forever fixed his place in movie history. He was killed in a car crash a month before the movie opened.

Moving to the Suburbs

Common sense might suggest that television alone precipitated the decline in post-World War II movie attendance, but the most dramatic drop actually occurred in the late 1940s—before most Americans even owned TV sets.[10]

The transformation from a wartime economy and a surge in consumer production had a significant impact on moviegoing. With industries turning from armaments to appliances, Americans started cashing in their wartime savings bonds for household goods and new cars. Discretionary income that formerly went to movie tickets now went to acquiring consumer products, and the biggest product of all was a new house in the suburbs—far from the downtown movie theaters. Relying on government help through Veterans Administration loans, people left the cities in record numbers to buy affordable houses in suburban areas where tax bases were lower. Home ownership in the United States doubled between 1945 and 1950, while the moviegoing public decreased just as quickly. According to census data, new home purchases, which had held steady at about 100,000 a year since the late 1920s, leaped to more than 930,000 in 1946 and peaked at 1,700,000 in 1950.

Additionally, after the war the average age for couples entering marriage dropped from twenty-four to nineteen. Unlike their parents, many postwar couples had their first child before they turned twenty-one. The combination of social and economic changes meant there were significantly fewer couples dating at the movies. Then, when television exploded in the late 1950s, there was even less discretionary income—and less reason to go to the movies.

Television Changes Hollywood

In the late 1940s, radio's popularity had a strong impact on film. Not only were 1948 and 1949 high points in radio listenership, but with the mass migration to the suburbs, radio offered Americans an inexpensive entertainment alternative to the movies (as it had during the Great Depression). As a result, many people stayed home and listened to radio programs until TV displaced both radio and movies as the medium of national entertainment in the mid-1950s. The movie industry responded in a variety of ways.

HOLLYWOOD STRETCHES ITS LIMITS
The explicit language and situations of *Who's Afraid of Virginia Woolf?* (1966), based on an Edward Albee play, led to the formation of the current ratings system in 1967.

> "So TV did not kill Hollywood. In the great Hollywood whodunit there is, after all, not even a corpse. The film industry never died. Only where we enjoy its latest products has changed, forever."
>
> DOUGLAS GOMERY, *WILSON QUARTERLY*, 1991

First, with growing legions of people gathering around their living-room TV sets, movie content slowly shifted toward more serious subjects. At first, this shift was a response to the war and an acknowledgment of life's complexity, but later movies focused on subject matter that television did not encourage. This shift began with film noir in the 1940s but continued into the 1950s, as commercial movies, for the first time, explored larger social problems such as alcoholism (*The Lost Weekend*, 1945), anti-Semitism (*Gentleman's Agreement*, 1947), mental illness (*The Snake Pit*, 1948), racism (*Pinky*, 1949), adult–teen relationships (*Rebel without a Cause*, 1955), drug abuse (*The Man with the Golden Arm*, 1955), and–perhaps most controversially–sexuality (*Peyton Place*, 1957; *Butterfield 8*, 1960; and *Lolita*, 1962).

These and other films challenged the authority of the industry's own prohibitive Motion Picture Production Code. Hollywood adopted the Code in the early 1930s to restrict film depictions of violence, crime, drug use, and sexual behavior and to quiet public and political concerns that the movie business was lowering the moral standards of America. (For more on the Code, see Chapter 16.) In 1967, after the Code had been ignored by producers for several years, the Motion Picture Association of America initiated the current ratings system, which rated films for age appropriateness, rather than censoring all adult content.

Second, just as radio worked to improve sound to maintain an advantage over television in the 1950s, the film industry introduced a host of technological improvements to sway Americans away from their TV sets. Technicolor, invented by an MIT scientist in 1917, had improved and was used in movies more often to draw people away from their black-and-white TVs. In addition, Cinerama, CinemaScope, and VistaVision all arrived in movie theaters, featuring striking wide-screen images, multiple synchronized projectors, and stereophonic sound. Then 3-D (three-dimensional) movies appeared, although they wore off quickly as a novelty. Finally, Panavision, which used special Eastman color film and camera lenses that decreased the fuzziness of images, became the wide-screen standard throughout the industry. These developments, however, generally failed to address the movies' primary problem: the middle-class flight to the suburbs, away from downtown theaters.

Hollywood Adapts to Home Entertainment

Just as nickelodeons, movie palaces, and drive-ins transformed movie exhibition in earlier times, the introduction of cable television and the videocassette in the 1970s transformed contemporary movie exhibition. Despite advances in movie exhibition, most people prefer the convenience of watching movies at home. In fact, almost 50 percent of domestic revenue for Hollywood studios now comes from the video/DVD rental and sales markets, leaving box-office receipts accounting for just 20 percent of total film revenue.

Although the video market has become a financial bonanza for the movie industry, Hollywood ironically tried to stall the arrival of the VCR in the 1970s–even filing lawsuits to prohibit customers from copying movies from television. The 1997 introduction of the DVD helped

FIGURE 7.1

GROSS REVENUES FROM BOX-OFFICE SALES, 1986–2007

Source: Motion Picture Association of America, U.S. Market Statistics, 2007, http://www.mpaa.org.

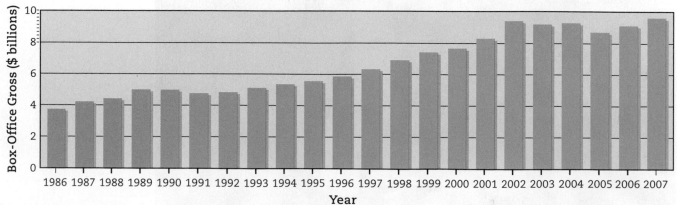

reinvigorate the flat sales of the home video market as people began to acquire new movie collections on DVD. The growing popularity of DVDs has also made sales of recorded movies outweigh rentals. Today, high-definition television sets are often enhanced with surround-sound audio home theater systems, making the experience feel even more like going to a movie theater.

However, movie rentals are still profitable and popular because of the large number of titles they offer. Blockbuster dominates this industry, with more than eight thousand stores internationally. Its nearest competitor, Movie Gallery/Hollywood Video, has about forty-five hundred stores. However, the total number of video/DVD stores has decreased in recent years due to competition from general retailers—Wal-Mart is now the number-one seller of DVDs. Online movie rental companies like Netflix have also claimed part of the DVD rental market and have influenced Blockbuster to introduce a similar rental program. But, by 2006, DVD sales had begun to slow, leading Hollywood to stake its future on a new format—Sony's Blu-ray discs, which in 2008 prevailed over Toshiba's competing HD-DVD format.[11]

The Economics of the Movie Business

Despite the development of network and cable television, pay-per-view, and DVDs, the movie business has continued to thrive. In fact, since 1963, Americans have purchased roughly 1 billion movie tickets each year; in 2007, 1.4 billion tickets were sold.[12] With first-run movie tickets in some areas rising to more than $11, gross revenues from box-office sales have climbed to a record $9.63 billion, up from $3.8 billion annually in the mid-1980s (see Figure 7.1). In addition, domestic video rentals and sales produced another $15.7 billion a year, easily surpassing box-office receipts. But to survive and flourish, the movie industry revamped its production, distribution, and exhibition system and consolidated its ownership.

Production, Distribution, and Exhibition Today

In the 1970s, attendance by young moviegoers at new suburban multiplex theaters made megahits of *The Godfather* (1972), *The Exorcist* (1973), *Jaws* (1975), *Rocky* (1976), and *Star Wars* (1977). During this period, *Jaws* and *Star Wars* became the first movies to gross more than $100 million at the U.S. box office in a single year. In trying to copy the success of these blockbuster hits, the major studios set in place economic strategies for future decades. (See "Media Literacy and the Critical Process: The Blockbuster Mentality" on page 238.)

Making Money on Movies Today

With 80 to 90 percent of newly released movies failing to make money at the box office, studios need at least one major hit each year to offset losses on other films. (See Table 7.2 on page 239 for a list of the highest-grossing films of all time.) The potential losses are great: In 2007, a major studio film, on average, cost $70.8 million to produce. Marketing, advertising, and print costs added an additional $35.9 million per film, bringing the total average cost to $106.6 million.[13]

BLOCKBUSTERS like *The Dark Knight* (2008) are sought after despite large budgets—$150 million for *Dark Knight*—because they can potentially bring in twice that in box-office sales, DVDs, merchandising, and licensing fees. *The Dark Knight* made back its budget its opening weekend, setting a record for a weekend opening ($158 million).

Media Literacy and the Critical Process

1 DESCRIPTION. Consider a list of the Top 25 all-time highest-grossing movies in the United States, such as the one on the Internet Movie Database, http://us.imdb.com/boxoffice/alltimegross.

2 ANALYSIS. Note patterns in the list. For example, of these twenty-five top-grossing films, twenty-three target young audiences (*Forrest Gump* and *The Passion of the Christ* are the only exceptions). Three-quarters of these top-grossing films feature animated or digitally composited characters (e.g., *Lion King; Shrek; Jurassic Park*) or extensive special effects (*Transformers; Spider-Man*). Three-quarters also either spawned or are a part of a series, like *The Lord of the Rings, The Dark Knight*, and *Harry Potter*. More than half of the films fit into the action movie genre. Nearly all of the Top 25 had intense merchandising campaigns that featured action figures, fast-food tie-ins, and an incredible variety of products for sale; that is, nearly all weren't "surprise" hits.

The Blockbuster Mentality

In the beginning of this chapter, we quoted film critic Roger Ebert, who noted Hollywood's shift toward a blockbuster mentality after the success of films like *Star Wars*. How pervasive is this blockbuster mentality, whose characteristics include young adults as the target audience, action-packed big-budget releases, heavy merchandising tie-ins, and the possibility of sequels?

3 INTERPRETATION. What do the patterns mean? It's clear, economically, why Hollywood likes to have successful blockbuster movie franchises. But what kinds of films get left out of the mix? Hits like *Forrest Gump*, which may have had big-budget releases but lack some of the other attributes of blockbusters, are clearly anomalies of the blockbuster mentality, although they illustrate that strong characters and compelling stories can carry a film to great commercial success.

4 EVALUATION. It is likely that we will continue to see an increase in youth-oriented, animated/action movie franchises that are heavily merchandised and intended for wide international distribution. Indeed, Hollywood does not have a lot of motivation to put out other kinds of movies that don't fit these categories. Is this a good thing? Can you think of a film that you thought was excellent and that would have likely been a bigger hit with better promotion and wider distribution?

5 ENGAGEMENT. Watch independent and foreign films and see what you're missing. Visit the Independent Film section in the IMDb.com or ForeignFilms.com and browse through the many films listed. See if your video store carries any of these titles, and request them if they don't. Make a similar request to your local theater chain. Write your cable company and request to have the Sundance Channel and the Independent Film Channel on your cable lineup. Organize an independent film night on your college campus and bring these films to a crowd.

"Hollywood may be the only industry that makes more money dumping failed products abroad than it does marketing successful ones at home."

DAVID KIPEN, AUTHOR OF *SCREENWRITING FOR A GLOBAL MARKET*, 2004

With climbing film costs, creating revenue from a movie is a formidable task. Studios make money on movies from six major sources: First, the studios get a portion of the theater box-office revenue—about 40 percent of the box-office take. Overall, box-office receipts provide studios with approximately 20 percent of a movie's domestic revenue.

Second, about four months after the theatrical release comes the DVD/video sales and rentals "window," which accounts for almost 50 percent of all domestic-film income for major studios. A small percentage of this market includes "direct-to-DVD" films, which don't have a theatrical release.

Third are the next "windows" of release for a film: cable and television outlets, including pay-per-view, video-on-demand, premium cable (such as HBO), network and basic cable, and, finally, the syndicated TV market. The price these cable and television outlets pay to the studios is negotiated on a film-by-film basis.

Fourth, studios earn profits from distributing films in foreign markets. In fact, international box-office gross revenues are almost double the U.S. and Canadian box-office receipts, and continue to climb annually, even as other countries produce more of their own films.

Rank	Title/Date	Domestic Gross** (millions)
1	*Titanic* (1997)	$601
2	*The Dark Knight* (2008)	522
3	*Star Wars* (1977)	461
4	*Shrek 2* (2004)	437
5	*E.T.: The Extra-Terrestrial* (1982)	435
6	*Star Wars: Episode I—The Phantom Menace* (1999)	431
7	*Pirates of the Caribbean: Dead Man's Chest* (2006)	423
8	*Spider-Man* (2002)	408
9	*Star Wars: Episode III—Revenge of the Sith* (2005)	380
10	*The Lord of the Rings: The Return of the King* (2003)	377

◀

TABLE 7.2

THE TOP 10 BOX-OFFICE CHAMPIONS, 2008*

Source: "All Time Top 100 Grossing Films," October 9, 2008, http://www.movieweb.com/ movies/box_office/alltime.phb. © 2008 MovieWeb. All Rights Reserved.

*Most rankings of the Top 10 most popular films are based on American box-office receipts. If these were adjusted for inflation, *Gone with the Wind* (1939) would become No. 1 in U.S. theater revenue.
**Gross is shown in absolute dollars based on box-office sales in the United States and Canada.

Fifth, studios make money by distributing the work of independent producers and filmmakers, who hire the studios to gain wider circulation. Independents pay the studios between 30 and 50 percent of the box-office and video rental money they make from movies.

Sixth, revenue is earned from merchandise licensing and *product placements* in movies. In the early days of television and film, characters generally used generic products, or product labels weren't highlighted in shots. For example, Bette Davis's and Humphrey Bogart's cigarette packs were rarely seen in their movies. But with soaring film production costs, product placements are adding extra revenues while lending an element of authenticity to the staging. Famous product placements in movies include Reese's Pieces in *E.T.: The Extra-Terrestrial* (1982), Pepsi-Cola in *Back to the Future II* (1989), and more than twenty-five products in *Casino Royale* (2006).

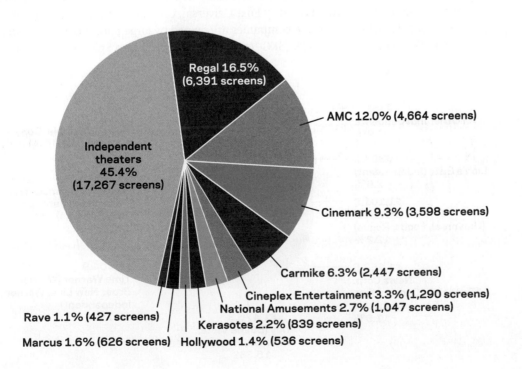

◀

FIGURE 7.2

TOP MOVIE THEATER CHAINS IN NORTH AMERICA

Source: National Association of Theatre Owners, 2008.

Theater Chains Consolidate Exhibition

Film exhibition is now controlled by a handful of theater chains; the leading seven companies operate more than 50 percent of U.S. screens. The major chains–Regal Cinemas, AMC Entertainment, Cinemark USA, Carmike Cinemas, Cineplex Entertainment, National Amusements (parent company of Viacom and CBS), and Kerasotes Theatres–own thousands of screens each in suburban malls and at highway crossroads, and most have expanded into international markets as well (see Figure 7.2 on page 239). Because distributors require access to movie screens, they do business with chains that control the most screens. In a multiplex, an exhibitor can project a potential hit on two or three screens at the same time; films that do not debut well are relegated to the smallest theaters or bumped quickly for a new release.

The strategy of the leading theater chains during the 1990s was to build more **megaplexes** (facilities with fourteen or more screens), but with upscale concession services and luxurious screening rooms with stadium-style seating and digital sound to make moviegoing a special event. Even with record box-office revenues, the major movie theater chains entered the 2000s in miserable financial shape. After several years of fast-paced building and renovations, the major chains had built an excess of screens and accrued enormous debt. But to further combat the home theater market, movie theater chains added IMAX screens and digital projectors in order to exhibit specially mastered and (with a nod to the 1950s) 3-D blockbusters.[14] By 2007, the movie exhibition business had grown to a record number (38,794) of indoor screens.

Still, theater chains sought to be less reliant on Hollywood's product, and with new digital projectors began to screen non-movie events, including live sporting events, rock concerts, and classic TV show marathons. One of the most successful theater events is the live HD simulcast of the New York Metropolitan Opera's performances, which began in 2007 and during its 2008-09 season screened eleven operas to more than eight hundred locations worldwide.

The Major Studio Players

The current Hollywood commercial film business is ruled primarily by six companies: Warner Brothers, Paramount, Twentieth Century Fox, Universal, Columbia Pictures, and Disney–the **Big Six**. Except for Disney, all these companies are owned by large parent conglomerates (see Figure 7.3). One studio, DreamWorks SKG–created in 1994 by Steven Spielberg, former Disney

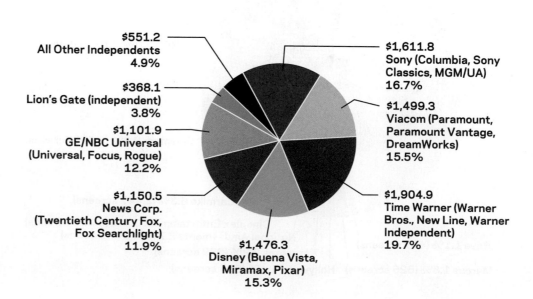

FIGURE 7.3

MARKET SHARE OF U.S. FILM STUDIOS AND DISTRIBUTORS, 2007 (IN $ MILLIONS)

Note: Based on gross box-office revenue, January 1, 2007–December 31, 2007. Overall gross for period: $9.664 billion.

Source: Box office Mojo, Studio Market Share, http://www .boxofficemojo.com/studio/.

$551.2
All Other Independents
4.9%

$368.1
Lion's Gate (independent)
3.8%

$1,101.9
GE/NBC Universal
(Universal, Focus, Rogue)
12.2%

$1,150.5
News Corp.
(Twentieth Century Fox,
Fox Searchlight)
11.9%

$1,476.3
Disney (Buena Vista,
Miramax, Pixar)
15.3%

$1,611.8
Sony (Columbia, Sony
Classics, MGM/UA)
16.7%

$1,499.3
Viacom (Paramount,
Paramount Vantage,
DreamWorks)
15.5%

$1,904.9
Time Warner (Warner
Bros., New Line, Warner
Independent)
19.7%

executive Jeffrey Katzenberg, and sound recording tycoon David Geffen—began to rival the production capabilities of the majors with films like *Shrek 2*, *Madagascar*, and *Anchorman*. Nevertheless, even DreamWorks could not sustain the high costs of distribution as an independent studio, and after an eleven-year run, was bought by Paramount (Viacom) in 2005. The six major studios account for more than 90 percent of the revenue generated by commercial films. They also control more than half the movie market in Europe and Asia.

In the 1980s, to offset losses resulting from box-office failures, the movie industry began to diversify, expanding into other product lines and other mass media. This expansion included television programming, print media, sound recordings, and home videos/DVDs, as well as cable and computers, electronic hardware and software, retail stores, and theme parks such as Universal Studios. To maintain the industry's economic stability, management strategies today rely on both heavy advance promotion (which can double the cost of a commercial film) and **synergy**—the promotion and sale of a product throughout the various subsidiaries of the media conglomerate. Companies promote not only the new movie itself but also its book form, soundtrack, calendars, T-shirts, Web site, and toy action figures, as well as "the-making-of" story for distribution on television, cable, and home video. The Disney studio, in particular, has been successful with its multiple packaging of youth-targeted movies, which includes comic books, toys, cable specials, fast-food tie-ins, and theme-park attractions. Since the 1950s, this synergy has been a key characteristic in the film industry and an important element in the flood of corporate mergers that have made today's Big Six even bigger.

The biggest corporate mergers have involved the internationalization of the American film business. Investment in American popular culture by the international electronics industry is particularly significant. This business strategy represents a new, high-tech kind of vertical integration—an attempt to control both the production of electronic equipment that consumers buy for their homes and the production/distribution of the content that runs on that equipment. This began in 1985 when Australia's News Corp. bought Twentieth Century Fox. Sony bought Columbia in 1989 for $4 billion and the neglected MGM/UA studio in 2005. Vivendi, a French utility, acquired Universal in 2000 but sold it to General Electric, the parent of NBC, in 2003. Finally, in 2006, Disney bought its animation partner, Pixar, while Viacom bought DreamWorks. (See "What Disney Owns.") Time Warner's basic and premium cable channels like CNN, TBS, and HBO also represent a new model of vertical integration in the movie industry, in which a company's films are distributed on its own cable channels for home viewing.

Movies Adjust to the Digital Age

The biggest challenge the movie industry faces today is the Internet. As broadband Internet service connects more households, movie fans are more likely to get movies from the Web. After witnessing the difficulties illegal file sharing brought on the music labels (some of which share the same corporate parent as film studios), the movie industry has more quickly embraced the Internet. Apple's iTunes store began selling digital downloads of a limited selection of movies in 2006, and in 2008, iTunes began renting new movies from all of the major studios for just $3.99. That same year, online DVD rental service Netflix began offering "instant viewing" of movies and videos by streaming some rentals to customers' computer screens. Also in 2008, NBC Universal (parent corporation of Universal Studios) and News Corp. (owner of Twentieth Century Fox) launched a joint Internet venture called Hulu. The site, which features full episodes and clips from hundreds of television shows and movies, is the studios' attempt to divert attention from YouTube and see if viewers will watch their free, ad-supported streaming movies and television shows online. Competition for viewers' attention is also coming from outside of Hollywood. Mobile phone makers like Nokia are attempting to market and position their phones as players of short movies that might be distributed via social networks.

Movies are not only being digitally distributed and exhibited for the small screens of computers and portable devices, but also for the large screens of theaters. By 2008, about five thousand theater screens in the United States used digital projection, but only about one thousand of those screens were advanced 3D projection systems capable of showing IMAX 3D versions of films. As Hollywood began making more 3D films (the latest form of product differentiation), the challenge for major studios has been to subsidize movie theater chains' installations of new projection systems, so there would be at least four thousand 3D screens across the country for major openings of 3D films.[15]

Alternative Voices

With the major studios exerting such a profound influence on the worldwide production, distribution, and exhibition of movies, new alternatives have helped open and redefine the movie industry. The digital revolution in movie production is the most recent opportunity to wrest some power away from the Hollywood studios. Substantially cheaper and more accessible than standard film equipment, **digital video** is a shift from celluloid film, and allows filmmakers to replace expensive and bulky 16-mm and 35-mm film cameras with less expensive, lightweight digital video cameras. For moviemakers, digital video also means seeing camera work instantly instead of waiting for film to be developed and being able to capture additional footage without concern for the high cost of film stock and processing.

By 2002, a number of major directors, including Steven Soderbergh, Spike Lee, Francis Ford Coppola, George Lucas, and Gus Van Sant, began testing the digital video format. British director Mike Figgis achieved the milestone of producing the first fully digital release from a major studio with his film *Time Code* (2000). But the greatest impact of digital technology is on independent filmmakers. Low-cost digital video opens up the creative process to countless new artists. With digital video camera equipment and computer-based desktop editors, movies can now be made for just a few thousand dollars, a fraction of what the cost would be on film. For example, the indie hit *The Blair Witch Project* (1999) was made for about $40,000 with mostly digital equipment and went on to gross more than $141 million in theaters. By 2006, independent filmmakers using digital cameras was the norm, and many directors at venues like the Sundance Film Festival had already upgraded to high-definition digital cameras, which rival film's visual quality. Ironically, both independent and Hollywood filmmakers have to contend with issues of preserving digital content: celluloid film stock can last a hundred years, whereas digital formats can be lost as storage formats fail and devices become obsolete.[16]

Because digital production puts movies in the same format as DVDs and the Internet, independent filmmakers have new distribution venues beyond film festivals or the major studios. For example, AtomFilms, IFILM, Vimeo, and YouTube have grown into leading Internet sites for the screening and distribution of short films and film festivals, providing filmmakers with their most valuable asset—an audience.

Popular Movies and Democracy

At the cultural level, movies function as **consensus narratives**, a term that describes cultural products that become popular and provide shared cultural experiences. These consensus narratives operate across different times and cultures. In this sense, movies are part of a long narrative tradition, encompassing "the oral formulaic of Homer's day, the theater of Sophocles,

the Elizabethan theater, the English novel from Defoe to Dickens, . . . the silent film, the sound film, and television during the Network Era."[17] Consensus narratives—whether they are dramas, romances, westerns, or mysteries—speak to central myths and values in an accessible language that often bridges global boundaries.

At the international level, countries continue to struggle with questions about the influence of American films on local customs and culture. Like other American mass media industries, the long reach of Hollywood movies is one of the key contradictions of contemporary life: Do such films contribute to a global village in which people throughout the world share a universal culture that breaks down barriers? Or does an American-based common culture stifle the development of local cultures worldwide and diversity in moviemaking? Clearly, the steady production of profitable action/adventure movies—whether they originate in the United States, Africa, France, or China—continues not only because these movies appeal to mass audiences, but also because they translate easily into other languages.

With the rise of international media conglomerates, it has become more difficult to awaken public debate over issues of movie diversity and America's domination of the film business. Consequently, issues concerning greater competition and a better variety of movies sometimes fall by the wayside. As critical consumers, those of us who enjoy movies and recognize their cultural significance must raise these broader issues in public forums as well as in our personal conversations. ▶

"Filmmaking, back when that meant real film, was a heinously expensive activity. Now anyone with access to digital equipment and some gullible friends, relatives, or investors can put their precious thoughts on a large screen for all to see."

DAVID CARR,
NEW YORK TIMES

CHAPTER REVIEW

REVIEW QUESTIONS

Early Technology and the Evolution of Movies

1. How did film go from the novelty stage to the mass medium stage?

2. Why were early silent films popular?

3. What contribution did nickelodeons make to film history?

The Rise of the Hollywood Studio System

4. Why did Hollywood end up as the center of film production?

5. Why did Thomas Edison and the patents Trust fail to shape and control the film industry, and why did Adolph Zukor of Paramount succeed?

6. How does vertical integration work in the film business?

The Studio System's Golden Age

7. Why did a certain structure of film—called classic Hollywood narrative—become so dominant in moviemaking?

8. Why are genres and directors important to the film industry?

9. Why are documentaries an important alternative to traditional Hollywood filmmaking? What contributions have they made to the film industry?

The Transformation of the Studio System

10. What political and cultural forces changed the Hollywood system in the 1950s?

11. How has home entertainment changed the film industry?

12. How has the movie industry used television to its advantage?

The Economics of the Movie Business

13. What are the various ways in which major movie studios make money from the film business?

14. How do a few large film studios manage to control more than 90 percent of the commercial industry?

15. Why is the Internet a potential threat to the movie industry, and how is the industry responding?

16. What is the impact of inexpensive digital technology on filmmaking?

Popular Movies and Democracy

17. Do films contribute to a global village in which people throughout the world share a universal culture? Or do U.S.-based films overwhelm the development of other cultures worldwide? Discuss.

QUESTIONING THE MEDIA

1. Describe your earliest memory of going to a movie. Do some research and compare this with a parent's or grandparent's earliest memory. Compare the different experiences.

2. Do you remember seeing a movie you were not allowed to see? Discuss the experience.

3. How often do you go to movie theaters today? How often do you play DVDs on a television at home, or watch movies on a computer? Which experience do you prefer and why?

4. If you were a Hollywood film producer or executive, what kinds of films would you like to see made? What changes would you make in what we see at the movies?

5. Look at the international film box-office statistics in the latest issue of *Variety* magazine. Note which films are the most popular worldwide. What do you think about the significant role U.S. movies play in global culture? Should their role be less significant? Explain your answer.

For review quizzes, chapter summaries, links to media-related Web sites, and more, go to bedfordstmartins.com/mediaculture.

COMMON THREADS

One of the Common Threads discussed in Chapter 1 is about mass media, cultural expression, and storytelling. The movie industry is a particularly potent example of this, as Hollywood movies dominate international screens. But Hollywood dominates our domestic screens as well. Does this limit our exposure to other kinds of stories?

Since the 1920s, after the burgeoning film industries in Europe lay in ruins from World War I, Hollywood gained an international dominance it has never relinquished. Critics have long cited America's *cultural imperialism*, flooding the world with our movies, music, television shows, fashion, and products. The strength of American cultural and economic power is evident when you witness a Thai man in a Tommy Hilfiger shirt watching *Transformers* at a Bangkok bar while eating a hamburger and drinking a Coke. Critics feel that American-produced culture overwhelms indigenous cultural industries, which will never be able to compete at the same level.

But other cultures are good at bending and blending our content. Hip-hop has been remade into regional music in places like Senegal, Portugal, Taiwan, and the Philippines. McDonald's is global, but in India you can get a McAlooTikki sandwich: a spicy fried potato and pea vegetarian patty. In Turkey, you can get a McTurco, a kebab with lamb or chicken. Or in France you can order a beer with your meal.

While some may be proud of the success of America's cultural exports, we might also ask ourselves this: What is the impact of our cultural dominance on our own media environment? Foreign films, for example, account for less than 2 percent of all releases in the United States. Is this because we find subtitles or other languages too challenging? At points in the twentieth century, American moviegoers were much more likely to see foreign films. Did our taste in movies change on our own accord, or did we simply forget how to appreciate different narratives and styles?

Of course, international content does make it to our shores. We exported rock and roll, and the British sent it back to us, with long hair. They also gave us *American Idol* and *The Office*. Japan gave us anime, Pokémon, *Iron Chef*, and Hello Kitty. Even the top four actors of the 2008 Academy Awards were Europeans: Daniel Day-Lewis (Britain/Ireland), Marion Cotillard (France), Javier Bardem (Spain), and Tilda Swinton (Britain), although two played Americans in their films.

But in a world where globalization is a key phenomenon, Hollywood doesn't show us the world through another's eyes. The burden falls to us to search out and watch those movies until Hollywood finally gets the message.

KEY TERMS

The definitions for the terms listed below can be found in the glossary at the end of the book. The page numbers listed with the terms indicate where the term is highlighted in the chapter.

8

Newspapers:

The Rise and Decline of Modern Journalism

In 1887, a young reporter left her job at the *Pittsburgh Dispatch* to seek her fortune in New York City. Only twenty-three years old, Elizabeth "Pink" Cochrane had grown tired of writing for the society pages and answering letters to the editor. She wanted to be on the front page. But at that time, it was considered "unladylike" for women journalists to use their real names, so the *Dispatch* editors, borrowing from a Stephen Foster song, had dubbed her "Nellie Bly."

After four months of persistent job-hunting and freelance writing, Nellie Bly earned a tryout at Joseph Pulitzer's *New York World*, the nation's biggest paper. Her assignment: to investigate the deplorable conditions at the Women's Lunatic Asylum on Blackwell's Island. Her method: to get herself declared mad and committed to the asylum. After practicing the look of a disheveled lunatic in front of mirrors, wandering city streets unwashed and seemingly dazed, and terrifying her fellow boarders in a New York rooming house by acting crazy, she succeeded in convincing doctors and officials to commit her. Other New York newspapers reported her incarceration, speculating on the identity of this "mysterious waif," this "pretty crazy girl" with the "wild, hunted look in her eyes."[1]

Ten days later, an attorney from the *World* went in to get her out. Her two-part story appeared in October 1887 and caused a sensation. She was the first reporter to pull off such a stunt. In the days before objective journalism, Nellie Bly's dramatic first-person accounts documented harsh cold baths ("three buckets of water over my head—ice cold water—into my eyes, my ears, my nose and my mouth"); attendants who abused and taunted patients; and newly arrived immigrant women, completely sane, who were committed to this "rat trap" simply because no one could understand them. After the exposé, Bly was famous. Pulitzer gave her a permanent job, and New York City committed $1 million toward improving its asylums.

Within a year, Nellie Bly had exposed a variety of shady scam artists, corrupt politicians and lobbyists, and unscrupulous business practices. Posing as an "unwed mother" with an unwanted child, she uncovered an outfit trafficking in newborn babies. Disguised as a sinner in need of reform, she revealed the appalling conditions at a home for "unfortunate women." And after stealing fifty dollars from another woman's purse, she got herself arrested and then reported on how women were treated in New York jails.

A lifetime champion of women and the poor, Nellie Bly pioneered what was then called *detective* or *stunt* journalism. Her work inspired the twentieth-century prac-

tice of investigative journalism—from Ida Tarbell's exposés of oil corporations in the early 1900s to the 2008 Pulitzer Prize for investigative reporting, which was shared by the *Chicago Tribune,* for a series about defective and ultimately fatal toys, and the *New York Times,* for stories on toxic products imported from China.[2]

But such journalism can also be dangerous. Working for Dublin's *Sunday Independent,* Veronica Guerin was the first reporter to cover in depth Ireland's escalating organized crime and drug problem. In 1995, a man forced his way into her home and shot her in the thigh. After the assault, she wrote about the incident, vowing to continue her reporting despite her fears. She was also punched in the face by the suspected head of Ireland's gang world, who threatened to hurt Guerin's son and kill her if she wrote about him. She kept writing. In December 1995, she flew to New York to receive the International Press Freedom Award from the Committee to Protect Journalists.

When Guerin returned to Dublin, she began writing stories naming gang members suspected of masterminding drug-related crimes and a string of eleven unsolved contract murders. In June 1996, while stopped in her car at a Dublin intersection, she was shot five times by two hired killers on a motorcycle. She had become contract murder victim number twelve. Ireland and the world's journalists mourned Veronica Guerin's death. After her funeral, the Irish government invoked her name, creating laws that allowed judges to deny bail to dangerous suspects and opening a bureau to confiscate money and property from suspected drug criminals and gang members.

▲ ALONG WITH THEIR INVESTIGATIVE ROLE, newspapers play many other roles in contemporary culture. As chroniclers of daily life, newspapers both inform and entertain. By reporting on scientific, technological, and medical issues, newspapers disseminate specialized knowledge to the public. In reviews of films, concerts, exhibits, books, and plays, they shape cultural trends and tastes. Opinion pages trigger public debates and offer differing points of view. Syndicated columnists provide everything from advice on raising children to opinions on the U.S. role as an economic and military superpower. Newspapers help readers make choices about everything from what kind of food to eat to what kind of leaders to elect.

Despite the pervasive importance of newspapers in daily life, in today's digital age, the industry is losing both papers and readers. Newspapers still garner a significant portion of the nation's advertising dollars, but they have lost their near monopoly on classified advertising, much of which has shifted to popular Web sites like craigslist.org. According to the annual "State of the News Media" study by the Project for Excellence in Journalism (PEJ), in 2007 total newspaper ad revenues fell 7 percent across the industry, despite a 20 percent rise in online ad sales (compared to a 30 percent rise the year before). Because of the switch to online advertising, many investors in publicly held newspapers don't believe print papers have much of a future. The PEJ reports that newspaper stocks fell 42 percent from the start of 2005 through 2007. The loss of papers, readers, advertising, and investor confidence raises significant concerns in a nation where daily news has historically functioned to "speak truth to power" by holding elected officials responsible and acting as a watchdog for democratic life.[3]

In this chapter, we trace the history of newspapers through a number of influential periods and styles. We explore the early political-commercial press, the penny press, and yellow journalism. Turning to the modern era, we examine the influence of the *New York Times* and twentieth-century journalism's embrace of objectivity. We also look at interpretive journalism, which emerged in the 1920s and 1930s, and the revival of literary journalism, which followed in the 1960s. Finally, we review issues of chain ownership, new technology, citizen journalism, and the crucial role of newspapers in our democracy.

The Evolution of American Newspapers

The idea of news is as old as language itself. The earliest news was passed along orally from family to family, from tribe to tribe, by community leaders and oral historians. The earliest known written news account, or news sheet, *Acta Diurna* (Latin for "daily events"), was developed by Julius Caesar and posted in public spaces and on buildings in Rome in 59 B.C.E. Even in its oral and early written stages, news informed people on the state of their relations with neighboring tribes and towns. The development of the printing press in the fifteenth century greatly accelerated a society's ability to send and receive information. Throughout history, news has satisfied our need to know things we cannot experience personally. Newspapers today continue to document daily life and bear witness to both ordinary and extraordinary events.

Colonial Newspapers and the Partisan Press

The novelty and entrepreneurial stages of media development first happened in Europe with the rise of the printing press. In North America the first newspaper, *Publick Occurrences, Both Foreign and Domestick*, was published on September 25, 1690, by Boston printer Benjamin Harris. The colonial government objected to Harris's negative tone regarding British rule,

> "There's almost no media experience sweeter ... than poring over a good newspaper. In the quiet morning, with a cup of coffee—so long as you haven't turned on the TV, listened to the radio, or checked in online—it's as comfortable and personal as information gets."
>
> JON KATZ, *WIRED*, 1994

> "Oral news systems must have arrived early in the development of language, some tens or even hundreds of thousands of years ago. ... And the dissemination of news accomplishes some of the basic purposes of language: informing others, entertaining others, protecting the tribe."
>
> MITCHELL STEPHENS, *A HISTORY OF NEWS*, 1988

and local ministers were offended by his published report that the king of France had an affair with his son's wife. The newspaper was banned after one issue.

In 1704, the first regularly published newspaper appeared in the American colonies—the *Boston News-Letter*, published by John Campbell. Considered dull, it reported on events that had taken place in Europe months earlier. Because European news took weeks to travel by ship, these early colonial papers were not very timely. In their more spirited sections, however, the papers did report local illnesses, public floggings, and even suicides. In 1721, also in Boston, James Franklin, the older brother of Benjamin Franklin, started the *New England Courant*. The *Courant* established a tradition of running stories that interested ordinary readers rather than printing articles that appealed primarily to business and colonial leaders. In 1729, Benjamin Franklin, at age twenty-four, took over the *Pennsylvania Gazette* and created, according to historians, the best of the colonial papers. Although a number of colonial papers operated solely on subsidies from political parties, the *Gazette* also made money by advertising products.

Another important colonial paper, the *New-York Weekly Journal*, appeared in 1733. John Peter Zenger had been installed as the printer of the *Journal* by the Popular Party, a political group that opposed British rule and ran articles that criticized the royal governor of New York. After a Popular Party judge was dismissed from office, the *Journal* escalated its attack on the governor. When Zenger shielded the writers of the critical articles, he was arrested in 1734 for *seditious libel*—defaming a public official's character in print. Championed by famed Philadelphia lawyer Andrew Hamilton, Zenger ultimately won his case in 1735. A sympathetic jury, in revolt against the colonial government, decided that newspapers had the right to criticize government leaders as long as the reports were true. After the Zenger case, the British never prosecuted another colonial printer. The Zenger decision would later provide a key foundation—the right of a democratic press to criticize public officials—for the First Amendment to the Constitution, adopted as part of the Bill of Rights in 1791. (See Chapter 16 for more on the First Amendment.)

By 1765, about thirty newspapers operated in the American colonies, with the first daily paper beginning in 1784. Newspapers were of two general types: political or commercial. Their development was shaped in large part by social, cultural, and political responses to British rule

Newspapers: The Rise and Decline of Modern Journalism

First Colonial Newspaper
In 1690, Boston printer Benjamin Harris publishes the first North American newspaper—*Publick Occurrences, Both Foreign and Domestick* (p. 249).

First Precedent for Libel and Press Freedom
In 1734, printer John Peter Zenger is arrested for seditious libel; jury rules in Zenger's favor in 1735—establishing freedom of press and newspapers' right to criticize government (p. 250).

First Native American Newspaper
The *Cherokee Phoenix* appears in Georgia in 1828, giving a voice to tribal concerns as settlers encroach and move west (p. 266).

Yellow Journalism
Joseph Pulitzer buys the *New York World* in 1883; William Randolph Hearst buys the *New York Journal* in 1895 and battles Pulitzer during the heyday of the yellow journalism era (pp. 254–255).

1650 • **1800** • **1850** •

First African American Newspaper
Freedom's Journal begins short-lived operation in 1827, establishing a tradition of newspapers speaking out against racism (p. 264).

Penny Press
Printer Benjamin Day founds the *New York Sun* in 1833 and sets the price at one cent, helping usher in the penny press era and news for the working and emerging middle class (p. 252).

Nellie Bly
In October 1887, the *New York World* prints Nellie Bly's first article on the conditions of women's insane asylums in New York City—an early effort in investigative journalism (p. 248).

and by its eventual overthrow. The gradual rise of political parties and the spread of commerce also influenced the development of early papers. Although the political and commercial papers carried both party news and business news, they had different agendas. Political papers, known as the **partisan press**, generally pushed the plan of the particular political group that subsidized the paper. The *commercial press*, by contrast, served business leaders, who were interested in economic issues. Both types of journalism left a legacy. The partisan press gave us the editorial pages, while the early commercial press was the forerunner of the business section.

From the early 1700s to the early 1800s, even the largest of these papers rarely reached a circulation of fifteen hundred. Readership was primarily confined to educated or wealthy men who controlled local politics and commerce. During this time, though, a few pioneering women operated newspapers, including Elizabeth Timothy, the first American woman newspaper publisher (and mother of eight children). After her husband died of smallpox in 1738, Timothy took over the *South Carolina Gazette*, established in 1734 by Benjamin Franklin and the Timothy family. Also during this period, Anna Maul Zenger ran the *New-York Weekly Journal* throughout her husband's trial and after his death in 1746.[4]

COLONIAL NEWSPAPERS
During the colonial period, New York printer John Peter Zenger was arrested for libel. He eventually won his case, which established the precedent that today allows U.S. journalists and citizens to criticize public officials. In this 1734 issue, Zenger's *New-York Weekly Journal* reported his own arrest and the burning of the paper by the city's "Common Hangman."

- **First U.S.-Based Spanish Paper**
  New York's *El Diario-La Prensa* is founded in 1913 to serve Spanish-language readers (p. 265).

- **Catholic Worker**
  In 1933, Dorothy Day cofounds a religious organization; its radical monthly paper, the *Catholic Worker*, opposes war and supports social reforms (p. 267).

- **First Underground Paper**
  In 1955, the *Village Voice* begins operating in Greenwich Village (p. 266).

- **Postmodern News**
  In 1982, the Gannett chain launches *USA Today*, ushering in the postmodern era in news with the first paper modeled on television (p. 261).

- **Online Growth**
  By 2008, most U.S. newspapers offer some kind of online news service (p. 274).

900   **1950**   **2000**   **2050**

Modern Journalism
Adolph Ochs buys the *New York Times* in 1896, transforming it into "the paper of record" and jump-starting modern "objective" journalism (p. 256).

Watergate
Investigative reporting by Bob Woodward and Carl Bernstein of the *Washington Post* uncovers the Watergate scandal and leads to the resignation of President Richard Nixon in 1974 (p. 260).

First Online Paper
Ohio's *Columbus Dispatch* in 1980 becomes the first newspaper to go online (p. 261).

Dominance of Chains
Led by Gannett, the Top 10 newspaper chains by 2001 control more than one-half of the nation's total daily newspaper circulation (p. 273).

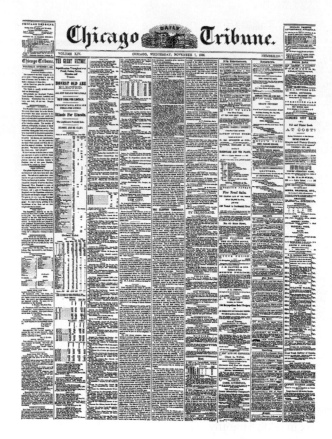

THE RISE OF THE DAILY NEWSPAPER
Launched in June 1847, the Midwest's first great newspaper was probably the *Chicago Tribune*. (In 1924, the *Tribune* launched Chicago's WGN Radio, its call letters reflecting the *Tribune* slogan, "World's Greatest Newspaper.") The headline from the paper above announces Abraham Lincoln's election as president in 1860.

The Penny Press Era: Newspapers Become Mass Media

By the late 1820s, the average newspaper cost six cents a copy and was sold through yearly subscriptions priced at ten to twelve dollars. Because that price was more than a week's salary for most skilled workers, newspaper readers were mostly affluent. By the 1830s, however, the Industrial Revolution made possible the replacement of expensive handmade paper with cheaper machine-made paper. During this time, the rise of the middle class spurred the growth of literacy, setting the stage for a more popular and inclusive press. In addition, breakthroughs in technology, particularly steam-powered presses replacing mechanical presses, permitted publishers to produce as many as four thousand newspapers an hour, which lowered the cost of newspapers. **Penny papers** soon began competing with six-cent papers. Though subscriptions remained the preferred sales tool of many penny papers, they began relying increasingly on daily street sales of individual copies.

Day and the *New York Sun*

In 1833, printer Benjamin Day founded the *New York Sun*. Day set the price at one penny and sold no subscriptions. The *Sun* (whose slogan was "It shines for all") highlighted local events, scandals, and police reports. It also ran serialized stories, making legends of frontiersmen Davy Crockett and Daniel Boone and blazing the trail for the media's enthusiasm for celebrity news. Like today's supermarket tabloids, the *Sun* fabricated stories, including the infamous moon hoax, which reported "scientific" evidence of life on the moon. Within six months, the *Sun's* lower price had generated a circulation of eight thousand, twice that of its nearest New York competitor.

The *Sun's* success initiated a wave of penny papers that favored **human-interest stories**: news accounts that focus on the daily trials and triumphs of the human condition, often featuring ordinary individuals facing extraordinary challenges. These kinds of stories reveal journalism's ties to literary traditions, which today can be found in everyday feature stories that chronicle the lives of remarkable people or in crime news that details the daily work of police and the misadventures of criminals. As was the case in the nineteenth century, crime stories remain popular and widely read.

Bennett and the *New York Morning Herald*

The penny press era also featured James Gordon Bennett's *New York Morning Herald*, founded in 1835. Bennett, considered the first U.S. press baron, freed his newspaper from political parties. He established an independent paper serving middle- and working-class readers as well as his own business ambitions. The *Herald* carried political essays and scandals, business stories, a letters section, fashion notes, moral reflections, religious news, society gossip, colloquial tales and jokes, sports stories, and, later, reports from the Civil War. In addition, Bennett's paper sponsored balloon races, financed safaris, and overplayed crime stories. Charles Dickens, after returning to Britain from his first visit to America in the early 1840s, used the *Herald* as a model for the sleazy *Rowdy Journal*, the fictional newspaper in his novel *Martin Chuzzlewit*. By 1860, the *Herald* reached nearly eighty thousand readers, making it the world's largest daily paper at the time.

Changing Economics and the Founding of the Associated Press

The penny papers were innovative. For example, they were the first to assign reporters to cover crime, and readers enthusiastically embraced the reporting of local news and crime. By gradu-

ally separating daily front-page reporting from overt political viewpoints on an editorial page, penny papers shifted their economic base from political parties to the market—to advertising revenue, classified ads, and street sales. Although many partisan papers took a moral stand against advertising some controversial products and services—such as medical "miracle" cures, the slave trade, and abortionists—the penny press became more neutral toward advertisers and printed virtually any ad. In fact, many penny papers regarded advertising as consumer news. The rise in ad revenues and circulation accelerated the growth of the newspaper industry. In 1830, 650 weekly and 65 daily papers operated in the United States, reaching a circulation of 80,000. By 1840, a total of 1,140 weeklies and 140 dailies attracted more than 300,000 readers.

In 1848, six New York newspapers formed a cooperative arrangement and founded the Associated Press (AP), the first major news wire service. **Wire services** began as commercial organizations that relayed news stories and information around the country and the world using telegraph lines and, later, radio waves and digital transmissions. In the case of the AP, the New York papers provided access to both their own stories and those from other newspapers. In the 1850s, papers started sending reporters to cover Washington, D.C., and in the early 1860s, more than a hundred reporters from northern papers went south to cover the Civil War, relaying their reports back to their home papers via telegraph and wire services. The news wire companies enabled news to travel rapidly from coast to coast and set the stage for modern journalism.

The marketing of news as a product and the use of modern technology to dramatically cut costs gradually elevated newspapers from an entrepreneurial stage to the status of a mass medium. By adapting news content, penny papers captured the middle- and working-class readers who could now afford the paper and also had more leisure time to read it. As newspapers sought to sustain their mass appeal, news and "factual" reports about crimes and other items of human interest eventually superseded the importance of partisan articles about politics and commerce.

The Age of Yellow Journalism: Sensationalism and Investigation

The rise of competitive dailies and the penny press triggered the next significant period in American journalism. In the late 1800s, **yellow journalism** emphasized profitable papers that

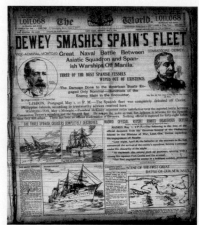

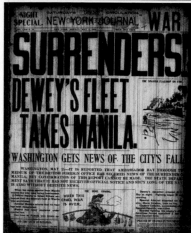

THE PENNY PRESS
The *World* (top) and the *New York Journal* (bottom) cover the same story in May 1898.

carried exciting human-interest stories, crime news, large headlines, and more readable copy. Generally regarded as sensationalistic and the direct forerunner of today's tabloid papers, reality TV, and newsmagazine shows like *Access Hollywood*, yellow journalism featured two major characteristics. First were the overly dramatic—or sensational—stories about crimes, celebrities, disasters, scandals, and intrigue. Second, and sometimes forgotten, are the legacy and roots that the yellow press provided for *investigative journalism*: news reports that hunted out and exposed corruption, particularly in business and government. Reporting increasingly became a crusading force for common people, with the press assuming a watchdog role on their behalf.

During this period, a newspaper circulation war pitted Joseph Pulitzer's *New York World* against William Randolph Hearst's *New York Journal*. A key player in the war was the first popular cartoon strip, *The Yellow Kid*, created in 1895 by artist R. F. Outcault, who once worked for Thomas Edison. The phrase *yellow journalism* has since become associated with the cartoon strip, which shuttled between the Hearst and Pulitzer papers during their furious battle for readers in the mid to late 1890s.

Pulitzer and the *New York World*

Joseph Pulitzer, a Jewish-Hungarian immigrant, began his career in newspaper publishing in the early 1870s as part owner of the *St. Louis Post*. He then bought the bankrupt *St. Louis Dispatch* for $2,500 at an auction in 1878 and merged it with the *Post*. The *Post-Dispatch* became known for stories that highlighted "sex and sin" ("A Denver Maiden Taken from Disreputable House") and satires of the upper class ("St. Louis Swells"). Pulitzer also viewed the *Post-Dispatch* as a "national conscience" that promoted the public good. He carried on the legacies of James Gordon Bennett: making money and developing a "free and impartial" paper that would "serve no party but the people." Within five years, the *Post-Dispatch* became one of the most influential newspapers in the Midwest.

In 1883, Pulitzer bought the *New York World* for $346,000. He encouraged plain writing and the inclusion of maps and illustrations to help immigrant and working-class readers understand the written text. In addition to running sensational stories on crime and sex, Pulitzer instituted advice columns and women's pages. Like Bennett, Pulitzer treated advertising as a kind of news that displayed consumer products for readers. In fact, department stores became major advertisers during this period. This contributed directly to the expansion of consumer culture and indirectly to the acknowledgment of women as newspaper readers. Eventually, because of pioneers like Nellie Bly, newspapers began employing women as reporters.

The *World* reflected the contradictory spirit of the yellow press. It crusaded for improved urban housing, better conditions for women, and equitable labor laws. It campaigned against monopoly practices by AT&T, Standard Oil, and Equitable Insurance. Such popular crusades helped lay the groundwork for tightening federal antitrust laws in the early 1910s. At the same time, Pulitzer's paper manufactured news events and staged stunts, such as sending star reporter Nellie Bly around the world in seventy-two days to beat the fictional "record" in the popular 1873 Jules Verne novel *Around the World in Eighty Days*. By 1887, the *World's* Sunday circulation had soared to more than 250,000, the largest anywhere.

Pulitzer created a lasting legacy by leaving $2 million to start the graduate school of journalism at Columbia University in 1912. In 1917, part of Pulitzer's Columbia endowment established the Pulitzer Prizes, the prestigious awards given each year for achievements in journalism, literature, drama, and music.

Hearst and the *New York Journal*

The *World* faced its fiercest competition when William Randolph Hearst bought the *New York Journal* (a penny paper founded by Pulitzer's brother Albert). Before moving to New York, the twenty-four-year-old Hearst took control of the *San Francisco Examiner* when his father, George

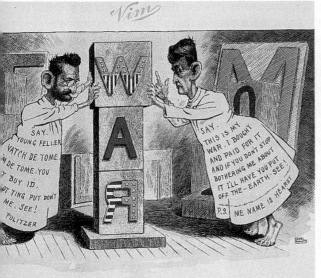

Hearst, was elected to the U.S. Senate in 1887 (the younger Hearst had recently been expelled from Harvard for playing a practical joke on his professors). In 1895, with an inheritance from his father, Hearst bought the ailing *Journal* and then raided Joseph Pulitzer's paper for editors, writers, and cartoonists.

Taking his cue from Bennett and Pulitzer, Hearst focused on lurid, sensational stories and appealed to immigrant readers by using large headlines and bold layout designs. To boost circulation, the *Journal* invented interviews, faked pictures, and encouraged conflicts that might result in a story. One tabloid account describes "tales about two-headed virgins" and "prehistoric creatures roaming the plains of Wyoming."[5] In promoting journalism as storytelling, Hearst reportedly said, "The modern editor of the popular journal does not care for facts. The editor wants novelty. The editor has no objection to facts if they are also novel. But he would prefer a novelty that is not a fact to a fact that is not a novelty."[6]

Hearst is remembered as an unscrupulous publisher who once hired gangsters to distribute his newspapers. He was also, however, considered a champion of the underdog, and his paper's readership soared among the working and middle classes. In 1896, the *Journal's* daily circulation reached 450,000, and by 1897, the Sunday edition of the paper rivaled the 600,000 circulation of the *World*. By the 1930s, Hearst's holdings included more than forty daily and Sunday papers, thirteen magazines (including *Good Housekeeping* and *Cosmopolitan*), eight radio stations, and two film companies. In addition, he controlled King Features Syndicate, which sold and distributed articles, comics, and features to many of the nation's dailies. Hearst, the model for Charles Foster Kane, the ruthless publisher in Orson Welles's classic 1940 film *Citizen Kane*, operated the largest media business in the world–the News Corp. of its day.

Competing Models of Modern Print Journalism

The early commercial and partisan presses were, to some extent, covering important events impartially. These papers often carried verbatim reports of presidential addresses and murder trials, or the annual statements of the U.S. Treasury. In the late 1800s, as newspapers pushed for greater circulation, newspaper reporting changed. Two distinct types of journalism

> "There is room in this great and growing city for a journal that is not only cheap but bright, not only bright but large ... that will expose all fraud and sham, fight all public evils and abuses— that will serve and battle for the people."
>
> JOSEPH PULITZER, PUBLISHER, *NEW YORK WORLD*, 1883

emerged: the story-driven model, dramatizing important events and used by the penny papers and the yellow press; and the "just the facts" model, an approach that appeared to package information more impartially, and was favored by the six-cent papers.[7] Underpinning these efforts is the question of whether, in journalism, there is an ideal, attainable objective model or whether the quest to be objective actually conflicts with journalists' traditional role of raising important issues about the abuses of power in a democratic society.

"Objectivity" in Modern Journalism

As the consumer marketplace expanded during the Industrial Revolution, facts and news became marketable products. Throughout the mid-1800s, the more a newspaper appeared not to take sides on its front pages, the more its readership base could be extended (although editorial pages were still often partisan). In addition, wire service organizations were serving a variety of newspaper clients in different regions of the country. To satisfy all their clients and the wide range of political views, newspapers began to look more impartial.

Ochs and the *New York Times*

The ideal of an impartial, or purely informational, news model was championed by Adolph Ochs, who bought the *New York Times* in 1896. The son of immigrant German Jews, Ochs grew up in Ohio and Tennessee, where at age twenty-one he took over the *Chattanooga Times* in 1878. Known more for his business and organizational ability than for his writing and editing skills, he transformed the Tennessee paper. Seeking a national stage and business expansion, Ochs moved to New York and invested $75,000 in the struggling *Times*. Through wise hiring, Ochs and his editors rebuilt the paper around substantial news coverage and provocative editorial pages. To distance the *Times* from the yellow press, the editors also downplayed sensational stories, favoring the documentation of major events or issues.

Partly as a marketing strategy, Ochs offered a distinct contrast to the more sensational Hearst and Pulitzer newspapers: an informational paper that provided stock and real estate reports to businesses, court reports to legal professionals, treaty summaries to political leaders, and theater and book reviews to educated general readers and intellectuals. Ochs's promotional gimmicks took direct aim at yellow journalism, advertising the *Times* under the motto "It does not soil the breakfast cloth." This strategy is similar to TV and Internet ads today that target upscale viewers who control a disproportionate share of consumer dollars.

With the Hearst and Pulitzer papers capturing the bulk of working- and middle-class readers, managers at the *Times* at first tried to use their straightforward, "no frills" reporting to appeal to more affluent and educated readers. In 1898, however, Ochs lowered the paper's price to a penny. He believed that people bought the *World* and the *Journal* primarily because they were cheap, not because of their stories. As a result, the *Times* began attracting middle-class readers who gravitated to the paper as a status marker for the educated and well informed. Between 1898 and 1899, its circulation rose from 25,000 to 75,000. By 1921, the *Times* had a daily circulation of 330,000, and 500,000 on Sunday. (For contemporary circulation figures, see Table 8.1.)

THE *NEW YORK TIMES* established itself as the official paper of record by the 1920s (below, the front page from 1865 declaring the end of the Civil War). The *Times* was the first modern newspaper, gathering information and presenting news in a straightforward way—without the opinion of the reporter. This continued when the *Times* went online (below, inset). On the Internet, reporters continue to present a short overview on the paper's home (or "front") page with links to the full story. As with print, though, the majority of readers do not read past the first "page" of an article.

Rank	Newspaper	Average Weekday Circulation
1	USA Today	2,284,219
2	Wall Street Journal	2,069,463
3	New York Times	1,077,256
4	Los Angeles Times	773,884
5	(New York) Daily News	703,137
6	New York Post	702,488
7	Washington Post	673,180
8	Chicago Tribune	541,663
9	Houston Chronicle	494,131
10	Arizona Republic	413,332

TABLE 8.1
THE NATION'S TEN LARGEST DAILY NEWSPAPERS, 2008
Source: Audit Bureau of Circulations FAS-FAX Report, March 31, 2008.

"Just the Facts, Please"

Early in the twentieth century, with reporters adopting a more "scientific" attitude to news- and fact-gathering, the ideal of objectivity began to anchor journalism. In **objective journalism**, which distinguishes factual reports from opinion columns, modern reporters strive to maintain a neutral attitude toward the issue or event they cover; they also search out competing points of view among the sources for a story.

The story form for packaging and presenting this kind of reporting has been traditionally labeled the **inverted-pyramid style**. Civil War correspondents developed this style by imitating the terse, compact press releases that came from President Abraham Lincoln's secretary of war, Edwin M. Stanton.[8] Often stripped of adverbs and adjectives, inverted-pyramid reports began—as they do today—with the most dramatic or newsworthy information. They answered who, what, where, when (and, less frequently, why or how) questions at the top of the story and then narrowed it down to less significant details. If wars or natural disasters disrupted the telegraph transmissions of these dispatches, the information the reporter chose to lead with had the best chance of getting through.

For much of the twentieth century, the inverted-pyramid style served as an efficient way to arrange a timely story. As one news critic pointed out, the wire services distributing stories to newspapers nationwide "had to deal with large numbers of newspapers with widely different political and regional interests. The news had to be 'objective' . . . to be accepted by such a heterogeneous group."[9] Among other things, the importance of objectivity and the reliance on the inverted pyramid signaled journalism's break from the partisan tradition. Although impossible to achieve (journalism is after all a literary practice, not a science), objectivity nonetheless became the guiding ideal of the modern press.

Despite the success of the *New York Times* and other modern papers, the more factual inverted-pyramid approach toward news has come under increasing scrutiny. As news critic and writing coach Roy Peter Clark has noted, "Some reporters let the pyramid control the content so that the news comes out homogenized. Traffic fatalities, three-alarm fires, and new city ordinances all begin to look alike. In extreme cases, reporters have been known to keep files of story forms. Fill in the blanks. Stick it in the paper."[10] Although the inverted-pyramid style has for years solved deadline problems for reporters and enabled editors to cut a story from the bottom to fit available space, it has also discouraged many readers from continuing beyond the key details in the opening paragraphs. Studies have demonstrated that the majority of readers do not follow a front-page story when it continues, or "jumps," inside the paper.

Interpretive Journalism

By the 1920s, there was a sense, especially after the trauma of World War I, that the impartial approach to reporting was insufficient for explaining complex national and global conditions. It was partly as a result of "drab, factual, objective reporting," one news scholar contended, that "the American people were utterly amazed when war broke out in August 1914, as they had no understanding of the foreign scene to prepare them for it."[11]

The Promise of Interpretive Journalism

Modern journalism had undermined an early role of the partisan press: offering analysis and opinion. But with the world becoming more complex, some papers began to re-explore the analytical function of news. The result was the rise of **interpretive journalism**, which aims to explain key issues or events and place them in a broader historical or social context. According to one historian, this approach, especially in the 1930s and 1940s, was a viable way for journalism to address "the New Deal years, the rise of modern scientific technology, the increasing interdependence of economic groups at home, and the shrinking of the world into one vast arena for power politics."[12] In other words, journalism took an analytic turn in a world grown more interconnected and complicated.

Noting that objectivity and factuality should serve as the foundation for journalism, by the 1920s editor and columnist Walter Lippmann insisted that the press should do more. He ranked three press responsibilities: (1) "to make a current record"; (2) "to make a running analysis of it"; and (3) "on the basis of both, to suggest plans."[13] Indeed, reporters and readers alike have historically distinguished between informational reports and editorial (interpretive) pieces, which offer particular viewpoints or deeper analyses of the issues. Since the boundary between information and interpretation can be somewhat ambiguous, American papers have traditionally placed news analysis in separate, labeled columns and opinion articles on certain pages so that readers do not confuse them with "straight news."

In the 1930s, the Great Depression and the Nazi threat to global stability helped news analysis take root in newsmagazines and radio commentary. First developed in the partisan era, editorial pages also made a strong comeback. More significant, however, was the growth of the political column. Although literary and humor columns existed prior to World War I, the political column was a new form. More than 150 syndicated columns developed between 1930 and 1934 alone. Moving beyond the informational and storytelling functions of news, journalists and newspapers began to extend their role as analysts.

The Challenge of Broadcast News

With the rise of radio in the 1930s, the newspaper industry became increasingly annoyed by broadcasters who took their news directly from papers and wire services. As a result, a battle developed between radio journalism and print news. Although they would eventually lose most of these cases in court, mainstream newspapers attempted to copyright facts reported in the news and even sued radio stations, which routinely used newspapers as their main news sources (a common practice to this day).

Editors and newspaper lobbyists argued that radio should be permitted to do only commentary. By conceding this interpretive role to radio, the print press tried to protect its dominion over "the facts." It was in this environment that radio analysis began to flourish as a form of interpretive news. Lowell Thomas delivered the first daily network analysis for CBS on September 29, 1930, attacking Hitler's rise to power in Germany. By 1941, twenty regular commentators—the forerunners of today's "talking heads" on cable, radio talk show hosts, and political bloggers—were explaining their version of the world to millions of listeners.

Some print journalists and editors came to believe that interpretive stories, rather than objective reports, could better compete with radio. They realized that interpretation was a way to counter radio's (and later television's) superior ability to report breaking news quickly. In 1933, the American Society of Newspaper Editors (ASNE) supported the idea of interpretive journalism. Newspapers, however, did not embrace probing analysis during the 1930s. Even Walter Lippmann believed that interpretation was misdirected without the foundation of facts and a "current record." As he put it, "the really important thing is to try and make opinion increasingly responsible to the facts."[14]

In most U.S. dailies, interpretation remained relegated to a few editorial and opinion pages. It wasn't until the 1950s—with the Korean War, the development of atomic power, tensions with the Soviet Union, and the anticommunist movement—that news analysis resurfaced on the newest medium: television. Interpretive journalism in newspapers grew at the same time, especially in such areas as the environment, science, agriculture, sports, health, politics, and business. Following the lead of the *New York Times*, many papers by the 1980s had developed an "op-ed" page—a page opposite the traditional editorial page that allowed a greater variety of columnists, news analyses, and letters to the editor.

Literary Forms of Journalism

By the late 1960s, many people were criticizing America's major social institutions. Political assassinations, Civil Rights protests, the Vietnam War, the drug culture, and the women's movement were not easily explained. Faced with so much change and turmoil, many individuals began to lose faith in the ability of institutions to oversee and ensure the social order. Members of protest movements as well as many middle- and working-class Americans began to suspect the privileges and power of traditional authority. As a result, key institutions—including journalism—lost some of their credibility.

Journalism as an Art Form

Throughout the first part of the twentieth century—journalism's modern era—journalistic storytelling was downplayed in favor of the inverted pyramid style and the separation of fact from opinion. Dissatisfied with these limitations, some reporters began exploring a new model of reporting. **Literary journalism**—sometimes dubbed "new journalism"—adapted fictional techniques, such as descriptive details and settings and extensive character dialogue, to nonfiction material and in-depth reporting. In the United States, literary journalism's roots are evident in nineteenth-century novelists like Mark Twain, Stephen Crane, and Theodore Dreiser, all of whom started out as reporters. In the late 1930s and 1940s, literary journalism surfaced: Journalists began to demonstrate how writing about real events could achieve an artistry often associated only with fiction.

In the 1960s, Tom Wolfe, a leading practitioner of new journalism, argued for mixing the *content* of reporting with the *form* of fiction to create "both the kind of objective reality of journalism" and "the subjective reality" of the novel.[15] Writers such as Wolfe (*The Electric Kool-Aid Acid Test*), Truman Capote (*In Cold Blood*), Joan Didion (*The White Album*),

"Journalists must make the significant interesting and relevant."

BILL KOVACH AND TOM ROSENSTIEL, *THE ELEMENTS OF JOURNALISM*, 2007

NEW JOURNALISM
Hunter S. Thompson (1937–2005), the most outrageous practitioner of new journalism, was a harsh critic of mainstream news and the ideal of objectivity. He was also the inspiration for the Uncle Duke character in the comic strip *Doonesbury* and for two Hollywood movies— *Where the Buffalo Roam* (1980) and *Fear and Loathing in Las Vegas* (1998). A longtime correspondent for *Rolling Stone*, he once called journalism "a cheap catch-all for . . . misfits—a false doorway to the backside of life." Much of his work, sometimes called gonzo journalism, tested the boundary between the objective and subjective.

Norman Mailer (*Armies of the Night*), and Hunter S. Thompson (*Hell's Angels*) turned to new journalism to overcome flaws they perceived in routine reporting. Their often self-conscious treatment of social problems gave their writing a perspective that conventional journalism did not offer.

After the 1960s' tide of intense social upheaval ebbed, new journalism subsided as well. However, literary journalism not only influenced magazines like *Mother Jones* and *Rolling Stone*, but it also affected daily newspapers by emphasizing longer feature stories on cultural trends and social issues with detailed description or dialogue. Today, writers such as Jon Krakauer (*Into the Wild*) and Adrian Nicole LeBlanc (*Random Family*) keep this tradition alive.

The Attack on Journalistic Objectivity

Former *New York Times* columnist Tom Wicker argued that in the early 1960s an objective approach to news remained the dominant model. According to Wicker, the "press had so wrapped itself in the paper chains of 'objective journalism' that it had little ability to report anything beyond the bare and undeniable facts."[16] Through the 1960s, attacks on the detachment of reporters escalated. News critic Jack Newfield condemned journalistic impartiality and argued that many reporters had become too trusting and uncritical of the powerful: "Objectivity is believing people with power and printing their press releases."[17] Eventually, the ideal of objectivity became suspect along with the authority of experts and professionals in various fields.

A number of reporters responded to the criticism by rethinking the framework of conventional journalism and adopting a variety of alternative techniques. One of these was *advocacy journalism*, in which the reporter actively promotes a particular cause or viewpoint. *Precision journalism*, another technique, attempted to make the news more scientifically accurate by using poll surveys and questionnaires. Throughout the 1990s, precision journalism became increasingly important. However, critics have charged that in every modern presidential campaign—including 2008—too many newspapers and TV stations became overly reliant on political polls, thus reducing campaign coverage to "race-horse" journalism, telling only "who's ahead" and "who's behind" stories rather than promoting substantial debates on serious issues. (See Table 8.2 for top works in American journalism.)

▶

TABLE 8.2

EXCEPTIONAL WORKS OF AMERICAN JOURNALISM

Working under the aegis of New York University's journalism department, thirty-six judges compiled a list of the Top 100 works of American journalism in the twentieth century. The list takes into account not just the newsworthiness of the event but the craft of the writing and reporting. What do you think of the Top 10 works listed here? What are some problems associated with making a list like this? Do you think newswriting should be judged in the same way we judge novels or movies?

Source: New York University, Department of Journalism, New York, N.Y., 1999.

	Journalists	Title or Subject	Publisher	Year
1	John Hersey	"Hiroshima"	*New Yorker*	1946
2	Rachel Carson	*Silent Spring*	Houghton Mifflin	1962
3	Bob Woodward/ Carl Bernstein	Watergate investigation	*Washington Post*	1972-73
4	Edward R. Murrow	Battle of Britain	CBS Radio	1940
5	Ida Tarbell	"The History of the Standard Oil Company"	*McClure's Magazine*	1902-04
6	Lincoln Steffens	"The Shame of the Cities"	*McClure's Magazine*	1902-04
7	John Reed	*Ten Days That Shook the World*	Random House	1919
8	H. L. Mencken	Coverage of the Scopes "monkey" trial	*Baltimore Sun*	1925
9	Ernie Pyle	Reports from Europe and the Pacific during World War II	Scripps-Howard newspapers	1940-45
10	Edward R. Murrow/ Fred Friendly	Investigation of Senator Joseph McCarthy	CBS Television	1954

Contemporary Journalism in the TV and Internet Age

In the early 1980s, a postmodern brand of journalism arose from two important developments. First, in 1980 the *Columbus Dispatch* became the first paper to go online. Today, nearly all U.S. papers offer some Web services. Second, the arrival of the colorful *USA Today* in 1982 radically changed the look of most major U.S. dailies.

USA Today Colors the Print Landscape

USA Today made its mark by incorporating features closely associated with postmodern forms, including an emphasis on visual style over substantive news or analysis and the use of brief news items that appealed to readers' busy schedules and shortened attention spans.

Now the most widely circulated paper in the nation, *USA Today* represents the only successful launch of a new major U.S. daily newspaper in the last several decades. Showing its marketing savvy, *USA Today* was the first paper to openly acknowledge television's central role in mass culture: The paper used TV-inspired color and designed its first vending boxes to look like color TVs. Even the writing style of *USA Today* mimics TV news by casting many reports in present tense rather than the past tense (which was the print-news norm throughout the twentieth century).

Writing for *Rolling Stone* in March 1992, media critic Jon Katz argued that the authority of modern newspapers suffered in the wake of a variety of "new news" forms that combined immediacy, information, entertainment, persuasion, and analysis. Katz claimed that the news supremacy of most prominent daily papers, such as the *New York Times* and the *Washington Post*, was being challenged by "news" coming from talk shows, television sitcoms, popular films, and even rap music. In other words, we were changing from a society in which the transmission of knowledge depended mainly on books, newspapers, and magazines to a society dominated by a mix of print, visual, and digital information.

Online Journalism Redefines News

These new forms of news began taking over the roles of traditional journalism, setting the nation's cultural, social, and political agendas. For instance, Matt Drudge, the conservative Internet news source and gossip behind *The Drudge Report*, hijacked the national agenda in January 1998 and launched a scandal when he posted a story claiming that *Newsweek* had backed off, or "spiked," a story about President Bill Clinton having an affair with White House intern Monica Lewinsky. Although Drudge's report was essentially accurate, *Newsweek* had delayed the story because its editors thought they needed more confirming sources before they could responsibly publish the allegations. Drudge effectively "outed" the *Newsweek* story prematurely, and critics debated whether his actions were legitimate or irresponsible.

Today, rather than subscribing to a traditional paper, many readers begin their day by logging on to the Internet and scanning a wide variety of news sources, including the sites of print papers, cable news channels, newsmagazines, bloggers, and online-only news sources.

USA TODAY—often called the first postmodern newspaper—began in 1982. It was the first daily newspaper to intentionally copy television, both in the TV-like look of its street vendor boxes and in its brief, compact stories.

This competition challenges newspapers, forcing their traditional role to change. For example, examine the way nontraditional TV and Internet media drove the story about the Reverend Jeremiah Wright during the 2008 Democratic campaign for president. As the former pastor of the Chicago church where candidate Barack Obama was a member, Wright had made several controversial statements—some of them highly critical of the U.S. government—that had been captured on video. After these clips spread on the Internet, mostly through YouTube, Obama criticized Wright's statements and delivered a major speech on race in America. However, the clips picked up momentum, and were aired on the 24/7 cable news channels for several months. In turn, the traditional TV network news and major newspapers felt obligated to cover the story, adding legitimacy and prolonging the media's attention. The Wright episode illustrates how a small story on the Internet can take on avalanche dimensions, picking up cable, network news, and newspapers as it careens downhill, forcing them to cover it.

Categorizing News and U.S. Newspapers

In the digital age, printed newspapers have to fight harder to keep their readers. By 2007, the nation's 1,430 daily papers were selling 53.5 million copies each weekday. This, however, was down from 2,600 dailies in 1910, the high-water mark for daily newspapers in the United States, and 1992, when weekday circulation was over 60 million.[18]

In the news industry today, there are several kinds of papers. *National newspapers* (such as the *Wall Street Journal*, the *New York Times*, the *Christian Science Monitor*, and *USA Today*) serve a broad readership across the country. Other papers primarily serve specific geographic regions. Roughly 100 *metropolitan dailies* have a circulation of 100,000 or more. About 35 of these papers have a circulation of more than 250,000. In addition, about 100 daily newspapers are classified as medium dailies, with circulations between 50,000 and 100,000. By far the largest number of U.S. dailies—about 1,200 papers—fall into the small daily category, with circulations under 50,000. While dailies serve urban and suburban centers, more than 8,000 nondaily and *weekly newspapers* (down from 14,000 back in 1910) serve smaller communities and average just over 5,000 copies per issue.[19]

Consensus vs. Conflict: Newspapers Play Different Roles

Smaller nondaily papers tend to promote social and economic harmony in their communities. Besides providing community calendars and meeting notices, nondaily papers focus on **consensus-oriented journalism**, carrying articles on local schools, social events, town government, property crimes, and zoning issues. Recalling the partisan spirit of an earlier era, small newspapers are often owned by business leaders who may also serve in local politics. Because consensus-oriented papers have a small advertising base, they are generally careful not to offend local advertisers, who provide the financial underpinnings for many of these papers. At their best, these small-town papers foster a sense of community; at their worst, they overlook or downplay discord and problems.

In contrast, national and metro dailies practice **conflict-oriented journalism**, in which front-page news is often defined primarily as events, issues, or experiences that deviate from social norms. Under this news orientation, journalists see their role not merely as neutral fact-gatherers but as observers who monitor their city's institutions and problems. They often maintain an adversarial relationship with local politicians and public officials. These papers offer competing perspectives on such issues as education, government, poverty, crime, and the

Media Literacy and the Critical Process

1 DESCRIPTION. Check a week's worth of business news in your local paper. Examine both the business pages and the front and local sections for these stories. Devise a chart and create categories for sorting stories (e.g., promotion news, scandal stories, earnings reports, home foreclosures, profit margins, and media-related news), and gauge whether these stories are positive or negative. If possible, compare this coverage to a week's worth of news from the business boom years of the 1990s. Or compare your local paper's coverage of the Enron trials, home foreclosures, or oil company profits to the coverage in one of the nation's dailies like the *New York Times*.

2 ANALYSIS. Look for patterns in the coverage. How many stories are positive? How many are negative? Do the stories show any kind of gender favoritism (such as more men covered than women) or class bias (management favored over workers)? Compared to the local paper, are there differences in the frequency and kinds of coverage offered in the national newspaper? Does your paper routinely cover the business of the parent company that owns the local paper? Does it cover national business stories? How many stories are there on the business of newspapers and media in general?

3 INTERPRETATION. What do some of the patterns mean? Did

Covering Business and Economic News

The 2001 collapse of Houston-based giant energy company Enron, the largest corporation ever to go bankrupt, put the spotlight on corporate corruption and journalism's coverage of such issues. Then in 2008 the subprime mortgage/home foreclosure crisis and record profits by oil companies led to new stories on lax government oversight of the banking and energy businesses. Over the years, critics have claimed that business news pages tend to favor issues related to management and downplay the role of everyday employees. Critics also charge that business news pages favor more positive business stories—such as manager promotions—and minimize negative business news (unlike the front pages, which usually emphasize routine crime news). In an era of corporate scandals, check the business coverage in your local daily paper to see if these charges are accurate or if business news coverage has changed.

you find examples where the coverage of business seems comprehensive and fair? If business news gets more positive coverage than political news, what might this mean? If managers get more coverage than employees, what does this mean, given that there are many more regular employees than managers at most businesses? What might it mean if men are more prominently featured than women in business stories? Considering the central role of media and news businesses in everyday life, what does it mean if these businesses are not being covered adequately by local and national news operations?

4 EVALUATION. Determine which papers and stories you would judge as good and which ones you would judge as weaker models for how business should be covered. Are some elements that should be included missing from coverage? If so, make suggestions.

5 ENGAGEMENT. Either write a letter to the editor reporting your findings or make an appointment with the editor to discuss what you discovered. Note what the newspaper is doing well and make a recommendation on how to improve coverage.

economy; and their publishers, editors, or reporters avoid playing major, overt roles in community politics. In theory, modern newspapers believe their role in large cities is to keep a wary eye fixed on recent local and state intrigue and events.

In telling stories about complex and controversial topics, conflict-oriented journalists often turn such topics into two-dimensional stories, pitting one idea or person against another. This convention, often called "telling both sides of a story," allows a reporter to take the position of a detached observer. Although this practice offers the appearance of balance, it usually functions to generate conflict and sustain a lively news story; sometimes reporters ignore the idea that there may be more than two sides to a story. But faced with deadline pressures, reporters often do not have the time—or the space—to develop a multifaceted and complex report or series of reports. (See "Media Literacy and the Critical Process: Covering Business and Economic News" on page 263.)

Ethnic, Minority, and Oppositional Newspapers

Historically, small-town weeklies and daily newspapers have served predominantly white, mainstream readers. However, since Benjamin Franklin launched the short-lived German-language *Philadelphische Zeitung* in 1732, newspapers aimed at ethnic groups have played a major role in initiating immigrants into American society. During the nineteenth century, Swedish- and Norwegian-language papers informed various immigrant communities in the Midwest. The early twentieth century gave rise to papers written in German, Yiddish, Russian, and Polish, assisting the massive influx of European immigrants.

Throughout the 1990s and into the twenty-first century, several hundred foreign-language daily and nondaily presses existed in at least forty different languages in the United States. Many are financially healthy today, supported by classified ads, local businesses, and increased ad revenue from long-distance phone companies and Internet services, which see the ethnic press as an ideal place to reach those customers most likely to need international communication services.[20]

Most of these weekly and monthly newspapers serve some of the same functions for their constituencies—minorities and immigrants, as well as disabled veterans, retired workers, gay and lesbian communities, and the homeless—as the "majority" papers do. These papers, however, are often published outside the social mainstream. Consequently, they provide viewpoints that are different from the mostly middle- and upper-class establishment attitudes that have shaped the media throughout much of America's history.

African American Newspapers

Between 1827 and the end of the Civil War in 1865, forty newspapers directed at black readers and opposed to slavery struggled for survival. These papers faced not only higher rates of illiteracy among readers but also hostility from white society and the majority press of the day. The first black newspaper, *Freedom's Journal*, operated from 1827 to 1829 and opposed the racism of many New York newspapers. In addition, it offered a voice for antislavery societies. Other notable papers included the *Alienated American* (1852-56) and the *New Orleans Daily Creole*, which began its short life in 1856 as the first black-owned daily in the South. The most influential oppositional newspaper at the time was Frederick Douglass's *North Star*, a weekly antislavery newspaper in Rochester, New York, which published from 1847 to 1860 and reached a circulation of three thousand. Douglass, a former slave, wrote essays on slavery and on a variety of national and international topics.

Since 1827, more than three thousand newspapers have been edited and owned by African Americans. These papers, with an average life span of nine years, took stands against race baiting, lynching, and the Ku Klux Klan. They also promoted racial pride long before the Civil Rights movement. The most widely circulated black-owned paper was Robert C. Vann's weekly *Pittsburgh Courier*, founded in 1910. Its circulation peaked at 350,000 in 1947—the year professional baseball was integrated by Jackie Robinson, thanks in part to relentless editorials in the *Courier* that denounced the color barrier in pro sports. As they have throughout their history, these papers offer oppositional viewpoints to the mainstream press and record the daily activities of black communities by listing weddings, births, deaths, graduations, meetings, and church functions. Today, there are more than 125 African American papers, including Baltimore's *Afro-American*, New York's *Amsterdam News*, and the *Chicago Defender*, which celebrated its one hundredth anniversary in 2005.

The circulation rates of most black papers dropped sharply, however, after the 1960s. The combined circulation of the local and national editions of the *Pittsburgh Courier*, for instance, dropped to only twenty thousand by the early 1980s.[21] Several factors contributed to these declines. First, television and black radio stations tapped into the limited pool of money that

FREDERICK DOUGLASS helped found the *North Star* in 1847. It was printed in the basement of the Memorial African Methodist Episcopal Zion Church, a gathering spot for abolitionists and "underground" activities in Rochester, New York. At the time, the white-owned *New York Herald* urged Rochester's citizens to throw the *North Star*'s printing press into Lake Ontario. Under Douglass's leadership, the paper came out weekly until 1860, addressing problems facing blacks around the country and offering a forum for Douglass to debate his fellow black activists.

"We wish to plead our own cause. Too long have others spoken for us."

FREEDOM'S JOURNAL, 1827

businesses allocated for advertising. Second, some advertisers, to avoid controversy, withdrew their support when the black press started giving favorable coverage to the Civil Rights movement in the 1960s. Third, the loss of industrial urban jobs in the 1970s and 1980s not only diminished readership but also hurt small neighborhood businesses, which could no longer afford to advertise in both the mainstream and the black press. Finally, after the enactment of Civil Rights and affirmative action laws, black papers were raided by mainstream papers seeking to integrate their newsrooms with good black journalists. Black papers could seldom match the offers from large white-owned dailies.

In siphoning off both ads and talent, a more integrated mainstream press diminished the status of many black papers—an ironic effect of the Civil Rights laws. In 2007, while one-third of the overall U.S. population was classified as part of a minority group, only 13.5 percent of the newsroom staffs at the nation's 1,400-plus daily papers were minorities, with blacks accounting for 2,790 or 5.3 percent of the newsroom workforce.[22]

AFRICAN AMERICAN NEWSPAPERS
This 1936 scene reveals the newsroom of Harlem's *Amsterdam News*, one of the nation's leading African American newspapers. Ironically, the Civil Rights movement and affirmative action policies in the 1960s served to drain talented reporters from the black press by encouraging them to work for mainstream white newspapers.

Spanish-Language Newspapers

Bilingual and Spanish-language newspapers have long served a variety of Mexican, Puerto Rican, Cuban, and other Hispanic readerships. New York's *El Diario-La Prensa* has been serving Spanish-language readers since 1913, while Los Angeles' *La Opinión* was founded in 1926 and was the nation's largest Spanish-language daily. The two papers merged in 2004.[23] Other prominent publications are in Miami (*La Voz* and *Diario Las Americas*), Houston (*La Información*), Chicago (*El Mañana Daily News* and *La Raza*), San Diego (*El Sol*), and New York (*Hoy, El Noticias del Mundo*). By the 2000s, more than fifteen hundred Spanish-language papers operated in the United States, reaching more than 17.6 million readers nationwide, an increase of 5 million since 1984.[24]

Until the late 1960s, Hispanic issues and culture were virtually ignored by mainstream newspapers. But with the influx of Mexican, Puerto Rican, and Cuban immigrants throughout the 1980s and 1990s, many mainstream papers began to feature weekly Spanish-language supplements. The first was the *Miami Herald*'s "El Nuevo Herald," introduced in 1976. Other mainstream papers also joined in, but many folded their Spanish-language supplements by the mid-1990s. In 1995, the *Los Angeles Times* discontinued its supplement, "Nuestro Tiempo," and the *Miami Herald* trimmed budgets and staff for "El Nuevo Herald." Spanish-language radio and television had beaten the papers to these potential customers and advertisers. By 2007, as the U.S. Hispanic population reached about 14 percent, Hispanic journalists accounted for only about 4.5 percent of the newsroom workforce at U.S. daily newspapers.[25]

EL DIARIO-LA PRENSA is the oldest Spanish-language newspaper in the United States. Dominant in the New York City market, the paper has almost 300,000 daily readers.

THE *WORLD JOURNAL* is a national daily paper that targets Chinese immigrants by focusing on news from China, Hong Kong, Taiwan, and other Southeast Asian communities.

Asian American Newspapers

In the 1980s, hundreds of small papers emerged to serve immigrants from Pakistan, Laos, Cambodia, and China. More than fifty small U.S. papers are now printed in Vietnamese. Ethnic papers like these help readers both adjust to foreign surroundings and retain ties to their traditional heritage. In addition, these papers often cover major stories that are downplayed in the mainstream press. For example, in the aftermath of 9/11, airport security teams detained thousands of Middle Eastern-looking men. The *Weekly Bangla Patrika*, a Long Island, New York, paper with a circulation of twelve thousand, not only reported in detail on the one hundred people the Bangladeshi community lost in the World Trade Center attacks but also took the lead in reporting on how it feels to be innocent yet targeted by ethnic profiling at New York's major airports.[26]

Native American Newspapers

An activist Native American press has provided oppositional voices to mainstream American media since 1828, when the *Cherokee Phoenix* appeared in Georgia. Another prominent early paper was the *Cherokee Rose Bud*, founded in 1848 by tribal women in the Oklahoma territory. The Native American Press Association has documented more than 350 different Native American papers, most of them printed in English but a few in tribal languages. Currently, two national papers are the *Native American Times*, which offers a Native American perspective on "sovereign rights, civil rights, and government-to-government relationships with the federal government," and *Indian Country Today*, owned by the Oneida nation in New York State.

To counter the neglect of their culture's viewpoints by the mainstream press, Native American newspapers have helped to educate various tribes about their heritage and build community solidarity. These papers also have reported on both the problems and the progress among tribes that have opened casinos and gambling resorts. Overall, these smaller papers provide a forum for debates on tribal conflicts and concerns, and they often signal the mainstream press on issues—such as gambling or hunting and fishing rights—that have significance for the larger culture.

The Underground Press

The mid to late 1960s saw an explosion of alternative newspapers. Labeled the *underground press* at the time, these papers questioned mainstream political policies and conventional values. Generally running on shoestring budgets, they often voiced radical opinions and were erratic in meeting publication schedules. Springing up on college campuses and in major cities, underground papers were inspired by the writings of socialists and intellectuals from the 1930s and 1940s and by a new wave of thinkers and artists. Particularly inspirational were poets and writers (such as Allen Ginsberg, Jack Kerouac, LeRoi Jones, and Eldridge Cleaver) and "protest" musicians (including Bob Dylan, Pete Seeger, and Joan Baez). In criticizing social institutions, alternative papers questioned the official reports distributed by public relations agents, government spokespeople, and the conventional press (see "Case Study–Alternative Journalism: Dorothy Day and I. F. Stone" on page 267).

During the 1960s, underground papers played a unique role in documenting social tension by including the voices of students, women, blacks, Native Americans, gay men and lesbians, and others whose opinions were often excluded from the mainstream press. The first and most enduring underground paper, the *Village Voice*, was founded in Greenwich Village in 1955. Today its circulation is 250,000 and it is still distributed free, surviving only through advertising. Among campus underground papers, the *Berkeley Barb* was the most influential, developing amid the free-speech movement in the mid-1960s. Despite their irreverent and often vulgar

Alternative Journalism:
Dorothy Day and I. F. Stone

Over the years, a number of unconventional reporters have struggled against the status quo to find a place for unheard voices and alternative ways to practice their craft. For example, Ida Wells fearlessly investigated violence against blacks for the *Memphis Free Speech* in the late 1800s. Newspaper lore also offers a rich history of alternative journalists and their publications, such as Dorothy Day's *Catholic Worker* and *I. F. Stone's Weekly*.

In 1933, Dorothy Day (1897–1980) cofounded a radical religious organization with a monthly newspaper, the *Catholic Worker*, that opposed war and supported social reforms. Like many young intellectual writers during World War I, Day was a pacifist; she also joined the Socialist Party. Quitting college at age eighteen to work as an activist reporter for socialist newspapers, Day participated in the ongoing suffrage movement to give women the right to vote. Throughout the 1930s, her Catholic Worker organization invested in thirty hospices for the poor and homeless, providing food and shelter for five thousand people a day. This legacy endures today, with the organization continuing to fund soup kitchens and homeless shelters throughout the country.

For more than seventy years, the *Worker* has consistently advocated personal activism to further social justice, opposing anti-Semitism, Japanese American internment camps during World War II, nuclear weapons, the Korean War, military drafts, and the communist witch-hunts of the 1950s. The *Worker's* circulation peaked in 1938 at 190,000, then fell dramatically during World War II, when Day's pacifism was at odds with much of America. Today the *Catholic Worker* has a circulation of 80,000.

I. F. Stone (1907–1989) shared Dorothy Day's passion for social activism. He also started early, publishing his own monthly paper at the age of fourteen and becoming a full-time reporter by age twenty. He worked as a Washington political writer for the *Nation* in the early 1940s and later for the *New York Daily Compass*. Throughout his career, Stone challenged the conventions and privileges of both politics and journalism. In 1941, for example, he resigned from the National Press Club when it refused to serve his guest, the nation's first African American federal judge. In the early 1950s, he actively opposed Joseph McCarthy's rabid search to rid government and the media of alleged communists.

When the *Daily Compass* failed in 1952, the radical Stone was unable to find a newspaper job and decided to create his own newsletter, *I. F. Stone's Weekly*, which he published for nineteen years. Practicing interpretive and investigative reporting, Stone became as adept as any major journalist at tracking down government records to discover contradictions, inaccuracies, and lies. Over the years, Stone questioned decisions by the Supreme Court, investigated the substandard living conditions of many African Americans, and criticized political corruption. He guided the *Weekly* to a circulation that reached 70,000 during the 1960s, when he probed American investments of money and military might in Vietnam.

I. F. Stone and Dorothy Day embodied a spirit of independent reporting that has been threatened by the decline in newspaper readership and the rise of chain ownership. Stone, who believed that alternative ideas were crucial to maintaining a healthy democracy, once wrote that "there must be free play for so-called 'subversive' ideas—every idea 'subverts' the old to make way for the new. To shut off 'subversion' is to shut off peaceful progress and to invite revolution and war."[1]

Willamette Week
Portland, Ore.

City Pages
Minneapolis/
St. Paul, Minn.

Pittsburgh
City Paper

Westword
Denver, Colo.

Chicago Reader

Boston Phoenix

San Francisco
Bay Guardian

Village Voice
New York City

Washington
City Paper

LA Weekly

Independent Weekly
Chapel Hill, N.C.

Salt Lake City Weekly

Creative Loafing
Atlanta, Ga.

Austin Chronicle
Austin, Tex.

Riverfront Times
St. Louis, Mo.

Gambit Weekly
New Orleans, La.

Miami New Times

FIGURE 8.1

**SELECTED ALTERNATIVE
NEWSPAPERS IN THE
UNITED STATES**

*Source: Association of Alternative
Newsweeklies, www.aan.org.*

"We received no
extra space for
9/11. We received
no extra space for
the Iraq war. We're
all doing this within
our budget. It is a
zero-sum game.
If something is
more important,
something else
may be a little less
important, a little
less deserving of
space."

JOHN GEDDES,
MANAGING EDITOR,
NEW YORK TIMES,
2006

tone, many underground papers turned a spotlight on racial and gender inequities and, on occasion, influenced mainstream journalism to examine social issues. Like the black press, though, many early underground papers folded after the 1960s. Given their radical outlook, it was difficult for them to generate sponsors or appeal to advertisers. In addition, like the black press, the underground press was raided by mainstream papers, which began expanding their own coverage of culture by hiring the underground's best writers. Still, today more than 120 papers are members of the Association of Alternative Newsweeklies (see Figure 8.1).

Newspaper Operations

Today a weekly paper might employ only two or three people, while a major metro daily might have a staff of more than one thousand, including workers in the newsroom and online operations, and in departments for circulation (distributing the newspaper), advertising (selling ad space), and mechanical operations (assembling and printing the paper). In either situation, however, most newspapers distinguish business operations from editorial or news functions. Journalists' and readers' praise or criticism usually rests on the quality of a paper's news and editorial components, but the business and advertising divisions drive today's industry.

Most major daily papers devote one-half to two-thirds of their pages to advertisements. Accounting for about 17-18 percent of all ad dollars spent annually in the United States, newspapers carry everything from expensive full-page spreads for department stores to classifieds, which consumers can purchase for a few dollars to advertise used cars, furniture, and old TVs. In most cases, ads are positioned in the paper first. The **newshole**–space not taken up by ads–accounts for the remaining 35 to 50 percent of the content of daily newspapers, including front-page news reports, horoscopes, and advice columns.

News and Editorial Responsibilities

The chain of command at most larger papers starts with the publisher and owner at the top and then moves, on the news and editorial side, to the editor in chief and managing editor, who are in charge of the daily news-gathering and writing processes. Under the main editors, assistant editors and news managers run different news divisions, including features, sports, photos, local news, state news, and wire service reports that contain much of the day's national and international news. In addition, copy editors check each story for accuracy, style, and grammar, and write the headlines for each report.

Reporters work for editors and are grouped into two broad categories: *general assignment reporters,* who handle all sorts of stories that might emerge–or "break"–in a given day, and *specialty reporters,* who are assigned to particular beats (police, courts, schools, government) or topics (education, religion, health, environment, technology). On large dailies, *bureau reporters* also file reports from other major cities, such as Washington, D.C., or their state's capital. Daily papers feature columnists and critics; these reporters have usually worked their way up the hierarchy and may review or analyze everything from fashion to foreign policy.

By the early 2000s, many newspapers employed a separate staff for their online operations, even though the vast majority of these operations were losing money. In recent years, media convergence has meant that most traditional print reporters are now expected to file online versions of their stories first. Many reporters are now also asked to carry digital cameras to

record images or video to complement their online stories. Such practices allow newspapers to make the news as timely as possible and better compete with the immediacy of radio and television. Still, online demands and newsroom cutbacks have put a strain on reporters and editors, who are increasingly being asked to do stories in multiple formats. According to the American Society of Newspaper Editors (ASNE), the workforce in daily U.S. newsrooms declined by 4.4 percent in 2007, the largest percentage decrease in the newsrooms since ASNE began its annual study in the late 1970s.[27]

Wire Services and Feature Syndication

Major daily papers might have between one hundred and two hundred local reporters and writers, but they still cannot cover the world or produce enough material to fill up the newshole each day. Newspapers also rely on wire services and syndicated feature services to supplement local coverage. A few major dailies, such as the *New York Times*, run their own wire services, selling their stories to other papers to reprint. Other agencies, such as the Associated Press (AP) and United Press International (UPI), have hundreds of staffers stationed throughout major U.S. cities and world capitals. They submit stories and photos each day for distribution to newspapers across the country. Some U.S. papers also subscribe to foreign wire services, such as Agence France-Presse in Paris or Reuters in London.

Daily papers generally pay monthly fees for access to all wire stories. Although they use only a fraction of what is available over the wires, editors carefully monitor wire services each day for important stories and ideas for local angles. Wire services have greatly expanded the national and international scope of news, as local editors put their trust in a handful of powerful wire firms when they select a newsworthy issue or event for reprinting.

In addition, **feature syndicates**, such as United Features and Tribune Media Services, are commercial outlets that contract

© MATSON ST. LOUIS POST-DISPATCH

STUBBORN AS A...

> "Teens have a greater interest in news than the generations before them. Newspapers have a great future as news organizations on the Web and perhaps elsewhere. Sadly, today in America when a newspaper reader dies, he or she is not replaced by a new reader."
>
> JEFFERY COLE, DIRECTOR, CENTER FOR THE DIGITAL FUTURE, USC ANNENBERG SCHOOL, 2006

with newspapers to provide work from the nation's best political writers, editorial cartoonists, comic-strip artists, and self-help columnists. These companies serve as brokers, distributing horoscopes and crossword puzzles as well as the political columns and comic strips that appeal to a wide audience. When a paper bids on and acquires the rights to a cartoonist or columnist, it signs exclusivity agreements with a syndicate to ensure that it is the only paper in the region to carry, say, *Dilbert*, Clarence Page, Maureen Dowd, Bob Herbert, George Will, Anna Quindlen, or cartoonist Tom Toles. Feature syndicates, like wire services, wield great influence in determining which writers and cartoonists gain national prominence.

Challenges Facing Newspapers

Publishers and journalists today face worrisome issues like the decline in newspaper readership and the failure of many papers to attract younger readers. However, other problems persist as well, including the inability of most cities to support competing newspapers and the capability of Web sites to vie with newspapers for lucrative classified advertising. Finally, the newspaper industry also struggles to find its place on the Internet, trying to figure out the future of digital news.

Readership Declines in the United States

The decline in newspaper readership began during the Depression, with the rise of radio. Between 1931 and 1939, six hundred newspapers ceased operation. Another big circulation crisis occurred from the late 1960s through the 1970s with the rise in network television viewing and greater competition from suburban weeklies. In addition, with an increasing number of women working full-time outside the home, newspapers could no longer consistently count on one of their core readership groups. (In fact, by 2007, women made up only 44 percent of all daily newspaper readers.) By the mid-2000s, circulation dropped by more than 20 percent in the nation's twenty largest cities (even though the population declined by only 6 percent in those areas).[28] The "State of the News Media 2008" report showed that readership since 2000 had declined 1 to 2 percent each year among most demographic groups, with the largest decline– 10 percent–among thirty-five-to-forty-four-year-olds. In 2000, 53 percent of that age group said they read a paper in a typical week, but that fell to 43 percent in 2007.[29]

Between 1970 and 1990, yearly circulation flattened out at just over 60 million copies per day. By 2007, though, only 52 million copies circulated each weekday and 54 million on Sunday. Although the overall population increased during that period, the percentage of adults who read a paper at least once a day dropped from 78 percent in 1970 to 51 percent by 2007 (58 percent on Sunday). In all, between 1950 and 2007, the number of daily papers in the United States dropped from 1,772 to fewer than 1,440. (For a new trend, see "Case Study: Newspaper Circulation Up! [for Free Papers]" on page 271.)

Remarkably, while the United States continues to experience declines in newspaper readership and advertising dollars, many other nations–where Internet news is still emerging– are experiencing increases. For example, in 2007 the World Association of Newspapers (WAN) reported that global newspaper sales were up 2.3 percent in 2006 and up 9.5 percent over the previous five years. Total newspaper sales increased in Asia, Europe, Africa, and South America, "with North America the sole continent to register a decline."[30] Worldwide, newspaper ad revenues were up 3.8 percent in 2006 and 15.8 percent over the previous five years. WAN reports that in 2007 "more than 515 million people buy a newspaper each day, up from 488 million in 2002."[31] The five top countries for daily newspaper sales for 2006 included China (99 million copies), India (89 million), Japan (69 million), United States (52 million), and Germany (21 million).

Newspaper Circulation Up! (for Free Papers)

The big story about the mainstream newspaper industry in the 2000s has been the decline of circulation and revenue for the print version, and the slow but promising growth of online editions. But in one segment of the newspaper industry—free newspapers—circulation is actually up; way up.

Unless you live in a large city with public transportation, you might not have even noticed. But take a trip to places like New York, Philadelphia, Baltimore, Washington, Boston, Chicago, Dallas, Denver, San Diego, or San Francisco, and you'll find free newspapers at newsracks, pushed by hawkers at entrances to subway and rail stations, and even delivered to certain neighborhoods.

There have been free alternative weekly newspapers in the United States since the 1950s. But the free newspapers that have emerged in the past decade are different: They're daily, they're widely available, and they're becoming immensely popular in the United States and worldwide.

Piet Bakker, a communications professor at the University of Amsterdam, is the leading expert on the free newspaper industry (see www.newspaperinnovation .com). He notes that 36 million copies of free dailies are now circulated in forty-nine countries, including Korea, Chile, Austria, and Botswana. The growth in Europe—where the world's first free commuter daily began in Sweden in 1995—has been especially phenomenal. The continent's total circulation of free dailies has grown five times over since 2000—to 125 titles with a combined circulation of 26.5 million by 2007. The market is highly competitive, with most of Europe's major cities having three or more free dailies. In at least a dozen European countries, the top paper is a free daily, and in Spain, Denmark, and Iceland, free dailies command a greater total market share than paid newspapers.

Free dailies are available in every major Canadian metro area, and now account for 20 percent of the nation's newspaper market share. In the United States, where growth has been steady but not quite as fast, there are now forty free newspapers with a combined circulation of more than 3 million.

New York has one of the liveliest free newspaper markets. Hawkers wearing green vests for *Metro New York* and red vests for *amNew York* plant themselves at opposite sides of sidewalk entrances to busy subway steps and press their papers into commuters' hands. The two newspapers illustrate ownership patterns in the free daily market, as some companies specialize in free dailies, while others develop free dailies to complement their established "paid" daily newspaper business. *Metro New York* is published by Metro International, a Luxembourg-based company that is the largest free daily publisher in the world, with newspapers in more than one hundred cities. The Tribune Company, publisher of the *Chicago Tribune* and several other newspapers, owns *amNewYork* as a way to maintain a presence in the New York market.

Although the free dailies don't make money on subscriptions, they are inexpensive to operate. They tend to be slim tabloids, with wire copy and short, easy-to-read stories developed by a small editorial staff. The newspapers are designed to be read in twenty minutes, the time of the average commute (in fact, some European free dailies call themselves "20 Minutes"). As Metro International says, their newspapers target "a high proportion of young and active, professional readers. This demographic group is not typically reading daily newspapers but is most attractive for advertisers." One company in the United States goes one step further in targeting upscale audiences. In 2004, Denver media billionaire Philip Anschutz bought the *San Francisco Examiner* (once the flagship newspaper of William Randolph Hearst) and converted it into a free daily. The company has since launched the *Washington Examiner* and *Baltimore Examiner*, and delivers them free to wealthy neighborhoods, a practice one Bay Area media critic likened to "a kind of 21st century journalistic redlining," where the poorer neighborhoods get excluded.[1]

But a study by the *New York Times* and Scarborough Research found encouraging news in the free newspaper trend for both traditional newspapers and democracy. First, it found that free dailies don't cannibalize paid newspapers. In fact, many paid newspaper readers use free dailies as a secondary newspaper source. Second, it discovered that free papers bring in new readers who have often shunned the paid papers—"the young, those from lower to moderate income households, and non-white ethnic groups."[2] Acculturating new people into the daily habit of newspaper readership is ultimately a good thing for the future health of the newspaper industry and for democracy. ◢

FREE NEWSPAPERS
The Tribune Company's *amNew York* and Metro International's *Metro New York* are distributed free in subway stations and other high pedestrian traffic locations.

India in particular is a growth area for newspapers, with "more than 150 million people" reading a paper each day, "compared to 97 million Americans and 48 million Germans."[32]

Joint Operating Agreements Combat Declining Competition

Although the regulation preventing newspaper monopolies has lessened, the government continues to monitor the declining number of newspapers in various American cities as well as mergers in cities where competition among papers might be endangered. In the mid-1920s, about five hundred American cities had two or more newspapers with separate owners. However, by 2008, fewer than fifteen cities had independent, competing papers. In 1995, for example, the *Houston Post* folded, leaving the nation's fourth-largest city with only one daily paper, the *Houston Chronicle*. In 1998, the *Nashville Banner* closed, leaving the Gannett-owned *Tennessean* as the dominant daily print game in town.

In 1970 Congress passed the Newspaper Preservation Act, which enabled failing papers to continue operating through a **joint operating agreement (JOA)**. Under a JOA, two competing papers keep separate news divisions while merging business and production operations for a period of years. Since the act, twenty-eight cities have adopted JOAs. In 2008, just nine JOAs remained in place—in Charleston, West Virginia; Denver; Detroit; Fort Wayne, Indiana; Las Vegas; Salt Lake City; Seattle; Tucson; and York, Pennsylvania. Although JOAs and mergers have monopolistic tendencies, they sometimes have been the only way to maintain competition between newspapers. The success of JOAs, though, is variable. When a JOA in Cincinnati expired in 2007, the *Cincinnati Post* couldn't survive on its own and folded, leaving only the Gannett-owned *Enquirer*.

In another example, Detroit was one of the most competitive newspaper cities in the nation until 1989. The *Detroit News* and the *Detroit Free Press* both ranked among the ten most widely circulated papers in the country and sold their weekday editions for just fifteen cents a copy. Faced with declining revenue, the papers' managers asked for and received a JOA in 1989. In the largest JOA to date, the *News*, then owned by Gannett, and the *Free Press*, then owned by Knight Ridder, began sharing business and production operations, while maintaining separate news and editorial departments. In 1995, a prolonged and bitter strike by several unions sharply reduced circulation. One union concern involved reduced competition under the JOA, which allowed both papers to cut jobs to sustain high profits for stockholders. Before the strike, Gannett and Knight Ridder had both reported profit margins of well over 15 percent on all their newspaper holdings.[33] In 2005,

NEWSROOMS
In this photo of the *Seattle Post-Intelligencer* newsroom, employees stop to watch a press conference on a dispute over its JOA with the *Seattle Times*. The *Post-Intelligencer* was started in 1863. Hearst bought the paper in 1921 and it remains part of the Hearst Corporation today.

Gannett sold the *News* to MediaNews Group and bought the *Free Press*. While both were ranked in the Top 10 circulated papers in the 1980s, neither paper was ranked in the Top 25 in 2008.

Newspaper Chains Consolidate Ownership

Edward Wyllis Scripps founded the first **newspaper chain**—a company that owns several papers throughout the country—in the 1890s. By the 1920s, there were about 30 chains in the United States, each one owning an average of five papers. The emergence of chains paralleled the major business trend during the twentieth century: the movement toward oligopolies in which fewer and fewer corporations control each industry.

By the 1980s, more than 130 chains owned an average of nine papers each, with the 12 largest chains accounting for 40 percent of the total circulation in the United States. By the early 2000s, the Top 10 chains controlled more than one-half of the nation's total daily newspaper circulation. Gannett, for example, the nation's largest chain, owns about eighty-five daily papers (and a thousand more nondailies), ranging from small suburban papers to the *Cincinnati Enquirer*, the *Nashville Tennessean*, and *USA Today*. (See "What Gannett Owns".)

Around 2005, the consolidation trend in newspaper ownership had leveled off. Despite the fact that most newspapers still generated 10 to 20 percent profit margins, the decline in newspaper circulation and ad sales led to panic with investors and major declines in the stock value for newspapers. Many newspaper chains responded by reducing their newsroom staffs significantly. The effects were nationwide as papers from the *Atlanta Journal-Constitution* to the *Minneapolis Star Tribune* and the *Seattle Times* suffered staff cuts. In fact, the "State of the News Media 2008" report says that since 1990, there are 25 percent fewer reporters now working in mainstream U.S. newsrooms.[34]

The cost cutting was particularly wrenching at the *Los Angeles Times*, which was bought by the Chicago-based Tribune Company in 2000. Continuing demands from the corporate offices for more cost reductions led to the resignation of editor John Carroll in 2005. In 2006, new editor Dean Baquet and publisher Jeffrey Johnson also resigned to protest demands for further cuts, which they said would damage the journalism capabilities of the *Times*. More cuts in 2007 resulted in the departures of some of the most talented staff members, including six Pulitzer Prize winners. The newsroom staff dropped to 850 from about 1,200 in 2000.[35] In 2007, the Tribune Company was bought by a private investor, Chicago real estate developer Sam Zell, who made the company private. This move insulated it from investors and stock market demands for unreasonably high profit margins. The Tribune Company took on $13 billion in debt at the time of the sale and sold the Long Island, N.Y.-based *Newsday* to Cablevision to earn some money. However, in 2008 the Tribune Company faced declining ad revenue and a tough economy and was forced to file for bankruptcy protection (excluding the Chicago Cubs baseball team). While the company continues to operate, this is an indicator of the type of troubles newspapers face.

About the same time, large chains started to break up, selling individual newspapers to private individuals and equity firms. For example, in 2006, Knight Ridder—the nation's second-leading chain with thirty-two daily newspapers—was sold for $4.5 billion to the McClatchy Company. McClatchy then resold twelve of the thirty-two papers, including the *San Jose Mercury News*, the *St. Paul Pioneer Press*, and the *Philadelphia Inquirer*, to several private buyers. McClatchy also sold its leading newspaper, the *Minneapolis Star Tribune*, to a private equity group for $530 million, less than half of what it had paid to buy the newspaper just eight years earlier.

Ownership of one of the nation's three national newspapers also changed hands. The *Wall Street Journal*, held by the Bancroft family for more than one hundred years, accepted a bid of nearly $5.8 billion dollars from News Corp. head Rupert Murdoch. News Corp. already owned the *New York Post*, one of the nation's Top 10 papers. At the time of this deal, critics raised serious concerns about the recent tendency in the newspaper business toward takeovers by large entertainment conglomerates. As small subsidiaries in large media empires, newspapers are increasingly treated as just another product line expected to perform in the same way that a movie or TV program does.

By 2008, a number of concerned journalists, economists, and citizens began calling for a new business model that would help protect newspapers in the transition to the digital era. One idea to insulate papers from stock market expectations is to mimic Sam Zell's model and take newspaper companies private. Another model is nonprofit ownership. For example, the Poynter Institute owns and operates the *St. Petersburg Times*, Florida's largest newspaper. As a nonprofit, the *St. Petersburg Times* is protected from the unrealistic 16 to 20 percent profit margins that publicly held newspapers have historically earned. National Public Radio (NPR) represents another nonprofit model where funding is provided by government subsidies and private contributions. Another nonprofit possibility is that wealthy universities like Harvard or Yale could use their billion-dollar endowments to buy and support newspapers, better insulating their public service and watchdog operations from the expectations of the marketplace. Finally, wealthy Internet companies like Microsoft and Google could also decide to get into the news business and start producing content for both print papers and online.

Newspapers Go Digital to Survive

Because of their local monopoly status, many newspapers were slower than other media to confront the challenges of the electronic and digital revolution. But faced with competition from cable, newspapers responded by developing online versions of their papers. While some observers think newspapers are on the verge of extinction as the digital age eclipses the print era, the industry is no dinosaur. In fact, the history of communication demonstrates that older mass media have always adapted. Actually, with more than fifteen hundred North American daily papers online in 2008, newspapers are solving one of the industry's major economic headaches: the cost of newsprint. After salaries, purchasing paper is the industry's largest expense, typically accounting for more than 25 percent of a newspaper's total cost.

Now, online newspapers are truly taking advantage of the flexibility the Internet offers. Because space is not an issue, newspapers can post online stories and reader letters that they weren't able to print in the paper edition. They can also run longer stories with more in-depth coverage, as well as offer immediate updates to breaking news. Also, most stories appear online before they appear in print, so they can be posted at any time and updated several times a day.

Online newspapers are also making themselves an invaluable resource to readers by offering hyperlinks to Web sites related to stories and by linking news reports to an archive of related articles. Free of charge or for a modest fee, a reader can search the newspaper's database from home and investigate the entire sequence and history of an ongoing story, such as a trial, over the course of several months. Taking advantage of the multimedia capabilities of the Internet, online newspapers offer readers the ability to download audio and video files—everything from presidential news conferences to sports highlights to original video reports. Today's online newspapers offer readers a dynamic rather than a static resource.

Despite these advances, online revenue accounted for only about 6 to 7 percent of U.S. newspaper advertising in 2007. Print newspapers are still among the media leaders in collecting advertising revenue, attracting about 17 to 18 percent of all ad revenues spent in the United States, down from a 27 percent share in the late 1980s (see Figure 8.2). Unfortunately, this means that the traditional printed newspaper will remain the big generator of revenue for the time being. To move this process forward faster, in 2008 more than four hundred daily newspapers collaborated with Yahoo! (the number one Web site where readers start their search for news) to begin an ad venture that promised to increase online papers' revenue by 10 to 20 percent.

Blogs Challenge Newspapers' Authority Online

The rise of blogs in the late 1990s and early 2000s brought amateurs into the realm of professional journalism. It was an awkward meeting. As National Press Club president Doug Harbrecht said to blogger Matt Drudge in 1998 while introducing him to the press club's members, "There aren't many in this hallowed room who consider you a journalist. Real journalists . . . pride themselves on getting it first and right; they get to the bottom of the story, they bend over backwards to get the other side. Journalism means being painstakingly thorough, even-handed, and fair." Harbrecht's suggestion, of course, was that untrained bloggers weren't as scrupulous as professionally trained journalists. In the following decade, though, as blogs like the Daily Kos, the Huffington Post, AndrewSullivan.com, and Talking Points Memo gained credibility and a large readership, traditional journalism began to slowly try blogging, allowing some reporters to write a blog in addition to their regular newspaper, television, or radio work. Some newspapers such as the *Washington Post* and the *New York Times* even hired journalists to blog exclusively for their Web sites.

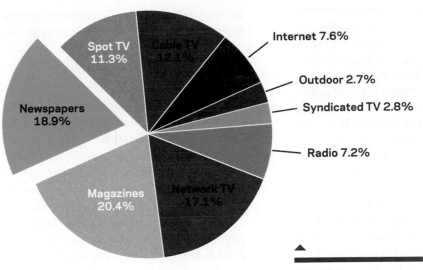

By 2005, the wary relationship between journalism and blogging began to change. Blogging became less a journalistic sideline and more a viable main feature. Established journalists left major news organizations to begin new careers in the blogosphere. For example, in 2007 top journalists John Harris and Jim VandeHei left the *Washington Post* to launch Politico.com, a national blog (and, secondarily, a local newspaper) about Capitol Hill politics. Eric Black—a veteran political writer for the *Minneapolis Star Tribune*, who wrote the highly regarded blog the Big Question for the paper—left during newsroom downsizing in 2007 to start his own blog for the Center for Independent Media. Nancy Cleeland, a labor reporter who won a Pulitzer Prize for a 2004 investigative team series on Wal-Mart's labor and outsourcing practices, left the *Los Angeles Times* during staff cuts in 2007.[36] Another breakthrough moment occurred when the Talking Points Memo blog, headed by Joshua Micah Marshall, won a George Polk Award for legal reporting in 2008. From Marshall's point of view, "I think of us as journalists; the medium

▲

FIGURE 8.2

NEWSPAPERS' SLICE OF THE U.S. ADVERTISING PIE, 2007

Source: Advertising Age, "100 National Leading Advertisers," June 23, 2008.

◀

EARLY NEWS BLOGS like The Drudge Report helped bring journalism and news commentary to the Web. (Left, Matt Drudge.)

> "Now, like hundreds of other mid-career journalists who are walking away from media institutions across the country, I'm looking for other ways to tell the stories I care about. At the same time, the world of online news is maturing, looking for depth and context. I think the timing couldn't be better."
>
> NANCY CLEELAND, ON WHY SHE WAS LEAVING THE *LOS ANGELES TIMES*, POSTED ON THE HUFFINGTON POST, 2007

we work in is blogging. We have kind of broken free of the model of discrete articles that have a beginning and end. Instead, there are an ongoing series of dispatches."[37]

Alternative Voices

The combination of the online news surge and traditional newsroom cutbacks has led to a new phenomenon known as **citizen journalism**, or *citizen media*, or *community journalism* (in those projects where the participants might not be actual citizens). As a grassroots movement, citizen journalism refers to people–activist amateurs and concerned citizens, not professional journalists–who use the Internet and blogs to disseminate news and information. In fact, with steep declines in newsroom staffs, many professional news media organizations–like CNN (iReport) and many regional newspapers–are increasingly trying to corral citizen journalists as an inexpensive way to make up for journalists lost to newsroom "downsizing."

A 2008 study by J-Lab: The Institute for Interactive Journalism reported that more than one thousand community-based Web sites were in operation, posting citizen stories on local government, police, and city development. This represented twice the number of community sites from a year earlier. J-Lab also operates the Knight Citizen News Network, "a Web site that advises citizens and traditional journalists on how to launch and operate community news and information sites."[38] These sites mostly use free software and target communities that get little media attention. Another example is the Philadelphia-based Media Mobilizing Project, which teaches community members, including immigrant rights groups and non-U.S. citizens, how to make community news using video and stream it on the Internet. In 2008, the group planned to produce stories on school violence, gun control, and neighborhood gentrification.[39]

Newspapers and Democracy

> "The danger is omnipresent for journalists in Iraq. There are few places to take refuge."
>
> JOEL CAMPAGNA, COMMITTEE TO PROTECT JOURNALISTS, 2006

Of all mass media, newspapers have played the longest and strongest role in sustaining democracy. Over the years, newspapers have fought heroic battles in places that had little tolerance for differing points of view. According to the Committee to Protect Journalists (CPJ), from 1992 through April 2008, 685 reporters from around the world were killed while doing their jobs. Of those 685, 72 percent were murdered, 17 percent were killed in combat assignments and war reporting, and 10 percent were killed performing "dangerous assignments."[40] Most of the recent deaths reported by the CPJ have come from the war in Iraq. From 2003 to mid-2008, more than 125 reporters had died in Iraq, along with 35 media workers and support staff. For comparison, 63 reporters were killed covering the Vietnam War; 17 died covering the Korean War; and 69 were killed during World War II.[41] Our nation is dependent on journalists willing to do this very dangerous reporting in order to keep us informed about what is going on around the world. (See Figure 8.3, "The Most Dangerous Countries for Journalists," on page 277.)

In addition to the physical danger, newsroom cutbacks, and closing of foreign bureaus, a number of smaller concerns remain as we consider the future of newspapers. For instance, some charge that newspapers have become so formulaic in their design and reporting styles that they may actually discourage new approaches to telling stories and reporting news. Another criticism is that many one-newspaper cities cover only issues and events of interest to middle- and upper-middle-class readers, thereby underreporting the experiences and events that affect poorer and working-class citizens. In addition, given the rise of newspaper chains,

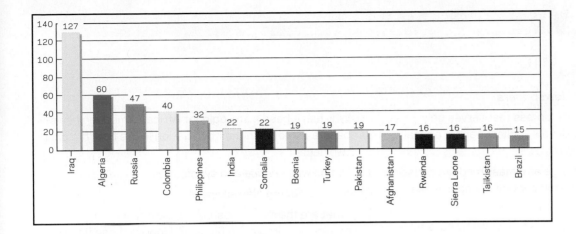

FIGURE 8.3

THE MOST DANGEROUS COUNTRIES FOR JOURNALISTS (NUMBER OF DEATHS 2003-2008)

Source: Committee to Protect Journalists

the likelihood of including new opinions, ideas, and information in mainstream daily papers may be diminishing. Moreover, chain ownership tends to discourage watchdog journalism and the crusading traditions of newspapers. Like other business managers, many news executives prefer not to offend investors or outrage potential advertisers by running too many investigative reports—especially business probes at a time in 2008 right before the financial crisis hit and few people seemed to know why. This may be most obvious in the fact that reporters have generally not reported adequately on the business and ownership arrangements in their own industry.

Finally, as print journalism shifts to digital culture, the greatest challenge is the upheaval of print journalism's business model. As print journalism loses readers and advertisers to a wide range of digital culture, what will become of newspapers, which do most of the nation's primary journalistic work? John Carroll presided over thirteen Pulitzer Prize-winning reports at the *Los Angeles Times* as editor from 2000 to 2005, but left the paper to protest deep corporate cuts to the newsroom. He lamented the future of newspapers and their unique role: "Newspapers are doing the reporting in this country. Google and Yahoo and those people aren't putting reporters on the street in any numbers at all. Blogs can't afford it. Network television is taking reporters off the street. Commercial radio is almost nonexistent. And newspapers are the last ones standing, and newspapers are threatened. And reporting is absolutely an essential thing for democratic self-government. Who's going to do it? Who's going to pay for the news? If newspapers fall by the wayside, what will we know?"[42] ▶

"The primary purpose of journalism is to provide citizens with the information they need to be free and self-governing."

BILL KOVACH AND TOM ROSENSTIEL, *THE ELEMENTS OF JOURNALISM*, 2007

CHAPTER REVIEW

REVIEW QUESTIONS

The Evolution of American Newspapers

1. What are the limitations of a press that serves only partisan interests? Why did the earliest papers appeal mainly to more privileged readers?

2. How did newspapers emerge as a mass medium during the penny press era? How did content changes make this happen?

3. What are the two main features of yellow journalism? How have Joseph Pulitzer and William Randolph Hearst contributed to newspaper history?

Competing Models of Modern Print Journalism

4. Why did objective journalism develop? What are its characteristics? What are its strengths and limitations?

5. Why did interpretive forms of journalism develop in the modern era? What are the limits of objectivity?

6. How would you define literary journalism? Why did it emerge in such an intense way in the 1960s? How is literary journalism an attack on objective news?

Categorizing News and U.S. Newspapers

7. What is the difference between consensus- and conflict-oriented newspapers?

8. What role have ethnic, minority, and oppositional newspapers played in the United States?

9. Why has it been a struggle for African American newspapers to maintain their circulation levels over the past two decades?

10. Define *wire service* and *syndication*.

Challenges Facing Newspapers

11. What are the major reasons for the decline in U.S. newspaper circulation figures? How do these figures compare with other nations?

12. What is the impact of a joint operating agreement (JOA) on the business and editorial divisions of competing newspapers?

13. Why did newspaper chains become an economic trend in the twentieth century?

14. What major challenges does new technology pose to the newspaper industry?

15. With traditional publicly owned newspapers in jeopardy today, what are some other business models for running a newspaper?

Newspapers and Democracy

16. What is a newspaper's role in a democracy?

17. What makes newspaper journalism different from the journalism of other mass media?

QUESTIONING THE MEDIA

1. What kinds of stories, topics, or issues are not being covered well by mainstream papers?

2. Why do you think people aren't reading U.S. daily newspapers as frequently as they once did? Why is newspaper readership going up in other countries?

3. Discuss whether newspaper chains are ultimately good or bad for the future of journalism.

4. Do newspapers today play a vigorous role as watchdogs of our powerful institutions? Why or why not?

5. Will blogs and other Internet news services eventually replace newspapers? Explain your response.

COMMON THREADS

One of the Common Threads discussed in Chapter 1 is about the role that media play in a democracy. The newspaper industry has always played a strong role in our democracy by reporting news and investigating stories. Even in the Internet age, newspapers remain our primary source for content. How will the industry's current financial struggles affect our ability to access (and demand) reliable news?

With the coming of radio and television, newspapers in the twentieth century surrendered their title as the mass medium shared by the largest audience. However, to this day newspapers remain the single most important source of news for the nation, even in the age of the Internet. Although many "readers" today cite Yahoo! and Google as the primary places they search for news, Yahoo! and Google are only directories that guide readers to other news stories—most often to online newspaper sites. This means that newspaper organizations are still the primary institutions doing the work of gathering and reporting the news. Even with all the newsroom cutbacks across the United States, newspapers remain the only journalistic organization in most towns and cities that still employs hundreds of people to report news and tell the community's stories.

Newspapers link people to what matters in their communities, their nation, and their world. No other journalistic institution serves society as well. But, with smaller news resources and the industry no longer able to sustain high profit margins, what will become of newspapers? Who will gather the information needed to sustain a democracy, to serve as the watchdog over our key institutions, and to document the comings and goings of everyday life? And, perhaps more importantly, who will act on behalf of the people who don't have the news media's access to authorities or the ability to influence them?

KEY TERMS

The definitions for the terms listed below can be found in the glossary at the end of the book. The page numbers listed with the terms indicate where the term is highlighted in the chapter.

partisan press, 251
penny papers, 252
human-interest stories, 252
wire services, 253
yellow journalism, 253
objective journalism, 257
inverted-pyramid style, 257
interpretive journalism, 258
literary journalism, 259

consensus-oriented journalism, 262
conflict-oriented journalism, 262
underground press, 266
newshole, 268
feature syndicates, 269
joint operating agreement (JOA), 272
newspaper chain, 273
citizen journalism, 276

9

Magazines in the Age of Specialization

Cosmopolitan didn't always have cover photos of women with plunging necklines, or cover lines like "67 New Sex Tricks" and "The Sexiest Things to Do after Sex." As the magazine itself says, "The story of how a '60s babe named Helen Gurley Brown (you've probably heard of her) transformed an antiquated general-interest mag called *Cosmopolitan* into the must-read for young, sexy single chicks is pretty damn amazing."[1]

In fact, *Cosmopolitan* had at least four format changes before Helen Gurley Brown came along. The magazine was launched in 1886 as an illustrated monthly for the modern family (meaning it was targeted at married women) with articles on cooking, child care, household decoration, and occasionally fashion, featuring illustrated images of women in the hats and high collars of late-Victorian fashion.[2]

But the magazine was thin on content and almost folded. *Cosmopolitan* was saved in 1889, when journalist and entrepreneur John Brisben Walker gave it a second chance as an illustrated magazine of literature and insightful reporting.

HELEN GURLEY BROWN in her office at *Cosmopolitan*.

The magazine featured writers like Edith Wharton, Rudyard Kipling, and Theodore Dreiser and serialized entire books, including H. G. Wells's *The War of the Worlds*. Walker, seeing the success of contemporary newspapers in New York, was not above stunt reporting either. When Joseph Pulitzer's *New York World* sent off reporter Nellie Bly to travel the world in less than eighty days in 1889 (challenging the premise of Jules Verne's fictional 1873 novel, *Around the World in Eighty Days*), Walker sent reporter Elizabeth Bisland around the world in the opposite direction for a more literary travel account.[3] Walker's leadership turned *Cosmopolitan* into a respected magazine with increased circulation and a strong advertising base.

Walker sold *Cosmopolitan* at a profit to William Randolph Hearst (Pulitzer's main competitor) in 1905. Under Hearst, *Cosmopolitan* had its third

rebirth—this time as a muckraking magazine. As magazine historians explain, Hearst was a U.S. representative who "had his eye on the presidency and planned to use his newspapers and the recently bought *Cosmopolitan* to stir up further discontent over the trusts and big business."[4] *Cosmopolitan*'s first big muckraking series, David Graham Phillips's "Treason of the Senate" in 1906, didn't help Hearst's political career, but it did boost the circulation of the magazine by 50 percent, and was reprinted in Hearst newspapers for even more exposure.

But by 1912, the progressive political movement that had given impetus to muckraking journalism was waning. *Cosmopolitan*, in its fourth incarnation and like a version of its former self, became an illustrated literary monthly targeted to women, with short stories and serialized novels by popular writers like Damon Runyon, Sinclair Lewis, and Faith Baldwin.

Cosmopolitan had great success as an upscale literary magazine, but by the early 1960s, the format had become outdated and readership and advertising had declined. At this point, the magazine had its most radical makeover. In 1962, Helen Gurley Brown, one of the country's top advertising copywriters, was recently married (at age forty), and wrote the best-selling book *Sex and the Single Girl*. When she proposed a magazine modeled on the book's vision of strong, sexually liberated women, the Hearst Corporation hired her in 1965 as editor in chief to reinvent *Cosmopolitan*. The new *Cosmopolitan* helped spark a sexual revolution and was marketed to the "Cosmo Girl": women age eighteen to thirty-four with an interest in love, sex, fashion, and their careers.

Brown's vision of *Cosmo* continues today with its "fun, fearless female" slogan. It's the top women's fashion magazine—surpassing competitors like *Glamour, InStyle, Self*, and *Vogue*—and has been the best-selling title in college bookstores for more than 25 years. Although its present format is far from its origins, *Cosmopolitan* endures based on its successful reinventions over the last 125 years.

▲ *SINCE THE 1740s,* magazines have played a key role in our social and cultural lives, becoming America's earliest national mass medium (ahead of newspapers, which were mainly local and regional in scope). They created some of the first spaces for discussing the broad issues of the age, including public education, the abolition of slavery, women's suffrage, literacy, and the Civil War. In addition, many leading literary figures used magazines to gain public exposure for their work, such as essays or fiction writing.

In the nineteenth century, magazines became an educational forum for women, who were barred from higher education and from the nation's political life. At the turn of the twentieth century, magazines' probing reports would influence investigative journalism, while their use of engraving and photography provided a hint of the visual culture to come. Economically, magazines brought advertised products into households, hastening the rise of a consumer society.

Today, more than nineteen thousand commercial, alternative, and noncommercial magazines are published in the United States annually. Like newspapers, radio, movies, and television, magazines reflect and construct portraits of American life. They are catalogues for daily events and experiences, but they also show us the latest products, fostering our consumer culture. We read magazines to learn something about our community, our nation, our world, and ourselves.

In this chapter, we investigate the history of the magazine industry, highlighting the colonial and early American eras, the arrival of national magazines, and the development of photojournalism. Turning to the modern American era, we focus on the age of muckraking and the rise of general-interest and consumer magazines. We then look at the decline of mass market magazines, TV's impact, and how magazines have specialized in order to survive in a fragmented market. Finally, we investigate the organization and economics of magazines and their function in a democracy.

> "Beauty can't amuse you, but brainwork— reading, writing, thinking—can."
>
> HELEN GURLEY BROWN

The Early History of Magazines

The first magazines appeared in seventeenth-century France in the form of bookseller catalogues and notices that book publishers inserted in newspapers. In fact, the word *magazine* derives from the French term *magasin*, meaning "storehouse." The earliest magazines were "storehouses" of writing and reports taken mostly from newspapers. Today, the word **magazine** broadly refers to collections of articles, stories, and advertisements appearing in nondaily (such as weekly or monthly) periodicals that are published in the smaller tabloid style rather than larger broadsheet newspaper style.

The First Magazines

The first political magazine, called the *Review*, appeared in London in 1704. Edited by political activist and novelist Daniel Defoe (author of *Robinson Crusoe*), the *Review* was printed sporadically until 1713. Like the *Nation*, the *National Review*, and the *Progressive* in the United States today, early European magazines were channels for political commentary and argument. These periodicals looked like newspapers of the time, but they appeared less frequently and were oriented toward broad domestic and political commentary rather than recent news.

Regularly published magazines or pamphlets, such as the *Tatler* and the *Spectator*, also appeared in England around this time. They offered poetry, politics, and philosophy for

COLONIAL MAGAZINES
The first issue of Benjamin Franklin's *General Magazine and Historical Chronicle* appeared in February 1741. While it only lasted six months, Franklin found success in other publications, like his annual *Poor Richard's Almanac,* starting in 1732 and lasting twenty-five years.

London's elite, and they served readerships of a few thousand. The first publication to use the term *magazine* was *Gentleman's Magazine*, which appeared in London in 1731 and consisted of reprinted articles from newspapers, books, and political pamphlets. Later the magazine began publishing original work by such writers as Defoe, Samuel Johnson, and Alexander Pope.

Magazines in Colonial America

Without a substantial middle class, widespread literacy, or advanced printing technology, magazines developed slowly in America. Like the partisan newspapers of the time, colonial magazines served politicians, the educated, and the merchant classes. Paid circulations of these magazines were slight—between one hundred and fifteen hundred copies. However, early magazines did serve the more widespread purpose of documenting a new nation coming to terms with issues of taxation, state versus federal power, Indian treaties, public education, and the end of colonialism. George Washington, Alexander Hamilton, and John Hancock all wrote for early magazines, and Paul Revere worked as a magazine illustrator for a time.

The first colonial magazines appeared in Philadelphia in 1741, about fifty years after the first newspapers. Andrew Bradford started it all with *American Magazine, or A Monthly View of the Political State of the British Colonies*. Three days later, Benjamin Franklin's *General Magazine and Historical Chronicle* appeared. Bradford's magazine lasted only three monthly issues, due to circulation and postal obstacles that Franklin, who had replaced Bradford as Philadelphia's postmaster, put in its way. For instance, Franklin mailed his magazine without paying the high postal rates that he subsequently charged others. Franklin's magazine primarily duplicated what was already available in local papers. After six months it, too, stopped publication.

Nonetheless, following the Philadelphia experiments, magazines began to emerge in the other colonies, beginning in Boston in the 1740s. The most successful magazines simply reprinted articles from leading London periodicals, keeping readers abreast of European events. These magazines included New York's *Independent Reflector* and *The Pennsylvania Magazine*, edited by activist Thomas Paine, which helped rally the colonies against British rule. By 1776, about

▼ **Magazines in the Age of Specialization**

National Magazines
The *Saturday Evening Post* is launched in 1821, becoming the first major magazine to appeal directly to women. It becomes the longest-running magazine in U.S. history (p. 285).

Postal Act of 1879
Both postal rates and rail transportation costs plummet, allowing magazine distribution to thrive (p. 287).

1700	1750	1800	1850

Colonial Magazines
First appearing in Philadelphia and Boston in 1741, these generally unsuccessful magazines reprint material from local newspapers (p. 284).

Engravings and Illustrations
By the mid-1850s, drawings, woodcuts, and other forms of illustration begin to fill the pages of magazines (p. 286).

a hundred colonial magazines had appeared and disappeared. Although historians consider them dull and uninspired for the most part, these magazines helped launch a new medium that caught on after the American Revolution.

U.S. Magazines in the Nineteenth Century

After the revolution, the growth of the magazine industry in the newly independent United States remained slow. Delivery costs remained high, and some postal carriers refused to carry magazines because of their weight. Only twelve magazines operated in 1800. By 1825, about a hundred magazines existed, although about another five hundred had failed between 1800 and 1825. Nevertheless, during the first quarter of the nineteenth century, most communities had their own weekly magazines. These magazines featured essays on local issues, government activities, and political intrigue, as well as material reprinted from other sources. They sold some advertising, but were usually in precarious financial straits because of their small circulations.

As the nineteenth century progressed, the idea of specialized magazines devoted to certain categories of readers developed. Many early magazines were overtly religious and boasted the largest readerships of the day. The Methodist *Christian Journal and Advocate*, for example, claimed twenty-five thousand subscribers by 1826. Literary magazines also emerged at this time. The *North American Review*, for instance, established the work of important writers such as Ralph Waldo Emerson, Henry David Thoreau, and Mark Twain. In addition to religious and literary magazines, specialty magazines that addressed various professions, lifestyles, and topics also appeared. Some of these magazines included the *American Farmer*, the *American Journal of Education*, the *American Law Journal*, *Medical Repository,* and the *American Journal of Science*. Such specialization spawned the modern trend of reaching readers who share a profession, a set of beliefs, cultural tastes, or a social identity.

The nineteenth century also saw the birth of the first general-interest magazine aimed at a national audience. In 1821, two young Philadelphia printers, Charles Alexander and Samuel Coate Atkinson, launched the *Saturday Evening Post*, which became the longest-running magazine in

> "They spring up as fast as mushrooms, in every corner, and like all rapid vegetation, bear the seeds of early decay within them . . . and then comes a 'frost, a killing frost,' in the form of bills due and debts unpaid. . . . The average age of periodicals in this country is found to be six months."
>
> *NEW-YORK MIRROR,* 1828

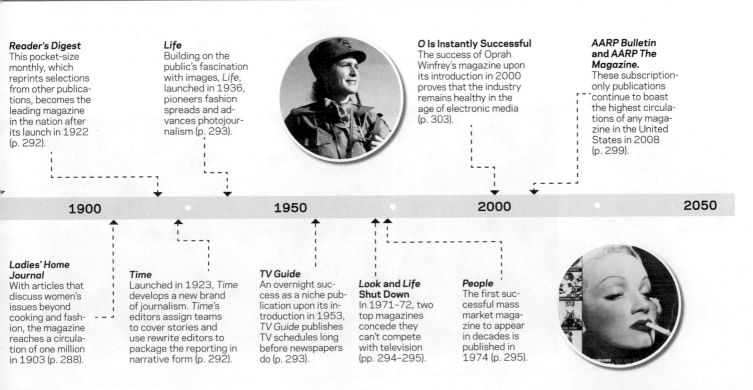

Reader's Digest
This pocket-size monthly, which reprints selections from other publications, becomes the leading magazine in the nation after its launch in 1922 (p. 292).

Life
Building on the public's fascination with images, *Life*, launched in 1936, pioneers fashion spreads and advances photojournalism (p. 293).

O Is Instantly Successful
The success of Oprah Winfrey's magazine upon its introduction in 2000 proves that the industry remains healthy in the age of electronic media (p. 303).

AARP Bulletin and AARP The Magazine.
These subscription-only publications continue to boast the highest circulations of any magazine in the United States in 2008 (p. 299).

1900   1950   2000   2050

Ladies' Home Journal
With articles that discuss women's issues beyond cooking and fashion, the magazine reaches a circulation of one million in 1903 (p. 288).

Time
Launched in 1923, *Time* develops a new brand of journalism. *Time's* editors assign teams to cover stories and use rewrite editors to package the reporting in narrative form (p. 292).

TV Guide
An overnight success as a niche publication upon its introduction in 1953, *TV Guide* publishes TV schedules long before newspapers do (p. 293).

Look and Life Shut Down
In 1971–72, two top magazines concede they can't compete with television (pp. 294–295).

People
The first successful mass market magazine to appear in decades is published in 1974 (p. 295).

U.S. history. Like most magazines of the day, the early *Post* included a few original essays but "borrowed" many pieces from other sources. Eventually, however, the *Post* grew to incorporate news, poetry, essays, play reviews, and more. The *Post* published the writings of such prominent popular authors as Nathaniel Hawthorne and Harriet Beecher Stowe. Although the *Post* was a general-interest magazine, it also was the first major magazine to appeal directly to women, via its "Lady's Friend" column, which addressed women's issues.

National, Women's, and Illustrated Magazines

With increases in literacy and public education, the development of faster printing technologies, and improvements in mail delivery (due to rail transportation), a market was created for more national magazines like the *Saturday Evening Post*. Whereas in 1825, one hundred magazines struggled for survival, by 1850 nearly six hundred magazines were being published regularly (thousands of others lasted less than a year). Significant national magazines of the era included *Graham's Magazine* (1840-58), one of the most influential and entertaining magazines in the country; *Knickerbocker* (1833-64), which published essays and literary works by Washington Irving, James Fenimore Cooper, and Nathaniel Hawthorne (preceding such national cultural magazines as the *New Yorker* and *Harper's*); the *Nation* (1865-present), which pioneered the national political magazine format; and *Youth's Companion* (1826-1929), one of the first successful national magazines for younger readers.

Besides the move to national circulation, other important developments in the magazine industry were underway. In 1828, Sarah Josepha Hale started the first magazine directed exclusively to a female audience: the *Ladies' Magazine*. In addition to general-interest articles, the magazine advocated for women's education, work, and property rights. After nine years and marginal success, Hale merged her magazine with its main rival, *Godey's Lady's Book* (1830-98), which she edited for the next forty years. By 1850, *Godey's*, known for its colorful fashion illustrations in addition to its advocacy, achieved a circulation of 40,000 copies—at the time, the biggest distribution ever for a U.S. magazine. By 1860, circulation swelled to 150,000. Hale's magazine played a central role in educating working- and middle-class women, who were denied access to higher education throughout the nineteenth century.

The other major development in magazine publishing during the mid-nineteenth century was the arrival of illustration. Like the first newspapers, early magazines were totally dependent on the printed word. By the mid-1850s, drawings, engravings, woodcuts, and other forms of illustration had become a major feature of magazines. During this time, *Godey's Lady's Book* employed up to 150 women to color-tint its magazine illustrations and stencil drawings by

COLOR ILLUSTRATIONS first became popular in the fashion sections of women's magazines in the mid-1800s. The color for this fashion image from *Godey's* was added to the illustrations by hand.

hand. Meanwhile, *Harper's New Monthly Magazine*, founded in 1850, offered extensive wood-cut illustrations with each issue. During the Civil War, many readers relied on *Harper's* for its elaborate battlefield sketches. Publications like *Harper's* married visual language to the printed word, helping to transform magazines into a mass medium. Bringing photographs into magazines took a bit longer. Mathew Brady and his colleagues, whose thirty-five hundred photos documented the Civil War, helped to popularize photography by the 1860s. But it was not until the 1890s that magazines and newspapers possessed the technology to reproduce photos in print media.

The Development of Modern American Magazines

In 1870, about twelve hundred magazines were produced in the United States; by 1890, that number reached forty-five hundred; and by 1905, more than six thousand magazines existed. Part of this surge in titles and readership was facilitated by the Postal Act of 1879, which assigned magazines lower postage rates and put them on an equal footing with newspapers delivered by mail, reducing distribution costs. Meanwhile, advances in mass-production printing, conveyor systems, assembly lines, and faster presses reduced production costs and made large-circulation national magazines possible.[5]

The combination of reduced distribution and production costs enabled publishers to slash magazine prices. As prices dropped from thirty-five cents to fifteen and then to ten cents, the working class was gradually able to purchase national publications. By 1905, there were about twenty-five national magazines, available from coast to coast and serving millions of readers.[6] As jobs and the population began shifting from farms and small towns to urban areas, magazines helped readers imagine themselves as part of a nation rather than as individuals with only local or regional identities. In addition, the dramatic growth of drugstores and dime stores, supermarkets, and department stores offered new venues and shelf space for selling consumer goods, including magazines.

As magazine circulation started to skyrocket, advertising revenue soared. The economics behind the rise of advertising was simple: A magazine publisher could dramatically expand circulation by dropping the price of an issue below the actual production cost for a single copy. The publisher recouped the loss through ad revenue, guaranteeing large readerships to advertisers who were willing to pay to reach more readers. Ad pages in national magazines soared. *Harper's*, for instance, devoted only seven pages to ads in the mid-1880s, nearly fifty pages in 1890, and more than ninety pages in 1900.[7]

By the turn of the century, advertisers increasingly used national magazines to capture consumers' attention and build a national marketplace. One magazine that took advantage of these changes was *Ladies' Home Journal*, begun in 1883 by Cyrus Curtis. The women's magazine began publishing more than the usual homemaking tips, including also popular fiction, sheet music, and—most importantly perhaps—the latest consumer ads. The magazine's broadened scope was a reflection of the editors' and advertisers' realization that women consumers constituted a growing and lucrative market. *Ladies' Home Journal* reached a circulation of over 500,000 by the early 1890s—the highest circulation of any magazine in the country. In 1903, it became the first magazine to reach a circulation of 1 million.

Social Reform and the Muckrakers

Better distribution and lower costs had attracted readers, but to maintain sales, magazines had to change content as well. While printing the fiction and essays of the best writers of the day was one way to maintain circulation, many magazines also engaged in one aspect of *yellow*

"Men with the muckrake are often indispensable to the well-being of society, but only if they know when to stop raking the muck."

TEDDY ROOSEVELT, 1906

A NAUSEATING JOB, BUT IT MUST BE DONE
(President Roosevelt takes hold of the investigating muck-rake himself in the packing-house scandal.)
From the *Saturday Globe* (Utica)

journalism–crusading for social reform on behalf of the public good. In the 1890s, for example, *Ladies' Home Journal* (*LHJ*) and its editor, Edward Bok, led the fight against unregulated patent medicines (which often contained nearly 50 percent alcohol), while other magazines joined the fight against phony medicines, poor living and working conditions, and unsanitary practices in various food industries.

The rise in magazine circulation coincided with rapid social changes in America. While hundreds of thousands of Americans moved from the country to the city in search of industrial jobs, millions of new immigrants also poured in. Thus, the nation that journalists had long written about had grown increasingly complex by the turn of the century. Many newspaper reporters became dissatisfied with the simplistic and conventional style of newspaper journalism and turned to magazines, where they were able to write at greater length and in greater depth about broader issues. They wrote about such topics as corruption in big business and government, urban problems faced by immigrants, labor conflicts, and race relations.

Booth Tarkington's serial "The Two Vanrevels" enhances the value of this issue of "McClure's Magazine."

MUCKRAKING MAGAZINES like *McClure's* and *Collier's* were the first to publish investigative stories on American institutions. The *Collier's* cover shown features a probe into patent medicines.

In 1902, *McClure's* magazine (1893-1933) touched off an investigative era in magazine reporting with a series of probing stories, including Ida Tarbell's "The History of the Standard Oil Company," which took on John D. Rockefeller's oil monopoly, and Lincoln Steffens's "Shame of the Cities," which tackled urban problems. In 1906, *Cosmopolitan* magazine joined the fray with a series called "The Treason of the Senate," and *Collier's* magazine (1888-1957) developed "The Great American Fraud" series, focusing on patent medicines (whose ads accounted for 30 percent of the profits made by the American press by the 1890s). Much of this new reporting style was critical of American institutions. Angry with so much negative reporting, in 1906 President Theodore Roosevelt dubbed these investigative reporters **muckrakers**, because they were willing to crawl through society's muck to uncover a story. Muckraking was a label that Roosevelt used with disdain, but it was worn with pride by reporters such as Ray Stannard Baker, Frank Norris, Lincoln Steffens, and Ida Tarbell.

Influenced by Upton Sinclair's novel *The Jungle*–a fictional account of Chicago's meatpacking industry–and by the muckraking reports of *Collier's* and *LHJ*, in 1906 Congress passed the Pure Food and Drug Act and the Meat Inspection Act. Other reforms stemming from muckraking journalism and the politics of the era include antitrust laws for increased government oversight of business, a fair and progressive income tax, and the direct election of U.S. senators.

The Rise of General-Interest Magazines

The heyday of the muckraking era lasted into the mid-1910s, when America was drawn into World War I. After the war and through the 1950s, **general-interest magazines** were the most prominent publications, offering occasional investigative articles but also covering a wide variety of topics aimed at a broad national audience. A key aspect of these magazines was **photojournalism**–the use of photos to document the rhythms of daily life (see "Case Study: The Evolution of Photojournalism" on pages 290-291). High-quality photos gave general-interest magazines a visual advantage over radio, which was the most popular medium of the day. In 1920, about fifty-five magazines fit the general-interest category; by 1946, more than one hundred such magazines competed with radio networks for the national audience.

The Evolution of Photojournalism

By Christopher R. Harris

What we now recognize as photojournalism started with the assignment of photographer Roger Fenton, of the *Sunday Times of London*, to document the Crimean War in 1856. Technical limitations did not allow direct reproduction of photodocumentary images in the publications of the day, however. Woodcut artists had to interpret the photographic images as black-and-white-toned woodblocks that could be reproduced by the presses of the period. Images interpreted by artists therefore lost the inherent qualities of photographic visual documentation: an on-site visual representation of facts for those who weren't present.

Woodcuts remained the basic method of press reproduction until 1880, when *New York Daily Graphic* photographer Stephen Horgan invented half-tone reproduction using a dot-pattern screen. This screen enabled metallic plates to directly represent photographic images in the printing process; now periodicals could bring exciting visual reportage to their pages.

In the mid-1890s, Jimmy Hare became the first photographer recognized as a photojournalist in the United States. Taken for *Collier's Weekly*, Hare's photoreportage on the sinking of the battleship *Maine* in 1898 near Havana, Cuba, established his reputation as a newsman traveling the world to bring back images of news events. Hare's images fed into growing popular support for Cuban independence from Spain and eventual U.S. involvement in the Spanish-American War.

In 1888, George Eastman opened photography to the working and middle classes when he introduced the first flexible-film camera from Kodak, his company in Rochester, New York. Gone were the bulky equipment and fragile photographic plates of the past. Now families and journalists could more easily and affordably document gatherings and events.

As photography became easier and more widespread, photojournalism began to take on an increasingly important social role. At the turn of the century, the documentary photography of Jacob Riis and Lewis Hine captured the harsh working and living conditions of the nation's many child laborers, including crowded ghettos and unsafe mills and factories. Reaction to these shockingly honest photographs resulted in public outcry and new laws against the exploitation of children. Photographs also brought the horrors of World War I to people far from the battlefields.

In 1923, visionaries Henry Luce and Britton Hadden published *Time*, the first modern photographic newsweekly; *Life* and *FORTUNE* soon followed. From coverage of the Roaring Twenties to the Great Depression, these magazines used images that changed the way people viewed the world.

Life, with its spacious 10-by-13-inch format and large photographs, became one of the most influential magazines in America, printing what are now classic images from World War II and the Korean War. Often, *Life* offered images that were unavailable anywhere else: Margaret Bourke-White's photographic proof of the unspeakably horrific concentration camps; W. Eugene Smith's gentle portraits of the humanitarian Albert Schweitzer in Africa; David Duncan's gritty images of the faces of U.S. troops fighting in Korea.

Television photojournalism made its quantum leap into the public mind as

JACOB RIIS
The Tramp, c. 1890. Riis, who emigrated from Denmark in 1870, lived in poverty in New York for several years before becoming a photojournalist. He spent much of his later life chronicling the lives of the poor in New York City. Courtesy: The Jacob A. Riis Collection, Museum of the City of New York.

it documented the assassination of President Kennedy in 1963. In televised images that were broadcast and rebroadcast, the public witnessed the actual assassination and the confusing aftermath, including live coverage of the murder of alleged assassin Lee Harvey Oswald and of President Kennedy's funeral procession. Photojournalism also provided visual documentation of the turbulent 1960s, including aggressive photographic coverage of the Vietnam War—its protesters and supporters. Pulitzer Prize–winning photographer Eddie Adams shook the emotions of the American public with his photographs of a South Vietnamese colonel's summary execution of a suspected Vietcong terrorist. Closer to home, shocking images of the Civil Rights movement culminated in pictures of Birmingham police and police dogs attacking civil rights protesters.

In the 1970s, new computer technologies emerged that were embraced by print and television media worldwide. By the late 1980s, computers could transform images into digital form, easily manipulated by sophisticated software programs. In addition, any photographer can now transmit images around the world almost instantaneously by using digital transmission, and the Internet allows publication of virtually any image, without censorship. In 1999, a reporter in war-torn Kosovo could take a picture and within minutes send that picture to news offices in Tokyo, Berlin, and New York; moments later, the image could be posted on the Internet or used in a late-breaking TV story. Digital technology is likely to revolutionize photojournalism, perhaps even more than the advent of roll film did in the late nineteenth century. Because of rapid delivery times, competition among print publications, television networks, and online news providers is heightened, as each can run late-breaking images transmitted from anywhere in the world.

There is a dark side to digital technology as well. Because of the absence of physical film, there is a resulting loss of proof, or veracity, of the authenticity of images. Original film has qualities that make it easy to determine whether it has been tampered with. Digital images, by contrast, can be easily altered, but such alteration can be very difficult to detect.

A recent example of image-tampering involved the *Men's Health* cover photo of tennis star Andy Roddick. Roddick, who is muscular but not bulky, didn't consent to the digital enhancement of his arms and later joked on his blog: "Little did I know I had 22-inch guns," referring to the size of his arms in the photo. (A birthmark on his right arm had also been erased.) A *Men's Health* spokesman said, "I don't see what the big issue is here."[1] Media critics have caught similar digital "improvements" of Angelina Jolie, Janet Jackson, America Ferrera, and Faith Hill in magazine photos. *Newsweek* magazine said "Airbrushing celebrity and model photos has become so common that it's a popular pastime for magazine readers to spot the digital manipulations," and then went on to ask: "But have photo editors gone too far?"[2]

Photojournalists and news sources are now confronted with unprecedented concerns over truth-telling. In the past, trust in documentary photojournalism rested solely on the verifiability of images as they were used in the media. Just as we must evaluate the words we read, at the start of a new century we must also view with a more critical eye these images that mean so much to so many.

Christopher R. Harris is a professor in the Department of Electronic Media Communication at Middle Tennessee State University.

Saturday Evening Post

Although it had been around since 1821, the *Saturday Evening Post* concluded the nineteenth century as only a modest success, with a circulation of about ten thousand. In 1897 Cyrus Curtis, who had already made *Ladies' Home Journal* the nation's top magazine, bought the *Post* and remade it into the first widely popular general-interest magazine. Curtis's strategy for reinvigorating the magazine included printing popular fiction and romanticizing American virtues through words and pictures (a *Post* tradition best depicted in the three-hundred-plus cover illustrations by Norman Rockwell). Curtis also featured articles that celebrated the business boom of the 1920s. This reversed the journalistic direction of the muckraking era, in which business corruption was often the focus. By the 1920s, the *Post* had reached two million in circulation, the first magazine to hit that mark.

Reader's Digest

The most widely circulated general-interest magazine during this period was *Reader's Digest*. Started in a Greenwich Village basement in 1922 by Dewitt Wallace and Lila Acheson Wallace, *Reader's Digest* championed one of the earliest functions of magazines: printing condensed versions of selected articles from other magazines. In the magazine's early years, the Wallaces refused to accept ads and sold the *Digest* only through subscriptions. With its inexpensive production costs, low price, and popular pocket-size format, the magazine's circulation climbed to over a million during the depths of the Great Depression, and by 1946, it was the nation's most popular magazine, with a circulation of more than nine million. By the mid-1980s it was the most popular magazine in the world. At its peak, *Reader's Digest* reached a circulation of twenty million in America and another ten to twelve million in 160 other countries.

Time

During the general-interest era, national newsmagazines such as *Time* were also major commercial successes. Begun in 1923 by Henry Luce and Britton Hadden, *Time* developed a magazine brand of interpretive journalism, assigning reporter-researcher teams to cover stories while a rewrite editor would put the article in narrative form with an interpretive point of view. *Time* had a circulation of 200,000 by 1930, increasing to more than 3 million by the mid-1960s. *Time*'s success encouraged prominent imitators, including *Newsweek* (1933-), *U.S. News & World Report* (1948-), and more recently the *Week* (2001-). When the major weekly general-interest magazines *Life* and *Look* failed in the 1970s, newsmagazines took over photojournalism's role in news reporting, visually documenting both national and international events. By 2008, the three major newsmagazines had circulations ranging from *Time*'s 3.3 million to *Newsweek*'s 3.1 million and *U.S. News*'s 2 million. *U.S. News* became a monthly magazine that year.

"Ford gave Everyman a car he could drive, [and] Wallace gave Everyman some literature he could read; both turned the trick with mass production."

JOHN BAINBRIDGE, MAGAZINE HISTORIAN, 1945

SATURDAY EVENING POST Norman Rockwell's 322 cover illustrations for the *Saturday Evening Post* between 1916 and 1963 included a series of 11 covers featuring a young World War II GI named Willie Gillis. The character was modeled after a Vermont neighbor of Rockwell's who posed for the artist and later went to war himself. In the final Willie Gillis cover illustration, in 1945, the soldier returns home to his mother.

Life

Despite the commercial success of *Reader's Digest* and *Time*, the magazines that really symbolized the general-interest genre during this era were the oversized pictorial weeklies *Look* and *Life*. More than any other magazine of its day, *Life* developed an effective strategy for competing with popular radio by advancing photojournalism. Launched as a weekly by Henry Luce in 1936, *Life* combined the public's fascination with images (invigorated by the movie industry), radio journalism, and the popularity of advertising and fashion photography. By the end of the 1930s, *Life* had a **pass-along readership**—the total number of people who come into contact with a single copy of a magazine—of more than seventeen million, rivaling the ratings of popular national radio programs.

Life's first editor, Wilson Hicks—formerly a picture editor for the Associated Press—built a staff of renowned photographer-reporters who chronicled the world's ordinary and extraordinary events from the late 1930s through the 1960s. Among *Life*'s most famous photojournalists was Margaret Bourke-White, the first woman war correspondent to fly combat missions during World War II, and Gordon Parks, who later became Hollywood's first African American director of major feature films.

The Fall of General-Interest Magazines

The decline of the weekly general-interest magazines, which had dominated the industry for thirty years, began in the 1950s. By 1957, both *Collier's* (founded in 1888) and *Woman's Home Companion* (founded in 1873) had folded. Each magazine had a national circulation of more than four million the year it died. No magazine with this kind of circulation had ever shut down before. Together, the two publications brought in advertising revenues of more than $26 million in 1956. Although some critics blamed poor management, both magazines were victims of changing consumer tastes, rising postal costs, falling ad revenues, and, perhaps most importantly, television, which began usurping the role of magazines as the preferred family medium.

TV Guide Is Born

While other magazines were just beginning to make sense of the impact of television on their readers, *TV Guide* appeared in 1953. Taking its cue from the pocket-size format of *Reader's Digest* and the supermarket sales strategy used by women's magazines, *TV Guide*, started by Walter Annenberg's Triangle Publications, soon rivaled the success of *Reader's Digest* by addressing the nation's growing fascination with television and by publishing TV listings. The first issue sold a

TABLE 9.1

THE TOP 10 MAGAZINES (RANKED BY PAID U.S. CIRCULATION AND SINGLE-COPY SALES, 1972 vs. 2008)

Source: Magazine Publishers of America, http://www.magazine .org, 2008.

1972		2008	
Rank/Publication	Circulation	Rank/Publication	Circulation
1 Reader's Digest	17,825,661	1 AARP The Magazine	24,204,313
2 TV Guide	16,410,858	2 AARP Bulletin	23,567,607
3 Woman's Day	8,191,731	3 Reader's Digest	9,684,759
4 Better Homes and Gardens	7,996,050	4 Better Homes and Gardens	7,681,722
5 Family Circle	7,889,587	5 National Geographic	5,051,999
6 McCall's	7,516,960	6 Good Housekeeping	4,686,152
7 National Geographic	7,260,179	7 Family Circle	3,967,065
8 Ladies' Home Journal	7,014,251	8 Woman's Day	3,924,195
9 Playboy	6,400,573	9 Ladies' Home Journal	3,918,472
10 Good Housekeeping	5,801,446	10 AAA Westways	3,764,966

record 1.5 million copies in ten urban markets. The next year, *TV Guide* featured twenty-seven regional editions, tailoring its listings to TV channels in specific areas of the country. Because many newspapers were not yet listing TV programs, *TV Guide*'s circulation soared to 2.2 million in its second year, and by 1962 the magazine became the first weekly to reach a circulation of 8 million with its seventy regional editions. (See Table 9.1 for the circulation figures of the Top 10 U.S. magazines.)

TV Guide's story illustrates a number of key trends that impacted magazines beginning in the 1950s. First, *TV Guide* highlighted America's new interest in specialized magazines. Second, it demonstrated the growing sales power of the nation's checkout lines, which also sustained the high circulation rates of women's magazines and supermarket tabloids. Third, *TV Guide* underscored the fact that magazines were facing the same challenge as other mass media in the 1950s: the growing power of television. *TV Guide* would rank among the nation's most popular magazines from the late 1950s into the twenty-first century.

In 1988, media baron Rupert Murdoch acquired Triangle Publications for $3 billion. Murdoch's News Corp. owned the new Fox network, and buying *TV Guide* ensured that the fledgling network would have its programs listed. Prior to this move, many predicted that no one would be able to start a new network because ABC, CBS, and NBC exercised so much control over television. By the mid-1990s, however, Fox was using *TV Guide* to promote the network's programming in the magazine's hundred-plus regional editions. Today, after years of declining circulation (TV schedules in local newspapers undermined its regional editions), *TV Guide* is now a full-size single-edition national magazine, dropping its smaller digest format and its 140 regional editions in 2005. The magazine now focuses on entertainment and life-style news and carries only limited listings of cable and network TV schedules. The TV Guide brand also lives on in the TV Guide Channel, an on-screen cable and satellite TV program guide since 1999.

Saturday Evening Post, Life, and *Look* Expire

Although *Reader's Digest* and women's supermarket magazines were not greatly affected by television, other general-interest magazines were. The *Saturday Evening Post* folded in 1969, *Look* in 1971, and *Life* in 1972. At the time, all three magazines were rated in the Top 10 in terms of paid circulation and each had a readership that exceeded 6 million per issue. Why did these magazines fold? First, to maintain these high circulation figures, their publishers were selling the magazines for far less than the cost of production. For example, a subscription to *Life* cost a consumer twelve cents an issue, yet it cost the publisher more than forty cents per copy to make and mail.

Second, the national advertising revenue pie that helped make up the cost differences for *Life* and *Look* now had to be shared with network television–and magazines' slices were getting smaller. *Life*'s high pass-along readership meant that it had a larger audience than many prime-time TV shows. But it cost more to have a single full-page ad in *Life* than it did to buy a minute of ad time during evening television. National advertisers were often forced to choose between the two, and in the late 1960s and early 1970s television seemed a better buy to advertisers looking for the biggest audience.

Third, dramatic increases in postal rates had a particularly negative effect on oversized publications (those larger than the 8-by-10.5-inch standard). In the 1970s, postal rates increased by more than 400 percent for these magazines. The *Post* and *Life* cut their circulations drastically to save money. The *Post* went from producing 6.8 million to 3 million copies per issue; *Life*, which lost $30 million between 1968 and 1972, cut circulation from 8.5 million to 7 million. The economic rationale here was that limiting the number of copies would reduce production and postal costs, enabling the magazines to lower their ad rates to compete with network television. But in fact, with decreased circulation, these magazines became less attractive to advertisers trying to reach the largest general audience.

The general magazines that survived the competition for national ad dollars tended to be women's magazines, such as *Good Housekeeping*, *Better Homes and Gardens*, *Redbook*, *Ladies' Home Journal*, and *Woman's Day*. These publications had smaller formats and depended primarily on supermarket sales rather than on expensive mail-delivered subscriptions (like *Life* and *Look*). However, the most popular magazines, *TV Guide* and *Reader's Digest*, benefited not only from supermarket sales but also from their larger circulations (twice that of *Life*), their pocket size, and their small photo budgets. The failure of the *Saturday Evening Post*, *Look*, and *Life* as oversized general audience weeklies ushered in a new era of specialization.

People Puts *Life* Back into Magazines

In March 1974, Time Inc. launched *People*, the first successful mass market magazine to appear in decades. With an abundance of celebrity profiles and human-interest stories, *People* showed a profit in two years and reached a circulation of more than two million within five years. *People* now ranks first in revenue from advertising and circulation sales–more than $1.4 billion a year.

The success of *People* is instructive, particularly because

THE RISE AND FALL OF *LOOK*

With large pages, beautiful photographs, and compelling stories on celebrities like Marlene Dietrich, *Look* entertained millions of readers from 1939 to 1971, emphasizing photojournalism to compete with radio. By the late 1960s, however, TV lured away national advertisers, postal rates increased, and production costs rose, forcing *Look* to fold despite a readership of more than eight million.

only two years earlier television had helped kill *Life* by draining away national ad dollars. Instead of using a bulky oversized format and relying on subscriptions, *People* downsized and generated most of its circulation revenue from newsstand and supermarket sales. For content, it took its cue from our culture's fascination with celebrities. Supported by plenty of photos, its short articles are about one-third the length of the articles in a typical newsmagazine.

Although *People* has not achieved the broad popularity that *Life* once commanded, it does seem to defy the contemporary trend of specialized magazines aimed at narrow but well-defined audiences, such as *Tennis World*, *Game Informer*, and *Hispanic Business*. One argument suggests that *People* is not, in fact, a mass market magazine but a specialized publication targeting people with particular cultural interests: a fascination with music, TV, and movie stars. If *People* is viewed as a specialty magazine, its financial success makes much more sense. It also helps to explain the host of magazines that try to emulate it, including *Us Weekly*, *Entertainment Weekly*, *In Touch Weekly*, *Star*, and *OK!*

The Domination of Specialization

The general trend away from mass market publications and toward specialty magazines coincided with radio's move to specialized formats in the 1950s. With the rise of television, magazines ultimately reacted the same way radio and movies did: They adapted. Radio developed formats for older and younger audiences, for rock fans and classical fans. At the movies, filmmakers focused on more adult subject matter that was off-limits to television's image as a family medium. And magazines traded their mass audience for smaller, discrete audiences that could be guaranteed to advertisers.

Magazines are now divided by advertiser type: *consumer magazines* (*Newsweek*; *Maxim*), which carry a host of general consumer product ads; *business* or *trade magazines* (*Advertising Age*; *Progressive Grocer*), which include ads for products and services for various occupational groups; and *farm magazines* (*Dairy Herd Management*; *Dakota Farmer*), which contain ads for agricultural products and farming lifestyles. Grouping by advertisers further distinguishes commercial magazines from noncommercial magazine-like periodicals. The noncommercial category includes everything from activist newsletters and scholarly journals to business newsletters created by companies for distribution to employees. Magazines such as *Ms.*, *Consumer Reports*, and *Cook's Illustrated*, which rely solely on subscription and newsstand sales, also accept no advertising, and fit into the noncommercial periodical category.

In addition to grouping magazines by advertising style, we can categorize popular consumer magazine styles by their target audience—such as gender, age, or ethnic group—or an audience interest area, such as entertainment, sports, literature, or tabloids.

Men's and Women's Magazines

One way the magazine industry competed with television was to reach niche audiences that were not being served by the new medium, including magazines focused on more adult subject matter. *Playboy*, started in 1953 by Hugh Hefner, was the first magazine to do this by undermining the conventional values of pre-World War II America and emphasizing previously taboo subject matter. Scraping together $7,000, Hefner published his first issue, which contained a nude calendar reprint of the actress Marilyn Monroe, along with male-focused articles that criticized alimony payments and gold-digging women. With the financial success of that first issue, which sold more than fifty thousand copies, Hefner was in business.

Playboy's circulation peaked in the 1960s at more than seven million, but fell gradually throughout the 1970s as the magazine faced competition from imitators and video, as well as criticism for "packaging" and objectifying women for the enjoyment of men. From the 1980s to today, *Playboy* and similar publications continue to publish, but newer men's magazines shifted their focus to include health (*Men's Health*) and lifestyle (*Details* and *Maxim*).

Women's magazines had long demonstrated that gender-based magazines were highly marketable, but during the era of specialization, the magazine industry aggressively sought the enormous market of magazine-reading women even more. *Better Homes and Gardens*, *Good Housekeeping*, *Ladies' Home Journal*, and *Woman's Day* focused on cultivating the image of women as homemakers and consumers. In the conservative 1950s and early 1960s, this formula proved to be enormously successful, but as the women's movement advanced in the late 1960s and into the 1970s, women's magazines grew more contemporary and sophisticated, incorporating content related to feminism (such as in Gloria Steinem's *Ms.* magazine, which first appeared in 1972), women's sexuality (such as in *Cosmopolitan* magazine, which became a women's magazine under the editorship of Helen Gurley Brown in the 1960s), and career and politics—topics previously geared primarily toward men.

Sports, Entertainment, and Leisure Magazines

The television age spawned not only *TV Guide* but also a number of specialized entertainment, leisure, and sports magazines. For example, *Soap Opera Digest* updates viewers on the latest plot twists and their favorite characters. In the age of specialization, magazine executives have developed multiple magazines for fans of soap operas, running, tennis, golf, hunting, quilting, antiquing, surfing, and gaming, to name only a few. Within categories, magazines specialize further, targeting older or younger runners, men or women golfers, duck hunters or birdwatchers, and midwestern or southern antique collectors.

The most popular sports and leisure magazine is *Sports Illustrated*, which took its name from a failed 1935 publication. Launched in 1954 by Henry Luce's Time Inc., *Sports Illustrated* was initially aimed at well-educated, middle-class men. It has become the most successful general sports magazine in history, covering everything from major-league sports and mountain

"The idea was there of a magazine that would paint the picture of a more entertaining, romantic life for a generation of men who had come back from World War II, were going to college in record numbers, and started to envision the possibilities of a life that was different and richer than what their fathers had lived."

CHRISTIE HEFNER, *PLAYBOY* EDITOR IN CHIEF, 2003

  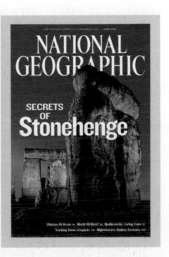

◄

SPECIALIZED MAGAZINES target a wide range of interests from mainstream sports to hobbies like making model airplanes. Some of the more successful specialized magazines include *Sports Illustrated*, *AARP The Magazine*, and *National Geographic*.

climbing to foxhunting and snorkeling. Although frequently criticized for its popular but exploitative yearly swimsuit edition, *Sports Illustrated* also has done major investigative pieces—for example, on racketeering in boxing and on land conservation. Its circulation rose to more than 3.2 million by 2008. *Sports Illustrated* competes directly with *ESPN The Magazine*, and indirectly with dozens of leisure and niche sports magazine competitors like *Golf Digest*, *Outside*, and *Pro Football Weekly*.

Another popular magazine type that fits loosely into the leisure category includes magazines devoted to music—everything from hip-hop's *Vibe* to country's *Country Weekly*. The all-time circulation champ in this category is *Rolling Stone*, started in 1967 as an irreverent, left-wing political and cultural magazine by twenty-one-year-old Jann Wenner. Once considered an alternative magazine, by 1982 *Rolling Stone* had paddled into the mainstream with a circulation approaching 800,000; by 2008, it had a circulation of more than 1.4 million. Many fans of the early *Rolling Stone*, however, disappointed with its move to increase circulation and reflect mainstream consumer values, turned to less high-gloss alternatives such as *Spin* and *Blender*.

Founded in 1888 by Boston lawyer Gardiner Green Hubbard and his famous son-in-law, Alexander Graham Bell, *National Geographic* promoted "humanized geography" and helped pioneer color photography in 1910. It was also the first publication to publish both undersea and aerial color photographs. In addition, many of *National Geographic*'s nature and culture specials on television, which began in 1965, rank among the most popular programs in the history of public television. *National Geographic*'s popularity grew slowly and steadily throughout the twentieth century, reaching 1 million in circulation in 1935 and 10 million in the 1970s. In the late 1990s, its circulation of paid subscriptions slipped to under 9 million. Other media ventures (for example, a cable channel and atlases) provided new revenue as circulation for the magazine continued to slide, falling to 5 million by 2008. Despite its falling circulation, *National Geographic* is often recognized as one of the country's best magazines for its reporting and photojournalism. Today, *National Geographic* competes with other travel and geography magazines like *Discover*, *Smithsonian*, *Travel & Leisure*, and *Condé Nast Traveler*.

Magazines for the Ages

In the age of specialization, magazines have further delineated readers along ever-narrowing age lines, appealing more and more to very young and to older readers, groups often ignored by mainstream television.

The first children's magazines appeared in New England in the late 1700s. Ever since, magazines such as *Youth's Companion*, *Boy's Life* (the Boy Scouts' national publication since 1912), *Highlights for Children*, and *Ranger Rick* have successfully targeted preschool and elementary-school children. The ad-free and subscription-only *Highlights for Children* topped the children's magazine category in 2008, with a circulation of more than two million.

In the popular arena, the leading female teen magazines have shown substantial growth; the top magazine for thirteen-to-nineteen-year-olds is *Seventeen*, with a circulation of 2 million in 2008. Several established magazines responded to the growing popularity of the teen market by introducing specialized editions, such as *Teen Vogue* and *Cosmo Girl!* (For a critical take on women's fashion magazines, see "Media Literacy and the Critical Process: Uncovering American Beauty" on page 299.)

Targeting young men in their twenties, *Maxim*, launched in 1997, was one of the fastest-growing magazines of the late 1990s, leveling off with a circulation of 2.5 million by 2005. *Maxim*'s covers boast the magazine's obsession with "sex, sports, beer, gadgets, clothes, fitness," a content mix that helped it eclipse rivals like *GQ* and *Esquire*. But by 2007, the lad fad had worn off, ad sales declined, and *Maxim* was reported to be for sale.

Media Literacy and the Critical Process

Uncovering American Beauty

How does the United States' leading fashion magazine define "beauty"? One way to explore this question is by critically analyzing the covers of *Cosmopolitan*.

1 DESCRIPTION. If you review a number of *Cosmopolitan* covers, you'll notice that they typically feature a body shot of a female model surrounded by blaring headlines often featuring the words "Hot" and "Sex" to usher a reader inside the magazine. The cover model is dressed provocatively and is positioned against a solid color background. She looks confident. Everything about the cover is loud and brassy.

2 ANALYSIS. What are some significant patterns here? One thing you'll notice is that all of these models look incredibly alike, particularly when it comes to race: *Cosmopolitan* has used only seven African American cover models from 1965 (when it became a women's fashion magazine) to 2008.[1] Things are improving somewhat in this regard; three of the seven models have appeared since 2002, and *Cosmo* has used several Hispanic cover models in recent years. (The July 2008 issue of *Italian Vogue* addressed the lack of racial diversity in fashion magazines by featuring only black models.) However, there is an even more consistent pattern regarding body type. Of its January 2008 cover

model Hillary Duff, *Cosmo* said, "at 20, with long honey-colored locks, a smokin' bod, and killer confidence, Hilary's looking every bit the hot Hollywood starlet." In *Cosmo*-speak, "smokin' bod" means ultrathin (sometimes made even more so with digital modifications).

3 INTERPRETATION. What does this mean? Although *Cosmo* doesn't provide height and weight figures for its models, it's likely that it's selling an unhealthy body weight (in fact, photos can be digitally altered to make the models look even more thin). In its guidelines for the fashion industry, the Academy for Eating Disorders suggests "for women and men over the age of 18, adoption of a minimum body mass index threshold of 18.5 kg/m2 (e.g., a female model who is 5'9" [1.75 m] must weigh more than 126 pounds [57.3 kg]), which recognizes that weight below this is considered underweight by the World Health Organization."[2]

4 EVALUATION. *Cosmopolitan* uses thin cover models as aspirational objects for its readers—that is, as women its readers would like to look

like. Thus, these cover models become the image of what a "terrific" body is for its readers, who—by *Cosmopolitan*'s own account—are women ages eighteen to twenty-four. *Cosmo* also notes that it's been the best-selling women's magazine in college bookstores for twenty-five years. But that target audience also happens to be the one most susceptible to body issues. As the Academy for Eating Disorders notes, "at any given time 10 percent or more of late adolescent and adult women report symptoms of eating disorders."

5 ENGAGEMENT. Contact *Cosmo*'s editor in chief, Kate White, and request representation of healthy body types on the magazine's covers. You can contact her and the editorial department via e-mail (cosmo_letters@hearst.com), telephone (212-649-3570), or U.S. mail: Kate White, Editor, *Cosmopolitan*, 224 West 57th Street, New York, NY 10019. Also, track body type issues with other fashion magazines.

In targeting audiences by age, the most dramatic success has come from magazines aimed at readers over age fifty, America's fastest-growing age segment. These publications have tried to meet the cultural interests of older Americans, who historically have not been prominently featured in mainstream consumer culture. The American Association of Retired Persons (AARP) and its magazine, *AARP The Magazine*, were founded in 1958 by retired California teacher Ethel Percy Andrus. Subscriptions to the bimonthly *AARP The Magazine* and the monthly *AARP Bulletin* come free when someone joins AARP and pays the modest membership fee ($12.50 in 2008). By the early 1980s, *AARP The Magazine*'s circulation approached 7 million. However, with the AARP signing up thirty thousand new members each week by the late 1980s, both *AARP The Magazine* and the newsletter overtook *TV Guide* and *Reader's Digest* as the top circulated magazines. By 2008, both had circulations of 23-24 million, far surpassing the circulations of all other magazines. Article topics in the magazine cover a range of lifestyle, travel, money, health, and entertainment issues, such as the effects of Viagra on relationships, secrets for spectacular vacations, and how poker can give you a sharper mind.

Elite Magazines

Although long in existence, *elite magazines* grew in popularity during the age of specialization. Elite magazines are characterized by their combination of literature, criticism, humor, and journalism and by their appeal to highly educated audiences, often living in urban areas. Among the numerous elite publications that grew in stature during the twentieth century were the *Atlantic Monthly, Vanity Fair,* and *Harper's.*

However, the most widely circulated elite magazine is the *New Yorker.* Launched in 1925 by Harold Ross, the *New Yorker* became the first city magazine aimed at a national upscale audience. Over the years, the *New Yorker* featured many of the twentieth century's most prominent biographers, writers, reporters, and humorists, including A. J. Liebling, Dorothy Parker, Lillian Ross, John Updike, E. B. White, and Garrison Keillor, as well as James Thurber's cartoons and Ogden Nash's poetry. It introduced some of the finest literary journalism of the twentieth century, devoting an entire issue to John Hersey's *Hiroshima* and serializing Truman Capote's *In Cold Blood.* By the mid-1960s, the *New Yorker*'s circulation hovered around 500,000; by 2008, the magazine's circulation rose to 1 million.

Minority-Targeted Magazines

Minority-targeted magazines, like newspapers, have existed since before the Civil War, including the African American antislavery magazines *Emancipator, Liberator,* and *Reformer.* One of the most influential early African American magazines, the *Crisis,* was founded by W. E. B. DuBois in 1910 and is the official magazine of the National Association for the Advancement of Colored People (NAACP).

In the modern age, the major magazine publisher for African Americans has been John H. Johnson, a former Chicago insurance salesman, who started *Negro Digest* in 1942 on $500 borrowed against his mother's furniture. By 1945, with a circulation of more than 100,000, the *Digest*'s profits enabled Johnson and a small group of editors to start *Ebony,* a picture text magazine modeled on *Life* but serving black readers. The Johnson Publishing Company also successfully introduced *Jet,* a pocket-size supermarket magazine, in 1951. By 2008, *Jet*'s circulation reached nearly 1 million, while *Ebony*'s circulation was 1.4 million. *Essence,* the first major magazine geared toward African American women, debuted in 1969, and by 2008 also had a circulation of over 1 million.

Other minority groups also have magazines aimed at their own interests. The *Advocate,* founded in 1967 as a twelve-page newsletter, was the first major magazine to address issues of interest to gay men and lesbians, and has in ensuing years published some of the best journalism about antigay violence, policy issues affecting the LGBT community, and AIDS, topics often not well-covered by the mainstream press. By the mid-1980s, the magazine had a circulation of nearly 90,000, and by 2008, its circulation had reached 168,000, just behind *Out,* a gay style magazine, with a circulation of 184,000.

With increases in Hispanic populations and immigration, magazines appealing to Spanish-speaking readers have developed rapidly since the 1980s. In 1983, the De Armas Spanish Magazine Network began distributing Spanish-language versions of mainstream American magazines, including *Cosmopolitan en Español; Harper's Bazaar en Español;* and *Ring,* the prominent boxing magazine. The bilingual *Latina* magazine was started with the help of Essence Communications in 1996, while recent magazine launches include *ESPN Deportes* and *Sports Illustrated en Español.* The new magazines target the most upwardly mobile segments of the growing American Hispanic population, which numbered more than 44 million–about 15 percent of the U.S. population–by 2008. Today, *People en Español, Latina,* and *Glamour en Español* rank as the Top 3 Hispanic magazines by ad revenue.

Although national magazines aimed at other minority groups were slow to arrive, magazines now target virtually every race, culture, and ethnicity, including *Asian Week, Native Peoples, Tikkun,* and many more.

Supermarket Tabloids

With headlines like "O.J. Caught with Drag Queen at 1 A.M.," "Extraterrestrials Follow the Teachings of Oprah Winfrey," and "Al Qaeda Breeding Killer Mosquitoes," **supermarket tabloids** push the limits of both decency and credibility. Although they are published on newsprint, the Audit Bureau of Circulations, which checks newspaper and magazine circulation figures to determine advertising rates, counts weekly tabloids as magazines. Tabloid history can be traced to newspapers' use of graphics and pictorial layouts in the 1860s and 1870s, but the modern U.S. tabloid began with the founding of the *National Enquirer* by William Randolph Hearst in 1926. The *Enquirer* struggled until it was purchased in 1952 by Generoso Pope, who originally intended to use it to "fight for the rights of man" and "human decency and dignity."[8] In the interest of profit, though, Pope settled on the "gore formula" to transform the paper's anemic weekly circulation of seven thousand: "I noticed how auto accidents drew crowds and I decided that if it was blood that interested people, I'd give it to them."[9]

By the mid-1960s, the *Enquirer*'s circulation had jumped to over 1 million through the publication of bizarre human-interest stories, gruesome murder tales, violent accident accounts, unexplained phenomena stories, and malicious celebrity gossip. By 1974, the magazine's weekly circulation topped 4 million. Its popularity inspired other tabloids like *Globe* (founded in 1954) and *Star,* founded by News Corp. in 1974, and the adoption of a tabloid style by general-interest magazines such as *People* and *Us Weekly.* Today, tabloid magazine sales are down from their peak in the 1980s, but continue to be extremely popular. American Media in Boca Raton, Florida, owns most of the supermarket tabloids today, including *Star, National Enquirer, Sun, Globe, National Examiner,* and now online-only *Weekly World News.*

LATINA, launched in 1996, has become the largest magazine targeted to Hispanic women in the United States. It counts a readership of 2 million bilingual, bicultural women and is also the top Hispanic magazine in advertising pages.

"Ah, *Weekly World News*, how could you make death so boring? You should shut down because ... your staff has been kidnapped by Elvis imitators from Mars.... Or because your Boca Raton, Fla., offices are being haunted by the noisy ghosts of dead rappers.... Or because giant radioactive cockroaches have eaten your computers.... But not because of 'challenges in the retail and wholesale magazine marketplace.' Not that."

THE *STATE* (COLUMBIA, SOUTH CAROLINA), 2007, ON THE CLOSING OF THE SUPERMARKET TABLOID *WEEKLY WORLD NEWS*

Online Magazines and Media Convergence

A more recent development in magazines is the growth of online magazines. With half of Americans linked to a broadband Internet connection, the Internet has become the place where print magazines like *Time* and *Entertainment Weekly* can extend their reach, where some magazines like *FHM* and *Elle Girl* can survive when their print version ends, or where online magazines like *Salon* and *Slate* can exist exclusively. Although the Internet was initially viewed as the death knell of print magazines, the industry now embraces it. Many online magazines now carry blogs, original video and audio podcasts, social networks, virtual fitting rooms, and other interactive components that could never work in print. For example, *PopularMechanics.com* has added interactive 3-D models for do-it-yourself projects, so that a reader can go over plans to make an Adirondack chair, examining joints and parts from every angle.

Webzines such as *Salon* and *Slate*, which are magazines that appear exclusively online, have made the Web a legitimate site for breaking news and discussing culture and politics. *Salon* was founded in 1995 by five former reporters from the *San Francisco Examiner* who wanted to break from the traditions of newspaper publishing and build "a different kind of newsroom" to create well-developed stories and commentary. With the help of positive word-of-mouth comments, *Salon* is the leading online magazine, claiming 5.8 million monthly unique visitors by 2008. Its main online competitor, *Slate*, founded in 1996 and now owned by the Washington Post Company, draws about 5 million monthly unique visitors. A new entrant to the field in 2007 was *Politico.com*, which garners about 2 million monthly unique visitors. *Politico* focuses on national politics and was started by a team of experienced political correspondents from several newspapers. Ironically, the Web version draws far more readers than *Politico*'s print newspaper, which circulates just 25,000 daily copies in the Washington, D.C., area.

In addition to Webzines, new print titles often publish with brand-extending synergies in mind. For example, in 1998, cable network ESPN started *ESPN The Magazine*. The brand familiarity helped *ESPN The Magazine* find readers in a segment already crowded with *Sports Illustrated*, the *Sporting News*, and dozens of niche sports publications. The magazine helps to cross-promote ESPN's growing business empire, including its cable channels, ESPN radio, the ESPN Web site, ESPN Zone restaurants, and the X Games. Other convergence-based magazines include Oprah Winfrey's *O: The Oprah Magazine*, and Reader's Digest's launch of *Everyday with Rachael Ray*, capitalizing on the Food Network's celebrity chef.

The Organization and Economics of Magazines

Given the great diversity in magazine content and ownership, it is hard to offer a common profile of a successful magazine. However large or small, most magazines deal with the same basic functions: production, content, ads, and sales. In this section, we discuss how magazines operate, the ownership structure behind major magazines, and how smaller publications fulfill niche areas that even specialized magazines do not reach.

Magazine Departments and Duties

Unlike a broadcast station or a daily newspaper, a small newsletter or magazine can begin cheaply via computer-based **desktop publishing**, which enables an aspiring publisher-editor to write, design, lay out, and print or post online a modest publication. For larger operations, however, the work is divided into departments.

Editorial and Production

The lifeblood of a magazine is the *editorial department*, which produces its content, excluding advertisements. Like newspapers, most magazines have a chain of command that begins with a publisher and extends to the editor in chief, the managing editor, and a variety of subeditors. These subeditors oversee such editorial functions as photography, illustrations, reporting and writing, copyediting, layout, and design. Magazine writers generally include contributing staff writers, who are specialists in certain fields, and freelance writers, nonstaff professionals who are assigned to cover particular stories or a region of the country. Many magazines, especially those with small budgets, also rely on well-written unsolicited manuscripts to fill their pages. Most commercial magazines, however, reject more than 95 percent of unsolicited pieces.

Despite the rise of inexpensive desktop publishing, most large commercial magazines still operate several departments, which employ hundreds of people. The *production and technology department* maintains the computer and printing hardware necessary for mass market production. Because magazines are printed weekly, monthly, or bimonthly, it is not economically practical for most magazine publishers to maintain expensive print facilities. As with *USA Today*, many national magazines digitally transport magazine copy to various regional printing sites for the insertion of local ads and for faster distribution.

Advertising and Sales

The advertising and sales department of a magazine secures clients, arranges promotions, and places ads. Like radio stations, network television stations, and basic cable television stations, consumer magazines are heavily reliant on advertising revenue. The more successful the magazine, the more they can charge for advertisement space. Magazines provide their advertisers with rate cards, which indicate how much they charge for a certain amount of advertising space

"Inevitably, fashion advertisers that prop up the glossies will, like everyone else, increasingly migrate to Web and mobile interactive advertising."

ADVERTISING AGE, 2006

"If you don't acknowledge your magazine's advertisers, you don't have a magazine."

ANNA WINTOUR, EDITOR OF *VOGUE*, 2000

on a page. A top-rated consumer magazine might charge $320,000 for a full-page color ad and $89,000 for a third of a page, black-and-white ad. However, in today's competitive world, most rate cards are not very meaningful: Almost all magazines offer 25 to 50 percent rate discounts to advertisers.[10] Although fashion and general-interest magazines carry a higher percentage of ads than do political or literary magazines, the average magazine contains about 50 percent ad copy and 50 percent editorial material, a figure that has remained fairly constant for the past twenty-five years.

A few contemporary magazines, such as *Highlights for Children*, have decided not to carry ads and rely solely on subscriptions and newsstand sales instead. To protect the integrity of their various tests and product comparisons, *Consumer Reports* and *Cook's Illustrated* carry no advertising. To strengthen its editorial independence, *Ms.* magazine abandoned ads in 1990 after years of pressure from the food, cosmetics, and fashion industries to feature recipes and more complementary copy. (See "Examining Ethics: *Ms.* Magazine's Latest Challenge" on page 305.)

Some advertisers and companies have canceled ads when a magazine featured an unflattering or critical article about a company or industry.[11] In some instances, this practice has put enormous pressure on editors not to offend advertisers. The cozy relationships between some advertisers and magazines have led to a dramatic decline in investigative reporting, once central to popular magazines during the muckraking era.

As television advertising siphoned off national ad revenues in the 1950s, magazines began introducing different editions of their magazines to attract advertisers. **Regional editions** are national magazines whose content is tailored to the interests of different geographic areas. For example, *Sports Illustrated* often prints five different regional versions of its College Football Preview and March Madness Preview editions, picturing regional stars on each of the five cov-

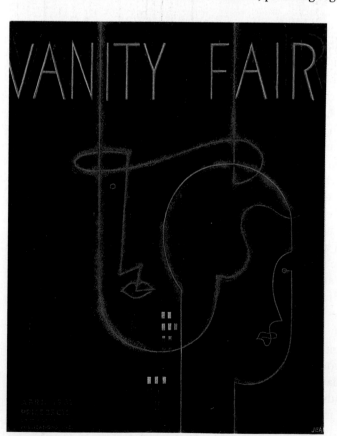

ers. In **split-run editions**, the editorial content remains the same, but the magazine includes a few pages of ads purchased by local or regional companies. Most editions of *Time, Newsweek,* and *Sports Illustrated*, for example, contain a number of pages reserved for regional ads. **Demographic editions**, meanwhile, are editions of magazines targeted at particular groups of consumers. In this case, market researchers identify subscribers primarily by occupation, class, and zip code. *Time* magazine, for example, developed special editions of its magazine for top management, high-income zip-code areas, and ultrahigh-income professional/managerial households. Demographic editions guarantee advertisers a particular magazine audience, one which enables them to pay lower rates for their ads because the ads would only

Ms. Magazine's Latest Challenge

In spring 1972, *Ms.* magazine jolted the U.S. magazine industry with the first issue of a magazine that took the feminist movement seriously. The magazine had its detractors, including network news anchor Harry Reasoner, who quipped, "I'll give it six months before they run out of things to say."

It turned out that *Ms.* had a lot of things to say. The magazine became a leading and award-winning voice on issues such as abortion, the Equal Rights Amendment, domestic violence, pornography, and date rape.

In 1990, *Ms.* magazine cofounder Gloria Steinem, surveying the state of women's magazines and the influence advertisers have over journalism, asked, "Can't we do better than this?" That was the beginning of another bold move for *Ms.* magazine, which subsequently stopped carrying advertisements (except for nonprofit and cause-related organizations).

Although its rejection of advertisers has enabled *Ms.* to be uniquely outspoken and independent in U.S. journalism, it has also made the magazine financially unstable at times, as it has had more than a half-dozen owners. In 2001, the Los Angeles–based Feminist Majority Foundation assumed ownership of the magazine and changed *Ms.* to a quarterly publication schedule.

In 2006, *Ms.* returned to the still audacious idea that its debut issue carried: a list of women who publicly declared that they had undergone abortions. In the article "We Had Abortions," *Ms.* argued for the need to once again "transform the public debate." More than five thousand people signed the new petition, and the editors reported that they were "flooded with letters." ◄

GLORIA STEINEM, cofounder of *Ms.*, regularly wrote for the magazine until 1987 and continues to sit on its advisory board today.

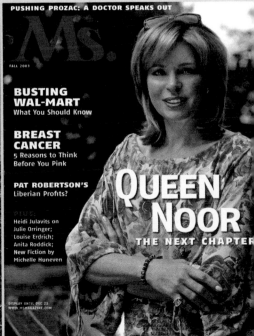

▶

TABLE 9.2

**MAJOR MAGAZINE
CHAINS**

Selected magazine titles
for each major chain. The
Top 20 magazines in 2007
(based on gross revenue of
ads and sales) are noted
with their rank.

*Source: Advertising Age, Ad Age
DataCenter, http://adage.com/
datacenter/article?article_
id=121567.*

ADVANCE PUBLICATIONS (Staten Island, N.Y.)	
Allure	Modern Bride
Architectural Digest	New Yorker
Bon Appétit	Parade (Rank: #5)
Bride's	Portfolio
Condé Nast Traveler	Self
Domino	Teen Vogue
Glamour (Rank: #19)	Vanity Fair
Gourmet	Vogue (Rank: #16)
GQ	W
House & Garden	Wired
Lucky	

HACHETTE FILIPACCHI, A SUBSIDIARY OF LAGARDÈRE GROUPE (Paris)	
Car and Driver	Metropolitan Home
Cycle World	Premiere
Elle	Road & Track
Elle Decor	Woman's Day (Rank: #10)

HEARST CORPORATION (New York, N.Y.)	
Cosmopolitan (Rank: #11)	Marie Claire
Country Living	O: The Oprah Magazine
Esquire	Popular Mechanics
Good Housekeeping (Rank: #7)	Redbook
Harper's Bazaar	Seventeen
House Beautiful	Town & Country

be run in a limited number of copies of the magazine. The magazine can then compete with advertising in regional television or cable markets and in newspaper supplements. Because of the flexibility of special editions, new sources of income opened up for national magazines. Ultimately, these marketing strategies permitted the massive growth of magazines in the face of predictions that television would cripple the magazine industry.

Circulation and Distribution

The circulation and distribution department of a magazine monitors single-copy and subscription sales. Toward the end of the general-interest magazine era in 1950, newsstand sales accounted for about 43 percent of magazine sales, and subscriptions constituted 57 percent. Today, newsstand sales have fallen to 13 percent, whereas subscriptions have risen to 87 percent. One tactic used by magazines' circulation departments to increase subscription sales is to encourage consumers to renew well in advance of their actual renewal dates. Magazines can thus invest and earn interest on early renewal money as a hedge against consumers who drop their subscriptions.

MEREDITH CORPORATION (Des Moines, Ia.)	
American Baby	Fitness
Better Homes and Gardens (Rank: #3)	Ladies' Home Journal (Rank: #15)
Child	Parents
Country Home	Ready Made
Family Circle (Rank #14)	Successful Farming

TIME, INC., A SUBSIDIARY OF TIME WARNER (New York, N.Y.)	
Cooking Light	Progressive Farmer
Entertainment Weekly	Real Simple
FORTUNE	Southern Living
Health	Sports Illustrated (Rank #4)
InStyle (Rank #13)	Sports Illustrated for Kids
Money	Sunset
Parenting	This Old House
People (Rank #1)	Time (Rank: #2)

Other strategies include **evergreen subscriptions**—those that automatically renew on a credit card account unless subscribers request that the automatic renewal be stopped—and *controlled circulations*, providing readers with the magazine at no charge by targeting captive audiences such as airline passengers or association members. These magazines' financial support comes solely from advertising or corporate sponsorship.

Major Magazine Chains

In terms of ownership, the commercial magazine industry most closely resembles the cable television business, which patterned its specialized channels on the consumer magazine market. Also, as in the cable industry, large companies or chains increasingly dominate the magazine business (see Table 9.2). Even though about seven hundred to one thousand new commercial magazine titles appear each year—many of them independently owned—it is a struggle to survive in the competitive magazine marketplace.

Long a force in upscale consumer magazines, Condé Nast is a division of Advance Publications, which operates the Newhouse newspaper chain (see "What Advance Publications Owns"). The Condé Nast group controls several key magazines, including *Vanity Fair*, *GQ*, and *Vogue*. Advance Publications also owns *Parade* magazine, the popular Sunday newspaper supplement that goes to thirty-two million homes each week. (Since *Parade* comes with newspaper subscriptions, it is not counted among most official magazine tallies.)

Time Warner, the world's largest media conglomerate, also runs a magazine subsidiary, Time Inc., a top player among magazine-chain operators with about thirty major titles including *People* and *Sports Illustrated*. Cross-division synergies at Time Warner have been particularly helpful to its magazines. For example, in 2008 the Warner Brothers Television group teamed up with *Essence* magazine to relaunch the Essence.com Web site and develop television content for African American women.

▶

WHAT ADVANCE PUBLICATIONS OWNS

Magazines
- American City Business Journals
- Condé Nast Publications (see Advance Publications in Table 9.2 for more)
  - Cookie
  - Details
  - Elegant Bride
  - Golf Digest
  - Golf World
  - Men's Vogue
- Fairchild Publications
  - Daily News Record (DNR)
  - Women's Wear Daily
  - Footwear News (FN)
- Parade magazine
- Home Furnishings News
- Executive Technology
- Supermarket News
- Brand Marketing
- Salon News
- Vitals
- Sporting News
- Tatler

Newspapers
- 19 newspapers
  - The Birmingham News (Ala.)
  - Patriot-News (Pa.)
  - Express-Times (Easton, Pa.)
  - Jersey Journal (Jersey City, N.J.)
  - Oregonian (Portland)
  - Staten Island Advance (N.Y.)
  - Post-Standard (Syracuse, N.Y.)
  - Times-Picayune (New Orleans)
  - Sun Newspapers (Ohio)
- Booth Newspapers of Michigan (8 local papers)

Books
- Fairchild Books

Cable Television
- Brighthouse Networks
- Cable Television Operations (with Time Warner)

Internet
- Advance.net
- CondéNet
  - Epicurious.com
  - Concierge.com
  - Reddit.com
- Advance Internet
  NJ.com
  - MassLive.com
  - NOLA.com
  - BestLocalJobs.com
  - BestLocalAutos.com

News Services
- Religion News Service
- Newhouse News Service

Other important commercial players include Rodale Press, a family-owned company that publishes health and wellness titles like *Prevention* and *Men's Health*, and the Meredith Corporation, which specializes in women's and home-related magazines. The Hearst Corporation, the leading magazine chain early in the twentieth century, still remains a formidable publisher with titles like *Cosmopolitan* and *Esquire*. The Paris-based Hachette Filipacchi owns more than two hundred magazine titles worldwide, including about twenty in the United States, such as *Elle* and *Car and Driver*.

In addition, a number of American magazines have carved out market niches worldwide. *Reader's Digest, Cosmopolitan, Newsweek*, and *Time*, for example, all produce international editions in several languages. In general, though, most American magazines are local, regional, or specialized and therefore less exportable than movies and television. Of the nearly nineteen thousand titles, only about two hundred magazines from the United States circulate routinely in the world market. Such magazines, however, like exported American TV shows and films, play a key role in determining the look of global culture.

Many major publishers, including Hearst, Meredith, Time, and Rodale, also generate additional revenue through custom publishing divisions, producing limited distribution publications, sometimes called **magalogs**, which combine glossy magazine style with the sales pitch of retail catalogs. Magalogs are often used to market goods or services to customers or employees. For example, Rodale produces the *little brown book* magalog for Bloomingdale's top 175,000 customers, while Time produces *myFord*, distributed by the automobile company to buyers of its vehicles.

Alternative Voices

With fewer than ninety of the almost nineteen thousand American magazines reaching circulations that top a million, most alternative magazines struggle to satisfy small but loyal groups of readers. At any given time, there are over two thousand alternative magazines in circulation, with many failing and others starting up every month.

Alternative magazines have historically defined themselves in terms of politics–published either by the Left (the *Progressive, In These Times*, the *Nation*) or the Right (the *National Review, American Spectator, Insight*). However, what constitutes an alternative magazine has broadened over time to include just about any publication considered "outside the mainstream," ranging from environmental magazines to alternative lifestyle magazines to punk-zines–the magazine world's answer to punk rock. (*Zines*, pronounced "zeens," is a term used to describe self-published magazines.) *Utne Reader*, widely regarded as "the *Reader's Digest* of alternative magazines," has defined *alternative* as any sort of "thinking that doesn't reinvent the status quo, that broadens issues you might see on TV or in the daily paper."

Occasionally, alternative magazines have become marginally mainstream. For example, during the conservative Reagan era in the 1980s, William F. Buckley's *National Review* saw its circulation swell to more than 100,000–enormous by alternative standards. In the late 1980s, the *Review* even ran slick TV ads featuring actors such as Charlton Heston and Tom Selleck, as well as former actor and president Ronald Reagan. On the Left, *Mother Jones* (named after labor organizer Mary Harris Jones), which champions muckraking and investigative journalism, had a circulation of about 225,000 in 2008.

Most alternative magazines, however, are content to swim outside the mainstream. These are the small magazines that typically include diverse political, cultural, religious, international, and environmental subject matter, such as *Against the Current, BadAzz MoFo, Buddhadharma, Home Education Magazine, Jewish Currents, Small Farmer's Journal*, and *Humor Times*.

Magazines in a Democratic Society

Like other mass media, magazines are a major part of the cluttered media landscape. To keep pace, the magazine industry has become fast-paced and high-risk. Of the seven hundred to one thousand new magazines that start up each year, fewer than two hundred will survive longer than a year.

As an industry, magazine publishing—like advertising and public relations—has played a central role in transforming the United States from a producer society to a consumer society. Since the 1950s, though, individual magazines have not had the powerful national voice they once possessed, uniting separate communities around important issues such as abolition and suffrage. Today, with so many specialized magazines appealing to distinct groups of consumers, magazines play a much-diminished role in creating a sense of national identity.

Contemporary commercial magazines provide essential information about politics, society, and culture, thus helping us think about ourselves as participants in a democracy. Unfortunately, however, these magazines have often identified their readers as consumers first and citizens second. With magazines growing increasingly dependent on advertising, and some of them (such as shopping magazines like *Lucky*) being primarily *about* the advertising, controversial content sometimes has difficulty finding its way into print. More and more, magazines define their readers merely as viewers of displayed products and purchasers of material goods.

At the same time, magazines have arguably had more freedom than other media to encourage and participate in democratic debates. More magazine voices circulate in the marketplace than do broadcast or cable television channels. Moreover, many new magazines still play an important role in uniting dispersed groups of readers, often giving cultural minorities or newly arrived immigrants or alternative groups a sense of membership in a broader community. In addition, because magazines are distributed weekly, monthly, or bimonthly, they are less restricted by the deadline pressures experienced by newspaper publishers or radio and television broadcasters. Good magazines can usually offer more analysis of and insight into society than other media outlets can. In the midst of today's swirl of images, magazines and their advertisements certainly contribute to the commotion. But good magazines also maintain our connection to words, sustaining their vital role in an increasingly electronic and digital culture. ▶

CHAPTER REVIEW

REVIEW QUESTIONS

The Early History of Magazines

1. Why did magazines develop later than newspapers in the American colonies?

2. Why did most of the earliest magazines have so much trouble staying financially solvent?

3. How did magazines become national in scope?

The Development of Modern American Magazines

4. How did magazines position women in the new consumer economy at the turn of the twentieth century?

5. What role did magazines play in social reform at the turn of the twentieth century?

6. When and why did general-interest magazines become so popular?

7. Why did some of the major general-interest magazines fail in the twentieth century?

The Domination of Specialization

8. What triggered the move toward magazine specialization?

9. What are the differences between regional and demographic editions?

10. What are the most useful ways to categorize the magazine industry? Why?

The Organization and Economics of Magazines

11. What are the four main departments at a typical consumer magazine?

12. What are the major magazine chains, and what is their impact on the mass media industry in general?

Magazines in a Democratic Society

13. How do magazines serve a democratic society?

14. How does advertising affect what gets published in the editorial side of magazines?

QUESTIONING THE MEDIA

1. What are your earliest recollections of magazines? Which magazines do you read regularly today? Why?

2. What role did magazines play in America's political and social shift from being colonies of Great Britain to becoming an independent nation?

3. Why is the muckraking spirit—so important in popular magazines at the turn of the twentieth century—generally missing from magazines today?

4. If you were the marketing director of your favorite magazine, how would you increase circulation?

5. Think of stories, ideas, and images (illustrations and photos) that do not appear in mainstream maga-

zines. Why do you think this is so? (Use the Internet, LexisNexis, or the library to compare your list with Project Censored, an annual list of the year's most underreported stories.)

6. Discuss whether your favorite magazines define you primarily as a consumer or as a citizen. Do you think magazines have a responsibility to educate their readers as both? What can they do to promote responsible citizenship?

7. Do you think the Internet will eventually displace magazines? Why or why not?

COMMON THREADS

One of the Common Threads discussed in Chapter 1 is about the commercial nature of the mass media. The magazine industry is an unusual example of this. Big media corporations control some of the most popular magazines, and commercialism runs deep in many consumer magazines. At the same time, magazines are one of the most democratic mass media. How can that be?

There are more than nineteen thousand magazine titles in the United States. But the largest and most profitable magazines are typically owned by some of the biggest media corporations. Time Warner, for example, counts *People, Time, Sports Illustrated, InStyle, FORTUNE, Southern Living,* and *Real Simple* among its holdings. Even niche magazines that seem small are often controlled by chains. Supermarket tabloids like *Star,* the *National Enquirer,* and *Globe* are all owned by Florida-based American Media, which also publishes *Shape, Muscle & Fitness, Men's Fitness, Fit Pregnancy,* and *Flex.*

High-revenue magazines, especially those focusing on fashion, fitness, and lifestyle, can also shamelessly break down the firewall between the editorial and business departments. "Fluff" story copy serves as a promotional background for cosmetic, clothing, and gadget advertisements. Digital retouching makes every model and celebrity thinner or more muscular, and always blemish-free. This altered view of their "perfection" becomes our ever-hopeful aspiration, spurring us to purchase the advertised products.

Yet, the huge number of magazine titles—more than the number of radio stations, TV stations, cable networks, or yearly Hollywood releases—means that magazines span a huge range of activities and thought. Each magazine sustains a community—although some may think of readers more as consumers, while others view them as citizens—and several hundred new launches each year bring new voices to the marketplace and search for their own community to serve.

So there is the glitzy, commercial world of the big magazine industry with *Time's* Person of the Year, the latest *Cosmo* girl, and the band on the cover of *Rolling Stone.* But the long list of smaller magazines—like *Multinational Monitor, Edutopia,* and *E-The Environmental Magazine*—account for the majority of magazine titles and the broad, democratic spectrum of communities that are their readers.

KEY TERMS

The definitions for the terms listed below can be found in the glossary at the end of the book. The page numbers listed with the terms indicate where the term is highlighted in the chapter.

magazine, 283
muckrakers, 289
general-interest magazines, 289
photojournalism, 289
pass-along readership, 293
supermarket tabloids, 301
Webzines, 302

desktop publishing, 303
regional editions, 304
split-run editions, 304
demographic editions, 304
evergreen subscriptions, 307
magalogs, 308
zines, 308

HOGWARTS EXPRESS
Zur Amazon.de
Harry Potter
und die Heiligtümer des Todes
CARLSEN
amazon.de

10

Books and the Power of Print

Two of the most successful original book series of this generation have been J. K. Rowling's Harry Potter and Philip Pullman's His Dark Materials. The series' "successes" are measured not only in actual book sales but in the profitable movie franchises and other merchandising they have inspired, as well as the new interest in fantasy literature they have spawned. As the British trade magazine *Bookseller* said, "Together with Philip Pullman's His Dark Materials trilogy, Harry Potter showed that fantasy could sell."[1]

Pullman started first, with the 1996 release of *The Golden Compass*, a story about 11-year-old Lyra Belaqua, an orphan ward of the fictional Jordan College in Oxford, England, who travels through parallel universes (Lyra's story continues in the *Subtle Knife*, 1997, and *The Amber Spyglass*, 2000). The series has sold more than 14 million copies, although it is probably best known in Great Britain, where the first volume won the Carnegie Award for children's fiction and the third volume was the first children's book to win the prestigious Whitbread Book of the Year.

In the Harry Potter series, each of the seven books follows a year in the life of orphan Harry Potter at Hogwarts School of Witchcraft and Wizardry. In terms of commercial success, the Harry Potter series has broken all records: More than 375 million copies of the books in sixty-five languages had been sold by 2008. The final book, *Harry Potter and the Deathly Hallows*, was released in July 2007 and sold 13.1 million copies that year, becoming the fastest-selling book in history. The Harry Potter books also occupied the *New York Times* best-seller list for ten years beginning in 1998. Although some critics like Jack Zipes, editor of the *Norton Anthology of Children's Literature*, chided the Potter books for being "conventional and mediocre," Rowling's books have received several honors, including a commendation from the Carnegie Awards and the Whitbread Children's Book of the Year award in 1999.[2]

Both book series have multiple similarities beyond their fantasy subject matter, awards, and British authors. Each has expanded across media platforms, most famously in movies, where the Harry Potter series has generated some of the highest-grossing movies of the past decade. In fact, Warner Brothers, which produces and distributes the movies, has an agreement with Rowling to split the final book into two movies, doubling the pleasure for the audiences and the payday for corporate parent Time Warner. Time Warner's New Line Cinema unit also released *The Golden Compass* movie. It premiered to mixed reviews but did well in international release, and more movies are anticipated.

While the books inspired people to see the movies, the movies also inspired people to read more than just those books. Pullman's and Rowling's successes revived interest in the older *Lord of the Rings* trilogy (also made into blockbuster movies) by J. R. R. Tolkien and C. S. Lewis's *Chronicles of Narnia* trilogy (spawning more blockbuster movies), while triggering a host of new fantasy books for children and adults.

Pullman's and Rowling's works also share controversy. The American Library Association reported that due to its religious viewpoints, *The Golden Compass* was one of 2007's most challenged books—books that receive formal complaints about being on classroom and library shelves because of potentially "offensive" content. Similar complaints about the Harry Potter series led to their being the most frequently challenged books so far in the twenty-first century.

In a world where digital media dominate our landscape, books—the oldest mass medium—still survive because they originate some of the biggest ideas and stories that resonate through the rest of the mass media. Many of these stories are timeless, but they are also copyrighted and—as Pullman's and Rowling's series demonstrate—can earn a lot of money in books and other media forms.

"In fifty years today's children will not remember who survived *Survivor* . . . but they will remember Harry [Potter]."

ANNA QUINDLEN,
NEWSWEEK, JULY 2000

◢ *IN THE 1950s AND 1960s,* cultural forecasters thought that the popularity of television might spell the demise of a healthy book industry, just as they thought television would replace the movie, sound recording, radio, newspaper, and magazine industries. Obviously, this did not happen. In 1950, more than 11,000 new book titles were introduced, and by 2007 publishers were producing over fifteen times that number—more than 170,000 titles per year (see Table 10.1). Despite the absorption of small publishing houses by big media corporations, more than twenty thousand different publishers—mostly small independents—issue at least one title a year in the United States alone.

The bottom line is that the book industry has met and survived many social and cultural challenges. For example, the book industry has managed to maintain a distinct cultural identity despite its convergence with other media. So, when Oprah Winfrey chooses a book for "Oprah's Book Club," it instantly appears on best-seller lists, in part because the book industry is willing to capitalize on TV's reach, and vice versa.

Our oldest mass medium is also still our most influential and diverse one. The portability and compactness of books make them the preferred medium in many situations (e.g., relaxing at the beach, resting in bed, traveling on buses or commuter trains), and books are still the main repository of history and everyday experience, passing along stories, knowledge, and wisdom from generation to generation.

In this chapter, we trace the history of books, from Egyptian papyrus to downloadable e-books. After examining the development of the printing press, we investigate the rise of the book industry

"A conservative reckoning of the number of books ever published is thirty-two million; Google believes that there could be as many as a hundred million."

NEW YORKER, 2007

TABLE 10.1

ANNUAL NUMBERS OF NEW BOOK TITLES PUBLISHED, SELECTED YEARS

Sources: Figures through 1945 from John Tebbel, A History of Book Publishing in the United States, 4 vols. (New York: R. R. Bowker, 1972-81); figures after 1945 from various editions of The Bowker Annual Library and Book Trade Almanac (Information Today, Inc.) and Bowker press releases.

*Changes in the Bowker Annual's methodology in 1997 and 2006 "more accurately track and report on these figures."

**Estimate based on percentage change between 2006 and 2007.

Year	Number of Titles
1778	461
1798	1,808
1880	2,076
1890	4,559
1900	6,356
1910	13,470 (peak until after World War II)
1915	8,202
1919	5,714 (low point as a result of World War I)
1925	8,173
1930	10,027
1935	8,766 (Great Depression)
1940	11,328
1945	6,548 (World War II)
1950	11,022
1960	15,012
1970	36,071
1980	42,377
1990	46,473
1996	68,175*
2001	114,487
2004	160,919
2006*	169,637
2007**	171,017

> "All good books are alike in that they are truer than if they had really happened and after you are finished reading one you will feel that all that happened... belongs to you: the good and the bad, the ecstasy, the remorse and sorrow, the people and the places and how the weather was."
>
> ERNEST HEMINGWAY, *ESQUIRE* MAGAZINE, 1934

from early publishers in Europe and colonial America to the development of publishing houses in the nineteenth and twentieth centuries. As part of this discussion, we review the various types of books and the economic issues facing the book industry as a whole, particularly the growth of bookstore chains and publishing conglomerates. Finally, we consider recent trends in the industry including books on tape, e-books, and book preservation, and explore how books play a pivotal role in our culture by influencing everything from educational curricula to popular movies.

The History of Books from Papyrus to Paperbacks

Before books, or writing in general, oral cultures passed on information and values through the wisdom and memories of a community's elders or tribal storytellers. Sometimes these rich traditions were lost. Print culture and the book, however, gave future generations different and often more enduring records of authors' words.

Ever since the ancient Babylonians and Egyptians began experimenting with alphabets some five thousand years ago, people have found ways to preserve their written symbols. These first alphabets mark the development stage for books. Initially, pictorial symbols and letters were drawn on wood strips or pressed with a stylus into clay tablets, and tied or stacked together to form the first "books." As early as 2400 B.C.E., the Egyptians wrote on **papyrus** (from which the word *paper* is derived), made from plant reeds found along the Nile River. They rolled these writings in scrolls, much as builders do today with blueprints. This method was adopted by the Greeks in 650 B.C.E. and by the Romans (who imported papyrus from Egypt) in 300 B.C.E. Gradually, **parchment**—treated animal skin—replaced papyrus in Europe. Parchment was stronger, smoother, more durable, and less expensive because it did not have to be imported from Egypt.

▼ **Books and the Power of Print**

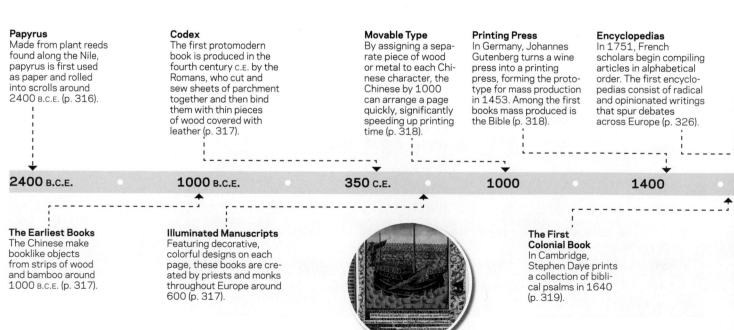

Papyrus
Made from plant reeds found along the Nile, papyrus is first used as paper and rolled into scrolls around 2400 B.C.E. (p. 316).

Codex
The first protomodern book is produced in the fourth century C.E. by the Romans, who cut and sew sheets of parchment together and then bind them with thin pieces of wood covered with leather (p. 317).

Movable Type
By assigning a separate piece of wood or metal to each Chinese character, the Chinese by 1000 can arrange a page quickly, significantly speeding up printing time (p. 318).

Printing Press
In Germany, Johannes Gutenberg turns a wine press into a printing press, forming the prototype for mass production in 1453. Among the first books mass produced is the Bible (p. 318).

Encyclopedias
In 1751, French scholars begin compiling articles in alphabetical order. The first encyclopedias consist of radical and opinionated writings that spur debates across Europe (p. 326).

2400 B.C.E.   **1000 B.C.E.**   **350 C.E.**   **1000**   **1400**

The Earliest Books
The Chinese make booklike objects from strips of wood and bamboo around 1000 B.C.E. (p. 317).

Illuminated Manuscripts
Featuring decorative, colorful designs on each page, these books are created by priests and monks throughout Europe around 600 (p. 317).

The First Colonial Book
In Cambridge, Stephen Daye prints a collection of biblical psalms in 1640 (p. 319).

At about the same time the Egyptians started using papyrus, the Babylonians recorded business transactions, government records, favorite stories, and local history on small tablets of clay. Around 1000 B.C.E., the Chinese also began creating booklike objects, using strips of wood and bamboo tied together in bundles. Although the Chinese began making paper from cotton and linen around 105 C.E., paper did not replace parchment in Europe until the thirteenth century because of questionable durability.

The first protomodern book was probably produced in the fourth century by the Romans, who created the **codex**, a type of book made of sheets of parchment and sewn together along the edge, then bound with thin pieces of wood and covered with leather. Whereas scrolls had to be wound, unwound, and rewound, a codex could be opened to any page, and its configuration allowed writing on both sides of a page.

The Development of Manuscript Culture

During the Middle Ages (400 to 1500 C.E.), the Christian clergy strongly influenced what is known as **manuscript culture**, a period in which books were painstakingly lettered, decorated, and bound by hand. This period also marks the entrepreneurial stage in the evolution of books. During this time, priests and monks advanced the art of bookmaking; in many ways, they may be considered the earliest professional editors. Known as *scribes*, they transcribed most of the existing philosophical tracts and religious texts of the period, especially versions of the Bible. Through tedious and painstaking work, scribes became the chief caretakers of recorded history and culture, promoting ideas they favored and censoring ideas that were out of line with contemporary Christian thought.

Many books from the Middle Ages were **illuminated manuscripts**. These books featured decorative, colorful designs and illustrations on each page, often made for churches or wealthy

ILLUMINATED MANUSCRIPTS were handwritten by scribes and illustrated with colorful and decorative images and designs.

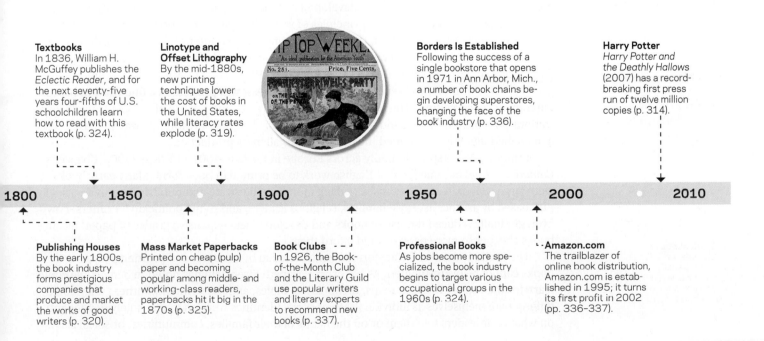

Textbooks
In 1836, William H. McGuffey publishes the *Eclectic Reader*, and for the next seventy-five years four-fifths of U.S. schoolchildren learn how to read with this textbook (p. 324).

Linotype and Offset Lithography
By the mid-1880s, new printing techniques lower the cost of books in the United States, while literacy rates explode (p. 319).

Borders Is Established
Following the success of a single bookstore that opens in 1971 in Ann Arbor, Mich., a number of book chains begin developing superstores, changing the face of the book industry (p. 336).

Harry Potter
Harry Potter and the Deathly Hallows (2007) has a record-breaking first press run of twelve million copies (p. 314).

1800   1850   1900   1950   2000   2010

Publishing Houses
By the early 1800s, the book industry forms prestigious companies that produce and market the works of good writers (p. 320).

Mass Market Paperbacks
Printed on cheap (pulp) paper and becoming popular among middle- and working-class readers, paperbacks hit it big in the 1870s (p. 325).

Book Clubs
In 1926, the Book-of-the-Month Club and the Literary Guild use popular writers and literary experts to recommend new books (p. 337).

Professional Books
As jobs become more specialized, the book industry begins to target various occupational groups in the 1960s (p. 324).

Amazon.com
The trailblazer of online book distribution, Amazon.com is established in 1995; it turns its first profit in 2002 (pp. 336–337).

clients. Their covers were made from leather, and some were embedded with precious gems or trimmed with gold and silver. During this period, scribes developed rules of punctuation, making distinctions between small and capital letters, and placing space between words to make reading easier. (Older Roman writing used all capital letters, and the words ran together on a page, making reading a torturous experience.) Hundreds of illuminated manuscripts still survive today in the rare book collections of museums and libraries.

The Innovations of Block Printing and Movable Type

While the work of the scribes in the Middle Ages led to advances in written language and the design of books, it did not lead to the mass proliferation of books, simply because each manuscript had to be painstakingly created one copy at a time. To make mechanically produced copies of pages, Chinese printers developed **block printing**—a technique in which sheets of paper were applied to blocks of inked wood with raised surfaces depicting hand-carved letters and illustrations—as early as the third century. This constituted the basic technique used in printing newspapers, magazines, and books throughout much of modern history. Although hand-carving each block, or "page," was time-consuming, this printing breakthrough enabled multiple copies to be printed and then bound together. The oldest dated printed book still in existence is China's *Diamond Sutra* by Wang Chieh, from 868 C.E. It consists of seven sheets pasted together and rolled up in a scroll. In 1295, explorer Marco Polo introduced these techniques to Europe after his excursion to China. The first block printed books appeared in Europe during the 1400s, and demand for them began to grow among the literate middle-class populace emerging in large European cities.

The next step in printing was the radical development of movable type, first invented in China around the year 1000. Movable type featured individual characters made from reusable pieces of wood or metal, rather than entire hand-carved pages. Printers arranged the characters into various word combinations, greatly speeding up the time it took to create block pages. This process, also used in Korea as early as the thirteenth century, developed independently in Europe in the 1400s.

The Gutenberg Revolution: The Invention of the Printing Press

A great leap forward in printing was developed by Johannes Gutenberg. In Germany, between 1453 and 1456, Gutenberg used the principles of movable type to develop a mechanical **printing press**, which he adapted from the design of wine presses. Gutenberg's staff of printers produced the first so-called modern books, including two hundred copies of a Latin Bible, twenty-one copies of which still exist. The Gutenberg Bible (as it's now known) required six presses, many printers, and several months to produce. It was printed on a fine calfskin-based parchment called **vellum**. The pages were hand-decorated, and the use of woodcuts made illustrations possible. Gutenberg and his printing assistants had not only found a way to make books a mass medium, but also formed the prototype for all mass production.

Printing presses spread rapidly across Europe in the late 1400s and early 1500s. Chaucer's *Canterbury Tales* became the first English work to be printed in book form. Many early books were large, elaborate, and expensive, taking months to illustrate and publish. They were usually purchased by aristocrats, royal families, religious leaders, and ruling politicians. Printers, however, gradually reduced the size of books and developed less expensive grades of paper, making books cheaper so more people could afford them.

The social and cultural transformations ushered in by the spread of printing presses and books cannot be overestimated. As historian Elizabeth Eisenstein has noted, when people could learn for themselves by using maps, dictionaries, Bibles, and the writings of others, they could differentiate themselves as individuals; their social identities were no longer solely dependent on what their leaders told them or on the habits of their families, communities, or social class.

> "A good book is the best of friends, the same today and forever."
>
> MARTIN FARQUHAR TUPPER, *PROVERBIAL PHILOSOPHY*, 1838

The technology of printing presses permitted information and knowledge to spread outside local jurisdictions. Gradually, individuals had access to ideas far beyond their isolated experiences, and this permitted them to challenge the traditional wisdom and customs of their tribes and leaders.[3]

The Birth of Publishing in the United States

In colonial America, English locksmith Stephen Daye set up a print shop in the late 1630s in Cambridge, Massachusetts. In 1640, Daye and his son Matthew printed the first colonial book, *The Whole Booke of Psalms* (known today as *The Bay Psalm Book*), marking the beginning of book publishing in the colonies. This collection of biblical psalms quickly sold out its first printing of 1,750 copies, even though fewer than thirty-five hundred families lived in the colonies at the time. By the mid-1760s, all thirteen colonies had printing shops.

In 1744, Benjamin Franklin, who had worked in printing shops, imported Samuel Richardson's *Pamela; or, Virtue Rewarded* (1740), from Britain, the first novel reprinted and sold in colonial America. Both *Pamela* and Richardson's second novel, *Clarissa; or, The History of a Young Lady* (1747), connected with the newly emerging and literate middle classes, especially with women, who were just starting to gain a social identity as individuals apart from their fathers, husbands, and employers. Richardson's novels portrayed women in subordinate roles; however, they also depicted women triumphing over tragedy, so he is credited as one of the first popular writers to take the domestic life of women seriously.

By the early 1800s, the demand for books was growing. To meet this demand, the cost of producing books needed to be reduced. By the 1830s, machine-made paper replaced more expensive handmade varieties, cloth covers supplanted more expensive leather ones, and **paperback books** with cheaper paper covers (introduced from Europe) all helped to make books more accessible to the masses. Further reducing the cost of books, Erastus and Irwin Beadle introduced paperback **dime novels** (so called because they sold for five or ten cents) in 1860. Ann Stephens authored the first dime novel, *Malaeska: The Indian Wife of the White Hunter*, a reprint of a serialized magazine story Stephens wrote in 1839 for the *Ladies' Companion* magazine.[4] By 1870, dime novels had sold seven million copies. By 1885, one-third of all books published in the United States were popular paperbacks and dime novels, sometimes identified as **pulp fiction**, a reference to the cheap, machine-made pulp paper they were printed on.

In addition, the printing process became quicker and more mechanized. In the 1880s, the introduction of **linotype** machines enabled printers to save time by setting type mechanically using a typewriter-style keyboard, while the introduction of steam-powered and high-speed rotary presses permitted the production of more books at lower costs. In the early 1900s, the development of **offset lithography** allowed books to be printed from photographic plates rather than from metal casts, greatly reducing the cost of color and illustrations and accelerating book production. With these developments, books disseminated further, preserving culture and knowledge and supporting a vibrant publishing industry.

PULP FICTION
The weekly paperback series *Tip Top Weekly*, which was published between 1896 and 1912, featured stories of the most popular dime novel hero of the day, the fictional Yale football star and heroic adventurer Frank Merriwell. This issue, from 1901, followed Frank's exploits in the wilds of the Florida Everglades.

Modern Publishing and the Book Industry

Throughout the 1800s, the rapid spread of knowledge and literacy as well as the Industrial Revolution spurred the emergence of the middle class. Their demand for books promoted the development of the publishing industry, which capitalized on increased literacy and widespread compulsory education. Many early publishers were mostly interested in finding quality authors and publishing books of importance. But with the growth of advertising and the rise of a market economy in the latter half of the nineteenth century, publishing gradually became more competitive and more concerned with sales.

The Formation of Publishing Houses

The modern book industry developed gradually in the 1800s with the formation of the early "prestigious" publishing houses: companies that tried to identify and produce the works of good writers.[5] Among the oldest American houses established at the time (all are now part of major media conglomerates) were J. B. Lippincott (1792); Harper & Bros. (1817), which became Harper & Row in 1962 and HarperCollins in 1990; Houghton Mifflin (1832); Little, Brown (1837); G. P. Putnam (1838); Scribner's (1842); E. P. Dutton (1852); Rand McNally (1856); and Macmillan (1869).

Between 1880 and 1920, as the center of social and economic life shifted from rural farm production to an industrialized urban culture, the demand for books grew. The book industry also helped assimilate European immigrants to the English language and American culture. In fact, 1910 marked a peak year in the number of new titles produced: 13,470, a record that would not be challenged until the 1950s. These changes marked the emergence of the next wave of publishing houses, as entrepreneurs began to better understand the marketing potential of books. These houses included Doubleday & McClure Company (1897), The McGraw-Hill Book Company (1909), Prentice-Hall (1913), Alfred A. Knopf (1915), Simon & Schuster (1924), and Random House (1925).

Despite the growth of the industry in the early twentieth century, book publishing sputtered from 1910 into the 1950s, as profits were adversely affected by the two world wars and the Great Depression. Radio and magazines fared better because they were generally less expensive and could more immediately cover topical issues during times of crisis. But after World War II, the book publishing industry bounced back.

Types of Books

The divisions of the modern book industry come from economic and structural categories developed both by publishers and by trade organizations such as the Association of American Publishers (AAP), the Book Industry Study Group (BISG), and the American Booksellers Association (ABA). The

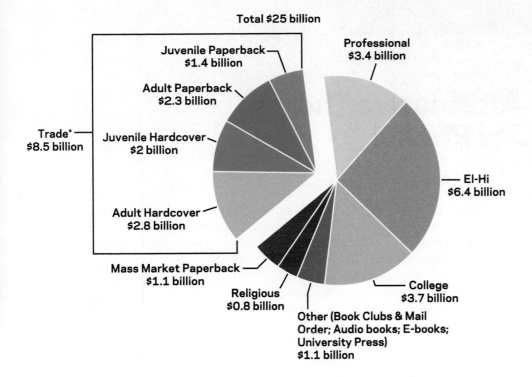

Total $25 billion

- Juvenile Paperback $1.4 billion
- Adult Paperback $2.3 billion
- Juvenile Hardcover $2 billion
- Trade* $8.5 billion
- Adult Hardcover $2.8 billion
- Mass Market Paperback $1.1 billion
- Religious $0.8 billion
- Other (Book Clubs & Mail Order; Audio books; E-books; University Press) $1.1 billion
- Professional $3.4 billion
- El-Hi $6.4 billion
- College $3.7 billion

FIGURE 10.1

ESTIMATED U.S. BOOK REVENUE, 2007

Source: "Association of American Publishers 2007 SI Report: Estimated Book Publishing Industry Net Sales 2002–2007," http://publishers.org/main/ IndustryStats/documents/ s12007Final.pdf.

*Estimates for juvenile hardbound and paperbound categories do not include sales of the Harry Potter series.

categories of book publishing that exist today include trade books (both adult and juvenile); professional books; elementary through high school (often called "el-hi") and college textbooks; mass market paperbacks; religious books; reference books; and university press books. (For sales figures for the book types, see Figure 10.1.)

Trade Books

One of the most lucrative parts of the industry, **trade books** include hardbound and paperback books aimed at general readers and are sold at commercial retail outlets. The industry distinguishes among adult trade, juvenile trade, and comics and graphic novels. Adult trade books include hardbound fiction; current nonfiction and biographies; literary classics; books on hobbies, art, and travel; popular science, technology, and computer publications; self-help books; and cookbooks. (*Betty Crocker's Cookbook*, first published in 1950, has sold more than twenty-two million hardcover copies.)

Juvenile book categories range from preschool picture books to young-adult or young-reader books, such as Dr. Seuss books, the Lemony Snicket series, the Fear Street series, and the Harry Potter series. In fact, the Harry Potter series alone provided an enormous boost to the industry, helping create record-breaking first-press runs: 10.8 million for *Harry Potter and the Half-Blood Prince* (2005) and 12 million for the final book in the series, *Harry Potter and the Deathly Hallows* (2007).

Since 2003, the book industry has also been tracking sales of comics and *graphic novels* (long-form stories with frame-by-frame drawings and dialogue, bound like books). As with the similar Japanese *manga* books, graphic novels appeal to both youth and adult, as well as male and female, readers. Will Eisner's *A Contract with God* (1978) is generally credited as the first graphic novel (and called itself so on its cover). Since that time interest in graphic novels has grown, and in 2006 their sales surpassed comic books. Given their strong stories and visual nature, many movies have been inspired by comics and graphic novels, including *X-Men*, *Sin City*, *300*, and *The Dark Knight*. But graphic novels aren't only about warriors and superheroes. Maira Kalman's *Principles of Uncertainty* and Rutu Modan's *Exit Wounds* are both acclaimed graphic novels, but their characters are regular mortals in real settings. (See "Case Study—Comic Books: Alternative Themes, but Superheroes Prevail" on pages 322–323.)

"For books, issuing from those primal founts of heresy and rebellion, the printing presses have done more to shape the course of human affairs than any other product of the human mind because they are the carriers of ideas and it is ideas that change the world."

JOHN TEBBEL, *A HISTORY OF BOOK PUBLISHING IN THE UNITED STATES*, 1972

Comic Books: Alternative Themes, but Superheroes Prevail

By Mark C. Rogers

At the precarious edge of the book industry are comic books, which are sometimes called *graphic novels* or simply *comix*. Comics have long integrated print and visual culture, and they are perhaps the medium most open to independent producers—anyone with a pencil and access to a Xerox machine can produce mini-comics. Nevertheless, two companies—Marvel and DC— have dominated the commercial industry for more than thirty years, publishing the routine superhero stories that have been so marketable.

Comics are relatively young, first appearing in their present format in the 1920s in Japan and in the 1930s in the United States. They began as simple reprints of newspaper comic strips, but by the mid-1930s most comic books featured original material. Comics have always been published in a variety of genres, but their signature contribution to American culture has been the superhero. In 1938, Jerry Siegel and Joe Shuster created Superman for DC comics. Bob Kane's Batman character arrived the following year. In 1941, Marvel comics introduced

Captain America to fight Nazis, and except for a brief period in the 1950s, the superhero genre has dominated the history of comics.

After World War II, comic books moved away from superheroes and began experimenting with other genres, most notably crime and horror (e.g., *Tales from the Crypt*). With the end of the war, the reading public was ready for more moral ambiguity than was possible in the simple good-versus-evil world of the superhero. Comics became increasingly graphic and lurid as they tried to compete with other mass media, especially television and mass market paperbacks.

In the early 1950s, the popularity of crime and horror comics led to a moral panic about their effects on society. Frederic Wertham, a prominent psychiatrist, campaigned against them, claiming they led to juvenile delinquency. Wertham was joined by many religious and parent groups, and Senate hearings were held on the issue. In October 1954, the Comics Magazine Association of America adopted a code of acceptable conduct for publishers of comic books. One of the most restrictive examples of industry self-censorship in mass-media history, the code kept the government from legislating its own code or restricting the sale of comic books to minors.

The code had both immediate and long-term effects on comics. In the short run, the number of comics sold in the United States declined sharply. Comic books lost many of their adult readers

because the code confined comics' topics to those suitable for children. Consequently, comics have rarely been taken seriously as a mass medium or as an art form; they remain stigmatized as the lowest of low culture—a sort of literature for the subliterate.

In the 1960s, Marvel and DC led the way as superhero comics regained their dominance. This period also gave rise to underground comics, which featured more explicit sexual, violent, and drug themes—for example, R. Crumb's *Mr. Natural* and Bill Griffith's *Zippy the Pinhead*. These alternative comics, like underground newspapers, originated in the 1960s counterculture and challenged the major institutions of the time. Instead of relying on newsstand sales, underground comics were sold through record stores, at alternative bookstores, and in a growing number of comic-book specialty shops.

In the 1970s, responding in part to the challenge of the underground form, "legitimate" comics began to increase the political content and relevance of their story lines. In 1974, a new method of distributing comics—direct sales—developed, catering to the increasing number of comic-book stores. This direct-sales method involved selling comics on a nonreturnable basis but with a higher discount than was available to newsstand distributors, who bought comics only on the condi-

tion that they could return unsold copies. The percentage of comics sold through specialty shops increased gradually, and by the early 1990s more than 80 percent of all comics were sold through direct sales.

The shift from newsstand to direct sales enabled comics to once again approach adult themes and also created an explosion in the number of comics available and in the number of companies publishing comics. Comic books peaked in 1993, generating more than $850 million in sales. That year the industry sold about 45 million comic books per month, but it then began a steady decline that led Marvel to declare bankruptcy in the late 1990s. After comic-book sales fell to $250 million in 2000 and Marvel reorganized, the industry rebounded. By 2007, sales reached $700 million, with several hundred million more generated through statue and action figure sales. Today, the industry releases 70 to 80 million comics a year. Marvel and DC control more than 70 percent of comic-book sales, but challengers like Dark Horse and Image plus another 150 small firms keep the industry vital by providing innovation and identifying new talent.

After the 1980s success of *Teenage Mutant Ninja Turtles* (which began life as an alternative comic book), many independent companies were purchased by or entered into alliances with larger media firms that want to exploit particular characters or superheroes. DC, for example, is owned by Time Warner, which has used the DC characters, especially Superman and Batman, to build successful film and television properties through its Warner Brothers division. Marvel also got into the licensing act with film versions of *SpiderMan* and *X-Men*.

Comics, however, are again more than just superheroes. In 1992, comics' flexibility was demonstrated in *Maus:*

Superman vs. The Amazing Spider-Man © 1976 DC Comics and Marvel Characters, Inc. All rights reserved. Superman is a registered Trademark of DC Comics.

A Survivor's Tale by Art Spiegelman, cofounder and editor of *Raw* (an alternative magazine for comics and graphic art). The first comic-style book to win a Pulitzer Prize, Spiegelman's two-book fable merged print and visual styles to recount his complex relationship with his father, a Holocaust survivor.

Although electronic comics may prove a way for comics to continue to flourish—as suggested by underground comic author Scott McCloud in his manifesto *Reinventing Comics*—comics are also making a resurgence through traditional book publishers. For example, DC Comics (owned by Time Warner) signed a distribution contract with Random House (owned by Bertelsmann) in 2007 to give its comics, graphic novels, and expensive comic collections editions a greater presence in bookstores like Barnes & Noble.

As other writers and artists continue to adapt the form to both fictional and nonfictional stories, comics endure as part of popular and alternative culture. ◢

Mark C. Rogers teaches communication at Walsh University. He writes about television and the comic-book industry.

"California has the ability to say, 'We want textbooks this way.'"

TOM ADAMS,
CALIFORNIA
DEPARTMENT OF
EDUCATION, 2004

Professional Books

The counterpart to professional trade magazines, **professional books** target various occupational groups and are not intended for the general consumer market. This area of publishing capitalizes on the growth of professional specialization that has characterized the job market, particularly since the 1960s. Traditionally, the industry has subdivided professional books into the areas of law, business, medicine, and technical-scientific works, with books in other professional areas accounting for a very small segment of the market. These books are sold mostly through mail order, the Internet, or sales representatives knowledgeable about various subject areas.

Textbooks

The most widely read secular book in U.S. history was *The Eclectic Reader*, an elementary-level reading textbook first written by William Holmes McGuffey, a Presbyterian minister and college professor. From 1836 to 1920, more than 100 million copies of this text were sold. Through stories, poems, and illustrations, *The Eclectic Reader* taught nineteenth-century schoolchildren to spell and read simultaneously—and to respect the nation's political and economic systems. Ever since the publication of the McGuffey reader (as it is often nicknamed), **textbooks** have served a nation intent on improving literacy rates and public education. Elementary school textbooks found a solid market niche in the nineteenth century, while college textbooks boomed in the 1950s, when the GI Bill enabled hundreds of thousands of working- and middle-class men returning from World War II to attend college. The demand for textbooks further accelerated in the 1960s, as opportunities for women and minorities expanded. Textbooks are divided into elementary through high school (el-hi) texts, college texts, and vocational texts.

In about half of the states, local school districts determine which el-hi textbooks are appropriate for their students. The other half of the states, including Texas and California, the two largest states, have statewide adoption policies that decide which texts can be used. If individual schools choose to use books other than those mandated, they are not reimbursed by the state for their purchases. Many teachers and publishers have argued that such sweeping authority undermines the autonomy of individual schools and local school districts, which have varied educational needs and problems. In addition, many have complained that the statewide system in Texas and California enables these two states to determine the content of all el-hi textbooks sold in the nation, because publishers are forced to appeal to the content demands of these states.

Unlike el-hi texts, which are subsidized by various states and school districts, college texts are paid for by individual students (and parents) and are sold primarily through college bookstores. The increasing cost of textbooks, the mark-up on used books, and the profit margins of local college bookstores (which in many cases face no on-campus competition) have caused disputes on most college campuses. For the 2007-08 school year, the average college student spent between $921 and $988 on textbooks and supplies.[6] (See Figure 10.2.)

As an alternative, some enterprising students have developed swap sites on the Web to trade, resell, and rent textbooks. Other students have turned to online purchasing, either through e-commerce sites like Amazon.com, BarnesandNoble.com, and eBay.com, or college textbook sellers like eCampus.com and textbooks.com. Those Web sites, plus college bookstores' own sites, now account for about one-quarter of college textbook purchases.[7]

Mass Market Paperbacks

Unlike the larger-sized trade paperbacks, which are sold mostly in bookstores, **mass market paperbacks** are sold on racks in drugstores, supermarkets, and airports as well as in bookstores. Contemporary mass market paperbacks—often the work of blockbuster authors such

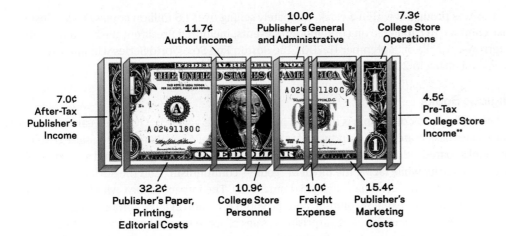

11.7¢
Author Income

10.0¢
Publisher's General
and Administrative

7.3¢
College Store
Operations

7.0¢
After-Tax
Publisher's
Income

4.5¢
Pre-Tax
College Store
Income**

32.2¢
Publisher's Paper,
Printing,
Editorial Costs

10.9¢
College Store
Personnel

1.0¢
Freight
Expense

15.4¢
Publisher's
Marketing
Costs

FIGURE 10.2

WHERE THE NEW TEXTBOOK DOLLAR GOES*

Source: © 2008 by the National Association of College Stores, www.nacs.org/common/research/textbook$.pdf.

*College store numbers are averages and reflect the most current data gathered by the National Association of College Stores. Publisher numbers are estimates based on data provided by the Association of American Publishers.

**Note: The amount of federal, state, and/or local tax, and therefore the amount and use of any after-tax profit, is determined by the store's ownership, and depends on whether the college store is owned by an institution of higher education, a contract management company, a cooperative, a foundation, or private individuals.

These numbers are averages and do not represent a particular publisher or store.

PAPERBACKS today are not only for new material but are a popular way to reprint older works. Shown is a collection of famed Japanese author Ryūnosuke Akutagawa's short stories, including *Rashomon* (originally published in 1914), and an introduction by modern author Haruki Murakami.

as Stephen King, Danielle Steel, Patricia Cornwell, and John Grisham—represent the largest segment of the industry in terms of units sold, but because the books are low priced (under $10), they generate less revenue than trade books. Moreover, mass market paperbacks have experienced declining sales in recent years because bookstore chains prefer to display and promote the more expensive trade paperback and hardbound books.

Paperbacks became popular in the 1870s, mostly with middle- and working-class readers. This phenomenon sparked fear and outrage among those in the professional and educated classes, many of whom thought that reading cheap westerns and crime novels might ruin civilization. Some of the earliest paperbacks ripped off foreign writers, who were unprotected by copyright law and did not receive royalties for the books they sold in the United States. This changed with the International Copyright Law of 1891, which mandated that any work by any author could not be reproduced without the author's permission.

The popularity of paperbacks hit a major peak in 1939 with the establishment of Pocket Books by Robert de Graff. Revolutionizing the paperback industry, Pocket Books lowered the standard book price of fifty or seventy-five cents to twenty-five cents. To accomplish this, de Graff cut bookstore discounts from 30 to 20 percent, the book distributor's share fell from 46 to 36 percent of the cover price, and author royalty rates went from 10 to 4 percent. In its first three weeks, Pocket Books sold 100,000 books in New York City alone. Among its first titles was *Wake Up and Live* by Dorothea Brande, a 1936 best-seller on self-improvement that ignited an early wave of self-help books. Pocket Books also published *The Murder of Roger Ackroyd* by Agatha Christie; *Enough Rope*, a collection of poems by Dorothy Parker; and *Five Great Tragedies* by Shakespeare. Pocket Books' success spawned a series of imitators, including Dell, Fawcett, and Bantam Books.[8]

A major innovation of mass market paperback publishers was the **instant book**, a marketing strategy that involved publishing a topical book quickly after a major event occurred. Pocket Books produced the first instant book, *Franklin Delano Roosevelt: A Memorial*, six days after FDR's death in 1945. Similar to made-for-TV movies and television programs that capitalize on contemporary events, instant books enabled the industry to better compete with newspapers and magazines. Such books, however, like their TV counterparts, have been accused of shoddy writing, exploiting tragedies, and avoiding in-depth analysis and historical perspective. Instant books have also made government reports into best-sellers. In 1964 Bantam published *The Report of the Warren Commission on the Assassination of President Kennedy*. After receiving the 385,000-word report on a Friday afternoon, Bantam staffers immediately began editing the Warren Report, and

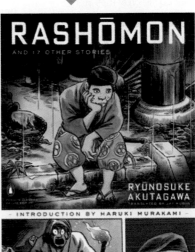

the book was produced within a week, ultimately selling over 1.6 million copies. Today, instant books continue to capitalize on contemporary events, including President Bush's address about the terrorist attacks of September 11, 2001, the Boston Red Sox World Series win in 2004, and Hurricane Katrina in 2005.

Religious Books

The best-selling book of all time is the Bible, in all its diverse versions. Over the years, the success of Bible sales has created a large industry for religious books. After World War II, sales of religious books soared. Historians attribute the sales boom to economic growth and a nation seeking peace and security while facing the threat of "godless communism" and the Soviet Union.[9] By the 1960s, though, the scene had changed dramatically. The impact of the Civil Rights struggle, the Vietnam War, the sexual revolution, and the youth rebellion against authority led to declines in formal church membership. Not surprisingly, sales of some types of religious books dropped as well. To compete, many religious-book publishers extended their offerings to include serious secular titles on such topics as war and peace, race, poverty, gender, and civic responsibility.

Throughout this period of change, the publication of fundamentalist and evangelical literature remained steady. It then expanded rapidly during the 1980s, when the Republican Party began making political overtures to conservative groups and prominent TV evangelists. After a record year in 2004 (twenty-one thousand new titles), there has been a slight decline in the religious book category. However, it continues to be an important part of the book industry, especially during turbulent social times.

Reference Books

Another major division of the book industry—**reference books**—includes dictionaries, encyclopedias, atlases, almanacs, and a number of substantial volumes directly related to particular professions or trades, such as legal casebooks and medical manuals.

The two most common reference books are encyclopedias and dictionaries. The idea of developing encyclopedic writings to document the extent of human knowledge is attributed to the Greek philosopher Aristotle. The Roman citizen Pliny the Elder (23–79 C.E.) wrote the oldest reference work still in existence, *Historia Naturalis*, detailing thousands of facts about animals, minerals, and plants. But it wasn't until the early 1700s that the compilers of encyclopedias began organizing articles in alphabetical order and relying on specialists to contribute essays in their areas of interest. Between 1751 and 1771, a group of French scholars produced the first multiple-volume set of encyclopedias.

The oldest English-language encyclopedia still in production, the *Encyclopaedia Britannica*, was first published in Scotland in 1768. U.S. encyclopedias followed, including *Encyclopedia Americana* (1829), *The World Book Encyclopedia* (1917), and *Compton's Pictured Encyclopedia* (1922). *Encyclopaedia Britannica* produced its first U.S. edition in 1908. This best-selling encyclopedia's sales dwindled in the 1990s due to competition from electronic encyclopedias (like Microsoft's *Encarta*), and it went digital too. *Encyclopaedia Britannica*, *Encarta*, and *World Book Encyclopedia* are now the leading online and CD-based encyclopedias, although even they struggle today, as young researchers increasingly rely on search engines such as Google or online resources like Wikipedia to find information (though many critics consider these sources inferior in quality).

Dictionaries have also accounted for a large portion of reference sales. The earliest dictionaries were produced by ancient scholars attempting to document specialized and rare

"Religion is just so much a part of the cultural conversation these days because of global terrorism and radical Islam. People want to understand those things."

LYNN GARRETT,
RELIGION EDITOR AT
PUBLISHERS WEEKLY,
2004

WIKIPEDIA Since its launch in 2001, Wikipedia has grown to include over 10 million entries in 253 languages. Despite controversies about bias, inconsistency, and incorrect information, the site is one of the most popular on the Web for "general information."

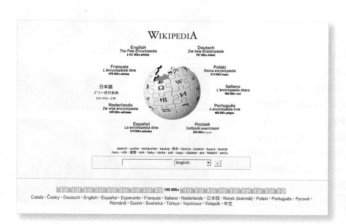

words. During the manuscript period in the Middle Ages, however, European scribes and monks began creating glossaries and dictionaries to help people understand Latin. In 1604, a British schoolmaster prepared the first English dictionary. In 1755, Samuel Johnson produced the *Dictionary of the English Language*. Describing rather than prescribing word usage, Johnson was among the first to understand that language changes—that words and usage cannot be fixed for all time. In the United States in 1828, Noah Webster, using Johnson's work as a model, published the *American Dictionary of the English Language*, differentiating between British and American usages and simplifying spelling (for example, *colour* became *color* and *musick* became *music*). As with encyclopedias, dictionaries have moved mostly to online formats since the 1990s, and they struggle to compete with free online or built-in word-processing software dictionaries.

University Press Books

The smallest market in the book industry is the nonprofit **university press**, which publishes scholarly works for small groups of readers interested in intellectually specialized areas such as literary theory and criticism, history of art movements, contemporary philosophy, etc. Professors often try to secure book contracts from reputable university presses to increase their chances for *tenure*, a lifetime teaching contract. Some university presses are very small, producing as few as ten titles a year. The largest—The University of Chicago Press—regularly publishes more than two hundred titles a year. One of the oldest and most prestigious presses is Harvard University Press, formally founded in 1913 but claiming roots that go back to 1640, when Stephen Daye published the first colonial book in a small shop located behind the house of Harvard's president.

University presses have not traditionally faced pressure to produce commercially viable books, preferring to encourage books about highly specialized topics by innovative thinkers. In fact, most university presses routinely lose money and are subsidized by their university. Even when they publish more commercially accessible titles, the lack of large marketing budgets prevents them from reaching mass audiences. While large commercial trade houses are often criticized for publishing only blockbuster books, university presses often suffer the opposite criticism—that they produce mostly obscure books that only a handful of scholars read. To offset costs and increase revenue, some presses are trying to form alliances with commercial houses to help promote and produce academic books that have wider appeal.

Trends and Issues in Book Publishing

Ever since Harriet Beecher Stowe's abolitionist novel *Uncle Tom's Cabin* sold fifteen thousand copies in fifteen days back in 1852 (and three million total copies prior to the Civil War), many American publishers have stalked the *best-seller*, or blockbuster (just like in the movie business). While most authors are professional writers, the book industry also reaches out to famous media figures, who may pen a best-selling book (Ellen DeGeneres, Jerry Seinfeld, and Bill Clinton) or a commercial failure (Whoopi Goldberg, Jay Leno). Other ways publishers attempt to ensure popular success is to pay rights to license popular film and television programs or experiment with formats like audio and e-books. In addition to selling new books, other industry issues include the preservation of older books and the history of banned books and censorship.

Influences of Television and Film

There are two major facets in the relationship among books, television, and film: how TV can help sell books and how books serve as ideas for TV shows and movies. Through the TV

"Wikipedia, or any free information resources, challenge reference publishers to be better than free.... It isn't enough for a publisher to simply provide information, we have to add value."

TOM RUSSELL, RANDOM HOUSE REFERENCE PUBLISHER, 2007

"The [university] presses are meant to be one of the few alternative sources of scholarship and information available in the United States.... Does the bargain involved in publishing commercial titles compromise that role?"

ANDRÉ SCHIFFRIN, *CHRONICLE OF HIGHER EDUCATION*, 1999

exposure, books by or about talk-show hosts, actors, and politicians such as Stephen Colbert, Julie Andrews, Barack Obama, and Hillary Clinton sell millions of copies–enormous sales in a business where 100,000 in sales constitutes remarkable success. In national polls conducted from the 1980s through today, nearly 30 percent of respondents said they had read a book after seeing the story or a promotion on television.

One of the most influential forces in promoting books on TV is Oprah Winfrey. Even before the development of Oprah's Book Club in 1996, Oprah's afternoon talk show had become a major power broker in selling books. In 1993, for example, Holocaust survivor and Nobel Prize recipient Elie Wiesel appeared on Oprah. Afterward, his 1960 memoir, *Night*, which had been issued as a Bantam paperback in 1982, returned to the best-seller lists. (Oprah "officially" chose *Night* for her book club in 2006.) In 1996, novelist Toni Morrison's nineteen-year-old book *Song of Solomon* became a paperback best-seller after Morrison appeared on Oprah. In 1998, after Winfrey brought Morrison's *Beloved* to movie screens, the book version was back on the best-seller lists. The success of Oprah's Book Club extends far beyond anyone's expectations. Each selection becomes an immediate best-seller, generating tremendous excitement within the book industry. Recent Oprah selections include Sidney Poitier's *The Measure of a Man*, Cormac McCarthy's *The Road*, and Gabriel Garcia Marquez's *Love in the Time of Cholera*.

The film industry gets many of its story ideas from books, which results in enormous movie rights revenues for the book industry and its authors. Michael Crichton's *Jurassic Park* and Ian McEwen's *Atonement*, for instance, became highly successful motion pictures. But the most profitable movie successes for the book industry in recent years emerged from the fantasy works of two British authors–J. K. Rowling and J. R. R. Tolkien. Rowling's best-selling Harry Potter books have become hugely popular movies, as has Peter Jackson's film trilogy of Tolkien's enduringly popular *Lord of the Rings* (first published in the 1950s). Even classic and *public domain* books (no longer subject to copyright law) can create profits for the book industry. For example, in 2005, a screen version of Jane Austen's 1813 novel *Pride and Prejudice* boosted paperback sales of the novel.

Audio Books

Another major development in publishing has been the merger of sound recording with publishing. *Audio books*–also known as talking books or books on tape–generally feature actors or authors reading abridged versions of popular fiction and nonfiction trade books. Indispensable to many sightless readers and older readers whose vision is diminished, audio books are also popular among regular readers who do a lot of commuter driving or who want to listen to a book at home while doing something else–like exercising. The number of audio books borrowed from libraries soared in the 1990s and early 2000s, and small bookstore chains developed to cater to the audio-book niche. By the early 2000s, audio books were also readily available on the Internet for downloading to iPods and other portable devices. The four hundred-plus new audio books available annually help generate more than $923 million in sales.

E-books

For several years, the biggest issue in the book industry is how to effectively take advantage of the digital age. Beyond digitizing the process of making books, publishers are exploring e-books and other virtual environments to attract readers who have strayed to other media forms.

At their most basic version, **e-books** are digital books accessed on a Web site and read on a computer. The more heralded consumer version involves electronic books that can be downloaded to portable e-book reading devices. Despite predictions that such e-books would garner at least 10 percent of publishing sales by 2005, this market has not yet materialized. Incarnations of e-book readers, such as the RCA eBook reader and the Sony Reader, failed to gain mass appeal. Readers just never warmed up to sitting down with a cup of tea and a lightweight LED monitor. However, in 2007, Amazon introduced a new e-book reader that it hoped would change the state of the e-book. The Kindle is a lightweight, thin reader with an easy-on-the-eyes electronic paper display. Unlike earlier e-book readers, Amazon's Kindle uses a wireless connection to directly buy and download from a selection of more than 120,000 books, newspapers, and blogs from its online store (a smaller version of Amazon's bookstore). Book downloads take less than a minute, and the Kindle can hold more than 200 books at a time. In the months following the introduction of the Kindle, Amazon increased manufacturing capacity to keep up with demand.

The publishing industry sees a future for e-books, but that market will develop slowly as engineers try to figure out how to make digital books an improvement on printed books. Until that time, distributors, publishers, and bookstores use digital technology to print books on demand, reviving books that would otherwise go out of print and avoiding the inconveniences of carrying unsold books or being unable to respond to limited demand for a book. Similarly, Internet-based publishing houses offer custom design and distribution for aspiring authors who want to self-publish a title.

Preserving and Digitizing Books

Another recent trend in the book industry involves the preservation of older books, especially those from the nineteenth century printed on acid-based paper, which gradually deteriorates. At the turn of the twentieth century, research initiated by libraries concerned with losing valuable older collections provided evidence that acid-based paper would eventually turn brittle and self-destruct. The paper industry, however, did not respond, so in the 1970s, leading libraries began developing techniques to halt any further deterioration (although this process could not restore books to their original state). Finally, by the early 1990s, motivated almost entirely by economics rather than by the cultural value of books, the paper industry finally began producing acid-free paper. Libraries and book conservationists, however, still had to focus attention on older, at-risk books. Some institutions began photocopying original books onto acid-free paper and made the copies available to the public. Libraries then stored the originals, which were treated to halt further wear. Today, research libraries are building secure, climate-controlled depositories for older books of permanent research value.

More recently, pioneering projects by Xerox and Cornell University have produced electronic copies of books through computer scanning. Other companies, such as netLibrary, have eschewed scanning, which they say produces too many errors, and have enlisted armies of typists in China, India, and the Philippines to convert books into electronic form. The Colorado-based company, a division of the nonprofit Online Computer Library Center, digitizes about 200 books a day. By 2008, netLibrary had more than 160,000 titles, and for a small fee more than sixteen thousand libraries worldwide subscribe to its service.

Finally, the Google Library Project, begun in 2004, features partnerships with the New York Public Library and several major university research libraries—including Harvard, Michigan, Oxford, and Stanford—to scan millions of books and make them available online. Google

THE KINDLE from Amazon is the latest, and arguably the most successful, attempt to transform books from paperbound purchases at a brick-and-mortar store to a completely online experience.

"Let's face it, a printed book is a very good technology for the transfer of information. It has taken hundreds of years to perfect."

ROBERT McCORMACK, PRESIDENT OF E-PUBLISHER AUTHORHOUSE, 2003

uses fully automated "robots" that safely, quickly, and accurately scan even fragile books. The scanned books are then available under Google's Book Search. The Authors Guild, the Association of American Publishers, and several publishing companies brought a lawsuit against Google in 2005, arguing that Google needs explicit permission to digitize the entire contents of copyrighted books. Google argues that its Book Search shows only a limited amount of content for copyrighted books, so it is legal under "fair use" rules.

An alternative group, dissatisfied by the Google Library Project restricting its scanned book content from use by other commercial search services, started a competing nonprofit service in 2007. The Open Content Alliance is working with the Boston Public Library, several New England university libraries, and Yahoo! to digitize millions of books with expired copyrights and make them freely available through the Internet Archive.

Censorship and Banned Books

Over time, the wide circulation of books gave many ordinary people the same opportunities to learn that were once available to only a privileged few. However, as societies discovered the power associated with knowledge and the printed word, books were subjected to a variety of censors. Imposed by various rulers and groups intent on maintaining their authority, the censorship of books often prevented people from learning about the rituals and moral standards of other cultures. Political censors sought to banish "dangerous" books that promoted radical ideas or challenged conventional authority. In various parts of the world, some versions of the Bible, Karl Marx's *Das Kapital* (1867), *The Autobiography of Malcolm X* (1965), and Salman Rushdie's *The Satanic Verses* (1989) have all been banned at one time or another. In fact, one of the triumphs of the Internet is that it allows the digital passage of banned books into nations where printed versions have been outlawed. (For more on banned books, see "Media Literacy and the Critical Process: Banned Books and 'Family Values'" on opposite page.)

Each year, the American Library Association (ALA) compiles a list of the most challenged books in the United States. Unlike an enforced ban, a **book challenge** is a formal complaint to have a book removed from a public or school library's collection. Common reasons for challenges include sexually explicit passages, offensive language, occult themes, violence, homosexual themes, promotion of a religious viewpoint, nudity, and racism. (The ALA defends the right of libraries to offer material with a wide range of views, and does not support removing material on the basis of partisan or doctrinal disapproval.) Some of the most challenged books of the past decade include *I Know Why the Caged Bird Sings* by Maya Angelou, *Forever* by Judy Blume, and the Captain Underpants series by Dav Pilkey. (See Table 10.2, "The Ten Most Challenged Books of the Twenty-first Century.")

> "We're out to help build the Library of Alexandria version 2, starting with humankind's published works, books, music, video, Web pages, software, and make it available to everyone anywhere at any time, and forever."
>
> BREWSTER KAHLE, CO-FOUNDER OF THE INTERNET ARCHIVE AND ITS OPEN CONTENT ALLIANCE, 2007

> "Most would-be censors object to the obvious 's' words—sex, suicide, Satanism, and swearing. The novels of J. D. Salinger and John Steinbeck, which deal with self-conscious teenagers and the rough edge of life, respectively, are perennial targets."
>
> MARY B. W. TAYLOR, *NEW YORK TIMES,* 1995

▶

TABLE 10.2

THE 10 MOST CHALLENGED BOOKS OF THE TWENTY-FIRST CENTURY (2000–05)

Source: American Library Association, http://www.ala.org/. The list is based on more than three thousand formal complaints to remove books from libraries between 2000 and 2005.

Rank	Title	Author
1	Harry Potter series	J. K. Rowling
2	*The Chocolate War*	Robert Cormier
3	Alice series	Phyllis Reynolds Naylor
4	*Of Mice and Men*	John Steinbeck
5	*I Know Why the Caged Bird Sings*	Maya Angelou
6	*Fallen Angels*	Walter Dean Myers
7	*It's Perfectly Normal*	Robie Harris
8	Scary Stories series	Alvin Schwartz
9	Captain Underpants series	Dav Pilkey
10	*Forever*	Judy Blume

Media Literacy and the Critical Process

1 DESCRIPTION. Identify two contemporary books that have been challenged or banned in two separate communities. (Check the American Library Association Web site [www.ala.org] for information on the most frequently challenged and banned books, or use the LexisNexis database.) Describe the communities involved and what sparked the challenges or bans. Describe the issues at stake and the positions students, teachers, parents, administrators, citizens, religious leaders, and politicians took with regard to the book. Discuss what happened and the final outcomes.

2 ANALYSIS. What patterns emerge? What are the main arguments given for censoring a book? What are the main arguments of those defending these particular books? Are there any middle-ground positions or unusual viewpoints raised in your book controversies? Did these communities take similar or different approaches when dealing with these books?

3 INTERPRETATION. Why did these issues arise? What do you think are the actual reasons why people would challenge or ban a book? (For example, can you tell if people seem genuinely concerned about protecting young readers, or are they really just personally offended by particular books?) How do people handle book banning and issues raised by First Amendment protections of printed materials?

4 EVALUATION. Who do you think is right and wrong in these controversies? Why?

5 ENGAGEMENT. Call or e-mail key players–teachers, librarians, or reporters–in the community for their views on what happened. Get their opinions on the resolution and how well they think the news media covered the issues. How well do you think the controversy was handled? How would you have handled it? What was done well? What might have been done differently?

Banned Books and "Family Values"

In *Free Speech for Me—But Not for Thee: How the American Left and Right Relentlessly Censor Each Other*, Nat Hentoff writes that "the lust to suppress can come from any direction." Indeed, *Ulysses* by James Joyce, *The Scarlet Letter* by Nathaniel Hawthorne, *Leaves of Grass* by Walt Whitman, *The Diary of a Young Girl* by Anne Frank, *Lolita* by Vladimir Nabokov, and *To Kill a Mockingbird* by Harper Lee have all been banned by some U.S. community, school, or library at one time or another. In fact, the most censored book in U.S. history is Mark Twain's *The Adventures of Huckleberry Finn*, the 1884 classic that still sells tens of thousands of copies each year. Often, the impulse behind calling for a book's banishment is to protect children in the name of a community's "family values."

The Organization and Ownership of the Book Industry

Compared with the revenues earned by other mass media industries, the steady growth of book publishing has been relatively modest. From the mid-1980s to 2007, total revenues went from $9 billion to about $25 billion. Within the industry, the concept of who or what constitutes a publisher varies widely. A publisher may be a large company that is a subsidiary of a global media conglomerate and occupies an entire office building, or a one-person home office operation using a desktop computer.

Ownership Patterns

Like most mass media, commercial publishing is dominated by a handful of major corporations with ties to international media conglomerates. And since the 1960s and 1970s–when CBS

FIGURE 10.3

FIVE LARGEST TRADE BOOK PUBLISHERS (NORTH AMERICAN REVENUE IN $MILLIONS)

Source: All revenues found in parent company SEC filings and annual reports for 2007 available on company Web sites and accessed on July 2, 2008.

*News Corp. revenues are estimated based on a claimed 3% increase from 2006. In its SEC filing, News Corp. combines worldwide book publishing revenue (including North America, the UK, and Australia) for a total of $1.3 billion.

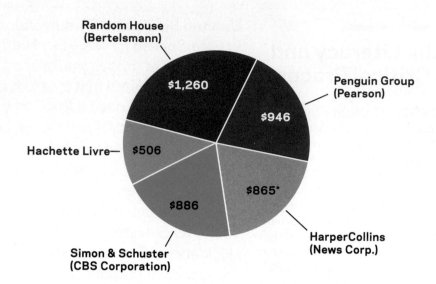

acquired Holt, Rinehart and Winston; Popular Library; and Fawcett—mergers and consolidations have driven the book industry. For example, the CBS Corporation (formerly Viacom) now also owns Simon & Schuster and its imprints, including Pocket Books; and News Corp. now owns HarperCollins and all of its imprints, including Avon (see Figure 10.3).

The largest publishing conglomerate is Germany's Bertelsmann. Starting in the late 1970s with its purchase of Dell for $35 million and its 1980s purchase of Doubleday for $475 million, Bertelsmann has been building a publishing dynasty. In 1998, Bertelsmann shook up the book industry by adding Random House, the largest U.S. book publisher, to its fold. With this $1.4 billion purchase, Bertelsmann gained control of about one-third of the U.S. trade book market (about 10 percent of the total U.S. book market) and became the world's largest publisher of English-language books.[10] Bertelsmann's book companies include Bantam Dell; Doubleday Broadway; Ballantine; Alfred A. Knopf; Random House and its imprints including Modern Library and Fodor's Travel; and more (see "What Bertelsmann Owns" on page 337).

A number of concerns have surfaced regarding the consolidation of the book industry. The distinctive styles of older houses and their associations with certain literary figures and book types no longer characterize the industry. Of special concern is the financial struggle of independent publishers and booksellers, who are often undercut in price and promotion by large corporations and bookstore chains. Large houses also tend to favor blockbusters or best-sellers and do not aggressively pursue more modest or unconventional books. From a corporate viewpoint, executives have argued that large companies can financially support a number of smaller struggling firms or imprints while allowing their editorial ideas to remain independent from the parent corporation. With thousands of independent presses able to make books using inexpensive production techniques or online options, book publishing appears healthy. Still, independents struggle as the large conglomerates define the industry's direction. (To learn about European book publishing, see "Global Village—Books: Cultural Status Defines Market" on page 333.)

The Structure of Book Publishing

A small publishing house may have a staff of a few to twenty people. Medium-size and large publishing houses employ hundreds of people. In the larger houses, divisions usually include acquisitions and development; copyediting, design, and production; marketing and sales; and administration and business. Unlike daily newspapers but similar to magazines, most publishing houses contract independent printers to produce their books.

Books: Cultural Status Defines Market

For decades, European countries have debated a fundamental question of the book industry: Should prices of books be fixed, or should they be able to float freely in a competitive market?

About half of Europe's countries, including Germany, France, Italy, Spain, Denmark, the Netherlands, Austria, and Hungary have retail price management (RPM) laws or publisher agreements that require retailers (including online vendors) to sell books at the price fixed by the publisher or importer. Other countries in Europe, including the United Kingdom, Ireland, Poland, Finland, and Sweden, allow retailers to freely set book prices.

The question has significant consequences, and not just for consumers. As noted in this chapter, book retailing has changed dramatically in the United States, where retailers can sell books at any price they wish. In the past two decades, book superstores, mass merchandisers, and online stores have used large sales volumes and product lines to offer discounts of 40 percent or more on certain book prices, greatly undercutting smaller booksellers'

prices. The effect has been a sharp drop in the market share and number of independent bookstores.

The United Kingdom, which abandoned its nearly one-hundred-year-old fixed-price agreement in 1995, has since witnessed a similar change in its book market, with mass merchandisers like Tesco and Asda (owned by Wal-Mart) offering deep discounts on books and driving many small and regional bookstores out of business. Popular bookstore chains like WH Smith expanded but now struggle to maintain profitability.

The argument for fixing prices is that books are not only consumer products but also cultural products. (Some countries, like Japan, extend fixed-pricing policies to newspapers and recorded music, too.) Fixed prices on cultural products, the argument goes, help to preserve diversity in book retailing and book publishing, as popular titles sold at full price help to subsidize the work of new authors and less popular titles.

The European Union (EU) advocates free trade and is pressing its members to give up their RPM laws. But the EU's biggest member, Germany, which has a high density of publishers and bookstores, is not inclined to change after more than a century of fixed prices and because books and neighborhood bookstores are part of German identity. Despite the EU's concern, fixed prices can help create more competition. Heike Fischer, a publisher from Köln (Cologne), says the idea behind the RPM is "equal protection. In this system everybody has the same chances, whether you're a small or big publisher

or bookseller, or a consumer in Berlin or some small town."[1]

Most European countries treat books with favor in regard to sales taxes, reducing or eliminating for books the typical 18–25 percent tax added to most retail sales. But beyond reduced taxation on book sales, it's hard to determine whether fixed prices foster more reading or less. In Norway, deemed the "world's most avid readers," there is no tax on books, but since 2005 there has been an agreement limiting store discounts to 12.5 percent off the list price.[2] But other Scandinavian nations have high reading rates as well, including Sweden (which abandoned RPM in 1970, but has a reduced tax and subsidizes Swedish literature), and Denmark (whose fixed-price rule dates all the way back to 1837, and which charges a 25 percent tax on books).

The prices of books may have less impact on reading than on the actual appearance of a city. In France, Lang's Law, named after then Minister of Culture Jack Lang, revived a national law for uniform book pricing in 1981 to protect small bookstores against large chain discounters. A stroll through Paris reveals the effects of the law on the city's composition: plenty of small specialty bookstores, and nothing in sight approaching the size and discounts of a Barnes & Noble superstore.

TABLE 10.3

HOW A PAPERBACK'S REVENUE IS DIVIDED

Source: Arianne Cohen, "A Publishing Company: Random House," New York, http://nymag.com/news/features/2007/profit/32906/.

Despite their low profit margins, mass market paperbacks remain an important segment of the book industry. For example, two-thirds of Random House's income comes from paperbacks. A Random House paperback, retail priced at $10, breaks down this way:	
Author royalty	$1.50
Publisher's costs	$2.00
Paper, printing, and binding	$1.00
Retailer	$5.00
Publisher Profit:	$.50

Most publishers employ **acquisitions editors** to seek out and sign authors to contracts. For fiction, this might mean discovering talented writers through book agents or reading unsolicited manuscripts. For nonfiction, editors might examine manuscripts and letters of inquiry or match a known writer to a project (such as a celebrity biography). Acquisitions editors also handle **subsidiary rights** for an author—that is, selling the rights to a book for use in other media, such as a mass market paperback or as the basis for a screenplay.

As part of their contracts, writers sometimes receive *advance money*, an early payment that is subtracted from royalties earned from book sales (see Table 10.3). Typically, an author's royalty is between 5 and 15 percent of the net price of the book. New authors may receive little or no advance from a publisher, but commercially successful authors can receive millions. For example, *Interview with a Vampire* author Anne Rice hauled in a $17 million advance from Knopf for three more vampire novels. Nationally recognized authors, such as political leaders, sports figures, or movie stars, can also command large advances from publishers who are banking on the well-known person's commercial potential. For example, in 2006, former chairman of the Federal Reserve Alan Greenspan received $8.5 million for his memoir, and, in 2007, Barbara Walters received $4 million for hers.

BOOK MARKETING
Barbara Walters signs her 2007 memoir, *Audition*. Book signings are a traditional and popular way to market a book, especially if the author is well-known.

After a contract is signed, the acquisitions editor may turn the book over to a **developmental editor** who provides the author with feedback, makes suggestions for improvements, and, in educational publishing, obtains advice from knowledgeable members of the academic community. If a book is illustrated, editors work with photo researchers to select photographs and pieces of art. Then the production staff enters the picture. While **copy editors** attend to specific problems in writing or length, production and **design managers** work on the look of the book, making decisions about type style, paper, cover design, and layout.

Simultaneously, plans are underway to market and sell the book. Decisions need to be made concerning the number of copies to print, how to reach potential readers, and costs for promotion and advertising. For trade books and some scholarly books, publishing houses may send advance copies of a book to appropriate magazines and newspapers with the hope of receiving favorable reviews that can be used in promotional material. Prominent trade writers typically have book signings and travel the radio and TV talk-show circuit to promote their books. Unlike trade publishers, college textbook firms rarely sell directly to bookstores. Instead, they contact instructors through direct-mail brochures or sales representatives assigned to geographic regions.

To help create a best-seller, trade houses often distribute large illustrated cardboard bins, called *dumps*, to thousands of stores to display a book in bulk quantity. Like food merchants who buy eye-level shelf placement for their products in supermarkets, large trade houses buy shelf space from major chains to ensure prominent locations in bookstores. For example, to have copies of one title placed in a front-of-the-store dump bin or table at all the Borders bookstore locations costs about $10,000 for two weeks.[11] Publishers also buy ad space in newspapers and magazines and on buses, billboards, television, radio, and the Web—all in an effort to generate interest in a new book.

Selling Books: Stores, Clubs, and Mail Order

The final part of the publishing process involves the business and order fulfillment stages—shipping books to thousands of commercial outlets and college bookstores. Warehouse inventories are monitored to ensure that enough copies of a book will be available to meet demand. Anticipating such demand, though, is a tricky business. No publisher wants to be caught short if a book becomes more popular than originally predicted or get stuck with books it cannot sell, as publishers must absorb the cost of returned books. Independent bookstores, which tend to order more carefully, return about 20 percent of books ordered; in contrast, mass merchandisers such as Wal-Mart, Sam's Club, Target, and Costco, which routinely overstock popular titles, often return up to 40 percent. Returns this high can seriously impact a publisher's bottom line. For years, publishers have talked about doing away with the practice of allowing bookstores to return unsold books to the publisher for credit. In 2008, HarperCollins started a new subsidiary that will sell popular trade book titles through bookstores, but on a nonreturnable basis. In terms of selling books, there are two main outlets: bookstores/book clubs and mail order.

Bookstores

About nineteen thousand outlets sell books in the United States, including traditional bookstores, department stores, drugstores, used-book stores, and toy stores. Book sales, however, are dominated by two large chains: Borders-Waldenbooks and Barnes & Noble, which includes B. Dalton stores. These chains operate hundreds of stores each and account for about one-quarter of all book sales.

Shopping-mall bookstores have boosted book sales since the late 1960s. But it was the development of book superstores in the 1980s that really reinvigorated the business. The idea

CITY LIGHTS is an independent bookstore in San Francisco. In business since 1953, the store was the first all-paperback bookstore and rose to prominence when it published Allen Ginsberg's *Howl and Other Poems* in 1956, enduring an obscenity trial as a result.

Year	Total # of bookstores	Total # of B&N and Borders Superstores (including Waldenbooks and B. Dalton)
1999	25,130	745
2001	25,916	2,160
2002	25,137	2,077
2003	23,643	2,038
2004	22,321	1,950
2007	18,456	1,925

"Large corporate booksellers, once an enemy of the little guy, now have enemies of their own: Amazon.com and big-box retailers like Costco and Target are taking on Borders with even deeper discounts than the chains used against the independents."

WASHINGTON POST, 2008

ONLINE BOOKSELLERS
Employees filling holiday orders in Amazon.com's Seattle distribution warehouse.

was to adapt the large retail store concept, such as Home Depot or Wal-Mart, to the book trade. Following the success of a single Borders store in Ann Arbor, Michigan, a number of book chains began developing book superstores that catered to suburban areas and to avid readers. A typical superstore now stocks up to 200,000 titles, compared with the 20,000 or 40,000 titles found in older mall stores. As superstores expanded, they began to sell recorded music and feature coffee shops and live performances. Borders had grown from 14 superstores in 1991 to more than 520 superstores and 460 Waldenbooks by 2008, but the company was losing money and put itself up for sale. The top bookstore chain, Barnes & Noble, was in better financial shape, operating more than 710 superstores and 85 smaller B. Dalton bookstores (see Table 10.4).

The rise of book superstores severely cut into independent bookstores' business, which dropped from a 31 percent market share in 1991 to about 10 percent by 2007.[12] Even more drastically, the number of independent bookstores has dropped from 5,100 in 1991 to just 1,000-plus today. Yet independents have successfully maintained their market share for several years, suggesting that their business has stabilized. To oppose chains, many independents have formed regional or statewide groups to plan survival tactics. For instance, independents in Madison, Wisconsin, once countered the arrival of a new Borders superstore by redecorating, extending hours and services, creating newsletters, and offering musical and children's performances.

Online Bookstores

Since the late 1990s, online booksellers have created an entirely new book distribution system on the Internet. The trailblazer is Amazon.com, established in 1995 by then-thirty-year-old Jeff Bezos, who left Wall Street to start a Web-based business. Bezos realized books were an untapped and ideal market for the Internet, with more than three million publications in print and plenty of distributors to fulfill orders. He moved to Seattle and started Amazon.com, so named because search engines like Yahoo! listed categories in alphabetical order, putting Amazon near the top of the list.

In 1997, Barnes & Noble, the leading retail store bookseller, launched the heavily invested and carefully researched bn.com (of which publishing giant Bertelsmann bought 50 percent in the following year, after it canceled plans to start its own online store). The Web site's success, however, remains dwarfed by Amazon. In 1999, the American Booksellers Association also launched BookSense.com to help more than one thousand independent bookstores create an online presence. By 2008, online booksellers controlled between 21 and 30 percent of consumer book sales.[13] The strength of online sellers lies in their convenience and low prices, and especially their ability to offer backlist titles and the works of less famous authors that even 200,000-volume superstores don't carry on their shelves. Online customers are also drawn to the interactive nature of these sites, which allow them to post their own book reviews, read those of fellow customers, and receive book recommendations based on book searches and past purchases. The chief business strategy of online booksellers is to buy exclusive listings with the most popular Internet portals. For example, bn.com signed a multimillion-dollar deal with Microsoft to be the "buy books" button on MSN.com, and it is the exclusive bookseller on AOL. Similarly, Amazon.com has a marketing agreement with Yahoo!

Book Clubs and Mail Order

Book clubs, similar to music clubs, entice new members with offers such as five books for one dollar, then require regular purchases from their list of recommended titles. Mail-order services also market specialized titles directly to readers. Originally, the two tactics helped the industry when bookstores were not as numerous as they are today. Modeled on the turn-of-the century catalogue sales techniques used by retailers such as Sears, direct-mail services brought books to rural and small-town areas that had no bookstores.

The Book-of-the-Month Club and the Literary Guild both started in 1926. Using popular writers and literary experts to recommend new books, the clubs were immediately successful. Book clubs have long served as editors for their customers, screening thousands of titles and recommending key books in particular genres. During the 1980s, book clubs began to experience declining sales. In 2000, the Book-of-the-Month Club, the Literary Guild, and Doubleday (the most active book club publisher) combined their online efforts with a partnership called Bookspan—owned jointly by Bertelsmann and Time Warner. This strategy was intended to make book clubs more competitive with online booksellers. However, in 2007, Time Warner sold out to Bertelsmann, which then merged the book club business with its DVD and music clubs. In 2008 Bertelsmann sold the North American parts of its book and music clubs to a private investment group.

Mail-order bookselling is used primarily by trade, professional, and university press publishers. Mail-order, like book clubs, immediately notifies readers about new book titles. Mail-order bookselling was pioneered in the 1950s by magazine publishers. They created special sets of books, including Time-Life Books, focusing on such areas as science, nature, household maintenance, and cooking. These series usually offered one book at a time and sustained sales through direct-mail flyers and other advertising. To enhance their perceived value, most of these sets could be obtained only through the mail. Although such sets are more costly due to advertising and postal charges, mail-order books still appeal to customers who prefer mail to the hassle of shopping or to those who prefer the privacy of mail order (particularly if they are ordering sexually explicit books or magazines).

Alternative Voices

Even though the book industry is dominated by large book conglomerates and superstores, there are still alternative options for both publishing and selling books. One alternative idea is to make books freely available to everyone. This idea is not a new one—in the late nineteenth and early twentieth centuries, industrialist Andrew Carnegie used millions of dollars from his vast steel fortune to build more than twenty-five hundred public libraries in the United States, Britain, Australia, and New Zealand. Carnegie believed that libraries created great learning opportunities for citizens, and especially for immigrants like himself. Indeed, public libraries may be some of the best venues for alternative voices—where a myriad of ideas exist side by side.

One Internet source, Newpages.com, is working on another alternative to conglomerate publishing and chain bookselling by trying to bring a vast array of alternative and university presses, independent bookstores, and guides to literary and alternative magazines together. Their 2008 listing of independent publishers, for example, included hundreds of publishers, mostly based in the United States and Canada, ranging from Academy Chicago Publishers (which publishes a range of fiction and nonfiction books) to Zephyr Press (which "publishes literary titles that foster deeper understanding of cultures and languages").

Finally, because e-books make publishing and distribution costs low, **e-publishing** has enabled authors to sidestep traditional publishers. A new breed of large Internet-based publishing houses, such as Xlibris, iUniverse, BookSurge, and AuthorHouse, design and distribute books for a comparatively small price for aspiring authors who want to self-publish a title. The companies then distribute the books in both print and e-book formats through Internet sellers. Although sales are typically low for such books, the low overhead costs allow higher royalty rates for the authors and lower retail prices for readers.

Books and the Future of Democracy

As we enter the digital age, the book-reading habits of children and adults have become a social concern. After all, books have played an important role not only in spreading the idea of democracy but also in connecting us to new ideas beyond our local experience. The impact of our oldest mass medium—the book—remains immense. Without the development of printing presses and books, the idea of democracy would be hard to imagine. From the impact of Harriet Beecher Stowe's *Uncle Tom's Cabin*, which helped bring an end to slavery in the 1860s, to Rachel Carson's *Silent Spring*, which led to reforms in the pesticide industry in the 1960s, books have made a difference. They have told us things that we wanted—and needed—to know, and inspired us to action. However, a 2007 National Endowment for the Arts (NEA) study, *To Read or Not To Read*, reported that "although there has been measurable progress in recent years in reading ability at the elementary school level, all progress appears to halt as children enter their teenage years." Less than one-third of thirteen-year-olds read daily, a 14 percent decline from 20 years earlier. Among first-year college students, 65 percent read for pleasure less than an hour a week or not at all (even as reading for pleasure strongly correlates with academic achievement). Moreover, the NEA report noted that people who read regularly were more active in civic and cultural life and more likely to perform volunteer and charity work, crucial activities in a democratic society.[14]

Yet other studies also suggest that reading habits are generally more evident among the young than among older people; 60 percent of all avid or regular book readers, for example, are under the age of forty. The Harry Potter phenomenon—the books have now been translated into sixty-five languages—has renewed reading among young people. One study in England reported that 60 percent of children surveyed said that the Potter books had improved their reading skills and 48 percent said the series is the main reason they read more.

In addition to a declining interest in books, the economic clout of publishing houses run by large multinational corporations has made it more difficult for new authors and new ideas to gain a foothold. Often, editors and executives prefer to invest in commercially successful authors or those who have a built-in television, sports, or movie audience. In his book *The Death of Literature*, Alvin Kernan argues that serious literary work has been increasingly overwhelmed by the triumph of consumerism. People jump at craftily marketed celebrity biographies and popular fiction, he argues, but seldom read serious works. He contends that cultural standards have been undermined by marketing ploys that divert attention away from serious books and toward mass-produced works that are more easily consumed.

Yet books and reading have survived the challenge of visual and digital culture. Developments such as word processing, audio books, children's pictorial literature, and online services have integrated aspects of print and electronic culture into our daily lives. Most of these new forms carry on the legacy of books: transcending borders to provide personal stories, world history, and general knowledge to all who can read. Also, despite a powerful commercial book industry, about a thousand new independent publishers enter the business each year.

Since the early days of the printing press, books have helped us to understand ideas and customs outside our own experiences. For democracy to work well, we must read. When we examine other cultures through books, we discover not only who we are and what we value but also who others are and what our common ties might be. ▶

"Universally priced at twenty-five cents in its early years, the paperback democratized reading in America."

KENNETH DAVIS,
TWO-BIT CULTURE, 1984

CHAPTER REVIEW

REVIEW QUESTIONS

The History of Books from Papyrus to Paperbacks

1. What distinguishes the manuscript culture of the Middle Ages from the oral and print eras in communication?

2. Why was the printing press such an important and revolutionary invention?

3. Why were books particularly important to women readers during the early periods of American history?

Modern Publishing and the Book Industry

4. Why did publishing houses develop?

5. Why is the trade book segment one of the most lucrative parts of the book industry?

6. What are the major issues that affect textbook publishing?

7. Why have instant books become important to the paperback market?

8. What has hampered the sales of printed and CD encyclopedias?

Trends and Issues in Book Publishing

9. What are the main ways in which digital technologies have changed the publishing industry?

10. Why did paper manufacturers convert to acid-free paper in the late 1980s and early 1990s?

11. What are the major issues in the debate over digitizing millions of books for Web search engines?

12. What's the difference between a book that is challenged and one that is banned?

The Organization and Ownership of the Book Industry

13. What are the current ownership patterns in the book industry? How do they affect the kinds of books published?

14. What are the general divisions within a typical publishing house?

15. What was the impact of the growth of book superstores on the rest of the bookstore industry?

16. What are the strengths of online bookstores?

17. What is Andrew Carnegie's legacy in regard to libraries in the United States and elsewhere?

Books and the Future of Democracy

18. Why is a declining interest in reading a threat to democratic life?

QUESTIONING THE MEDIA

1. What are your earliest recollections of books? Do you read for pleasure? If yes, what kinds of books do you enjoy? Why?

2. What can the book industry do better to ensure that we are not overwhelmed by a visual and electronic culture?

3. If you were opening an independent bookstore in a town with a chain store, such as a Barnes & Noble, how would you compete?

4. Imagine that you are on a committee that oversees book choices for a high school library in your town. What policies do you think should guide the committee's selection of controversial books?

5. Why do you think the availability of television and cable hasn't substantially decreased the number of new book titles available each year? What do books offer that television doesn't?

6. Would you read a book on an iPod or a Kindle? Why or why not?

COMMON THREADS

One of the Common Threads discussed in Chapter 1 is about the developmental stages of the mass media. Books have been a mass medium since at least the mid-1500s, but with the advent of digital technologies, will books be the same mass medium? That is, does paper make the medium?

Except for their earliest incarnation as clay tablets, books have been printed on various forms of paper—papyrus, parchment, or pulp. But as the printed word becomes digital, it actually isn't *printed* on anything, just represented on a screen. In this case, will the content still be considered a book? Think about how newspapers and magazines are changing, how Facebook has rendered the college yearbook almost extinct, how digital photos have done the same to bound photo albums, or what a recorded music "album" means in the era of the music download. How have content and accessibility changed with these evolutions?

In light of this, what is the meaning of the bound book in our culture? How do we interpret a lush paneled room full of literary classics, a large glossy "coffee-table" book, or a well-worn textbook? Will we still buy books based on their covers if there is no actual paper cover? If the primary reading medium becomes a screen, will we want to read text on a screen that reminds us of a book, or will the small screen of an iPod or mobile phone suffice?

In his review of Amazon's Kindle, Ezra Klein wrote in the *Columbia Journalism Review* that "just as the early television shows were really radio programs with moving images, the early electronic books are simply printed text uploaded to a computer."[15] If that is the case, what will the coming generation make of books? Will the "solitary pursuit" of reading, as Klein notes, become a social activity, with immediate connections to other readers and the author? Will a book purchase be an admission fee for an ongoing relationship, with updates or new chapters from the author?

Printed words on paper, bound together, create a natural enclosure to the communication of reading—it is just the individual reader interpreting an author's story, long after it has been written. Is that activity the essential nature of the book as a mass medium? Or can the book, with words released from paper, evolve into an entirely new communicative practice?

KEY TERMS

The definitions for the terms listed below can be found in the glossary at the end of the book. The page numbers listed with the terms indicate where the term is highlighted in the chapter.

Google

B40 & B43

Advertising and Commercial Culture

Back in 1993, the trade magazine *Adweek* wrote about "The Ultimate Network"— something called the Internet: "Advertisers and agencies take note: It has the potential to become the next great mass/personal medium."[1]

The prediction was correct, if not understated. The Internet has become a huge medium for advertisers, targeting audiences more precisely than any medium before it. Yet, none of the venerable ad agencies at that time could have guessed that an Internet start-up—Google— would become bigger than the leading multi-national advertising holding companies like Omnicom, WPP, Interpublic, and Publicis. Nearly 99 percent of Google's $16.6 billion revenue in 2007 came from advertising.

However, Google is different from the Madison Avenue agencies. It doesn't design witty, slick ad campaigns. Instead, it facilitates the dull but effective text-based sponsored links that appear in Google searches or on affiliated sites. "We are in the really boring part of the business…the boring big business," Google's CEO Eric Schmidt says.[2]

What Google's ads lack in creativity, they make up in precision. Google's AdWords advertising system has made advertising both targeted (by keyword or geographically) and inexpensive (ad buyers can preset daily spending limits). This has revolutionized advertising and enabled millions of new small advertisers to afford their own customized advertising plan along with traditional big advertisers. Google also notes that "we will do our best to provide the most relevant and useful advertising." Google doesn't like ads that create an "annoying interruption."[3] The company's own Google Toolbar blocks pop-up advertising—a kind of annoying Internet advertising it doesn't make (but its competitors do).

Looking beyond text-only Internet ads, Google is expanding to other advertising media, with subsidiaries to automate and target sales of radio broadcasting ads (through its acquisition of dMarc Advertising), newspaper ads (Google is already placing ads in more than 650 newspapers), click-to-play video ads (particularly in conjunction with its YouTube property), and television ads. Google is also testing ad placements in mobile phone search (advertising's "third screen," after television and computer screens).

All of Google's advertising ventures are based on the Internet, Google's analytical tools, and its enormous computer system. "These new platforms, new

innovations, and new services in fact create new opportunities for advertisers," Google's Schmidt told a conference of the American Association of Advertising Agencies in 2008 that also included presentations by Apple, Microsoft, and Yahoo! The targeted Internet approaches will be central to the future direction of advertising, Schmidt added. "I think these models are going to be the ones that will really evolve to be the defining models for advertising over the next 10 to 20 years."[4]

The current shift of advertising to more measurable, Internet-based forms marks the most wide-sweeping changes in the business since the advent of television. As billions of ad dollars continue to move to new advertising platforms, and as Google's revenue comes close to eclipsing the total ad revenue of the four major TV networks, history suggests that the advertising-based mass media are sure to change as well.

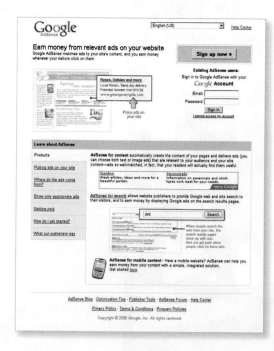

◢ **TODAY, ADVERTISEMENTS ARE EVERYWHERE AND IN EVERY MEDIA FORM.** Ads take up more than half the space in most daily newspapers and consumer magazines. They are inserted into trade books and textbooks. They clutter Web sites on the Internet. They fill our mailboxes and wallpaper the buses we ride. Dotting the nation's highways, billboards promote fast-food and hotel chains, while neon signs announce the names of stores along major streets and strip malls. Ads are even found in the restrooms of malls, restaurants, and bars.

At local theaters and on DVDs, ads now precede the latest Hollywood movie trailers. Corporate sponsors spend millions for **product placement**: buying spaces for particular goods to appear on a TV show or in a movie. Ads are part of a deejay's morning patter, and ads routinely interrupt our favorite TV and cable programs. By 2007, an average of fifteen minutes of each hour of prime-time network television carried commercials, program promos, and public service announcements—an increase from thirteen minutes an hour in 1992. According to the Food Marketing Institute, the typical supermarket's shelves are filled with thirty thousand to fifty thousand different brand-name packages, all functioning like miniature billboards. By some research estimates, the average American comes into contact with two thousand forms of advertising each day.

Advertising comes in many forms, from classified ads to business-to-business ads, providing detailed information on specific products. However, in this chapter we concentrate on the more conspicuous advertisements that shape product images and brand-name identities. Because so much consumer advertising intrudes into daily life, ads are often viewed in a negative light. Although business managers agree that advertising is the foundation of a healthy media economy—far preferable to government-controlled media—citizens routinely complain about how many ads they are forced to endure, and they increasingly find ways to avoid them, like zipping through television ads with Tivo and blocking pop-up ads with Web browsers. Without consumer advertisements, however, mass communication industries would cease to function in their present forms. Advertising is the economic glue that holds most media industries together.

In this chapter, we examine the historical development and role of advertising—an industry that helped transform numerous nations into consumer societies. We look at the first U.S. ad agencies; early advertisements; and the emergence of packaging, trademarks, and brand-name recognition. Then we consider the growth of advertising in the last century, scrutinizing the increasing influence of ad agencies and the shift to a more visually oriented culture. In keeping with our goal of developing critical skills, we outline the key persuasive techniques used in consumer advertising. In addition, we investigate ads as a form of commercial speech and discuss the measures aimed at regulating advertising. Finally, we look at political advertising and its impact on democracy.

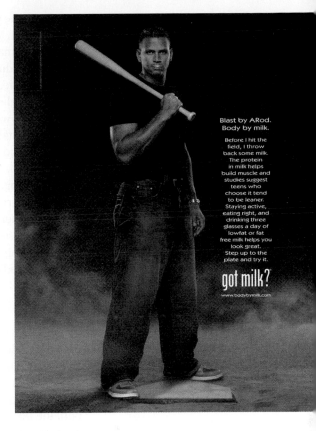

THE "GOT MILK?" advertising campaign was originally designed by Goodby, Silverstein & Partners for the California Milk Processor Board in 1993. Since 1998, the National Milk Processor Board has licensed the "got milk?" slogan for their celebrity milk moustache ads like this one.

Early Developments in American Advertising

Advertising has existed since 3000 B.C.E., when shop owners in ancient Babylon hung outdoor signs carved in stone and wood so that customers could spot their stores. Merchants in early Egyptian society hired town criers to walk through the streets, announcing the arrival of ships and listing the goods on board. Archaeologists searching Pompeii, the ancient Italian city destroyed when Mount Vesuvius erupted in 79 C.E., found advertising messages painted on walls. By 900 C.E., many European cities featured town criers who not only called out the news of the day but also directed customers to various stores.

The earliest media ads were on handbills, posters, and broadsides (long, newsprint-quality posters). English booksellers printed brochures and bills announcing new publications as early as the 1470s, when posters advertising religious books were tacked on church doors. In 1622, print ads imitating the oral style of criers appeared in the first English newspapers. Announcing land deals and ship cargoes, the first newspaper ads in colonial America ran in the *Boston News-Letter* in 1704.

To distinguish their approach from the commercialism of newspapers, early magazines refused to carry advertisements. By the mid-1800s, though, most magazines contained ads and most publishers started magazines hoping to earn advertising dollars. About 80 percent of these early advertisements covered three subjects: land sales, transportation announcements (stagecoach and ship schedules), and "runaways" (ads placed by farm and plantation owners whose slaves had fled).

The First Advertising Agencies

Until the 1830s, little need existed for elaborate advertising, as few goods and products were even available for sale. Before the Industrial Revolution, 90 percent of Americans lived in isolated areas and produced most of their own tools, clothes, and food. The minimal advertising that did exist usually featured local merchants selling goods and services in their own communities. National advertising, which initially focused on patent medicines, didn't start in earnest until the 1850s, when railroads linking the East Coast to the Mississippi River Valley began carrying newspapers, handbills, and broadsides—as well as national consumer goods—across the country.

> "You can tell the ideals of a nation by its advertisements."
>
> NORMAN DOUGLAS, *SOUTH WIND*, 1917

▼ Advertising and Commercial Culture

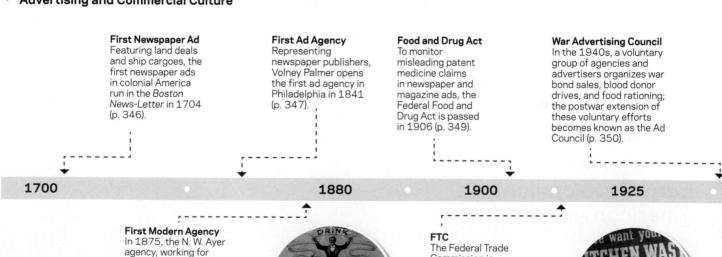

First Newspaper Ad
Featuring land deals and ship cargoes, the first newspaper ads in colonial America run in the *Boston News-Letter* in 1704 (p. 346).

First Ad Agency
Representing newspaper publishers, Volney Palmer opens the first ad agency in Philadelphia in 1841 (p. 347).

Food and Drug Act
To monitor misleading patent medicine claims in newspaper and magazine ads, the Federal Food and Drug Act is passed in 1906 (p. 349).

War Advertising Council
In the 1940s, a voluntary group of agencies and advertisers organizes war bond sales, blood donor drives, and food rationing; the postwar extension of these voluntary efforts becomes known as the Ad Council (p. 350).

1700   1880   1900   1925

First Modern Agency
In 1875, the N. W. Ayer agency, working for advertisers and product companies rather than publishers, opens in Philadelphia (p. 347).

FTC
The Federal Trade Commission is established by the federal government in 1914 to help monitor advertising abuses (p. 351).

The first American advertising agencies were newspaper **space brokers**: individuals who purchased space in newspapers and sold it to various merchants. Newspapers, accustomed to a 25 percent nonpayment rate from advertisers, welcomed the space brokers, who paid upfront. Brokers usually received discounts of 15 to 30 percent but sold the space to advertisers at the going rate. In 1841, Volney Palmer opened the first ad agency in Boston; for a 25 percent commission from newspaper publishers, he sold space to advertisers.

Advertising in the 1800s

The first so-called modern ad agency, N. W. Ayer, worked primarily for advertisers and product companies rather than for newspapers. Opening in 1875 in Philadelphia, the agency helped create, write, produce, and place ads in selected newspapers and magazines. The traditional payment structure at this time had the agency collecting a fee from its advertising client for each ad placed; the fee covered the price that each media outlet charged for placement of the ad, plus a 15 percent commission for the agency. The more ads an agency placed, the larger the agency's revenue. Thus agencies had little incentive to buy fewer ads on behalf of their clients. Nowadays, however, many advertising agencies work for a flat fee, and some will agree to be paid on a performance basis.

Trademarks and Packaging

During the mid-1800s, most manufacturers served retail store owners, who usually set their own prices by purchasing goods in large quantities. Manufacturers, however, came to realize that if their products were distinctive and associated with quality, customers would ask for them by name. This would allow manufacturers to dictate prices without worrying about being undersold by stores' generic products or bulk items. Advertising let manufacturers establish a special identity for their products, separate from their competitors.

> "The American apparatus of advertising is something unique in history[;] . . . it is like a grotesque, smirking gargoyle set at the very top of America's sky-scraping adventure in acquisition ad infinitum."
>
> JAMES RORTY, *OUR MASTER'S VOICE*, 1934

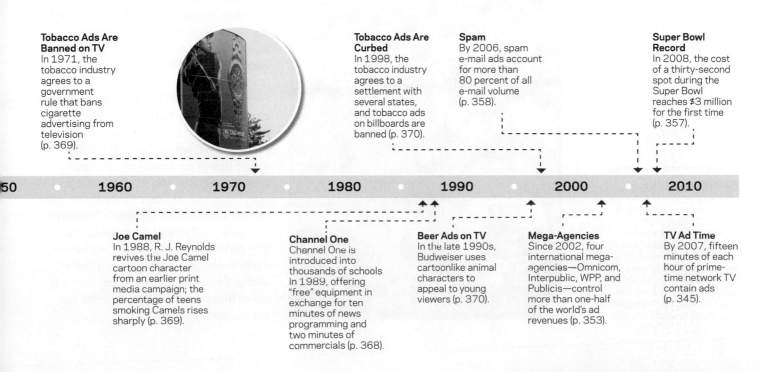

Tobacco Ads Are Banned on TV
In 1971, the tobacco industry agrees to a government rule that bans cigarette advertising from television (p. 369).

Tobacco Ads Are Curbed
In 1998, the tobacco industry agrees to a settlement with several states, and tobacco ads on billboards are banned (p. 370).

Spam
By 2006, spam e-mail ads account for more than 80 percent of all e-mail volume (p. 358).

Super Bowl Record
In 2008, the cost of a thirty-second spot during the Super Bowl reaches $3 million for the first time (p. 357).

50 — 1960 — 1970 — 1980 — 1990 — 2000 — 2010

Joe Camel
In 1988, R. J. Reynolds revives the Joe Camel cartoon character from an earlier print media campaign; the percentage of teens smoking Camels rises sharply (p. 369).

Channel One
Channel One is introduced into thousands of schools In 1989, offering "free" equipment in exchange for ten minutes of news programming and two minutes of commercials (p. 368).

Beer Ads on TV
In the late 1990s, Budweiser uses cartoonlike animal characters to appeal to young viewers (p. 370).

Mega-Agencies
Since 2002, four international mega-agencies—Omnicom, Interpublic, WPP, and Publicis—control more than one-half of the world's ad revenues (p. 353).

TV Ad Time
By 2007, fifteen minutes of each hour of prime-time network TV contain ads (p. 345).

BRAND NAMES
Originally called the Joseph A. Campbell Preserve Company back in 1869, the Campbell Soup Co. introduced its classic red-and-white soup can labels in 1897 after an employee was inspired by the uniforms of the Cornell University football team. Today, the label is updated, but Campbell's red and white cans remain one of the most recognized brands in the country.

Like many ads today, nineteenth-century advertisements often created the impression of significant differences among products when in fact very few differences actually existed. But when consumers began demanding certain products—either because of quality or because of advertising—manufacturers were able to control the prices of their goods. With ads creating and maintaining brand-name recognition, retail stores had to stock the desired brands.

One of the first brand names, Smith Brothers, has been advertising cough drops since the early 1850s. Quaker Oats, the first cereal company to register a trademark, has used the image of William Penn, the Quaker who founded Pennsylvania in 1681, to project a company image of honesty, decency, and hard work since 1877. Other early and enduring brands include Campbell Soup, which came along in 1869; Levi Strauss overalls in 1873; Ivory Soap in 1879; and Eastman Kodak film in 1888. Many of these companies packaged their products in small quantities, thereby distinguishing them from the generic products sold in large barrels and bins.

Product differentiation associated with brand-name packaged goods represents the single biggest triumph of advertising. Studies suggest that although most ads are not very effective in the short run, over time they create demand by leading consumers to associate particular brands with quality. Not surprisingly, building or sustaining brand-name recognition is the focus of many product-marketing campaigns. But the costs that packaging and advertising add to products generate many consumer complaints. The high price of many contemporary products results from advertising costs. For example, designer jeans that cost $150 (or more) today are made from roughly the same inexpensive denim that has outfitted farm workers since the 1800s. The difference now is that more than 90 percent of the jeans' costs goes toward advertising and profit.

PATENT MEDICINES
Unregulated patent medicines, such as the one represented in this ad, created a bonanza for nineteenth-century print media in search of advertising revenue. After several muckraking magazine reports about deceptive patent medicine claims, Congress created the Food and Drug Administration in 1906.

Patent Medicines and Department Stores

By the end of the 1800s, patent medicines and department stores accounted for half of the revenues taken in by ad agencies. Meanwhile, one-sixth of all print ads came from patent medicine and drug companies. Such ads ensured the financial survival of numerous magazines as "the role of the publisher changed from being a seller of a product to consumers to being a gatherer of consumers for the advertisers."[5] Bearing names like Lydia Pinkham's Vegetable Compound, Dr. Lin's Chinese Blood Pills, and William Radam's Microbe Killer, patent medicines were often made with water and 15 to 40 percent concentrations of ethyl alcohol. One patent medicine—Mrs. Winslow's Soothing Syrup—actually contained morphine. The powerful drugs in these medicines explain why people felt "better" after taking them; at the same time, they triggered lifelong addiction problems for many customers.

Many contemporary products, in fact, originated as medicines. Coca-Cola, for instance, was initially sold as a medicinal tonic and even contained traces of cocaine until 1903, when it was replaced by caffeine. Early Post and Kellogg's cereal ads promised to cure stomach and digestive problems. Many patent medicines made outrageous claims about what they could cure, leading to increased public cynicism. As a result, advertisers began to police their ranks and develop industry codes to restore customer confidence. Partly to monitor patent medicine claims, the Federal Food and Drug Act was passed in 1906.

Along with patent medicines, department store ads were also becoming prominent in newspapers and magazines. By the early 1890s, more than 20 percent of ad space was devoted to department stores. At the time, these stores were frequently criticized for undermining small shops and businesses, where shopkeepers personally served customers. The more impersonal department stores allowed shoppers to browse and find brand-name goods themselves. Because these stores purchased merchandise in large quantities, they could generally sell the same products for less. With increased volume and less money spent on individualized service, department store chains, like Target and Wal-Mart today, undercut small local stores and put more of their profits into ads.

Advertising's Impact on Newspapers

With the advent of the Industrial Revolution, "continuous-process machinery" kept company factories operating at peak efficiency, helping to produce an abundance of inexpensive packaged consumer goods.[6] The companies that produced those goods–Procter & Gamble, Colgate-Palmolive, Heinz, Borden, Pillsbury, Eastman Kodak, Carnation, and American Tobacco–were some of the first to advertise, and they remain major advertisers today (although many of these brand names have been absorbed by larger conglomerates; see Table 11.1).

The demand for newspaper advertising by product companies and retail stores significantly changed the ratio of copy at most newspapers. While newspapers in the mid-1880s featured 70 to 75 percent news and editorial material and only 25 to 30 percent advertisements, by the early 1900s, more than half the space in daily papers was devoted to advertising. This trend continues today, with more than 60 percent of the space in large daily newspapers consumed by ads.

Promoting Social Change and Dictating Values

As U.S. advertising became more pervasive, it contributed to major social changes in the twentieth century. First, it significantly influenced the transition from a producer-directed

"Consumption, Asthma, Bronchitis, Deafness, cured at HOME!"

AD FOR CARBOLATE OF TAR INHALANTS, 1883

TABLE 11.1
THE TOP 10 NATIONAL ADVERTISERS, 2007

Source: Advertising Age, "100 Leading National Advertisers," http://adage.com/datacenter/article?article_id=127791. Accessed July 23, 2008.

Rank	Advertiser	Headquarters	2007 Advertising Expenditures (in $ millions)	% Change from 2006
1	Procter & Gamble	Cincinnati, Ohio	$5,230.1	+7.1
2	AT&T	San Antonio, Tex.	3,207.3	-4.1
3	Verizon	New York, N.Y.	3,016.1	+8.0
4	General Motors Corp.	Detroit, Mich.	3,010.1	-8.7
5	Time Warner	New York, N.Y.	2,962.1	-3.6
6	Ford Motor Company	Dearborn, Mich.	2,525.2	-2.0
7	GlaxoSmithKline	Brentford, Middlesex, U.K.	2,456.9	-1.9
8	Johnson & Johnson	New Brunswick, N.J.	2,408.8	+0.3
9	Walt Disney Co.	Burbank, Calif.	2,293.3	-0.3
10	Unilever	London/Rotterdam	2,245.8	+7.0

to a consumer-driven society. By stimulating demand for new products, advertising helped manufacturers create new markets and recover product start-up costs quickly. From farms to cities, advertising spread the word—first in newspapers and magazines and later on radio and television.

Second, advertising promoted technological advances by showing how new machines, such as vacuum cleaners, washing machines, and cars, could improve daily life. Third, advertising encouraged economic growth by increasing sales. To meet the demand generated by ads, manufacturers produced greater quantities, which reduced their costs per unit, although they did not always pass these savings along to consumers.

Appealing to Female Consumers

By the early 1900s, advertisers and ad agencies believed that women, who constituted 70 to 80 percent of newspaper and magazine readers, controlled most household purchasing decisions. (This is still a fundamental principle of advertising today.) Ironically, more than 99 percent of the copywriters and ad executives at that time were men, primarily based in Chicago and New York. They emphasized stereotyped appeals to women, believing that simple ads with emotional and even irrational content worked best. Thus early ad copy featured personal tales of "heroic" cleaning products and household appliances. The intention was to help consumers feel good about defeating life's problems—an advertising strategy that endured throughout much of the twentieth century.

Dealing with Criticism

Although ad revenues fell during the Great Depression in the 1930s, World War II brought a rejuvenation for advertising. For the first time, the federal government bought large quantities of advertising space to promote U.S. involvement in a war. These purchases helped offset a decline in traditional advertising, as many industries had turned their attention and production facilities to the war effort.

Also during the 1940s, the industry began to actively deflect criticism that advertising created consumer needs that ordinary citizens never knew they had. Criticism of advertising grew as the industry appeared to be dictating values as well as driving the economy. To promote a more positive image, the industry developed the War Advertising Council—a voluntary group of agencies and advertisers that organized war bond sales, blood donor drives, and the rationing of scarce goods.

The postwar extension of advertising's voluntary efforts became known as the Ad Council, praised over the years for its Smokey the Bear campaign ("Only you can prevent forest fires"); its fund-raising campaign for the United Negro College Fund ("A mind is a terrible thing to waste"); and its "crash dummy" spots for the Department of Transportation, which substantially increased seat belt use. Choosing a dozen worthy causes annually, the Ad Council continues to produce pro bono *public service announcements* (PSAs) on a wide range of topics, including literacy, homelessness, drug addiction, smoking, and AIDS education.

WAR ADVERTISING COUNCIL
During World War II, the federal government engaged the advertising industry to create messages to support the U.S. war effort. Advertisers promoted the sale of war bonds, conservation of natural resources such as tin and gasoline, and even saving kitchen waste so it could be fed to farm animals.

Early Ad Regulation

The early 1900s saw the formation of several watch-dog organizations. Partly to keep tabs on deceptive advertising, advocates in the business community in 1913 created the nonprofit Better Business Bureau, which now has more than one hundred branch offices in the United States. At the same time, advertisers wanted a formal service that tracked newspaper readership, guaranteed accurate audience measures, and ensured that papers would not overcharge agencies and their clients. As a result, publishers formed the Audit Bureau of Circulation (ABC) in 1914.

That same year, the government created the Federal Trade Commission (FTC), in part to help monitor advertising abuses. Thereafter, the industry urged self-regulatory measures in order to keep government interference at bay. The American Association of Advertising Agencies (AAAA), for example—established in 1917—tried to minimize government oversight by urging ad agencies to refrain from making misleading product claims.

Finally, the advent of television dramatically altered advertising. With this new visual medium, ads increasingly intruded on daily life. Critics also discovered that some agencies used **subliminal advertising**. This term, coined in the 1950s, refers to hidden or disguised print and visual messages that allegedly register on the subconscious and fool people into buying products. Noted examples of subliminal ads from the time include a "Drink Coca-Cola" ad embedded in a few frames of a movie and alleged hidden sexual activity drawn into liquor ads; but research suggests that such ads are no more effective than regular ads. Nevertheless, the National Association of Broadcasters banned the use of subliminal ads in 1958.

The "It's Not Like I'm Drunk" Cocktail

2 oz. tequila
1 oz. triple sec
1/2 ounce lime juice
Salt
1 too many
1 automobile
1 missed red light
1 false sense of security
1 lowered reaction time

Combine ingredients. Shake.
Have another. And another.

Never underestimate 'just a few.'
Buzzed driving is drunk driving.

AdCouncil.org

U.S. Department of Transportation

The Shape of U.S. Advertising Today

Until the 1960s, the shape and pitch of most U.S. ads were determined by a **slogan**, the phrase that attempts to sell a product by capturing its essence in words. With slogans such as "A Diamond Is Forever" (which DeBeers first used in 1948), the visual dimension of ads was merely a complement. Eventually, however, through the influence of European design, television, and, now, multimedia devices, images asserted themselves, and visual style began to dominate U.S. advertising and ad agencies.

PUBLIC SERVICE ANNOUNCEMENTS
The Ad Council has been creating public service announcements (PSAs) since 1942. Supported by contributions from individuals, corporations, and foundations, the council's PSAs are produced pro bono by ad agencies. This recent PSA is part of a drunk-driving prevention campaign.

The Influence of Visual Design

Just as a postmodern design phase developed in art and architecture during the 1960s and 1970s, a new design era began to affect advertising at the same time. Part of this visual revolution was imported from non-U.S. schools of design; indeed, ad-rich magazines such as *Vogue* and *Vanity Fair* increasingly hired European designers as art directors. These directors tended to be less tied to U.S. word-driven radio advertising because most European countries had government-sponsored radio systems with no ads.

By the early 1970s, agencies had developed teams of writers and artists, thus granting equal status to images and words in the creative process. By the mid-1980s, the visual techniques of MTV, which initially modeled its style on advertising, influenced many ads and most agencies. MTV promoted a particular visual aesthetic—rapid edits, creative camera angles, compressed narratives, and staged performances. Video-style ads soon saturated television and featured such prominent performers as Paula Abdul, Ray Charles, Michael Jackson, Elton John, and Madonna. The popularity of MTV's visual style also started a trend in the 1980s to license hit songs for commercial tie-ins. By the early part of the twenty-first century, a wide range of short, polished musical performances and familiar songs—including the work of Fergie (Verizon), The Shins (McDonald's), the Brazilian Girls (Axe), Mary J. Blige (Propel), and classic Afrika Bambaataa (Visa)—were routinely used in TV ads to encourage consumers not to click the remote control.

Most recently, the Internet and multimedia devices, such as computers, mobile phones, and portable media players, have had a significant impact on visual design in advertising. As the Web became a mass medium in the 1990s, TV and print designs often mimicked the drop-down menu of computer interfaces. In the twenty-first century, visual design has evolved in other ways, becoming more three-dimensional, as full-motion, 3-D animation becomes a high-bandwidth multimedia standard. At the same time, design is also more simple, as ads and logos need to appear clearly on the small screens of mobile phones and portable media players, and more international, as agencies need to appeal to the global audiences of many companies and therefore need to reflect styles from anywhere in the world.

MAD MEN
AMC's hit series *Mad Men* depicts the male-dominated world of Madison Avenue in 1960, as the U.S. consumer economy kicked into high gear and agencies developed ad campaigns for cigarettes, exercise belts, and presidential candidates. In 2008, the drama was nominated for sixteen Emmys and won six.

Types of Advertising Agencies

There are more than thirteen thousand ad agencies that currently operate in the United States. In general, these agencies are either classified as **mega-agencies**–large ad firms that are formed by merging several individual agencies and that maintain worldwide regional offices–or small **boutique agencies** that devote their talents to only a handful of select clients. Both types of agencies wield great control over the type of advertising we see daily.

Mega-Agencies

Mega-agencies provide a full range of services from advertising and public relations to operating their own in-house radio and TV production studios. In 2008, the top four mega-agencies were Omnicom, WPP, Interpublic, and Publicis.[7]

Omnicom, formed in 1986 and based in New York, has 70,000 employees in more than 100 countries and owns the global advertising firms BBDO Worldwide, DDB Worldwide, and TBWA\ Worldwide. The company also owns three leading public relations agencies: Fleishman-Hillard, Ketchum, and Porter Novelli. The London-based WPP Group grew quickly in the 1980s with the purchases of J. Walter Thompson, the largest U.S. ad firm at the time; Hill & Knowlton, one of the largest U.S. public relations agencies; and Ogilvy & Mather Worldwide. In the 2000s, WPP Group continued its growth and acquired Young & Rubicam and Grey Global–both major U.S. ad firms. By 2008, WPP had more than 102,000 employees and offices in 106 countries.

The Interpublic Group, based in New York with 43,000 employees worldwide, holds global agencies like McCann Erickson (the top U.S. ad agency), Draftfcb, and Lowe Worldwide, and public relations firms GolinHarris and Weber Shandwick. The Paris-based Publicis Groupe has global reach through agencies like Leo Burnett Worldwide, British agency Saatchi & Saatchi, Digitas, and public relations firm Manning Selvage & Lee. Publicis employed more than 43,000 people worldwide in 2008 (see Figure 11.1).

This mega-agency trend has stirred debate among consumer and media watchdog groups. Some consider large agencies a threat to the independence of smaller firms, which are slowly being bought out. An additional concern is that these four firms now control more than half the distribution of advertising dollars globally. As a result, the cultural values represented by U.S. and European ads may undermine or overwhelm the values and products of developing countries.

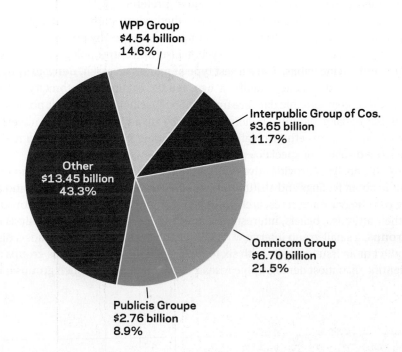

FIGURE 11.1

THE WORLD'S FOUR LARGEST AGENCIES, U.S. REVENUES, 2008 (INCOME IN BILLIONS)

Source: "Agency Report, 2008," May 5, 2008, htttp://adage.com/ agencyfamilytrees08.

*Note: Based on $31.1 billion U.S. revenue from all agency activities. Non-advertising revenue is excluded.

WPP Group
$4.54 billion
14.6%

Interpublic Group of Cos.
$3.65 billion
11.7%

Other
$13.45 billion
43.3%

Omnicom Group
$6.70 billion
21.5%

Publicis Groupe
$2.76 billion
8.9%

Boutique Agencies

The visual revolutions in advertising during the 1960s elevated the standing of designers and graphic artists, who became closely identified with the look of particular ads. Breaking away from bigger agencies, many of these creative individuals formed small boutique agencies. Offering more personal services, the boutiques prospered, bolstered by innovative ad campaigns and increasing profits from TV accounts. By the 1980s, large agencies had bought up many of the boutiques. Nevertheless, these boutiques continue to operate as fairly autonomous subsidiaries within multinational corporate structures.

One independent boutique agency in Minneapolis, Peterson Milla Hooks, has made its name with a boldly graphic national branding ad campaign for Target department stores. The series of ads plays on the red and white Target bull's-eye, which is recognized by 96 percent of U.S. consumers.[8] The agency employs about fifty people but counts Mattel, Turner Classic Movies, and Anheuser-Busch among its other clients.

The Structure of Ad Agencies

Traditional ad agencies, regardless of their size, generally divide the labor of creating and maintaining advertising campaigns among four departments: account planning, creative development, media coordination, and account management. Expenses incurred for producing the ads are part of a separate negotiation between the agency and the advertiser. As a result of this commission arrangement, it generally costs most large-volume advertisers no more to use an agency than it does to use their own staff.

Account Planning, Market Research, and VALS

The account planner's role is to develop an effective advertising strategy by combining the views of the client, creative team, and consumers. Consumers' views are the most difficult to understand, so account planners coordinate **market research** to assess the behaviors and attitudes of consumers toward particular products long before any ads are created. Researchers may study everything from possible names for a new product to the size of the copy for a print ad. Researchers also test new ideas and products with consumers to get feedback before developing final ad strategies. In addition, some researchers contract with outside polling firms to conduct regional and national studies of consumer preferences.

Agencies have increasingly employed scientific methods to study consumer behavior. In 1932, Young & Rubicam first used statistical techniques developed by pollster George Gallup. By the 1980s, most large agencies retained psychologists and anthropologists to advise them on human nature and buying habits. The earliest type of market research, **demographics**, mainly studied and documented audience members' age, gender, occupation, ethnicity, education, and income. Today, demographic data are much more specific. They make it possible to locate consumers in particular geographic regions—usually by zip code. This enables advertisers and product companies to target ethnic neighborhoods or affluent suburbs for direct mail, point-of-purchase store displays, or specialized magazine and newspaper inserts.

Demographic analyses provide advertisers with data on people's behavior and social status but reveal little about feelings and attitudes. By the 1960s and 1970s, advertisers and agencies began using **psychographics**, a research approach that attempts to categorize consumers according to their attitudes, beliefs, interests, and motivations. Psychographic analysis often relies on **focus groups**, a small-group interview technique in which a moderator leads a discussion about a product or an issue, usually with six to twelve people. Because focus groups are small and less scientific than most demographic research, the findings from such groups may be suspect.

> "The best advertising artist of all time was Raphael. He had the best client —the papacy; the best art director— the College of Cardinals; and the best product— salvation. And we never disparage Raphael for working for a client or selling an idea."
>
> MARK FENSKE, CREATIVE DIRECTOR, N. W. AYER, 1996

In 1978, the Stanford Research Institute (SRI), now called SRI Consulting Business Intelligence, instituted its **Values and Lifestyles (VALS)** strategy. Using questionnaires, VALS researchers measured psychological factors and divided consumers into types. VALS research assumes that not every product suits every consumer and encourages advertisers to vary their sales slants to find market niches.

Over the years, the VALS system has been updated to reflect changes in consumer orientations (see Figure 11.2 on page 356). The most recent system classifies people by their primary consumer motivations: ideals, achievement, or self-expression. The ideals-oriented group, for instance, includes *thinkers*–"mature, satisfied, comfortable, and reflective people who value order, knowledge, and responsibility." VALS and similar research techniques ultimately provide advertisers with microscopic details about which consumers are most likely to buy which products.

Agencies and clients–particularly auto manufacturers–have relied heavily on VALS to determine the best placement for ads. VALS data suggest, for example, that *achievers* and *experiencers* watch more sports and news programs; these groups prefer luxury cars or sport-utility vehicles. *Thinkers*, on the other hand, favor TV dramas and documentaries and like the functionality of minivans or the gas efficiency of hybrids.

VALS researchers do not claim that most people fit neatly into a category. But many agencies believe that VALS research can give them an edge in markets where few differences in quality may actually exist among top-selling brands. Consumer groups, wary of such research, argue that too many ads promote only an image and provide little information about a product's price, its content, or the work conditions under which it was produced.

Creative Development

Teams of writers and artists–many of whom regard ads as a commercial art form–make up the nerve center of the advertising business. The creative department outlines the rough sketches for print and online ads and then develops the words and graphics. For radio, the creative side prepares a working script, generating ideas for everything from choosing the narrator's voice to determining background sound effects. For television, the creative department develops a **storyboard**, a sort of blueprint or roughly drawn comic-strip version of the potential ad. For digital media, the creative team may develop Web sites, interactive tools, flash games, downloads, and **viral marketing**–short videos or other content that (marketers hope) quickly gains widespread attention as users share it with friends online, or by word of mouth.

Often the creative side of the business finds itself in conflict with the research side. In the 1960s, for example, both Doyle Dane Bernbach (DDB) and Ogilvy & Mather downplayed research; they championed the art of persuasion and what "felt right." Yet DDB's simple ads for Volkswagen Beetles in the 1960s were based on weeks of intensive interviews with VW workers as well as on creative instincts. The campaign was remarkably successful in establishing the first niche for a foreign car manufacturer in the United States. Although sales of the VW "bug" had been growing before the ad campaign started, the successful ads helped Volkswagen preempt the Detroit auto industry's entry into the small-car field.

Both the creative and the strategic sides of the business acknowledge that they cannot predict with any certainty which ads and which campaigns will succeed. Agencies say ads work best by slowly creating brand-name identities–by associating certain products over time with quality and reliability in the minds of consumers. Some economists, however, believe that much of the money spent on advertising is ultimately wasted because it simply encourages consumers to change from one brand name to another. Such switching may lead to increased profits for a particular manufacturer, but it has little positive impact on the overall economy.

> "Alcohol marketers appear to believe that the prototypical college student is (1) male; (2) a nitwit; and (3) interested in nothing but booze and 'babes.'"
>
> MICHAEL F. JACOBSON AND LAURIE ANN MAZUR, *MARKETING MADNESS*, 1995

> "Ads seem to work on the very advanced principle that a very small pellet or pattern in a noisy, redundant barrage of repetition will gradually assert itself."
>
> MARSHALL MCLUHAN, *UNDERSTANDING MEDIA*, 1964

FIGURE 11.2

VALS TYPES AND CHARACTERISTICS

Source: SRI Consulting Business intelligence, 2006, http://www.sric-bi.com/VALS.

▼

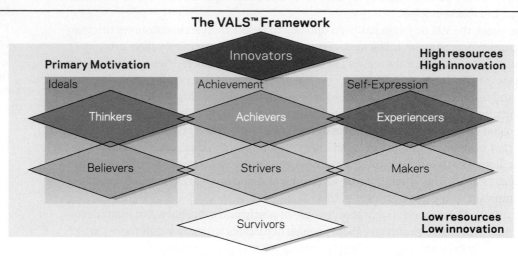

The VALS™ Framework

VALS™ Types and Characteristics

Innovators Innovators are successful, sophisticated, take-charge people with high self-esteem and abundant resources. They exhibit all three primary motivations in varying degrees. They are change leaders and are the most receptive to new ideas and technologies. They are very active consumers, and their purchases reflect cultivated tastes for upscale, niche products and services.

Thinkers Thinkers are motivated by ideals. They are mature, satisfied, comfortable, and reflective people who value order, knowledge, and responsibility. They tend to be well educated and actively seek out information in the decision-making process. They are well informed about world and national events and are alert to opportunities to broaden their knowledge.

Achievers Motivated by the desire for achievement, Achievers have goal-oriented lifestyles and a deep commitment to career and family. Their social lives reflect this focus and are structured around family, their place of worship, and work. Achievers live conventional lives, are politically conservative, and respect authority and the status quo. They value consensus, predictability, and stability over risk, intimacy, and self-discovery.

Experiencers Experiencers are motivated by self-expression. As young, enthusiastic, and impulsive consumers, Experiencers quickly become enthusiastic about new possibilities but are equally quick to cool. They seek variety and excitement, savoring the new, the offbeat, and the risky. Their energy finds an outlet in exercise, sports, outdoor recreation, and social activities.

Believers Like thinkers, Believers are motivated by ideals. They are conservative, conventional people with concrete beliefs based on traditional, established codes; family, religion, community, and the nation. Many Believers express moral codes that are deeply rooted and literally interpreted. They follow established routines, organized in large part around home, family, community, and social or religious organizations to which they belong.

Strivers Strivers are trendy and fun loving. Because they are motivated by achievement, Strivers are concerned about the opinions and approval of others. Money defines success for Strivers, who don't have enough of it to meet their desires. They favor stylish products that emulate the purchases of people with greater material wealth. Many see themselves as having a job rather than a career, and a lack of skills and focus often prevents them from moving ahead.

Makers Like Experiencers, Makers are motivated by self-expression. They express themselves and experience the world by working on it—building a house, raising children, fixing a car, or canning vegetables—and have enough skill and energy to carry out their projects successfully. Makers are practical people who have constructive skills and value self-sufficiency. They live within a traditional context of family, practical work, and physical recreation and have little interest in what lies outside that context.

Survivors Survivors live narrowly focused lives. With few resources with which to cope, they often believe that the world is changing too quickly. They are comfortable with the familiar and are primarily concerned with safety and security. Because they must focus on meeting needs rather than fulfilling desires, Survivors do not show a strong primary motivation.

Media Coordination: Planning and Placing Advertising

The media department is staffed by media planners and **media buyers**: people who choose and purchase the types of media that are best suited to carry a client's ads, reach the targeted audience, and measure the effectiveness of those ad placements. For instance, a company like Procter & Gamble, one of the world's leading advertisers, displays its more than three hundred major brands—most of them household products like Crest toothpaste and Huggies diapers—on TV shows viewed primarily by women. To reach male viewers, however, media buyers encourage beer advertisers to spend their ad budgets on cable and network sports programming, evening talk radio, or sports magazines.

Along with commissions or fees, advertisers often add incentive clauses to their contracts with agencies, raising the fee if sales goals are met and lowering it if goals are missed. Incentive clauses can sometimes encourage agencies to conduct repetitive **saturation advertising**, in which a variety of media are inundated with ads aimed at target audiences. The initial Miller Lite beer campaign ("Tastes great, less filling"), which used humor and retired athletes to reach its male audience, became one of the most successful saturation campaigns in media history. It ran from 1973 to 1991 and included television and radio spots, magazine and newspaper ads, and billboards and point-of-purchase store displays. The excessive repetition of the campaign helped light beer overcome a potential image problem: being viewed as watered-down beer unworthy of "real" men.

The cost of advertising, especially on network television, increases each year. The Super Bowl remains the most expensive program for purchasing television advertising, with thirty seconds of time costing up to $3 million in 2008. Running a thirty-second ad during a national prime-time TV show can cost from $100,000 to more than $700,000 depending on the popularity and ratings of the program. All this factors in to where and when media buyers place ads.

CREATIVE ADVERTISING
The New York ad agency Doyle Dane Bernbach created a famous series of print and television ads for Volkswagen beginning in 1959 (below, left), and helped to usher in an era of creative advertising that combined a single-point sales emphasis with bold design, humor, and honesty. Arnold Worldwide, a Boston agency, continued the highly creative approach with its clever, award-winning "Drivers Wanted" campaign for the New Beetle (below).

Lemon.

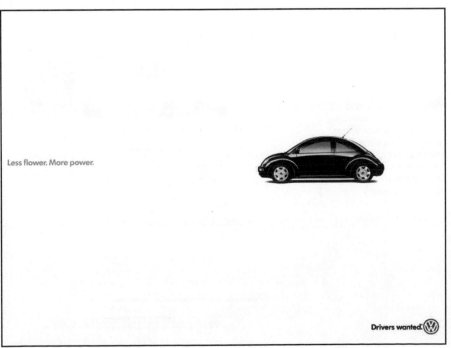

Less flower. More power.

Drivers wanted.

Account and Client Management

Client liaisons, or **account executives**, are responsible for bringing in new business and managing the accounts of established clients, including overseeing budgets and the research, creative, and media planning work done on their campaigns. This department also oversees new ad campaigns in which several agencies bid for a client's business: coordinating the presentation of a proposed campaign and various aspects of the bidding process, such as determining what a series of ads will cost a client. Account executives function as liaisons between the advertiser and the agency's creative team. Because most major companies maintain their own ad departments to handle everyday details, account executives also coordinate activities between their agency and a client's in-house personnel.

The advertising business is volatile, and account departments are especially vulnerable to upheavals. One industry study conducted in the mid-1980s indicated that client accounts stayed with the same agency for about seven years on average, but since the late 1980s, clients have changed agencies much more often. Clients routinely conduct **account reviews**, the process of evaluating and reinvigorating a product's image by reviewing an ad agency's existing campaign or by inviting several new agencies to submit new campaign strategies, which may result in the product company switching agencies.[9]

Business Trends in Internet Advertising

The earliest form of Web advertising appeared in the mid-1990s and featured banner ads, the printlike display ads that load across the top or side of a Web page. Since that time, other formats have emerged, including pop-up ads, pop-under ads, flash multimedia ads, and **interstitials**, which pop up in new screen windows as a user clicks to a new Web page. Other forms of Internet advertising include classified ads and unsolicited e-mail ads—known as **spam**—which now account for more than 80 percent of e-mail.

More recently, paid search advertising has become the dominant format of Web advertising. Even though their original mission was to provide impartial search results, search sites such as Google, MSN, and Yahoo! have quietly morphed into advertising companies, selling sponsored links associated with search terms and distributing online ads to affiliated Web pages.[10]

ONLINE ADS are mostly placed by large Internet companies like Google, Yahoo!, Microsoft, and AOL. Such services have allowed small businesses access to more customers than traditional advertising because the online ads can be cheaper and only shown to targeted users.

Online Advertising Agencies

By 2007, the threat of online companies to traditional advertising agencies was real. Internet ads accounted for at least 7 percent of all advertising spending in the United States, and that share was expected to rise to more than 10 percent by 2010, particularly as companies begin shifting their ad budgets away from newspapers, radio, and television.[11] For advertisers, the Web, more than any other medium, has the ability to target ads precisely to relevant consumers—for example, sending hotel and tour package ads to someone looking for information on London vacations.

Internet ads are generally placed by Internet advertising agencies and served to hundreds of client sites by the agencies' computers. The agencies track ad impressions (how often ads are seen) and click-throughs, and develop consumer profiles that direct targeted advertisements to Web site visitors. Internet user information is gained through cookies and online surveys—for example, an ESPN.com contest requires users to fill out a survey to be eligible to win sports tickets—or through sites, like nytimes.com, that require users to provide demographic information for free access to the site. Agencies can add online and retail sales data to user profiles to create an unprecedented database, largely without the consumer's knowledge. Such a database is a boon to marketers, but troubling to privacy advocates.

New Challenges to Traditional Agencies

The leading Internet companies aggressively expanded into the advertising market by acquiring smaller Internet advertising agencies. Google bought DoubleClick, the biggest online ad server; Yahoo! purchased Right Media, which auctions online ad space; AOL bought Third Screen Media, a mobile-phone ad network; and Microsoft acquired aQuantive, an online ad server and network that enables potential advertisers to place ads on many Web sites with a single buy. After all that consolidation, the *Wall Street Journal* drew this conclusion: "The online-ad market is maturing around an oligopoly of huge companies that sell and place the ads users see online. Placing those ads is increasingly seen as the business model that will fund almost everything on the Internet—from search portals, news sites, and video downloads to Web-based software services such as word processing."[12]

With their deep pockets and broad reach, the Internet oligopoly also began to move beyond the $11 billion Internet ad market and become ad brokers for other mass media. As mentioned in the beginning of the chapter, Google has ventured into selling ads for newspaper, television, and radio. Meanwhile, the traditional advertising conglomerates countered by expanding their Internet capabilities. Among their biggest investments: WPP bought 24/7 Real Media, a leading online ad network; Publicis acquired Internet marketing firm Digitas; Interpublic grabbed Reprise Media, a search-engine advertising company; and Omnicom bought digital agencies Organic and Agency.com.

Of increasing importance are mobile phones, the "third screen" for advertisers. Mobile phones offer effective targeting to individuals, as does Internet advertising, but also offers the bonus (to advertisers) of tailoring ads to be appropriate to a specific geographic location (e.g., a restaurant ad goes to someone in close proximity) or according to the user demographic (mobile phone companies already have that information). Advertising offers mobile phone service providers a great potential source of revenue, but they have been slow to adopt it, fearing a consumer backlash.

> "It's clear that digital services have become a way of life (or a way to avoid death) for agencies of all disciplines."
>
> *ADVERTISING AGE,* 2008

Persuasive Techniques in Contemporary Advertising

Ad agencies and product companies often argue that the main purpose of advertising is to inform consumers about available products in a straightforward way. Most consumer ads, however, merely create a mood or tell stories about products without revealing much else. Because national advertisers generally choose to buy a one-page magazine ad or a thirty-second TV spot to deliver their pitch, consumers get little information about how a product was made, how much it costs, or how it compares with similar brands. In managing space and time constraints, advertising agencies engage in a variety of persuasive techniques.

"[Tiger Wood's]
earnings and
endorsement-
money total of
$769,440,709
puts him on pace
to become the first
$1 billion athlete."

GOLF DIGEST, 2008

Conventional Persuasive Strategies

One of the most frequently used advertising approaches is the **famous-person testimonial**, in which a product is endorsed by a well-known person. For example, Tiger Woods has become the leading sports spokesperson, providing endorsements for a growing list of companies, including Nike, American Express, Electronic Arts, Golf Digest, Rolex, Wheaties, CBS SportsLine, ABC, ESPN, Warner Books, TLC Laser Eye Centers, Buick, and Asahi Beverages in Japan. Now the most recognizable sports figure on the planet, Woods amassed $100 million in 2007, far more than the $45 million that basketball star Michael Jordan made in his best year of endorsements.

Another technique, the **plain-folks pitch**, associates a product with simplicity. Over the years, Volkswagen ("Drivers wanted"), General Electric ("We bring good things to life"), and Microsoft ("Where do you want to go today?") have each used slogans that stress how new technologies fit into the lives of ordinary people.

By contrast, the **snob-appeal approach** attempts to persuade consumers that using a product will maintain or elevate their social status. Advertisers selling jewelry, perfume, clothing, and luxury automobiles often use snob appeal. For example, the pricey bottled water brand Fiji ran ads in *Esquire* and other national magazines that said "The label says Fiji because it's not bottled in Cleveland"—a jab intended to favorably compare the water bottled in the South Pacific to the drinking water of an industrial city in Ohio. (Fiji ended up withdrawing the ad after the Cleveland Water Department released test data that found its water was more pure than Fiji water.)

Another approach, the **bandwagon effect**, points out in exaggerated claims that everyone is using a particular product. Brands that refer to themselves as "America's favorite" or "the best" imply that consumers will be "left behind" if they ignore these products. A different technique, the **hidden-fear appeal**, plays on consumers' sense of insecurity. Deodorant, mouthwash, and shampoo ads frequently invoke anxiety, pointing out that only a specific product could relieve embarrassing personal hygiene problems and restore a person to social acceptability.

A final ad strategy, used more in local TV and radio campaigns than in national ones, has been labeled **irritation advertising**: creating product-name recognition by being annoying or obnoxious. Although both research and common sense suggest that irritating ads do not work very well, there have been exceptions. In the 1950s and 1960s, for instance, an aspirin company ran a TV ad illustrating a hammer pounding inside a person's brain. Critics and the product's own agency suggested that people bought the product, which sold well, to get relief from the ad as well as from their headaches. On the regional level, irritation ads are often used by appliance discount stores or local car dealers, who dress in outrageous costumes and yell at the camera.

The Association Principle

Historically, American car advertisements have shown automobiles in natural settings—on winding roads that cut through rugged mountain passes or across shimmering wheat fields—but rarely on congested city streets or in other urban settings where most driving actually occurs. Instead, the car—an example of advanced technology—merges seamlessly into the natural world.

This type of advertising exemplifies the **association principle**, a persuasive technique used in most consumer ads that associates a product with a positive cultural value or image even if it has little connection to the product. For example, many ads displayed visual symbols of American patriotism in the wake of the 9/11 terrorist attacks in an attempt to associate products and companies with national pride. In trying "to convince us that there's an innate relationship between a brand name and an attitude,"[13] advertising may associate products with nationalism, happy families, success at school or work, natural scenery, or humor.

One of the more controversial uses of the association principle has been the linkage of products to stereotyped caricatures of women. In numerous instances, women have been portrayed either as sex objects or as clueless housewives who, during many a daytime TV commercial, needed the powerful off-screen voice of a male narrator to instruct them in their own kitchens (see "Case Study–Idiots and Objects: Stereotyping in Advertising" on page 362).

Another popular use of the association principle is to claim that products are "real" and "natural"—possibly the most familiar adjectives associated with advertising. For example, Coke sells itself as "the real thing," and the cosmetics industry offers synthetic products that make us look "natural." The adjectives—*real* and *natural*—saturate American ads, yet almost always describe processed or synthetic goods. "Green" marketing has a similar problem, as it is associated with goods and services that aren't always environmentally friendly.

Philip Morris's Marlboro brand has used the association principle to completely transform its product image. In the 1920s, Marlboro began as a fashionable woman's cigarette. Back then, the company's ads equated smoking with a sense of freedom, attempting to appeal to women who had just won the right to vote. Marlboro, though, did poorly as a women's product, and new campaigns in the 1950s and 1960s transformed the brand into a man's cigarette. Powerful images of active, rugged men dominated the ads. Often, Marlboro associated its product with nature: an image of a lone cowboy roping a calf, building a fence, or riding over a snow-covered landscape. By 2008, the branding consultancy BrandZ (a division of WPP) called Marlboro the world's tenth "most powerful brand," having an estimated worth of $37 billion. (Google and General Electric were the Top 2 rated brands; see Table 11.2.)

Rank	Brand	Brand Value ($ millions)	Brand Value Change
1	Google	$86,057	+30%
2	GE (General Electric)	71,379	+15%
3	Microsoft	58,208	+29%
4	Coca-Cola*	57,225	+17%
5	China Mobile	57,225	+39%
6	IBM	55,335	+65%
7	Apple	55,206	+123%
8	McDonald's	49,499	+49%
9	Nokia	43,975	+39%
10	Marlboro	37,324	-5%

"In a mobile society, commercial products with familiar [brand] names provide people with some sense of identity and continuity in their lives."

MICHAEL SCHUDSON, *ADVERTISING, THE UNEASY PERSUASION*, 1984

TABLE 11.2

THE TOP 10 GLOBAL BRANDS

Source: "BrandZ Top 100 Most Powerful Brands 08," Millward Brown Optimor, April 21, 2008, http://www.millwardbrown.com/sites/optimor/media/pdfs/en/BrandZ/BrandZ-2008-Report.pdf.

*Coca-Cola includes Diet Coke.

Idiots and Objects: Stereotyping in Advertising

Over the years, critics and consumers alike have complained about stereotyping in mainstream advertising. *Stereotyping* refers to the process of assigning people to abstract groups, whose members are assumed to act as a single entity—rather than as individuals with distinct identities—and to display shared characteristics, which often have negative connotations.

Today, particularly in beer ads, men are often stereotyped as inept or stupid, incapable of negotiating a routine day or a normal conversation unless fortified—or dulled—by the heroic product. Throughout advertising history, men have often been portrayed as doofuses and idiots when confronted by ordinary food items or a simple household appliance.

On the other hand, in the early history of product ads on television, women were often stereotyped as naïve or emotional, needing the experienced voice of a rational male narrator to guide them around their own homes. Ads have also stereotyped women as brainless or helpless or offered them as a man's reward for drinking a particular beer, wearing cool jeans, or smoking the right cigarette. Worst of all, women, or even parts of women—with their heads cut from the frame—have been used as objects, merely associated with a particular product (e.g., a swimsuit model holding a new car muffler or wrapped around a bottle of Scotch). Influenced by the women's movement and critiques of advertising culture, such as Betty Friedan's *The Feminine Mystique* (1963), ads depicting women have changed. Although many sexist stereotypes still persist in advertising, women today are portrayed in a variety of social roles.

In addition to ads that have stereotyped men and women, there is also invisible stereotyping. This occurs when whole segments of the population are ignored—particularly African, Arab, Asian, Latin, and Native Americans. Advertising—especially in its early history—has often faced criticism that many segments of the varied and multicultural U.S. population have been missing or underrepresented in the ads and images that dominate the landscape. In the last several years, however, conscious of how diverse the United States has become, many companies have been doing a better job of representing various cultures in their product ads. ◢

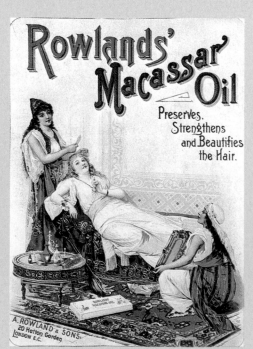

Disassociation as an Advertising Strategy

As a response to corporate mergers and public skepticism toward impersonal and large companies, a *disassociation corollary* emerged in advertising. The nation's largest winery, Gallo, pioneered the idea in the 1980s by establishing a dummy corporation, Bartles & Jaymes, to sell jug wine and wine coolers, thereby avoiding the Gallo corporate image in ads and on its bottles. The ads featured Frank and Ed, two low-key, grandfatherly types, as "co-owners" and ad spokesmen. On the one hand, the ad was "a way to connect with younger consumers who yearn for products that are handmade, quirky, and authentic."[14] On the other hand, this technique, by concealing the Gallo tie-in, also allowed the wine giant to disassociate from the negative publicity of the 1970s—a period when labor leader Cesar Chavez organized migrant workers in a long boycott of Gallo.

In the 1990s, the disassociation strategy was used by General Motors. Reeling from a declining corporate reputation, GM "disassociate[d] itself from its innovative offspring, the Saturn," and tried to package the Saturn as "a small-town enterprise, run by folks not terribly unlike Frank and Ed" who provide caring, personal service.[15] As an ad strategy, disassociation links new brands in a product line to eccentric or simple regional places rather than to images conjured up by multinational conglomerates.

Advertising as Myth

Another way to understand ads is to use **myth analysis**, which provides insights into how ads work at a general cultural level. Here, the term *myth* does not refer to an untrue story or outright falsehood. Rather, myths help us to define people, organizations, and social norms. According to myth analysis, most ads are narratives with stories to tell and social conflicts to resolve. Three common mythical elements are found in many types of ads:

1. Ads incorporate myths in ministory form, featuring characters, settings, and plots.
2. Most stories in ads involve conflicts, pitting one set of characters or social values against another.
3. Such conflicts are negotiated or resolved by the end of the ad, usually by applying or purchasing a product. In advertising, the product and those who use it often emerge as the heroes of the story.

Even though the stories ads tell are usually compressed into thirty seconds or onto a single page, they still include the traditional elements of narrative. For instance, many SUV ads ask us to imagine ourselves driving out into the raw, untamed wilderness, to a quiet, natural place that only a Jeep or Hummer can take us. The audience implicitly understands that the SUV can somehow, almost magically, take us out of our fast-paced, freeway-wrapped urban world plagued with long commutes, traffic jams, and automobile exhaust. This implied conflict between the natural world and the manufactured world is apparently resolved by the image of the SUV in a natural setting. Although SUVs typically pack our urban and suburban highways, burn gasoline, and create tons of air pollution particulates, the ads ignore those facts. Instead, they offer an alternative story about the wonders of nature, and the SUV literally becomes the vehicle that negotiates the conflict between city/suburban blight and the unspoiled wilderness.

MYTH ANALYSIS
Ads for SUVs or Jeeps like this one want us to believe that the conflict between our world and the natural one can be solved by purchasing a car. What does the ad leave out?

Media Literacy and the Critical Process

The Branded You
To what extent are you influenced by brands?

1 **DESCRIPTION.** Take a look around your home or dormitory room and list all the branded products you've purchased, including food, electronics, clothes, shoes, toiletries, and cleaning products.

2 **ANALYSIS.** Now organize your branded items into categories. For example, how many of your clothes are branded with athletic, university, or designer logos? What patterns emerge and what kind of psychographic profile do these brands suggest about you?

3 **INTERPRETATION.** Why did you buy each particular product? Was it because you thought it was of superior quality? Was it because it was cheaper? Was it because your parents used this product, so it was tried, trusted, and familiar? Was it because it made you feel a certain way about yourself, and you wanted to project this image toward others? Have you ever purchased items without brands or removed logos once you bought the product? Why?

4 **EVALUATION.** If you're more conscious of our branded environment (and your participation in it), what is your assessment of U.S. consumer culture? Is there too much conspicuous branding? What is good and bad about the ubiquity of brand names in our culture? How does branding relate to the common American ethic of individualism?

5 **ENGAGEMENT.** Visit Adbusters .org and read about action projects that confront commercialism, including Buy Nothing Day, Media Carta, TV Turn-off, the Culturejammers Network, the Blackspot non-brand sneaker, and Un-brand America. Also visit the home page for the advocacy organization Commercial Alert (http://www.commercialalert .org) to learn about the most recent commercial incursions into everyday life and what can be done about them. Or write a letter to a company about a product or ad that you think is a problem. How did the company respond?

Most advertisers do not expect consumers to accept without question the stories or associations they make in ads; they do not "make the mistake of asking for belief."[16] Instead, ads are most effective when they create attitudes and reinforce values. Then they operate like popular fiction, encouraging us to suspend our disbelief. Although most of us realize that ads create a fictional world, we often get caught up in their stories and myths. Indeed, ads often work because the stories offer comfort about our deepest desires and conflicts–between men and women, nature and technology, tradition and change, the real and the artificial. Most contemporary consumer advertising does not provide much useful information about products. Instead, it tries to reassure us that through the use of familiar brand names, everyday tensions and problems can be managed (see "Media Literacy and the Critical Process: The Branded You").

Product Placement

Product companies and ad agencies have become adept in recent years at *product placement*: strategically placing ads or buying space–in movies, TV shows, comic books, and most recently video games–so they appear as part of a story's set environment (see "Tracking Technology: Dynamic and 'Baked-in' Ads Hit Video Games" on the opposite page). For example, the 2008 movie *Iron Man* featured product placements from Burger King, Audi, and LG mobile phones (making their product placement debut). Also in 2008, McDonald's placed its iced coffee on the set of local morning news shows on stations owned by the Meredith Corporation.

For many critics, product placement has gotten out of hand. What started out as subtle appearances in realistic settings–like Reese's Pieces in the 1982 movie *E.T.*–has turned into Coca-Cola being almost an honorary "cast member" on Fox's *American Idol* set. The practice is now so pronounced that it was a subject of Hollywood parody in the 2006 film *Talladega Nights: The Ballad of Ricky Bobby*, starring Will Ferrell.

"The level of integration on- and off-screen in *Talladega Nights* is unprecedented. I can't remember ever seeing this much product placement displayed, from the commercials to the trailers for the film to the publicity and press events. It's pretty incredible, and it's pretty unheard of . . . a new and great thing for the brands involved."

AARON GORDON, MARKETING EXECUTIVE, 2006

TRACKING TECHNOLOGY

Dynamic and "Baked-in" Ads Hit Video Games

By Abbey Klaassen

Sony is opening up its in-game advertising platform, likely providing a boost to the already burgeoning $400 million in-game-ad market and sparking a battle among the three key players who sell these ads.

The maker of the PlayStation3 system will offer an open platform, meaning in-game-ad-serving companies like Double Fusion, IGA, and Google-owned AdScape all will be able to sell ads in games that run on PS3, according to people familiar with Sony's plans. The three companies will strike deals with the major game publishers creating PS3 games, such as Electronic Arts, Activision, and Ubisoft. Increasingly, those who score the plum publisher deals will turn out to be the winners

IN-GAME ADVERTISING Is this the new background for video games?

in the competitive and fast-growing space.

"It'll come down to games and who has the largest catalog of games," said one person familiar with Sony's plans, but who did not have authorization to speak about it publicly.

Sony is just starting to sell in-game ads and has its own PlayStation Network sales force to sell dynamic ads in Sony-produced games, such as the "Pain" title. While the ad-serving companies might have hoped for an exclusive contract to sell ads in PS3 games, analysts said that a more competitive model could benefit marketers and the in-game market in general. "Making things open only makes things better for marketers or people who want to place ads because they aren't at the mercy of a given network," said James Belcher, a longtime video-game writer and senior writer at eMarketer. He said the market is already hypercompetitive. "Everyone's playing around with the best model—how to charge, what gamers will and will not put up with." According to eMarketer data, video-game advertising is a $400 million category this year and is expected to grow during the next five years at a compound annual growth rate of nearly 23 percent.

Dynamic in-game advertising refers to ads that are changed in and out of games post-development, from interactive placements to signage to sponsorships. Video-game advertising also includes ads that are "baked in" to games—meaning they are an integral part of the game's development and cannot be switched out once they're created—and ads that run on the console communities, such as XBox Live and the Sony Home network, which is in private beta. Dynamic ads are considered less risky than baked-in integrations because they don't require a marketer to speculate whether a game will be a hit. Marketers can wait, see how a game performs, and then buy ads in it.

Sony's open platform is a clear departure from how things are done on Microsoft's Xbox, whose exclusive model means all dynamic in-game ads must be brokered through Massive, a company the software giant acquired in May 2006. That acquisition essentially closed off the opportunity for other in-game ad brokers to sell inventory in games that run on its Xbox and Xbox 360 consoles—and it elevated the bet they are placing on Sony.

Of course, one potential complication of an open philosophy is that, at least initially, Sony's decision will make in-game advertising harder to buy, as an advertiser could have to buy through as many as three different parties to place ads in a single game—Massive for the title's Xbox version, another for dynamic ads in the version that runs on Sony's PS3, and a third for baked-in product placement in the game. ◢

Source: Abbey Klaassen, "Game-ad Boom Looms as Sony Opens Up PS3," Advertising Age, February 25, 2008, p. 1.

▶

PRODUCT PLACEMENT
in movies is more prevalent
today than when it first
became popular in the
1980s in movies like *E.T.*

In 2005, watchdog organization Commercial Alert asked both the FTC and the FCC to mandate that consumers be warned about product placement on television. The FTC rejected the petition, and the FCC had still made no formal response by 2008. But FCC Commissioner Jonathan S. Adelstein said that he believed undisclosed product placement might constitute a form of illegal payola, particularly in sponsored shows that disguised themselves as news programs.

Commercial Speech and Regulating Advertising

> "There's no law that says we have to sell you time or space. We sell time for many, many different things, but not controversial issues of social importance."
>
> JULIE HOOVER, VICE PRESIDENT OF ADVERTISING, ABC, 2004

In 1791, Congress passed and the states ratified the First Amendment to the U.S. Constitution, promising, among other guarantees, to "make no law . . . abridging the freedom of speech, or of the press." Over time, we have developed a shorthand label for the First Amendment, misnaming it the free-speech clause. The amendment ensures that citizens and journalists can generally say and write what they want, but it says nothing directly about **commercial speech**—any print or broadcast expression for which a fee is charged to organizations and individuals buying time or space in the mass media.

While freedom of speech refers to the right to express thoughts, beliefs, and opinions in the abstract marketplace of ideas, commercial speech is about the right to circulate goods, services, and images in the concrete marketplace of products. For most of the history of mass media, only very wealthy citizens (like Bill Gates or Steve Forbes), established political parties, and multinational companies could routinely afford to purchase speech spaces that reached millions. The Internet, however, has helped to level that playing field. Political speech like a cleverly edited mash-up video, or entertaining speech like a WebCam video of a New Jersey resident lip synching to a Moldovan dance song (the infamous Numa Numa guy on YouTube) can go viral and quickly reach millions, rivaling the most expensive commercial speech.

Less cars, more world. **D**rivers wanted.®

Although the mass media have not hesitated to carry product and service-selling advertisements and have embraced the concepts of infomercials and cable home shopping channels, they have also refused certain issue-based advertising that might upset their traditional advertisers. For example, although corporations have easy access in placing paid ads, many labor unions have had their print and broadcast ads rejected as "controversial." The nonprofit Adbusters Media Foundation, based in Vancouver, Canada, has had difficulty getting networks to air its "uncommercials." One of its spots promotes the Friday after Thanksgiving (traditionally, the beginning of the holiday buying season) as "Buy Nothing Day."

Critical Issues in Advertising

In his 1957 book *The Hidden Persuaders*, Vance Packard expressed concern that advertising was manipulating helpless consumers, attacking our dignity, and invading "the privacy of our minds."[17] According to this view, the advertising industry was considered to be all-powerful. Although consumers have historically been regarded as dupes by many critics, research reveals that the consumer mind is not as easy to predict as some advertisers once thought. In the 1950s, for example, Ford could not successfully sell its midsize car, the Edsel, which was aimed at newly prosperous Ford customers looking to move up to the latest in push-button window wipers and antennas. After a splashy and expensive ad campaign, Ford sold only 63,000 Edsels in 1958 and just 2,000 in 1960, when the model was discontinued.

One of the most disastrous campaigns ever featured the now famous "This is not your father's Oldsmobile" spots that began running in 1989 and starred celebrities like former Beatles drummer Ringo Starr and his daughter. Oldsmobile (which became part of General Motors in 1903) and its ad agency, Leo Burnett, decided to market to a younger generation after sales declined from a high of 1.1 million vehicles in 1985 to only 715,000 in 1988. But the campaign backfired, apparently alienating its older loyal customers (who may have felt abandoned by Olds and its catchy new slogan) and failing to lure younger buyers (who probably still had trouble getting past the name "Olds"). In 2000, Oldsmobile sold only 260,000 cars, and GM phased out its Olds division by 2005.[18]

As these examples illustrate, most people are not easily persuaded by advertising. Over the years, studies have suggested that between 75 and 90 percent of new consumer products typically fail because they are not embraced by the buying public.[19] But despite public resistance to many

ADVERTISING TO CHILDREN is an ongoing concern for parents and activist groups. With television turned on an average of eight hours a day, children are exposed to hundreds of hours of commercials each year.

"It isn't enough to advertise on television. . . . [Y]ou've got to reach kids throughout the day—in school, as they're shopping in the mall . . . or at the movies. You've got to become part of the fabric of their lives."

CAROL HERMAN, SENIOR VICE PRESIDENT, GREY ADVERTISING, 1996

new products, the ad industry has made contributions, including raising the American standard of living and financing most media industries. Yet serious concerns over the impact of advertising remain. Watchdog groups worry about the expansion of advertising's reach, and critics continue to condemn ads that stereotype or associate products with sex appeal, youth, and narrow definitions of beauty. Some of the most serious concerns involve children, teens, and health.

Children and Advertising

Children and teenagers, living in a culture dominated by TV ads, are often viewed as "consumer trainees." For years, groups such as Action for Children's Television (ACT) worked to limit advertising aimed at children. In the 1980s, ACT fought particularly hard to curb program-length commercials: thirty-minute cartoon programs (such as *G.I. Joe*, *My Little Pony and Friends*, *The Care Bear Family*, and *He-Man and the Masters of the Universe*) developed for television syndication primarily to promote a line of toys. This commercial tradition continued with programs such as *Pokémon* and *SpongeBob SquarePants*.

In addition, parent groups have worried about the heavy promotion of products like sugar-coated cereals during children's programs. Pointing to European countries, where children's advertising is banned, these groups have pushed to limit advertising directed at children. Congress, hesitant to rein in the protection that the First Amendment offers commercial speech, and faced with the lobbying of the advertising industry, has responded weakly. The Children's Television Act of 1990 mandated that networks provide some educational and informational children's programming, but the act has been difficult to enforce and did little to restrict advertising aimed at kids.

Because children and teenagers influence up to $500 billion a year in family spending—on everything from snacks to cars—they are increasingly targeted by advertisers.[20] A Stanford University study found that a single thirty-second TV ad can influence the brand choices of children as young as age two. In addition, very young children cannot distinguish between a commercial and the TV program that the ad interrupts. Still, methods for marketing to children have become increasingly seductive as product placement and merchandising tie-ins become more prevalent.

Advertising in Schools

A controversial development in advertising was the introduction of Channel One into thousands of schools during the 1989-90 school year. The brainchild of Whittle Communications, Channel One offered "free" video and satellite equipment (tuned exclusively to Channel One) in exchange for a twelve-minute package of current events programming that included two minutes of commercials. In 2007, Alloy Media + Marketing, a New York-based marketing company that targets young audiences, bought Channel One. By 2008, Channel One reached a captive audience of approximately six million U.S. students in eight thousand middle schools and high schools each day.

Over the years, the National Dairy Council and other organizations have also used schools to promote products, providing free filmstrips, posters, magazines, folders, and study guides adorned with corporate logos. Teachers, especially in underfunded districts, have usually been grateful for the support. Channel One, however, has been viewed as a more intrusive threat, violating the implicit cultural border between an entertainment situation (watching commercial television) and a learning situation (going to school). One study showed that schools with a high concentration of low-income students were more than twice as likely as affluent schools to receive Channel One.[21]

Some individual school districts have banned Channel One, as have the states of New York and California. These school systems have argued that Channel One provides students with only slight additional knowledge about current affairs; but students find the products advertised–sneakers, cereal, and soda, among others– more worthy of purchase because they are advertised in educational environments.[22] A 2006 study found that students remember "more of the advertising than they do the news stories shown on Channel One."[23]

Health and Advertising

Eating Disorders.   Advertising has a powerful impact on the standards of beauty in our culture. A long-standing trend in advertising is the association of certain products with ultrathin female models, promoting a style of "attractiveness" that girls and women are invited to emulate. Even today, despite the popularity of resistance training and more shapely bodies, most fashion models are much thinner than the average woman. Some forms of fashion and cosmetics advertising actually pander to individuals' insecurities and low self-esteem by promising the ideal body. Such advertising suggests standards of style and behavior that may be not only unattainable but also harmful, leading to eating disorders such as anorexia and bulimia and an increase in cosmetic surgeries.

If advertising has been criticized for promoting skeleton-like beauty, it has also been blamed for the tripling of obesity rates in the United States since the 1980s, with a record 66 percent of adult Americans overweight or obese (about one-third of children are overweight or obese). Corn syrup-laden soft drinks, fast food, junk food, and processed food are the staples of media advertising and are major contributors to the nationwide weight problem. More troubling is that an overweight and obese nation is good for business (creating a multibillion-dollar market for diet products, exercise equipment, self-help books, and larger clothing sizes), so media outlets see little reason to change current ad practices. The food and restaurant industry has denied any connection between its advertising and the rise of U.S. obesity rates, instead blaming individuals who make bad choices.

Tobacco.   One of the most sustained criticisms of advertising is its promotion of tobacco consumption. Opponents of tobacco advertising have become more vocal in the face of grim statistics: Each year, an estimated 438,000 Americans die from diseases related to nicotine addiction and poisoning. Tobacco ads disappeared from television in 1971, under pressure from Congress and the FCC. However, over the years numerous ad campaigns have targeted teenage consumers of cigarettes. In 1988, for example, R. J. Reynolds, a subdivision of RJR Nabisco, updated its Joe Camel cartoon character, outfitting him with hipper clothes and sunglasses. Spending $75 million annually, the company put Joe on billboards and store posters and in sports stadiums and magazines. One study revealed that before 1988 fewer than 1 percent of teens under age eighteen smoked Camels. After the ad blitz, however, 33 percent of this age group preferred Camels.

In addition to young smokers, the tobacco industry has targeted other groups. In the 1960s, for instance, the advertising campaigns for Eve and Virginia Slims cigarettes (reminiscent of ads during the suffrage movement in the early 1900s) associated their products with women's liberation, equality, and slim fashion models. And in 1989, Reynolds introduced a cigarette called Uptown, targeting African American consumers. The ad campaign fizzled due to public protests by black leaders and government officials. When these leaders pointed to the high concentration of cigarette billboards in poor urban areas and the high mortality rates among black male smokers, the tobacco company withdrew the brand.

> "We have to sell cigarettes to your kids. We need half a million new smokers a year just to stay in business. So we advertise near schools, at candy counters."
>
> CALIFORNIA ANTI-CIGARETTE TV AD. TOBACCO COMPANIES FILED A FEDERAL SUIT AGAINST THE AD AND LOST WHEN THE U.S. SUPREME COURT TURNED DOWN THEIR APPEAL IN 2006

The government's position regarding the tobacco industry began to change in the mid-1990s, when new reports revealed that tobacco companies had known that nicotine was addictive as early as the 1950s and had withheld that information from the public. In 1998, after four states won settlements against the tobacco industry and the remaining states threatened to bring more expensive lawsuits against the companies, the tobacco industry agreed to an unprecedented $206 billion settlement that carried significant limits on advertising and marketing tobacco products.

The agreement's provisions banned cartoon characters in advertising, thus ending the use of the Joe Camel character; prohibited the industry from targeting young people in ads and marketing, including free samples, tobacco-brand clothing, and other merchandise; and ended outdoor billboard and transit advertising. The agreement also banned tobacco company sponsorship of concerts and athletic events, and it strictly limited other corporate sponsorships by tobacco companies. These agreements, however, do not apply to tobacco advertising abroad (see "Global Village: Smoking Up the Global Market" on opposite page). Today, tobacco companies still spend about $13.1 billion annually on U.S. advertisements—more than twenty times the amount spent on anti-tobacco ads.

Alcohol.   Every year, 105,000 people die from alcohol-related diseases, and another 16,000 to 17,000 die in car crashes involving drunk drivers. As you can guess, many of the same complaints regarding tobacco advertising are also being directed at alcohol ads. (The hard liquor industry has voluntarily banned TV and radio ads for decades.) For example, one of the most popular beer ad campaigns of the late 1990s, featuring the trio of Budweiser frogs (which croak Bud-weis-errrr), has been accused of using cartoonlike animal characters to appeal to young viewers. In fact, the Budweiser ads would be banned under the standards of the tobacco settlement, which prohibits the attribution of human characteristics to animals, plants, or other objects.

Alcohol ads have also targeted minority populations. Malt liquors, which contain higher concentrations of alcohol than beers do, have been touted in high-profile television ads for such labels as Colt 45, PowerMaster, and Magnum. There is also a trend toward marketing high-end liquors to African American and Hispanic male populations. In two separate 2006 marketing campaigns, Hennessey targeted African American populations in ads featuring musical icons Marvin Gaye and Miles Davis and the tagline "Never Blend In." Similarly, another ad campaign featured the Colombian-born American actor-comedian John Leguizamo and the tagline "Pure Character," with the ads printed in English and Spanish.

College students, too, have been heavily targeted by alcohol ads, particularly by the beer industry. Although colleges and universities have outlawed "beer bashes" hosted and supplied directly by major brewers, both Coors and Miller still employ student representatives to help "create brand awareness." These students notify brewers of special events that might be sponsored by and linked to a specific beer label. The images and slogans in alcohol ads often

Smoking Up the Global Market

By 2000, the status of tobacco companies and their advertising in the United States had hit a low point. A $206 billion settlement between tobacco companies and state attorneys general ended tobacco advertising on billboards and severely limited the ways in which cigarette companies can promote their products in the United States. Advertising bans and antismoking public service announcements contributed to a growing disfavor about tobacco in America, with smoking rates dropping from a high of 42.5 percent of the population in 1965 to just 25 percent more than thirty years later.

As Western cultural attitudes have turned against tobacco, the large tobacco multinationals have shifted their global marketing focus, targeting Asia in particular. So while smoking has declined by 13 percent in developed countries over the last decade, it has increased by 20 percent in China, which now boasts an estimated 350 million smokers.[1] Underfunded government health programs and populations that generally admire American and European cultural products make Asian nations ill-equipped to deal with cigarette marketing efforts. For example, even though Vietnam strengthened its ban on print, broadcast, and billboard ads in 1994, nearly three-fourths of Vietnamese men smoke, the highest smoking rate for men in the world. In China, 63 percent of males over age eighteen now smoke; and across Asia in general, 40,000 to 50,000 teens a day light up for the first time.

Advertising bans have actually forced tobacco companies to find alternative and, as it turns out, better ways to promote smoking. Philip Morris, the largest private tobacco company, and its global rival, British American Tobacco (BAT), practice "brand stretching"—linking their logos to race-car events, soccer leagues, youth festivals, disco parties, rock concerts, TV shows, and popular cafés. The higher price for Western cigarettes in Asia has the effect of increasing their prestige, and it makes packs of Marlboros symbols of middle-class aspirations.

The unmistakable silhouette of the Marlboro Man is ubiquitous throughout developing countries, particularly in Asia. In Hanoi, Vietnam, almost every corner boasts a street vendor with a trolley cart, the bottom half of which carries the Marlboro logo or one of the other premium foreign brands. Vietnam's Ho Chi Minh City has two thousand such trolleys. Children in Malaysia are especially keen on Marlboro clothing, which, along with watches, binoculars, radios, knives, and backpacks, they can win by collecting a certain number of empty Marlboro packages. (It is now illegal to sell tobacco-brand clothing and merchandise in the United States.)

Sporting events have proved to be an especially successful brand-stretching technique with men, who smoke the majority of cigarettes in Asia. Many observers argue that much of the popularity of Marlboro cigarettes in China derives from Philip Morris's sponsorship of the Marlboro soccer league there. Throughout Asia, attractive young women wearing tight red Marlboro outfits cruise cities in red Marlboro minivans, frequently stopping to distribute free cigarettes, even to minors.

Some critics suggest that the same marketing strategies will make their way into the United States and other Western countries, but that's unlikely. Tobacco companies are mainly interested in developing regions like Asia for two reasons. First, China alone accounts for nearly a third of the world's cigarette smoking, with people there consuming 1.9 trillion cigarettes in 2005. Because only one in twenty cigarettes now sold in China is a foreign brand, the potential market is staggering. Second, the majority of smokers in countries like China—whose government officially bans tobacco advertising—are unaware that smoking causes diseases like lung cancer. In fact, 3.5 million people—nearly 10,000 per day—now die from tobacco-related diseases.

LIFESTYLE AD APPEALS
TBWA (now a unit of Omnicom) introduced Absolut Vodka's distinctive advertising campaign in 1980. The campaign marketed a little-known Swedish vodka as an exclusive lifestyle brand, an untraditional approach that parlayed it into one of the world's best-selling spirits. The long-running ad campaign ended in 2006, with more than 1,450 ads having maintained the brand's premium status by referencing fashion, artists, and contemporary music.

associate the products with power, romance, sexual prowess, or athletic skill. In reality, though, alcohol is a chemical depressant; it diminishes athletic ability and sexual performance, triggers addiction in roughly 10 percent of the U.S. population, and factors into many domestic abuse cases. A national study released in 2006 demonstrated "that young people who see more ads for alcoholic beverages tend to drink more."[24]

Prescription Drugs.   Another area of concern is the recent surge in prescription drug advertising. According to a study by the Kaiser Family Foundation, spending on direct-to-consumer advertising for prescription drugs increased ninefold, from $266 million in 1994 to $4.7 billion in 2005, largely because of growth in television advertising, which accounts for about two-thirds of such ads. The advertisements have made household words out of prescription drugs such as Nexium, Claritin, Paxil, Viagra, Celebrex, and Flonase. The ads have been effective for the pharmaceutical companies: A survey found that nearly one in three adults has talked to a doctor and one in eight has received a prescription in response to seeing an ad for a prescription drug.

With the tremendous growth of prescription drug ads—affecting billions of dollars in prescription drug sales—there is the potential for false and misleading claims, particularly because a brief TV advertisement can't possibility communicate all of the cautionary information. But as spending on direct-to-consumer prescription drug advertisements has risen, federal enforcement is on the decline. A House Government Reform Committee report in 2004 found that responses by the Food and Drug Administration (FDA) to false and misleading advertisements were not timely, and that pharmaceutical companies who were repeat violators did not face tougher enforcement actions.

Watching over Advertising

A few nonprofit watchdog and advocacy organizations—Commercial Alert, as well as the Better Business Bureau and the National Consumers League—compensate in many ways for some of the shortcomings of the Federal Trade Commission (FTC) and other government agencies in monitoring the excesses of commercialism and false and deceptive ads.

Excessive Commercialism

Since 1998, Commercial Alert has been working to "limit excessive commercialism in society." For example, in 2008, HarperCollins Children's Books announced a new book series called Mackenzie Blue for girls ages eight to twelve. The Mackenzie character would be "fun and eco-conscious" and would be a role model for encouraging tween girls to "make good choices." The series announcement also included "dynamic corporate partnerships"—that is, product placements woven into the stories—and the author is also the founder of a marketing group aimed at teens.

Commercial Alert responded to HarperCollins by requesting that they drop or revise the book project. "Books should educate and entertain children, not serve as a vehicle to deliver hidden marketing messages encouraging them to buy a particular brand of shoe or soft drink or cosmetics," the organization wrote. Commercial Alert also notified book reviewers about the Mackenzie Blue project, and asked them: "Will you treat this book as a novel to be reviewed, or as an advertisement, which is suitable for discussion in the business pages?"[25]

Founded in part by longtime consumer advocate Ralph Nader, Commercial Alert is a Portland, Oregon-based nonprofit organization and a lonely voice in checking the commercialization of U.S. culture. Some of its other activities have included challenges to specific marketing tactics, such as when the clothing retailer Limited Too enlisted with the Girl Scouts' "Fashion Adventure" project, which encouraged girls to shop, try on clothes, and model them in front of others. In constantly questioning the role of advertising in democracy, the organization has aimed to strengthen noncommercial culture and limit the amount of corporate influence on publicly elected government bodies.

The FTC Takes on Puffery and Deception

Since the days when Lydia Pinkham's Vegetable Compound promised "a sure cure for all female weakness," false and misleading claims have haunted advertising. Over the years, the FTC, through its truth-in-advertising rules, has played an investigative role in substantiating the claims of various advertisers. A certain amount of *puffery*—ads featuring hyperbole and exaggeration—has usually been permitted, particularly when a product says it is "new and improved." However, ads become deceptive when they are likely to mislead reasonable consumers based on statements in the ad, or because they omit information. Moreover, when a product claims to be "the best," "the greatest," or "preferred by four out of five doctors," FTC rules require scientific evidence to back up the claims.

A typical example of deceptive advertising is the Campbell Soup ad in which marbles in the bottom of a soup bowl push more bulky ingredients—and less water—to the surface. In another instance, a 1990 Volvo commercial featured a monster truck driving over a line of cars and crushing all but the Volvo; the company later admitted that the Volvo had been specially reinforced and the other cars' support columns had been weakened. A more subtle form of deception featured the Klondike Lite ice-cream bar—"the 93 percent fat-free dessert with chocolate-flavored coating." The bars were indeed 93 percent fat-free, but only after the chocolate coating was removed.[26]

In 2003, the FTC brought enforcement actions against companies marketing the herbal weight-loss supplement ephedra. Ephedra has a long-standing connection to elevated blood pressure, strokes, and heart attacks and has contributed to numerous deaths. Nevertheless, companies advertised ephedra as a safe and miraculous weight-loss supplement and, incredibly, as "a beneficial treatment for hypertension and coronary disease." According to the FTC, one misleading ad said: "Teacher loses 70 pounds in only eight weeks. . . . This is how over one million people have safely lost millions of pounds! No calorie counting! No hunger! Guaranteed to work for you too!" As the director of the FTC's Bureau of Consumer Protection summed up, "There is no such thing as weight loss in a bottle. Claims that you'll lose substantial amounts of weight and still eat everything you want are simply false."[27] In 2004, the United States banned ephedra.

When the FTC discovers deceptive ads, it usually requires advertisers to change or remove them from circulation. The FTC can also impose monetary civil penalties for consumers, and it occasionally requires an advertiser to run spots to correct the deceptive ads.

CONTROVERSIAL ADS
From 1983 to 2000, former fashion photographer Oliviero Toscani developed one of the most talked-about ad campaigns of the late twentieth century. As creative director for clothing manufacturer Benetton, Toscani used "United Colors of Benetton" poster-style images featuring few words and no Benetton clothing. Instead, the ads carried frank, often controversial sociopolitical images, such as a white infant nursing at a black woman's breast, a nun kissing a priest, Jewish and Arab boys embracing, dying AIDS patients, and U.S. death row prisoners.

"Clinically proven to increase fat-loss by an unprecedented 1,700 percent."

DECEPTIVE AD CLAIM BY DIET-PILL MAKER NUTRAQUEST (FILED FOR BANKRUPTCY IN 2003)

Alternative Voices

One of the provisions of the government's multibillion-dollar settlement with the tobacco industry in 1998 established a nonprofit organization with the mission to counteract tobacco marketing and reduce youth tobacco use. That mission became a reality in 2000, when the American Legacy Foundation launched its antismoking/anti-tobacco-industry ad campaign called "Truth."

Working with a coalition of ad agencies, a group of teenage consultants, and a $300 million budget, the foundation has created a series of stylish, gritty print and television ads that deconstruct the images that have long been associated with cigarette ads—macho horse country, carefree beach life, sexy bar scenes, and daring skydives. These ads show teens dragging, piling, or heaving body bags across the beach or onto a horse, and holding up signs that say "What if cigarette ads told the Truth?" Other ads show individuals with lung cancer ("I worked where people smoked. I chose not to. But I got lung cancer anyway") or illustrate how many people are indirectly touched by tobacco deaths ("Yeah, my grandfather died April last year").

The TV and print ads all prominently reference the foundation's Web site, www.thetruth .com, which offers statistics, discussion forums, and outlets for teen creativity. For example, the site provides facts about addiction (more than 80 percent of all adult smokers started smoking before they turned eighteen) and tobacco money (tobacco companies make $1.8 billion from underage sales), and urges site visitors to organize the facts in their own customized folders. By 2007, with its jarring messages and cross-media platform, the "Truth" anti-tobacco campaign was recognized by 80 percent of teens and was ranked in the Top 10 "most memorable teen brands."[28]

ALTERNATIVE ADS
In 2005, "Truth," the national youth smoking prevention campaign, won a national Emmy Award in the National Public Service Announcement category. "Truth" ads were created by the ad firms of Arnold Worldwide of Boston and Crispin Porter & Bogusky of Miami. Here a "Truth" ad reimagines a common image found in Marlboro cigarette ads.

Advertising, Politics, and Democracy

Advertising as a profession came of age in the twentieth century, facilitating the shift of U.S. society from production-oriented small-town values to consumer-oriented urban lifestyles. With its ability to create consumers, advertising became the central economic support system for our mass media industries. Through its seemingly endless supply of pervasive and persuasive strategies, advertising today saturates the cultural landscape. Products now blend in as props or even as "characters" in TV shows and movies. In addition, almost every national consumer product now has its own Web site to market itself to a global audience 365 days a year. With today's digital technology, ad images can be made to appear in places where they don't really exist. For example, advertisements can be superimposed on the backstop wall behind the batter during a nationally televised baseball broadcast. Viewers at home see the ads, but the ads can't be seen by fans at the game.

Advertising's ubiquity raises serious questions about our privacy and the ease with which companies can gather data on our consumer habits. But an even more serious issue is the influence of advertising on our lives as democratic citizens. With fewer and fewer large media conglomerates controlling advertising and commercial speech, what is the effect on free speech and political debate? In the future, how easy will it be to get heard in a marketplace where only a small number of large companies control access to that space?

Advertising's Role in Politics

Since the 1950s, political consultants have been imitating market-research and advertising techniques to sell their candidates, giving rise to **political advertising**, the use of ad techniques to promote a candidate's image and persuade the public to adopt a particular viewpoint. In the early days of television, politicians running for major offices either bought or were offered half-hour blocks of time to discuss their views and the issues of the day. As advertising time became more valuable, however, local stations and the networks became reluctant to give away time in large chunks. Gradually, TV managers began selling thirty-second spots to political campaigns, just as they sold time to product advertisers.

During the 1992 and 1996 presidential campaigns, third-party candidate Ross Perot restored the use of the half-hour time block when he ran political infomercials on cable and the networks. Barack Obama also ran a half-hour infomercial in 2008. However, only very wealthy or well-funded candidates can afford such promotional strategies, because television does not usually provide free airtime to politicians. Questions about political ads continue to be asked: Can serious information on political issues be conveyed in thirty-second spots? Do repeated attack ads, which assault another candidate's character, so undermine citizens' confidence in the electoral process that they stop voting?[29] And how does a society ensure that alternative political voices, which are not well financed or commercially viable, still receive a hearing in a democratic society?

Although broadcasters use the public's airwaves, they have long opposed providing free time for political campaigns and issues, since political advertising is big business for television stations. TV broadcasters earned $400 million in 1996 and took in more than $1.5 billion from political ads during the presidential and congressional elections in 2004. In 2008, the long, competitive presidential nominating season for candidates stretching from January to June led to estimates of a record $3 billion in spending on political advertising by Election Day in November.[30]

The Future of Advertising

Although commercialism–through packaging both products and politicians–has generated cultural feedback that is often critical of advertising's pervasiveness, the growth of the industry has not diminished. Ads continue to fascinate. Many consumers buy magazines or watch the Super Bowl just for the advertisements. Adolescents decorate their rooms with their favorite ads and identify with the images certain products convey. In 2007, $280 billion was spent on U.S. advertising (about one-third of the money spent on ads worldwide)–enough money to finance the budgets of several small countries.

A number of factors have made possible advertising's largely unchecked growth. Many Americans tolerate advertising as a necessary "evil" for maintaining the economy, but many dismiss advertising as not believable and even trivial. As a result, unwilling to downplay its centrality to global culture, many citizens do not think advertising is significant enough to monitor or reform. Such attitudes have ensured advertising's pervasiveness and suggest the need to escalate our critical vigilance.

As individuals and as a society, we have developed an uneasy relationship with advertising. Favorite ads and commercial jingles remain part of our cultural world for a lifetime, but we detest irritating and repetitive commercials. We realize that without ads, many mass media would need to reinvent themselves. At the same time, we should remain critical of what advertising has come to represent: the overemphasis on commercial acquisitions and cultural images, and the disparity between those who can afford to live comfortably in a commercialized society and those who cannot. ▶

"One is tempted to ask, can a candidate buy the presidency? Let's hope not. But successful fundraising does separate political haves from have nots."

MACON (GA.) TELEGRAPH EDITORIAL, 2007

"Corporations put ads on fruit, ads all over the schools, ads on cars, ads on clothes. The only place you can't find ads is where they belong: on politicians."

MOLLY IVINS, SYNDICATED COLUMNIST, 2000

"Mass advertising flourished in the world of mass media. Not because it was part of God's Natural Order, but because the two were mutually sustaining."

BOB GARFIELD, ADVERTISING AGE, 2007

CHAPTER REVIEW

REVIEW QUESTIONS

Early Developments in American Advertising

1. Whom did the first ad agents serve?

2. How did packaging and trademarks influence advertising?

3. Explain why patent medicines and department stores figured so prominently in advertising in the late 1800s.

4. What role did advertising play in transforming America into a consumer society?

The Shape of U.S. Advertising Today

5. What influences did visual culture exert on advertising?

6. What are the differences between boutique agencies and mega-agencies?

7. What are the major divisions at most ad agencies? What is the function of each department?

8. What causes the occasional tension between the research and creative departments at some agencies?

Persuasive Techniques in Contemporary Advertising

9. How do the common persuasive techniques used in advertising work?

10. How does the association principle work, and why is it an effective way to analyze advertising?

11. What is the disassociation corollary?

Commercial Speech and Regulating Advertising

12. What is commercial speech?

13. What are four serious contemporary issues regarding health and advertising? Why is each issue controversial?

14. What is product placement? Cite examples.

15. What aspect of Internet advertising concerns privacy advocates?

Advertising, Politics, and Democracy

16. What are some of the major issues involving political advertising?

17. What role does advertising play in a democratic society?

QUESTIONING THE MEDIA

1. What is your earliest recollection of watching a television commercial? Do you have a favorite ad? A most-despised ad? What is it about these ads that you particularly like or dislike?

2. Why are so many people critical of advertising?

3. If you were (or are) a parent, what strategies would you use to explain an objectionable ad to your child or teenager? Use an example.

4. Should advertising aimed at children be regulated? Support your response.

5. Should tobacco (or alcohol) advertising be prohibited? Why or why not? How would you deal with First Amendment issues regarding controversial ads?

6. Would you be in favor of regular advertising on public television and radio as a means of financial support for these media? Explain your answer.

7. Is advertising at odds with the ideals of democracy? Why or why not?

For review quizzes, chapter summaries, links to media-related Web sites, and more, go to bedfordstmartins.com/mediaculture.

COMMON THREADS

One of the Common Threads discussed in Chapter 1 is the commercial nature of the mass media. The U.S. media system, due to policy choices made in the early twentieth century, is built largely on a system of commercial sponsorship. This acceptance was based on a sense that media content and sponsors should remain independent of each other. Today, is that line between media content and advertising shifting–or completely disappearing?

Although media consumers have not always been comfortable with advertising, they developed a resigned acceptance of it because it "pays the bills" of the media system. Yet media consumers have their limits. Moments in which sponsors stepped over the usual borders of advertising into the realm of media content—including the TV quiz show and radio payola scandals, complimentary newspaper reports about advertisers' businesses, and product placement in TV and movies—have generated the greatest legal and ethical debates about advertising.

Still, as advertising has become more pervasive and consumers more discriminating, ad practitioners have searched for ways to weave their work more seamlessly into the social and cultural fabric. Products now blend in as props or even as "characters" in TV shows and movies. Search engines deliver "paid" placements along with regular search results. Product placements—some permanent, some networked to change with the user—are woven into video games.

Among the more intriguing efforts to become enmeshed in the culture are the ads that exploit, distort, or transform the political and cultural meanings of popular music. When Nike used the Beatles' song "Revolution" (1968) to promote Nike shoes in 1987 ("Nike Air is not a shoe . . . it's a revolution," the ad said), many music fans were outraged to hear the Beatles' music being used for the first time to sell products.

That was more than twenty years ago. These days, having a popular song used in a TV commercial is considered a good career move—even better than radio airplay. Similarly, while product placement in TV and movies was hotly debated in the 1980s and 1990s, the explosive growth of paid placements in video games hardly raises an eyebrow today. Even the lessons of the quiz show scandals, which forced advertisers out of TV program production in the late 1950s, are forgotten or ignored today as advertisers have been warmly invited to help develop TV programs.

Are we as a society giving up on trying to set limits on the neverending onslaught of advertising? Are we weary of trying to keep advertising out of media production? Or are we now less concerned about the integration of advertising into the core of media culture?

KEY TERMS

The definitions for the terms listed below can be found in the glossary at the end of the book. The page numbers listed with the terms indicate where the term is highlighted in the chapter.

12

Public Relations and Framing the Message

In the mid-1950s, the blue jeans industry was in deep trouble. After hitting a postwar peak in 1953, jeans sales began to slide. The durable one-hundred-year-old denim product had become associated with rock and roll and teenage troublemakers. Popular movies, especially *The Wild One* and *Blackboard Jungle*, featured emotionally disturbed, blue jeans–wearing "young toughs" terrorizing adult authority figures. A Broadway play about juvenile delinquency was even titled *Blue Denim*. The worst was yet to come, however. In 1957, the public school system in Buffalo, New York, banned the wearing of blue jeans for all high school students. Formerly associated with farmers, factory workers, and an adult work ethic, jeans had become a reverse fashion statement for teenagers—something many adults could not abide.

◀

THE DELINQUENT IN JEANS Marlon Brando in *The Wild One* (1953).

In response to the crisis, the denim industry waged a public relations (PR) campaign to eradicate the delinquency label and rejuvenate denim's image. In 1956, the nation's top blue jeans manufacturers formed the national Denim Council "to put schoolchildren back in blue jeans through a concerted national public relations, advertising, and promotional effort."[1] First the council targeted teens, but its promotional efforts were unsuccessful. The manufacturers soon realized that the problem was not with the teens but with the parents, administrators, teachers, and school boards. It was the adults who felt threatened by a fashion trend that seemed to promote disrespect through casualness. In response, the council hired a public relations firm to turn the image of blue jeans around. Over the next five years, the firm did just that.

The public relations team determined that mothers were refusing to outfit their children in jeans because of the product's association with delinquency. To change this perception among

women, the team encouraged fashion designers to update denim's image by producing new women's sportswear styles made from the fabric. Media outlets and fashion editors were soon inundated with news releases about the "new look" of durable denim.

The PR team next enlisted sportswear designers to provide new designs for both men's and women's work and utility clothes, long the backbone of denim sales. Targeting business reporters as well as fashion editors, the team transformed the redesign effort into a story that appealed to writers in both areas. They also planned retail store promotions nationwide, including "jean queen" beauty contests, and advanced positive denim stories in men's publications.

The team's major PR coup, however, involved an association with the newly formed national Peace Corps. The brainchild of the Kennedy administration, the Peace Corps encouraged young people to serve their country by working with people from developing nations.

BLUE JEANS successfully reinvented their image and were (and still are) accepted and worn by the volunteers who work for the Peace Corps.

Envisioning the Peace Corps as the flip side of delinquency, the Denim Council saw its opening. In 1961, it agreed to outfit the first group of two hundred corps volunteers in denim. As a result of all these PR efforts, by 1963 manufacturers were flooded with orders, and sales of jeans and other denim goods were way up. The delinquency tag disappeared, and jeans gradually became associated with a more casual, though not antisocial, dress ethic.

▲ *THE BLUE JEANS STORY ILLUSTRATES A MAJOR DIFFERENCE* between advertising and public relations: Advertising is controlled publicity that a company or an individual buys; public relations attempts to secure favorable media publicity (which is more difficult to control) to promote a company or client. The transformation of denim in the public's eye was primarily achieved not by purchasing advertising but by restyling denim's image through friendly relations with reporters, who subsequently wrote stories associating the fabric with a casual, dedicated, youthful America.

Public relations (PR) covers a wide array of practices, such as shaping the public image of a politician or celebrity, establishing or repairing communication between consumers and companies, and promoting government agencies and actions, especially during wartime. Broadly defined, **public relations** refers to the total communication strategy conducted by a person, a government, or an organization attempting to reach and persuade an audience to adopt a point of view.[2] While public relations may sound very similar to advertising, which also seeks to persuade audiences, it is a different skill in a variety of ways. Advertising uses simple and fixed messages (e.g., "our appliance is the most efficient and affordable") that are transmitted directly to the public through the purchase of ads. Public relations involves more complex messages that may evolve over time (e.g., a political campaign or a long-term strategy to dispel unfavorable reports about "fatty processed foods") and may be transmitted to the public indirectly, often through the news media.

The social and cultural impact of public relations has been immense. In its infancy, PR helped convince many American businesses of the value of nurturing the public, who became purchasers rather than producers of their own goods after the Industrial Revolution. PR set the tone for the corporate image-building that characterized the economic environment of the twentieth century and for the battles of organizations taking sides in today's environmental, energy, and labor issues. Perhaps PR's most significant effect, however, has been on the political process where individuals and organizations—on both the Right and the Left—hire spin doctors to shape their media images.

In this chapter, we examine the impact of public relations and the historical conditions that affected its development as a modern profession. We begin by looking at nineteenth-century press agents and the role that railroad and utility companies played in developing corporate PR. We then consider the rise of modern PR, particularly the influences of former reporters Ivy Lee and Edward Bernays. In addition, we explore the major practices and specialties of public relations, the reasons for the long-standing antagonism between journalists and members of the PR profession, and the social responsibilities of public relations in a democracy.

Early Developments in Public Relations

At the beginning of the twentieth century, the United States shifted to a consumer-oriented, industrial society that fostered the development of new products and services as people moved to cities to find work. During this transformation from farm to factory, advertising and PR emerged as professions. While advertising drew attention and customers to new products, PR partly began to help businesses fend off increased scrutiny from the muckraking journalists and emerging labor unions of the time.[3]

The first PR practitioners were simply theatrical **press agents**: those who sought to advance a client's image through media exposure, primarily via stunts staged for newspapers.

> "An image . . . is not simply a trademark, a design, a slogan, or an easily remembered picture. It is a studiously crafted personality profile of an individual, institution, corporation, product, or service."
>
> DANIEL BOORSTIN, *THE IMAGE*, 1961

> "Public relations developed in the early part of the twentieth century as a profession which responded to, and helped shape, the public, newly defined as irrational, not reasoning; spectatorial, not participant; consuming, not productive."
>
> MICHAEL SCHUDSON, *DISCOVERING THE NEWS*, 1978

EARLY PUBLIC RELATIONS
Buffalo Bill's Wild West and Congress of Rough Riders of the World show, depicted in this 1899 poster, was internationally popular as a touring show for more than thirty years. William Frederick Cody (1846–1917) became popularly known as "Buffalo Bill" through dime-store novel stories adapted from his life by E. Z. C. Judson (under the pen name Ned Buntline). Prior to his fame as an entertainer, Cody worked as a Pony Express rider at age fourteen, and later as a buffalo hunter for the Kansas Pacific Railroad.

The advantages of these early PR techniques soon became obvious. For instance, press agents were used by people like Daniel Boone, who engineered various land-grab and real estate ventures, and Davy Crockett, who in addition to heroic exploits was also involved in the massacre of Native Americans. Such individuals often wanted press agents to repair and reshape their reputations as cherished frontier legends or as respectable candidates for public office.

P. T. Barnum and Buffalo Bill

The most notorious press agent of the 1800s was Phineas Taylor (P. T.) Barnum, who used gross exaggeration, fraudulent stories, and staged events to secure newspaper coverage for his clients; his American Museum; and, later, his circus. Barnum's circus, dubbed "The Greatest Show on Earth," included the "midget" General Tom Thumb, Swedish soprano Jenny Lind, Jumbo the Elephant, and Joice Heth (who Barnum claimed was the 161-year-old nurse of George Washington, but was actually 80 when she died). These performers became some of the earliest nationally known celebrities because of Barnum's skill in using the media for promotion. Decrying outright fraud and cheating, Barnum understood that his audiences liked to be tricked. In newspapers and on handbills, he later often revealed the strategies behind his more elaborate hoaxes.

From 1883 to 1916, William F. Cody, who once killed buffalo for the railroads, promoted himself and his traveling show: "Buffalo Bill's Wild West and Congress of Rough Riders of the World." Cody's troupe–which featured Bedouins, Cossacks, and gauchos, as well as "cowboys and Indians"–re-created dramatic gunfights, the Civil War, and battles of the Old West. The show employed sharpshooter Annie Oakley and Lakota medicine man Sitting Bull, whose legends were partially shaped by Cody's nine press agents. These agents were led by John Burke, who successfully promoted the show for its entire thirty-four-year run. Burke was one of the first

---

▼ Public Relations and Framing the Message

Early Promotions through Media
In a career that spans the 1840s to the 1880s, theatrical agent P. T. Barnum employs early PR tactics to promote his many acts, including the Swedish soprano Jenny Lind and Jumbo, the twelve-foot-high African elephant (p. 382).

"Poison Ivy" Lee
After opening one of the first PR firms in New York in the early 1900s, Lee, in 1914, works for the wealthy Rockefeller family, transforming the senior Rockefeller's reputation as a stingy curmudgeon into that of a child-loving philanthropist (p. 385).

Walter Lippmann
In 1922, the newspaper columnist publishes the book *Public Opinion* and illustrates how slogans, stereotypes, and other media messages can shape public perception (p. 386).

| 1840 | 1860 | 1880 | 1900 | 1920 |

The Railroads
PR practice of bribing reporters for positive news stories and deadheading (giving reporters free rail passes) reaches its height (p. 383).

Edward Bernays
In 1923, Bernays teaches the first public relations course at New York University and writes the first PR textbook (p. 386).

press agents to use a wide variety of media channels to generate publicity: promotional newspaper stories, magazine articles and ads, dime novels, theater marquees, poster art, and early films. Burke and Buffalo Bill shaped many of the lasting myths about rugged American individualism and frontier expansion that were later adopted by books, radio programs, and Hollywood films about the American West. Along with Barnum, they were among the first to use **publicity**—a type of PR communication that uses various media messages to spread information about a person, corporation, issue, or policy—to elevate entertainment culture to an international level.

Big Business and Press Agents

As P. T. Barnum, Buffalo Bill, and John Burke demonstrated, utilizing the press brought with it an enormous power to sway the public and to generate business. So it is not surprising that during the 1800s, America's largest industrial companies, particularly the railroads, also employed press agents to win favor in the court of public opinion.

The railroads began to use press agents to help them obtain federal funds. Initially, local businesses raised funds to finance the spread of rail service. Around 1850, however, the railroads began pushing for federal subsidies, complaining that local fund-raising efforts took too long. For example, Illinois Central was one of the first companies to use government *lobbyists* (people who try to influence the voting of lawmakers) to argue that railroad service between the North and the South was in the public interest and would ease tensions, unite the two regions, and prevent a war.

The railroad press agents successfully gained government support by developing some of the earliest publicity tactics. Their first strategy was simply to buy favorable news stories about rail travel from newspapers through direct bribes. Another practice was to engage in *deadheading*—giving reporters free rail passes with the tacit understanding that they would write glowing reports about rail travel. Eventually, wealthy railroads received the federal subsidies they wanted and increased their profits, while the American public shouldered much of the financial burden of rail expansion.

> "For setting forth of virtues (actual or alleged) of presidents, general managers, or directors, $2 per line. . . . Epic poems, containing descriptions of scenery, dining cars, etc., will be published at special rates."
>
> CHICAGO NEWS REPORTER'S FICTIONAL RATES FOR THE BRIBES OFFERED TO JOURNALISTS FOR FAVORABLE RAILROAD COVERAGE, LATE 1880S

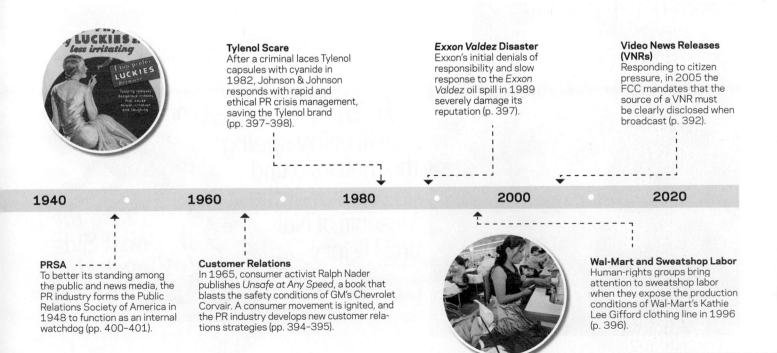

Tylenol Scare
After a criminal laces Tylenol capsules with cyanide in 1982, Johnson & Johnson responds with rapid and ethical PR crisis management, saving the Tylenol brand (pp. 397–398).

Exxon *Valdez* Disaster
Exxon's initial denials of responsibility and slow response to the *Exxon Valdez* oil spill in 1989 severely damage its reputation (p. 397).

Video News Releases (VNRs)
Responding to citizen pressure, in 2005 the FCC mandates that the source of a VNR must be clearly disclosed when broadcast (p. 392).

1940 1960 1980 2000 2020

PRSA
To better its standing among the public and news media, the PR industry forms the Public Relations Society of America in 1948 to function as an internal watchdog (pp. 400–401).

Customer Relations
In 1965, consumer activist Ralph Nader publishes *Unsafe at Any Speed*, a book that blasts the safety conditions of GM's Chevrolet Corvair. A consumer movement is ignited, and the PR industry develops new customer relations strategies (pp. 394–395).

Wal-Mart and Sweatshop Labor
Human-rights groups bring attention to sweatshop labor when they expose the production conditions of Wal-Mart's Kathie Lee Gifford clothing line in 1996 (p. 396).

Having obtained construction subsidies, the larger rail companies turned their attention to bigger game—persuading the government to control rates and reduce competition, especially from smaller, aggressive regional lines. Railroad lobbyists argued that federal support would lead to improved service and guaranteed quality, because the government would be keeping a close watch. These lobbying efforts, accompanied by favorable publicity, led to passage of the Interstate Commerce Act in 1881, authorizing railroads "to revamp their freight classification, raise rates, and eliminate fare reduction."[4] Historians have argued that, ironically, the PR campaign's success actually led to the decline of the railroads: Artificially maintained higher rates and burdensome government regulations forced smaller firms out of business and eventually drove many customers to other modes of transportation.

Along with the railroads, utility companies such as Chicago Edison and AT&T also used PR strategies in the late 1800s to derail competition and eventually attain monopoly status. In fact, AT&T's PR and lobbying efforts were so effective that they eliminated all telephone competition—with the government's blessing—until the 1980s. In addition to buying the votes of key lawmakers, the utilities hired third-party editorial services, which would send favorable articles about utilities to newspapers; assigned company managers to become leaders in community groups; produced ghostwritten articles (often using the names of prominent leaders and members of women's social groups, who were flattered to see their names in print); and influenced textbook authors to write histories favorable to the utilities.[5] The tactics of the 1880s and 1890s, however, would haunt public relations as it struggled to become a respected profession.

The Birth of Modern Public Relations

By the early 1900s, reporters and muckraking journalists began investigating the promotional practices behind many companies. As an informed citizenry paid more attention, it became more difficult for large firms to fool the press and mislead the public. With the rise of the middle class, increasing literacy among the working classes, and the spread of information through print media, democratic ideals began to threaten the established order of business and

IVY LEE, a founding father of public relations (below), did more than just crisis work with large companies and business magnates. His PR work also included clients like transportation companies in New York City (below right) and Charles Lindbergh.

politics—and the elite groups who managed them. Two pioneers of public relations—Ivy Lee and Edward Bernays—emerged in this atmosphere to popularize an approach that emphasized shaping the interpretation of facts and "engineering consent."

Ivy Ledbetter Lee

Most nineteenth-century corporations and manufacturers cared little about public sentiment. By the early 1900s, though, executives realized that their companies could sell more products if they were associated with positive public images and values. Into this public space stepped Ivy Ledbetter Lee, considered one of the founders of modern public relations. Lee understood that the public's attitude toward big corporations had changed. He counseled his corporate clients that honesty and directness were better PR devices than the deceptive practices of the 1800s, which had fostered suspicion and an anti-big-business sentiment.

A minister's son, an economics student at Princeton University, and a former reporter, Lee opened one of the first PR firms in the early 1900s with George Park. Lee quit the firm in 1906 to work for the Pennsylvania Railroad, which, following a rail accident, hired him to help downplay unfavorable publicity. Lee's advice, however, was that Penn Railroad admit its mistake, vow to do better, and let newspapers in on the story. These suggestions ran counter to the then-standard practice of hiring press agents to manipulate the media, yet Lee argued that an open relationship between business and the press would lead to a more favorable public image. In the end, Penn adopted Lee's ultimately successful strategies.

In 1914, Lee went to work for John D. Rockefeller, who by the 1880s controlled 90 percent of the nation's oil industry. Rockefeller suffered from periodic image problems, particularly after Ida Tarbell's powerful muckraking series about the ruthless business tactics practiced by Rockefeller and his Standard Oil Company appeared in *McClure's Magazine* in 1904. The Rockefeller and Standard Oil reputations reached a low point in April 1914, when tactics to stop union organizing erupted in tragedy at a coal company in Ludlow, Colorado. During a violent strike, fifty-three workers and their family members, including thirteen women and children, died.

Lee was hired to contain the damaging publicity fallout. He immediately distributed a series of "fact" sheets to the press, telling the corporate side of the story and discrediting the tactics of the United Mine Workers, who organized the strike. As he had done for Penn Railroad, Lee also brought in the press and staged photo opportunities. John D. Rockefeller Jr., who now ran the company, donned overalls and a miner's helmet and posed with the families of workers and union leaders. Lee's tactics ultimately helped facilitate improved conditions for the Ludlow workers and resuscitated the Rockefeller family's image. However, his PR campaign also kept the union out of the Ludlow coal mines. This was probably the first use of a PR campaign in a labor-management dispute. Over the years, Lee completely transformed the wealthy family's image, urging the discreet Rockefellers to publicize their charitable work. To improve his image, the senior Rockefeller took to handing out dimes to children wherever he went—a strategic ritual that historians attribute to Lee.

Called "Poison Ivy" by newspaper critics and corporate foes, Lee had a complex understanding of facts. He realized, better than most journalists of his day, that facts were open to various interpretations. For Lee, facts were elusive and malleable, begging to be forged and shaped. In the Ludlow case, for instance, Lee noted that the women and children who died while retreating from the charging company-backed militia had overturned a stove, which caught fire and caused their deaths. His PR fact sheet implied that they had, in part, been victims of their own carelessness.

PHOTO OPPORTUNITIES like this one showing Rockefeller Jr. with coal mine workers were an important part of Lee's PR strategy to help improve the Rockefeller image after the Ludlow massacre.

Beat back the HUN with LIBERTY BONDS

PR SERVES THE GOVERNMENT
During World War I, PR pioneer Edward Bernays (1891–1995) worked for the federal Committee on Public Information (CPI). One of the main functions of the CPI was to create the poster art and print ads that would persuade reluctant or isolationist Americans to support the war effort against Germany.

Edward Bernays

The nephew of Sigmund Freud, former reporter Edward Bernays inherited the public relations mantle from Ivy Lee. Beginning in 1919 when he opened his own office, Bernays was the first person to apply the findings of psychology and sociology to public relations, referring to himself as a "public relations counselor" rather than a "publicity agent." Over the years, Bernays's client list included General Electric, the American Tobacco Company, General Motors, *Good Housekeeping* and *Time* magazines, Procter & Gamble, RCA, the government of India, the city of Vienna, and President Coolidge.

Bernays also worked for the Committee on Public Information (CPI) during World War I, developing propaganda that supported America's entry into that conflict and promoting the image of President Woodrow Wilson as a peacemaker. Both efforts were among the first full-scale governmental attempts to mobilize public opinion. In addition, Bernays made key contributions to public relations education, teaching the first class called "public relations"–at New York University in 1923–and writing the field's first textbook, *Crystallizing Public Opinion*. For many years, his definition of PR was the standard: "Public relations is the attempt, by information, persuasion, and adjustment, to engineer public support for an activity, cause, movement, or institution."[6]

In the 1920s, Bernays was hired by the American Tobacco Company to develop a campaign to make smoking more publicly acceptable for women. Among other strategies, Bernays staged an event: placing women smokers in New York's 1929 Easter parade. He labeled cigarettes "torches of freedom" and encouraged women to smoke as a symbol of their newly acquired suffrage and independence from men. He also asked the women he placed in the parade to contact newspaper and newsreel companies in advance–to announce their symbolic protest. The campaign received plenty of free publicity from newspapers and magazines. Within weeks of the parade, men-only smoking rooms in New York theaters began opening up to women.

Through much of his writing, Bernays suggested that emerging freedoms threatened the established hierarchical order. He thought it was important for experts and leaders to control the direction of American society: "The duty of the higher strata of society–the cultivated, the learned, the expert, the intellectual–is therefore clear. They must inject moral and spiritual motives into public opinion."[7] For the cultural elite to maintain order and control, they would have to win the consent of the larger public. As a result, he termed the shaping of public opinion through PR as the "engineering of consent." Like Ivy Lee, Bernays thought that public opinion was malleable and not always rational: In the hands of the right experts, leaders, and PR counselors, public opinion could be shaped into forms people could rally behind.[8] However, journalists like Walter Lippmann, who wrote the famous book *Public Opinion* in 1922, worried that PR professionals with hidden agendas, rather than journalists with professional detachment, held too much power over American public opinion.

Throughout Bernays's most active years, his business partner and later his wife, Doris Fleischman, worked with him on many of his campaigns as a researcher and coauthor. Beginning in the 1920s, she was one of the first women to work in public relations, and she

introduced PR to America's most powerful leaders through a pamphlet she edited called *Contact*. Because she opened up the profession to women from its inception, PR emerged as one of the few professions—apart from teaching and nursing—accessible to women who chose to work outside the home at that time. Today, women outnumber men by more than three to one in the profession.

The Practice of Public Relations

Today, there are more than 2,900 PR firms worldwide, including 1,900 in the United States; thousands of companies and organizations also have in-house departments devoted to PR. Since the 1980s, the formal study of public relations has grown significantly at colleges and universities. By 2008, the Public Relations Student Society of America (PRSSA) had nearly ten thousand members and 297 chapters in colleges and universities. As certified PR programs have expanded (often requiring courses or a minor in journalism), the profession has relied less and less on its traditional practice of recruiting journalists for its workforce. At the same time, new courses in professional ethics and issues management have expanded the responsibility of future practitioners. In this section, we discuss the differences between public relations agencies and in-house PR services and the various practices involved in performing PR.

Approaches to Organized Public Relations

The Public Relations Society of America (PRSA) offers this simple and useful definition of PR: "Public relations helps an organization and its publics adapt mutually to each other." To carry out this mutual communication process, the PR industry uses two approaches. First, there are independent PR agencies whose sole job is to provide clients with PR services. Second, most companies, which may or may not also hire the independent PR firms, maintain their own in-house PR staffs to handle routine tasks, such as writing press releases, managing various media requests, staging special events, and dealing with internal and external publics.

About 1,900 U.S. companies identify themselves as public relations firms. Many large ones are owned by, or are affiliated with, multinational communications holding companies like WPP, Omnicom, and Interpublic (see Figure 12.1). Two of the largest PR agencies, Burson-Marsteller and Hill & Knowlton, generated part of the $1.28 billion in PR revenue for their parent corporation, the WPP Group, in 2008. Founded in 1953, Burson-Marsteller has 103 offices in fifty-nine countries and lists the U.S. Bureau of Engraving & Printing, Johnnie Walker whiskey, Old Navy, Sony, and the United Arab Emirates among its clients. Hill & Knowlton, founded in 1927, has 71 offices in forty countries and includes American Express, Baidu.com (China's largest search engine), Procter & Gamble, Starbucks, and the United Kingdom on its client list. Most independent PR firms are smaller and are operated locally or regionally. New York-based Edelman, the largest independent firm, is an exception, with global operations and clients like the American Beverage Association, Burger King, General Electric, Microsoft, Samsung, and Unilever/Dove.

FIGURE 12.1

THE TOP 6 HOLDING FIRMS, WITH PUBLIC RELATIONS SUBSIDIARIES, 2008 (BY WORLDWIDE REVENUE IN U.S.$)

Source: "Agency Family Trees 2008," Advertising Age, May 5, 2008, http://adage.com/agencyfamilytrees08.

Note: Revenue represents total company income including PR agencies.

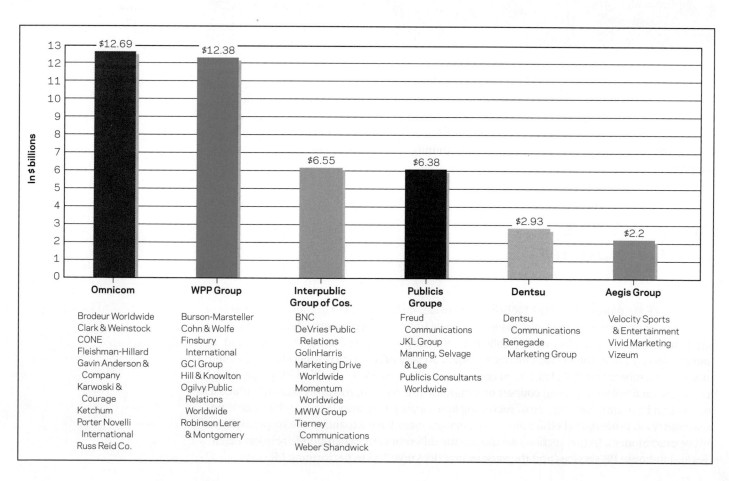

In contrast to these external agencies, most PR work is done in-house at companies and organizations. Although America's largest companies typically retain external PR firms, almost every company involved in the manufacturing and service industries has an in-house PR department. Such departments are also a vital part of many professional organizations, such as the American Medical Association, the AFL-CIO, and the National Association of Broadcasters, as well as large nonprofit organizations, such as the American Cancer Society, the Arthritis Foundation, and most universities and colleges.

Performing Public Relations

Public relations, like advertising, pays careful attention to the needs of its clients—politicians, small businesses, industries, and nonprofit organizations—and to the perspectives of its targeted audiences: consumers and the general public, company employees, shareholders, media organizations, government agencies, and community and industry leaders. To do so, PR involves providing a multitude of services, including publicity, communication, public affairs, issues management, government relations, financial PR, community relations, industry relations, minority relations, advertising, press agentry, promotion, media relations, and propaganda. This last service, **propaganda**, is communication strategically placed, either as advertising or as publicity, to gain public support for a special issue, program, or policy, such as a nation's war effort.

In addition, PR personnel (both PR technicians, who handle daily short-term activities, and PR managers, who counsel clients and manage activities over the long term) produce employee newsletters, manage client trade shows and conferences, conduct historical tours, appear on news programs, organize damage control after negative publicity, analyze complex issues and trends that may affect a client's future, and much more. Basic among these activities, however, are formulating a message through research; conveying the message through various channels; sustaining public support through community and consumer relations; and maintaining client interests through government relations.

Research: Formulating the Message

Before anything else begins, one of the most essential practices in the PR profession is doing research. Just as advertising is driven today by demographic and psychographic research, PR uses similar strategies to project messages to appropriate audiences. Because it has historically been difficult to determine why particular PR campaigns succeed or fail, research has become the key ingredient in PR forecasting. Like advertising, PR makes use of mail, telephone, and Internet surveys and focus group interviews to get a fix on an audience's perceptions of an issue, policy, program, or client's image.

Research also helps PR firms focus the campaign message. For example, the Liz Claiborne Foundation has been combating domestic violence with its "Love Is Not Abuse" campaign

"It was the astounding success of propaganda during the war which opened the eyes of the intelligent few in all departments of life to the possibilities of regimenting the public mind."

EDWARD BERNAYS, *PROPAGANDA*, 1928

WHAT YOU NEED TO KNOW ABOUT DATING VIOLENCE

love is respect.org

LIZ CLAIBORNE
WOMEN'S WORK

▲

MESSAGE FORMULATION can help ensure that the right message is reaching the audience, as it did with the Claiborne "Love Is Not Abuse" message.

for more than a decade, but without much media visibility. In 2005, however, the company turned its focus to a subset of domestic violence—teen dating abuse—and hired Ruder Finn, a leading independent PR firm, to help shape its campaign. The research phase began with a national survey of 683 teens between the ages of thirteen and eighteen. The results were sobering: One in three teenagers reported knowing someone who had been physically hurt by a partner; 13 percent of teenage girls reported being physically hurt in a relationship; and 80 percent of teenagers regarded verbal abuse as a serious issue for their age group. Ruder Finn helped its client develop a "Love Is Not Abuse" curriculum for high school students, and released the survey results and new curriculum in partnership with *Marie Claire* magazine. Through newspaper, television, and radio talk show coverage about the new anti-abuse curriculum, the message reached an estimated fifty million people, a number of schools adopted the curriculum, and not only the Liz Claiborne Foundation but also its parent company received strong favorable publicity in the media. The foundation advanced the campaign with additional research surveys in 2007 and 2008 on teen and tween (ages eleven to fourteen) dating abuse, and the establishment of the National Teen Dating Abuse Helpline.[9]

Conveying the Message

One of the chief day-to-day functions in public relations is creating and distributing PR messages for the news media or the public. There are several possible message forms, including press releases, VNRs, and various online options.

Press releases, or news releases, are announcements, written in the style of news reports that give new information about an individual, a company, or an organization and pitch a story idea to the news media. In issuing press releases, PR agents hope that their client information will be picked up by the news media and transformed into news reports. Through press releases, PR firms manage the flow of information, controlling which media get what material in which order. (A PR agent may even reward a cooperative reporter by strategically releasing information.) News editors and broadcasters sort through hundreds of releases daily to determine which ones contain the most original ideas or are the most current. Most large media institutions rewrite and double-check the releases, but small media companies often use them verbatim because of limited editorial resources. Usually, the more closely a press release resembles actual news copy, the more likely it is to be used. (See Figure 12.2.)

Since the introduction of portable video equipment in the 1970s, PR agencies and departments have also been issuing **video news releases (VNRs)**—thirty- to ninety-second visual press releases designed to mimic the style of a broadcast news report. Although networks and large TV news stations do not usually broadcast VNRs, news stations in small TV markets regularly use material from VNRs. On occasion, news stations have been criticized for using video footage from a VNR without acknowledging the source. (See "Case Study—Video News Releases: Manufacturing the News" on page 392.) As with press releases, VNRs give PR firms some control over what constitutes "news" and a chance to influence what the general public thinks about an issue, a program, or a policy.

The equivalent of VNRs for nonprofits are **public service announcements (PSAs):** fifteen- to sixty-second audio or video reports that promote government programs, educational projects, volunteer agencies, or social reform. As part of their requirement to serve the public interest, broadcasters have been encouraged to carry free PSAs. Since the deregulation of

broadcasting began in the 1980s, however, there has been less pressure and no minimum obligation for TV and radio stations to air PSAs. When PSAs do run, they are frequently scheduled between midnight and 6 A.M., a less commercially valuable time slot.

Today, the Internet is an essential avenue for transmitting PR messages. The Internet can be used to send electronic press releases and VNRs, download PR press kits, post YouTube videos, and host PR-based Web sites (for instance, the official Web sites of political candidates). At Edelman Public Relations, blogs by company executives are used to increase the dialogue between PR firms and the public and promote transparency in public relations. (See http://www .edelman.com/landingblog.) Other Internet-based PR strategies include Fleishman-Hillard Public Relations' promotional YouTube and Flash videos to introduce text-message ordering for the pizza chain Papa John's (an award-winning campaign) and the viral marketing campaign for the 2008 movie *Cloverfield* that included a MySpace site for Robby Hawkins (a character), a Web site

▲

FIGURE 12.2

DIFFERENCES BETWEEN A PRESS RELEASE AND A NEWS STORY

News reporters can be heavily dependent on public relations for story ideas. At right above is a press release written by the News & Public Information Office at Miami University about students who started a finance business, and the magazine and newspaper articles inspired by the release (above left and center).

Video News Releases:
Manufacturing the News

You may have seen these seemingly innocuous stories on your local TV news over the summer: tips for staying in motels/hotels with pets; the importance of getting rental-car insurance; or how-to instructions for taking great digital photos of your vacation. These may not sound like traditional news stories, but they were broadcast because (1) a company called Medialink promoted them with text, photos, and digital video downloads from their Web site, and (2) companies—like Motel 6, Allstate Insurance, and Fuji Photo Film—paid Medialink to promote these stories (which subtly mention their products) as news. Medialink, a $33-million business headquartered in New York City, specializes in video news releases (VNRs), a form of public relations that they pioneered in 1986.

Oftentimes, these VNRs aren't labeled as company sponsored material, so local TV stations mistakenly treat them as real news. Other times, local affiliates are just plain understaffed or sloppy, and either take the VNRs as is or repackage them. Since the late 1980s, television stations across the country have been bombarded with VNRs from Medialink and other sources. Medialink distributes the VNRs and even tracks the number of "plays" their clients' VNRs get on television stations around the world, providing a return on their clients' investment.

The obvious question might be: Why don't Motel 6, Allstate, Fuji, and other companies spend their money on advertising instead? The answer is simple: the news has more credibility.

The success of VNRs to disguise marketing as news hasn't been lost on government officials, either. As reports in the *New York Times* and elsewhere in March 2005 revealed, the federal government has become a major originator of VNRs. During the first four years of George W. Bush's administration, $254 million in taxpayers' dollars was spent on public relations contracts, almost double the amount spent in the previous four years. A significant part of this spending was for VNRs—sometimes with PR officials posing as reporters—emanating from at least twenty different federal agencies, promoting the Bush agenda on issues such as the Medicare prescription drug law, post-invasion Iraq, military prison guard training, and agriculture programs.

This production of "good news" from the White House has one little problem: It's illegal. As Congress's General Accounting Office (GAO) noted, the federal government can't use *covert propaganda*—that is, VNRs that don't identify themselves as the work of government agencies. In fact, the GAO issued three opinions on the illegality of such VNRs and notified the White House to stop using them. The Bush administration told its federal agencies to ignore the GAO, Congress's investigative arm.

With the pressure of more than forty thousand citizen petitions to stop government VNRs, the Federal Communications Commission (FCC) responded on April 13, 2005, with a public notice that stated, "Whenever broadcast stations and cable operators air VNRs, licensees and operators generally must clearly disclose to members of their audiences the nature, source and sponsorship of the material that they are viewing." As FCC Commissioner Jonathan Adelstein noted at the time, "People have a legal right to know the

VIDEO NEWS RELEASES
Medialink publicist Kate Brookes (*top*) posing as a reporter in a video news release. KTNV, Channel 13, in Las Vegas (*bottom*), airing the VNR and making it appear as if Kate Brookes is a real reporter.

real source when they see something on TV that is disguised as 'news.'"

Yet in a study from June 2005 to March 2006, the Center for Media and Democracy found that at least seventy-seven television stations across the country had used VNRs but failed to provide disclosure to viewers. A follow-up report in 2007 revealed a continued use of unattributed VNRs across the country.[1]

Whether produced by the government or a company, VNRs are a pressing problem for local markets. Why? Local news directors often get their video from other larger news services, such as CNN Newsource, NBC News Channel, or ABC. These TV news services supply the video for national and international news stories that air on local TV. The problem is that these services are also sometimes paid to distribute VNRs in their news feeds as well. "If you're going to take that video, you're trusting that they went out and generated that video," Becky Lutgen-Gardner, news director at KCRG-TV in Cedar Rapids, Iowa, says. But, "unless they flag it, I wouldn't know." ◢

(www.1-18-08.com), and YouTube videos to help build the movie's "mystery." These tactics helped to create a record-breaking opening for the horror film.

Media Relations

PR managers specializing in media relations promote a client or an organization by securing publicity or favorable coverage in the news media. This often requires an in-house PR person to speak on behalf of an organization or to direct reporters to experts who can provide information. Media-relations specialists also perform damage control or crisis management when negative publicity occurs. Occasionally, in times of crisis—such as a scandal at a university or a safety recall by a car manufacturer—a PR spokesperson might be designated as the only source of information available to news media. Although journalists often resent being cut off from higher administrative levels and leaders, the institution or company wants to ensure that rumors and inaccurate stories do not circulate in the media. In these situations, a game often develops between PR specialists and the media in which reporters attempt to circumvent the spokesperson and induce a knowledgeable insider to talk off the record, providing background details without being named directly as a source.

PR agents who specialize in media relations also recommend advertising to their clients when it seems appropriate. Unlike publicity, which is sometimes outside a PR agency's control, paid advertising may help to focus a complex issue or a client's image. Publicity, however, carries the aura of legitimate news and thus has more credibility than advertising. In addition, media specialists cultivate associations with editors, reporters, freelance writers, and broadcast news directors to ensure that press releases or VNRs are favorably received. (See "Examining Ethics: Improving the Credibility Gap" on page 396.)

Special Events and Pseudo-Events

Another public relations practice involves coordinating *special events* to raise the profile of corporate, organizational, or government clients. Since 1967, for instance, the city of Milwaukee has run Summerfest, a ten-day music and food festival that attracts about a million people each year and now bills itself as "The World's Largest Music Festival." As the festival's popularity grew, various companies sought to become sponsors of the event. Today, Milwaukee's Miller Brewing Company sponsors one of the music festival's stages, which carries the Miller name and promotes Miller Lite as the "official beer" of the festival. Briggs & Stratton and Harley Davidson are also among the local companies that sponsor stages at the event. In this way, all three companies receive favorable publicity by showing a commitment to the city in which their corporate headquarters are located.[10]

More typical of special-events publicity is a corporate sponsor aligning itself with a cause or an organization that has positive stature among the general public. For example, John Hancock Financial has been the primary sponsor of the Boston Marathon since 1986 and funds the race's prize money. The company's corporate communications department also serves as the PR office for the race, operating the pressroom and creating the marathon's media guide and other press

PUBLIC SERVICE ANNOUNCEMENTS also include print and Web components (not just TV or radio ads). The National Youth Anti-Drug Media Campaign created the Above the Influence brand to help teens resist pressure to use drugs.

PSEUDO-EVENTS like turning 7-Eleven stores into "Kwik-E Marts" to promote *The Simpsons Movie* are a popular way to attract media attention without directly buying advertising.

materials. Eighteen other sponsors, including Adidas, Gatorade, PowerBar, and jetBlue Airways, also pay to affiliate themselves with the Boston Marathon. At the local level, companies often sponsor a community parade or a charitable fund-raising activity.

In contrast to a special event, a **pseudo-event** is any circumstance created for the sole purpose of gaining coverage in the media. Historian Daniel Boorstin coined the term in his influential book *The Image* when pointing out the key contributions of PR and advertising in the twentieth century. Typical pseudo-events are press conferences, TV and radio talk show appearances, or any other staged activity aimed at drawing public attention and media coverage. The success of such events depends on the participation of clients, sometimes on paid performers, and especially on the media's attention to the event. In business, pseudo-events extend back at least as far as P. T. Barnum's publicity stunts, such as parading Jumbo the Elephant across the Brooklyn Bridge in the 1880s. One of the most successful pseudo-events in recent years was the temporary transformation of selected 7-Eleven convenience stores into "Kwik-E Marts" in 2007 to promote the release of *The Simpsons Movie*. The campaign generated millions in free publicity and attracted thousands to take photos and buy Squishees and Simpsons Sprinkalicious donuts. In politics, Theodore Roosevelt's administration set up the first White House pressroom and held the first presidential press conferences in the early 1900s. By the 2000s, presidential pseudo-events had evolved to a multimillion-dollar White House Communications Office.

As powerful companies, savvy politicians, and activist groups became aware of the media's susceptibility to pseudo-events, these activities proliferated. For example, to get free publicity, companies began staging press conferences to announce new product lines. During the 1960s, antiwar and Civil Rights protesters began their events only when the news media were assembled. One anecdote from that era aptly illustrates the principle of a pseudo-event: A reporter asked a student leader about the starting time for a particular protest; the student responded, "When can you get here?" Today, politicians running for national office have become particularly adept at scheduling press conferences and interviews around 5:00 or 6:00 P.M. They realize that local TV news is live during these times, so they stage pseudo-events to take advantage of TV's appetite for live remote feeds and breaking news.

Community and Consumer Relations

Another responsibility of PR is to sustain goodwill between its clients and the public. The public is often seen as two distinct audiences: communities and consumers.

Companies have learned that sustaining close ties with their communities and neighbors not only enhances their image and attracts potential customers, but also promotes the idea that the companies are good citizens. As a result, PR firms encourage companies to participate in community activities such as hosting plant tours and open houses, making donations to national and local charities, and participating in town events like parades and festivals. In addition, more progressive companies may also get involved in unemployment and job-retraining programs, or donate equipment and workers to urban revitalization projects such as Habitat for Humanity.

In terms of consumer relations, PR has become much more sophisticated since 1965, when Ralph Nader's groundbreaking book, *Unsafe at Any Speed*, revealed safety problems concerning the Chevrolet Corvair. Not only did Nader's book prompt the discontinuance of the Corvair line, it also lit the fuse that ignited a vibrant consumer movement. After the success of Nader's book, along with a growing public concern over corporate mergers and their lack of accountability to the public, consumers became less willing to readily accept the claims of corporations. As a result of the consumer movement, many newspapers and TV stations hired consumer reporters to track down the sources of customer complaints and embarrass companies by putting them in the media spotlight. Public relations specialists responded by encouraging companies to pay more attention to customers, establish product service and safety guarantees, and ensure that all calls and mail from customers were answered promptly. Today, PR professionals routinely advise clients that satisfied customers mean not only repeat business but also new business, based on a strong word-of-mouth reputation about a company's behavior and image.

Government Relations and Lobbying

While sustaining good relations with the public is a priority, so is maintaining connections with government agencies that have some say in how companies operate in a particular community, state, or nation. Both PR firms and the PR divisions within major corporations are especially interested in making sure that government regulation neither becomes burdensome nor reduces their control over their businesses.

Government PR specialists monitor new and existing legislation, create opportunities to ensure favorable publicity, and write press releases and direct-mail letters to persuade the public about the pros and cons of new regulations. In many industries, government relations has developed into **lobbying**: the process of attempting to influence lawmakers to support and vote for an organization or industry's best interests. In seeking favorable legislation, some lobbyists contact government officials on a daily basis. In Washington, D.C., alone, there are more than thirty-four thousand registered lobbyists—up from only eleven thousand lobbyists in 1995.[11] That translates to at least sixty-three lobbyists for each member of Congress.

Lobbying can often lead to ethical problems, as in the case of earmarks and astroturf lobbying. *Earmarks* are specific spending directives that are slipped into bills to accommodate the interests of lobbyists and are often the result of political favors or outright bribes. In 2006, lobbyist Jack Abramoff (dubbed "The Man Who Bought Washington" in *Time*) and several of his associates were convicted of corruption related to earmarks, leading to the resignation of leading House members. (Earmarks jumped from 1,000 in 1995 to 15,832 in 2006.)

Astroturf lobbying is phony grassroots public-affairs campaigns engineered by public relations firms. PR firms deploy massive phone banks and computerized mailing lists to drum up support and create the impression that millions of citizens back their client's side of an issue. For instance, the Center for Consumer Freedom (CCF), an organization that appears to serve the interests of consumers, is actually a creation of the Washington, D.C.-based PR firm Berman & Co. and is funded by the restaurant, food, alcohol, and tobacco industries. According to Sourcewatch.org, which tracks astroturf lobbying, "Anyone who criticizes tobacco, alcohol, fatty foods or soda pop is likely to come under attack from CCF."

PUBLIC RELATIONS FOR NONPROFITS
The nonprofit Rainforest Action Network uses public relations campaigns to "align the policies of multinational corporations with widespread public support for environmental protection." The group has worked to protect millions of acres of forests in Chile, Brazil, Indonesia, and Canada and has convinced companies like Home Depot, Citigroup, Boise Cascade, and Goldman Sachs to change their practices.

"I get in a lot of trouble if I'm quoted, especially if the quotes are accurate."

A CONGRESSIONAL STAFF PERSON, EXPLAINING TO THE *WALL STREET JOURNAL* WHY HE CAN SPEAK ONLY "OFF THE RECORD," 1999

Improving the Credibility Gap

In the 1990s, a growing tide of Americans focused on the problems of outsourcing: using the production, manufacturing, and labor resources of foreign companies to produce American brand-name products, sometimes under deplorable working conditions. Outsourcing was pushed into the public eye in 1996 after major media attention focused on morning talk show host Kathie Lee Gifford when investigations by the National Labor Committee revealed that part of her clothing line, made and distributed by Wal-Mart, came from sweatshops in New York and Honduras. The sweatshops paid less than minimum wage, and some employed child laborers. Human-rights activists claimed that in overseas sweatshops in particular, children were being exploited in violation of international child-labor laws.

Although some companies like Levi Strauss have distinguished themselves by pioneering public relations programs to guard against sweatshop practices, many leading clothing labels and retailers continue to ignore pressure from consumer and labor groups; these companies still tolerate sweat-

shop conditions in which workers take home minimal pay, sometimes less than a dollar an hour for working ten- to twelve-hour shifts six days a week.

Gap Inc.—one of the world's largest clothing retailers with more than 3,100 Gap, Banana Republic, Old Navy, and Forth & Towne stores (and an online shoe store)—made a huge statement in the industry by publicizing its efforts to watch over labor conditions at its overseas factories, an enormous policy shift from the company's past defensiveness against allegations of worker exploitation. Gap issued its first Social Responsibility Report in 2004—the first time any company has ever publicly detailed the production and labor information of the factories with which it contracts.

In explaining the genesis of the Social Responsibility Report, Paul Pressler, then-president and CEO of Gap, noted "When I decided to join Gap Inc. in the fall of 2002, one of the first things my teenage daughter asked was 'Doesn't Gap use sweatshops?' I was able to tell her how the company was working to fight sweatshop practices and improve garment factory conditions around the world. Her question didn't surprise me, though. Our company hasn't done enough to tell people about our efforts."[1]

The report is Gap's effort at improved transparency and better communication with its employees, shareholders, and those concerned about garment industry operations. The company now employs a team of more than ninety people to inspect and improve working conditions in its approximately three thousand contracted garment factories in fifty countries, and continues to issue progress reports. In most cases, Gap is able to improve labor conditions, but it also cancels contracts when needed. Gap terminated seventy factory contracts in 2004 and another sixty-two in 2005. Typical violations include lack of compliance with child-labor laws, pay below minimum wage, work weeks in excess of sixty hours, psychological coercion and verbal abuse, locked or inaccessible exits, and lack of access to potable water.

Gap's social responsibility efforts also involve co-sponsorship of the global (PRODUCT) RED campaign, founded in part by rock singer Bono to raise awareness and money for HIV/AIDS in Africa. Gap's role includes spending millions in advertising dollars to sell (PRODUCT) RED clothing to support HIV/AIDS relief and helping to develop a sustainable garment industry in Lesotho. The campaign also included other consumer product manufacturers, such as Converse, Giorgio Armani, American Express, Motorola, and Apple. Social responsibility has sprung up in entire new clothing lines as well. Edun, for example, is a collection established by Bono; his wife, Ali Hewson; and designer Rogan Gregory to create fair, sustainable micro-industries in developing countries, particularly in Africa. As Hewson says, "People are reading the labels on their clothes. They're asking themselves if they want to wear something that was made out of someone else's despair."[2]

Public relations firms do not always work for the interests of corporations, however. They also work for other clients, including consumer groups, labor unions, professional groups, religious organizations, and even foreign governments. In 2005, for example, the California Center for Public Health Advocacy, a nonpartisan, nonprofit organization, hired Brown-Miller Communications, a small California PR firm, to rally support for landmark legislation that would ban junk food and soda sales in the state's public schools. Brown-Miller helped state legislators see obesity not as a personal choice issue but as a public policy issue, cultivated the editorial support of newspapers to compel legislators to sponsor the bills, and ultimately succeeded in getting the bill passed.

U.S. public relations firms even lobby on behalf of foreign governments. After the September 11, 2001, terrorist attacks on the United States, the Saudi Arabian government hired the PR firm Qorvis Communications to help repair its image with American citizens.[12] The administration of George W. Bush also engaged in extensive and sophisticated PR practices with its establishment of the White House Office of Global Communications (OGC). The bureau was created to repackage the image of U.S. Middle East policies and actions at home and abroad. The government also funded multimillion-dollar PR campaigns in Iraq. One government contractor, the Lincoln Group of Washington, D.C., was investigated by the Pentagon in 2006 for secretly paying Iraqi newspapers to publish stories written by the U.S. military.[13]

Public Relations during a Crisis

Since the Ludlow strike, one important duty of PR is helping a corporation handle a public crisis or tragedy, especially if the public assumes the company is at fault. Disaster management may reveal the best and the worst attributes of the company and its PR firm. Let's look at two significant examples of crisis management and the different ways they were handled.

One of the largest environmental disasters of the twentieth century occurred when, in 1989, the *Exxon Valdez* spilled eleven million gallons of crude oil into Prince William Sound, contaminating fifteen hundred miles of Alaskan coastline and killing countless birds, otters, seals, and fish. In one of the biggest PR blunders of that century, Exxon was slow to react to the crisis and even slower to accept responsibility. Although its PR advisers had encouraged a quick response, the corporation failed to send any of its chief officers immediately to the site. Many critics believed that Exxon was trying to duck responsibility by laying the burden of the crisis on the shoulders of the tanker's captain. Despite changing the name of the tanker to *Mediterranean* and other image-salvaging strategies, the company's outlay of $2 billion to clean up both its image and the spill was not a success. As a former president of NBC News, William Small, said: "[Exxon] lost the battle of public relations" and suffered "one of the worst tarnishings of its corporate image in American history."[14]

A decidedly different approach was taken in the 1982 tragedy involving Tylenol pain-relief capsules. Seven people died in the Chicago area after someone tampered with several bottles and laced them with poison. Discussions between the parent company, Johnson & Johnson, and its PR representatives focused on whether or not withdrawing all Tylenol capsules from store shelves might send a signal that corporations could be intimidated by a single deranged person. Nevertheless, Johnson & Johnson's chairman, James E. Burke, and the company's PR agency, Burson-Marsteller, opted for full disclosure to the media and the immediate recall of the capsules nationally, costing the company an estimated $100 million and cutting its market share in half. As part of its PR strategy to overcome the negative publicity and to restore Tylenol's market share, Burson-Marsteller tracked public opinion nightly through telephone surveys and organized satellite press conferences to debrief the news media. In addition, emergency phone lines were set up to take calls from consumers and health-care providers. When the company reintroduced Tylenol three months later, it did so with tamper-resistant

"We're proud of the work we do for Saudi Arabia. It's a very challenging assignment."

MIKE PETRUZZELLO, QORVIS COMMUNICATIONS

"Managing the outrage is more important than managing the hazard."

THOMAS BUCKMASTER, HILL & KNOWLTON, 1997

"The *Exxon Valdez* Story: How to Spend a Billion or Two and Still Get a Black Eye in Public."

BUSINESS SCHOOL CONFERENCE TITLE, FORDHAM UNIVERSITY, 1990

bottles that were soon copied by almost every major drug manufacturer. Burson-Marsteller, which received PRSA awards for its handling of the crisis, found that the public thought Johnson & Johnson had responded admirably to the crisis and did not hold Tylenol responsible for the deaths. In fewer than three years, Tylenol recaptured its former (and dominant) share of the market.

Tensions between Public Relations and the Press

In 1932, Stanley Walker, an editor at the *New York Herald Tribune*, identified public relations agents as "mass-mind molders, fronts, mouthpieces, chiselers, moochers, and special assistants to the president."[15] Walker added that newspapers and PR firms would always remain enemies, even if PR professionals adopted a code of ethics (which they did in the 1950s) to "take them out of the red-light district of human relations."[16] Walker's tone captures the spirit of one of the most mutually dependent—and antagonistic—relationships in all of mass media.

Much of this antagonism, directed at public relations from the journalism profession, is historical. Journalists have long considered themselves part of a public service profession, but some regard PR as having emerged as a pseudo-profession created to distort the facts that reporters work hard to gather. Over time, reporters and editors developed the derogatory term **flack** to refer to a PR agent. The term, derived from the military word *flak*, meaning an antiaircraft artillery shell or a protective military jacket, symbolizes for journalists the protective barrier PR agents insert between their clients and the press. Today, the Associated Press manual for editors defines flack simply as "slang for press agent." Yet this antagonism belies journalism's dependence on public relations. Many editors, for instance, admit that more than half of their story ideas each day originate with PR people. In this section, we take a closer look at the relationship between journalism and public relations, which can be both adversarial and symbiotic.

"PR expands the public discourse, helps provide a wide assortment of news, and is essential in explaining the pluralism of our total communication system."

JOHN C. MERRILL,
MEDIA DEBATES, 1991

Elements of Professional Friction

The relationship between journalism and PR is important and complex. Although journalism lays claim to independent traditions, the news media have become ever more reliant on public relations because of the increasing amount of information now available. Newspaper staff cutbacks, combined with television's need for local news events, have expanded the news media's need for PR story ideas.

Another cause of tension is that PR firms often raid the ranks of reporting for new talent. Because most press releases are written to imitate news reports, the PR profession has always sought good writers who are well connected to sources and savvy about the news business. For instance, the fashion industry likes to hire former style or fashion news writers for its PR staff, and university information offices seek reporters who once covered higher education. However, although reporters frequently move into PR, public relations practitioners seldom move into journalism; the news profession rarely accepts prodigal sons or daughters back into the fold once they have left reporting for public relations. Nevertheless, the professions remain co-dependent: PR needs journalists for publicity, and journalism needs PR for story ideas and access.

Public relations, by making reporters' jobs easier, has often enabled reporters to become lazy. PR firms now supply what reporters used to gather for themselves. Instead of trying to get a scoop, many journalists have become content to wait for a PR handout or a good tip before following up on a story. Some members of the news media, grateful for the reduced workload that occurs when they are provided with handouts, may be hesitant to criticize a particular PR firm's clients. Several issues shed light on this discord and on the ways in which different media professions interact.

Undermining Facts and Blocking Access

Journalism's most prevalent criticism of public relations is that it works to counter the truths reporters seek to bring to the public. Modern public relations redefined and complicated the notion of what "facts" are. PR professionals demonstrated that the facts can be spun in a variety of ways, depending on what information is emphasized and what is downplayed. As Ivy Lee noted in 1925: "The effort to state an absolute fact is simply an attempt to achieve what is humanly impossible; all I can do is to give you my interpretation of the facts."[17] With practitioners like Lee showing the emerging PR profession how the truth could be interpreted, the journalist's role as a custodian of accurate information became much more difficult.

Journalists have also objected that PR professionals block press access to key business leaders, political figures, and other newsworthy people. Before the prevalence of PR, reporters could talk to such leaders directly and obtain quotable information for their news stories. Now, however, journalists complain that PR agents insert themselves between the press and the newsworthy, thus disrupting the journalistic tradition in which reporters would vie for interviews with top government and business leaders. Journalists further argue that PR agents are now able to manipulate reporters by giving exclusives to journalists who are likely to cast a story in a favorable light or by cutting off a reporter's access to a newsworthy figure altogether if that reporter has written unfavorably about the PR agency's client in the past.

Promoting Publicity and Business as News

Another explanation for the professional friction between the press and PR involves simple economics. PR agents help companies "promote as news what otherwise would have been purchased in advertising."[18] As Ivy Lee wrote to John D. Rockefeller after he gave money to Johns Hopkins University: "In view of the fact that this was not really news, and that the newspapers

"The reason companies or governments hire oodles of PR people is because PR people are trained to be slickly untruthful or half-truthful. Misinformation and disinformation are the coin of the realm, and it has nothing to do with being a Democrat or a Republican."

RICHARD COHEN, LEGAL ANALYST, CBS NEWS, 2008

"Cohen's . . . misguided comments are indicative of the way the public still feels about the PR profession. From Enron to the Iraq war, the public has been deceived, and, for whatever insensible reason, blame the conduits rather than the decision makers."

PRWEEK, 2008

gave so much attention to it, it would seem that this was wholly due to the manner in which the material was 'dressed up' for newspaper consumption. It seems to suggest very considerable possibilities along this line."[19] News critics worry that this type of PR is taking media space and time away from those who do not have the financial resources or the sophistication to become visible in the public eye. There is another issue: If public relations can secure news publicity for clients, the added credibility of a journalistic context gives clients a status that the purchase of advertising cannot offer.

Another criticism is that PR firms with abundant resources clearly get more client coverage from the news media than their lesser-known counterparts. For example, a business reporter at a large metro daily sometimes receives as many as a hundred press releases a day—far outnumbering the fraction of handouts generated by organized labor or grassroots organizations. Workers and union leaders have long argued that the money that corporations allocate to PR leads to more favorable coverage for management positions in labor disputes. Therefore, standard news reports may feature subtle language choices, with "rational, cool-headed management making offers" and "hot-headed workers making demands." Walter Lippmann saw such differences in 1922 when he wrote: "If you study the way many a strike is reported in the press, you will find very often that [labor] issues are rarely in the headlines, barely in the leading paragraph, and sometimes not even mentioned anywhere."[20] This imbalance is particularly significant in that the great majority of workers are neither managers nor CEOs, and yet these workers receive little if any media coverage on a regular basis. Most newspapers now have business sections that focus on the work of various managers, but few have a labor, worker, or employee section.[21]

Shaping the Image of Public Relations

Dealing with both a tainted past and journalism's hostility has often preoccupied the public relations profession, leading to the development of several image enhancing strategies. In 1948,

TABLE 12.1

PUBLIC RELATIONS SOCIETY OF AMERICA ETHICS CODE

In 2000, the PRSA approved a completely revised Code of Ethics, which included core principles, guidelines, and examples of improper conduct. Here is one section of the code.

Source: The full text of the PRSA Code of Ethics is available at http://www.prsa.org.

PRSA Member Statement of Professional Values
This statement presents the core values of PRSA members and, more broadly, of the public relations profession. These values provide the foundation for the Member Code of Ethics and set the industry standard for the professional practice of public relations. These values are the fundamental beliefs that guide our behaviors and decision making process. We believe our professional values are vital to the integrity of the profession as a whole.
ADVOCACY We serve the public interest by acting as responsible advocates for those we represent. We provide a voice in the marketplace of ideas, facts, and viewpoints to aid informed public debate.
HONESTY We adhere to the highest standards of accuracy and truth in advancing the interests of those we represent and in communicating with the public.
EXPERTISE We acquire and responsibly use specialized knowledge and experience. We advance the profession through continued professional development, research, and education. We build mutual understanding, credibility, and relationships among a wide array of institutions and audiences.
INDEPENDENCE We provide objective counsel to those we represent. We are accountable for our actions.
LOYALTY We are faithful to those we represent, while honoring our obligation to serve the public interest.
FAIRNESS We deal fairly with clients, employers, competitors, peers, vendors, the media and the general public. We respect all opinions and support the right of free expression.

the PR industry formed its own professional organization, the PRSA (Public Relations Society of America). The PRSA functions as an internal watchdog group that accredits PR agents and firms, maintains a code of ethics, and probes its own practices, especially those pertaining to its influence on the news media. Most PRSA local chapters and national conventions also routinely invite reporters and editors to speak to PR practitioners about the news media's expectations of PR. In addition to the PRSA, independent agencies devoted to uncovering shady or unethical public relations activities publish their findings in publications like *Public Relations Tactics*, *PR Week*, and *PR Watch*. Ethical issues have become a major focus of the PR profession, with self-examination of these issues routinely appearing in PR textbooks as well as in various professional newsletters (see Table 12.1).

Over the years, as PR has subdivided itself into specialized areas, it has used more positive phrases, such as *institutional relations*, *corporate communications*, and *news and information services* to describe what it does. Public relations' best press strategy, however, may be the limitations of the journalism profession itself. For most of the twentieth century, many reporters and editors clung to the ideal that journalism is, at its best, an objective institution that gathers information on behalf of the public. Reporters have only occasionally turned their pens, computers, and cameras on themselves to examine their own practices or their vulnerability to manipulation. Thus, by not challenging PR's more subtle strategies, many journalists have allowed PR professionals to interpret "facts" to their clients' advantage.

Alternative Voices

Because public relations professionals work so closely with the press, their practices are not often the subject of media reports or investigations. Indeed, the multibillion-dollar industry remains virtually invisible to the public, most of whom have never heard of Burson-Marsteller, Hill & Knowlton, or Ketchum. John Stauber and Sheldon Rampton, investigative reporters who work for the Center for Media and Democracy in Washington, D.C., are concerned about the invisibility of PR practices and have sought to expose the hidden activities of large PR firms. As editors of *PR Watch*, a quarterly publication they launched in 1995, they publish investigative reports on the PR industry that never appear in mainstream mass media outlets. "*PR Watch* seeks to serve the public rather than PR," they explain. "With the assistance of whistleblowers and a few sympathetic insiders, we report about

THE INVISIBILITY OF PUBLIC RELATIONS is addressed in a series of books by John Stauber and Sheldon Rampton.

the secretive activities of an industry which works behind the scenes to control government policy and shape public opinion."[22] (See "Media Literacy and the Critical Process: The Invisible Hand of PR" on the opposite page.)

Stauber and Rampton have also written books targeting public relations practices having to do with the Republican Party's lobbying establishment (*Banana Republicans*), U.S. propaganda on the Iraq War (*The Best War Ever*), industrial waste (*Toxic Sludge Is Good for You*), mad cow disease (*Mad Cow USA*), and PR uses of scientific research (*Trust Us, We're Experts!*). Their work helps bring an alternative angle to the well-moneyed battles over public opinion. "You know, we feel that in a democracy, it's very, very critical that everyone knows who the players are, and what they're up to," Stauber says.[23]

Public Relations and Democracy

From the days of PR's origins in the early 1900s, many people—especially journalists—have been skeptical of communications originating from public relations professionals. The bulk of the criticism leveled at public relations argues that the crush of information produced by PR professionals overwhelms traditional journalism. However, PR's most significant impact may be on the political process, especially when organizations hire spin doctors to favorably shape or reshape a candidate's media image. In one example, former president Richard Nixon, who resigned from office in 1974 to avoid impeachment hearings regarding his role in the Watergate scandal, hired Hill & Knowlton to restore his post-presidency image. Through the firm's guidance, Nixon's writings, mostly on international politics, began appearing in Sunday op-ed pages. Nixon himself started showing up on television news programs like *Nightline* and spoke frequently before such groups as the American Newspaper Publishers Association and the Economic Club of New York. In 1984, after a media blitz by Nixon's PR handlers, the *New York Times* announced: "After a decade, Nixon is gaining favor," and *USA Today* trumpeted: "Richard Nixon is back." Before his death in 1994, Nixon, who never publicly apologized for his role in Watergate, saw a large portion of his public image shift from that of an arrogant, disgraced politician to that of a revered elder statesman.[24] Many media critics have charged that the press did not counterbalance this PR campaign and treated Nixon too reverently.

In terms of its immediate impact on democracy, the information crush delivered by public relations is at its height during national election campaigns. In 2008, some of the behind-the-scenes work of PR in presidential campaigns was revealed. First, Mark Penn, the chief strategist of Hillary Clinton's campaign to be the Democratic nominee, became a news story himself when he resigned from her campaign over a conflict of interest. Penn worked for Clinton while he maintained his position as chief executive of Burson-Marsteller, where he lobbied on behalf of Colombia for a trade treaty opposed by Clinton. Second, Scott McClellan, President George W. Bush's press secretary from 2003 to 2006, disclosed in his 2008 book that the White House had a "carefully orchestrated campaign to shape and manipulate sources of public approval" and decided to "turn away from honesty and candor" in the lead-up to and during the Iraq War.[25] Both instances illustrate the centrality of public relations—and the temptation of stepping over ethical boundaries—in shaping politicians.

Media Literacy and the Critical Process

The Invisible Hand of PR

John Stauber, of the industry watchdog *PR Watch*, has described the PR industry as "a huge, invisible industry . . . that's really only available to wealthy individuals, large multinational corporations, politicians and government agencies."[1] How true is this? Is the PR industry so invisible?

1 DESCRIPTION. Test the so-called invisibility of the PR industry by seeing how often, and in what way, PR firms are discussed in the print media. Using LexisNexis, search U.S. newspapers–over the last six months–for any mention of three prominent PR firms: Weber Shandwick, Fleishman-Hillard, and Burson-Marsteller.

2 ANALYSIS. What patterns emerge from the search? Possible patterns may have to do with personnel: someone was hired or fired. (These articles may be extremely brief, with only a quick mention of the firms.) Or these personnel-related articles may reveal connections between politicians or corporations and the PR industry. What about specific PR campaigns or articles that quote "experts" who work for Weber Shandwick, Fleishman-Hillard, or Burson-Marsteller?

3 INTERPRETATION. What do these patterns tell you about how the PR industry is covered by the news media? Was the coverage favorable? Was it critical or analytical? Did you learn anything about how the industry operates? Is the industry itself, its influencing strategies, and its wide reach across the globe visible in your search?

4 EVALUATION. PR firms–such as the three major firms in this search–have enormous power when it comes to influencing the public image of corporations, government bodies, and public policy initiatives in the United States and abroad. PR firms also have enormous influence over news content. Yet the U.S. media are silent on this influence. Public relations firms aren't likely to reveal their power, but should journalism be more forthcoming about its role as a publicity vehicle for PR?

5 ENGAGEMENT. Visit the Center for Media and Democracy's Web site (prwatch.org) and begin to learn about the unseen operations of the public relations industry. Sign up for the organization's free weekly e-newsletter, the *Weekly Spin*. Read some of the organization's books, join forum discussions, or attend a *PR Watch* event. Visit the organization's wiki site, Source Watch (sourcewatch.org), and, if you can, do some research of your own on PR and contribute an entry.

Though public relations often provides political information and story ideas, the PR profession bears only part of the responsibility for "spun" news; after all, it is the job of a PR agency to get favorable news coverage for the individual or group it represents. PR professionals police their own ranks for unethical or irresponsible practices, but the news media should also monitor the public relations industry, as they do other government and business activities. Journalism itself also needs to institute changes that will make it less dependent on PR and more conscious of how its own practices play into the hands of spin strategies. A positive example of change on this front is that many major newspapers and news networks now offer regular critiques of the facts and falsehoods contained in political advertising. This media vigilance should be on behalf of citizens, who are entitled to robust, well-rounded debates on important social and political issues.

Like advertising and other forms of commercial speech, PR campaigns that result in free media exposure raise a number of questions regarding democracy and the expression of ideas. Large companies and PR agencies, like well-financed politicians, have money to invest to figure out how to obtain favorable publicity. The question is not how to prevent that but how to ensure that other voices, less well financed and less commercial, also receive an adequate hearing. To that end, journalists need to become less willing conduits in the distribution of publicity. PR agencies, for their part, need to show clients that participating in the democratic process as responsible citizens can serve them well and enhance their image. ▶

> **"In politics, image [has] replaced action."**
>
> RANDALL ROTHENBERG, *WHERE THE SUCKERS MOON*, 1994

CHAPTER REVIEW

REVIEW QUESTIONS

Early Developments in Public Relations

1. What did people like P. T. Barnum and Buffalo Bill Cody contribute to the development of modern public relations in the twentieth century?

2. How did railroads and utility companies give the early forms of corporate public relations a bad name?

3. What contributions did Ivy Lee make toward the development of modern PR?

4. How did Edward Bernays affect public relations?

The Practice of Public Relations

5. What are two approaches to organizing a PR firm?

6. What are press releases, and why are they important to reporters?

7. What is the difference between a VNR and a PSA?

8. What is a pseudo-event? How does it relate to the manufacturing of news?

9. What special events might a PR firm sponsor to build stronger ties to its community?

10. Why have research and lobbying become increasingly important to the practice of PR?

11. What are some socially responsible strategies that a PR specialist can use during a crisis to help a client manage unfavorable publicity?

Tensions between Public Relations and the Press

12. Explain the historical background of the antagonism between journalism and public relations.

13. How did PR change old relationships between journalists and their sources?

14. In what ways is conventional news like public relations?

15. How does journalism as a profession contribute to its own manipulation at the hands of competent PR practitioners?

Public Relations and Democracy

16. In what ways does the profession of public relations serve the process of election campaigns? In what ways can it impede election campaigns?

QUESTIONING THE MEDIA

1. What do you think of when you hear the term *public relations*? What images come to mind? Where did these impressions come from?

2. What might a college or university do to improve public relations with homeowners on the edge of a campus who have to deal with noisy student parties and a shortage of parking spaces?

3. What steps can reporters and editors take to monitor PR agents who manipulate the news media?

4. Can and should the often hostile relationship between the journalism and PR professions be mended? Why or why not?

5. Besides the *Exxon Valdez* and Tylenol cases cited in this chapter, investigate and research a PR crisis (such as the Bridgestone/Firestone–Ford Explorer tire problems, the spinach E. coli scare, the recall of laptop batteries, or any number of campaigns described by prwatch.org). How was the crisis handled?

For review quizzes, chapter summaries, links to media-related Web sites, and more, go to bedfordstmartins.com/mediaculture.

COMMON THREADS

One of the Common Threads in Chapter 1 is about the need for critical analysis of the mass media. One key ethical contradiction that can emerge in PR is that (according to the PRSA Code of Ethics) PR should be honest and accurate in disclosing information while at the same time being loyal and faithful to clients and their requests for confidentiality and privacy. In this case, how does the general public know when public communications are the work of paid advocacy?

The goal of most public relations campaigns is to have communication gently seep into the mass media, causing a desired shift in attitudes and behaviors. But for media consumers who want to be media literate, we must understand and analyze the role of public relations in everyday life.

This is not easy. As noted in the "Media Literacy" exercise in this chapter, PR tends to operate with an invisible hand. There are hundreds of PR firms working for thousands of clients. Yet their public communication messages rarely reveal their PR origins, and sometimes they don't even make clear who the beneficiary (the paying client) is.

The key may be, as the anonymous source in *All the President's Men* famously said, to "follow the money." As a media literacy student, you can do this through the critical process. First, describe a potential PR communication, which could come via the news or entertainment media, social networking sites, or public policy discussions. Second, analyze patterns in communication and connect them with the originators of the ideas. Public records like lobbying reports, annual reports, organizational Web sites, and watchdog Web sites may also yield clues. Third, interpret the messages. Advocacy communication with transparent origins is likely to be more reliable than that which cannot be identified. Fourth, based on the transparency of the communication and additional fact-checking against other sources, determine the truthfulness of the information.

Fifth, share your findings with the public. Engage with your community by publicly supporting honest and accurate advocacy information and disclosing the facts behind advocacy communications that fall short of those ideals. None of this is easy work. But, through critical analysis, it is possible to have a positive impact on public debates influenced by public relations.

KEY TERMS

The definitions for the terms listed below can be found in the glossary at the end of the book. The page numbers listed with the terms indicate where the term is highlighted in the chapter.

public relations, 381
press agents, 381
publicity, 383
propaganda, 389
press releases, 390
video news releases (VNRs), 390

public service announcements (PSAs), 390
pseudo-events, 394
lobbying, 395
astroturf lobbying, 395
flack, 398

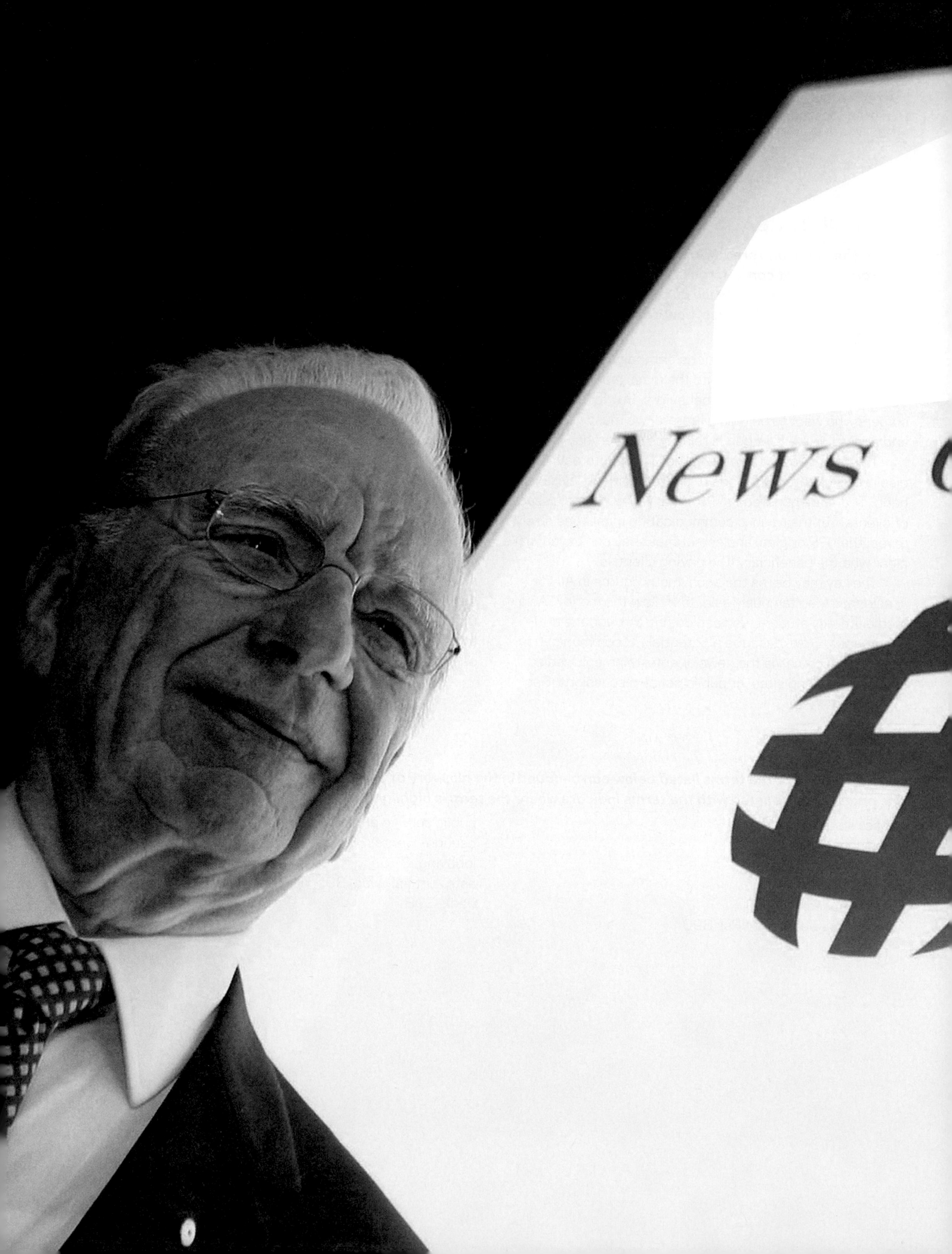
News

13

Media Economics and the Global Marketplace

Throughout the book, we discuss the influence of major media conglomerates and the consolidation of media industries. One company, News Corp.—and the powerful Australian family behind it, the Murdochs—has become a major player in this changing world of global media. What started in 1952, when Rupert Murdoch inherited two Australian newspapers from his father, had grown to become the world's third largest media empire, after Time Warner and Disney, by 2008. In the 1970s, Murdoch first entered the U.S. market by buying the *San Antonio Express-News* and the *New York Post* and founding the *Star*, a supermarket gossip tabloid. After purchasing the London *Times* in 1981, he made another big move in the mid-1980s by buying the Twentieth Century Fox film studio and several U.S. TV stations. He then launched the Fox network—the first successful TV network start-up since 1948. He even bought *TV Guide* magazine to promote his new network, which helped programs like *The Simpsons* and *The X-Files* find big audiences in the 1990s. Today popular programs like *American Idol* and *House* have

helped make Fox the most-watched TV network in 2007–08, ahead of CBS, NBC, and ABC. Starting in the mid-1990s, News Corp. also launched several cable channels, including Fox News, FX, and Fox Business Channel.

Now, News Corp. is working to change the way TV shows reach audiences. In 2008, MySpaceTV partnered with British-based ShineReveille International, a global TV program and DVD distributor, to turn the popular Internet site—with more than 110 million members—into a major player and "content laboratory" for premiering TV programs. (Elizabeth Murdoch, a daughter of Rupert Murdoch, is the chief executive of Shine Group, which owns ShineReveille.) Purchased in 2005 by News Corp. for $580 million, MySpace—in addition to social networking, signing bands, and distributing new music—has been running experimental TV programs such as *Quarterlife*, *Roommates*, and *Special Delivery*. NBC tried to move *Quarterlife* to the traditional network in February 2008, but the program drew only three million viewers and was shipped back to cyberspace, where it routinely draws five to six million views. However, the extended writers' strike in 2007–08 encouraged big entertainment companies like News Corp. "to reconsider the time-honored tradition of paying for expensive pilots only to reject many of them."[1]

Another recent News Corp. acquisition was stock market giant Dow Jones and its flagship financial newspaper the *Wall Street Journal*, for $5.6 billion in 2006. Media industry observers think that Murdoch's plan is to use the *Journal* to create an international news rival to the *New York Times*, often considered the world's best general-interest newspaper. After first promising to keep the *Journal*'s top editor, Marcus Brauchli, Murdoch in 2008 replaced him with Robert Thomson, another Australian native, who had spent five years as the top editor for Murdoch's London *Times*. Thomson fired an early shot at the *New York Times*, calling it "skewed" and announcing that the *Times* "fetishes prizes" and "believes that length of a story is a measure of its worth."[2]

With their sights set on becoming the world's top media empire, Murdoch and News Corp. have advanced a business strategy that aims to make its content a centerpiece in American popular culture—especially its movies, music, and TV programs. But at the same time, News Corp. pays attention to how these media will be distributed globally, purchasing new media upstarts like MySpace and old media stalwarts like the *Wall Street Journal*, which also had one of the more successful paid Internet subscription services—and under Murdoch's ownership was one of the few U.S. newspapers to gain in circulation in 2007 and 2008.

◢ THE MEDIA TAKEOVERS, MULTIPLE MERGERS, AND CORPORATE CONSOLIDATION over the last two decades have made our modern world very distinct from that of earlier generations—at least in economic terms. What's at the heart of this "Brave New Media World" is not just the emergence of a handful of media giants—from News Corp. to Google—but a media landscape that has been forever altered by the emergence of the Internet. As News Corp. and MySpace demonstrate, the Internet is shifting the terrain; by threatening the classified ads of newspapers and altering distribution for music, movies, and TV programs, the Internet has forced almost all media businesses to rethink not only the content they provide but the entire economic structure under which our capitalist media system operates.

In this chapter, we explore the issues and tensions that have contributed to the current economic conditions. We look at the rise of the Information Age, distinguished by flexible, specialized, and global markets. We discuss the breakdown of economic borders, focusing on media consolidation, corporate mergers, synergy, deregulation, and the emergence of an economic global village. We also take up ethical and social issues in media economics, investigating the limits of antitrust laws, the concept of consumer control, and the threat of cultural imperialism. Finally, after examining the role of journalism in monitoring media economics, we consider the impact of media consolidation on democracy and on the diversity of the marketplace.

Analyzing the Media Economy

Given the sprawling scope of the mass media, the study of their economic conditions poses a number of complicated questions. For example, does the government need to play a stronger role in determining who owns the mass media and what kinds of media products are manufactured? Or should the government step back and let competition and market forces dictate what happens to mass media industries? Should citizen groups play a larger part in demanding that media organizations help maintain the quality of social and cultural life? Does the influence of American popular culture worldwide smother or encourage the growth of democracy and local cultures? Does the increasing concentration of economic power in the hands of several international corporations too severely restrict the number of players and voices in the media?

Answers to such questions span the economic and social spectrums. On the one hand, critics express concerns about the increasing power and reach of large media conglomerates. On the other hand, many free-market advocates maintain that as long as these structures ensure efficient operation and generous profits, they measure up as quality media organizations. In order to probe these issues fully, we need to understand key economic concepts across two broad areas: media structure and media performance.[3]

The Structure of the Media Industry

In most media industries, three common structures characterize the economics of the business: monopoly, oligopoly, and limited competition.

A **monopoly** occurs when a single firm dominates production and distribution in a particular industry, either nationally or locally. For example, at the national level, AT&T ran a rare government-approved and -regulated monopoly—the telephone business—for more than a hundred years until its breakup in the mid-1980s. In a suit brought by the Justice Department and twenty states, software giant Microsoft was accused of monopolistic practices for controlling more than

MEDIA CONGLOMERATES
Richard Parsons, Time Warner chairman of the board and CEO from 2002 to 2007, with Bugs Bunny, part of Time Warner's lucrative Looney Tunes franchise.

80 percent of computer operating systems worldwide and was ordered to split into two separate companies. Microsoft, however, appealed, and in 2002 agreed to a court settlement that imposed restrictions only on its business dealings with personal computer makers but left the company intact.

On the local level, monopoly situations have been more plentiful, occurring in any city that has only one newspaper or one cable company. While the federal government has encouraged owner diversity since the 1970s by prohibiting a newspaper from operating a broadcast or cable company in the same city, many individual local media monopolies have been purchased by national and international firms. For instance, Time Warner owns hundreds of small cable monopolies and in 2008 began considering making its cable division a freestanding company, much the way that Viacom spun off CBS as a separate company (but CBS is still owned primarily by Viacom stockholders like Sumner Redstone). Likewise, in the newspaper business, chain operators like Gannett own hundreds of newspapers, most of which constitute a newspaper monopoly in their communities.

▼ Media Economics and the Global Marketplace

Clayton Antitrust Act
Congress strengthens antitrust law in 1914 by prohibiting companies from selling only to dealers who agree to reject rival products (p. 414).

Disney Founded in Hollywood
The future media conglomerate begins as a small animation studio in 1928 (p. 422).

| 1880 | 1900 | 1920 | 1930 |

Sherman Antitrust Act
Congress passes an act in 1890 that outlaws monopoly practices and corporate trusts that fix prices (p. 414).

Busting the Big Boys
In 1911, the federal government uses antimonopoly laws to break up both American Tobacco Co. and Rockefeller's Standard Oil Co. into smaller firms (p. 414).

In an **oligopoly,** just a few firms dominate an industry. For example, the book publishing and feature-film businesses are both oligopolies. Each has five or six major players that control the majority of the production and distribution in the industry. The production and distribution of the world's music is basically controlled by just four international corporations–Time Warner (U.S.), Sony/BMG (Japan/Germany), Universal-Vivendi (France), and EMI (Great Britain). Usually conducting business only in response to each other, such companies face little economic competition from small independent firms. Oligopolies often add new ideas and product lines by purchasing successful independent companies.

Sometimes called *monopolistic competition,* **limited competition** characterizes a media market with many producers and sellers but only a few products within a particular category.[4] For instance, hundreds of independently owned radio stations operate in the United States. Most of these commercial stations, however, feature a limited number of formats–such as country, classic rock, or contemporary hits. Because commercial broadcast radio is now a difficult market to enter–requiring an FCC license and major capital investment–most stations only play one of the few formats that attract sizable audiences. Under these circumstances, fans of blues, alternative country, or classical music may not be able to find a radio station that matches their interests. Given the high start-up costs of launching a commercial business in any media industry, companies offering alternative products are becoming rare in the twenty-first century.

The Performance of Media Organizations

In analyzing the behavior and performance of media companies, economists pay attention to a number of elements–from how media make money to how they set prices and live up to society's expectations. In addition, many corporations now adapt their practices to new Internet standards. For example, most large regional newspapers by 2008 had lost a high percentage of classified ad revenue to Internet companies and were adjusting to the slow shift of advertising dollars from newsprint to online.

> "Rapid consolidation, evidenced most recently by the breakup of the once-venerable Knight-Ridder newspapers, the sale of the Tribune Company and its media properties and the swallowing of the *Wall Street Journal* by Murdoch's News Corp. continues the steady replacement of civic and democratic values by commercial and entertainment priorities."
>
> ROBERT McCHESNEY AND JOHN NICHOLS, *THE NATION,* 2008

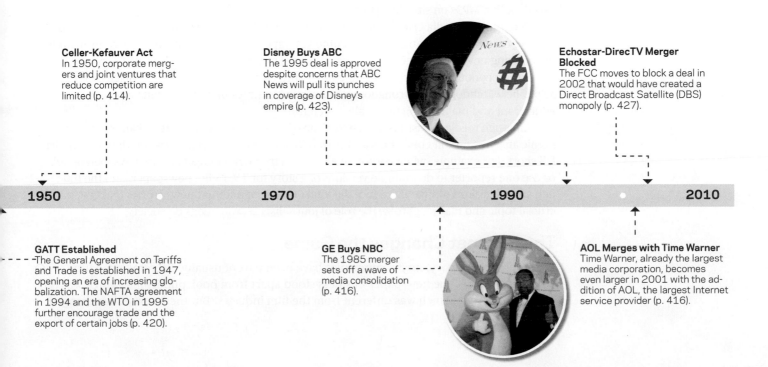

Celler-Kefauver Act
In 1950, corporate mergers and joint ventures that reduce competition are limited (p. 414).

Disney Buys ABC
The 1995 deal is approved despite concerns that ABC News will pull its punches in coverage of Disney's empire (p. 423).

Echostar-DirecTV Merger Blocked
The FCC moves to block a deal in 2002 that would have created a Direct Broadcast Satellite (DBS) monopoly (p. 427).

1950   **1970**   **1990**   **2010**

GATT Established
The General Agreement on Tariffs and Trade is established in 1947, opening an era of increasing globalization. The NAFTA agreement in 1994 and the WTO in 1995 further encourage trade and the export of certain jobs (p. 420).

GE Buys NBC
The 1985 merger sets off a wave of media consolidation (p. 416).

AOL Merges with Time Warner
Time Warner, already the largest media corporation, becomes even larger in 2001 with the addition of AOL, the largest Internet service provider (p. 416).

Collecting Revenue

The media collect revenues in two ways: through direct and indirect payments. **Direct payment** involves media products supported primarily by consumers, who pay directly for a book, a CD, a movie, or an Internet or cable TV service. **Indirect payment** involves media products supported primarily by advertisers, who pay for the quantity or quality of audience members that a particular medium delivers. Over-the-air radio and TV broadcasting, daily newspapers, consumer magazines, and most Web sites rely on indirect payments for the majority of their revenue.

Through direct payments, consumers communicate their preferences immediately. Through the indirect payments of advertising, "the client is the advertiser, not the viewer or listener or reader."[5] Advertisers, in turn, seek media channels that persuade customers to acquire new products or switch brand loyalties. Many forms of mass media, of course, generate revenue both directly and indirectly, including newspapers, magazines, online services, and cable systems, which charge subscription fees in addition to selling commercial time to advertisers.

Commercial Strategies and Social Expectations

When evaluating the media, economists also look at other elements of the commercial process, including program or product costs, price setting, marketing strategies, and regulatory practices. For instance, marketers and media economists determine how high a local newspaper can raise its weekly price before enough disgruntled readers drop their subscriptions and offset the profits made from the price increase. Or, as in 1996, critics and government agencies began reviewing the inflated price of CDs. They demonstrated that the **economies of scale** principle—the practice of increasing production levels to reduce the cost for each product—should have driven down the price of a CD in the same way that the price of videotapes dropped in the 1980s. Yet it wasn't until October 2003 that any of the major recording companies dropped their CD prices. At that time, Universal, trying to generate consumer demand in the face of illegal file-sharing of music, cut the recommended retail price of music CDs by a third—to $12.98 each (in 2008 the price dropped to an average $10 at discount retailers and on Amazon but a new CD from a popular artist still cost $14-$15; this does not include downloading MP3s on sites like iTunes).

Economists, media critics, and consumer organizations have also asked the mass media to meet certain performance criteria. Some key expectations of media organizations include introducing new technologies to the marketplace; making media products and services available to all economic classes; facilitating free expression and robust political discussion; acting as public watchdogs over wrongdoing; monitoring in times of crisis; playing a positive role in education; and maintaining the quality of culture.[6]

Although media industries live up to some of these expectations better than others, economic analyses permit consumers and citizens to examine the instances when the mass media fall short. For example, when corporate executives trim news budgets or fire news personnel, or use one reporter to do multiple versions of a story for TV, radio, newspaper, and the Internet, such decisions ultimately reduce the total number of different news stories that cover a crucial topic and may jeopardize the role of journalists as watchdogs on society.

The Internet Changes the Game

For much of its history, media companies have been part of usually discrete or separate industries—that is, the newspaper business stood apart from book publishing, which was different from radio, which was different from the film industry. But the Internet has changed that—not only by offering a portal to view or read older media forms—but also by requiring virtually all older media companies to establish an online presence. Today newspapers, magazines, book publishers, music companies, radio and TV stations, and film studios all have Web sites that offer online versions of their product or Web services that enhance their original media form. Interestingly, this allows new opportunities for ad revenue for non-commercial public broadcasters. Public radio and TV stations, which are prohibited by FCC regulations from taking advertising, face no such prohibitions online and are rethinking the methods they use for raising money by having advertisements on their Web sites.

However, the ease of putting up and locating information on the Internet can be problematic. Traditional broadcast and cable services have challenged Internet sites like Google's YouTube for displaying content that appears online without permission. In 2007, Viacom, owner of MTV and Comedy Central, sued Google and YouTube for $1 billion for the unauthorized posting of more than 150,000 video clips—including episodes of *Sponge-Bob SquarePants*, *South Park*, *The Daily Show*, and *MTV Unplugged*. For its part, Google said YouTube has lived up to the requirements of the 1998 Digital Millennium Copyright Act, noting that "the federal law was intended to protect companies like YouTube as long as they responded properly to content owners' claims of infringement."[7] In response, Viacom noted that Google/YouTube had done "little or nothing" to stop copyright infringement. Viacom's lawyers argued that copyright violations appeared to be central to the Google/YouTube business model: "the availability on the YouTube site of a vast library of the copyrighted works of plaintiffs and others is the cornerstone of defendants' business plan."[8] As the suit moved forward in 2008, the Internet's ability to disrupt old business models continued to present challenges for traditional media companies who are still uncertain whether this type of Internet exposure actually works as a form of promotion for their content, drawing new viewers and readers.

The Transition to an Information Economy

The first half of the twentieth century emphasized mass production, the rise of manufacturing plants, and the intense rivalry of U.S.-based businesses competing against products from other nations. By the 1990s, however, car parts for both Japanese- and American-based firms were being manufactured in plants all over the world. The transition to this new cooperative global economy actually began taking shape back in the 1950s—a period in which the machines that drove the Industrial Age changed gears for the new Information Age. With offices displacing factories as major work sites, centralized mass production declined and often gave way to internationalized, decentralized, and lower-paid service work.

The major shift to an information-based economy emphasized information distribution and retrieval as well as transnational economic cooperation. As part of this trend, in the 1950s various mass media industries began marketing music, movies, television programs, and computer software on a global level. The emphasis on mass production shifted to the cultivation of specialized niche markets. In the 1960s, serious national media consolidation began, escalating into the global media mergers that have continued since the 1980s.

"Had anyone in 1975 predicted that the two oldest and most famous corporate producers and marketers of American recorded music [the RCA and CBS labels] would end up in the hands of German printers and publishers [Bertelsmann] and Japanese physicists and electronic engineers [Sony], the reaction in the industry would have been astonishment."

BARNET AND CAVANAGH, *GLOBAL DREAMS*, 1994

ANTITRUST REGULATION
During the late 1800s, John D. Rockefeller, Sr., considered the richest businessman in the world, controlled more than 90 percent of the U.S. oil refining business. But antitrust regulations were used in 1911 to bust Rockefeller's powerful Standard Oil into more than thirty separate companies. He later hired PR guru Ivy Lee to refashion his negative image as a greedy corporate mogul.

Deregulation Trumps Regulation

During the rise of industry in the nineteenth century, entrepreneurs such as John D. Rockefeller in oil, Cornelius Vanderbilt in shipping and railroads, and Andrew Carnegie in steel created monopolies in their respective industries. In 1890, Congress passed the Sherman Antitrust Act, outlawing the monopoly practices and corporate trusts that often fixed prices to force competitors out of business. In 1911, the government used this act to break up both the American Tobacco Company and Rockefeller's Standard Oil Company, which was divided into thirty smaller competing firms.

In 1914, Congress passed the Clayton Antitrust Act, prohibiting manufacturers from selling only to dealers and contractors who agreed to reject the products of business rivals. The Celler-Kefauver Act of 1950 further strengthened antitrust rules by limiting any corporate mergers and joint ventures that reduced competition. Today, these laws are enforced by the Federal Trade Commission and the antitrust division of the Department of Justice.

The Escalation of Deregulation

Until the financial banking, credit, and mortgage crises erupted in fall 2008, government regulation had often been denounced as a barrier to the more flexible flow of capital. Although the administration of President Carter (1977-81) actually initiated deregulation, under President Reagan (1981-89) most controls on business were drastically weakened. Sometimes the deregulation and the decline in government oversight had severe consequences—such as the savings and loan industry scandal, which cost consumers billions—but until late 2008 many businesses flourished in this new pro-commerce climate. Deregulation also led to easier mergers, corporate diversification, and increased tendencies in some sectors (airlines, energy, communications, and financial services) toward oligopolies.[9]

In the broadcast industry, the Telecommunications Act of 1996 (under President Clinton) lifted most restrictions on how many radio and TV stations one corporation could own. The act further welcomed the seven powerful regional telephone companies, known as the Baby Bells, into the cable TV business. In addition, cable operators not only regained the right to raise cable rates with less oversight but also were authorized to compete in the local telephone business (although high costs kept cable out of the phone business at the time). Some economists thought the new competition would initially bring down consumer prices. But others predicted more mergers and an oligopoly owning *both* the telephone and the cable industries in which two or three mega-corporations would control most of the wires entering a home and dictate both phone and cable TV pricing.

By 2006, the main battle for this control featured phone companies (already permitted by the 1996 Telecommunications Act to buy cable companies) lobbying for permission to home-deliver video and television through phone lines along with their Internet and telephone services. In 2007 the U.S. Senate passed a bill that allowed telephone companies like AT&T to enter into the video market and compete with cable. Cable companies responded by claiming that they were the one competitor standing in the way of the reemergence of phone giants like AT&T. However, by 2008 cable companies had successfully entered the phone business, and giant cable firms like Time Warner and Comcast were offering consumers three-way "bundled" services–high-speed Internet, digital phone service, and cable.

Media Deregulation Marches On

Since the 1980s, a spirit of deregulation and special exemptions has guided communication legislation. For example, in 1995, despite complaints from NBC, Rupert Murdoch's Australian company News Corp. received a special dispensation from the FCC and Congress allowing the firm to continue owning and operating the Fox network and a number of local TV stations. The Murdoch decision ran counter to government decisions made after World War I. At that time, the government feared outside owners and thus limited foreign investment in U.S. broadcast operations to 20 percent. To make things easier, Murdoch became a U.S. citizen, and in 2004, News Corp. moved its headquarters to the United States, where the company was doing about 80 percent of its business.

FCC rules were further relaxed in late 2007, when the agency modified the newspaper-broadcast cross-ownership rule, allowing a company located in a Top 20 market to own one TV station and one newspaper as long as there were at least eight TV stations in the market. Previously, a company could not own a newspaper and a broadcast outlet–either a TV or radio station–in the same market (although if a media company had such cross-ownership prior to the early 1970s, the FCC usually granted waivers to let it stand). Murdoch had already been granted a permanent waiver from the FCC to own the *New York Post* and the New York TV station WNYW. So with the change, the FCC actually restructured the cross-ownership rule to accommodate News Corp. The U.S. Senate in 2008 did vote nearly unanimously on a resolution to oppose the new rule, but this battle was carried over into the Obama presidency since the Bush administration supported the relaxed rule and threatened to veto any opposing legislation. (Earlier in 2006, when News Corp. bought the New York-based *Wall Street Journal*, the FCC declared that the *Journal* was a national newspaper, not a local one that fell under the cross-ownership rule.)

Deregulation returned media economics to nineteenth-century principles, which suggested that markets can take care of themselves with little government interference. In this context, one of the ironies in broadcast history is that more than eighty years ago commercial radio broadcasters demanded government regulation to control technical interference and amateur competition. By the mid-1990s, however, the original impetus for regulation had reversed course. With new cable channels, DBS, and the Internet, broadcasting was no longer regarded as a scarce resource–once a major rationale for regulation as well as government funding of noncommercial and educational stations. Almost fourteen thousand commercial and educational radio stations and nearly eighteen hundred commercial and educational television stations now operate in the United States.

Media Powerhouses: Consolidation, Partnerships, and Mergers

The antitrust laws of the twentieth century, despite their strength, have been unevenly applied, especially in terms of the media. When International Telephone & Telegraph (ITT) tried to acquire ABC in the 1960s, loud protests and government investigations sank the deal. Even though the Justice Department broke up AT&T's century-old monopoly in the mid-1980s–creating telephone competition–at the same time the government was also authorizing a number of mass media mergers that consolidated power in the hands of a few large companies. For

> "Big is bad if it stifles competition . . . but big is good if it produces quality programs."
>
> MICHAEL EISNER, THEN-CEO, DISNEY, 1995

> "It's a small world, after all."
>
> THEME SONG, DISNEY THEME PARKS

▶

MEDIA PARTNERSHIPS
like the one between NBC
and Microsoft, which resulted in the creation of MSNBC,
are one of the ways media
conglomerates work together
to consolidate power. Here
Chris Matthews (left) of
Hardball with Chris Matthews
interviews a guest on his
talking-head-style show on
MSNBC.

"In antitrust, as in
many other areas
involving economic
regulation, there is
a general percep-
tion today that
businesses have
slipped the traces
of public control
and that unregu-
lated market
forces will not
ensure a just, or
even efficient,
economy."

HARRY FIRST,
DIRECTOR, TRADE
REGULATION
PROGRAM, NYU, 2008

example, when General Electric purchased RCA/NBC in the 1980s, the FTC, the FCC, and the
Justice Department found few problems. Then, in 1996, computer giant Microsoft partnered
with NBC to create a CNN alternative, MSNBC: a twenty-four-hour news channel available on
both cable and the Internet. In 2005 NBC Universal acquired control of the cable channel
while remaining a 50-50 joint partner in MSNBC.com, one of the nation's leading online news
sources.

In 1995, Disney acquired ABC for $19 billion. To ensure its rank as the world's largest me-
dia conglomerate, Time Warner countered and bought Turner Broadcasting in 1995 for $7.5 bil-
lion. In 2001, AOL acquired Time Warner for $106 billion–the largest media merger in history
at the time. For a time the company was called AOL Time Warner. However, when the online
giant saw its subscription service decline in the face of new high-speed broadband services
from cable companies, the company went back to the Time Warner name (see "What Time
Warner Owns" on opposite page). Also in 2001, the federal government approved a $72 billion
deal uniting AT&T's cable division with Comcast, creating a cable company twice the size of its
nearest competitor (AT&T would quickly leave the merger, selling its cable holdings to Comcast
for $47 billion late in 2001).

Until the 1980s, antitrust rules attempted to ensure diversity of ownership among competing businesses. Sometimes this happened, as in the breakup of AT&T, and sometimes it did
not, as in the cases of local newspaper and cable monopolies. What has occurred consistently,
though, is that media competition has been usurped by media consolidation. Today, the same
anticompetitive mindset exists that once allowed a few utility and railroad companies to control their industries in the days before antitrust laws.

Most media companies have skirted monopoly charges by purchasing diverse types of
mass media rather than trying to control just one medium. For example, Disney, rather than
trying to dominate one area, provides programming to TV, cable, and movie theaters. In 1995,
then-Disney CEO Michael Eisner defended the company's practices, arguing that as long as

large companies remain dedicated to quality–and as long as Disney did not try to buy the phone lines and TV cables running into homes–such mergers benefit America.

But Eisner's position raises questions: How is the quality of cultural products determined? If companies cannot make money on quality products, what happens? If ABC News cannot make a substantial profit, should Disney's managers cut back their national or international news staff? What are the potential effects of such layoffs on the public mission of news media and consequently on our political system? How should the government and citizens respond?

Business Tendencies in Media Industries

In addition to the consolidation trend, a number of other factors characterize the economics of mass media businesses. These are general trends or tendencies that cut across most business sectors and demonstrate how larger global contemporary economies operate.

Flexible Markets and the Decline of Labor Unions

Today's information culture is characterized by what business executives call flexibility– a tendency to emphasize "the new, the fleeting . . . and the contingent in modern life, rather than the more solid values implanted" during Henry Ford's day, when relatively stable mass production drove mass consumption.[10] The new elastic economy features the expansion of the service sector (most notably in health care, banking, real estate, fast food, Internet ventures, and computer software) and the need to serve individual consumer preferences. This type of economy has relied on cheap labor–sometimes exploiting poor workers in sweatshops–and on quick, high-volume sales to offset the costs of making so many niche products for specialized markets.

Given that 80 to 90 percent of new consumer and media products typically fail, a flexible economy has demanded rapid product development and efficient market research. Companies need to score a few hits to offset investments in failed products. For instance, during the peak summer movie season, studios premiere dozens of new feature films, such as *Iron Man* and the fourth *Indiana Jones* movie in the summer of 2008. A few are hits but many more miss, and studios hope to recoup their losses via merchandising tie-ins and DVD rentals and sales. Similarly, TV networks introduce scores of new programs each year but quickly replace those that fail to attract a large audience or the "right" kind of affluent viewers. This flexible media system, of course, heavily favors large companies with greater access to capital funds over small businesses that cannot easily absorb the losses incurred from failed products.

The era of flexible markets also coincided with the decline of workers who belong to labor unions. Having made strong gains on behalf of workers after World War II, labor unions represented 35 percent of U.S. workers in 1955 at their peak. Then, manufacturers and other large industries began to look for ways to cut the rising cost of labor. With the shift to an information economy, many jobs, such as making computers, CD players, TV sets, VCRs, and DVDs, were exported to avoid the high price of U.S. unionized labor. (Today, in fact, many of the technical and customer support services for these kinds of product lines are outsourced to nations like India.) As large companies bought up small companies across national boundaries, commerce developed rapidly at the global level. According to the U.S. Department of Labor, union membership fell to 20.1 percent in 1983 and 12.1 percent in 2007 (versus more than 30 percent in Canada).

Downsizing and the Wage Gap

With the apparent advantage to large companies in this flexible age, who is disadvantaged? The U.S. Department of Labor reported in 2005 that "30 million full-time American employees have gotten pink slips" since that department "belatedly started to count them in 1984." This

▶

WHAT TIME WARNER OWNS

Books/Magazines
- DC Comics
- MAD Magazine
- Time Inc.
  - *Entertainment Weekly*
  - *Essence*
  - *FORTUNE*
  - *Golf*
  - *InStyle*
  - *Money*
  - *People / People en Español*
  - *Real Simple*
  - *Sports Illustrated*
  - *This Old House*
  - *Time*
- Southern Progress Corporation
  - *Coastal Living*
  - *Cooking Light*
  - *Health*
  - *Southern Living*

Internet
- AOL
  - Mapquest
  - Moviefone
  - Netscape
  - AIM
  - Winamp
  - CompuServe
  - Weblogs, Inc.
  - TMZ.com

Television/Cable
- HBO
  - HBO
  - Cinemax
- Turner Broadcasting System
  - Cartoon Network
  - CNN
  - TBS
  - TCM
  - TNT
- Time Warner Cable
  - Road Runner
  - Digital Phone
  - Time Warner Cable
- Local Channels (9)
  - News 8 Austin, Austin, Tx.
  - News 10 Now-Syracuse, Syracuse, N.Y.
  - NY1 News New York, N.Y.
- Warner Bros. Television Group
  - Warner Bros. Television
  - Warner Bros. Animation
  - The CW Network

Movies
- Warner Bros. Pictures
- Warner Independent Pictures
- Warner Bros. Home Entertainment Group
- Warner Bros. Theatre Ventures

phenomenon has been related to corporate "downsizing"—a euphemism for laying off workers—which is supposed to make companies "more productive, more competitive, more flexible."[11]

This trend, spurred by government deregulation and a decline in worker protection, means that many employees today scramble for jobs, often working two or three part-time positions. In his 2006 book *The Disposable American*, Louis Uchitelle reports that as of 2004 more than 45 percent of U.S. workers earned $13.45 an hour or less—or roughly $26,000 per year at the high end.[12] (Wal-Mart—the largest private employer in the world with 1.4 million workers—reported its average hourly pay in 2007 at $10.51—roughly $21,000 per year.) Uchitelle also noted two side effects of downsizing: businesses that can no longer compete well because of fewer employees, and a decline in innovation. In the news media, the "downsizing" of traditional newsrooms—reporting staffs are down by more than 25 percent since the early 1990s—has led to the emergence of online news sites, blogs, and other ventures (e.g., the Huffington Post or Talking Points Memo) that compete head-on with traditional news media. In addition, layoffs and buyouts in newsrooms mean there are fewer reporters and editors to develop new ideas and innovative techniques to compete with the online onslaught.

The main beneficiaries of downsizing have been corporate CEOs—many of whom have overseen the layoffs. The 2008 Nobel economist and *New York Times* columnist Paul Krugman reported in 2002 on the growing gap between CEOs and average workers:

Over the past 30 years most people have seen only modest salary increases: the average annual salary in America, expressed in 1998 dollars (that is, adjusted for inflation), rose from $32,522 in 1970 to $35,864 in 1999. That's about a 10 percent increase over 29 years—progress, but not much. Over the same period, however, according to Fortune *magazine, the average real annual compensation of the top 100 CEOs went from $1.3 million—39 times the pay of an average worker—to $37.5 million, more than 1,000 times the pay of ordinary workers.*[13]

Beyond being part of this wage disparity, CEOs in media industries ultimately control how widely this kind of economic news becomes public, how often its implications are circulated, and what this all might mean for democracy.

Economics, Hegemony, and Storytelling

To understand why our society hasn't (until recently) participated in much public discussion about wealth disparity and salary gaps, it is helpful to understand the concept of *hegemony*. The word *hegemony* has roots in ancient Greek, but in the 1920s and 1930s, Italian philosopher and activist Antonio Gramsci worked out a modern understanding of *hegemony*: how a ruling class in a society maintains its power—not simply by military or police force, but more commonly by citizens' consent and deference to power. He explained that people who are without power—the disenfranchised, the poor, the disaffected, the unemployed, exploited workers—do not routinely rise up against those in power because "the rule of one class over another does not depend on economic or physical power alone but rather on persuading the ruled to accept the system of beliefs of the ruling class and to share their social, cultural, and moral values."[14] **Hegemony**, then, is the acceptance of the dominant values in a culture by those who are subordinate to those who hold economic and political power.

How then does this process actually work in our society? How do lobbyists, the rich, and our powerful two-party political system convince regular citizens that they should go along with the status quo? Edward Bernays, one the founders of modern public relations (see Chapter 12), wrote in his 1947 article "The Engineering of Consent" that companies and rulers couldn't lead people—or get them to do what the ruling class wanted—until the people consented to what those companies or rulers were trying to do, whether it was convincing the public to support women smoking cigarettes or to go to war. To pull this off, Bernays would convert a client's goals into "common sense"; that is, he tried to convince consumers and citizens that his clients' interests were the "natural" or normal way things worked.

So if companies or politicians convinced consumers and citizens that the interests of the powerful were common sense and therefore normal or natural, they also created an atmosphere and context in which there was less chance for challenge and criticism. Common sense, after all, repels self-scrutiny ("that's just plain common sense–end of discussion"). In this case, status quo values and "conventional wisdom" (e.g., hard work and religious belief are rewarded with economic success) and political arrangements (e.g., the traditional two-party system serves democracy best) become taken for granted as normal and natural ways to organize and see the world.

To argue that a particular view or value is common sense is often an effective strategy for stopping conversation and debate. Yet common sense is socially and symbolically constructed and shifts over time. For example, it was once common sense that the world was flat and that people who were not property-owning white males shouldn't be allowed to vote. Common sense is particularly powerful because it contains no abstract strategies for criticizing elite or dominant points of view and therefore certifies class, race, or sexual orientation divisions or mainstream political views as natural and given.

To buy uncritically into concepts presented as common sense inadvertently serves to maintain such concepts as natural, shutting down discussions about the ways in which economic divisions or political hierarchies are *not* natural and given. So when Democratic and Republican candidates run for office, the stories they tell about themselves espouse their connection to Middle American common sense and "down home" virtues–for example, a photo of George W. Bush in blue jeans clearing brush on his Texas ranch or a video of Barack Obama playing basketball in a small Indiana high school gym. These ties to ordinary commonsense values and experience connect the powerful to the everyday, making their interests and ours seamless.

To understand how hegemony works as a process, let's examine how common sense is practically and symbolically transmitted. Here it is crucial to understand the central importance of storytelling to culture. The narrative–as the dominant symbolic way we make sense of experience and articulate our values–is a vehicle for delivering "common sense." Therefore, ideas, values, and beliefs are carried in our mainstream stories–the stories we tell and find in daily conversations, in the local paper, in political ads, on the evening news, or in books, magazines, movies, and favorite TV shows. The narrative, then, is the normal and familiar structure that aids in converting ideas, values, and beliefs to common sense–normalizing them into "just the way things are."

The reason that common narratives "work" is that they identify with a culture's dominant values; "Middle American" virtues include allegiances to family, honesty, hard work, religion, capitalism, health, democracy, moderation, loyalty, fairness, authenticity, modesty, and so forth. These kinds of Middle American virtues are the ones that our politicians most frequently align themselves with in the political ads that tell their stories. These virtues lie at the heart of powerful American Dream stories that for centuries now have told us that if we work hard and practice such values, we will triumph and be successful. Hollywood, too, distributes these shared narratives, celebrating characters and heroes who are loyal, honest, and hardworking. Through this process, the media (and the powerful companies that control them) provide the commonsense narratives that keep the economic status quo relatively unchallenged and leave little room for alternatives.

AMERICAN DREAM STORIES are distributed through our media. This is especially true of early television shows in the 1950s like *The Adventures of Ozzie and Harriet,* which idealized the American nuclear family as central to the American Dream.

In the end, hegemony helps explain why we occasionally support economic plans and structures that may not be in our best interest. We may do this out of altruism, as when wealthy people or companies support programs that would tax them more because of a sense of obligation to give back to those who are less fortunate. But more often, the American Dream story is so powerful in our media and popular culture that many of us believe that we too can become rich and therefore successful and happy. So why do anything to disturb the economic structures that the dream is built upon? In fact, in many versions of our American Dream story–from Hollywood films to political ads–the government often plays the role of villain, seeking to raise our taxes or undermine rugged individualism and hard work. Pitted against the government in these stories, the protagonist is the "little guy" at odds with burdensome regulation and bureaucratic oversight. However, many of these stories are produced and distributed by large media corporations and political leaders who rely on us to consent to the shared power of the American Dream narrative to keep their position as the status quo–the "common sense" way the world works.

Specialization and Global Markets

In today's complex and often turbulent economic environment, global firms have sought greater profits by moving labor to less economically developed countries that need jobs but have poor health and safety regulations for workers. The continuous outsourcing of many U.S. jobs and the breakdown of global economic borders accompanied this transformation. Bolstered by the passage in 1947 of GATT (General Agreement on Tariffs and Trade) and the WTO (World Trade Organization), which succeeded GATT in 1995, and NAFTA (North American Free Trade Agreement) in 1994, global cooperation fostered transnational media corporations and business deals across international terrain.

But in many cases this global expansion by U.S. companies ran counter to America's early-twentieth-century vision of itself. Henry Ford, for example, followed his wife's suggestion to lower prices so workers could afford Ford cars. In many countries today, however, most workers cannot afford the stereo equipment and TV sets they are making primarily for U.S. and European markets.

The Rise of Specialization and Synergy

The new globalism coincided with the rise of specialization. The magazine, radio, and cable industries sought specialized markets both in the United States and overseas, in part to counter television's mass appeal. By the 1980s, however, even television–confronted with the growing popularity of home video and cable–began niche marketing, targeting affluent eighteen- to thirty-four-year-old viewers, whose buying habits were not as stable or predictable as those of older consumers. Younger and older audiences, abandoned by the networks, were sought by other media outlets and advertisers. Magazines such as *Seventeen* and *AARP The Magazine* now flourish. Cable channels such as Nickelodeon and the Cartoon Network serve the under-eighteen market, while A&E and Lifetime address viewers over age fifty and female; in addition, cable channel BET targets young African Americans, helping to define them as a consumer group. (See "Case Study: Co-opting Consumers of Color" on opposite page.)

CASE STUDY

Co-opting Consumers of Color

By Makani Themba-Nixon

They call it penetration—as in market penetration. The tentacles of the transnational mediopolies reach deeper into racial and ethnic communities than ever before. For some, this is a triumph in diversity. Big corporations reaching consumers of color is something they say we should celebrate. However, this market penetration has gone hand in hand with decreasing media ownership by people of color, resulting in loss of industry voice and jobs. Flagship properties that were once trumpeted as success stories in black ownership—BET and *Essence* magazine—have become little more than shadows of their parent companies. The outlets' makeovers were designed to garner greater "synergy" and brand recognition for their corporate masters. As a result, BET looks more and more like VH1, complete with dog-eat-dog "reality" shows, cloying countdown lists,

EVERYBODY HATES CHRIS

▼

and decade retrospectives that work to remake history—even black history—into trivia. In fact, BET was the last place to tune in for Black History Month programming. Its main commemorative offering: a VH1 adaptation hosted by comedian Paul Mooney titled *BET's Top 25 Most @#%! Moments in Black History*. To many, it was fitting, as BET regularly programs what some regard as the most @#%! moments in black popular culture.

The remaking of *Essence* magazine has been more subtle. Celebrity profiles and gossipy features increase in page share, à la *People* magazine (both are Time Warner publications), while the names of *Essence* veterans have been disappearing from the masthead—mostly as a result of "restructuring" under editor and *Teen People* import Angela Burt-Murray.

The loss of *Essence's* expert leadership is but one example of how diversity in staffing (especially at the top) is closely tied to diversity in ownership. According to a 2002 study by the Minority Media and Telecommunications Council, only 4.2 percent of radio outlets are minority-owned, yet these outlets employ more than half of all the people of color in radio. Fewer minority-owned outlets has meant fewer minorities in media. And changes in regulation, like the elimination of tax incentives for outlet sales to minorities, are making things worse.

Television-staffing diversity has also been taking a real blow, especially since the merger of UPN with WB. According to a study commissioned by the Writers Guild of America west, before the merger UPN had the single highest concentration of writers of color—63 percent of television writers of color in 2005–06 were employed by UPN. This was part of a conscious marketing strategy aimed at cornering the young black market to carve out a bankable niche. Some of the most controversial black programming on the air, including a short-lived, much-protested sitcom on slavery, was on CBS-owned UPN. But UPN [has merged] with WB to create a new network called CW. CW's fall scheduling plans show a safe mix of both networks' main stalwarts, which bodes deep cuts in UPN's black programming: Only a few appear to have survived, including *Girlfriends* and *Everybody Hates Chris*.

From Fox Sports en Español to the growing proliferation of affinity groups of color on MySpace (News Corporation's mega "e-community"), there are few spaces that Big Media hasn't invaded. And if that's not enough to keep you up at night, consider this: If public discourse in our communities becomes completely corporatized, what will become of our voices, our points of view, our interests? As history has shown, communities without access to media in their interest are vulnerable indeed. ◢

Source: Makani Themba-Nixon, "The National Entertainment State," Nation, July 3, 2006. Themba-Nixon is executive director of the Praxis Project, a media and policy advocacy center based in Washington, D.C.

Beyond specialization, though, what really distinguishes current media economics is the extension of **synergy** to international levels. *Synergy* typically refers to the promotion and sale of different versions of a media product across the various subsidiaries of a media conglomerate (e.g., a Time Warner HBO cable special about "the making of" a Warner Brothers movie reviewed in *Time* magazine). However, it also refers to global companies like Sony buying up popular culture–movie studios and record labels–to play on its various electronic products. Today, synergy is the default business mode of most media companies.

Disney: A Postmodern Media Conglomerate

To understand the contemporary story of media economics and synergy, we need only examine the transformation of Disney from a struggling cartoon producer to one of the world's largest media conglomerates.

The Early Years

After Walt Disney's first cartoon company, Laugh-O-Gram, went bankrupt in 1922, Disney moved to Hollywood and found his niche. He created Mickey Mouse (originally named Mortimer) for the first sound cartoons in the late 1920s and developed the first feature-length cartoon, *Snow White and the Seven Dwarfs*, completed in 1937.

For much of the twentieth century, the Disney company set the standard for popular cartoons and children's culture. The *Silly Symphonies* series (1929-39) established the studio's reputation for high-quality hand-drawn cartoons. Although Disney remained a minor studio, *Fantasia* and *Pinocchio*–the two top-grossing films of 1940–each made more than $40 million. Nonetheless, the studio barely broke even because cartoon projects took time–four years for *Snow White*–and commanded the company's entire attention.

The Company Diversifies

The 1950s and early 1960s were marked by corporate diversification. With the demise of the cartoon film short in movie theaters, Disney expanded into other areas, with its first nature documentary short, *Seal Island* (1949); its first live-action feature, *Treasure Island* (1950); and its first feature documentary, *The Living Desert* (1953).

Disney was also among the first film studios to embrace television. In 1954, the company launched a long-running prime-time show, an even more popular venue than theaters for displaying its products. Then, in 1955, Disneyland opened in Southern California. Eventually, Disney's theme parks would produce the bulk of the studio's revenues (Walt Disney World in Orlando, Florida, began operation in 1971).

In 1953, Disney started Buena Vista, a distribution company. This was the first step in making the studio into a major player. The company also began exploiting the power of its early cartoon features. *Snow White,* for example, was successfully re-released in theaters to new generations of children before eventually going to videocassette and much later to DVD.

Global Expansion

The death of Walt Disney in 1966 triggered a period of decline for the studio. But in 1984 a new management team, led by Michael Eisner, initiated a turnaround. The newly created Touchstone movie division reinvented the live-action cartoon for adults as well as children in *Who Framed Roger Rabbit* (1988). A string of hand-drawn animated hits followed, including *The Little Mermaid* (1989), *Beauty and the Beast* (1991), *The Lion King* (1994), *Mulan* (1998), *Fantasia 2000*, and *Lilo + Stitch* (2002). In a partnership with Pixar Animation Studios, Disney also distributed a string of computer-animated blockbusters, including *Toy Story* (1995), *Monsters, Inc.* (2001), *Finding Nemo* (2003), *The Incredibles* (2004), and *Ratatouille* (2007).

Disney also came to epitomize the synergistic possibilities of media consolidation. It can produce an animated feature for both theatrical release and DVD distribution. With its ABC network (purchased in 1995), it can place a cartoon version of the movie on ABC's Saturday-morning schedule. A book version can be released through Disney's publishing arm, Hyperion, and "the-making-of" versions can appear on cable's Disney Channel or ABC Family, as well as in *Disney Adventures,* the company's popular children's magazine. Characters can become attractions at Disney's theme parks, which themselves have spawned Hollywood movies such as the lucrative *Pirates of the Caribbean* trilogy. Some Disney films have had upwards of seventeen thousand licensed products, from clothing to toys to dog-food bowls.

DISNEY'S EXPANSION has led the company to new frontiers like adapting some of its hit movies to the Broadway stage. Starting with *The Lion King,* this strategy also currently includes *The Little Mermaid* and *Mary Poppins.*

Throughout the 1990s, Disney continued to find new sources of revenue in both entertainment and distribution. Through its purchase of ABC, Disney also became the owner of the cable sports channels ESPN and ESPN2, and later expanded the brand with ESPNews and ESPN Classic channels, *ESPN The Magazine,* ESPN Radio, ESPN.com, and ESPN Zone—a sports-themed restaurant chain. In New York City, Disney renovated several theaters and launched versions of *Beauty and the Beast* and *The Lion King* as successful Broadway musicals.

Building on the international appeal of its cartoon features, in 1983 Disney extended its global reach by opening a successful theme park in Japan. In 1986, the company started marketing cartoons to Chinese television, attracting an estimated 300 million viewers per week. Disney also started a magazine in Chinese; opened several Disney stores and a theme park in Hong Kong; and signed a deal with Russian television, where Disney received exclusive rights to sell ads during the airing of its programs. Disney continued its international expansion in the 1990s, but to less success.

In 1991, EuroDisney (now called Disneyland Resort Paris) opened outside Paris. Many Europeans criticized the company for pushing out and vulgarizing classical culture. (The park lost millions of dollars a month until the mid-1990s.) On the home front, a proposed historical park in Virginia, Disney's America, suffered defeat at the hands of citizens who raised concerns about Disney misinterpreting or romanticizing American history. In 1995, shortly after the company purchased ABC, Disney suffered criticism for running a flattering company profile one evening on ABC's evening news program.

Despite criticism, little slowed Disney's global expansion. Orbit—a Saudi-owned satellite relay station based in Rome—introduced Disney's twenty-four-hour premium cable channel to twenty-three countries in the Middle East and North Africa in 1997. Disney exemplifies the formula for becoming a "great media conglomerate" as defined by the book *Global Dreams*: "Companies able to use visuals to sell sound, movies to sell books, or software to sell hardware would become the winners in the new global commercial order."[15]

Corporate Shake-ups and Disney Today

Even as Disney grew into the world's No. 2 media conglomerate in the early 2000s, the cartoon pioneer experienced the multiple shocks of a recession, failed films and Internet ventures, and declining theme park attendance. In addition, CEO Eisner's business moves had damaged Disney's relationships with a number of partners and subsidiaries, including Pixar (which had surpassed Disney in making highly profitable animated cartoons) and the film studio Miramax, which had produced a string of Oscar-winning movies including *Shakespeare in Love, Chicago,* and *The Aviator.*

In 2004 Eisner and Disney refused to distribute Michael Moore's controversial Iraq war documentary *Fahrenheit 9/11,* which Miramax had financed; the movie cost $7 million to make and went on to earn $119 million in U.S. theaters. By 2005, Disney had fallen to No. 5 among movie studios in U.S. box office sales–down from No. 1 in 2003. A divided and unhappy board of directors forced Eisner out in 2005 after twenty-one years as CEO.[16] In 2006, new CEO Robert Iger repaired the relationship between Disney and Pixar by merging the companies and making Pixar and Apple Computer founder and CEO Steve Jobs a Disney board member. (In 2008, Jobs was listed as Disney's largest individual stockholder with a 7 percent holding.)

The Pixar deal showed that Disney was ready to embrace the digital age and the new millennium. In an effort to focus on television, movies, and its new online initiatives, Disney sold its twenty-two radio stations and the ABC Radio Network to Citadel Broadcasting for $2.7 billion in 2007. Disney also made its (and ABC's) movies and TV programs available for download at Apple's iTunes store and redesigned its Web site as a destination for kids to play games, watch videos, and join a social network.

Global Audiences Expand Media Markets

As Disney's story shows, international expansion has allowed media conglomerates some advantages, including secondary markets to earn profits and advance technological innovations. First, as media technologies get cheaper and more portable (from the original Walkman to the latest iPod), American media proliferate both inside and outside national boundaries. Today, greatly facilitated by the Internet, media products easily flow into the eyes and ears of the world. Second, this globalism also permits companies that lose money on products at home to profit in the international market. Roughly 80 percent of American movies, for instance, do not earn back their costs in U.S. theaters and thus depend on foreign circulation as well as home video formats to make up for early losses.

The same is true for the television industry. Consider the 1990s phenomenon *Baywatch,* which went into first-run syndication in 1991 after being canceled by NBC. The program's producers claimed that by the late 1990s, *Baywatch,* a show about the adventures of underdressed lifeguards who make beaches safer for everyone, was the most-watched program in the world, with more than a billion viewers. The dialogue in the series, like that of action movies, was limited and fairly simple, which made it easy and inexpensive to translate the program into other languages.

In addition, satellite transmission has made North American and European TV available at the global level. Cable services such as CNN and MTV quickly took their national acts to the international stage, and by the twenty-first century, CNN and MTV were available in more than two hundred countries. (For contrast, see "Media Literacy and the Critical Process: Newspaper Readership in India and the United States" on page 425 about the rise of India's newspapers.) Today, of course, the swapping of music, TV shows, and movies on the Internet (both legally and illegally) has expanded the global flow of popular culture even further.

Social Issues in Media Economics

As the Disney-ABC merger suggests, recent years have brought a surplus of billion-dollar takeovers and mergers, including those between Time Inc. and Warner Communication, Viacom and Paramount, Time Warner and Turner, AOL and Time Warner, AT&T and Bell South, UPN and WB, GE and Universal, and News Corp. and Dow Jones. This mergermania has

Media Literacy and the Critical Process

Newspaper Readership in India and the United States

Newspaper readership is rising in India but declining in the United States. Why? Do newspaper media companies in India better serve their cities? To find out, investigate a U.S. newspaper and a newspaper that is serving one or more of India's largest cities—like Mumbai, Calcutta, or New Delhi. Do some general research to choose your cities and papers (if you can, try to find stories about the newspapers and the cities for background context). After choosing your papers, find out what each is doing to serve its readers.

1 DESCRIPTION. In a LexisNexis search, locate recent articles on your newspapers. Find out if they have a parent corporation or if they own other media properties. Using the newspapers' Web sites, read the papers for a three-day period and log a typical day's news coverage. (Work with your instructor to limit which sections of the paper's site you will use for your analysis.) Most major Indian newspapers offer an online English version. Create categories of news and information based on what you read. How much local and national information is there? How much do the two papers cover parts of the world outside their region and nation?

2 ANALYSIS. What patterns did you find in the papers' coverage of their cities and nations? What kind of news is offered, and what kind of information is available about local and national events? What patterns did you find in the stories devoted to events and issues from

abroad? What other nations and what kinds of issues tended to get covered? Are things missing from the coverage?

3 INTERPRETATION. Based on what you have discovered, what does it mean? Can you make an argument about whether or not the cities represented by these papers are well served by their newspapers? Just from looking at the three days of coverage, can you offer any reason why the U.S. paper may be in decline while the Indian paper might be on the rise? Provide evidence.

4 EVALUATION. Based on what you have found, are the companies running these papers doing a good or bad job? What are they doing well? What are they doing poorly?

5 ENGAGEMENT. Try to interview (via e-mail) editors from one or both of the papers. Ask them how well they think they are serving their cities. Ask them about readership and who their customers are. Why do these editors think readership is going up or down? How is the Internet affecting their readership?

---

accompanied stripped-down regulation, which has virtually suspended most ownership limits on media industries. As a result, a number of consumer advocates and citizen groups have raised questions about deregulation and ownership consolidation.

One longtime critic of media mergers, Ben Bagdikian, author of *The Media Monopoly,* has argued that although there are abundant products in the market–"1,700 daily papers, more than 8,000 weeklies, 10,000 radio and television stations, 11,000 magazines, 2,500 book publishers"–only a limited number of companies are in charge of those products.[17] Bagdikian and others fear that this represents a dangerous anti-democratic tendency in which a handful of media moguls wield a disproportionate amount of economic control. (See "Case Study: From Fifty to a Few: The Most Dominant Media Corporations" on page 426.)

The Limits of Antitrust Laws

Although meant to ensure multiple voices and owners, American antitrust laws have been easily subverted since the 1980s as companies expanded by diversifying holdings, merging product lines with other big media firms, and forming local monopolies, especially in newspapers and

From Fifty to a Few: The Most Dominant Media Corporations

When Ben Bagdikian wrote the first edition of *The Media Monopoly*, published in 1983, he warned of the chilling control wielded by the fifty elite corporations that owned most of the U.S. mass media. By the publication of the book's seventh edition in 2004, the number of corporations controlling most of America's daily newspapers, magazines, radio, television, books, and movies had dropped from fifty to five. Today, most of the leading corporations have a high profile in the United States, particularly through ownership of television networks: Time Warner (CW), Disney (ABC), News Corp. (Fox), CBS Corporation (CBS and CW), and GE/NBC Universal (NBC).

The creep of consolidation over the past few decades requires us to think differently about how we experience the mass media on a daily basis. Potential conflicts of interest abound. For example, should we trust how NBC News covers GE or how ABC News covers Disney? Should we be wary if *Time* magazine hypes a Warner Brothers film? More importantly, what actions can we take to ensure that the mass media function not just as successful businesses for stockholders but also as a necessary part of our democracy?

To help you get a better understanding of how our media landscape is changing, look at the table below that lists the Top 10 media companies for 1980, 1997, and 2007. What patterns do you notice? How does this reflect larger trends in the media? For example, seven of the major companies in 1980 were mostly print businesses, but in 2007, only one was. Why? Most of the large media companies have been profiled here and in Chapters 2 to 10 (illustrating their principal holdings). While the subsidiaries of these companies often change, the charts demonstrate the wide reach of today's large conglomerations. To get a better understanding of how the largest media corporations relate to each other and the larger world, see the folded insert at the beginning of the book. ◢

TOP 10 U.S. MEDIA COMPANIES, 1980, 1997, 2007*

1980			1997			2007		
Rank	Company	Revenue in $millions	Rank	Company	Revenue in $millions	Rank	Company	Revenue in $millions
1	American Broadcasting Cos.	$2,204.5	1	Time Warner	$11,851.1	1	Time Warner	$33,993
2	CBS Inc.	2,001.0	2	Walt Disney Co.	6,555.9	2	Comcast Corp.	27,392
3	RCA Corp.	1,521.8	3	Tele-Communications Inc.	5,954.0	3	Walt Disney Co.	16,838
4	Time Inc.	1,348.5	4	NBC TV (General Electric Co.)	5,230.0	4	News Corp.	14,091
5	S. I. Newhouse & Sons	1,250.0	5	CBS Corp.	4,333.5	5	DirecTV Group	13,744
6	Gannett Co.	1,195.0	6	Gannett Co.	4,214.4	6	NBC TV (General Electric Co.)	13,240
7	Times Mirror Co.	1,128.4	7	News Corp.	4,005.0	7	CBS Corp.	12,183
8	Hearst Corp.	1,100.0	8	Advance Publications	3,385.0	8	Cox Enterprises	10,385
9	Knight-Ridder Newspapers	1,099.0	9	Cox Enterprises	3,075.3	9	EchoStar Communications Corp.	9,456
10	Tribune Co.	1,048.7	10	Knight-Ridder	2,851.9	10	Viacom	8,444

Source: Ad Age's 100 Leading Media Companies report, December 7, 1981; "100 Companies by Media Revenue," Advertising Age, August 18, 1997; "100 Leading Media Companies," Advertising Age, October 2007.

*Note: The revenue in $millions is based on Total Net U.S. Media Revenue and does not include non-media and international revenue.

cable. The resulting consolidation of media owners has limited the number of independent voices in the market and reduced the number of owners who might be able to innovate and challenge established economic powers.

Diversification

Most media companies diversify among different media products (such as television stations and film studios), never fully dominating a particular media industry. Time Warner, for example, spreads its holdings among television programming, film, publishing, cable channels, and its Internet divisions. However, the media giant really only competes with a few other big companies like Disney, Viacom, and News Corp.

Such diversification promotes oligopolies in which a few behemoth companies control most media production and distribution. This kind of economic arrangement makes it difficult for products offered outside an oligopoly to compete in the marketplace. For instance, in broadcast TV, the few networks that control prime time—all of them now owned by or in league with film studios—offer programs that are selected from known production companies that the networks either contract with regularly or own outright. Thus even with a very good program or series idea, an independent production company—especially one that operates outside Los Angeles or New York—has a very difficult time entering the national TV market. The film giants even prefer buying from each other before dealing with independents. So, for example, in 2008 CBS sold syndication rights for its drama *Ghost Whisperer* to NBC Universal's SciFi channel. And for years, CBS's *Without a Trace* and NBC's *Law and Order* were both running in syndication on cable's TNT channel, owned by Time Warner, which also co-owns the CW network with CBS.

Local Monopolies

Because antitrust laws aim to curb national monopolies, most media monopolies today operate locally. For instance, although Gannett owns ninety daily newspapers, it controls less than 10 percent of daily U.S. newspaper circulation. Nonetheless, almost all Gannett papers are monopolies—that is, they are the only papers in their various towns. Virtually every cable company has been granted monopoly status in its local community; these firms alone often decide which channels are made available and what rates are charged.

Furthermore, antitrust laws have no teeth globally. Although international copyright laws offer some protection to musicians and writers, no international antitrust rules exist to prohibit transnational companies from buying up as many media companies as they can afford. Still, as legal scholar Harry First points out, antitrust concerns in 2008 are "alive and well and living in Europe."[18] For example, when Sony and Bertelsmann's BMG unit joined their music businesses, only the European Union (EU) raised questions about the merger on behalf of the independent labels and musicians worried about the oligopoly nature of the music business. The EU has frequently reviewed the merger, which started in 2004, and was looking at it again in 2008.

Occasionally, independent voices raise issues that aid the Justice Department and the FTC in their antitrust cases. For example, when Echostar proposed to purchase DirecTV in 2001, a number of rural, consumer, and Latino organizations spoke out against the merger for several reasons. Latino organizations opposed the merger because in many U.S. markets, Direct Broadcast Satellite (DBS) service offers the only available Spanish-language television programming. The merger would have left the United States with just one major DBS company and created a virtual monopoly for Echostar, which had fewer Spanish-language offerings than DirecTV. In 2002, the FCC declined to approve the merger, saying it would not serve the public interest, convenience, and necessity.

The Fallout from a Free Market

Since the wave of media mergers began with gusto in the 1980s, a number of consumer critics have pointed to the lack of public debate surrounding the tightening oligopoly structure of international media. Economists and media critics have traced the causes and history of this void to two major issues: a reluctance to criticize capitalism and the debate over how much control consumers have in the marketplace.

Equating Free Markets with Democracy

In the 1920s and 1930s, commercial radio executives, many of whom befriended FCC members, succeeded in portraying themselves as operating in the public interest while labeling their noncommercial radio counterparts in education, labor, or religion as mere voices of propaganda. In these early debates, corporate interests succeeded in aligning the political ideas of democracy, misleadingly, with the economic structures of capitalism.

Throughout the Cold War period in the 1950s and 1960s, it became increasingly difficult to even criticize capitalism, which had become a synonym for democracy in many circles. In this context, any criticism of capitalism became an attack on the free marketplace. This, in turn, appeared to be a criticism of free speech, because the business community often sees its right to operate in a free marketplace as an extension of its right to buy commercial speech in the form of advertising. As longtime CBS chief William Paley told a group of educators in 1937: "He who attacks the fundamentals of the American system" of commercial broadcasting "attacks democracy itself."[19]

Broadcast historian Robert McChesney, discussing the rise of commercial radio in the 1930s, has noted that leaders like Paley "equated capitalism with the free and equal marketplace, the free and equal marketplace with democracy, and democracy with 'Americanism.'"[20] The collapse of the former Soviet Union's communist economy in the 1990s is often portrayed as a triumph for democracy. As we now realize, however, it was primarily a victory for capitalism and free-market economies.

Consumer Choice versus Consumer Control

As many economists point out, capitalism is not structured democratically but arranged vertically, with powerful corporate leaders at the top and hourly wage workers at the bottom. But democracy, in principle, is built on a more horizontal model in which each individual has an equal opportunity to have his or her voice heard and vote counted. In discussing free markets, economists distinguish between similar types of consumer power: *consumer control* over marketplace goods and freedom of *consumer choice*: "The former requires that consumers participate in deciding what is to be offered; the latter is satisfied if [consumers are] free to select among the options chosen for them by producers."[21] Most Americans and the citizens of other economically developed nations clearly have *consumer choice*: options among a range of media products. Yet consumers and even media employees have limited *consumer control*: power in deciding what kinds of media get created and circulated.

One promising development concerns the role of independent and alternative producers, artists, writers, and publishers. Despite the movement toward economic consolidation, the fringes of media industries still offer a diversity of opinions, ideas, and alternative products. In fact, when independent companies become even marginally popular, they are often pursued by large companies that seek to make them subsidiaries. For example, alternative music often taps into social concerns that are not normally discussed in the recording industry's corporate boardrooms. Moreover, business leaders "at the top" depend on independent ideas "from below" to generate new product lines. A number of transnational corporations encourage the development of local artists—talented individuals who might have the capacity to transcend the regional or national level and become the next global phenomenon.

> "[AOL Time Warner] turned into one of the biggest corporate disasters in U.S. history: America Online's business collapsed, synergies failed to materialize, the company missed its financial targets, and the stock price plunged."
>
> WALL STREET JOURNAL, 2003

> "What they were really looking forward to was creating the biggest shopping mall in the world."
>
> BEN BAGDIKIAN, AUTHOR OF *THE MEDIA MONOPOLY*, ON THE AOL-TIME WARNER MERGER, 2000

Cultural Imperialism

The influence of American popular culture has created considerable debate in international circles. On the one hand, the notion of freedom that is associated with innovation and rebellion in American culture has been embraced internationally. The global spread of and access to media have made it harder for political leaders to secretly repress dissident groups because police and state activity (such as the torture of illegally detained citizens) can now be documented digitally and easily dispatched by satellite, the Internet, and cell phones around the world.

On the other hand, American media are shaping the cultures and identities of other nations. American styles in fashion and food, as well as media fare, dominate the global market–a process known as **cultural imperialism**. Today, many international observers contend that the idea of consumer control or input is even more remote in countries inundated by American movies, music, television, and images of beauty. For example, consumer product giant Unilever sells Dove soap with its "Campaign for Real Beauty" in the United States, but markets Fair & Lovely products– a skin-lightening line–to poor women in India.

Although many indigenous forms of media culture–such as Brazil's *telenovela* (a TV soap opera), Jamaica's reggae, and Japan's animé–are extremely popular, U.S. dominance in producing and distributing mass media puts a severe burden on countries attempting to produce their own cultural products. For example, American TV producers have generally recouped their production costs by the time their TV shows are exported. This enables American distributors to offer these programs to other countries at bargain rates, undercutting local production companies trying to create original programs.

Defenders of American popular culture argue that because some aspects of our culture challenge authority, national boundaries, and outmoded traditions, they create an arena in which citizens can raise questions. Supporters also argue that a universal popular culture creates a *global village* and fosters communication across national boundaries.

Critics, however, believe that although American popular culture often contains protests against social wrongs, such protests "can be turned into consumer products and lose their bite. Protest itself becomes something to sell."[22] The harshest critics have also argued that American cultural imperialism both hampers the development of native cultures and negatively influences teenagers, who abandon their own rituals to adopt American tastes. The exportation of U.S. entertainment media is sometimes viewed as "cultural dumping," because it discourages the development of original local products.

Perhaps the greatest concern regarding a global village is the cultural disconnection for people whose standards of living are not routinely portrayed in contemporary media. About two-thirds of the world's population cannot afford most of the products advertised on American, Japanese, and European television. Yet more and more of the world's populations are able to glimpse consumer abundance and middle-class values through television, magazines, and the Internet.

As early as the 1950s, media managers feared political fallout–"the revolution of rising expectations"–in that ads and products would raise the hopes of poor people but not keep pace with their actual living conditions.[23] Furthermore, the conspicuousness of consumer culture makes it difficult for many of us to even imagine other ways of living that are not heavily dependent on the mass media and brand-name products.

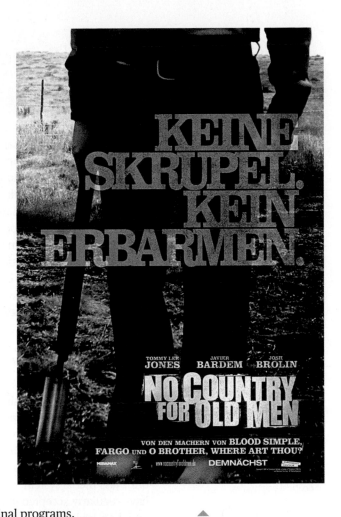

CULTURAL IMPERIALISM
Ever since Hollywood gained an edge in film production and distribution during World War I, U.S. movies have dominated the box office in Europe, in some years accounting for more than 80 percent of the revenues taken in by European theaters.

The Media Marketplace and Democracy

In the midst of today's major global transformations of economies, cultures, and societies, the best way to monitor the impact of transnational economies is through vigorous news attention and lively public discussion. Clearly, however, this process is hampered. Starting in the 1990s, for example, news organizations, concerned about the bottom line, severely cut back the number of reporters assigned to cover international developments. This occurred–especially after 9/11–just as global news became critical to an informed citizenry.

We live in a society in which often-superficial or surface consumer concerns, stock market quotes, and profit aspirations, rather than broader social issues, increasingly dominate the media agenda. In response, critics have posed some key questions: As consumers, do we care who owns the media as long as most of us have a broad selection of products? Do we care who owns the media as long as multiple voices *appear* to exist in the market?

The Effects of Media Consolidation on Democracy

Merged and multinational media corporations will continue to control more aspects of production and distribution. Of pressing concern is the impact of mergers on news operations, particularly the influence of large corporations on their news subsidiaries. These companies have the capacity to use major news resources to promote their products and determine national coverage.

Because of the growing consolidation of mass media, it has become increasingly difficult to sustain a public debate on economic issues. From a democratic perspective, the relationship of our mass media system to politics has been highly dysfunctional. Politicians in Washington, D.C., have regularly accepted millions of dollars in contributions from large media conglomerates and their lobbying groups to finance their campaigns. This changed in 2008 when the Obama campaign raised the bulk of its financing from small donors and citizens. Still, media conglomerates will try to influence deregulation to grow larger. But this will be more difficult because of the 2008-09 financial crisis and President Obama's promise of more oversight and regulation.

Politicians have turned to local television stations, spending record amounts during each election period to get their political ads on the air. By 2000, politicians had become the third-best advertising client for network-affiliated local TV stations, just behind automobiles and retail stores. In 2004, local TV stations reaped an estimated $1.6 billion from political advertising during the election season; in 2006, broadcasters earned $2 billion from political campaigns. Estimates for the entire 2008 election cycle–including primaries–were more than $3 billion, with

BILL MOYERS, one of the most recognized and respected journalists in the United States, returned to television in 2007 with *Bill Moyers' Journal*. The revived series, which Moyers started 35 years earlier, is a weekly hour-long public service journalism program on PBS.

Moyers has been one of the few broadcast journalists to discuss media economics on a regular basis. His program is funded almost completely by nonprofit foundations. Some of his initial programs discussed the mainstream news media's coverage of the run-up to the Iraq war, Rupert Murdoch's bid to buy the *Wall Street Journal*, and the relationship between the mass media and the financing of political campaigns.

over $100 million going to Internet advertising. But although broadcasters have been happy to take political ad money, they have been poor public citizens in covering their regional U.S. congressional candidates. According to a Lear Center Local News Study,

the amount of time given to presidential news coverage [in 2004] was in most cases roughly equivalent to the amount of presidential advertising time, even in markets where the presidential race was competitive. By contrast, in races for the U.S. Senate, ads outnumbered news by as much as 17-to-one, and in U.S. House races by as much as seven-to-one.[24]

The Media Reform Movement

In 2008, Robert McChesney and John Nichols described in the *Nation* the current state of concern about the gathering consolidation of mainstream media power: "'Media Reform' has become a catch-all phrase to describe the broad goals of a movement that says consolidated ownership of broadcast and cable media, chain ownership of newspapers, and telephone and cable-company colonization of the Internet pose a threat not just to the culture of the Republic but to democracy itself."[25] While our current era has spawned numerous grassroots organizations that challenge media to do a better job for the sake of democracy, there has not been a large outcry from the general public for the kinds of concerns described by McChesney and Nichols. There is a reason for that. One key paradox of the Information Age is that for such economic discussions to be meaningful and democratic, they must be carried out in the popular media as well as in educational settings. Yet public debates and disclosures about the structure and ownership of the media are often not in the best economic interests of media owners.

Still, in some places, local groups and consumer movements are trying to address media issues that affect individual and community life. Such movements—like the annual National Conference for Media Reform—are usually united by geographic ties, common political backgrounds, or shared concerns about the state of the media. The Internet has also made it possible for media reform groups to form globally, uniting around such issues as contesting censorship or monitoring the activities of multinational corporations. The movement was also largely responsible for the success of preserving "network neutrality," which prevents Internet service providers from censoring or penalizing particular Web sites and online services (see Chapter 2).

With this reform victory, perhaps we are more ready now to question some of the hierarchical and undemocratic arrangements of what McChesney, Nichols, and other reform critics call "Big Media." Even in the face of so many media mergers, the general public today seems open to such examinations, which might improve the global economy, improve worker conditions, and also serve the public good. By better understanding media economics, we can make a contribution to critiquing media organizations and evaluating their impact on democracy. ▶

"The top management of the networks, with a few notable exceptions, has been trained in advertising, research, or show business. But by the nature of the corporate structure, they also make the final and crucial decisions having to do with news and public affairs. Frequently they have neither the time nor the competence to do this."

EDWARD R. MURROW, BROADCAST NEWS PIONEER, 1958

CHAPTER REVIEW

REVIEW QUESTIONS

Analyzing the Media Economy

1. How are the three basic structures of mass media organizations—monopoly, oligopoly, and limited competition—different from one another?

2. What are the differences between direct and indirect payments for media products?

3. What are some of society's key expectations of its media organizations?

The Transition to an Information Economy

4. Why has the federal government emphasized deregulation at a time when so many media companies are growing so large?

5. How have media mergers changed the economics of mass media?

Specialization and Global Markets

6. How do global and specialized markets factor into the new media economy? How are regular workers affected?

7. Using Disney as an example, what is the role of synergy in the current climate of media mergers?

Social Issues in Media Economics

8. What are the differences between freedom of consumer choice and consumer control?

9. What is cultural imperialism, and what does it have to do with the United States?

The Media Marketplace and Democracy

10. What do critics and activists fear most about the concentration of media ownership? How do media managers and executives respond to these fears?

11. What are some promising signs regarding the relationship between media economics and democracy?

QUESTIONING THE MEDIA

1. Are you exposed to popular culture from other countries? Why or why not? Give some examples.

2. Do you read international news? Why or why not?

3. What steps can reporters and editors take to cover media ownership issues in a better way?

4. How does the concentration of media ownership limit the number of voices in the marketplace? Do we need rules limiting media ownership?

5. Is there such a thing as a global village? What does this concept mean to you?

COMMON THREADS

One of the Common Threads discussed in Chapter 1 is the commercial nature of the mass media. In thinking about media ownership regulations, it is important to consider how the media wield their influence.

Back during the 2000 presidential election, two marginal candidates, Pat Buchanan on the Right, and Ralph Nader on the Left, shared a common view that both major party candidates largely ignored. They warned of the increasing power of corporations to influence the economy and our democracy. In fact, between 2000 and 2005 alone, registered lobbyists grew from about fifteen thousand to thirty-five thousand—most of these working for commercial companies.[26] (See Chapter 12 for more on lobbyists.)

These warnings generally have gone unnoticed and unreported by mainstream media, whose reporters, editors, and pundits often work for the giant media corporations that are not only well represented by Washington lobbyists but also give millions of dollars in campaign contributions to the major parties. Their hope in doing so is to influence legislation that governs media ownership and commercial speech.

Fast-forward to 2008. With the economy doing poorly, both major parties campaigned against lobbyists and made various versions of corporate reform part of their platforms.

Democratic candidate Barack Obama not only declined to take money from lobbyists but asked the Democratic Party to do the same for the 2008 general election. Meanwhile, Republican candidate John McCain let go a number of campaign workers and advisers who had ties to corporate lobbying.

What both Buchanan and Nader argued in 2000 was that corporate influence is a bipartisan concern that we share in common—that all of us in a democracy need to be vigilant about how powerful and influential corporations become. This is especially true for the media companies that report the news and distribute many of our cultural stories. As media-literate consumers, we need to demand that the media serve as watchdogs over the economy and our democratic values. And when they fall down on the job, we need to demand accountability (through alternative media channels or the Internet), especially from those mainstream media—radio, television, and cable—that are licensed to operate in the public interest.

KEY TERMS

The definitions for the terms listed below can be found in the glossary at the end of the book. The page numbers listed with the terms indicate where the term is highlighted in the chapter.

monopoly, 409
oligopoly, 411
limited competition, 411
direct payment, 412
indirect payment, 412

economies of scale, 412
hegemony, 418
synergy, 422
cultural imperialism, 429

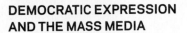

14

The Culture of Journalism:

Values, Ethics, and Democracy

In 2008, a former press secretary for outgoing president George W. Bush dropped a literary bomb on the White House in the form of a political memoir. In *What Happened: Inside the Bush White House and Washington's Culture of Deception*, Scott McClellan (pictured) told the story of a broken Washington political system that was too partisan and too focused on winning elections. He described Washington as "the home of the permanent campaign, a game of endless politicking based on the manipulation of shades of truth, partial truths, twisting of the truth, and spin. Governing has become an appendage of politics rather than the other way around. . . . That means shaping the narrative before it shapes you. Candor and honesty are pushed to the side in the battle to win the latest news cycle."[1] The Bush administration fired back by stating that the book was untruthful and McClellan was a disgruntled ex-employee. Later that year McClellan endorsed Democrat Barack Obama for president.

McClellan also criticized the mainstream media as "complicit enablers" in the political system, especially in the run-up to the Iraq war. Many in the traditional news media—particularly in network news—disagreed with McClellan on this point and defended their coverage. However, both the *Washington Post* and the *New York Times* had issued apologies in 2004 for not being more skeptical of the White House's rationale for the Iraq war.[2]

By 2006, the relations between the administration and the press had grown hostile. The Bush White House criticized the *New York Times* for publishing a story that "disclosed a secret Bush administration program to monitor" bank records of suspected terrorists— and those of millions of others.[3] While the *Los Angeles Times* and the *Wall Street Journal* had also disclosed the program, the White House condemned only the *Times* (which takes more liberal positions in its editorials), calling the report "disgraceful" and "very dangerous." Despite calls to prosecute the paper for treason, the U.S. government has "never once prosecuted the press for publishing government secrets."[4]

At that time, NBC's *Meet the Press* featured a roundtable debate on tensions between the government and the press, and on the government's tendency to attack the news media when White House initiatives do poorly. Among other guests, the program featured conservative *Times* columnist William Safire, the *Post's* Dana Priest, and William Bennett, a conservative spokesman for Republicans.

The *Meet the Press* program was a healthy debate about how the press has to weigh the public good against an administration's desire for secrecy. In the end, the debate revealed two differing conservative camps. Opposing the publication of the *Times's* banking story, William Bennett claimed that an elected president had the right to carry out a war as he saw fit. On the other side, supporting the story's publication, William Safire said the decision to publish was difficult but served the public's best interests.

Safire argued that, with the First Amendment, our founders enabled the press to "act as a check and balance on government." And historically the Supreme Court has agreed with Safire. As Justice Hugo Black wrote in 1971, "The government's power to censor the press was abolished so that the press would remain forever free to censure the government. The press was protected so that it could bare the secrets of the government and inform the people." What McClellan and other news media critics remind us about the coverage of the Iraq war is that too often the news media did not use all of the tools at their disposal to "inform the people" about the war and how we got there.

"Our liberty depends on the freedom of the press, and that cannot be limited without being lost."
THOMAS JEFFERSON

▲ **JOURNALISM IS THE ONLY MEDIA ENTERPRISE** that democracy absolutely requires–and it is the only media practice and business that is specifically mentioned and protected by the U.S. Constitution. However, with the gradual decline in traditional news audiences, the growing criticism of East Coast celebrity journalists, and the rise of twenty-four-hour cable news channels and Internet news blogs, mainstream journalists are searching for ways to reconnect with the public.

In this chapter, we examine the changing news landscape and definitions of journalism. We also look at the implicit values underlying news practice and the ethical problems confronting journalists. Next, we study the legacy of print-news conventions and rituals. We then turn to the impact of television and the Internet on news. Finally, we take up recent controversial developments in journalism and democracy, specifically examining the public journalism movement, satirical forms of news, and citizen journalism.

Modern Journalism in the Information Age

In modern America, serious journalism has sought to provide information that enables citizens to make intelligent decisions. Today, this guiding principle has been partially derailed. Why? First, we may just be producing too much information. According to social critic Neil Postman, as a result of developments in media technology, society has developed an "information glut" that transforms news and information into "a form of garbage."[5] Postman believed that scientists, technicians, managers, and journalists merely pile up mountains of new data, which add to the problems and anxieties of everyday life. As a result, too much unchecked data–especially on the Internet–and too little thoughtful discussion emanate from too many channels of communication.

A second, related problem suggests that the amount of information the media now provide has made little impact on improving public and political life. Many people feel cut off from our major institutions, including journalism. As a result, some citizens are looking to take part in public conversations and civic debates–to renew a democracy in which many voices participate. For example, one of the benefits of the controversial 2000 presidential post-election story was the way its legal and political complications engaged the citizenry at a much deeper level than the predictable, staged campaigns themselves did.

What Is News?

In a 1963 staff memo, NBC news president Reuven Frank outlined the narrative strategies integral to all news: "Every news story should . . . display the attributes of fiction, of drama. It should have structure and conflict, problem and denouement, rising and falling action, a beginning, a middle, and an end."[6] Despite Frank's candid insights, many journalists today are uncomfortable thinking of themselves as storytellers. Instead, they tend to describe themselves mainly as information-gatherers.

News is defined here as the process of gathering information and making narrative reports–edited by individuals for news organizations–that offer selected frames of reference; within those frames, news helps the public make sense of prominent people, important events, and unusual happenings in everyday life.

"DEEP THROAT"
The major symbol of
twentieth-century
investigative journalism,
Carl Bernstein and Bob
Woodward's (*above right*)
coverage of the Watergate
scandal for the *Washington
Post* helped topple the
Nixon White House. In *All
the President's Men*, the
newsmen's book about
their investigation, a major
character is Deep Throat,
the key unidentified source
for much of Woodward's
reporting. Deep Throat's
identity was protected by
the two reporters for more
than thirty years. Then in
summer 2005 he revealed
himself as Mark Felt (*above*),
the former No. 2 official in
the FBI during the Nixon
administration. (Felt passed
away in 2008.)

Characteristics of News

Over time, a set of conventional criteria for determining **newsworthiness**–information most worthy of transformation into news stories–has evolved. Journalists are taught to select and develop news stories with one or more of these criteria: timeliness, proximity, conflict, prominence, human interest, consequence, usefulness, novelty, and deviance.[7]

Most issues and events that journalists select as news are *timely* or *new*. Reporters, for example, cover speeches, meetings, crimes, and court cases that have just happened. In addition, most of these events have to occur close by, or in *proximity* to, readers and viewers. Although local papers usually offer some national and international news, readers and viewers expect to find the bulk of news devoted to their own towns and communities.

Most news stories are narratives and thus contain a healthy dose of *conflict*–a key ingredient in narrative writing. In developing news narratives, reporters are encouraged to seek contentious quotes from those with opposing views. For example, stories on presidential elections almost always feature the most dramatic opposing Republican and Democratic positions. And stories in the aftermath of the terrorist attacks of September 11, 2001, pitted the values of other cultures against those of Western culture–for example, Islam versus Christianity or premodern traditional values versus contemporary consumerism.

Reader and viewer surveys indicate that most people identify more closely with an individual than with an abstract issue. Therefore, the news media tend to report stories that feature *prominent*, powerful, or influential people. Because these individuals often play a role in shaping the rules and values of a community, journalists have traditionally been responsible for keeping a watchful eye on them.

But reporters also look for the *human-interest* story: extraordinary incidents that happen to "ordinary" people. In fact, reporters often relate a story about a complicated issue (such as unemployment, war, tax rates, health care, or homelessness) by illustrating its impact on one "average" person or family.

Two other criteria for newsworthiness are *consequence* and *usefulness*. Stories about isolated or bizarre crimes, even though they might be new, near, or notorious, often have little impact on our daily lives. To balance these kinds of stories, many editors and reporters believe that some news must also be of consequence to a majority of readers or viewers. For example, stories about issues or events that affect a family's income or change a community's laws have consequence. Likewise, many people look for stories with a practical use: hints on buying a used car or choosing a college, strategies for training a pet or removing a stain.

Finally, news is often about the *novel* and the *deviant*. When events happen that are outside the routine of daily life, such as a seven-year-old girl trying to pilot a plane across the country or an ex-celebrity involved in a drug deal, the news media are there. Reporters also cover events that appear to deviate from social norms, including murders, rapes, fatal car crashes, fires, political scandals, and gang activities. For example, as the war in Iraq escalated, any suicide bombing in the Middle East represented the kind of novel and deviant behavior that qualified as major news.

Values in American Journalism

Although newsworthiness criteria are a useful way to define news, they do not reveal much about the cultural aspects of news. News is both a product and a process. It is both the morning paper or evening newscast and a set of subtle values and shifting rituals that have been adapted to historical and social circumstances, such as the partisan press ideals of the 1700s or the informational standards of the twentieth century.

For example, in 1841, Horace Greeley described the newly founded *New York Tribune* as "a journal removed alike from servile partisanship on the one hand and from gagged, mincing neutrality on the other."[8] Greeley feared that too much neutrality would make reporters into wimps who stood for nothing. Yet the neutrality Greeley warned against is today a major value of conventional journalism, with mainstream reporters assuming they are acting as detached and all-seeing observers of social experience, along with other modern news values.

Neutrality Boosts Credibility ... and Sales

As journalism professor and former reporter David Eason notes: "Reporters . . . have no special method for determining the truth of a situation nor a special language for reporting their findings. They make sense of events by telling stories about them."[9]

Even though journalists transform events into stories, they generally believe that they are—or should be—neutral observers who present facts without passing judgment on them. Conventions such as the inverted-pyramid news lead, the careful attribution of sources, the minimal use of adverbs and adjectives, and a detached third-person point of view all help reporters perform their work in a supposedly neutral way.

Like lawyers, therapists, and other professionals, many modern journalists believe that their credibility derives from personal detachment. Yet the roots of this view reside in less noble territory. Jon Katz, media critic and former CBS News producer, discusses the history of the neutral pose:

The idea of respectable detachment wasn't conceived as a moral principle so much as a marketing device. Once newspapers began to mass market themselves in the mid-1880s, . . . publishers ceased being working, opinionated journalists. They mutated instead into businessmen eager to reach the broadest number of readers and antagonize the fewest. . . . Objectivity works well for publishers, protecting the status quo and keeping journalism's voice militantly moderate.[10]

To reach as many people as possible across a wide spectrum, publishers and editors realized as early as the 1840s that softening their partisanship might boost sales.

Other Cultural Values in Journalism

Neutral journalism remains a selective process. Reporters and editors turn some events into reports and discard many others. This process is governed by a deeper set of subjective beliefs

> "The 'information' the modern media provide leaves people feeling useless not because it's so bleak but because it's so trivial. It doesn't inform at all; it only bombards with random data bits, faux trends, and surveys that reinforce preconceptions."
>
> SUSAN FALUDI, *NATION*, 1996

> "Real news is bad news—bad news about somebody, or bad news for somebody."
>
> MARSHALL MCLUHAN, *UNDERSTANDING MEDIA*, 1964

SMALL-TOWN PASTORALISM is one of the values sociologist Herbert Gans found in American journalism. Stories that feature the "goodness" of small-town America—like communities pulling together to sandbag river banks during the floods in the Midwest in 2008—are a favorite among reporters.

that are not neutral. Sociologist Herbert Gans, who studied the newsroom cultures of CBS, NBC, *Newsweek,* and *Time* in the 1970s, generalized that several basic "enduring values" have been shared by most American reporters and editors. The most prominent of these values, which endure to this day, are ethnocentrism, responsible capitalism, small-town pastoralism, and individualism.[11]

By **ethnocentrism** Gans means that, in most news reporting, especially foreign coverage, reporters judge other countries and cultures on the basis of how "they live up to or imitate American practices and values." Critics outside the United States, for instance, point out that CNN's international news channels portray world events and cultures primarily from an American point of view rather than through some neutral, global lens.

Gans also identified **responsible capitalism** as an underlying value, contending that journalists sometimes naively assume that businesspeople compete with one another not primarily to maximize profits but "to create increased prosperity for all." Gans points out that although most reporters and editors condemn monopolies, "there is little implicit or explicit criticism of the oligopolistic nature of much of today's economy."[12] In fact, by the 1990s, most journalists worked in monopoly newspaper towns or for oligopoly parent companies. Thus writing about the limitations of such economic structures constituted "biting the hand that fed you."

Another value that Gans found was the romanticization of **small-town pastoralism**: favoring the small over the large and the rural over the urban. Many journalists equate small-town life with innocence and harbor suspicions of cities, their governments, and urban experiences. Consequently, stories about rustic communities with crime or drug problems have often been framed as if the purity of country life had been contaminated by mean city values.

Finally, **individualism**, according to Gans, remains the most prominent value underpinning daily journalism. Many idealistic reporters are attracted to this profession because it rewards the rugged tenacity needed to confront and expose corruption. Beyond this, individuals who overcome personal adversity are the subjects of many enterprising news stories.

Often, however, journalism that focuses on personal triumphs fails to explain how large organizations and institutions work or fail. Many conventional reporters and editors are unwilling or unsure of how to tackle the problems raised by institutional decay. In addition, because they value their own individualism and are accustomed to working alone, many journalists dislike cooperating on team projects or participating in forums in which community members discuss their own interests and alternative definitions of news.[13]

Facts, Values, and Bias

Traditionally, reporters have aligned facts with an objective position and values with subjective feelings.[14] Within this context, news reports offer readers and viewers details, data, and description. It then becomes the citizen's responsibility to judge and take a stand about the social problems represented by the news. Given these assumptions, reporters are responsible only for adhering to the traditions of the trade—"getting the facts." As a result, many reporters view themselves as neutral "channels" of information rather than selective storytellers or citizens actively involved in public life.

Still, most public surveys have shown that, while journalists may work hard to claim and defend their neutrality, most people regard them as politically biased. Not surprisingly, conservatives tend to see the media as liberally biased, while liberals tend to see the media as favoring conservative positions. (See "Case Study: Bias in the News," page 442). But political bias is complicated. During the 2008 presidential campaign, Senator Hillary Clinton's campaign argued that the press was biased in favor of Barack Obama. Meanwhile, media critics said that the press "took it easy" on Republican presidential candidate John McCain because he was a war hero and relatively open to talking to reporters.

According to Evan Thomas of *Newsweek* magazine, "the suspicion of press bias" comes from two assumptions or beliefs that the public holds about news media: "The first is that reporters are out to get their subjects. The second is that the press is too close to its subjects. . . ."[15] Thomas argues that the "press's real bias is for conflict." He says that editors and reporters really value scandals, "preferably sexual," and "have a weakness for war, the ultimate conflict." Thomas claims that in the end journalists "are looking for narratives that reveal something of character. It is the human drama that most compels our attention."[16]

Ethics and the News Media

The story at the beginning of this chapter speaks to a profound ethical dilemma that national journalists occasionally face, especially in the aftermath of 9/11: When is it right to protect government secrets, and when should those secrets be revealed to the public? How must editors weigh such decisions when national security bumps up against citizens' need for information?

In 2006, Dean Baquet, then-editor of the *Los Angeles Times*, and Bill Keller, executive editor of the *New York Times*, wrestled with and wrote about this dilemma:

Finally, we weigh the merits of publishing against the risks of publishing. There is no magic formula. . . . We make our best judgment.

When we come down on the side of publishing, of course, everyone hears about it. Few people are aware when we decide to hold an article. But each of us, in the past few years, has had the experience of withholding or delaying articles when the administration convinces us that the risk of publication outweighed the benefits. . . .

We understand that honorable people may disagree . . . to publish or not to publish. But making those decisions is a responsibility that falls to editors, a corollary to the great gift of our independence. It is not a responsibility we take lightly. And it is not one we can surrender to the government.[17]

What makes the predicament of these national editors so tricky is that in the war against terrorism, the government claimed that one value terrorists truly hate is "our freedom"; and yet what is more symbolic of liberty than the freedom of an independent press—so independent that for more than two hundred years U.S. courts have protected the news media's right to criticize our political leaders and reveal government secrets?

> "There's a fine line between show biz and news biz. The trick is to walk up to that line and touch it with your toe but don't cross it. And some people stay so far away from the line that nobody wants to watch what they do. And other people keep crossing the line. . . . But there has to be a line because the line is called truth. And the difference between what we do is, we tell true stories and other people tell make-believe stories."
>
> DON HEWITT, CREATOR OF *60 MINUTES*

Bias in the News

All news is biased. News, after all, is primarily selective storytelling, not objective science. Editors choose certain events to cover and ignore others; reporters choose particular words or images to use and reject others. The news is also biased in favor of storytelling, drama, and conflict; in favor of telling "two sides of a story"; in favor of powerful and connected sources; and in favor of practices that serve journalists' space and time limits.

In terms of overt political bias, public perception says that mainstream news media operate mostly with a liberal bias. A June 2006 Harris Poll found 38 percent of adults surveyed detected a liberal bias in news coverage while 25 percent sensed a conservative bias (31 percent were "not sure" and 5 percent said there was "no bias").[1] This would seem to be supported by a 2004 Pew Research Center survey that found that 34 percent of national journalists self-identify as liberal, 7 percent as conservative, and 54 percent as moderate.[2]

Given primary dictionary definitions of *liberal* (adj., "favorable to progress or reform, as in political or religious affairs") and *conservative* (adj., "disposed to preserve existing conditions, institutions, etc., or to restore traditional ones,

and to limit change"), it is not surprising that a high percentage of liberals and moderates gravitate to mainstream journalism.[3] A profession that honors documenting change, checking power, and reporting wrongdoing would attract fewer conservatives, who are predisposed to "limit change." As sociologist Herbert Gans demonstrated in *Deciding What's News*, most reporters are socialized into a set of work rituals—especially getting the story first and telling it from "both sides" to achieve a kind of balance.[4] In fact, this commitment to political "balance" mandates that if journalists interview someone on the Left, they must also interview someone on the Right. Ultimately, such a balancing act makes conventional news a middle-of-the-road or moderate proposition.

Still, the "liberal bias" narrative persists. In 2001, Bernard Goldberg, a former producer at CBS News, published *Bias*. Using anecdotes from his days at CBS, he maintained that national news slanted to the left.[5] In 2003, Eric Alterman, a columnist for the *Nation*, countered with *What Liberal Media?* Alterman admitted that mainstream news media do reflect more liberal views on social issues, but that they had become more conservative on politics and economics—displayed

in their support for deregulated media and concentrated ownership.[6] Alterman says the liberal bias tale persists because conservatives keep repeating that story in the major media. Conservative voices have been so successful that a study in *Communication Research* reported "a fourfold increase over the past dozen years in the number of Americans telling pollsters that they discerned a liberal bias in the news. But a review of the media's actual ideological content, collected and coded over a 12-year period, offered no corroboration whatever for this view."[7]

Since journalists are primarily storytellers, and not scientists, searching for liberal or conservative bias should not be the main focus of our criticism. Under time and space constraints, most journalists serve the routine process of their profession, which calls on them to moderate their own political agendas. News reports, then, are always "biased," given human imperfection in storytelling and in communicating through the lens of language, images, and institutional values. Fully critiquing news stories depends, then, on whether they are fair, represent an issue's complexity, provide verification and documentation, represent multiple views, and serve democracy. ◢

IS THERE A BIAS IN REPORTING THE NEWS?

	Political Party Affiliation				Political Philosophy		
	Total %	Republican %	Democrat %	Independent %	Conservative %	Moderate %	Liberal %
There is a liberal bias in the media.	38	66	18	36	62	35	10
There is no bias in the media.	5	1	8	7	3	5	9
There is a conservative bias in the media.	25	13	37	26	13	24	47
Not at all sure.	31	20	36	31	22	36	34

Note: Percentages add up to more than 100 percent due to multiple responses accepted.
Source: The Harris Poll® #52, June 30, 2006, http://www.harrisinteractive.com/harris_poll.

Ethical Predicaments

What is the moral and social responsibility of journalists, not only for the stories they report but also for the actual events or issues they are shaping for millions of people? Wrestling with such media ethics involves determining the moral response to a situation through critical reasoning. Although national security issues raise problems for a few of our largest news organizations, the most frequent ethical dilemmas encountered in most newsrooms across the United States involve intentional deception, privacy invasions, and conflicts of interest.

Deploying Deception

Ever since Nellie Bly faked insanity to get inside an asylum in the 1880s, investigative journalists have used deception to get stories. Today, journalists continue to use disguises and assume false identities to gather information on social transgressions. Beyond legal considerations, though, a key ethical question comes into play: Does the end justify the means? For example, can a newspaper or TV newsmagazine use deceptive ploys to go undercover and expose a suspected fraudulent clinic that promises miracle cures at a high cost? Are news professionals justified in posing as clients desperate for a cure?

In terms of ethics, there are at least two major positions and multiple variations. First, *absolutist ethics* suggest that a moral society has laws and codes, including honesty, that everyone must live by. This means citizens, including members of the news media, should tell the truth at all times and in all cases. In other words, the ends (exposing a phony clinic) never justify the means (using deception to get the story). An editor who is an absolutist would cover this story by asking a reporter to find victims who have been ripped off by the clinic, telling the story through their eyes. At the other end of the spectrum is *situational ethics,* which promotes ethical decisions on a case-by-case basis. If a greater public good could be served by using deceit, journalists and editors who believe in situational ethics would sanction deception as a practice.

Should a journalist withhold information about his or her professional identity to get a quote or a story from an interview subject? Many sources and witnesses are reluctant to talk with journalists, especially about a sensitive subject that might jeopardize a job or hurt another person's reputation. Journalists know they can sometimes obtain information by posing as someone other than a journalist, such as a curious student or a concerned citizen.

Most newsrooms frown on such deception. In particular situations, though, such a practice might be condoned if reporters and their editors believed that the public needed the information. The ethics code adopted by the Society of Professional Journalists (SPJ) is fairly silent on issues of deception. The code "requires journalists to perform with intelligence, objectivity, accuracy, and fairness," but it also says that "truth is our ultimate goal." (See Figure 14.1, "SPJ Code of Ethics," on page 444.)

Invading Privacy

To achieve "the truth" or to "get the facts," journalists routinely straddle a line between "the public's right to know" and a person's right to privacy. For example, journalists may be sent to hospitals to gather quotes from victims who have been injured. Often there is very little the public might gain from such information, but journalists worry that if they don't get the quote, a competitor might. In these instances, have the news media responsibly weighed the protection of individual privacy against the public's right to know? Although the latter is not constitutionally guaranteed, journalists invoke the public's right to know as justification for many types of stories.

Privacy issues also affect corporations and institutions. For example, in 1998 a *Cincinnati Enquirer* reporter got into trouble for illegally gaining access to the voice-mail system at Chiquita, a company best known for selling bananas. The reporter used voice-mail information

FIGURE 14.1

SOCIETY OF PROFESSIONAL JOURNALISTS' CODE OF ETHICS

Source: Society of Professional Journalists.

▼

Code Of Ethics

Preamble

Members of the Society of Professional Journalists believe that public enlightenment is the forerunner of justice and the foundation of democracy. The duty of the journalist is to further those ends by seeking truth and providing a fair and comprehensive account of events and issues. Conscientious journalists from all media and specialties strive to serve the public with thoroughness and honesty. Professional integrity is the cornerstone of a journalist's credibility.

Members of the Society share a dedication to ethical behavior and adopt this code to declare the Society's principles and standards of practice.

Seek Truth and Report It

Journalists should be honest, fair and courageous in gathering, reporting and interpreting information.

Journalists should:

- Test the accuracy of information from all sources and exercise care to avoid inadvertent error. Deliberate distortion is never permissible.
- Diligently seek out subjects of news stories to give them the opportunity to respond to allegations of wrongdoing.
- Identify sources whenever feasible. The public is entitled to as much information as possible on sources' reliability.
- Always question sources' motives before promising anonymity. Clarify conditions attached to any promise made in exchange for information. Keep promises.
- Make certain that headlines, news teases and promotional material, photos, video, audio, graphics, sound bites and quotations do not misrepresent. They should not oversimplify or highlight incidents out of context.
- Never distort the content of news photos or video. Image enhancement for technical clarity is always permissible. Label montages and photo illustrations.
- Avoid misleading re-enactments or staged news events. If re-enactment is necessary to tell a story, label it.
- Avoid undercover or other surreptitious methods of gathering information except when traditional open methods will not yield information vital to the public. Use of such methods should be explained as part of the story.
- Never plagiarize.
- Tell the story of the diversity and magnitude of the human experience boldly, even when it is unpopular to do so.
- Examine their own cultural values and avoid imposing those values on others.
- Avoid stereotyping by race, gender, age, religion, ethnicity, geography, sexual orientation, disability, physical appearance or social status.
- Support the open exchange of views, even views they find repugnant.
- Give voice to the voiceless; official and unofficial sources of information can be equally valid.
- Distinguish between advocacy and news reporting. Analysis and commentary should be labeled and not misrepresent fact or context.
- Distinguish news from advertising and shun hybrids that blur the lines between the two.
- Recognize a special obligation to ensure that the public's business is conducted in the open and that government records are open to inspection.

Minimize Harm

Ethical journalists treat sources, subjects and colleagues as human beings deserving of respect.

Journalists should:

- Show compassion for those who may be affected adversely by news coverage. Use special sensitivity when dealing with children and inexperienced sources or subjects.
- Be sensitive when seeking or using interviews or photographs of those affected by tragedy or grief.
- Recognize that gathering and reporting information may cause harm or discomfort. Pursuit of the news is not a license for arrogance.
- Recognize that private people have a greater right to control information about themselves than do public officials and others who seek power, influence or attention. Only an overriding public need can justify intrusion into anyone's privacy.
- Show good taste. Avoid pandering to lurid curiosity.
- Be cautious about identifying juvenile suspects or victims of sex crimes.
- Be judicious about naming criminal suspects before the formal filing of charges.
- Balance a criminal suspect's fair trial rights with the public's right to be informed.

Act Independently

Journalists should be free of obligation to any interest other than the public's right to know.

Journalists should:

- Avoid conflicts of interest, real or perceived.
- Remain free of associations and activities that may compromise integrity or damage credibility.
- Refuse gifts, favors, free travel and special treatment, and shun secondary employment, political involvement, public office and service in community organizations if they compromise journalistic integrity.
- Disclose unavoidable conflicts.
- Be vigilant and courageous about holding those with power accountable.
- Deny favored treatment to advertisers and special interests and resist their pressure to influence news coverage.
- Be wary of sources offering information for favors or money; avoid bidding for news.

Be Accountable

Journalists are accountable to their readers, listeners, viewers and each other.

Journalists should:

- Clarify and explain news coverage and invite dialogue with the public over journalistic conduct.
- Encourage the public to voice grievances against the news media.
- Admit mistakes and correct them promptly.
- Expose unethical practices of journalists and the news media.
- Abide by the same high standards to which they hold others.

to report on the company's business practices. Although a few journalists applauded the reporter's resourcefulness, many critics said it was a violation of the company's privacy rights. Today, in the digital age, when reporters can gain access to private e-mail messages as well as voice mail, such practices raise serious questions about how far a reporter should go to get information.

Reporters and editors should always ask the ethical questions: What public good is being served here? What significant public knowledge will be gained through the exploitation of a tragic private moment? Although journalism's code of ethics says, "The news media must guard against invading a person's right to privacy," this clashes with another part of the code: "The public's right to know of events of public importance and interest is the overriding mission of the mass media."[18] When these two ethical standards collide, journalists usually err on the side of the public's right to know.

Conflict of Interest

Journalism's code of ethics also warns reporters and editors not to place themselves in positions that produce a **conflict of interest**–that is, any situation in which journalists may stand to benefit personally from stories they produce. "Gifts, favors, free travel, special treatment or privileges," the code states, "can compromise the integrity of journalists and their employers. Nothing of value should be accepted."[19]

For instance, large newspapers or broadcast stations usually pay for the game tickets of their sportswriters and for the meals of their restaurant critics. Small newspapers, however, with limited resources and poorly paid reporters, might accept such "freebies" from a local business or interview subject. This practice may be an economic necessity, but it does increase the likelihood of a conflict of interest that produces favorable or uncritical coverage.

On a broader level, ethical guidelines at many news outlets attempt to protect journalists from compromising positions. For instance, in most cities, U.S. journalists do not actively participate in politics or support social causes. Some journalists will not reveal their political affiliations, and some even decline to vote.

For these journalists, the rationale behind their decisions is straightforward: Journalists should not place themselves in a situation in which they might have to report on the misdeeds of an organization or a political party to which they belong. If a journalist has a tie to any group, and that group is later suspected of involvement in shady or criminal activity, the reporter's ability to report on that group would be compromised–along with the credibility of the news outlet for which he or she works.

Conversely, other journalists believe that not actively participating in politics or social causes means abandoning their civic obligations. They believe that fairness in their reporting, not total detachment from civic engagement, is their primary obligation.

Resolving Ethical Problems

When a journalist is criticized for ethical lapses or questionable reporting tactics, a typical response might be "I'm just doing my job" or "I was just getting the facts." Such explanations are troubling, though, because in responding this way, reporters are transferring personal responsibility for the story to a set of institutional rituals.

There are, of course, ethical alternatives to self-justifications such as "I'm just doing my job" that force journalists to think through complex issues. With the crush of deadlines and daily duties, most media professionals deal with ethical situations only on a case-by-case basis as issues arise. However, examining major ethical models and theories provides a common strategy for addressing ethics on a general rather than a situational basis. The most well-known ethical standard, the Judeo-Christian command to "love your neighbor as

ETHICS AND REPORTING
For almost three months, security guard Richard Jewell was the FBI's main suspect in the July 1996 Olympic Park bombing that killed one person. When the FBI finally exonerated Jewell, he filed libel suits against the *Atlanta Journal-Constitution*, CNN, and NBC. In 2005, serial bomber Eric Rudolph pleaded guilty to the Olympics bombing and three other bomb attacks.

yourself," provides a foundation for constructing ethical guidelines. Although we cannot address all major moral codes here, a few key precepts can guide us.

Aristotle, Kant, Bentham, and Mill

The Greek philosopher Aristotle offered an early ethical concept, the "golden mean"—a guideline for seeking balance between competing positions. For Aristotle, this was a desirable middle ground between extreme positions, usually one regarded as deficient, the other excessive. For example, Aristotle saw ambition as the balance between sloth and greed.

Another ethical principle entails the "categorical imperative," developed by German philosopher Immanuel Kant (1724-1804). This idea maintains that a society must adhere to moral codes that are universal and unconditional, applicable in all situations at all times. For example, the Golden Rule ("Do unto others as you would have them do unto you") is articulated in one form or another in most of the world's major religious and philosophical traditions, and operates as an absolutist moral principle. The First Amendment, which prevents Congress from abridging free speech and other rights, is an example of a national unconditional law.

British philosophers Jeremy Bentham (1748-1832) and John Stuart Mill (1806-1873) promoted an ethical principle derived from "the greatest good for the greatest number," directing us "to distribute a good consequence to more people rather than to fewer, whenever we have a choice."[20]

Developing Ethical Policy

Arriving at ethical decisions involves several stages. These include laying out the case; pinpointing the key issues; identifying involved parties, their intent, and their competing values; studying ethical models; presenting strategies and options; and formulating a decision.

One area that requires ethics is covering the private lives of people who have become prominent in the news. Consider Richard Jewell, the Atlanta security guard who, for eighty-eight days, was the FBI's prime suspect in the park bombing at the 1996 Olympics. The FBI never charged Jewell with a crime, and he later successfully sued several news organizations for libel. The news media competed to be the first to report important developments in the case, and with the battle for newspaper circulation and broadcast ratings adding fuel to a complex situation, editors were reluctant to back away from the story once it began circulating.

At least two key ethical questions emerged: (1) Should the news media have named Jewell as a suspect even though he was never charged with a crime? (2) Should the media have camped out daily in front of his mother's house in an attempt to interview him and his mother? The Jewell case pitted the media's right to tell stories and earn profits against a person's right to be left alone.

Working through the various ethical stages, journalists formulate policies grounded in overarching moral principles.[21] Should reporters, for instance, follow the Golden Rule and be willing to treat themselves, their families, or their friends the way they treated the Jewells? Or should they invoke Aristotle's "golden mean" and seek moral virtue between extreme positions?

In Richard Jewell's situation, journalists could have developed guidelines to balance Jewell's interests and the news media's. For example, in addition to apologizing for using Jewell's name in early accounts, reporters might have called off their stakeout and allowed Jewell to set interview times at a neutral site, where he could talk with a small pool of journalists designated to relay information to other media outlets.

Reporting Rituals and the Legacy of Print Journalism

Unfamiliar with being questioned themselves, many reporters are uncomfortable discussing their personal values or their strategies for getting stories. Nevertheless, a stock of rituals, derived from basic American values, underlie the practice of reporting. These include focusing on the present, relying on experts, balancing story conflict, and acting as adversaries toward leaders and institutions.

Focusing on the Present

In the 1840s, when the telegraph first enabled news to crisscross America instantly, modern journalism was born. To complement the new technical advances, editors called for a focus on the immediacy of the present. Modern front-page print journalism de-emphasized political analysis and historical context, accenting instead the new and the now.

As a result, the profession began drawing criticism for failing to offer historical, political, and social analyses. This criticism continues today. For example, urban drug stories heavily dominated print and network news during the 1986 and 1988 election years. Such stories, however, virtually disappeared from the news by 1992, although the nation's serious drug and addiction problems had not diminished.[22] For many editors and reporters at the time, drug stories became "yesterday's news."

Modern journalism tends to reject "old news" for whatever new event or idea disrupts today's routines. During the 1996 elections, when statistics revealed that drug use among middle-class high school students was rising, reporters latched on to new versions of the drug story, but their reports made only limited references to the 1980s. And although drug problems and addiction rates did not diminish in subsequent years, these topics were virtually ignored by journalists during the 2000, 2004, and 2008 national elections. Indeed, given the space and time constraints of current news practices, reporters seldom link stories to the past or to the ebb and flow of history. (To analyze current news stories, see "Media Literacy and the Critical Process: Telling Stories and Covering Disaster" on page 449.)

Getting a Good Story

Early in the 1980s, the Janet Cooke hoax demonstrated the difference between the mere telling of a good story and the social responsibility to tell the truth.[23] Cooke, a former *Washington Post* reporter, was fired for fabricating an investigative report for which she initially won a Pulitzer Prize (it was later revoked). She had created a cast of characters, featuring a mother who contributed to the heroin addiction of her eight-year-old son.

At the time the hoax was exposed, Chicago columnist Mike Royko criticized conventional journalism for allowing narrative conventions—getting a good story—to trump journalism's responsibility to the daily lives it documents: "There's something more important than a

GETTING THE STORY
The pressure on journalists to tell great stories and get them first has led to occasional problems. In May 2003, the *New York Times* revealed that one of its reporters, twenty-seven-year-old Jayson Blair (*left*), made up facts; invented sources; stole quotes from other newspapers; and, in short, plagiarized dozens of articles. He even pretended to be reporting from Texas when he was actually at home in Brooklyn. In a fourteen-thousand-word report and self-examination, the *Times* called the episode "a low point" in the paper's storied history. Both the chief editor and managing editor of the *Times* resigned shortly after Blair's dismissal.

"[M]arathon mourning is now a hit show biz formula for generating ratings and news-stand sales....
The treacly theme music, the cheesy greeting-card art graphics, the New Age vocabulary of 'closure,' the ritual-istically repeated slo-mo video clips."

FRANK RICH,
NEW YORK TIMES
COLUMNIST,
CRITICIZING THE
EXCESSIVE COVERAGE
OF THE 1999 PLANE
CRASH THAT KILLED
JFK JR., CAROLYN
BESSETTE KENNEDY,
AND LAUREN
BESSETTE

story here. This eight-year-old kid is being murdered. The editors should have said forget the story, find the kid. . . . People in any other profession would have gone right to the police."[24] Had editors at the *Post* demanded such help, Cooke's hoax would not have gone as far as it did.

According to Don Hewitt, the creator and longtime executive producer of *60 Minutes*, "There's a very simple formula if you're in Hollywood, Broadway, opera, publishing, broadcasting, newspapering. It's four very simple words—tell me a story."[25] For most journalists, the bottom line is "Get the story"—an edict that overrides most other concerns. It is the standard against which reporters measure themselves and their profession.

Getting a Story First

In a discussion on public television about the press coverage of a fatal airline crash in Milwaukee in the 1980s, a news photographer was asked to discuss his role in covering the tragedy. Rather than take up the poignant, heartbreaking aspects of witnessing the aftermath of such an event, the excited photographer launched into a dramatic recounting of how he had slipped behind police barricades to snap the first grim photos, which later appeared in the *Milwaukee Journal*. As part of their socialization into the profession, reporters often learn to evade authority figures to secure a story ahead of the competition.

The photographer's recollection points to the important role journalism plays in calling public attention to serious events and issues. Yet he also talked about the news-gathering process as a game that journalists play. It's now routine for local television stations, 24/7 cable news, and newspapers to run self-promotions about how they beat competitors to a story. In addition, during political elections, local television stations and networks project winners in particular races and often hype their projections when they are able to forecast results before the competition does. This practice led to the fiasco in November 2000 when the major networks and cable news services badly flubbed their predictions regarding the outcome of voting in Florida in the presidential election.

Journalistic *scoops* and exclusive stories attempt to portray reporters in a heroic light: They have won a race for facts, which they have gathered and presented ahead of their rivals. It is not always clear, though, how the public is better served by a journalist's claim to have gotten a story first. In some ways, the 24/7 cable news, the Internet, and bloggers have intensified the

Media Literacy and the Critical Process

1 **DESCRIPTION.** Find print and broadcast news versions of the *same* disaster story from two different days of the week. Make copies of each story, and note the pictures chosen to tell the story.

2 **ANALYSIS.** Find patterns in the coverage. How are the stories treated differently in print and on television? Are there similarities in the words chosen or images used? What kinds of experience are depicted? Who are the sources the reporters use to verify their information?

3 **INTERPRETATION.** What do these patterns suggest? Can you make any interpretations or arguments based on the kinds of disaster covered, sources used, areas covered, or words/images chosen? How are the stories told in relation to their importance to the entire community or nation? How complex are the stories?

Telling Stories and Covering Disaster

Covering difficult stories—such as natural disasters or tragedies—may present challenges to journalists about how to frame their coverage. The opening sections—or leads—from news stories can vary depending on the source—whether it is print, broadcast, or online news—or even the editorial style of the news organization (e.g., some story leads are straightforward, some are very dramatic). And, although modern journalists claim objectivity as a goal, it is unlikely that a profession in the storytelling business can approximate any sort of scientific objectivity. The best journalists can do is be fair, reporting and telling stories to their communities and nation by explaining the complicated and tragic experiences they convert into words or pictures. To explore this type of coverage, try this exercise with examples from recent disaster coverage from a regional or national event.

4 **EVALUATION.** Which stories are the strongest? Why? Which are the weakest? Why? Make a judgment on how well these disaster stories serve your interests as a citizen and the interests of the larger community or nation.

5 **ENGAGEMENT.** In an e-mail or letter to the editor, report your findings to relevant editors and TV news directors. How did they respond?

race for getting a story first. With a fragmented audience and more media competing for news, the mainstream news often feels more pressure to lure an audience with exclusive, and often sensational, stories. Although readers and viewers might value the tenacity of reporters, the earliest reports are not necessarily better, more accurate, or as complete as stories written later with more context and perspective.

On occasion, scoop behavior leads to pack or **herd journalism**, which occurs when reporters stake out a house, chase celebrities in packs, or follow a story in such herds that the entire profession comes under attack for invading people's privacy and exploiting their personal problems. For example, in spring 2008, after Barack Obama clinched the Democratic presidential nomination, his wife Michelle gave him an affectionate "fist bump" that was caught on camera. Despite many people recognizing it as a congratulatory gesture signifying a job well done, some in the news media were apparently baffled by its meaning, or worse. For example, one pundit, E. D. Hill of Fox News, speculated: "A fist bump? A pound? A terrorist fist jab? The gesture everyone seems to interpret differently?" For several weeks, the news media covered the story and unearthed other video examples of the gesture, including President Bush exchanging fist bumps with soldiers. One *New York Times* reporter called the whole affair a "media dorkathon." E. D. Hill was forced to apologize, which drew more media coverage, and shortly thereafter

HERD JOURNALISM often leads to the overexposure of a story or incident that should not merit extreme amounts of attention, such as the fist bump between then–Democratic presidential nominee Barack Obama and his wife, Michelle.

> "I made a special effort to come on the show today because I have . . . mentioned this show as being bad . . . as it's hurting America."
>
> JON STEWART, ON CNN'S *CROSSFIRE*, 2004

lost her program on Fox (although cable executives said it had nothing to do with her terrorist symbol comments).

Relying on Experts

Another ritual of modern print journalism–relying on outside sources– has made reporters heavily dependent on experts. Reporters, though often experts themselves in certain areas by virtue of having covered them over time, are not typically allowed to display their expertise overtly. Instead, they must seek outside authorities to give credibility to seemingly neutral reports. Basically, *what* daily reporters know is generally subordinate to *whom* they know.

During the early 1900s, progressive politicians and leaders of opinion such as President Woodrow Wilson and Walter Lippmann believed in the cultivation of strong ties among national reporters, government officials, scientists, business managers, and researchers. They wanted journalists supplied with expertise across a variety of areas. Today, the widening gap between those with expertise and those without it has created a need for public mediators. Reporters have assumed this role as surrogates who represent both leaders' and readers' interests. With their access to experts, reporters transform specialized and insider knowledge into the everyday commonsense language of news stories.

Reporters also frequently use experts to create narrative conflict by pitting a series of quotes against one another, or on occasion use experts to support a particular position. In addition, the use of experts enables journalists to distance themselves from daily experience; they are able to attribute the responsibility for the events or issues reported in a story to those who are quoted.

To use experts, journalists must make direct contact with a source–by phone or e-mail or in person. Journalists do not, however, heavily cite the work of other writers; that would violate reporters' desire not only to get a story first but to get it on their own. Telephone calls and face-to-face interviews, rather than extensively researched interpretations, are the stuff of daily journalism.

Newsweek's Jonathan Alter once called expert sources the "usual suspects." Alter contended that "the impression conveyed is of a world that contains only a handful of knowledgeable people. . . . Their public exposure is a result not only of their own abilities, but of deadlines and a failure of imagination on the part of the press."[26]

In addition, expert sources have historically been predominantly white and male. Fairness and Accuracy in Reporting (FAIR) conducted a major study of the 14,632 sources used on the 2001 evening news programs on ABC, CBS, and NBC. FAIR found that only 15 percent of sources were women–and 52 percent of these women represented "average citizens" or "non-experts." By contrast, of the male sources, 86 percent were cast in "authoritative" or "expert" roles. Among "U.S. sources" where race could be determined, the study found the following: "[W]hites made up 92 percent of the total, blacks 7 percent, Latinos and Arab-Americans 0.6 percent each, and Asian Americans 0.2 percent. (According to the 2000 census, the U.S.

population [stood at] 69 percent non-Hispanic white, 13 percent Hispanic, 12 percent black, and 4 percent Asian.).”[27] So as mainstream journalists increased their reliance on a limited pool of experts, they alienated many viewers, who may have felt excluded from participation in day-to-day social and political life.

In the late 1990s, many journalists were criticized for blurring the line between remaining neutral and being an expert. The boom in twenty-four-hour cable news programs at this time led to a news vacuum that eventually was filled with talk shows and interviews with journalists willing to give their views. During events with intense media coverage, such as the 2000, 2004, and 2008 presidential elections, 9/11, and the Iraq war, many print journalists appeared several times a day on various cable programs acting as experts on the story, sometimes providing factual information, but mostly offering opinion and speculation.

Some editors even encourage their reporters to go on these shows for marketing reasons. Reporters and columnists from the *Washington Post*, for example, routinely appear in remote TV shots with the paper's logo prominently displayed in the background. Today, many big city newspapers have spaces set aside for reporters to use for cable, TV, and Internet interviews. Many critics contend that these practices erode the credibility of the profession by blending journalism with celebrity culture and commercialism.

Balancing Story Conflict

For most journalists, *balance* means presenting all sides of an issue without appearing to favor any one position. The quest for balance presents problems for journalists. On the one hand, time and space constraints do not always permit representing *all* sides; in practice this value has often been reduced to "telling *both* sides of a story." In recounting news stories as two-sided dramas, reporters often misrepresent the multifaceted complexity of social issues. The abortion controversy, for example, is often treated as a story that pits two extreme positions (staunchly pro-life vs. resolutely pro-choice) against each other. Yet people whose views fall somewhere between these positions are seldom represented (studies show this group actually represents the majority of Americans). In this manner, "balance" becomes a narrative device to generate story conflict.

On the other hand, although many journalists claim to be detached, they often stake out a moderate or middle-of-the-road position between the two sides represented in a story. In claiming neutrality and inviting readers to share their detached point of view, journalists offer a distant, third-person, all-knowing point of view (a narrative device that many novelists use as well), enhancing the impression of neutrality by making the reporter appear value-free (or valueless).

The claim for balanced stories, like the claim for neutrality, disguises journalism's narrative functions. After all, when reporters choose quotes for a story, these are usually the most dramatic or conflict-oriented words that emerge from an interview, press conference, or public meeting. Choosing quotes sometimes has more to do with enhancing drama than with being fair, documenting an event, or establishing neutrality.

The balance claim is also in the financial interest of modern news organizations that stake out the middle ground. William Greider, a former *Washington Post* editor, makes the connection between good business and balanced journalism: "If you're going to be a mass circulation journal, that means you're going to be talking simultaneously to lots of groups that have opposing views. So you've got to modulate your voice and pretend to be talking to all of them."[28]

Acting as Adversaries

The value that many journalists take the most pride in is their adversarial relationship with the prominent leaders and major institutions they cover. The prime narrative frame for portraying this relationship is sometimes called a *gotcha story,* which refers to the moment when, through questioning, the reporter nabs "the bad guy" or wrongdoer.

> "Cable news is full of spin doctors shouting at each other. . . . Jerry Springer without the hair pulling."
>
> TOM RAWLINS, EDITOR, *ST. PETERSBURG TIMES*, 1998

> "Opinion journalism can be more honest than objective-style journalism, because it doesn't have to hide its point of view."
>
> MICHAEL KINSLEY, WASHINGTONPOST.COM, 2006

This narrative strategy–part of the *tough questioning style* of some reporters–is frequently used in political reporting. Many journalists assume that leaders are hiding something and that the reporter's main job is to ferret out the truth through tenacious fact-gathering and "gotcha" questions. An extension of the search for balance, this stance locates the reporter in the middle, between "them" and "us," between political leaders and the people they represent.

Critics of the tough-question style of reporting argue that, while it can reveal significant information, when overused, it fosters a cynicism among journalists that actually harms the democratic process. Although journalists need to guard against becoming too cozy with their political sources, they sometimes go to the other extreme. By constantly searching for what politicians may be hiding, some reporters may miss other issues or other key stories.

When journalists employ the gotcha model to cover news, being tough often becomes an end in itself. Thus reporters believe they have done their job just by roughing up an interview subject or by answering the limited "What is going on here?" question. Yet the Pulitzer Prize, the highest award honoring journalism, often goes to the reporter who asks ethically charged and open-ended questions, such as "Why is this going on?" and "What ought to be done about it?"

EDWARD R. MURROW
was one of the pioneers of the U.S. television news documentary. Murrow's program *See It Now*, which ran sporadically on CBS from 1951 to 1958, tackled a number of controversial topics, including the connection between smoking and cancer and the threat to free expression posed by the anticommunist witch-hunter Senator Joseph McCarthy.

Journalism in the Age of TV and the Internet

The rules and rituals governing American journalism began shifting in the 1950s. At the time, former radio reporter John Daly hosted the CBS game show *What's My Line?* When he began moonlighting as the evening TV news anchor on ABC, the network blurred the entertainment and information border, foreshadowing what was to come.

In the early days, the most influential and respected television news program was CBS's *See It Now*. Coproduced by Fred Friendly and Edward R. Murrow, *See It Now* practiced a kind of TV journalism lodged somewhere between the neutral and narrative traditions. Generally regarded as "the first and definitive" news documentary on American television, *See It Now* sought "to report in depth–to tell and show the American audience what was happening in the world using film as a narrative tool."[29] Murrow worked as both the program's anchor and its main reporter, introducing the investigative model of journalism to television–a model that programs like *60 Minutes, 20/20,* and *Dateline* would later imitate.

Differences between Print and TV News

Although TV news reporters share many values, beliefs, and conventions with their print counterparts, television transformed journalism in a number of ways. First, broadcast news is driven by its technology. If a camera crew and news van are dispatched to a remote location for a live broadcast, reporters are expected to justify the expense by developing a story, even if nothing significant is occurring. For instance, when a national political candidate does not arrive at the local airport in time for an interview on the evening news, the reporter may cover a flight delay instead. Print reporters, in contrast, slide their notebooks or laptops back into their bags and report on a story when it occurs. However, with print reporters now posting regular online updates to their stories, they offer the same immediacy that live television news does.

Second, although print editors cut stories to fit the physical space around ads, TV news directors have to time stories to fit between commercials. Despite the fact that a much higher percentage of space is devoted to print ads (about 60 percent at most dailies), TV ads (which take up less than 25 percent of a typical thirty-minute news program) generally seem more intrusive to viewers, perhaps because TV ads take up time rather than space.

Third, while modern print journalists are expected to be detached, TV news derives its credibility from live, on-the-spot reporting; believable imagery; and viewers' trust in the reporters and anchors. In fact, since the early 1970s, the annual Roper polls have indicated that the majority of viewers find television news a more credible resource than print news. Viewers tend to feel a personal regard for the local and national anchors who appear each evening on TV sets in their living rooms.

By the mid-1970s, the public's fascination with the Watergate scandal, combined with the improved quality of TV journalism, helped local news departments realize profits. In an effort to retain high ratings, stations began hiring consultants, who advised news directors to invest in national prepackaged formats, such as Action News or Eyewitness News. Traveling the country, viewers noticed similar theme music and opening graphic visuals from market to market. Consultants also suggested that stations lead their newscasts with *crime blocks*: a group of TV stories that recount the worst local criminal transgressions of the day. A cynical slogan soon developed in the industry: "If it bleeds, it leads."

Few stations around the country have responded to viewers and critics who complain about overemphasizing crime. (In reality, FBI statistics reveal that crime and murder rates have fallen or leveled off in most major urban areas since the 1990s.) In 1996, the news director at KVUE-TV in Austin, Texas, created a new set of criteria that had to be met for news reports to qualify as responsible crime stories. She asked that her reporters answer the following questions: Do citizens or officials need to take action? Is there an immediate threat to safety? Is there a threat to children? Does the crime have significant community impact? Does the story lend itself to a crime prevention effort? With KVUE's new standards, the station eliminated many routine crime stories. Instead, the station provided a context for understanding crime rather than a mindless running tally of the crimes committed each day.[30]

Sound Bitten

Beginning in the 1980s, the term **sound bite** became part of the public lexicon. The TV equivalent of a quote in print news, a sound bite is the part of a broadcast news report in which an expert, a celebrity, a victim, or a person-on-the-street responds to some aspect of an event or issue. With increasing demands for more commercial time, there is less time for interview subjects to explain their views, and sound bites became the focus of intense criticism. Studies revealed that during political campaigns the typical sound bite from candidates had shrunk from an average duration of forty to fifty seconds in the 1950s and 1960s to fewer than eight seconds by the late 1990s. With shorter comments from interview subjects, TV news sometimes seemed like dueling sound bites, with reporters creating dramatic tension by editing competing viewpoints together as if interviewees had actually been in the same location speaking to one another. Of course, print news also pits one quote against another in a story, even though the actual interview subjects may never have met. Once again, these reporting techniques are evidence of the profession's reliance on storytelling devices to replicate or create conflict.

"It's the job of journalists to make complicated things interesting. The shame of American journalism is that [PBS's] *Frontline*, with its limited resources, has been doing infinitely better, more thoughtful, more creative reporting on places like Afghanistan or Rwanda than the richest networks in the world. If it is a glory for *Frontline*, it is a shame for those big networks and the [people] at the top of the corporate structure who run them."

DAVID HALBERSTAM, JOURNALIST, OCTOBER 2001

Pretty-Face and Happy-Talk Culture

In the early 1970s, at a Milwaukee TV station, consultants advised the station's news director that the evening anchor looked too old. The anchor, who showed a bit of gray, was replaced and went on to serve as the station's editorial director. He was thirty-two years old at the time. In the late 1970s, a reporter at the same station was fired because of a "weight problem," although that was not given as the official reason. Earlier that year, she had given birth to her first child. In 1983, Christine Craft, a former Kansas City television news anchor, was awarded $500,000 in damages in a sex discrimination suit against station KMBC (she eventually lost the monetary award when the station appealed). She had been fired because consultants believed she was too old, too unattractive, and not deferential enough to men.

Such stories are rampant in the annals of TV news. They have helped create a stereotype of the half-witted but physically attractive news anchor, reinforced by popular culture images (from Ted Baxter on TV's *Mary Tyler Moore Show* to Ron Burgundy in the film *Anchorman*). Although the situation has improved slightly, national news consultants set the agenda for what local reporters should cover (lots of crime) as well as how they should look (young, attractive, pleasant, and with no regional accent). Essentially, news consultants—also known as *news doctors*—have tried to replicate the predominant male and female advertising images of the 1960s and 1970s in modern local TV news.

Another news strategy favored by news consultants has been *happy talk*: the ad-libbed or scripted banter that goes on among local news anchors, reporters, meteorologists, and sports reporters before and after news reports. During the 1970s, consultants often recommended such chatter to create a more relaxed feeling on the news set and to foster the illusion of conversational intimacy with viewers. Some also believed that happy talk would counter much of that era's "bad news," which included coverage of urban riots and the Vietnam War. A strategy still used today, happy talk often appears forced and may create awkward transitions, especially when anchors report on events that are sad or tragic.

The Internet Enhances and Challenges Journalism

For mainstream print and TV reporters and editors, online news has added new dimensions to journalism. Both print and TV news can continually update breaking stories online, and many reporters now post their online stories first and then work on traditional versions. This means that readers and viewers no longer have to wait until the next day for the morning paper or for the local evening newscast for important stories. To enhance the online reports, which do not have the time or space constraints of television or print, newspaper reporters are increasingly required to also provide video or audio for their stories. This allows readers and viewers to see full interviews rather than just the selected print quotes in the paper or the sound bites on the TV report.

However, online news comes with a special set of problems. Print reporters, for example, can do e-mail interviews rather than leaving the office to question a subject in person. Many editors discourage this practice and allow e-mail interviews only when a phone or live interview is impossible. These editors think relying on e-mail gives interviewees the chance to control and shape their answers. While some might argue this provides more thoughtful answers, traditional journalists say it takes the elements of surprise and spontaneity out of the news interview, during which a subject might accidentally reveal information–something less likely to occur in an online setting.

Another problem for journalists is the enormous resources of the Internet. This includes access to versions of stories from other papers or broadcast stations. Journalists have to be careful not to copy story ideas or quotes (a mistake that can cost reporters their jobs). In addition, access to databases and other informational sites can keep reporters at their computers rather than out tracking down information, cultivating sources, and getting a sense of their communities.

The Power of Visual Language

The shift from a print-dominated culture to an electronic-digital culture requires that we look carefully at differences among various approaches to journalism. For example, how do the visual language of TV news and the Internet capture events more powerfully than words? Over the past fifty years, television news has dramatized America's key events. Civil Rights activists, for instance, acknowledge that the movement benefited enormously from televised news that documented the plight of southern blacks in the 1960s. The news footage of southern police officers turning powerful water hoses on peaceful Civil Rights demonstrators or the news images of "white only" and "colored only" signs in hotels and restaurants created a context for understanding the disparity between black and white in the 1950s and 1960s.

Other enduring TV images are also embedded in our collective memory: the Kennedy and King assassinations in the 1960s; the turmoil of Watergate in the 1970s; the first space shuttle disaster and the Chinese student uprisings in the 1980s; the Oklahoma City federal building bombing and the Clinton impeachment hearings in the 1990s; the terrorist attacks on the Pentagon and World Trade Center in 2001; Hurricane Katrina in 2005; the Virginia Tech shootings in 2007; and the historic 2008 presidential election. During these critical events, TV news has been a cultural reference point marking the strengths and weaknesses of a nation.

Today, the Internet functions as a repository for news images and video, for good or bad, allowing us to catch up on stories we may have missed or to be overexposed to controversial clips. After 24/7 cable news and various Internet sites ran endless loops of Barack Obama's former Chicago pastor delivering provocative sermons, Obama was forced to respond. On the campaign trail in Philadelphia in March 2008, he delivered a speech on U.S. race relations and his biracial heritage that critics and supporters at the time compared favorably to Martin Luther King's famous 1964 "I Have a Dream" speech. While Obama's speech drew relatively small audiences on cable when he delivered it live, it became an Internet phenomenon on YouTube, viewed by millions of people. And in the days after, 24/7 cable and other Internet sites once again played endless loops of excerpts.

NEWS IN THE DIGITAL AGE
Al-Jazeera, the Arab satellite news service originating in the small Persian Gulf nation of Qatar, was formed in 1996 to fill the gap after the British Broadcasting Corporation (BBC) closed its Arabic news service in Saudi Arabia. Although some have charged al-Jazeera with an anti-U.S. bias, it is actually the most independent news service in the Arab world and regularly covers controversial issues and dissenting political views in the region. In 2003, the news service launched its English-language Web site at http://english.al-jazeera .net, and in 2006 started an English-language TV station.

Alternative Models: Public Journalism and Fake News

In 1990, Poland was experiencing growing pains as it shifted from a state-controlled economic system to a more open market economy. The country's leading newspaper, *Gazeta Wyborcza*, the first noncommunist newspaper to appear in Eastern Europe since the 1940s, was also undergoing challenges. Based in Warsaw with a circulation of about 350,000 at the time, *Gazeta Wyborcza* had to report on and explain the new economy and the new crime wave that accompanied it. Especially troubling to the news staff and Polish citizens were gangs that robbed American and Western European tourists at railway stations, sometimes assaulting them in the process. The stolen goods would then pass to an outer circle, whose members transferred the goods to still another exterior ring of thieves. Even if the police caught the inner circle members, the loot disappeared.

These developments triggered heated discussions in the newsroom. A small group of young reporters, some of whom had recently worked in the United States, argued that the best way to cover the story was to describe the new crime wave and relay the facts to readers in a neutral manner. Another group, many of whom were older and more experienced, felt that the paper should take an advocacy stance and condemn the criminals through interpretive columns on the front page. The older guard won this particular debate, and more interpretive pieces appeared.[31]

This story illustrates the two competing models that have influenced American and European journalism since the early 1900s. The first—the *informational* or *modern model*—emphasizes describing events and issues from a seemingly neutral point of view. The second—a more *partisan* or *European model*—stresses analyzing occurrences and advocating remedies from an acknowledged point of view.

In most American newspapers today, the informational model dominates the front page, while the partisan model remains confined to the editorial pages and an occasional front-page piece. However, alternative models of news—from the serious to the satirical—have emerged to challenge modern journalistic ideals. (To learn about how the press works in China, see "Global Village: The Newsroom in China" on the opposite page.)

The Public Journalism Movement

From the late 1980s through the 1990s, a number of papers experimented with ways to involve readers more actively in the news process. These experiments surfaced primarily at midsize daily papers, including the *Charlotte Observer*, the *Wichita Eagle*, the *Virginian-Pilot*, and the *Minneapolis Star Tribune*. Davis "Buzz" Merritt, editor and vice president of the *Wichita Eagle* at the time, defined key aspects of **public journalism**:

- It moves beyond the limited mission of "telling the news" to a broader mission of helping public life go well, and acts out that imperative. . . .
- It moves from detachment to being a fair-minded participant in public life. . . .
- It moves beyond only describing what is "going wrong" to also imagining what "going right" would be like. . . .
- It moves from seeing people as consumers—as readers or nonreaders, as bystanders to be informed—to seeing them as a public, as potential actors in arriving at democratic solutions to public problems.[32]

> "We need to see people not as readers, nonreaders, endangered readers, not as customers to be wooed or an audience to be entertained, but as a public, citizens capable of action."
>
> DAVIS "BUZZ" MERRITT, *WICHITA EAGLE*, 1995

The Newsroom in China

Publishing and broadcasting have been growth industries in China. Since 1979, when the sale of advertisements in state-controlled newspapers became legal, the media industry has undergone dramatic commercial reform. The state has weaned the media from subsidies and pushed outlets to rely on advertising revenue, all while keeping control over news content through financial incentives, administrative measures, and the threat of punishment. Since Hu Jintao became president in 2003, journalists say, these restrictions have become more stringent.

Though the Chinese constitution protects freedom of the press, speech, and expression, there are institutional barriers to the free distribution of news in China. All news outlets must be authorized by the State Council and must comply with specific media regulations guarding almost every aspect of operation: hiring and training practices, amount of registered capital, location of premises, ties to any sponsoring state agency, and number of news bureaus.

PRESS FREEDOMS
In the aftermath of the deadly Sichuan earthquake in 2008, the Chinese government temporarily allowed a bit more journalistic freedom.

Regulations for operating broadcast, print, and Internet news outlets also list broad categories of unacceptable content, including anything that "disrupts the social order or undermines social stability" or is "detrimental to social morality or to the finer cultural traditions of the nation." Outlets that violate regulations can be punished with fines or shutdowns. By law, all news outlets must be affiliated with a state entity, but the degree of direct party oversight, the level of financial pressure, and the influence of reporters and editors vary across regions and types of media. National state-controlled media such as the Xinhua News Agency, *Guangming Daily, People's Daily*, and China Central Television, for instance, enjoy the backing of the central party leadership and are known to do critical reporting at the local level even as they praise the Beijing elite. Print and Internet media tend to have more leeway than broadcast news outlets.

For chief editors, though, miscalculating official reaction carries significant risk. No case illustrates this more clearly than the crackdown at *Nanfang Dushi Bao* in 2004. Cheng Yizhong led the newspaper as it investigated the death in police custody of college graduate Sun Zhigang. The newspaper's powerful reporting resonated with the public, forcing the government to make nationwide changes in detention policies. Yet the very same reporting caused the newspaper itself to come under investigation. Cheng was subsequently held in police custody for five months, and two colleagues served several years in prison on corruption charges.

In addition, journalists understand they have to stay away from stories about the military, ethnic conflict, and religion (particularly Falun Gong and underground churches), along with articles on the inner workings of the party and, to a lesser extent, the government.

The penalties for crossing the censors' line are mostly administrative. Serious infractions are noted in a journalist's employment record. Seeing a pattern of controversial reports, propaganda authorities may close down a publication or "reorganize" its personnel. Each year, several high-profile publications disappear, or have offending staff demoted and shuttled off to publications where they have less impact.

In China's commercial press, the payment system for journalists has emerged as a central method of content control. At most papers, reporters receive bonuses when their articles are published, and those bonuses make up the bulk of their income. The end result is that staff reporters are more likely to go after stories that will make it into print, or at least cover them in a way that will not offend the censors.

While authorities effectively keep unwanted news from reaching mass audiences, journalists know they can troll the Web for hidden treasures. Thus, they say, the scope of news and commentary has broadened over nearly three decades of commercial reform and information revolution. That the government's system of media control has effectively stayed the same is a source of optimism for some journalists.

Source: Committee to Protect Journalists, "Falling Short: Olympic Promises Go Unfulfilled as China Falters on Press Freedoms," Chapter 5, "Censorship at Work: The Newsroom in China," June 5, 2008, http://cpj.org/Briefings/2007/Falling_Short/China/5_2.html.

CITIZEN JOURNALISM
One way technology has allowed citizens to become involved in the reporting of news is through cell phone photos and videos. Witnesses can now pass on what they have captured to major mainstream news sources.

"The idea is to frame stories from the citizen's view, rather than inserting man-in-the-street quotes into a frame dominated by professionals."

JAY ROSEN, NYU, 1995

Public journalism might best be imagined as a conversational model for journalistic practice. Modern journalism draws a distinct line between reporter detachment and community involvement; public journalism—driven by citizen forums, community conversations, and even talk shows—obscures this line.

In the 1990s—before the full impact of the Internet—public journalism served as a response to the many citizens who felt alienated from participating in public life in a meaningful way. This alienation arose, in part, as viewers watched passively as the political process played out in the mainstream news media that seemed to involve only party operatives and media pundits. Public journalism was a way to involve both the public and journalists more centrally in civic and political life. Editors and reporters interested in addressing citizen alienation—and reporter cynicism—began devising ways to engage people as conversational partners in determining the news. In an effort to draw the public into discussions about community priorities, these journalists began sponsoring reader and citizen forums, where readers were supposed to have a voice in shaping aspects of the news that directly affected them.

An Early Public Journalism Project

Although isolated citizen projects and reader forums are sprinkled throughout the history of journalism, the public journalism movement began in earnest in 1987 in Columbus, Georgia. The city was suffering from a depressed economy, an alienated citizenry, and an entrenched leadership. In response, a team of reporters from the *Columbus Ledger-Enquirer* surveyed and talked with community leaders and other citizens about the future of the city. The paper then published an eight-part series based on the findings.

When the provocative series evoked little public response, the paper's leadership realized there was no mechanism or forum for continuing the public discussions about the issues raised in the series. Consequently, the paper created such a forum by organizing a town meeting. The editor of the paper, Jack Swift, organized a follow-up cookout at his own home at which concerned citizens created a new civic organization called United Beyond 2000 to tackle issues such as racial tension and teenage behavior.

The committee spurred the city's managers and other political leaders into action. The Columbus project generated public discussion, involved more people in the news process, and eased race and class tensions by bringing various groups together in public conversations. In the newsroom, the *Ledger-Enquirer* reimagined the place of journalists in politics: "Instead of standing outside the political community and reporting on its pathologies, they took up residence within its borders."[33]

Criticizing Public Journalism

By 2000, more than a hundred newspapers, many teamed with local television and public radio stations, had practiced some form of public journalism. Yet many critics and journalists remained skeptical of the experiment, raising a number of concerns including loss of editorial control, loss of credibility, loss of balance, and loss of diverse views.[34]

First, some editors and reporters argue that public journalism was co-opted by the marketing department, merely pandering to what readers wanted and taking editorial control away from newsrooms. They believe that focus group samples and consumer research—tools of marketing, not journalism—blurred the boundary between the editorial and business functions of a paper. Some journalists also feared that, as they become more active in the community, they may have been perceived as community boosters rather than as community watchdogs.

Second, critics worry that public journalism compromises the profession's credibility, which many believe derives from detachment. They argue that public journalism turns reporters into participants rather than observers. However, as the *Wichita Eagle*'s editor Davis Merritt points out, professionals who have credibility "share some basic values about life, some common ground about common good." Yet many journalists insist they "don't share values with anyone; that [they] are value-neutral."[35] Merritt argues that, as a result, modern journalism actually has little credibility with the public.

This view is buoyed by polls that reveal the public's distrust of newspapers. Research studies in 1988, for instance, indicated that 50 percent of surveyed respondents had "a great deal of confidence in newspapers"; by 1993 and into the early 2000s, similar polls showed that confidence had dropped to less than 25 percent.[36] But two years into the Iraq war, in 2005, this figure rose to 28 percent,[37] which some critics attributed to the work war correspondents were doing as embedded journalists covering the Iraqi and Afghan wars. But a Gallup Poll released in 2007 found only 22 percent of Americans said they had "confidence in newspapers," down from 30 percent in a 2006 Gallup survey. TV reporters fared a bit better, with 23 percent of respondents saying they had confidence, down from 33 percent in 2006.[38]

Third, critics also contend that public journalism undermines the both-sides-of-a story convention by constantly seeking common ground and community consensus; therefore, it runs the risk of dulling the rough edges of democratic speech. Public journalists counter that they are trying to set aside more room for centrist positions. Such positions are often representative of many in the community but are missing in the mainstream news, which is more interested in the extremist views that make for a gripping story.

Fourth, many traditional reporters assert that public journalism, which they consider merely a marketing tool, has not addressed the changing economic structure of the news business. With more news outlets in the hands of fewer owners, both public journalists and traditional reporters need to raise tough questions about the disappearance of competing daily papers and newsroom staff cutbacks at local monopoly newspapers. Facing little competition, in 2008 newspapers continued to cut reporting staffs and expensive investigative projects and reduced the space for news. While such a trend may help profits and satisfy stockholders, it also limits the voices and views in a community.

Fake News and Satiric Journalism

For many young people, it is especially disturbing that two wealthy, established political parties–beholden to special interests and their lobbyists–control the nation's government. After all, 98 percent of congressional incumbents get reelected each year–not always because they've done a good job but often because they've made promises and done favors for the lobbyists and interests that helped get them elected in the first place.

Why shouldn't people, then, be cynical about politics? It is this cynicism that has drawn increasingly larger audiences to "fake news" shows like *The Daily Show with Jon Stewart* and *The Colbert Report* on cable's Comedy Central. Following in the tradition of *Saturday Night Live (SNL)*, which began in 1975, news satires tell their audiences something that seems truthful about politicians and how they try to manipulate media and public opinion. But most importantly, these shows critique the news media and our political system. *SNL*'s sketches on GOP VP candidate Sarah Palin in 2008 drew large audiences and shaped the way younger viewers thought about the election.

The Colbert Report satirizes cable "star" news hosts, particularly Fox's Bill O'Reilly and MSNBC's Chris Matthews, and the bombastic opinion-argument culture promoted by their programs.

SATIRIC JOURNALISM
The persona of Stephen
Colbert on *The Colbert
Report* is partially based
on Fox's Bill O'Reilly. In
2007, Colbert was a guest
on O'Reilly's *No Spin Zone*,
where the two traded jabs
about the parody.

**"There's no
journalist today,
real or fake, who is
more significant
for people 18 to 25."**

SETH SIEGEL,
ADVERTISING AND
BRANDING
CONSULTANT, TALKING
ABOUT JON STEWART

In critiquing the limits of news stories and politics, *The Daily Show*, "anchored" by Stewart, parodies the narrative conventions of the regular evening news programs: the clipped eight-second "sound bite" that limits meaning and the formulaic shot of the TV news "stand up," which depicts reporters "on location," establishing credibility by revealing that they were really there.

On *The Daily Show*, a cast of fake reporters are digitally superimposed in front of exotic foreign locales, Washington, D.C., or other U.S. locations. In a 2004 exchange with "political correspondent" Rob Corrdry, Stewart asked him for his opinion about presidential campaign tactics. "My opinion? I don't have opinions," Corrdry answered. "I'm a reporter, Jon. My job is to spend half the time repeating what one side says, and half the time repeating the other. Little thing called objectivity; might want to look it up."

As news court jester, Stewart exposes the melodrama of TV news that nightly depicts the world in various stages of disorder while offering the stalwart, comforting presence of celebrity-anchors overseeing it all from their high-tech command centers. Even before CBS's Walter Cronkite signed off the evening news with "And that's the way it is," network news anchors offered a sense of order through the reassurance of their individual personalities.

As a satirist, Stewart is not so reassuring, arguing that things are a mess and in need of repair. For example, while a national news operation like MSNBC thought nothing of adopting the Pentagon slogan "Operation Iraqi Freedom" as its own graphic title, *The Daily Show* countered with "Mess O' Potamia." Even as a fake anchor, Stewart displays a much greater range of emotion—a range that may match our own—than we get from our detached "hard news" anchors: more amazement, irony, outrage, laughter, and skepticism.

Much of what fake news shows critique has to do with the way news producers repeat familiar formulas rather than inventing new story forms. Although the world has changed, local TV news story formulas (except for splashy opening graphics and Doppler weather radar) have virtually gone unaltered since the 1970s, when *SNL*'s "Weekend Update" first started making fun of TV news. Newscasts still limit reporters' stories to two minutes or less and promote stylish anchors, a sports "guy," and a certified meteorologist as familiar personalities whom we invite into our homes each evening. Now that a generation of viewers has been raised on the TV satire and political cynicism of "Weekend Update," Jay Leno, David Letterman, Conan O'Brien, *The Daily Show*, and *The Colbert Report*, the slick, formulaic packaging of political ads and the canned, cautious sound bites offered in news packages are simply not so persuasive.

More importantly, journalism needs to break free from tired formulas—especially in TV news—and reimagine better ways to tell stories. In fictional TV, storytelling has evolved over time, becoming increasingly complex. Although the Internet and 24/7 cable have introduced new models of journalism and commentary, why has TV news remained virtually unchanged over the past forty years? Aren't there new ways to report the news? Maybe audiences want news that matches the complicated storytelling that surrounds them in everything from TV dramas to interactive video games to their own conversations. We should demand news stories that better represent the complexity of our world.

Democracy and Reimagining Journalism's Role

Journalism is central to democracy: Both citizens and the media must have access to the information that we need to make important decisions. As this chapter illustrates, however, this is a complicated idea. For example, in the aftermath of 9/11, some government officials claimed that reporters or columnists who raised questions about fighting terrorism, invading Iraq, or developing secret government programs were being unpatriotic. Yet the basic principles of democracy require citizens and the media to question our leaders and government. Isn't this, after all, what the American Revolution was all about?

Conventional journalists will fight ferociously for the overt principles that underpin journalism's basic tenets–questioning government, freedom of the press, the public's right to know, and two sides to every story. These are all worthy ideals, but they do have limitations. These tenets, for example, generally do not acknowledge any moral or ethical duty for journalists to improve the quality of daily life. (See "Examining Ethics: Reporting Violence on Campus" on page 462.) Rather, conventional journalism values its news-gathering capabilities and the well-constructed news narrative, leaving the improvement of civic life to political groups, nonprofit organizations, business philanthropists, individual citizens, and practitioners of Internet activism.

Social Responsibility

Although reporters have traditionally thought of themselves first and foremost as observers and recorders, some journalists have acknowledged a social responsibility. Among them was James Agee in the 1930s. In his book *Let Us Now Praise Famous Men*, which was accompanied by the Depression-era photography of Walker Evans, Agee regarded conventional journalism as dishonest, partly because the act of observing intruded on people and turned them into story characters that newspapers and magazines exploited for profit.

Agee also worried that readers would retreat into the comfort of his writing–his narrative–instead of confronting what for many families was

"Information these days is like steam. It escapes through the tiniest cracks. The notion that any piece of information even can be sealed away, I think, is a relic of the past."

JON KLEIN, CNN PRESIDENT, APRIL 2007

THE SOCIAL ROLE OF JOURNALISM
In *Let Us Now Praise Famous Men*, which begins with haunting photos taken by Walker Evans, author James Agee questioned the basic honesty of daily journalism in the late 1930s. He thought that professional journalists could too easily exploit interview subjects simply as news stories that serve a business enterprise without actively engaging in changing the conditions of social life.

Reporting Violence on Campus

On April 16, 2007, a twenty-three-year-old Virginia Tech student killed thirty-two people and then himself—the largest mass shooting in modern U.S. history. Between murdering two students in a dorm and massacring thirty more students and teachers in another building, the shooter—remarkably—sent a package to NBC that contained "more than 45 photographs, more than 23 minutes of videotape, and 23 . . . pages of written materials."[1] After informing authorities and sending them copies, NBC News decided on April 18 to run a number of the photos and videos of the killer, Seung-Hui Cho. NBC also shared the killer's "manifesto" with other news networks and newspapers—in exchange for the NBC logo appearing on the images.

Media saturation of these chilling materials lasted only a day or so. In protest, families of two victims canceled scheduled appearances on NBC's

SOCIALLY RESPONSIBLE NEWS

While journalists have to report on major national events like the April 2007 killings at Virginia Tech or the August 2007 highway bridge collapse in Minneapolis, they often have a tendency—especially on TV—to turn tragedy into melodrama, complete with dramatic theme music and graphic titles like "Massacre at Virginia Tech" or "Road to Ruin."

▼

morning *Today* program. A poster on the campus soon announced, "VT Stay Strong—Media Stay Away." The next day, NBC cut displays of the images to "10 percent" of its overall coverage on both its broadcast and cable news services. Fox News decided to quit running the images altogether.

Soon, the Canadian newspaper *Ottawa Citizen* asked a key ethical question: "How should the media handle the public manifesto of a killer?"[2] Under scrutiny from the public and critics, mainstream news media asserted their positions. Steve Capus, president of NBC News, said that the "decision was not taken lightly. . . . We selectively chose certain limited passages and material to release. We believe it provides some answers to the critical question, 'Why did this man carry out these awful murders?'"[3] NBC's decision was backed by many journalists. But Harry Smith, CBS's *Early Show* anchor, said his own program ran too much footage, and at some point he stopped producers from airing more: "To be brutally honest, I felt manipulated by the fact [that Cho] was getting exactly what he wanted."[4] Several journalists wrestled with the same problem as they—in apparent contradiction— showed footage while acknowledging they were giving the killer what he wanted: having his "demented" but carefully prepared materials distributed widely to the public.

Bob Steele, an ethics scholar from the Poynter Institute, ultimately backed Capus and NBC: "The pieces of the tape we see give the public more understanding of what went on in this demented individual's mind. . . . These are pieces of a 1,000-piece jigsaw puzzle—a painful puzzle we don't want to look at but

have to."[5] Brian Williams, anchor of the *NBC Nightly News*, agreed: "I don't know of a reputable news organization in this country that, upon receipt of that package, would have . . . slipped it in a drawer and not shared its contents. It is beyond disturbing. It is beyond horrifying. It is also news, and the news is our role, however unpleasant the stories are at times."[6]

At the other end of the spectrum, CBC—Canada's main TV news service—chose not to run anything from the manifesto. CBC news chief Tony Burman criticized NBC's decision: "Sickened as I'm sure most viewers were, I imagined what kind of impact this broadcast would have on similarly deranged people."[7] Kevin Cameron, an Alberta risk-assessment specialist, backed the CBC stance: "The video should have never been released. It adds to the justification of other people like him."[8] He pointed out that the videos made by student killers Eric Harris and Dylan Klebold in their 1999 rampage that killed fourteen—including themselves—at Colorado's Columbine High School remain sealed even though some news media are working to get those videos released.

So what would you do as a TV news director or managing editor in this situation? In the end, Al Tompkins, a former TV news director who teaches broadcast news and ethics courses at Poynter, said that refusing to air this controversial material "would have been an easy thing to do. . . . People would have said, 'Good for you.' But that doesn't . . . enlighten us. That only protects us. And the job of the journalist is not to protect us from the truth; it's to tell us the truth, no matter how repugnant it is."[9] Do you agree? Is there a way to tell such a tragic story—to tell the truth about what happened—without showing images from the killer's "multimedia manifesto"?[10] ◢

the horror of the Great Depression. For Agee, the question of responsibility extended not only to journalism and himself but to the readers of his stories as well: "The reader is no less centrally involved than the authors and those of whom they tell."[39] Agee's self-conscious analysis provides insights into journalism's hidden agendas and the responsibility of all citizens to make public life better.

Deliberative Democracy

According to advocates of public journalism, when reporters are chiefly concerned with maintaining their antagonistic relationship to politics and are less willing to improve political discourse, news and democracy suffer. *Washington Post* columnist David Broder thinks that national journalists like him—through rising salaries, prestige, and formal education—have distanced themselves "from the people that we are writing for and have become much, much closer to people we are writing about."[40] Broder believes that journalists need to become activists, not for a particular party but for the political process and in the interest of re-energizing public life. In some ways this happened with the intense coverage, especially on the Internet and 24/7 cable, of the Obama/McCain presidential race in 2008. But this might also involve mainstream media spearheading voter registration drives or setting up pressrooms or news bureaus in public libraries or shopping malls, where people converge in large numbers.

Public journalism offers people models for how to deliberate in forums, and then it covers those deliberations. This kind of community journalism aims to reinvigorate a *deliberative democracy* in which citizen groups, local government, and the news media together work more actively to shape social, economic, and political agendas. In a more deliberative democracy, a large segment of the community discusses public life and social policy before advising or electing officials who represent the community's interests.

In 1989, the historian Christopher Lasch argued that "the job of the press is to encourage debate, not to supply the public with information."[41] Although he overstated his case—journalism does both and more—Lasch made a cogent point about how conventional journalism has lost its bearings. Adrift in data, mainstream journalism has lost touch with its partisan roots. The early mission of journalism—to advocate opinions and encourage public debate—has been relegated to alternative magazines, the editorial pages, news blogs, and cable news channels starring elite reporters. Ironically, Lasch connected the gradual decline in voter participation, which began in the 1920s, to more professionalized conduct on the part of journalists. With a modern "objective" press, he contended, the public increasingly began to defer to the "more professional" news media to watch over civic life on its behalf.

As the advocates of public journalism acknowledge, people have grown used to letting their representatives think and act for them. More community-oriented journalism and other civic projects offer citizens an opportunity to deliberate and to influence their leaders. This may include broadening the story models and frames they use to recount experiences; paying more attention to the historical and economic contexts of these stories; doing more investigative reports that analyze both news conventions and social issues; taking more responsibility for their news narratives; participating more fully in the public life of their communities; admitting to their cultural biases and occasional mistakes; and defending themselves better when they are attacked for performing their watchdog role.

Arguing that for too long journalism has defined its role only in negative terms, news scholar Jay Rosen notes: "To be adversarial, critical, to ask tough questions, to expose scandal and wrongdoing . . . these are necessary tasks, even noble tasks, but they are negative tasks." In addition, he suggests, journalism should assert itself as a positive force, not merely as a watchdog or as a neutral information conduit to readers but as "a support system for public life."[42] ▶

"Neither journalism nor public life will move forward until we actually rethink, redescribe, and reinterpret what journalism is; not the science of information of our culture but its poetry and conversation."

JAMES CAREY, *KETTERING REVIEW*, 1992

CHAPTER REVIEW

REVIEW QUESTIONS

Modern Journalism in the Information Age

1. What are the drawbacks of the informational model of journalism?
2. What is news?
3. What are some of the key values that underlie modern journalism?

Ethics and the News Media

4. How do issues such as deception and privacy present ethical problems for journalists?
5. Why is getting a story first important to reporters?
6. What are the connections between so-called neutral journalism and economics?

Reporting Rituals and the Legacy of Print Journalism

7. Why have reporters become so dependent on experts?
8. Why do many conventional journalists (and citizens) believe firmly in the idea that there are two sides to every story?

Journalism in the Age of TV and the Internet

9. How is credibility established in TV news as compared with print journalism?

10. With regard to TV news, what are sound bites and happy talk?
11. In what ways has the Internet influenced traditional forms of journalism?

Alternative Models: Public Journalism and Fake News

12. What is public journalism? In what ways is it believed to make journalism better?
13. What are the major criticisms of the public journalism movement, and why do the mainstream national media have concerns about public journalism?
14. What role do satirical news programs like *The Daily Show* and *The Colbert Report* play in the world of journalism?

Democracy and Reimagining Journalism's Role

15. What is deliberative democracy, and what does it have to do with journalism?

QUESTIONING THE MEDIA

1. What are your main criticisms of the state of news today? In your opinion, what are the news media doing well?
2. If you were a reporter or an editor, would you quit voting in order to demonstrate your ability to be neutral? Why or why not?
3. Is there political bias in most front-page news stories? If so, cite examples.

4. How would you go about formulating an ethical policy with regard to using deceptive means to get a story?
5. For a reporter, what are the dangers of both detachment from and involvement in public life?
6. Do satirical news programs make us more cynical about politics and less inclined to vote? Why or why not?
7. What steps would you take to make journalism work better in a democracy?

COMMON THREADS

One of the Common Threads discussed in Chapter 1 is the role that media play in a democracy. Today, one of the major concerns about the media is the proliferation of multiple news sources. How well is our society being served by this trend—especially on cable and the Internet—compared with the time when just a few major news media sources dominated journalism?

Historians, media critics, citizens, and even many politicians argue that a strong democracy is only possible with a strong, healthy, skeptical press. In the "old days," a few legacy media—key national newspapers, three major networks, and three newsmagazines—provided most of the journalistic common ground for discussing major issues confronting U.S. society.

In today's online and 24/7 cable world, though, the legacy or mainstream media have ceded some of their power and many of their fact-checking duties to new media forms, especially the blogosphere. As discussed in this chapter and in Chapter 8, this loss is partly economic, driven by severe cutbacks in newsroom staffs due to substantial losses in advertising (which has gone to the Internet) and because bloggers, 24/7 cable news media, and news satire shows like *The Daily Show* and *The Colbert Report* are fact-checking the media as well as reporting traditional stories that used to be the domain of professional news organizations.

The case before us then goes something like this: In the "old days," the major news media provided us with major news narratives to share, discuss, and argue about. But in today's explosion of news and information, that common ground has eroded or is shifting. Instead, today we often rely only on those media sources that match our comfort level, cultural values, or political affiliations; increasingly these are blog sites, radio talk shows, or cable channels. Sometimes these opinion channels and sites are not supported with the careful fact-gathering and verification that has long been a pillar of the best kinds of journalism.

So in today's media environment, how severely has the "common ground" role of mainstream media been undermined by technological and cultural transformations? And, are these changes ultimately good or bad for democracy?

KEY TERMS

The definitions for the terms listed below can be found in the glossary at the end of the book. The page numbers listed with the terms indicate where the term is highlighted in the chapter.

news, 437
newsworthiness, 438
ethnocentrism, 440
responsible capitalism, 440
small-town pastoralism, 440

individualism, 440
conflict of interest, 445
herd journalism, 449
sound bite, 453
public journalism, 456

FREE
DIE HARD

EVERY killer lives ne

disturbia

april 13   disturbia.com

15

Media Effects and Cultural Approaches to Research

In 1966, NBC showed the Rod Serling made-for-television thriller *The Doomsday Flight*, the first movie to depict an airplane hijacking. In the story, a man plants a bomb and tries to extract ransom money from an airline. In the days following the telecast, the nation's major airlines reported a dramatic rise in anonymous bomb threats, some of them classified as teenage pranks. The network agreed not to run the film again.

In 1985, the popular heavy-metal band Judas Priest made headlines when two Nevada teenagers shot themselves after listening to the group's allegedly subliminal suicidal message on their 1978 *Stained Class* album. One teen died instantly; the other lived for three more years, in constant pain from severe facial injuries. The teenagers' parents lost a civil product liability suit against the British metal band and CBS Records.

In 1995, an eighteen-year-old woman and her boyfriend went on a killing spree in Louisiana after reportedly watching Oliver Stone's 1994 film *Natural Born Killers* more than twenty times. The family of one of the victims filed a lawsuit against Stone and Time Warner, charging that the film—starring Juliette Lewis and Woody Harrelson as a demented, celebrity-craving young couple on a murderous rampage—irresponsibly incited real-life violence. Part of the family's case was based on a 1996 interview in which Stone said: "The most pacifist people in the world said they came out of this movie and wanted to kill somebody." Stone and Time Warner argued that the lawsuit should be dismissed on the grounds of free speech, and the case was finally thrown out in 2001. There was no evidence, according to the judge, that Stone had intended to incite violence.

In 1999, two heavily armed students wearing trench coats attacked Columbine High School in Littleton, Colorado. They planted as many as fifty bombs and murdered twelve fellow students and a teacher before killing themselves. In the wake of this tragedy, many people blamed the mass media, speculating that the killers had immersed themselves in the dark lyrics of shock rocker Marilyn Manson and were desensitized to violence by "first-person shooter" video games such as *Doom*. Still others looked to the influence of films like *The Basketball Diaries*, in which a drug-using, trench-coated teenager (played by Leonardo DiCaprio) imagines shooting a teacher and his classmates.

In April 2007, a student massacred thirty-two people on the Virginia Tech campus before killing himself. Gunman Seung-Hui Cho was mentally disturbed and praised "martyrs like Eric and Dylan," the infamous Columbine killers. Cho's rampage included a twist: during the attack, he sent a package of letters, videos, and photos of himself to NBC News. The images and ramblings of his "multimedia manifesto" became a major part of the news story (as did ethical questions about the news media broadcasting clips of his videos) while the country tried to make sense of the tragedy.

Each of these events has renewed longstanding cultural debates over the suggestive power of music, visual imagery, and screen violence. Since the emergence of popular music, movies, television, and video games as influential mass media, the relationship between make-believe stories and real-life imitation has drawn a great deal of attention. Concerns have been raised not only by parents, teachers, and politicians but also by several generations of mass communication researchers.

". . . the relationship between make-believe stories and real-life imitation has drawn a great deal of attention."

▲ *AS THESE TRAGIC TALES OF VIOLENCE ILLUSTRATE,* many believe that media have a powerful effect on individuals and society. This belief has led media researchers to focus most of their efforts on two types of research: media effects research and cultural studies research.

Media effects research attempts to understand, explain, and predict the effects of mass media on individuals and society. The main goal of this type of research is to uncover whether or not there is a connection between aggressive behavior and violence in the media, particularly in children and teens. In the late 1960s, government leaders–reacting to the social upheavals of that decade–first set aside $1 million to examine this potential connection. Since that time, thousands of studies have told us what most teachers and parents believe instinctively: Violent scenes on television and in movies stimulate aggressive behavior in children and teens–especially young boys.

The other major area of mass media research is **cultural studies**. This research approach focuses on how people make meaning, apprehend reality, articulate values, and order experience through their use of cultural symbols. Cultural studies scholars also examine the way status quo groups in society, particularly corporate and political elites, use media to circulate their messages and sustain their interests. This research has attempted to make daily cultural experience the focus of media studies, keying on the subtle intersections among mass communication, history, politics, and economics.

In this chapter, we examine the evolution of media research over time. After looking at early research efforts, we focus on the two major strains of media research, investigating the strengths and limitations of each. Finally, we conclude with a discussion of how media research interacts with democratic ideals.

Early Media Research Methods

In the early days of the United States, philosophical and historical writings tried to explain the nature of news and print media. For instance, the French political philosopher Alexis de Tocqueville, author of *Democracy in America,* noted differences between French and American newspapers in the early 1830s:

In France the space allotted to commercial advertisements is very limited, and . . . the essential part of the journal is the discussion of the politics of the day. In America three quarters of the enormous sheet are filled with advertisements and the remainder is frequently occupied by political intelligence or trivial anecdotes; it is only from time to time that one finds a corner devoted to the passionate discussions like those which the journalists of France every day give to their readers.[1]

During most of the nineteenth century, media analysis was based on moral and political arguments, as noted in the de Tocqueville quote above.[2]

More scientific approaches to mass media research did not begin to develop until the late 1920s and 1930s. In 1920, Walter Lippmann's *Liberty and the News* called on journalists to operate more like scientific researchers in gathering and analyzing factual material. Lippmann's next book, *Public Opinion* (1922), was the first to apply the principles of psychology to journalism. Considered by many academics to be "the founding book in American media studies,"[3] it led to an expanded understanding of the effects of the media, emphasizing data collection and numerical measurement. According to media historian Daniel Czitrom, by the 1930s

"The pictures inside the heads of these human beings, the pictures of themselves, of others, of their needs, purposes, and relationships, are their public opinions."

WALTER LIPPMANN,
PUBLIC OPINION, 1922

UNITED WE WIN

EFFECTS OF PROPAGANDA
One of the earliest forms of U.S. mass communication research—propaganda analysis—was prominent during the twentieth century's two world wars. Researchers studied the impact of war posters and other government information campaigns to determine how audiences could be persuaded through stirring media messages about patriotism and duty.

"an aggressively empirical spirit, stressing new and increasingly sophisticated research techniques, characterized the study of modern communication in America."[4] Czitrom traces four trends between 1930 and 1960 that contributed to the rise of modern media research: propaganda analysis, public opinion research, social psychology studies, and marketing research.

Propaganda Analysis

After World War I, some media researchers began studying how governments used propaganda to advance the war effort. They found that, during the war, governments routinely relied on propaganda divisions to spread "information" to the public. Though propaganda was considered a positive force for mobilizing public opinion during the war, researchers after the war labeled propaganda negatively, calling it "partisan appeal based on half-truths and devious manipulation of communication channels."[5] Harold Lasswell's important 1927 study *Propaganda Technique in the World War* focused on propaganda in the media, defining propaganda as "the control of opinion by significant symbols, . . . by stories, rumors, reports, pictures and other forms of social communication."[6] **Propaganda analysis** thus became a major early focus of mass media research.

Public Opinion Research

Researchers soon went beyond the study of war propaganda and began to focus on more general concerns about how the mass media filtered information and shaped public attitudes. In the face of growing media influence, Walter Lippmann distrusted the public's ability to function as knowledgeable citizens as well as journalism's ability to help the public separate truth from lies. In promoting the place of the expert in modern life, Lippmann celebrated the social scientist as part of a new expert class that could best make "unseen facts intelligible to those who have to make decisions."[7]

Today, social scientists conduct *public opinion research* or citizen surveys; these have become especially influential during political elections. On the upside, public opinion research on diverse populations has provided insights into citizen behavior and social differences, especially during election periods or following major national events. For example, in 2008, the level of enthusiasm for voting in national elections was higher among Democrats than among Republicans. Polls showed that more than 50 percent of Democrats were enthusiastic about voting versus about 30 percent for Republicans, a reverse of the Republican voter excitement leading up to the 1994 election in which Republicans gained control of Congress.

On the downside, journalism has become increasingly dependent on polls, particularly for political insight. Some critics argue that this heavy reliance on measured public opinion has begun to adversely affect the active political involvement of American citizens. Many people do not vote because they have seen or read poll projections and have decided that

SOCIAL AND PSYCHOLOGICAL EFFECTS OF MEDIA
Concerns about film violence are not new. This 1930 movie, *Little Caesar*, follows the career of gangster Rico Bandello (played by Edward G. Robinson, shown), who kills his way to the top of the crime establishment and gets the girl as well. The Motion Picture Production Code, which was established a few years after this movie's release, reined in sexual themes and profane language, set restrictions on film violence, and attempted to prevent audiences from sympathizing with bad guys like Rico.

their votes would not make a difference. Furthermore, some critics of incessant polling argue that the public is just passively responding to surveys that mainly measure opinions on topics of interest to business, government, academics, and the mainstream news media. A final problem is the pervasive use of unreliable **pseudo-polls**, typically call-in, online, or person-in-the-street polls that the news media use to address a "question of the day." The National Council of Public Opinion Polls notes that "unscientific pseudo-polls are widespread and sometimes entertaining, if always quite meaningless," and discourages news media from conducting them.[8]

Social Psychology Studies

While opinion polls measure public attitudes, *social psychology studies* measure the behavior and cognition of individuals. The most influential early social psychology study, the Payne Fund Studies, encompassed a series of thirteen research projects conducted by social psychologists between 1929 and 1932. Named after the private philanthropic organization that funded the research, the Payne Fund Studies were a response to a growing national concern about the effects of motion pictures, which had become a particularly popular pastime for young people in the 1920s. These studies, which were later used by some politicians to attack the movie industry, linked frequent movie attendance to juvenile delinquency, promiscuity, and other antisocial behaviors, arguing that movies took "emotional possession" of young filmgoers.[9]

In one of the Payne studies, for example, children and teenagers were wired with "electrodes" and "galvanometers," mechanisms that detected any heightened response via the subject's skin. The researchers interpreted changes in the skin as evidence of emotional arousal. In retrospect, the findings hardly seem surprising: The youngest subjects in the group had the

"Motion pictures are not understood by the present generation of adults. They are new; they make an enormous appeal to children; and they present ideas and situations which parents may not like."

MOTION PICTURES AND THE SOCIAL ATTITUDES OF CHILDREN: A PAYNE FUND STUDY, 1933

FIGURE 15.1

TV PARENTAL GUIDELINES

The TV industry continues to study its self-imposed rating categories, promising to fine-tune them to ensure that the government keeps its distance. These standards are one example of a policy that was shaped in part by media research. Since the 1960s, research has attempted to demonstrate links between violent TV images and increased levels of aggression among children and adolescents.

Source: TV Parental Guidelines Monitoring Board, http://www.tvguidelines.org, 7/10/06.

The following categories apply to programs designed solely for children:

 All Children. *This program is designed to be appropriate for all children.*

 Note: For those programs where fantasy violence may be more intense or more combative than other programs in this category, such programs will be designated **TV-Y7-FV.**

 Directed to Older Children. *This program is designed for children age 7 and above.*

The following categories apply to programs designed for the entire audience:

 General Audience. *Most parents would find this program suitable for all ages.*

 Parents Strongly Cautioned. *This program contains some material that many parents would find unsuitable for children under 14 years of age.*

 Parental Guidance Suggested. *This program contains material that parents may find unsuitable for younger children.*

 Mature Audiences Only. *This program is specifically designed to be viewed by adults and therefore may be unsuitable for children under 17.*

For programs rated **TV-PG, TV-14,** and **TV-MA,** labels are included to provide more information about contents, where appropriate:

D — **suggestive dialogue**
L — **coarse language**
S — **sexual situations**
V — **violence**

strongest reaction to violent or tragic movie scenes, while the teenage subjects reacted most strongly to scenes with romantic and sexual content. The researchers concluded that films could be dangerous for young children and might foster sexual promiscuity among teenagers. The conclusions of this and other Payne Fund Studies contributed to the establishment of the film industry's production code, which tamed movie content from the 1930s through the 1950s (see Chapter 16). As forerunners of today's TV violence and aggression research, the Payne Fund Studies became the model for media research. (See Figure 15.1 for one example of a contemporary policy that has developed from media research. Also see "Examining Ethics: What to Do about Television Violence?" on the opposite page for more on the problems inherent in tackling violence on television.)

Marketing Research

A fourth influential area of early media research, *marketing research,* developed when advertisers and product companies began conducting surveys on consumer buying habits in the 1920s. The emergence of commercial radio led to the first ratings systems that measured how many people were listening on a given night. By the 1930s, radio networks, advertisers, large stations, and advertising agencies all subscribed to ratings services. However, compared with print media, whose circulation departments kept careful track of customers' names and addresses, radio listeners were more difficult to trace. This problem precipitated the development of increasingly sophisticated marketing research methods to determine consumer preferences and media use, such as direct-mail diaries, television meters, phone surveys, telemarketing, and eventually Internet tracking. In many instances, product companies looking for participation in their surveys paid consumers nominal amounts of money to take part in these studies.

What to Do about Television Violence?

The debate over violent television programming is almost as old as television, with the first congressional hearings on the matter occurring in 1952. More than a half-century later, the debate continues. In 2007, the FCC released a lengthy report, "Violent Television Programming and Its Impact on Children," and recommended action to address violent programming.

The commission agreed with research that suggests "exposure to violence in the media can increase aggressive behavior in children, at least in the short term." Yet as the report tried to make conclusive statements about violent programming, it only raised more questions about what to do. The FCC cited several troubling statistics:

- An average American household has the television set turned on eight hours, eleven minutes, daily.
- Children watch on average between two and four hours of television every day.
- Depending on their age, one- to two-thirds of children have televisions in their bedrooms.

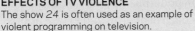

EFFECTS OF TV VIOLENCE
The show *24* is often used as an example of violent programming on television.

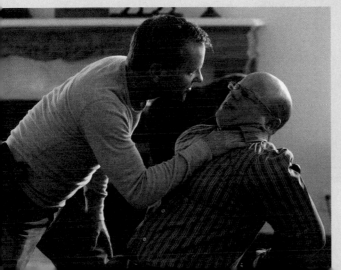

- By the time most children begin the first grade, they will have spent the equivalent of three school years in front of the television set.
- By the time the average child is eighteen years old, he or she will have watched more than ten thousand hours of television.
- By age eighteen, an American child will have seen upwards of fifteen thousand simulated murders and about two hundred thousand acts of violence on television.[1]

The report also identified a number of prime-time broadcast shows with violent content, including, of course, *24*, *CSI*, and *WWE Smackdown* but also, and less obviously, *Grey's Anatomy*, *Law & Order*, and *Desperate Housewives*.

But dealing with television violence has been persistently confounded by several problems. First is the problem of defining violent content, at least in a way that could be used in government policies. Courts have struck down vague definitions that call for regulating excessive violence, noting that many classic stories from the Bible, Greek mythology, and fairy tales are filled with gruesome violence.

A second problem is determining which television programming to regulate. Most proposals include prime-time programming, but what about news, sports, commercials, and promotional announcements? And how should regulations treat cable and satellite television providers, who aren't subject to the same level of FCC oversight as broadcasters? Third is the issue of free speech. Courts have ruled that the First Amendment protects depictions of

violence and violent speech. Although broadcasters have less First Amendment protection than other mass media and are subject to daytime restrictions on indecent content to protect children (see "The FCC Regulates Broadcasting" on pages 515–516), it's not clear that similar rules could be applied to violent content. As FCC Commissioner Jonathan S. Adelstein stated in the report, "I do not even like my kids watching a cartoon of an anvil falling on the coyote's head, but I do not think any court would let us ban it."

Fourth, although a majority of Americans think there is too much violence on television, nearly all parties have fallen short in using existing tools to deal with it. The FCC charged that broadcast networks are inconsistent in how they voluntarily rate and label programs for violent content, and often "underlabel" programs with less restrictive ratings to increase advertiser incentives. Although the ratings have been around since 1997, many parents don't understand them. One in five parents has never heard of the ratings system, and only 8 percent can correctly identify the categories. Moreover, the V-chip, which has been built into television sets since 2000 to enable parents to block violent programming, is rarely used.

Finally, for all of the research suggesting that TV violence causes violent behavior, there are still significant questions that such effects even exist. Although the FCC sided with effects researchers, the report also noted that controlled laboratory environments and experimental measures of aggression (e.g., hitting dolls, "killing" characters in video games) can't be generalized to the real world and that there is—at least as yet—no demonstrable correlation between media violence and crime statistics.

Research on Media Effects

As concern about public opinion, propaganda, and the impact of the media merged with the growth of journalism and mass communication departments in colleges and universities, media researchers looked more and more to behavioral science as the basis of their research. Between 1930 and 1970, "Who says what to whom with what effect?" became the key question "defining the scope and problems of American communications research."[10] In addressing this question specifically, media effects researchers asked follow-up questions such as this: If children watch a lot of TV cartoons (stimulus or cause), will this repeated act influence their behavior toward their peers (response or effect)? For most of the twentieth century, media researchers and news reporters used different methods to answer similar sets of questions—who, what, when, and where—about our daily experiences.

Early Explanations of Media Effects

A major goal of scientific research is to develop theories or laws that can consistently explain or predict human behavior. The varied impacts of the mass media and the diverse ways in which people make popular culture, however, tend to defy predictable rules. Historical, economic, and political factors influence media industries, making it difficult to develop systematic theories that explain communication. Researchers developed a number of small theories, or models, that help explain individual behavior rather than the impact of the media on large populations. But before these small theories began to emerge in the 1970s, mass media research followed several other models. Developing between the 1930s and the 1970s, these major approaches included the hypodermic-needle, minimal-effects, and uses and gratifications models.

The Hypodermic-Needle Model

One of the earliest media theories attributed powerful effects to the mass media. A number of intellectuals and academics were fearful of the influence and popularity of film and radio in the 1920s and 1930s. Some social psychologists and sociologists who arrived in the United States after fleeing Germany

EFFECTS OF MASS MEDIA
Early media researchers were concerned about Adolf Hitler's use of national radio to control information and indoctrinate the German people throughout the 1930s. Germany's wartime international broadcasts, however, were considered failures. Trying to undermine morale using broadcasts aimed at Allied soldiers and British citizens, Germany hired British defector William Joyce ("Lord Haw Haw") and Ohioan Mildred Gillars ("Axis Sally"). Because so many media messages competed with Nazi propaganda in democratic countries, these radio traitors had little impact.

and Nazism in the 1930s had watched Hitler use radio, film, and print media as propaganda tools. They worried that the popular media in America also had a strong hold over vulnerable audiences. This concept of powerful media affecting weak audiences has been labeled the **hypodermic-needle model**, sometimes also called the *magic bullet theory* or the *direct effects model*. It suggests that the media shoot their potent effects directly into unsuspecting victims.

One of the earliest challenges to this theory involved a study of Orson Welles's legendary October 30, 1938, radio broadcast of *War of the Worlds*, which presented H. G. Wells' Martian invasion novel in the form of a news report and frightened millions of listeners who didn't realize it was fictional (see Chapter 4). In a 1940 book-length study of the broadcast, *The Invasion from Mars: A Study in the Psychology of Panic*, radio researcher Hadley Cantril argued that contrary to expectations according to the hypodermic-needle model, not all listeners thought the radio program was a real news report. Instead, Cantril, after conducting personal interviews and a nationwide survey of listeners and analyzing newspaper reports and listener mail to CBS Radio and the FCC, noted that although some did believe it to be real (mostly those who missed the disclaimer at the beginning of the broadcast), the majority reacted out of collective panic, not out of a gullible belief in anything transmitted through the media. Although the hypodermic-needle model over the years has been disproved by social scientists, many people still attribute direct effects to the mass media, particularly in the case of children.

The Minimal-Effects Model

Cantril's research helped to lay the groundwork for the **minimal-effects model**, or *limited model*. With the rise of empirical research techniques, social scientists began discovering and demonstrating that media alone cannot cause people to change their attitudes and behaviors. Based on tightly controlled experiments and surveys, researchers argued that people generally engage in **selective exposure** and **selective retention** with regard to the media. That is, people expose themselves to the media messages that are most familiar to them, and they retain the messages that confirm the values and attitudes they already hold. Minimal effects researchers have argued that in most cases mass media reinforce existing behaviors and attitudes rather than change them. The findings from the first comprehensive study of children and television–by Wilbur Schramm, Jack Lyle, and Edwin Parker in the late 1950s–best capture the minimal-effects theory:

For some *children, under* some *conditions, some television is harmful. For other children under the same conditions, or for the same children under other conditions, it may be beneficial. For most children, under most conditions, most television is probably neither particularly harmful nor particularly beneficial.*[11]

In addition, Joseph Klapper's important 1960 research study, *The Effects of Mass Communication*, found that the mass media only influenced individuals who did not already hold strong views on an issue and that the media had a greater impact on poor and uneducated audiences. Solidifying the minimal-effects argument, Klapper concluded that strong media effects occur largely at an individual level and do not appear to have large-scale, measurable, and direct effects on society as a whole.[12]

The minimal-effects theory furthered the study of the relationship between the media and human behavior, but it still assumed that audiences were passive and were acted upon by the media. Schramm, Lyle, and Parker suggested that there were problems with the position they had taken on effects:

In a sense the term "effect" is misleading because it suggests that television "does something" to children. The connotation is that television is the actor, the children are acted upon. Children are thus made to seem relatively inert; television, relatively active. Children are sitting victims; television bites them. Nothing can be further from the fact. It is the children who are most active in this relationship. It is they who use television, rather than television that uses them.[13]

"Theories abound, examples multiply, but convincing facts that specific media content is reliably associated with particular effects have proved quite elusive."

GUY CUMBERBATCH, *A MEASURE OF UNCERTAINTY*, 1989

"If we're a nation possessed of a murderous imagination, we didn't start the bloodletting. Look at Shakespeare, colossus of the Western canon. His plays are written in blood."

SCOT LEHIGH, *BOSTON GLOBE*, 2000

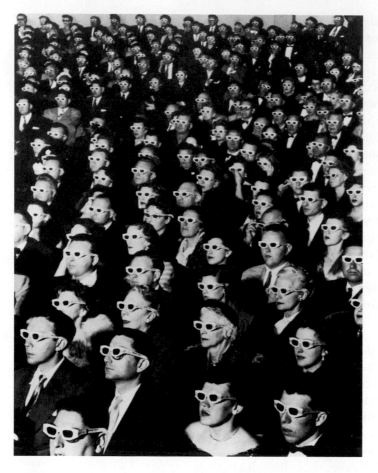

Indeed, as the authors observed, numerous studies have concluded that viewers—especially young children—are often *actively* engaged in using media.

The Uses and Gratifications Model

A response to the minimal-effects theory, the **uses and gratifications model** was proposed to contest the notion of a passive media audience. Under this model, researchers—usually using in-depth interviews to supplement survey questionnaires—studied the ways in which people used the media to satisfy various emotional or intellectual needs. Instead of asking, "What effects do the media have on us?" researchers asked, "Why do we use the media?" Asking the *why* question enabled media researchers to develop inventories cataloguing how people employed the media to fulfill their needs. For example, researchers noted that some individuals used the media to see authority figures elevated or toppled, to seek a sense of community and connectedness, to fulfill a need for drama and stories, and to confirm moral or spiritual values.[14]

Although the uses and gratifications model addressed the *functions* of the mass media for individuals, it did not address important questions related to the impact of the media on society. Once researchers had accumulated substantial inventories of the uses and functions of media, they often did not move in new directions. Consequently, uses and gratifications never became a dominant or enduring theory in media research.

Conducting Media Effects Research

Media research generally comes from the private or public sector—each type with distinguishing features. *Private research,* sometimes called *proprietary research,* is generally conducted for a business, a corporation, or even a political campaign. It is usually applied research in the sense that the information it uncovers typically addresses some real-life problem or need. *Public research,* on the other hand, usually takes place in academic and government settings. It involves information that is often more *theoretical* than applied; it tries to clarify, explain, or predict the effects of mass media rather than to address a consumer problem.

Most media research today focuses on the effects of the media in such areas as learning, attitudes, aggression, and voting habits. This research employs the **scientific method**, a blueprint long used by scientists and scholars to study phenomena in systematic stages. These steps in the scientific method include:

1. identifying the research problem
2. reviewing existing research and theories related to the problem
3. developing working hypotheses or predictions about what the study might find
4. determining an appropriate method or research design
5. collecting information or relevant data
6. analyzing results to see if the hypotheses have been verified
7. interpreting the implications of the study to determine whether they explain or predict the problem

The scientific method relies on *objectivity* (eliminating bias and judgments on the part of researchers); *reliability* (getting the same answers or outcomes from a study or measure during repeated testing); and *validity* (demonstrating that a study actually measures what it claims to measure).

In scientific studies, researchers pose one or more **hypotheses**: tentative general statements that predict the influence of an *independent variable* on a *dependent variable*. For example, a researcher might hypothesize that frequent TV viewing among adolescents (independent variable) causes poor academic performance (dependent variable). Or, another researcher might hypothesize that playing first-person-shooter video games (independent variable) is associated with aggression in children (dependent variable).

Broadly speaking, the methods for studying media effects on audiences have taken two forms—experiments and survey research. To supplement these approaches, researchers also use content analysis to count and document specific messages that circulate in mass media.

Experiments

Like all studies that use the scientific method, **experiments** in media research isolate some aspect of content; suggest a hypothesis; and manipulate variables to discover a particular medium's impact on attitude, emotion, or behavior. To test whether a hypothesis is true, researchers expose an *experimental group*—the group under study—to a selected media program or text. To ensure valid results, researchers also use a *control group*, which serves as a basis for comparison; this group is not exposed to the selected media content. Subjects are picked for each group through **random assignment**, which simply means that each subject has an equal chance of being placed in either group. Random assignment ensures that the independent variables researchers want to control are distributed to both groups in the same way.

For instance, to test the effects of violent films on pre-adolescent boys, a research study might take a group of ten-year-olds and randomly assign them to two groups. Researchers expose the experimental group to a violent action movie that the control group does not see. Later, both groups are exposed to a staged fight between two other boys so that the researchers can observe how each group responds to an actual physical confrontation. Researchers then determine whether or not there is a statistically measurable difference between the two groups' responses to the fight. For example, perhaps the control subjects tried to break up the fight but the experimental subjects did not. Because the groups were randomly selected and the only measurable difference between them was the viewing of the movie, researchers may conclude that under these conditions the violent film caused a different behavior. (See the "Bobo doll" experiment photos on page 480.)

When experiments carefully account for independent variables through random assignment, they generally work well to substantiate direct cause-effect hypotheses. Such research takes place both in laboratory settings and in field settings, where people can be observed using the media in their everyday environments. In field experiments, however, it is more difficult for researchers to control variables. In lab settings, researchers have more control, but other problems may occur. For example, when subjects are removed from the environments in which they regularly use the media, they may act differently—often with fewer inhibitions—than they would in their everyday surroundings.

Experiments have other limitations as well. One, they are not generalizable to a larger population; they cannot tell us whether cause-effect results can be duplicated outside of the laboratory. Two, most academic experiments today are performed on college students, who are convenient subjects for research but are not representative of the general public. Finally, while most experiments are fairly good at predicting short-term media effects under controlled conditions, they do not predict how subjects will behave months or years later in the real world.

> "Writing survey questions and gathering data are easy; writing good questions and collecting useful data are not."
>
> MICHAEL SINGLETARY, *MASS COMMUNICATION RESEARCH*, 1994

Survey Research

In the simplest terms, **survey research** is collecting and measuring data taken from a group of respondents. Using random sampling techniques that give each potential subject an equal chance to be included in the survey, this research method draws on much larger populations than those used in experimental studies. Surveys may be conducted through direct mail, personal interviews, telephone calls, e-mail, and Web sites, enabling survey researchers to accumulate large amounts of information by surveying diverse cross sections of people. These data help to examine demographic factors such as educational background, income level, race, ethnicity, gender, age, sexual orientation, and political affiliations, along with questions directly related to the survey topic.

Two other benefits of surveys are that they are usually generalizable to the larger society and that they enable researchers to investigate populations in long-term studies. For example, survey research can measure subjects when they are ten, twenty, and thirty years old to track changes in how frequently they watch television and what kinds of programs they prefer at different ages. In addition, large government and academic survey databases are now widely available and contribute to the development of more long-range or **longitudinal studies**, which make it possible for social scientists to compare new studies with those conducted years earlier.

Like experiments, surveys have several drawbacks. First, survey investigators cannot account for all the variables that might affect media use; therefore, they cannot show cause-effect relationships. Survey research can, however, reveal **correlations**—or associations—between two variables. For example, a random questionnaire survey of ten-year-old boys might demonstrate that a correlation exists between aggressive behavior and watching violent TV programs. Such a correlation, however, does not explain what is the cause and what is the effect—that is, do violent TV programs cause aggression or are more aggressive ten-year-old boys simply drawn to violent television? Second, the validity of survey questions is a chronic problem for survey practitioners. Surveys are only as good as the wording of their questions and the answer choices they present. For example, as NPR reported recently, "[I]f you ask people whether they support or oppose the death penalty for murderers, about two-thirds of Americans say they support it. If you ask whether people prefer that murderers get the death penalty or life in prison without parole, then you get a 50-50 split."[15]

Content Analysis

Over the years, researchers recognized that experiments and surveys focused on general topics (violence) while ignoring the effects of specific media messages (gun violence, fist fights, etc.). As a corrective, researchers developed a method known as **content analysis** to study these messages. Such analysis is a systematic method of coding and measuring media content.

Although content analysis was first used during World War II for radio, more recent studies have focused on television and film. Probably the most influential content analysis studies have been conducted by George Gerbner and his colleagues at the University of Pennsylvania. Since the late 1960s, they have coded and counted acts of violence on network television. Combined with surveys, these annual "violence profiles" have shown that heavy watchers of television, ranging from children to retired Americans, tend to overestimate the amount of violence that exists in the actual world.[16]

The limits of content analysis, however, have been well documented. First, this technique does not measure the effects of the messages on audiences nor explain how those messages are presented. For example, a content analysis sponsored by the Kaiser Family Foundation that examined more than eleven hundred television shows found that 70 percent featured sexual content.[17] But the study doesn't explain how viewers interpreted the content or the context of the messages. (See "Media Literacy and the Critical Process: Counting Sexual Scenes on TV" on the opposite page.)

Media Literacy and the Critical Process

1 DESCRIPTION. Central to any study using content analysis is developing a working definition of terms. For the Kaiser study, "sex is defined as any depiction of sexual activity, sexually suggestive behavior, or talk about sexuality or sexual activity." What would you include or not include in a definition of sexual content?

2 ANALYSIS. The study analyzed a sample of more than eleven hundred programs, covering a range of television genres but excluding daily newscasts, children's shows, and sporting events. The main sample included shows from ABC, CBS, NBC, Fox, an independent WB affiliate, a PBS affiliate, Lifetime, TNT, USA Network, and HBO. The sample also included daytime soap operas, one of the genres with the highest percentage of sexual content. Do these genres represent the viewing environment of twelve- to seventeen-year-olds, the age group of greatest concern to the researchers? In reviewing the study online, what are the significant patterns that emerged?

3 INTERPRETATION. Do jokes about a newlywed couple's sexual encounters (*Scrubs*), bedroom banter between a married couple (*According to Jim*), depictions of flirting (*House*), scenes of intimate touching (*CSI: New*

Counting Sexual Scenes on TV

Every few years since 1999, the Kaiser Family Foundation, a nonprofit private foundation dedicated to "providing information and analysis on health care issues to policymakers, the media, the health care community, and the general public," releases a major study of sexual content on television. In 2005, the foundation released *Sex on TV 4* and reported that the number of sexual scenes on television had nearly doubled since 1998.[1] But what does "sexual content" actually mean, and what do the study's results suggest to policymakers? To address these questions, we will use the critical process to analyze the study.

York), dramatic discussions about sexually transmitted diseases (*Law & Order: Special Victims Unit*), a comment about oral sex (*The View*), and implied (*Boston Legal*) or actual (*General Hospital*) depictions of sexual intercourse all have the same impact and meaning? This study treats them all as sex scenes. Do you think viewers would interpret these scenes the same way? How would audience studies–focusing on how people actually use and interpret this television content–help to clarify the interpretation of the content analysis?

4 EVALUATION. The *Sex on TV 4* study notes that over the past decade "fewer teens are having sex, and more of those who are having intercourse are using protection–and the teen pregnancy rate is going down as a result." Does this admission undermine

the study's concerns that "the amount of sexual content on television continues to increase" and it "may be contributing to perceptions about peer norms regarding both sexual behavior (e.g., 'everybody is doing it') and safer sex practices"? How is it that sexual content, as measured by this study, is increasing on television, while teen sexual behavior is declining and becoming more safe?

5 ENGAGEMENT. This series of studies has had a big impact on the way policymakers understand media effects. There's bipartisan support in Congress to fund more studies that would analyze media effects on the health and development of children. How would you undertake this kind of study? To make an informed recommendation, critically read the studies for yourself at www.kff.org/entmedia/index.cfm.

Second, problems of definition occur in content analysis. For instance, in the case of coding and counting acts of violence, how do researchers distinguish slapstick cartoon aggression from the violent murders or rapes in an evening police drama? Critics point out that such varied depictions may have diverse and subtle effects on viewers that are not differentiated by content analysis. Finally, critics point out that as content analysis grew to be a primary tool in media research, it sometimes pushed to the sidelines other ways of thinking about television and media content. Broad questions concerning the media as a popular art form, as a measure of culture, as a democratic influence, or as a force for social control are difficult to address through strict

measurement techniques. Critics of content analysis, in fact, have objected to the kind of social science that reduces culture to acts of counting. Such criticism has addressed the tendency by some researchers to favor measurement accuracy over intellectual discipline and inquiry.[18]

Contemporary Media Effects Theories

By the 1960s, the first departments of mass communication began graduating Ph.D.-level researchers schooled in experiment and survey research techniques, as well as content analysis. These researchers began documenting consistent patterns in mass communication and devel-oping new theories. Four of the most influential contemporary theories that help explain media effects are social learning theory, agenda-setting, the cultivation effect, and the spiral of silence.

Social Learning Theory

Some of the most well-known studies that suggest a link between the mass media and behavior are the "Bobo doll" experiments, conducted on children by psychologist Albert Bandura and his colleagues at Stanford University in the 1960s. Bandura concluded that the experiments demonstrated a link between violent media programs, such as those on television, and aggres-sive behavior. Bandura developed **social learning theory** as a four-step process: *attention* (the subject must attend to the media and witness the aggressive behavior), *retention* (the subject must retain the memory for later retrieval), *motor reproduction* (the subject must be able to physically imitate the behavior), and *motivation* (there must be a social reward or reinforcement to encourage modeling of the behavior).

Supporters of social learning theory often cite real-life imitations of media aggression (see the beginning of the chapter) as evidence of social learning theory at work. Yet critics note that many studies conclude just the opposite—that there is no link between media content and aggression. For example, millions of people have watched episodes of *CSI* and *The Sopranos* without subsequently exhibiting aggressive behavior. As critics point out, social learning theory simply makes television, film, and other media scapegoats for larger social problems relating to violence. Others suggest that experiencing media depictions of aggression can actually help viewers let off steam peacefully through a catharsis effect.

Agenda-Setting

A key phenomenon posited by contemporary media effects researchers is **agenda-setting**: the idea that when the mass media focus their attention on particular events or issues, they determine—that is, set the agenda for—the major topics of discussion for individuals and society. Essentially, agenda-setting researchers have argued that the mass media do not so much tell us what to think as *what to think about*. Traceable to Walter Lippmann's notion in the early 1920s that the media "create pictures in our heads," the first investigations into agenda-setting began in the 1970s.[19]

Over the years, agenda-setting research has demonstrated that the more stories the news media do on a particular subject, the more importance audiences attach to that subject. For instance, when the media seriously began to cover ecology issues after the first Earth Day in 1970, a much higher percentage of the population began listing the environment as a primary social concern in surveys. When *Jaws* became a blockbuster in 1975, the news media started featuring more shark attack stories; even landlocked people in the Midwest began ranking sharks as a major problem, despite the rarity of such incidents worldwide. More recently, the extensive news media coverage of the Hurricane Katrina disaster in fall 2005 sparked a corresponding increase in public concern about preparedness for natural disasters. Today, however, even with the affected areas far from rebuilt, as the national news coverage has dropped, so has much of the public interest in the region's recovery.

The Cultivation Effect

Another mass media phenomenon—the **cultivation effect**—suggests that heavy viewing of television leads individuals to perceive the world in ways that are consistent with television portrayals. This area of media effects research has pushed researchers past a focus on how the media affects individual behavior and toward a focus on larger ideas about the impact on perception.

The major research in this area grew from the TV violence profiles of George Gerbner and his colleagues, who attempted to make broad generalizations about the impact of televised violence. The cultivation effect suggests that the more time individuals spend viewing television and absorbing its viewpoints, the more likely their views of social reality will be "cultivated" by the images and portrayals they see on television.[20] For example, Gerbner's studies concluded that, although fewer than 1 percent of Americans are victims of violent crime in any single year, people who watch a lot of television tend to overestimate this percentage. Such exaggerated perceptions, Gerbner and his colleagues argued, are part of a "mean world" syndrome, in which viewers with heavy, long-term exposure to television violence are more likely to believe that the external world is a mean and dangerous place.

According to the cultivation effect, media messages interact in complicated ways with personal, social, political, and cultural factors; they are one of a number of important factors in determining individual behavior and defining social values. Some critics have charged that cultivation research has provided limited evidence to support its findings. In addition, some have argued that the cultivation effects recorded by Gerbner's studies have been so minimal as to be benign and that, when compared side-by-side, the perceptions of heavy television viewers and nonviewers in terms of the "mean world" syndrome are virtually identical.

Spiral of Silence

Developed by German communication theorist Elisabeth Noelle-Neumann in the 1970s and 1980s, the **spiral of silence** theory links the mass media, social psychology, and the formation of public opinion. The theory proposes that those who believe that their views on controversial issues are in the minority will keep their views to themselves—i.e., become silent—for fear of social isolation. As those in the minority voice their views less often, alternative and minority perspectives are diminished and even silenced. The theory is based on social psychology studies, such as the classic conformity research studies of Solomon Asch in 1951. In Asch's study on the effects of group pressure, he demonstrated that a test subject is more likely to give clearly wrong answers to questions about line lengths if all other people in the room (all secret confederates of the experimenter) unanimously state an incorrect answer. Noelle-Neumann argued that this effect is exacerbated by the mass media, particularly television, which can communicate a real or presumed majority public opinion widely and quickly. For example, one researcher noted that from the 1970s through the 1990s, the political Right in the United States was effective in using the media to frame liberals as an elite minority who protected special-interest groups such as atheists and criminals. At the same time, the Right was expounding the existence of a conservative Christian "moral majority" in the country. Instead of offering additional models of morality or protesting a narrow narrative frame that was too restrictive, some liberals—apparently finding themselves portrayed as a minority—chose to remain silent.[21]

According to the theory, the mass media can help create a false, overrated majority; that is, a true majority of people holding a certain position can grow silent when they sense an opposing majority in the media. One criticism of the theory is that some people may not fall into a spiral of silence because they don't monitor the media, or they mistakenly perceive that more people hold their position than really do. Noelle-Neumann acknowledges that in many cases, "hard-core nonconformists" exist and remain vocal even in the face of social isolation and can ultimately prevail in changing public opinion.

Evaluating Research on Media Effects

The mainstream models of media research have made valuable contributions to our under-standing of the mass media, submitting content and audiences to rigorous testing. This wealth of research exists partly because funding for studies on the effects of the media on young people remains popular among politicians and has drawn ready government support since the 1960s. Media critic Richard Rhodes argues that media effects research is inconsistent and often flawed but continues to resonate with politicians and parents because it offers an easy-to-blame social cause for real-world violence.

> "Many studies currently published in mainstream communication journals seem filled with sophisticated treatments of trivial data, which, while showing effects . . . make slight contributions to what we really know about human mass-mediated communication."
>
> WILLARD ROWLAND AND BRUCE WATKINS, *INTERPRETING TELEVISION*, 1984

Funding restricts the scope of some media effects and survey research, particularly if the government, business, or other administrative agendas do not align with researchers' interests. Other limits also exist, including the inability to address how media affect communities and social institutions. Because most media research operates best in examining media and individual behavior, fewer research studies explore media's impact on community and social life. Some research has begun to address these deficits and also to turn more attention to the increasing impact of media technology on international communication.

Cultural Approaches to Media Research

During the rise of modern media research, approaches with a stronger historical and interpretive edge developed as well, often in direct opposition to the scientific models. In the late 1930s, some social scientists began to warn about the limits of "gathering data" and "charting trends," particularly when these kinds of research projects served only advertisers and media organizations and tended to be narrowly focused on individual behavior, ignoring questions like "Where are institutions taking us?" and "Where do we want them to take us?"[22]

In the United States in the 1960s, an important body of research—loosely labeled *cultural studies*—arose to challenge mainstream media effects theories. Since that time, cultural studies research has focused on how people make meaning, understand reality, and order experience by using cultural symbols that appear in the media. This research has attempted to make everyday culture the centerpiece of media studies, focusing on how subtly mass communication shapes and is shaped by history, politics, and economics. Other cultural studies work examines the relationships between elite individuals and groups in government and politics and how media play a role in sustaining the authority of elites and, occasionally, in challenging their power.

Early Developments in Cultural Studies Research

In Europe, media studies have always favored interpretive rather than scientific approaches; in other words, researchers there have approached the media as if they were literary or cultural critics rather than experimental or survey researchers. These approaches were built on the writings of political philosophers such as Karl Marx and Antonio Gramsci, who investigated how mass media support existing hierarchies in society. They examined how popular culture and sports distract people from redressing social injustices, and they addressed the subordinate status of particular social groups, something emerging media effects researchers were seldom doing.

In the United States, early criticism of media effects research came from the Frankfurt School, a group of European researchers who emigrated from Germany to America to escape Nazi persecution in the 1930s. Under the leadership of Max Horkheimer, T. W. Adorno, and Leo Lowenthal, this group pointed to at least three inadequacies of traditional scientific approaches to media research, arguing that they (1) reduced large "cultural questions" to measurable and "verifiable categories"; (2) depended on "an atmosphere of rigidly enforced neutrality"; and (3) refused to place "the phenomena of modern life" in a "historical and moral context."[23] The researchers of the Frankfurt School did not completely reject the usefulness of measuring and counting data. They contended, however, that historical and

"When people say to you, 'of course that's so, isn't it?' that 'of course' is the most ideological moment, because that's the moment at which you're least aware that you are using a particular framework."

STUART HALL, 1983

cultural approaches were also necessary to focus critical attention on the long-range effects of the mass media on audiences.

Since the time of the Frankfurt School, criticisms of the media effects tradition and its methods have continued, with calls for more interpretive studies of the rituals of mass communication. Academics who have embraced a cultural approach to media research try to understand how media and culture are tied to the actual patterns of communication in daily life. For example, in the 1970s, Stuart Hall and his colleagues studied the British print media and the police, who were dealing with an apparent rise in crime and mugging incidents. Arguing that the close relationship between the news and the police created a form of urban surveillance, the authors of *In Policing the Crisis* demonstrated that the mugging phenomenon was exacerbated, and in part created, by the key institutions assigned the social tasks of controlling crime and reporting on it.[24]

Contemporary Cultural Studies Theories

Cultural research focuses on the investigation of daily experience, especially on issues of race, gender, class, and sexuality, and on the unequal arrangements of power and status in contemporary society. Such research emphasizes how some social and cultural groups have been marginalized and ignored throughout history. Consequently, cultural studies have attempted to recover lost or silenced voices, particularly among African American, Native American, Asian and Asian American, Arabic, Latino, Appalachian, gay and lesbian, immigrant, and women's cultures. The major analytical approaches in cultural studies research today are textual analysis, audience studies, and political economy studies.

Textual Analysis

In cultural studies research, **textual analysis** highlights the close reading and interpretation of cultural messages, including those found in books, movies, and TV programs. It is the equivalent of measurement methods like experiments and surveys and content analysis. While media effects research approaches media messages with the tools of modern science–replicability, objectivity, and data–textual analysis looks at rituals, narratives, and meaning. (See "Case Study: Labor Gets Framed" on the opposite page.)

Although textual analysis has a long and rich history in film and literary studies, it became significant to media in 1974 when Horace Newcomb's book *TV: The Most Popular Art,* became the first serious academic book to analyze television shows. Newcomb studied why certain TV programs and formats became popular, especially comedies, westerns, mysteries, soap operas, news reports, and sports programs. Newcomb took television programs seriously, examining patterns in the most popular programs at the time, such as the *Beverly Hillbillies, Bewitched,* and *Dragnet,* which traditional researchers had usually snubbed or ignored. Trained as a literary scholar, Newcomb argued that content analysis and other social science approaches to popular media often ignored artistic traditions and social context. For Newcomb, "the task for the student of the popular arts is to find a technique through which many different qualities of the work–aesthetic, social, psychological–may be explored" and to discover "why certain formulas . . . are popular in American television."[25]

Before Newcomb's work, textual analysis generally focused only on "important" or highly regarded works of art–debates, films, poems, and books. But by the end of the 1970s a new generation of media studies scholars, who had grown up on television and rock and roll, began to study less elite forms of culture. They extended the concept of what a "text" is to include architecture, fashion, tabloid magazines, pop icons like Madonna, rock music, hip-hop, soap operas and telenovelas, movies, cockfights, shopping malls, reality TV, Martha Stewart, and professional wrestling, trying to make sense of the most taken-for-granted aspects of everyday

Labor Gets Framed

Labor union membership in the United States dropped from a high of 34.7 percent of the workforce in 1954 to less than 12 percent (less than 8 percent in the private sector) by 2007. In a world where economic and social forces increasingly separate the "haves" from the "have-nots" and popular media such as entertainment television and film rarely address labor issues, the news media remain one of the few places to find stories about the decline in labor unions and the working class.

Could the way in which news stories frame labor unions have an impact on how people in the United States understand them?

Analyzing the frames of news stories—that is, the ways in which journalists present them—is one form of textual analysis. Unfortunately, if one looks at how the news media frame their reports about labor unions, one has to conclude that news coverage of labor is not at all good.

PROTESTORS during the December 2005 Transit Workers Union (TWU) strike in New York City (TWU members operate the city's public transportation system, the largest in the country). The reasons behind the strike got less news coverage because the news focused on the millions of stranded commuters instead.

In a major study,[1] hundreds of network television news (ABC, CBS, and NBC) and national newspaper (*New York Times* and *USA Today*) reports involving labor over a ten-year period were analyzed to get a sense of how such stories are framed.

An interesting pattern emerged. Instead of discovering a straightforward bias against labor, the study found that news stories frame labor in a way that selects the consumer perspective (as opposed to a citizen or worker perspective). That is, labor unions aren't portrayed as inherently bad, but any kind of collective action by workers, communities, and even consumers that upsets the American consumer economy and its business leaders and entrepreneurs is framed as a bad thing.

The classic example is the strike story. Even though less than 2 percent of all contract negotiations result in strikes, news stories seem to show union members regularly wielding picket signs. The real stars of strike stories, though, are the inconvenienced consumers—sour-faced people who are livid about missed flights, late package delivery, or canceled ball games. And usually the reports don't explain why a strike is occurring; viewers and readers mainly learn that the hallowed American consumer is upset and if those darned workers would just be a little more agreeable, then none of this inconvenience would have happened.

The frame carries an interesting underlying assumption: If collective action is bad, then economic intervention by citizens should happen only at the individual level (e.g., tell your boss to "take this job and shove it" if you are dissatisfied, or "vote with your pocketbook" if you don't like something). Of course,

individual action would preempt collective action on the part of organizations such as labor unions, which, as organized groups, hold the promise of offering more democratic and broader solutions to problems that affect not one but many workers.

Corporate news that appears in many newspaper business sections frames labor stories in ways that are in harmony with the media corporations' own economic priorities. (Corporations like General Electric, Disney, Gannett, and Wal-Mart all have long track records of either trying to weaken their unions or break them completely.) But such stories do so without giving the appearance of bias, which would undermine their credibility. So they frame these stories from the perspective of the consumer (indeed, in an advertising- and corporate sponsor-based media system, this is the familiar environment in which all media stories are framed).

With such framing, the news media's stories undercut a legal institution—labor unions—that might serve as a useful remedy for millions of American workers who want independent representation in their workplace for collective bargaining and dispute resolution, as well as a voice in the economy. In fact, national surveys have shown that the majority of American workers would like a stronger voice in their workplaces but have negative opinions about unions, so they aren't likely to consider joining them.[2]

And that's the disconnect that the framing study illustrates: People want independent workplace representation, but—according to the news—labor unions and similar forms of collective action are hardly a viable option. ◢

CULTURAL APPROACHES TO MEDIA
James W. Carey, who spent many years teaching at the University of Illinois and Columbia University, was an influential figure in cultural and critical communication studies. Carey's most well-known contributions envisioned communication as a cultural ritual rather than a mechanistic process of transmission. Carey died in 2006.

"I take culture ... and the analysis of it to be therefore not an experimental science in search of law but an interpretive one in search of meaning."

CLIFFORD GEERTZ, CULTURAL ANTHROPOLOGIST, 1973

media culture. Often the study of these seemingly minor elements of popular culture provides insight into broader meanings within our society. By shifting the focus to daily popular culture artifacts, cultural studies succeeded in focusing scholarly attention—not just on significant presidents, important religious leaders, prominent political speeches, or military battles—but on the more ordinary ways that "normal" people organize experience and understand their daily lives.

Audience Studies

Cultural studies research that focuses on how people use and interpret cultural content is called **audience studies**, or *reader-response research*. Audience studies differs from textual analysis because the subject being researched is the audience for the text, not the text itself. For example, in *Reading the Romance: Women, Patriarchy and Popular Literature*, Janice Radway studied a group of midwestern women who were fans of romance novels. Using her training in literary criticism and employing interviews and questionnaires, Radway investigated the meaning of romance novels to the women. She argued that reading romance novels functions as personal time for some women, whose complex family and work lives leave them very little time for themselves. The study also suggested that these particular romance-novel fans identified with the active, independent qualities of the romantic heroines they most admired. As a cultural study, Radway's work did not claim to be scientific, and her findings are not generalizable to all women. Rather, Radway was interested in investigating and interpreting the relationship between reading popular fiction and ordinary life.[26]

Radway's influential cultural research used a variety of interpretive methods, including literary analysis, interviews, and questionnaires. Most important, these studies helped to define culture in broad terms, as being made up of both the *products* a society fashions and the *processes* that forge those products.

Political Economy Studies

A focus on the production of popular culture and the forces behind it is the topic of **political economy studies**, which specifically examine interconnections among economic interests, political power, and how that power is used. Among the major concerns of political economy studies is the increasing conglomeration of media ownership. The increasing concentration of ownership means that the production of media content is being controlled by fewer and fewer organizations, investing those companies with more and more power. Moreover, the domination of public discourse by for-profit corporations may mean that the bottom line for all public communication and popular culture is money, not democratic expression.

Political economy studies work best when combined with textual analysis and audience studies, which provide context for understanding the cultural content of a media product, its production process, and how the audience responds. For example, a major media corporation may, for commercial reasons, create a film and market it through a number of venues (political economy), but the film's meaning or popularity makes sense only within the historical and narrative contexts of the culture (textual analysis), and it may be interpreted by various audiences in ways both anticipated and unexpected (audience studies).

Evaluating Cultural Studies Research

In opposition to media effects research, cultural studies research involves interpreting written and visual "texts" or artifacts as symbolic representations that contain cultural, historical, and political meaning. For example, the wave of police and crime TV shows that appeared in the mid-1960s can be interpreted as a cultural response to concerns and fears people had about urban unrest and income disparity. Audiences were drawn to the heroes of these dramas, who often exerted control over forces that, among society in general, seemed out of control. Similarly, people today who participate in radio talk shows, Internet forums, and TV reality shows can be viewed, in part, as responding to feeling disconnected from economic success or political power. Taking part in these forums represents a popular culture avenue for engaging with media in ways that are usually reserved for professional actors or for the rich, famous, and powerful. As James Carey put it, the cultural approach, unlike media effects research, which is grounded in the social sciences, "does not seek to explain human behavior, but to understand it. . . . It does not attempt to predict human behavior, but to diagnose human meanings."[27] In other words, a cultural approach does not provide explanations for laws that govern how mass media behave. Rather, it offers interpretations of the stories, messages, and meanings that circulate throughout our culture.

One of the main strengths of cultural studies research is the freedom it affords to broadly interpret the impact of the mass media. Because cultural work is not bound by the precise control of variables, researchers can more easily examine the ties between media messages and the broader social, economic, and political world. For example, media effects research on politics has generally concentrated on election polls and voting patterns, while cultural research has broadened the discussion to examine class, gender, and cultural differences among voters and the various uses of power by individuals and institutions in authority. Following Horace Newcomb's work, cultural investigators have expanded the study of media content beyond "serious" works. They have studied many popular forms, including music, movies, and prime-time television.

CULTURAL STUDIES researchers are interested in the production, meaning, and audience response to a wide range of elements within communication culture, including the meaning and reception of sports figures like Barry Bonds, who was caught in a media controversy over performance-enhancing drugs. (*Below left*, Bonds in 1992; *below*, Bonds in 2006.)

Just as media effects research has its limits, so does cultural studies research. Sometimes cultural studies have focused exclusively on the meanings of media programs or "texts," ignoring their effect on audiences. Some cultural studies, however, have tried to address this deficiency by incorporating audience studies. Both media effects and cultural studies researchers today have begun to look at the limitations of their work more closely, borrowing ideas from each other to better assess the complexity of the media's meaning and impact.

Media Research and Democracy

One charge frequently leveled at academic studies is that they fail to address the everyday problems of life; they often seem to have little practical application. The growth of mass media departments in colleges and universities has led to an increase in specialized jargon, which tends to alienate and exclude nonacademics. Although media research has built a growing knowledge base and dramatically advanced what we know about the effect of mass media on individuals and societies, the academic world has paid a price. That is, the larger public has often been excluded from access to the research process even though cultural research tends to identify with marginalized groups. The scholarship is self-defeating if its complexity removes it from the daily experience of the groups it addresses. Researchers themselves have even found it difficult to speak to one another across disciplines because of discipline-specific language used to analyze and report findings. For example, understanding the elaborate statistical analyses used to document media effects requires special training.

In some cultural research, the language used is often incomprehensible to students and to other audiences who use the mass media. A famous hoax in 1996 pointed out just how

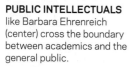

PUBLIC INTELLECTUALS
like Barbara Ehrenreich
(center) cross the boundary
between academics and the
general public.

inaccessible some academic jargon can be. Alan Sokal, a New York University physics professor, submitted an impenetrable article, "Transgressing the Boundaries: Toward a Transformative Hermeneutics of Quantum Gravity," to a special issue of the academic journal *Social Text* devoted to science and postmodernism. As he had expected, the article–a hoax designed to point out how dense academic jargon can sometimes mask sloppy thinking–was published. According to the journal's editor, about six reviewers had read the article but didn't suspect that it was phony. A public debate ensued after Sokal revealed his hoax. Sokal said he worries that jargon and intellectual fads cause academics to lose contact with the real world and "undermine the prospect for progressive social critique."[28]

In addition, increasing specialization in the 1970s began isolating many researchers from life outside of the university. Academics were locked away in their "ivory towers," concerned with seemingly obscure matters to which the general public couldn't relate. Academics across many fields, however, began responding to this isolation and became increasingly active in political and cultural life in the 1980s and 1990s. For example, literary scholar Henry Louis Gates Jr. began writing essays for *Time* and the *New Yorker* magazines. Linguist Noam Chomsky has written for decades about excessive government and media power; he was also the subject of an award-winning documentary, *Manufacturing Consent: Noam Chomsky and the Media*. Steven D. Levitt, an economics professor at the University of Chicago, worked with journalist coauthor Stephen Dubner to popularize his unconventional economics studies (asking questions like "If drug dealers make so much money, why do they still live with their mothers?") in the 2005 book *Freakonomics*. Essayist and cultural critic Barbara Ehrenreich has written often about labor and economic issues in magazines such as *Time* and the *Nation*. In her 2008 book *This Land Is Their Land: Reports from a Divided Nation,* she investigates incidents of poverty among recent college graduates, undocumented workers, and Iraq war military families, documenting the wide divide between rich and poor. Finally, Georgetown University sociology professor Michael Eric Dyson, author of the book *April 4, 1968: Martin Luther King, Jr.'s Death and How It Changed America*, made frequent appearances on network and cable news channels during the 2008 presidential campaign to speak on the issues of race and the meaning of Barack Obama's historic candidacy.

In recent years, public intellectuals have also encouraged discussion about media production in a digital world. Stanford University law professor Lawrence Lessig has been a leading advocate of efforts to rewrite the nation's copyright laws to enable noncommercial "amateur culture" to flourish on the Internet. He publishes his work both in print and online. American University's Pat Aufderheide, longtime media critic for the alternative magazine *In These Times*, worked with independent filmmakers to develop the *Documentary Filmmakers' Statement of Best Practices in Fair Use*, which calls for documentary filmmakers to have reasonable access to copyrighted material for their work.

Like public journalists, public intellectuals based on campuses help carry on the conversations of society and culture, actively circulating the most important new ideas of the day and serving as models for how to participate in public life. ▶

"In quantum gravity, as we shall see, the space-time manifold ceases to exist as an objective reality; geometry becomes relational and contextual; and the foundational conceptual categories of prior science—among them, existence itself—become problematized and relativized. This conceptual revolution, I will argue, has profound implications for the content of a future postmodern and liberatory science."

FROM ALAN SOKAL'S PUBLISHED JARGON-RIDDLED HOAX, 1996

"My idea of a good time is using jargon and citing authorities."

MATT GROENING, *SCHOOL IS HELL*, 1987

CHAPTER REVIEW

REVIEW QUESTIONS

Early Media Research Methods

1. What were the earliest types of media studies, and why weren't they more scientific?

2. What were the major influences that led to scientific media research?

Research on Media Effects

3. What are the differences between experiments and surveys as media research strategies?

4. What is content analysis, and why is it significant?

5. What are the differences between the hypodermic-needle model and the minimal-effects model in the history of media research?

6. What are the main ideas behind social learning theory, agenda-setting, the cultivation effect, and the spiral of silence?

7. What are some strengths and limitations of modern media research?

Cultural Approaches to Media Research

8. Why did cultural studies develop in opposition to media effects research?

9. What are the features of cultural studies?

10. How is textual analysis different from content analysis?

11. What are some of the strengths and limitations of cultural research?

Media Research and Democracy

12. How has specialization in academic research influenced universities?

13. How can public intellectuals and academics improve the relationship between campuses and the general public?

QUESTIONING THE MEDIA

1. What are your main concerns or criticisms about the state of media studies at your college or university?

2. One charge that has been leveled against a lot of media research—both the effects and the cultural models—is that it has very little impact on changing our media institutions. Do you agree or disagree, and why?

3. Can you think of an issue that media industry and academic researchers could study together? Explain.

4. In looking at media courses in a college curriculum, what do you think the relationship is between theory and practice? Do hands-on, practical-skills courses such as news reporting, advertising copywriting, or TV production belong in a liberal arts college or in a separate mass communication college? Explain your answer.

For review quizzes, chapter summaries, links to media-related Web sites, and more, go to bedfordstmartins.com/mediaculture.

COMMON THREADS

One of the Common Threads discussed in Chapter 1 focuses on the commercial nature of the mass media. In controversies about media content, how much of what society finds troubling in the mass media is due more to the commercial nature of the media than to any intrinsic quality of the media themselves?

For some media critics, such as former advertising executive Jerry Mander in his popular book *Four Arguments for the Elimination of Television* (1978), the problems of the mass media (in his case, television) are inherent in the technology of the medium (e.g., the hypnotic lure of a light-emitting screen) and can't be fixed or reformed. Other researchers focus primarily on the effects of media on individual behavior.

But how much of what critics dislike about television and other mass media—including violence, indecency, immorality, inadequate journalism, and unfair representations of people and issues—derives from the way in which the mass media are organized in our culture rather than anything about the technologies themselves or their effects on behavior? In other words, are many criticisms of television and other mass media merely masking what should be broader criticisms of capitalism?

One of the keys to accurately analyzing television and the other mass media is to tease apart the effects of a capitalist economy (which organizes media industries and relies on advertising, corporate underwriting, and other forms of sponsorship to profit from them) from the effects of the actual medium (television, movies, the Internet, radio,

newspapers, etc.). If our media system wasn't commercial in nature—wasn't controlled by large corporations—would the same "effects" exist? Would the content change? Would different kinds of movies fill theaters? Would radio play the same music? What would the news be about? Would search engines generate other results?

Basically, would society be learning other things if the mass media were organized in a noncommercial way? Would a noncommercial mass media set the same kind of political agenda, or would it cultivate a different kind of reality? What would the spiral of silence theory look like in a noncommercial media system?

Perhaps a noncommercial mass media would have its own problems. Indeed, there may be effects that can't be unhitched from the technology of a mass medium, no matter what the economy is. But it's worth considering whether any effects are due to the economic system that brings the content to us. If we determine that the commercial nature of the media is a source of negative effects, then we should also reconsider our policy solutions for trying to deal with those effects.

KEY TERMS

The definitions for the terms listed below can be found in the glossary at the end of the book. The page numbers listed with the terms indicate where the term is highlighted in the chapter.

media effects research, 469
cultural studies, 469
propaganda analysis, 470
hypodermic-needle model, 475
minimal-effects model, 475
selective exposure, 475
selective retention, 475
uses and gratifications model, 476
scientific method, 476
hypotheses, 477
experiments, 477
random assignment, 477

survey research, 478
longitudinal studies, 478
correlations, 478
content analysis, 478
social learning theory, 480
agenda-setting, 481
cultivation effect, 481
spiral of silence, 482
textual analysis, 484
audience studies, 486
political economy studies, 486

16

Legal Controls and Freedom of Expression

"So I was at my office/studios in downtown Atlanta and about 5:30, I was outside about to do an interview when about two or three Tahoes pulled up on the side of our street. You know, about 15 to 20 cops jumped out of the cars, you know, full gear on, M-16s drawn, you know, pointed directly at us. They put me under arrest."[1]

—DJ Drama

On the evening of January 16, 2007, police raided the offices of twenty-eight-year-old Tyree Simmons (aka DJ Drama), confiscated nearly everything of value, and charged him and an associate with racketeering. Their crime? Being hip-hop music mixtape artists.

Mixtape artists produce compilation digital recordings, which contain "unreleased remixes, sneak previews from coming CDs, casual free-style rhymes, never-to-be-released goofs."[2] DJ Drama is one of the best, and he helped launch the southern hip-hop sound and the careers of Lil Wayne, Young Jeezy, Willie the Kid, and Lil KeKe with his *Gangsta Grillz* mixtapes.

The arrest was at the urging of the Recording Industry Association of America, which considers mixtapes pirated work, violating copyright law. Ironically, mixtapes are often helpful promotional tools for music labels, and major stars like 50-Cent, P. Diddy, and Jay-Z have used mixtapes to further their careers.

Mixtapes are just one form of digital music under fire for copyright violations. Another is sampling. As University of Iowa communication studies professor Kembrew McLeod explains, in the late 1980s, sampling "was a creative window that had been forced open by hip-hop artists" but "by the early 1990s, the free experimentation was over. . . . [E]veryone had to pay for the sounds that they sampled or risk getting sued."[3] The cost for most acts was far too prohibitive. Fees to use snippets of copyrighted sounds in the Beastie Boys' 1989 sample-rich *Paul's Boutique* recording cost $250,000.[4] Today, a recording based on creative mash-ups of samples probably couldn't even be made, as some copyright owners demand up to $50,000 for sampling just a few seconds of their song.

Some artists are still trying nevertheless. Pittsburgh-based mash-up DJ Girl Talk (Gregg Gillis) has no problem performing his sample-heavy music, where he remixes a dozen or more samples on his laptop with some of his own beats to create a new song. Copyright royalties are covered for his live public performances, since venues already have public performance agreements with copyrights management agencies BMI, ASCAP, and SESAC. (These are the same agencies that collect fees from restaurants and radio stations for publicly performed music.) But—and this is one of the many inconsistencies in copyright law—if Gillis wants to make a recording of his music, the cost of the copyright royalty payments (should they even be granted by the copyright holder) would exceed the revenue generated by the CD. But, if he doesn't get copyright permission for the samples used, he risks hundreds of thousands of dollars in penalties. In this kind of situation, McLeod argues, copyright ends up acting like a censor, because it makes recordings of creative work like Girl Talk's impossible.

Despite the threat of lawsuits, Gillis and an independent label—appropriately named Illegal Art—released the acclaimed *Night Ripper* album in 2006 and *Feed the Animals* in 2008. In defending the recording against potential lawsuits, Gillis and his label argue that they are protected from copyright infringement by the fair use exemption, which allows for *transformative use*—creating new work from bits of copyrighted work.[5]

The uneven and unclear rules for the use of sound, images, video, and text have become one of the most contentious issues of today's digital culture. As digital media make it easier than ever to create and re-create cultural content, copyright law has yet to catch up with these new forms of expression. Revisions to copyright law—which likely will not be made for several more years—will determine whether artists like DJ Drama and Girl Talk are able to legally borrow a little, borrow a lot, or borrow nothing at all in creating their works.

"Mixtapes are just one form of digital music under fire for copyright violations."

▲ **THE CULTURAL AND SOCIAL STRUGGLES OVER WHAT CONSTITUTES "FREE SPEECH"** or "free expression" have defined American democracy. In 1989, when Supreme Court Justice William Brennan Jr. was asked to comment on his favorite part of the Constitution, he replied, "The First Amendment, I expect. Its enforcement gives us this society. The other provisions of the Constitution really only embellish it." Of all the issues that involve the mass media and popular culture, none is more central–or explosive–than freedom of expression and the First Amendment. Our nation's historical development can often be traced to how much or how little we tolerated speech during particular periods.

The current era is as volatile a time as ever for free speech issues. Contemporary free speech debates include copyright issues, hate-speech codes on college and university campuses, explicit lyrics in music, violent images in film and television, the swapping of media files on the Internet, and the right of the press to publish government secrets.

In this chapter, we will examine free expression issues, focusing on the implications of the First Amendment for a variety of mass media. We investigate the models of expression, the origins of free expression, and the First Amendment. Next, we examine the prohibition of censorship and how the First Amendment has been challenged and limited throughout American history. Focusing on the impact of gag orders, shield laws, and the use of cameras in the courtroom, we then examine some of the clashes between the First Amendment and the Sixth Amendment. With regard to film, we review the social and political pressures that gave rise to early censorship boards and the current film ratings system. We then turn to issues in broadcasting and examine why it has been treated differently from print media. Finally, we explore the newest frontier in free expression–the Internet.

> "Congress shall make no law respecting an establishment of religion, or prohibiting the free exercise thereof; or abridging the freedom of speech, or of the press; or the right of the people peaceably to assemble, and to petition the Government for a redress of grievances."
>
> FIRST AMENDMENT, U.S. CONSTITUTION, 1791

The Origins of Free Expression and a Free Press

When students from other cultures attend school in the United States, many are astounded by the number of books, news articles, editorials, cartoons, films, TV shows, and Web sites that make fun of U.S. presidents, the military, and the police. Many countries' governments throughout history have jailed, even killed, their citizens for such speech "violations." For instance, between 1992 and late 2008, 713 international journalists have been killed in the line of duty, often because someone disagreed with what they wrote or reported.[6] In the United States, however, we

◄

JOURNALISTS AT RISK
According to the Committee to Protect Journalists, thirty-four journalists around the world were killed in the line of duty between January and October 2008. The war in Iraq accounted for ten of those deaths, with experienced war correspondents labeling the "postwar" period as their most dangerous assignment.

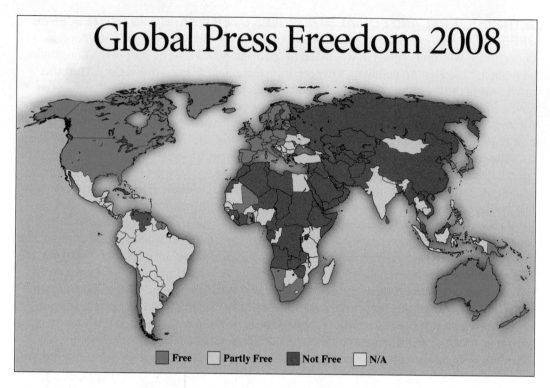

Global Press Freedom 2008

■ Free   □ Partly Free   ■ Not Free   □ N/A

have generally taken for granted our right to criticize and poke fun at the government and other authority figures. Moreover, many of us are unaware of the ideas that underpin our freedoms and don't realize the extent to which those freedoms surpass those in most other countries.

In fact, a recent international survey of the news media in 195 countries, conducted by the human rights organization Freedom House, reported that about 63 percent of the world's people live in countries where the press is significantly less than free. This 2008 survey related that sixty-four nations allowed virtually no freedom of the press, with those governments exercising tight control over the news media and even intimidating, jailing, and executing journalists.

Models of Expression

Since the mid-1950s, four conventional models for speech and journalism have been used to categorize the widely differing ideas underlying free expression.[7] These models include the authoritarian, communist, libertarian, and social responsibility concepts. They are distinguished by the levels of freedom permitted and by the attitudes of the ruling and political classes toward the freedoms granted to the average citizen. Today, given the diversity among nations, the experimentation of journalists, and the collapse of many communist press systems, these categories are no longer as relevant. Nevertheless, they offer a good point of departure for discussing the press and democracy.

The **authoritarian model** developed at about the time the printing press first arrived in sixteenth-century England. Its advocates held that the general public, largely illiterate in those days, needed guidance from an elite, educated ruling class. Government criticism and public dissent were not tolerated, especially if such speech undermined "the common good"—an ideal that elites and rulers defined and controlled. Censorship was also frequent, and the government issued printing licenses primarily to publishers who were sympathetic to government and ruling-class agendas.

Today, many authoritarian systems operate in developing countries throughout Asia, Latin America, and Africa, where journalism often joins with government and business to foster economic growth, minimize political dissent, and promote social stability. The leaders in these systems generally believe that too much outspoken speech and press freedom would undermine the delicate stability of their social and political infrastructures. In these societies, criticizing government programs may be viewed as an obstacle to keeping the peace, and both reporters and citizens may be punished if they question leaders and the status quo too fiercely.

In the authoritarian model, the news is controlled by private enterprise. But under the **communist** or **state model**, the press is controlled by the government because state leaders believe the press should serve the goals of the state. Although some government criticism is tolerated under this model, ideas that challenge the basic premises of state authority are not. Although state media systems were in decline throughout the 1990s, there are still a few countries using this model, including Myanmar (Burma), China, Cuba, and North Korea.

The **social responsibility model** characterizes the ideals of mainstream journalism in the United States. The concepts and assumptions behind this model were outlined in 1947 by the Hutchins Commission, which was formed to examine the increasing influence of the press. The commission's report called for the development of press watchdog groups because the mass media had grown too powerful and needed to become more socially responsible. Key recommendations encouraged comprehensive news reports that put issues and events in context; more news forums for the exchange of ideas; better coverage of society's range of economic classes and social groups; and stronger overviews of our nation's social values, ideals, and goals.

A socially responsible press is usually privately owned (although the government technically operates the broadcast media in most European democracies). In this model, the press functions as a **Fourth Estate**—that is, as an unofficial branch of government that monitors the legislative, judicial, and executive branches for abuses of power. In theory, private ownership keeps the news media independent of government. Thus, they are better able to watch over the system on behalf of citizens. Under this model, the press supplies information to citizens so that they can make informed decisions regarding political and social issues.

The flip side of the state and authoritarian models and a more radical extension of the social responsibility model, the **libertarian model** encourages vigorous government criticism and supports the highest degree of individual and press freedoms. In the libertarian model, no restrictions are placed on the mass media or on individual speech. Libertarians tolerate the expression of everything, from publishing pornography to advocating anarchy. In North America and Europe, many alternative newspapers and magazines operate on such a model. Placing a great deal of trust in citizens' ability to distinguish truth from fabrication, libertarians maintain that speaking out with absolute freedom is the best way to fight injustice and arrive at the truth.

The First Amendment of the U.S. Constitution

To understand the development of free expression in the United States, we must first understand how the idea for a free press came about. In various European countries throughout the 1600s, in order to monitor—and punish, if necessary—the speech of editors and writers, governments controlled the circulation of ideas through the press by requiring printers to obtain licenses from them. However, in 1644, English poet John Milton, author of *Paradise Lost*, published his essay *Areopagitica*, which opposed government licenses for printers and defended a free press. Milton argued that all sorts of ideas, even false ones, should be allowed to circulate freely in a democratic society, because eventually the truth would emerge. In 1695, England stopped licensing newspapers, and most of Europe followed. In many democracies today, publishing a newspaper, magazine, or newsletter remains one of the few public or service enterprises that requires no license.

Less than a hundred years later, the writers of the Constitution were ambivalent about the freedom of the press. In fact, the U.S. Constitution as originally ratified in 1788 didn't include a guarantee of freedom of the press. Constitutional framer Alexander Hamilton thought it impractical to attempt to define "liberty of the press," and that whatever declarations might be added to the Constitution, its security would ultimately depend on public opinion. At that time, though, nine of the original thirteen states had charters defending the freedom of the press, and the states pushed to have federal guarantees of free speech and press approved at the first

session of the new Congress. The Bill of Rights, which contained the first ten amendments to the Constitution, was adopted in 1791.

The commitment to freedom of the press, however, was not resolute. In 1798, the Federalist Party, which controlled the presidency and Congress, passed the Sedition Act to silence opposition to an anticipated war against France. Led by President John Adams, the Federalists believed that defamatory articles by the opposition Democratic-Republican party might stir up discontent against the government and undermine its authority. Over the next three years, twenty-five individuals were arrested and ten were convicted under the act, which was also used to prosecute anti-Federalist newspapers. After failing to curb opposition, the Sedition Act expired in 1801 during Thomas Jefferson's presidency. Jefferson, a Democratic-Republican who had challenged the act's constitutionality, pardoned all defendants convicted under it.[8] Ironically, the Sedition Act, the first major attempt to constrain the First Amendment, became the defining act in solidifying American support behind the notion of a free press. As journalism historian Michael Schudson explained, "Only in the wake of the Sedition Act did Americans boldly embrace a free press as a necessary bulwark of a liberal civil order."[9]

Censorship as Prior Restraint

In the United States, the First Amendment has theoretically prohibited censorship. Over time, Supreme Court decisions have defined censorship as **prior restraint**. This means that courts and governments cannot block any publication or speech before it actually occurs, on the principle that a law has not been broken until an illegal act has been committed. In 1931, for example, the Supreme Court determined in *Near v. Minnesota* that a Minneapolis newspaper could not be stopped from publishing "scandalous and defamatory" material about police and law officials who they felt were negligent in arresting and punishing local gangsters.[10] However, the Court left open the idea that the news media could be ordered to halt publication in exceptional cases. During a declared war, for instance, if a U.S. court judged that the publication of an article would threaten national security, such expression could be restrained prior to its printing. In fact, during World War I the U.S. Navy seized all wireless radio transmitters. This was done to ensure control over critical information about weather conditions and troop movements that might inadvertently aid the enemy. In the 1970s, though, the Pentagon Papers decision and the *Progressive* magazine case tested important concepts underlying prior restraint.

The Pentagon Papers Case

In 1971, with the Vietnam War still in progress, Daniel Ellsberg, a former Defense Department employee, stole a copy of the forty-seven-volume report "History of U.S. Decision-Making Process on Vietnam Policy." A thorough study of U.S. involvement in Vietnam since World War II, the report was classified by the government as top secret. Ellsberg and a friend leaked the study—nicknamed the Pentagon Papers—to the *New York Times* and the *Washington Post*. In June 1971, the *Times* began publishing articles based on the study. To block any further publications, the Nixon administration applied for and received a federal court injunction against the *Times*, arguing that the publication of these documents posed "a clear and present danger" to national security.

A lower U.S. district court supported the newspaper's right to publish, but the government's appeal put the case before the Supreme Court less than three weeks after the first article was published. In a 6-3 vote, the Court sided with the newspaper. Justice Hugo Black, in his majority opinion, attacked the government's attempt to suppress publication: "Both the history and language of the First Amendment support the view that the press must be left free to publish news, whatever the source, without censorship, injunctions, or prior restraints."[11] (See "Media Literacy and the Critical Process: Who Knows the First Amendment?" on page 500.)

The *Progressive* Magazine Case

The issue of prior restraint for national security surfaced again in 1979, when an injunction was issued to block publication of the *Progressive*, a national left-wing magazine, in which the editors planned to publish an article entitled "The H-Bomb Secret: How We Got It, Why We're Telling It." The dispute began when the editor of the magazine sent a draft to the Department of Energy to verify technical portions of the article. Believing that the article contained sensitive data that might damage U.S. efforts to halt the proliferation of nuclear weapons, the Energy Department asked the magazine not to publish it. When the magazine said it would proceed anyway, the government sued the *Progressive* and asked a federal district court to block publication.

Judge Robert Warren sought to balance the *Progressive*'s First Amendment rights against the government's claim that the article would spread dangerous information and undermine national security. In an unprecedented action, Warren sided with the government, deciding that "a mistake in ruling against the United States could pave the way for thermonuclear annihilation for us all. In that event, our right to life is extinguished and the right to publish becomes moot."[12] During appeals and further litigation, several other publications, including the *Milwaukee Sentinel* and *Scientific American*, published their own articles related to the H-bomb, getting much of their information from publications already in circulation. None of these articles, including the one eventually published in the *Progressive*–after the government dropped the case during an appeal–contained the precise technical details needed to actually design a nuclear weapon, nor did they provide information on where to obtain the sensitive ingredients.

Even though the article was eventually published, Warren's decision stands as the first time in American history that a prior-restraint order imposed in the name of national security actually stopped the initial publication of a controversial news report.

Unprotected Forms of Expression

Despite the First Amendment's provision that "Congress shall make no law" restricting speech, the federal government has made a number of laws that do just that, especially concerning false or misleading advertising, expressions that intentionally threaten public safety, and certain speech restrictions during times of war or other national security concerns.

Beyond the federal government, state laws and local ordinances have on occasion curbed expression, and over the years the court system has determined that some kinds of expression

PRIOR RESTRAINT
In 1971, Daniel Ellsberg surrendered to government prosecutors in Boston. Ellsberg was a former Pentagon researcher who turned against America's military policy in Vietnam and leaked information to the press. He was charged with unauthorized possession of top-secret federal documents. Later called the Pentagon Papers, the documents contained evidence on the military's bungled handling of the Vietnam War. In 1973, an exasperated federal judge dismissed the case when illegal government-sponsored wiretaps of Ellsberg's psychoanalyst came to light during the Watergate scandal.

Media Literacy and the Critical Process

1 DESCRIPTION. Working alone or in small groups, find eight to ten people you know from two different age groups: (1) from your peers and friends or younger siblings; (2) from your parents' and/or grandparents' generations. (Do not choose students from your class.) Interview your subjects individually, either in person, by phone, or by e-mail, and ask them this question: If Congress were considering the following law–then read or type the First Amendment (see page 495), but don't tell them what it is–would they approve? Then ask them to respond to the following series of questions, adding any other questions that you think would be appropriate:

1. Do you agree or disagree with the freedoms? Explain.
2. Which do you support, and which do you think are excessive or provide too much freedom?
3. Ask them if they recognize the law. Note how many identified it as the First Amendment to the U.S. Constitution and how many did not. Note the percentage from each age group.
4. Optional: Find out each person's political leanings–Republican, Democrat,

Who Knows the First Amendment?

Enacted in 1791, the First Amendment supports not just press and speech freedoms but also religious freedom and the right of people to protest and to "petition the government for a redress of grievances." It also says that "Congress shall make no law" abridging or prohibiting these five freedoms. To investigate some critics' complaint that many citizens don't exactly know the protections offered in the First Amendment, conduct your own survey. Discuss with friends, family, or colleagues what they know or think about the First Amendment.

Independent, not sure, disaffected, apathetic, other, etc.

2 ANALYSIS. What patterns emerge in the answers from the two groups? Are their answers similar or different? How? Note any differences in the answers based on gender, level of education, or occupation.

3 INTERPRETATION. What do these patterns mean? Are your interview subjects supportive or unsupportive of the First Amendment? What are their reasons?

4 EVALUATION. How do your interviewees judge the freedoms? In general, what did your interview

subjects know about the First Amendment? What impressed you about your subjects' answers? Did you find anything alarming or troubling in their answers? Explain.

5 ENGAGEMENT. Research free expression and locate any national studies that are similar to this assignment. Then, check the recent national surveys on attitudes toward the First Amendment at either www.freedomforum.org or www.firstamendmentcenter.org. Write a letter to a local TV station news director and a newspaper editor and find out what limits they would or do place on themselves. Share your study and research with your teacher and the class.

do not merit protection under the Constitution, including seditious expression, copyright infringement, libel, obscenity, privacy rights, and expression that interferes with the Sixth Amendment.

Seditious Expression

For more than a century after the Sedition Act of 1798, Congress passed no laws prohibiting dissenting opinion. But the sentiments of the Sedition Act reappeared by the twentieth century in times of war. For instance, the Espionage Acts of 1917 and 1918, which were enforced during World Wars I and II, made it a federal crime to disrupt the nation's war effort, authorizing severe punishment for seditious statements.

In the landmark *Schenck v. United States* (1919) appeal case during World War I, the Supreme Court upheld the conviction of a Socialist Party leader, Charles T. Schenck, for distributing leaflets urging American men to protest the draft, in violation of the recently passed

Espionage Act. In upholding the conviction, Justice Oliver Wendell Holmes wrote two of the more famous interpretations and phrases in the First Amendment's legal history:

But the character of every act depends upon the circumstances in which it is done. The most stringent protection of free speech would not protect a man in falsely shouting fire in a theater and causing a panic.

The question in every case is whether the words used are used in such circumstances and are of such a nature as to create a clear and present danger that they will bring about the substantive evils that Congress has a right to prevent.

In supporting Schenck's sentence–a ten-year prison term–Holmes noted that the Socialist leaflets were entitled to First Amendment protection, but only during times of peace. In establishing the "clear and present danger" criterion for expression, the Supreme Court demonstrated the limits of the First Amendment.

And in 2006, after the *New York Times*, *Wall Street Journal*, and *Los Angeles Times* all published articles about the Bush administration's secret program to track the banking records of suspected terrorists, one congressman called for the *Times* "to be prosecuted for violating the 1917 Espionage Act."[13] Although no prosecutions occurred, it demonstrated that some politicians still want to curtail the political dissent guaranteed by the First Amendment during wartime.

Copyright Infringement

Appropriating a writer's or an artist's words or music without consent or payment is also a form of expression that is not protected as speech. A **copyright** legally protects the rights of authors and producers to their published or unpublished writing, music, lyrics, TV programs, movies, or graphic art designs. When Congress passed the first Copyright Act in 1790, it gave authors the right to control their published works for fourteen years, with the opportunity for a renewal for another fourteen years. After the end of the copyright period, the work enters the **public domain**, which gives the public free access to the work. The idea was that a period of copyright control would give authors financial incentive to create original works, and that the public domain gives others incentive to create derivative works.

Over the years, as artists lived longer, and–more importantly, as corporate copyright owners became more common–copyright periods were extended by Congress. In 1976, Congress extended the copyright period to the life of the author plus fifty years, or seventy-five years for a corporate copyright owner. In 1998 (as copyrights on works such as Disney's Mickey Mouse were set to expire), Congress again extended the copyright period for twenty additional years. As Stanford Law professor Lawrence Lessig observed, this was the eleventh time in forty years that the terms for copyright had been extended.[14]

Corporate owners have millions of dollars to gain by keeping their properties out of the public domain. Disney, a major lobbyist for the 1998 extension, would have lost its copyright to Mickey Mouse in 2004, but now continues to earn millions on its movies, T-shirts, and Mickey Mouse watches through 2024. Warner/Chappell Music, which owns the copyright to the popular "Happy Birthday to You" song, will keep generating money on the song at least through 2030, and even longer if corporations successfully pressure Congress for another extension.

As discussed earlier, hip-hop performers have faced a number of battles over copyright infringement; they have been accused of stealing other musicians' work by sampling, a technique fundamental to the genre. *File-swapping*

THE LIMITS OF COPYRIGHT In a 1994 landmark case, the Supreme Court ruled that the rap group 2 Live Crew's 1989 song "Pretty Woman" was a legitimate parody of the 1964 Roy Orbison song and was thus covered by the fair use exception to copyright.

on the Internet has raised an entirely new class of copyright concerns, in every media sector. The Recording Industry Association of American (RIAA) has been particularly aggressive in fighting file-swapping that violates music copyrights, and has sent letters to college students who are caught file-swapping, urging them to pay fines or risk prosecution. In 2008, a jury rendered the first-ever guilty verdict in an online music copyright infringement trial. One of the major enforcement tools of the RIAA and other media industry trade groups is the Digital Millennium Copyright Act of 1998, which outlaws technology or actions that circumvent copyright protection systems. In other words, it may be illegal to merely create or distribute technology that enables someone to make illegal copies of digital content, such as a music CD or a DVD.

Libel

The biggest single legal worry that haunts editors and publishers is the issue of libel, a form of expression that, unlike political expression, is not protected as free speech under the First Amendment. **Libel** refers to defamation of character in written or broadcast form; libel is different from **slander**, which is spoken language that defames a person's character. Inherited from British common law, libel is generally defined as a false statement that holds a person up to public ridicule, contempt, or hatred or injures a person's business or occupation. Examples of libelous statements include falsely accusing someone of professional dishonesty or incompetence (such as medical malpractice); falsely accusing a person of a crime (such as drug dealing); falsely stating that someone is mentally ill or engages in unacceptable behavior (such as public drunkenness); or falsely accusing a person of associating with a disreputable organization or cause (such as the Mafia or a neo-Nazi military group). (See "Case Study: A False Wikipedia 'Biography'" on the opposite page.)

Since 1964, the *New York Times v. Sullivan* case has served as the standard for libel law. The case stems from a 1960 full-page advertisement placed in the *New York Times* by the Committee to Defend Martin Luther King and the Struggle for Freedom in the South. Without naming names, the ad criticized the law-enforcement tactics used in southern cities—including Montgomery, Alabama—to break up Civil Rights demonstrations. The ad condemned "southern violators of the Constitution" bent on destroying King and the movement. Taking exception, the city commissioner of Montgomery, L. B. Sullivan, sued the *Times* for libel, claiming the ad defamed him indirectly. Although Alabama civil courts awarded Sullivan $500,000, the newspaper's lawyers appealed to the Supreme Court, which unanimously reversed the ruling, holding that Alabama libel law violated the *Times*' First Amendment rights.[15]

As part of the *Sullivan* decision, the Supreme Court asked future civil courts to distinguish whether plaintiffs in libel cases are public officials or private individuals. Citizens with more "ordinary" jobs, such as city sanitation employees, undercover police informants, nurses, or unknown actors, are normally classified as private individuals. Private individuals have to prove (1) that the public statement about them was false; (2) that damages or actual injury occurred (such as the loss of a job, harm to reputation, public humiliation, or mental anguish); and (3) that the publisher or broadcaster was negligent in failing to determine the truthfulness of the statement.

There are two categories of public figures: (1) public celebrities (movie or sports stars) or people who "occupy positions of such pervasive power and influence that they are deemed public figures for all purposes" (such as presidents, senators, mayors, etc.) and (2) individuals who have thrown themselves—usually voluntarily but sometimes involuntarily—into the middle of "a significant public controversy," such as a lawyer defending a prominent client, an advocate for an antismoking ordinance, or a labor union activist.

Public officials also have to prove falsehood, damages, negligence, and **actual malice** on the part of the news medium; actual malice means that the reporter or editor knew the statement

CASE STUDY

A False Wikipedia "Biography"

by John Seigenthaler

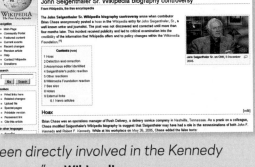

"John Seigenthaler Sr. was the assistant to Attorney General Robert Kennedy in the early 1960's. For a brief time, he was thought to have been directly involved in the Kennedy assassinations of both John, and his brother, Bobby. Nothing was ever proven." – **Wikipedia**

This is a highly personal story about Internet character assassination. It could be your story. I have no idea whose sick mind conceived the false, malicious "biography" that appeared under my name for 132 days on Wikipedia, the popular, online, free encyclopedia whose authors are unknown and virtually untraceable. There was more: "John Seigenthaler moved to the Soviet Union in 1971, and returned to the United States in 1984," Wikipedia said. "He started one of the country's largest public relations firms shortly thereafter."

At age 78, I thought I was beyond surprise or hurt at anything negative said about me. I was wrong. One sentence in the biography was true. I was Robert Kennedy's administrative assistant in the early 1960s. I also was his pallbearer. It was mind-boggling when my son, John Seigenthaler, journalist with NBC News, phoned later to say he found the same scurrilous text on Reference.com and Answers.com. I had heard for weeks from teachers, journalists, and historians about "the wonderful world of Wikipedia," where millions of people worldwide visit daily for quick reference "facts," composed and posted by people with no special expertise or knowledge—and sometimes by people with malice.

At my request, executives of the three websites now have removed the false content about me. I phoned Jimmy Wales, Wikipedia's founder, and asked, "Do you . . . have any way to know who wrote that?"

"No, we don't," he said. Representatives of the other two websites said their computers are programmed to copy data verbatim from Wikipedia, never checking whether it is false or factual. Naturally, I want to unmask my "biographer." And, I am interested in letting many people know that Wikipedia is a flawed and irresponsible research tool. But searching cyberspace for the identity of people who post spurious information can be frustrating. I traced the registered IP (Internet Protocol) number of my "biographer" to a customer of BellSouth Internet. That company advertises a phone number to report "Abuse Issues." An electronic voice said all complaints must be e-mailed. My two e-mails were answered by identical form letters, advising me that the company would conduct an investigation but might not tell me the results. It was signed "Abuse Team."

After three weeks, hearing nothing further about the Abuse Team investigation, I phoned BellSouth's Atlanta corporate headquarters, which led to conversations between my lawyer and BellSouth's counsel. My only remote chance of getting the name, I learned, was to file a "John or Jane Doe" lawsuit against my "biographer." Major communications Internet companies are bound by federal privacy laws that protect the identity of their customers, even those who defame online. Only if a lawsuit resulted in a court subpoena would BellSouth give up the name.

Federal law also protects online corporations—BellSouth, AOL, MCI, Wikipedia, etc.—from libel lawsuits. Section 230 of the Communications Decency Act, passed in 1996, specifically states that "no provider or user of an interactive computer service shall be treated as the publisher or speaker." That legalese means that, unlike print and broadcast companies, online service providers cannot be sued for disseminating defamatory attacks on citizens posted by others. Recent low-profile court decisions document that Congress effectively has barred defamation in cyberspace.

Wikipedia's website acknowledges that it is not responsible for inaccurate information, but Wales, in a C-Span interview with Brian Lamb, insisted that his website is accountable and that his community of thousands of volunteer editors (he said he has only one paid employee) corrects mistakes within minutes.

My experience refutes that. My "biography" was posted May 26 [2005]. For four months, Wikipedia depicted me as a suspected assassin before Wales erased it from his website's history Oct. 5. The falsehoods remained on Answers.com and Reference.com for three more weeks. And so we live in a universe of new media with phenomenal opportunities for worldwide communications and research—but populated by volunteer vandals with poison-pen intellects. Congress has enabled them and protects them. ◢

Note: In 2006, Seigenthaler, with the help of some intrepid reporters, tracked down the man who posted the libelous content. Seigenthaler, however, chose not to sue him, deciding instead to speak out about the experience and to call on Wikipedia to require those who post entries to sign their names and take responsibility for their work. The controversy is now a part of his online Wikipedia bio and also has its own entry (pictured).

Source: John Seigenthaler, "A False Wikipedia 'Biography,'" USA Today, November 30, 2005, p. 11A.

LIBEL AND THE MEDIA
This is the 1960 *New York Times* advertisement that triggered one of the most influential and important libel cases in U.S. history.

was false and printed or broadcast it anyway, or acted with a reckless disregard for the truth. Because actual malice against a public official is hard to prove, it is difficult for public figures to win libel suits. The *Sullivan* decision allowed news operations to aggressively pursue legitimate news stories without fear of continuous litigation. However, the mere threat of a libel suit still scares off many in the news media. Plaintiffs may also belong to one of many vague classification categories, such as public high school teachers, police officers, and court-appointed attorneys. Individuals from these professions end up as public or private citizens depending on a particular court's ruling.

Defenses against Libel Charges

Since the 1730s, the best defense against libel in American courts has been the truth. In most cases, if libel defendants can demonstrate that they printed or broadcast statements that were essentially true, such evidence usually bars plaintiffs from recovering any damages–even if their reputations were harmed.

In addition, there are other defenses against libel. Prosecutors, for example, who would otherwise be vulnerable to being accused of libel, are granted *absolute privilege* in a court of law so that they are not prevented from making accusatory statements towards defendants. The reporters who print or broadcast statements made in court are also protected against libel; they are granted conditional or **qualified privilege**, allowing them to report judicial or legislative proceedings even though the public statements being reported may be libelous.

Another defense against libel is the rule of **opinion and fair comment**. Generally, libel applies only to intentional misstatements of factual information rather than opinion, and therefore opinions are protected from libel. However, the line between fact and opinion is often hazy. For this reason, lawyers advise journalists first to set forth the facts on which a viewpoint is based and then to state their opinion based on those facts. In other words, journalists should make it clear that a statement is a criticism and not an allegation of fact.

One of the most famous tests of opinion and fair comment occurred in 1983 when Larry Flynt, publisher of *Hustler* magazine, published a spoof of a Campari advertisement depicting conservative minister and political activist Jerry Falwell as a drunk and as having had sexual relations with his mother. In fine print at the bottom of the page, a disclaimer read: "Ad parody–not to be taken seriously." Often a target of Flynt's irreverence and questionable taste, Falwell sued for libel, asking for $45 million in damages. In the verdict, the jury rejected the libel suit but found that Flynt had intentionally caused Falwell emotional distress, awarding Falwell $200,000. The case drew enormous media attention and raised concerns about the erosion of the media's right to free speech. However, Flynt's lawyers appealed, and in 1988 the Supreme Court unanimously overturned the verdict. Although the Court did not condone the *Hustler* spoof, the justices did say that the magazine was entitled to constitutional protection. In affirming *Hustler*'s speech rights, the Court suggested that even though parodies and insults of public figures might indeed cause emotional pain, denying the right to publish them and awarding damages for emotional reasons would violate the spirit of the First Amendment.[16]

Libel laws also protect satire, comedy, and opinions expressed in reviews of books, plays, movies, and restaurants. Such laws may not, however, protect malicious statements in which plaintiffs can prove that defendants used their free-speech rights to mount a damaging personal attack.

Obscenity

For most of this nation's history, legislators have argued that **obscenity** does not constitute a legitimate form of expression protected by the First Amendment. The problem, however, is that little agreement has existed on how to define an obscene work. In the 1860s, a court could judge an entire book obscene if it contained a single passage believed capable of "corrupting" a person. In fact, throughout the 1800s, certain government authorities outside the courts–especially U.S. post office and customs officials–held the power to censor or destroy material they deemed obscene.

This began to change in the 1930s during the trial involving the celebrated novel *Ulysses* by Irish writer James Joyce. Portions of *Ulysses* had been serialized in the early 1920s in an American magazine, *Little Review*, copies of which were later seized and burned by postal officials. The publishers of the magazine were fined $50 and nearly sent to prison. Because of the four-letter words contained in the novel and the book-burning and fining incidents, British and American publishing houses backed away from the book, and in 1928, the U.S. Customs Office officially banned *Ulysses* as an obscene work. Ultimately, however, Random House agreed to publish the work in the United States if it was declared "legal." Finally, in 1933, a U.S. judge ruled that an important literary work such as *Ulysses* was a legitimate, protected form of expression, even if portions of the book were deemed objectionable by segments of the population.

In a landmark 1957 case, *Roth v. United States*, the Supreme Court offered this test of obscenity: whether to an "average person," applying "contemporary standards," the major thrust or theme of the material "taken as a whole" appealed to "prurient interest" (in other

"You cannot hold us to the same [libel] standards as a newscast or you kill talk radio. If we had to qualify everything we said, talk radio would cease to exist."

LIONEL, WABC TALK-RADIO MORNING HOST, 1999

LIBEL AND THE COURTS
Prior to his 1984 libel trial, *Hustler* magazine publisher Larry Flynt was also convicted of pandering obscenity. Here, Flynt answers questions from newsmen on February 9, 1977, as he is led to jail.

words, was intended to "incite lust"). By the 1960s, based on *Roth*, expression was not obscene if only a small part of the work lacked "redeeming social value."

The current legal definition of obscenity derives from the 1973 *Miller v. California* case, which stated that to qualify as obscenity, the material must meet three criteria: (1) the average person, applying contemporary community standards, would find that the material as a whole appeals to prurient interest; (2) the material depicts or describes sexual conduct in a patently offensive way; and (3) the material, as a whole, lacks serious literary, artistic, political, or scientific value. The *Miller* decision contained two important ideas not present in *Roth*. First, it acknowledged that different communities and regions of the country have different values and standards with which to judge obscenity. Second, it required that a work be judged *as a whole*, so that publishers could not use the loophole of inserting a political essay or literary poem into pornographic materials to demonstrate in court that their publications contained redeeming features.

Since the *Miller* decision, courts have granted great latitude to printed and visual obscenity. By the 1980s and 1990s, major prosecutions had become rare—aimed mostly at child pornography—as the legal system accepted the concept that a free and democratic society must tolerate even repulsive kinds of speech. Most battles over obscenity are now online, where the concept of community standards has been eclipsed by the global reach of the Internet. The most recent incarnation of the Child Online Protection Act—originally formed in 1998 to make it illegal to post "material that is harmful to minors"—was found unconstitutional in 2007 because it would infringe on the right to free speech on the Internet. The presiding judge also stated that the act would be ineffective, as it wouldn't apply to pornographic Web sites from overseas, which account for up to half of pornographic sites. The most recent ruling suggested that the best protections for children are parental supervision and software filters.

The Right to Privacy

Whereas libel laws safeguard a person's character and reputation, the right to privacy protects an individual's peace of mind and personal feelings. In the simplest terms, the **right to privacy** addresses a person's right to be left alone, without his or her name, image, or daily activities becoming public property. Invasions of privacy occur in different situations, the most common of which are intrusion into someone's personal space via unauthorized tape recording, photographing, wiretapping, etc.; making available to the public personal records such as health and phone records; disclosing personal information such as religion, sexual activities, or personal activities; and the unauthorized appropriation of someone's image or name for advertising or other commercial purpose. In general, the news media have been granted wide protections under the First Amendment to do their work. For instance, the names and pictures of both private individuals and public figures can usually be used without their consent in most news stories. Additionally, if private citizens become part of public controversies and subsequent news stories, the courts have usually allowed the news media to treat them like public figures (i.e., record their quotes and use their images without the individuals' permission). The courts have even ruled that accurate reports of criminal and court records, including the identification of rape victims, do not normally constitute privacy invasions. Nevertheless, most newspapers and broadcast outlets use their own internal guidelines and ethical codes to protect the privacy of victims and defendants, especially in cases involving rape and child abuse.

Public figures have received some legal relief as many local municipalities and states have passed "anti-paparazzi" laws that protect individuals from unwarranted scrutiny and surveillance of personal activities on private property or outside public forums. Some courts have ruled that photographers must keep a certain distance away from celebrities, although powerful zoom lens technology usually overcomes this obstacle. However, every year brings a few stories of a Hollywood actor or sports figure punching a tabloid photographer or TV cameraman who got too close. And in 2004, the Supreme Court ruled—as an exception to the Freedom of

Information Act—that families of prominent figures who have died have the right to object to the release of autopsy photos, so that the images may not be exploited.

A number of laws also protect the privacy of regular citizens. For example, the Privacy Act of 1974 protects individuals' records from public disclosure unless individuals give written consent. The Electronic Communications Privacy Act of 1986 extended the law to computer-stored data and the Internet, although subsequent court decisions ruled that employees have no privacy rights in electronic communications conducted on their employer's equipment. The USA PATRIOT Act of 2001, however, weakened the earlier laws, and gave the federal government more latitude in searching private citizens' records and intercepting electronic communications without a court order.

First Amendment versus Sixth Amendment

Over the years, First Amendment protections of speech and the press have often clashed with the Sixth Amendment, which guarantees an accused individual in "all criminal prosecutions . . . the right to a speedy and public trial, by an impartial jury." In 1954, for example, the Sam Sheppard case garnered enormous nationwide publicity and became the inspiration for the TV show and film *The Fugitive*. Featuring lurid details about the murder of Sheppard's wife, the press editorialized in favor of Sheppard's quick arrest; some papers even pronounced him guilty. A prominent and wealthy osteopath, Sheppard was convicted of the murder, but twelve years later, Sheppard's new lawyer, F. Lee Bailey, argued before the Supreme Court that his client had not received a fair trial because of prejudicial publicity in the press. The Court overturned the conviction and freed Sheppard.

Gag Orders and Shield Laws

A major criticism of recent criminal cases concerns the ways in which lawyers use the news media to comment publicly on cases that are pending or are in trial. After the Sheppard reversal

"[Jailed *New York Times* reporter Judith Miller] does not believe, nor do we, that reporters are above the law, but instead holds that the work of journalists must be independent and free from government control if they are to effectively serve as government watchdogs."

REPORTERS COMMITTEE FOR FREEDOM OF THE PRESS, 2005

in the 1960s, the Supreme Court introduced safeguards that judges could employ to ensure fair trials in heavily publicized cases. These included sequestering juries (Sheppard's jury was not sequestered), moving cases to other jurisdictions, limiting the number of reporters, and placing restrictions, or **gag orders**, on lawyers and witnesses. In some countries, courts have issued gag orders to prohibit the press from releasing information or giving commentary that might prejudice jury selection or cause an unfair trial. In the United States, however, especially since a Supreme Court review in 1976, gag orders have been struck down as a prior-restraint violation of the First Amendment.

In opposition to gag rules, **shield laws** have favored the First Amendment rights of reporters, protecting them from having to reveal their sources for controversial information used in news stories. The news media have argued that protecting the confidentiality of key sources maintains a reporter's credibility, protects a source from possible retaliation, and serves the public interest by providing information citizens might not otherwise receive. In the 1960s, when the First Amendment rights of reporters clashed with Sixth Amendment fair-trial concerns, judges usually favored the Sixth Amendment arguments. In 1972, a New Jersey journalist became the first reporter jailed for contempt of court for refusing to identify sources in a probe of the Newark housing authority. After this case, a number of legal measures emerged to protect the news media. Thirty-five states and the District of Columbia now have some type of shield law. There is no federal shield law in the United States, though, leaving journalists exposed to subpoenas from federal prosecutors and courts. (See "Examining Ethics: Cartoons, T-shirts, and More: Why We Must Protect What Offends" on the opposite page.)

Cameras in the Courtroom

The debates over limiting intrusive electronic broadcast equipment and photographers in the courtroom actually date to the sensationalized coverage of the Bruno Hauptmann trial in the mid-1930s. Hauptmann was convicted and executed for the kidnap-murder of the nineteen-month-old son of Anne and Charles Lindbergh (the aviation hero who made the first solo flight across the Atlantic Ocean in 1927). During the trial, Hauptmann and his attorney complained that the circus atmosphere fueled by the presence of radio and flash cameras prejudiced the jury and turned the public against him.

"The day you see a camera come into our courtroom, it's going to roll over my dead body."

SUPREME COURT
JUSTICE DAVID
SOUTER, 1996

Cartoons, T-shirts, and More: Why We Must Protect What Offends

by Gene Policinski

Why does the First Amendment protect those who are showing and saying things many of us would rather not see or hear? That question was raised recently in three very different situations:

- News reports [in spring 2008] said that among the offerings on the ubiquitous YouTube, the free electronic video-sharing site that lets virtually anyone post clips, home movies and such, was a series of racially offensive cartoons that had been out of public view for four decades.

- A reporter for a French online news service called the First Amendment Center to inquire why U.S. law protected the right of self-styled American Nazi skinheads to march within sight of the U.S. Capitol in April [2008], carrying signs that the reporter said contained racial slurs against illegal immigrants.

- In Illinois on April 27 [2008], the 7th U.S. Circuit Court of Appeals voted to allow a high school student to wear a "Be Happy, Not Gay" T-shirt to school while his case proceeds, over the objection of school officials, who said the shirt's message offended some students and faculty.

Let's consider each circumstance.

The cartoons—a series of 11 produced by Warner Brothers in the 1940s, according to a *New York Times* story—were controversial even when they were originally released. In 1943, the *Times* reported, the NAACP protested the stereotyped images and language as demeaning portrayals of black citizens. Withdrawn from public view in 1968, according to several sources, the series surfaced on YouTube and prompted an online debate on many sites about whether the clips should be available to a new generation of viewers.

The French reporter's inquiry was rooted in a bit of history, too. Don't Americans realize, she said, that permitting racist groups even a moment in the public consciousness could lead to horrible developments? Europeans, she noted, had "experience" with such things—and in most nations on that continent, public displays raising Nazi memories would be banned.

"I disapprove of what you say, but I will defend to the death your right to say it."

VOLTAIRE (ATTRIBUTED)

The Illinois T-shirt case and others like it in recent years pit student-speech rights against school administrators' claims that offensive images and words disrupt teaching, interfere with order, or impinge on other students' rights. Other clothing-and-accessory disputes have arisen over images recalling the Confederate battle flag, seen as racist by some and simply historical by others, and over religious symbols worn as pendants or pins.

Yes, there may be momentary appeal to the notion that life in America would be better if we didn't offend each other so often. And an "orderly" school process would seem to advance education.

But think again. Hearing ideas and experiencing different points of view can, at the very least, alert citizens to what political opponents or social opposites are thinking. Those same First Amendment protections that shield the offensive speech from government censorship also protect those who would speak out in opposition.

And the give-and-take among ideas and those who express them is fundamental to the very-American concept that "truth" will, in the long run, win out in a free and open marketplace of ideas.

The nation's founders had experience with a system that decided, in advance and sometimes with a royal claim to divine guidance, what was "truth" and what was not. They designed a system that not only keeps the government from controlling our speech, but that also challenges us to speak out—to go on the offensive against that which offends.

T-shirts, protest signs and even bigoted cartoons from an earlier, insensitive generation not only offend, but also prod us to take stock of the ideas they advance—and what we might say in opposition. And that's how free speech works. ◢

Source: Gene Policinski, "Cartoons, T-shirts, and More: Why We Must Protect What Offends," First Amendment Center, May 18, 2008, http://www.firstamendmentcenter.org/commentary.aspx?id=20058.

**MEDIA IN THE
COURTROOM**
Photographers surround
aviator Charles A. Lindbergh
(without hat) as he leaves the
courthouse in Flemington,
N.J., during the trial of Bruno
Hauptmann on charges of
kidnapping and murdering the
Lindbergh baby boy in 1935.

After the trial, the American Bar Association amended its professional ethics code, Canon 35, stating that electronic equipment in the courtroom detracted "from the essential dignity of the proceedings." Calling for a ban on photographers and radio equipment, the association believed that if such elements were not banned, lawyers would begin playing to audiences and negatively alter the judicial process. For years after the Hauptmann trial, almost every state banned photographic, radio, and TV equipment from courtrooms.

As broadcast equipment became more portable and less obtrusive, however, and as television became the major news source for most Americans, courts gradually reevaluated their bans on broadcast equipment. In fact, in the early 1980s the Supreme Court ruled that the presence of TV equipment did not make it impossible for a fair trial to occur, leaving it up to each state to implement its own system. The ruling opened the door for the debut of Court TV in 1991 and the televised O.J. Simpson trial of 1994 (the most publicized case in history). All states today allow television coverage of cases, although most states place certain restrictions on coverage of courtrooms, often leaving it up to the discretion of the presiding judge. While U.S. federal courts now allow limited TV coverage of their trials, the Supreme Court continues to ban TV from its proceedings, but in 2000 the Court broke its anti-radio rule by permitting delayed radio broadcasts of the hearings on the Florida vote recount case that determined the winner of the 2000 presidential election.

As libel law and the growing acceptance of courtroom cameras indicate, the legal process has generally, though not always, tried to ensure that print and other news media are able to cover public issues broadly without fear of reprisals.

Film and the First Amendment

When the First Amendment was ratified in 1791, even the most enlightened leaders of our nation could not have predicted the coming of visual media such as film and television. Consequently, new communication technologies have not always received the same kinds of protection under the First Amendment as those granted to speech or print media like newspapers, magazines, and books. Movies, in existence since the late 1890s, only earned legal speech protection after a 1952 Supreme Court decision. Prior to that, social and political pressures led to both censorship and self-censorship in the movie industry.

Social and Political Pressure on the Movies

During the early part of the twentieth century, movies rose in popularity among European immigrants and others from modest socioeconomic groups. This, in turn, spurred the formation of censorship groups, which believed that the movies would undermine morality. During this time, according to media historian Douglas Gomery, criticism of movies converged on four areas: "the effects on children, the potential health problems, the negative influences on morals and manners, and the lack of a proper role for educational and religious institutions in the development of movies."[17]

Public pressure on movies came both from conservatives, who saw them as a potential threat to the authority of traditional institutions, and from progressives, who worried that children and adults were more attracted to movie houses than to social organizations and urban education centers. As a result, civic leaders publicly escalated their pressure, organizing local *review boards* that screened movies for their communities. In 1907, the Chicago City Council created an ordinance that gave the police authority to issue permits for the exhibition of movies. By 1920, more than ninety cities in the United States had some type of movie censorship board made up of vice squad officers, politicians, or citizens. By 1923, twenty-two states had established such boards.

Meanwhile, social pressure began to translate into law as politicians, wanting to please their constituencies, began to legislate against films.

Support mounted for a federal censorship bill. When Jack Johnson won the heavyweight championship in 1908, boxing films became the target of the first federal censorship law aimed at the motion-picture industry. In 1912, the government outlawed the transportation of boxing movies across state lines. The laws against boxing films, however, had more to do with Johnson's race than with concern over violence in movies. The first black heavyweight champion, he was perceived as a threat to some in the white community.

The first Supreme Court decision regarding film's protection under the First Amendment was handed down in 1915 and went against the movie industry. In *Mutual v. Ohio*, the Mutual Film Company of Detroit sued the state of Ohio, whose review board had censored a number of the distributor's films. On appeal, the case arrived at the Supreme Court, which unanimously ruled that motion pictures were not a form of speech but "a business pure and simple" and, like a circus, merely a "spectacle" for entertainment with "a special capacity for evil." This ruling would stand as a precedent for thirty-seven years, although a movement to create a national censorship board failed.

Self-Regulation in the Movie Industry

As the film industry expanded after World War I, the impact of public pressure and review boards began to affect movie studios and executives who wanted to ensure control over their economic well-being. In the early 1920s, a series of scandals rocked Hollywood: actress Mary

SOCIAL PRESSURES IN THE FILM INDUSTRY
Silent film comedian Roscoe "Fatty" Arbuckle never served jail time for the death of Virginia Rappe, but his career was ruined. Paramount canceled its $3 million contract with him, and he was blacklisted in Hollywood.

Pickford's divorce and quick marriage to actor Douglas Fairbanks; director William Desmond Taylor's unsolved murder; and actor Wallace Reid's death from a drug overdose. But the most sensational scandal involved aspiring actress Virginia Rappe, who died a few days after a wild party in a San Francisco hotel hosted by popular silent-film comedian Fatty Arbuckle. After Rappe's death, the comedian was indicted for rape and manslaughter, in a case that was sensationalized in the press. Although two hung juries could not reach a verdict, Arbuckle's career was ruined. Censorship boards across the country banned his films. Even though he was acquitted at his third trial in 1922, the movie industry tried to send a signal about the kinds of values and lifestyles it would tolerate: Arbuckle was banned from acting in Hollywood. He later resurfaced to direct several films under the name Will B. Goode.

In response to the scandals, particularly the first Arbuckle trial, the movie industry formed the Motion Picture Producers and Distributors of America (MPPDA) and hired as its president Will Hays, a former Republican National Committee chair. Hays's $100,000 salary, a huge sum at the time, was for cleaning up "sin city." Also known as the Hays Office, the MPPDA attempted to smooth out problems between the public and the industry. Hays blacklisted promising actors or movie extras with even minor police records. He also developed an MPPDA public relations division, which stopped a national movement for a federal law censoring movies.

The Motion Picture Production Code

During the 1930s, the movie business faced a new round of challenges. First, various conservative and religious groups—including the influential Catholic Legion of Decency—increased their scrutiny of the industry. Second, deteriorating economic conditions during the Great Depression forced the industry to tighten self-regulation in order to maintain profits and keep harmful public pressure at bay. In 1927, the Hays Office had developed a list of "Don'ts and Be Carefuls" to steer producers and directors away from questionable sexual, moral, and social themes. Nevertheless, pressure for a more formal and sweeping code mounted. As a result, in the early 1930s, the Hays Office established the Motion Picture Production Code, whose overseers were charged with officially stamping Hollywood films with a moral seal of approval.

The code laid out its mission in its first general principle: "No picture shall be produced which will lower the moral standards of those who see it. Hence the sympathy of the audience shall never be thrown to the side of crime, wrong-doing, evil or sin." The code dictated how producers and directors should handle "methods of crime," "repellent subjects," and "sex hygiene." A section on profanity outlawed a long list of phrases and topics, including "toilet gags" and "traveling salesmen and farmer's daughter jokes." Under "scenes of passion," the code dictated that "excessive and lustful kissing, lustful embraces, suggestive postures and gestures are not to be shown," and it required that "passion should be treated in such a manner as not to stimulate the lower and baser emotions." The section on religion revealed the influences of a Jesuit priest and a Catholic publisher, who helped write the code: "No film or episode may throw ridicule on any religious faith," and "ministers of religion . . . should not be used as comic characters or as villains."

Adopted by 95 percent of the industry, the code influenced nearly every commercial movie made between the mid-1930s and the early 1950s. It also gave the industry a relative degree of freedom, enabling the major studios to remain independent of outside regulation. When television arrived, however, competition from the new family medium forced movie producers to explore more adult subjects.

The Miracle Case

In 1952, the Supreme Court heard the *Miracle* case—officially *Burstyn v. Wilson*—named after Roberto Rossellini's film *Il Miracolo* (*The Miracle*). The movie's distributor sued the head of the New York Film Licensing Board for banning the film. A few New York City religious and political leaders considered the 1948 Italian film sacrilegious and pressured the film board for the ban. In the film, an unmarried peasant girl is impregnated by a scheming vagrant who tells her that he is St. Joseph and she has conceived the baby Jesus. The importers of the film argued that censoring it constituted illegal prior restraint under the First Amendment. Because such an action could not be imposed on a print version of the same story, the film's distributor argued that the same freedom should apply to the film. The Supreme Court agreed, declaring movies "a significant medium for the communication of ideas." The decision granted films the same constitutional protections as those enjoyed by the print media and other forms of speech. Even more importantly, the decision rendered most activities of film review boards unconstitutional, because these boards had been engaged in prior restraint. Although a few local boards survived into the 1990s to handle complaints about obscenity, most of them had disbanded by the early 1970s.

The MPAA Ratings System

The current voluntary movie rating system—the model for the advisory labels for music, television, and video games—developed in the late 1960s after discontent again mounted over movie content, spurred on by such films as 1965's *The Pawnbroker*, which contained brief female nudity, and 1966's *Who's Afraid of Virginia Woolf?*, which featured a level of profanity and sexual frankness that had not been seen before in a major studio film. In 1966, the movie industry hired Jack Valenti to run the MPAA (the Motion Picture Association of America, formerly the MPPDA), and in 1968 he established an industry board to rate movies. Eventually, G, PG, R, and X ratings emerged as guideposts for the suitability of films for various age groups. In 1984, prompted by

"No approval by the Production Code Administration shall be given to the use of . . . *damn* [or] *hell* (excepting when the use of said last two words shall be essential and required for portrayal, in proper historical context, of any scene or dialogue based upon historical fact or folklore, or for the presentation in proper literary context of a Biblical, or other religious quotation, or a quotation from a literary work provided that no such use shall be permitted which is intrinsically objectionable or offends good taste)."

MOTION PICTURE PRODUCTION CODE, 1934

TABLE 16.1

**THE VOLUNTARY MOVIE
RATING SYSTEM**

*Source: Motion Picture Associa-
tion of America, "What Do the
Ratings Mean?" http://www
.mpaa.org/FlmRat_Ratings.asp
(accessed November 20, 2007).*

Rating	Description
G	**General Audiences:** All ages admitted; contains nothing that would offend parents when viewed by their children.
PG	**Parental Guidance Suggested:** Parents urged to give "parental guidance" as it may contain some material not suitable for young children.
PG-13	**Parents Strongly Cautioned:** Parents should be cautious because some content may be inappropriate for children under the age of 13.
R	**Restricted:** The film contains some adult material. Parents/guardians are urged to learn more about it before taking children under the age of 17 with them.
NC-17	**No one 17 and under admitted:** Adult content. Children are not admitted.

the releases of *Gremlins* and *Indiana Jones and the Temple of Doom*, the MPAA added the PG-13 rating and sandwiched it between PG and R to distinguish slightly higher levels of violence or adult themes in movies that might otherwise qualify as PG-rated films (see Table 16.1).

The MPAA copyrighted all ratings designations as trademarks, except for the X rating, which was gradually appropriated as a promotional tool by the pornographic film industry. In fact, between 1972 and 1989, the MPAA stopped issuing the X rating. In 1990, however, based on protests from filmmakers over movies with adult sexual themes that they did not consider pornographic, the industry copyrighted the NC-17 rating—no children age seventeen or under. In 1995, *Showgirls* became the first movie to intentionally seek an NC-17 to demonstrate that the rating was commercially viable. However, many theater chains refused to carry NC-17 movies, fearing economic sanctions and boycotts by their customers or religious groups. Many newspapers also refused to carry ads for NC-17 films. Panned by the critics, *Showgirls* flopped at the box office. Since then, the NC-17 rating has not proved commercially viable, and distributors avoid releasing films with the rating, preferring to label such films "unrated" or to cut the film to earn an R rating, as happened with *Clerks* (1994), *Eyes Wide Shut* (1999), *Team America: World Police* (2004), and *Zack and Miri Make a Porno* (2008). Today, there is mounting protest against the MPAA, which many argue is essentially a censorship board that limits the First Amendment rights of filmmakers.

Expression in the Media:
Print, Broadcast, and Online

During the Cold War, a vigorous campaign led by Joseph McCarthy, an ultraconservative senator from Wisconsin, tried to rid both government and the media of so-called communist subversives who were allegedly challenging the American way of life. In 1950, a publication called *Red Channels: The Report of Communist Influence in Radio and Television* aimed "to show how the Communists have been able to carry out their plan of infiltration of the radio and television industry." *Red Channels*, inspired by McCarthy and produced by a group of former FBI agents, named 151 performers, writers, and musicians who were "sympathetic" to communist or left-wing causes. Among those named were Leonard Bernstein, Will Geer, Dashiell Hammett, Lillian Hellman, Lena Horne, Burgess Meredith, Arthur Miller, Dorothy Parker, Pete Seeger, Irwin Shaw, and Orson Welles. For a time, all were banned from working in television and radio even though no one on the list was ever charged with a crime.[18]

Although the First Amendment protects an individual's right to hold controversial political views, network executives either sympathized with the anticommunist movement or feared losing ad revenue. At any rate, the networks did not stand up to the communist witch-hunters.

In order to work, a blacklisted or "suspected" performer required the support of the program's sponsor. Though *I Love Lucy*'s Lucille Ball, who in sympathy with her father once registered to vote as a communist in the 1930s, retained Philip Morris's sponsorship of her popular program, other performers were not as fortunate. Although no evidence was ever introduced to show how entertainment programs circulated communist propaganda, by the early 1950s the TV networks were asking actors and other workers to sign loyalty oaths denouncing communism—a low point for the First Amendment.

The communist witch-hunts demonstrated key differences between print and broadcast protection under the First Amendment. On the one hand, licenses for printers and publishers have been outlawed since the eighteenth century. On the other hand, in the late 1920s, commercial broadcasters themselves asked the federal government to step in and regulate the airwaves. At that time, they wanted the government to clear up technical problems, channel noise, noncommercial competition, and amateur interference. Ever since, most broadcasters have been trying to free themselves from the government intrusion they once demanded.

► ISSUES OF EXPRESSION IN THE MEDIA
In 1950, the 215-page *Red Channels*, published by American Business Consultants (a group of former FBI agents), placed 151 prominent writers, directors, and performers from radio, movies, and television on a blacklist, many of them simply for sympathizing with left-wing democratic causes. Although no one on the list was ever charged with a crime, many of the talented individuals targeted by *Red Channels* did not work in their professions for years.

The FCC Regulates Broadcasting

Drawing on the argument that limited broadcast signals constitute a scarce national resource, the Communications Act of 1934 mandated that radio broadcasters operate in "the public interest, convenience, and necessity." Since the 1980s, however, with cable and, later, DBS increasing channel capacity, station managers have lobbied to own their airwave assignments. Although the 1996 Telecommunications Act did not grant such ownership, stations continue to challenge the "public interest" statute. They argue that, because the government is not allowed to dictate content in newspapers, it should not be allowed to control broadcasting via licenses or mandate any broadcast programming.

Two cases—*Red Lion Broadcasting Co. v. FCC* (1969) and *Miami Herald Publishing Co. v. Tornillo* (1974)—demonstrate the historic legal differences between broadcast and print. The *Red Lion* case began when WGCB, a small-town radio station in Red Lion, Pennsylvania, refused to give airtime to Fred Cook, author of a book that criticized Barry Goldwater, the Republican Party's presidential candidate in 1964. A conservative radio preacher and Goldwater fan, the Reverend Billy James Hargis, verbally attacked Cook on-air. Cook asked for response time from the two hundred stations that carried the Hargis attack. Most stations complied, granting Cook free reply time. But WGCB offered only to sell Cook time. He appealed to the FCC, which ordered the station to give Cook free time. The station refused, claiming that its First Amendment rights granted it control over its program content. On appeal, the Supreme Court sided with the FCC, deciding that, whenever a broadcaster's rights conflict with the public interest, the public interest must prevail. In interpreting broadcasting as different from print, the

"It is the right of the viewers and listeners, not the right of the broadcasters, which is paramount."

SUPREME COURT DECISION IN *RED LION BROADCASTING CO. V. FCC*, 395 U.S. 367, JUNE 9, 1969

"A responsible press is an undoubtedly desirable goal, but press responsibility is not mandated by the Constitution and like many other virtues it cannot be legislated."

SUPREME COURT DECISION IN *MIAMI HERALD PUBLISHING CO. V. TORNILLO*, 418 U.S. 241, JUNE 25, 1974

Supreme Court upheld the 1934 Communications Act by reaffirming that broadcasters' responsibilities to program in the public interest may outweigh their right to program whatever they want.

In contrast, five years later, in *Miami Herald Publishing Co. v. Tornillo*, the Supreme Court sided with the newspaper. A political candidate, Pat Tornillo Jr., requested space to reply to an editorial opposing his candidacy. Previously, Florida had a right-to-reply law, which permitted a candidate to respond, in print, to editorial criticisms from newspapers. Counter to the *Red Lion* decision, the Court in this case struck down the Florida state law as unconstitutional. The Court argued that mandating that a newspaper give a candidate space to reply violated the paper's First Amendment rights to control what it chose to publish. The two decisions demonstrate that the unlicensed print media receive protections under the First Amendment that have not always been available to licensed broadcast media.

Dirty Words, Indecent Speech, and Hefty Fines

In theory, communication law prevents the government from censoring broadcast content. Accordingly, the government may not interfere with programs or engage in prior restraint, although it may punish broadcasters for **indecency** or profanity after the fact. Over the years, a handful of radio stations have had their licenses suspended or denied after an unfavorable FCC review of past programming records. Concerns over indecent broadcast programming began in 1937 when NBC was scolded by the FCC for running a sketch featuring comedian actress Mae West on ventriloquist Edgar Bergen's network program. West had the following conversation with Bergen's famous wooden dummy, Charlie McCarthy:

WEST: *That's all right. I like a man that takes his time. Why don't you come home with me? I'll let you play in my woodpile . . . you're all wood and a yard long. . . .*

CHARLIE: *Oh, Mae, don't, don't . . . don't be so rough. To me love is peace and quiet.*

WEST: *That ain't love—that's sleep.*[19]

After the sketch, West did not perform on radio for years. Ever since, the FCC has periodically fined or reprimanded stations for indecent programming, especially during times when children might be listening.

In the 1960s, *topless radio* featured deejays and callers discussing intimate sexual subjects in the middle of the afternoon. The government curbed the practice in 1973, when the chairman of the FCC denounced topless radio as "a new breed of air pollution . . . with the suggestive, coaxing, pear-shaped tones of the smut-hustling host."[20] After an FCC investigation, a couple of stations lost their licenses, some were fined, and topless radio was temporarily over. It reemerged in the 1980s, this time with doctors and therapists—instead of deejays—offering intimate counsel over the airwaves.

The current precedent for regulating broadcast indecency stems from a complaint to the FCC in 1973. In the middle of the afternoon, WBAI, a nonprofit Pacifica network station in New York, aired George Carlin's famous comedy sketch about the seven dirty words that could not be uttered by broadcasters. A father, riding in a car with his fifteen-year-old son, heard the program and complained to the FCC, which sent WBAI a letter of reprimand. Although no fine was issued, the station appealed on principle and won its case in court. The FCC, however, appealed to the Supreme Court. Although no court had legally defined indecency (and still hasn't), the Supreme Court's unexpected ruling in the 1978 *FCC v. Pacifica Foundation* case sided with the FCC and upheld the agency's authority to require broadcasters to air adult programming at times when children were not likely to be listening. The Court ruled that so-called indecent programming, though not in violation of federal obscenity laws, was a nuisance and could be restricted to late-evening hours. As a result, the FCC banned indecent programs from most stations between 6:00 A.M. and 10:00 P.M. In 1990, the FCC tried to ban such programs entirely.

Although a federal court ruled this move unconstitutional, it still upheld the time restrictions intended to protect children.

This ruling lies at the heart of the indecency fines that the FCC has frequently leveled against programs and stations that have carried indecent programming during daytime and evening hours. While Howard Stern and his various bosses own the record for racking up FCC indecency fines in the years before he moved to unregulated satellite radio, the largest-ever fine was for $3.6 million, leveled in 2006 against 111 TV stations that broadcast a 2004 episode of the popular CBS program *Without a Trace* that depicted teenage characters taking part in a sexual orgy.

After the FCC fined two broadcasts of *Billboard Music Awards* shows on Fox and an *NYPD Blue* episode on ABC, the four major networks sued the FCC on grounds that their First Amendment rights had been violated. (The FCC later dropped the fines against Fox and ABC.) In their

INDECENT SPEECH
The sexual innuendo of an "Adam and Eve" radio sketch between sultry film star Mae West and dummy Charlie McCarthy (voiced by ventriloquist Edgar Bergen) on a Sunday evening in December 1937 enraged many listeners of Bergen's program. The networks banned West from further radio appearances for what was considered indecent speech.

INDECENT PROGRAMMING
The current precedent for indecency is based on a complaint about comedian George Carlin's sketch about the seven dirty words that could not be aired.

fining flurry, a conservative FCC was partly responding to organized campaigns aimed at Howard Stern's vulgarity and at the Janet Jackson exposed-breast incident during the 2005 Superbowl half-time show. The FCC's power to curb indecency, however, continues: In 2006, President Bush signed a law that substantially increased the FCC's maximum allowable fine to $325,000 per incident of indecency.

Political Broadcasts and Equal Opportunity

In addition to indecency rules, another law that the print media do not encounter is **Section 315** of the 1934 Communications Act, which mandates that, during elections, broadcast stations must provide equal opportunities and response time for qualified political candidates. In other words, if broadcasters give or sell time to one candidate, they must give or sell the same opportunity to others. Local broadcasters and networks have fought this law for years, complaining that it has required them to give poorly funded third-party candidates equal airtime in political discussions. Broadcasters claim that because no similar rule applies to newspapers or magazines, the law violates their First Amendment right to control content. In fact, because of this rule, many stations avoided all political programming, ironically reversing the rule's original intention. The TV networks managed to get the law amended in 1959 to exempt newscasts, press conferences, and other events—such as political debates—that qualify as news. For instance, if a senator running for office appears in a news story, opposing candidates cannot invoke Section 315 and demand free time. The FCC has subsequently ruled that interview portions of programs like the *700 Club* and *TMZ* also count as news.

Due to Section 315, many stations from the late 1960s through the 1980s refused to air movies starring Ronald Reagan. Because his film appearances did not count as bona fide news stories, politicians opposing Reagan as a presidential candidate could demand free time in markets that ran old Reagan movies. For the same reason, in 2003, TV stations in California banned the broadcast of Arnold Schwarzenegger movies when he became a candidate for governor, and dozens of stations nationwide preempted an episode of *Saturday Night Live* that was hosted by Al Sharpton, a Democratic presidential candidate.

However, supporters of the equal opportunity law argue that it has provided forums for lesser-known candidates representing views counter to those of the Democratic and Republican parties. They further note that one of the few ways for alternative candidates to circulate their messages widely is to buy political ads, thus limiting serious outside contenders to wealthy candidates, such as Ross Perot, Steve Forbes, or members of the Bush or Clinton families.

The Demise of the Fairness Doctrine

Considered an important corollary to Section 315, the **Fairness Doctrine** was to controversial issues what Section 315 is to political speech. Initiated in 1949, this FCC rule required stations (1) to air and engage in controversial-issue programs that affected their communities, and (2) to provide competing points of view when offering such programming. Antismoking activist John Banzhaf ingeniously invoked the Fairness Doctrine to force cigarette advertising off television in 1971. When the FCC mandated antismoking public service announcements to counter "controversial" smoking commercials, tobacco companies decided not to challenge an outright ban rather than tolerate a flood of antismoking spots authorized by the Fairness Doctrine.

Over the years, broadcasters argued that mandating opposing views every time a program covered a controversial issue was a burden not required of the print media, and that it forced many of them to refrain from airing controversial issues. As a result, the Fairness Doctrine ended with little public debate in 1987 after a federal court ruled that it was merely a regulation rather than an extension of Section 315 law.

Since 1987, however, periodic support for reviving the Fairness Doctrine surfaces. Its supporters argue that broadcasting is fundamentally different from—and more pervasive than—print media, requiring greater accountability to the public. Although many broadcasters disagree, supporters of fairness rules insist that as long as broadcasters are licensed as public trustees of the airwaves—unlike newspaper or magazine publishers—legal precedent permits the courts and the FCC to demand responsible content and behavior from radio and TV stations.

Communication Policy and the Internet

Because the Internet is not regulated by the government, is not subject to the Communications Act of 1934, and has done little in regard to self-regulation, many have looked to it as the one true venue for free, unlimited free speech under the First Amendment. (See "Examining Ethics: Cartoons, T-shirts, and More: Why We Must Protect What Offends" on page 509.) Its current global expansion is comparable to the early days of broadcasting, when economic and technological growth outstripped law and regulation. At that time, noncommercial experiments by amateurs and engineering students provided a testing ground that commercial interests later exploited for profit. In much the same way, "amateurs," students, and various interest groups have explored and extended the communication possibilities of the Internet. They have experimented so successfully that commercial vendors have raced to buy up pieces of the Internet since the 1990s.

Public conversations about the Internet have not typically revolved around ownership. Instead, the debates have focused on First Amendment issues such as civility and pornography. Not unlike the public's concern over television's sexual and violent images, the scrutiny of the Internet is mainly about harmful images and information online, not about who controls it and for what purposes. However, as we watch the rapid expansion of the Internet, an important question confronts us: Will the Internet continue to develop as a democratic medium, evading government or corporate plans to contain it, change it, and closely monitor who has access? In the early days of broadcasting, commercial interests became dominant partly because the companies running radio (such as the Hearst Corporation, which also owned chains of newspapers and magazines) did not report on ownership questions as serious news stories. It was not in their economic interest to do so. Today, once again, it has not been in the news media's economic interest to organize or lead the Internet ownership debate; the major print and broadcast owners, after all, are heavily invested in the Internet.

> "There is no doubt about the unique impact of radio and television. But this fact alone does not justify government regulation. In fact, quite the contrary. We should recall that the printed press was the only medium of mass communication in the early days of the republic—and yet this did not deter our predecessors from passing the First Amendment to prohibit abridgement of its freedoms."
>
> CHIEF JUDGE DAVID BAZELON, U.S. COURT OF APPEALS, 1972

> "Internet service providers should not be able to favor some content over others. . . . [Net neutrality] is vital to preserve the Internet's role in promoting entrepreneurship and free expression."
>
> EDITORIAL, *NEW YORK TIMES*, 2007

Critics and observers hope that a vigorous debate about ownership will develop—a debate that will go beyond First Amendment issues. The promise of the Internet as a democratic forum encourages the formation of all sorts of regional, national, and global interest groups. In fact, many global movements use the Internet to fight political forms of censorship. Human Rights Watch, for example, encourages free expression advocates to use blogs "for disseminating information about, and ending, human rights abuses around the world."[21] Where oppressive regimes have tried to monitor and control Internet communication, Human Rights Watch suggests bloggers post anonymously to safeguard their identity. Just as fax machines, satellites, and home videos helped to document and expedite the fall of totalitarian regimes in Eastern Europe in the late 1980s, the Internet helps spread the word and activate social change today.

The First Amendment and Democracy

"One thing is clear:
media reform will
not be realized
until politicians
add it to their list
of issues like the
environment,
education, the
economy, and
health care."

ROBERT McCHESNEY,
FREEPRESS.NET, 2004

For most of our nation's history, citizens have counted on journalism to monitor abuses in government and business. During the muckraking period, writers like Upton Sinclair, Ida Tarbell, and Sinclair Lewis made strong contributions in reporting corporate expansion and social change. Unfortunately, however, news stories about business issues today are usually reduced to consumer affairs reporting. In other words, when a labor strike or a factory recall is covered, the reporter mainly tries to answer the question "How do these events affect consumers?" Although this is an important news angle, discussions about media ownership or labor management ethics are not part of the news that journalists typically report. Similarly, when companies announce mergers, reporters do not routinely question the economic wisdom or social impact of such changes but instead focus on how consumers will be affected.

At one level, journalists have been compromised by the ongoing frenzy of media mergers involving newspapers, TV stations, radio stations, and Internet corporations. As Bill Kovach, former curator of Harvard's Nieman Foundation for Journalism, pointed out, "This rush to merge mainly entertainment organizations that have news operations with companies deeply involved in doing business with the government raises ominous questions about the future of watchdog journalism."[22] In other words, how can journalists adequately cover and lead discussions on issues of media ownership when the very companies they work for are the prime buyers and sellers of major news-media outlets?

As a result, it is becoming increasingly important that the civic role of watchdog be shared by both citizens and journalists. Citizen action groups like Free Press, the Media Access Project, and the Center for Digital Democracy have worked to bring media ownership issues into the mainstream. However, it is important to remember that the First Amendment protects not only the news media's free-speech rights but also the rights of all of us to speak out. Mounting concerns over who can afford access to the media go to the heart of free expression. As we struggle to determine the future of converging print, electronic, and digital media and to broaden the democratic spirit underlying media technology, we need to stay engaged in spirited public debates about media ownership and control, about the differences between commercial speech and free expression. As citizens, we need to pay attention to who is included and excluded from opportunities not only to buy products but also to speak out and shape the cultural landscape. To accomplish this, we need to challenge our journalists and our leaders. More importantly, we need to challenge ourselves to become watchdogs—critical consumers and engaged citizens—who learn from the past, care about the present, and map mass media's future. ▶

FREE SPEECH rights include our right to protest decisions that we believe infringe on our First Amendment rights. Here students protest in front of the U.S. Supreme Court in 2007 in the "Bong Hits 4 Jesus" case that started in 2002 in Juneau, Alaska.

CHAPTER REVIEW

REVIEW QUESTIONS

The Origins of Free Expression and a Free Press

1. Explain the various models of the news media that exist under different political systems.

2. What is the basic philosophical concept that underlies America's notion of free expression?

3. What happened with the passage of the Sedition Act of 1798, and what was its relevance to the United States' new First Amendment?

4. How has censorship been defined historically?

5. What is the significance of the Pentagon Papers and the *Progressive* magazine cases?

6. What is the public domain, and why is it an important element in American culture?

7. Why is the case of *New York Times v. Sullivan* so significant in First Amendment history?

8. What does a public figure have to do to win a libel case? What are the main defenses that a newspaper can use to thwart a charge of libel?

9. What is the legal significance of the *Falwell v. Flynt* case?

10. What issues are at stake when First Amendment and Sixth Amendment concerns clash?

Film and the First Amendment

11. Why were films not constitutionally protected as a form of speech until 1952?

12. Why did film review boards develop, and why did they eventually disband?

13. How did both the Motion Picture Production Code and the current movie rating system come into being?

Expression in the Media: Print, Broadcast, and Online

14. The government and the courts view print and broadcasting as different forms of expression. What are the major differences?

15. What's the difference between obscenity and indecency?

16. What is the significance of Section 315 of the Communications Act of 1934?

17. Why didn't broadcasters like the Fairness Doctrine?

The First Amendment and Democracy

18. What are the similarities and differences between the debates over broadcast ownership in the 1920s and Internet ownership today?

19. Why is the future of watchdog journalism in jeopardy?

QUESTIONING THE MEDIA

1. Have you ever had an experience in which you thought personal or public expression went too far and should be curbed? Explain. How might you remedy this situation?

2. If you owned a community newspaper and had to formulate a policy for your editors about which letters from readers could appear in a limited space on your editorial page, what kinds of letters would you eliminate and why? Would you be acting as a censor in this situation? Why or why not?

3. The writer A. J. Liebling once said that freedom of the press belonged only to those who owned one. Explain why you agree or disagree.

4. Who is Judith Miller? Should the United States have a federal shield law to protect reporters?

5. What do you think of the current movie rating system? Should it be changed? Why or why not?

6. Should the Fairness Doctrine be revived? Why or why not?

COMMON THREADS

One of the Common Threads discussed in Chapter 1 is about the role that media play in a democracy. Is a free media system necessary for democracy to exist, or must democracy first be established to enable a media system to operate freely? What do the mass media do to enhance or secure democracy?

In 1787, as the Constitution was being formed, Thomas Jefferson famously said "Were it left to me to decide whether we should have a government without newspapers, or newspapers without a government, I should not hesitate a moment to prefer the latter." Jefferson supported the notion of a free press and free speech. He stood against the Sedition Act, which penalized free speech, and did not support its renewal when he became president in 1801.

Nevertheless, as president, Jefferson had to withstand the vitriol and allegations of a partisan press. In 1807, near the end of his second term, Jefferson's idealism about the press had cooled, as he remarked, "The man who never looks into a newspaper is better informed than he who reads them, inasmuch as he who knows nothing is nearer the truth than he whose mind is filled with falsehoods and errors."

Today, we contend with a mass media that extends far beyond newspapers—a media system that is among the biggest and most powerful institutions in the country. Unfortunately, it is also a media system that too often envisions us as consumers of capitalism, not citizens of a democracy. Media sociologist Herbert Gans argues that the media alone can't guarantee a democracy.[23] "Despite much disingenuous talk about citizen empowerment by politicians and merchandisers, citizens have never had much clout. Countries as big as America operate largely through organizations," Gans explains.

But in a country as big as America, the media constitute one of those critical organizations that can help or hurt us in creating a more economically and politically democratic society. At their worst, the media can distract or misinform us with falsehoods and errors. But, at their Jeffersonian best, the media can shed light on the issues, tell meaningful stories, and foster the discussions that can help a citizens' democracy flourish.

KEY TERMS

The definitions for the terms listed below can be found in the glossary at the end of the book. The page numbers listed with the terms indicate where the term is highlighted in the chapter.

authoritarian model, 496
communist or state model, 497
social responsibility model, 497
Fourth Estate, 497
libertarian model, 497
prior restraint, 498
copyright, 501
public domain, 501
libel, 502
slander, 502

actual malice, 502
qualified privilege, 504
opinion and fair comment, 504
obscenity, 505
right to privacy, 506
gag orders, 508
shield laws, 508
indecency, 516
Section 315, 518
Fairness Doctrine, 519

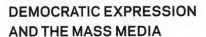

Extended Case Study:

Analyzing Coverage of the Financial Crisis

In the September before the historic presidential election of 2008, a major financial crisis hit the U.S. and foreign markets. By mid-October, most observers agreed that this international crisis was the worst financial disaster since the Great Depression. The U.S. stock market fell more than five hundred points on September 15 (the biggest drop since 9/11) and by the end of October had lost 14 percent of its value, erasing hundreds of billions from investment portfolios, retirement accounts, and government pensions. Major financial institutions also began to falter. The giant investment firm Lehman Brothers, established in 1850 and a survivor of the Great Depression, folded. Merrill Lynch was forced to sell out to the Bank of America, while the government seized Washington Mutual in the largest bank failure in U.S. history. The federal government also provided billions to bail out two giant mortgage companies, Fannie Mae and Freddie Mac, and the world's largest insurance company, American International Group (AIG).

Credit froze up, and many banks stopped lending money. Home foreclosures accelerated, and by the end of October one in five homes in the United States was valued at less than what its owner owed on the mortgage. Congress voted to provide $700 billion to help unfreeze credit and get banks lending again.

But what did all this mean? To help the public understand what was happening, talking heads on cable's Fox Business News, CNBC's *Squawk Box*, and Jim Kramer's *Mad Money* took varying positions on the problems, evaluated the government responses, and offered their own remedies. Business sections and opinion columnists in newspapers and magazines also weighed in on the crisis, as did a slew of business-related Web sites, blogs, and radio shows. In the end, lots of vague descriptions of the financial problems and much contradictory advice circulated. It was hard to know what to believe and what to do.

Looking for someone to explain the complexity of the economic meltdown, many people expected the news media coverage to be really strong and clear about exactly what was happening. After all, as we discussed in Chapters 8 and 14, one role of journalism is to act as a watchdog for our society. However, as Jon Stewart on Comedy Central's *The Daily Show* pointed out, some TV news media outlets were oversimplifying the complexity of the issues for viewers: using a cartoon to explain the crisis or spreading out sheets of construction paper on a coffee table to show viewers how many zeroes were in a trillion dollars.

The truth about the 2008 financial crisis was that few people saw it coming and even experts from the business world seemed amazed by how it happened and by the extent of its global impact. While

the mainstream news media cannot be expected to predict such crises or even to know more about business than business experts do, individuals and societies depend on journalism to help sort out crises and determine what happened. As we discussed in Chapter 14, daily news is good at telling stories about what's happening right now and not so good at providing historical perspective, social context, and future planning. In addition to these traditional limitations, the current economic instability of the news business was exacerbated by the world financial crisis. Many traditional newspapers, broadcast networks, and local TV stations had already been cutting reporting staffs in the face of declining advertising revenue and dropping stock prices, following a belief among many investors that newspapers, and even traditional TV news, had a questionable future because of the Internet. This means that during the crisis there were fewer reporters to cover business and economic news and very few reporters doing long-term investigative stories on our banking, credit, and loan systems. This also partly explains why so many people were caught off guard by the crisis—there were not enough journalists paying close attention.

"The economy has been the No. 2 story so far in 2008 in the U.S. media, moving ahead of the Iraq war. But coverage has not come close to that of the presidential campaign."
PROJECT FOR EXCELLENCE IN JOURNALISM, 2008

◢ *THE CASE BEFORE US IS TO INVESTIGATE HOW WELL THE TRADITIONAL NEWS MEDIA COVERED THE ECONOMIC CRISIS* that began in the fall of 2008. To do so, choose a week from mid-September 2008 or one of the weeks following to study; a period with significant economic developments would be best. Choose two news sources to compare—for example, news stories from both your local newspaper and a national newspaper (such as the *New York Times, Wall Street Journal,* or *USA Today*); from two business magazines (such as *FORTUNE, Forbes,* or *Business Week*); or from two national news networks (ABC, CBS, NBC, or PBS). Or you could pick one media source from each category (a local paper, a business magazine, a national newspaper, and a TV network) and compare how each performed during your week. To focus our study a bit more, let's concentrate on critiquing how well these news media explained complex business and economic terms and processes to help everyday readers and viewers understand what was going on.

As you think about the job the media did during the period you chose, consider these key questions: How well did each outlet explain the unfamiliar terms and often complicated issues surrounding the crisis? Let's focus attention here on how well the news sources defined and explained recurring terms and concepts by choosing one of the following to help organize your study: (1) subprime mortgages, Fannie Mae, Freddie Mac, and the housing market collapse; (2) credit cards and credit contractions; (3) financial instruments, derivatives, and stock market fluctuations; (4) the difference between investment banks and traditional banks; and (5) employment statistics, worker wages, and CEO salaries. Are the stories that use these terms clear and helpful? Are there stories that seem confusing? Are these terms defined well?

In addition to focusing on specific terms above, your study should also look broadly at the stories in your weekly sample. Why wasn't there more of a warning before the crisis hit? How well did the news media perform their watchdog role? Did the news media provide context and historical overviews (such as comparing the recent crisis to the Great Depression or other economic crises)? What did business coverage look like immediately before the crisis? Studying a week's worth of news stories and using these questions as guidelines can help you use your critical skills to make sense of these stories and shed light on the ways traditional media cover an economic crisis.

LEHMAN BROTHERS was one of the many banks to collapse during the financial crisis. Here former Lehman CEO Richard Fuld Jr. leaves Capitol Hill after testifying before the House Oversight and Government Reform Committee. How did the media cover the executives and leaders of the failed companies?

As developed in Chapter 1, a media-literate perspective involves mastering five overlapping critical stages that build on each other: (1) *description*: paying close attention, taking notes, and researching the subject under study—in this case, media coverage of an economic crisis; (2) *analysis*: discovering and focusing on significant patterns that emerge from the description stage; (3) *interpretation*: asking and answering the "What does that mean?" and "So what?" questions about one's findings; (4) *evaluation*: arriving at a judgment about whether something is good, bad, or mediocre, which involves subordinating one's personal taste to the critical assessment resulting from the first three stages; and (5) *engagement*: taking some action that connects our critical interpretations and evaluations with our responsibility to question not only our news organizations but our government representatives and our financial institutions, adding our own voice to the process of shaping the cultural and economic environment.

Step 1:
Description

For the **description** phase, you will need to take a lot of notes on the different stories you read or watch. To research the news services you are studying, try an archival or LexisNexis search for newspaper, magazine, and/or TV news transcripts. Try to find accounts and stories that will allow you to trace the economic issue over a week. Create categories of news and information based on what you read and the terms/phrases you have chosen to study–for example, *general overviews* of the economy, *historical comparisons, mortgage and housing, jobs and employment, the stock market, credit cards and tightening credit, consumer confidence,* and stories on *particular companies.* Consider also *political-economic* stories (the financial crisis was a major issue for the presidential candidates in 2008: What did the candidates say they would do to solve particular problems?) and any other relevant categories. (See Figure 1.)

You might also explore your specific terms/phrases. How well are these terms explained in your stories? For example, a September 16, 2008, story from *USA Today*, "Markets in Turmoil," mentions "complex financial arrangements called derivatives" but does not define *derivatives.* The article also discusses subprime mortgages and defines them as "loans made to borrowers with poor credit." (Check such media definitions against the definitions of key terms and concepts you find in Internet or library searches on your own.) You might also want to check the Project for Excellence in Journalism site (www.journalism.org) for sample studies about media coverage of the economy to get ideas on categories of coverage and data to support your own findings and insights.

From the notes taken at this stage, you will be able to develop a sense of how media stories frame and represent the financial crisis. Identify any central characters, conflicts, topics, and themes that emerge in the stories you are examining. Does a certain kind of narrative emerge from the stories? How about characters? That is, what types of experts or people-on-the-street are interviewed or quoted in these stories? How well do the stories explain their topics and issues? In this stage, also document what might be missing from the stories, such as the definition of *derivative* from the *USA Today* story. Are there other concepts and claims in your articles that are poorly explained? For example, the *USA Today* story, in explaining the crisis,

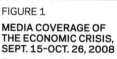

FIGURE 1

**MEDIA COVERAGE OF
THE ECONOMIC CRISIS,
SEPT. 15–OCT. 26, 2008**

*Source: Project for Excellence
in Journalism, "The Meltdown
and the Media," journalism
.org/node/13371. Accessed
November 4, 2008.*

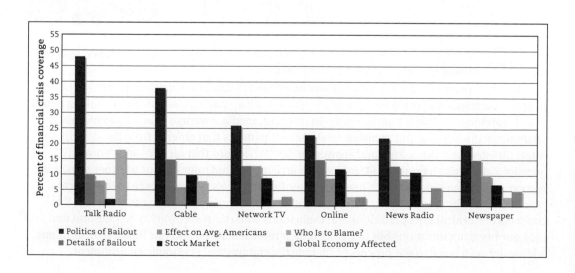

reports that "analysts say too many companies have borrowed too much to buy high risk assets" without explaining what that means. Are there other aspects of your stories that your chosen news media don't consider or recognize, or that they quickly brush over? Do the articles describe how the crisis might affect the global market or us as individuals and as a nation?

Step 2: Analysis

In the second stage of the critical process–**analysis**–isolate patterns that call for closer attention. For example, do you see a pattern in the kinds of stories told about the crisis? How are the ups and downs in the stock market treated in your stories? How much explanation is there in terms of what these fluctuations actually mean to readers and viewers? As the crisis grew, a narrative developed in the media (and even surrounded the presidential election) to frame the crisis: Wall Street vs. Main Street. These opposing ideas came to embody much of the tension between "greedy" corporations and bankers and the average, struggling American homeowner. In fact, a LexisNexis search for stories that contained both Wall Street and Main Street turned up over three thousand newspaper articles between September 15 and November 1, 2008. How useful was this story construction in explaining the crisis? What role did this narrative fill?

Do you also see a pattern in terms of who the news media go to for information, analysis, and quotes (or sound bites in the case of television)? How are experts represented in the stories? How are ordinary people represented? What kinds of information and insights do these story "characters" and interview subjects provide? Who seems to be portrayed as heroes or

WALL STREET VS. MAIN STREET

villains? How are both financial executives and everyday homeowners characterized in stories using the Wall Street vs. Main Street narrative? In your analysis, look also for other repeated narrative themes or conflicts that emerge, but choose only three or four to focus on.

Step 3:
Interpretation

In the **interpretation** stage, you try to determine the meanings of the patterns you have analyzed. The most difficult stage in criticism, interpretation demands an answer to the questions "So what?" and "What does this all mean?" In looking at the patterns that emerged in the analysis stage, what do you think these patterns might mean? For example, why was the particular Wall Street vs. Main Street narrative pattern so pervasive in many of these stories? What kinds of stories seemed strong and clear to you and what kinds did not? You might compare NPR's *This American Life* episodes "Giant Pool of Money" (May 9, 2008) and "Another Frightening Show about the Economy" (October 3, 2008) with overview stories from national newspapers. Can you make an argument about whether you are being well served by the ways in which news media covered this crisis? Provide evidence to support your views.

You may also want to consider these questions: What does it mean that particular kinds or categories of stories dominated in the news? If you found a wide variety of story types during the crisis, what does that mean? Did these stories assume you had a lot of economic knowledge, or did they assume you had a little economic or financial knowledge? What does it mean that characters and sources for stories were depicted in particular ways? What role do competing narratives—Wall Street vs. Main Street, CEOs vs. workers—play, if any?

Step 4:
Evaluation

The **evaluation** stage of the critical process is about making informed judgments. Building on description, analysis, and interpretation, you are now better able to evaluate the fairness, accuracy, sense, and substance of the media stories you have investigated. Which kinds of stories served readers and viewers well and which did not? Did the stories discuss how the large global crisis would actually affect local finances or "average" people? For example, a November 1, 2008, *New York Times* article, "From Midwest to M.T.A., Pain from Global Gamble," explained how banks in Scotland and Germany were linked to some school boards in Wisconsin and the transportation authority in New York City through a complex series of loans, investments, and insurance policies. After the economy declined and debt mounted on all sides, the school boards lost millions of dollars and had to cut back on school services and improvements, and they may also lose some of their retirement funds. The German government was forced to make its own billion-dollar bailout to save one of its major banks as a result. Did your stories have concrete examples of the local, national, and international effects of the crisis?

For your examination, offer insights into which kinds of stories were the most and least effective based on the evidence you gathered and the interpretations you made. You could also

judge whether the stories were fair, accurate, and representative of the complex issues at stake. Finally, based on what you found and your judgment, which news outlet did the best job? What did the media do well to cover the crisis? What did they do poorly? Provide evidence. What suggestions would you make to improve business and economic news coverage?

Step 5: Engagement

The fifth stage in the critical process—**engagement**—encourages you to take action, adding your own voice to the process of shaping our cultural and economic world. For this part of your study, get into the community. Show your findings to finance, marketing, and economics professors at your school and to local business leaders, regular consumers, small-business owners, bankers, realtors, or other people who are affected directly by the crisis to see what they think is strong or weak in the media's coverage. Invite a speaker to your class to talk about these issues and to clear up any vague information or terms from the stories.

With regard to further action and additional study, are there alternative ways to tell stories about economic crises? That is, can you offer ideas about how traditional media might cover business and the economy better? You might also develop strategies for pitching your ideas to the mainstream media (hint: appeal to media's appetite for dramatic and unusual stories).

Throughout this process, remember that the point of media literacy and a critical approach is acknowledging that a healthy democracy requires the active participation of engaged readers and viewers. This involves paying attention to the multiple versions of stories being told in our media. Our task, then, as engaged citizens and active critics, is to read and view widely in order to understand the narrative process that media industries use, hold them accountable for the substance of the stories they tell, and offer alternative points of view and narrative frames. Remember especially that right now, as students, you are outsiders to this process, and you may have a great idea that could transform the way media work.

PHOTOJOURNALISM
In addition to what is written or said about the recent economic crisis, how do the media portray the story through photos and videos? That is, what message do the images send? Also, consider any differences or similarities between the photos used to show previous financial crises like the Great Depression (above left) and the current one (above).

Notes

1 Mass Communication: A Critical Approach

1. See Anna Quindlen, "Youth Vote Turnout Bodes Well for U.S.," *Chicago Sun-Times*, November 6, 2008, editorial, p. 29. Quindlen is a columnist for *Newsweek* magazine.

2. Clark Hoyt, "Urgent Issues, Buried in the Mud," *New York Times*, October 12, 2008, "Week in Review," p. 10.

3. See Jo Mannies, "Obama's Missouri Ad Advantage over McCain Was 5-1 in Final Week," *St. Louis Post-Dispatch*, November 8, 2008, p. A7.

4. Neil Postman, *Amusing Ourselves to Death: Public Discourse in the Age of Show Business* (New York: Penguin Books, 1985), 19.

5. James W. Carey, *Communication as Culture: Essays on Media and Society* (Boston: Unwin Hyman, 1989), 203.

6. Postman, *Amusing Ourselves to Death*, 65. See also Elizabeth Eisenstein, *The Printing Press as an Agent of Change*, 2 vols. (Cambridge: Cambridge University Press, 1979).

7. Roger Rosenblatt, "I Am Writing Blindly," *Time*, November 6, 2000, 142.

8. See Plato, *The Republic*, Book II, 377B.

9. For a historical discussion of culture, see Lawrence Levine, *Highbrow/Lowbrow: The Emergence of Cultural Hierarchy in America* (Cambridge: Harvard University Press, 1988).

10. For an example of this critical position, see Allan Bloom, *The Closing of the American Mind: How Higher Education Has Failed Democracy and Impoverished the Souls of Today's Students* (New York: Simon & Schuster, 1987).

11. For overviews of this position, see Postman, *Amusing Ourselves to Death*; and Stuart Ewen, *Captains of Consciousness: Advertising and the Social Roots of the Consumer Culture* (New York: McGraw-Hill, 1976).

12. See Carey, *Communication as Culture*.

13. Walter Lippmann, *Public Opinion* (1922; reprint New York: Free Press Paperbacks, 1997), 11, 19, 246-47.

14. For more on this idea, see Cecelia Tichi, *Electronic Hearth: Creating an American Television Culture* (New York: Oxford University Press, 1991), 187-88.

15. See Jon Katz, "Rock, Rap and Movies Bring You the News," *Rolling Stone*, March 5, 1992, 33.

◢ EXAMINING ETHICS Covering the War, p. 14

1. Bill Carter, "Some Stations to Block 'Nightline' War Tribute," *New York Times*, April 30, 2004, p. A13.

2. For reference and guidance on media ethics, see Clifford Christians, Mark Fackler, and Kim Rotzoll, *Media Ethics: Cases and Moral Reasoning*, 4th ed. (White Plains, N.Y.: Longman, 1995); and Thomas H. Bivins, "A Worksheet for Ethics Instruction and Exercises in Reason," *Journalism Educator* (Summer 1993): 4-16.

◢ CASE STUDY The Sleeper Curve, p. 20

1. Steven Johnson, *Everything Bad Is Good for You: How Today's Popular Culture Is Actually Making Us Smarter* (New York: Riverhead Books, 2005). See book's subtitle.

2. Neil Postman, *Amusing Ourselves to Death: Public Discourse in the Age of Show Business* (New York: Penguin Books, 1985).

3. Ibid., 3-4.

4. Ibid., 129-31.

5. Steven Johnson, "Watching TV Makes You Smarter," *New York Times Magazine*, April 24, 2005, 55ff. Article adapted from Johnson's book *Everything Bad Is Good for You*. All subsequent quotations are from this article.

◢ GLOBAL VILLAGE Bedouins, Camels, Transistors, and Coke, p. 30

1. Václav Havel, "A Time for Transcendence," *Utne Reader*, January/February 1995, 53.

2. Dan Rather, "The Threat to Foreign News," *Newsweek*, July 17, 1989, 9.

Extended Case Study Video Games and Storytelling, p. 35

1. Micah Mertes, "Experts Say Simplicity the Key to Wii's Genius," *Lincoln Journal Star* (Nebraska), February 28, 2008, p. E1.

2. Stephen Poole, *Trigger Happy: Videogames and the Entertainment Revolution* (New York: Arcade Publishing, 2000), 208.

3. See Jordan Miller, "U-M Study Tracks Kids; Recheck in Adulthood Finds More Violence," *Ann Arbor News*, November 28, 2007, p. 1.

4. Susan Gonzales, "Video Games Score Points with Researchers," *Evening Sun* (Hanover, Pa.), February 10, 2008, Local section, p. 1.

5. Poole, *Trigger Happy*, 236.

6. See John M. Broder, "Bill Is Signed to Restrict Video Games in California," *New York Times*, October 8, 2005, www.nytimes.com.

7. See Steve Geissinger, "Governor Distances Self from 'Conan' Video Game," *Inside Bay Area* (California), December 12, 2007, p. 1.

8. "Essential Facts about the Video and Computer Game Industry," Entertainment Software Association (ESA), www.theESA.com, 2005.

9. Mike Musgrove, "Granny Got Game; Wii's Move-Around Style Appeals to a New Demographic," *Washington Post*, December 15, 2007, p. D1.

10. See Eric Nagourney, "A Video Game, an M.R.I and What Men's Brains Do," *New York Times*, p. F6.

2 The Internet and New Technologies: The Media Converge

1. Federal Communications Commission, "Statement of Chairman Kevin J. Martin," July 31, 2007, http://hraunfoss.fcc.gov/edocs_public/attachmatch/DOC-275669A2.pdf.

2. Google, "Industry Leaders Announce Open Platform for Mobile Devices," November 5, 2007, http://www.google.com/intl/en/press/pressrel/20071105_mobile_open.html.

3. David Landis, "World Wide Web Helps Untangle Internet's Labyrinth," *USA Today*, August 3, 1994, p. D10.

4. Enid Burns, "U.S. Search Engine Rankings, December 2007," Search Engine Watch, February 5, 2008, http://searchenginewatch.com/showPage.html?page=3628341.

5. Pew Internet & American Life Project, "The State of Blogging," January 2005, http://www.pewinternet.org/PPF/r/144/report_display.asp.

6. Wikipedia contributors, "John Seigenthaler Sr. Wikipedia Biography Controversy," *Wikipedia, The Free Encyclopedia*, http://en.wikipedia.org/w/index.php?title=John_Seigenthaler_Sr._Wikipedia_biography_controversy&oldid=45268872 (accessed March 3, 2008).

7. Jim Giles, "Internet Encyclopaedias Go Head to Head," *Nature.com*, December 14, 2005, http://www.nature.com/news/2005/051212/full/438900a.html (accessed March 24, 2006).

8. The Smoking Gun, "College Sued over 'Drunken Pirate' Sanctions," http://www.thesmokinggun.com/archive/years/2007/0426072pirate1.html (accessed March 3, 2008).

9. Tim Berners-Lee, James Hendler, and Ora Lassila, "The Semantic Web," *Scientific American*, May 17, 2001.

10. Steven Musil, "Week in Review: Windows Woes," *New York Times*, February 29, 2008, http://www.nytimes.com/cnet/CNET_2100-1083_3-6232545.html? (accessed March 3, 2008).

11. Katie Hafner, "Libraries Shun Deals to Place Books on the Web," *New York Times*, October 22, 2008, http://www.nytimes.com/2007/10/22/technology/22library.html (accessed March 3, 2008).

12. David Bollier, "Saving the Information Commons," Remarks to American Library Association convention, Atlanta, June 15, 2002, http://www.lita.org/ala/acrlbucket/copyrightcommitt/copyrightcommitteepiratesbollier.cfm (accessed March 3, 2008).

13. See Federal Trade Commission, *Privacy Online: Fair Information Practices in the Electronic Marketplace*, May 2000, http://www.ftc.gov/reports/privacy2000.pdf.

14. American Library Association, "CIPA Questions and Answers," July 16, 2003 http://www.ala.org/ala/washoff/woissues/civilliberties/cipaweb/adviceresources/CIPAQA.pdf (accessed March 3, 2008).

15. "Demographics of Internet Users," Pew Internet & American Life Project, February 15, 2008, http://www.pewinternet.org/trends/User_Demo_2.15.08.htm (accessed March 3, 2008).

16. Susannah Fox, Pew Internet & American Life Project, "Digital Divisions," October 5, 2005, http://www.pewinternet.org/PPF/r/165/report_display.asp. Also see Nielsen/Netratings, "Two-thirds of Active U.S.Web Populations Using Broadband," March 14, 2006, http://www.nielsen-netratings.com/pr/pr_060314.pdf.

17. ClickZ, " Stats - Web Worldwide," http://www.clickz.com/showPage.html?page=stats/web_worldwide (accessed March 3, 2008).

18. Douglas Gomery, "In Search of the Cybermarket," *Wilson Quarterly* (Summer 1994): 10.

GOOGLE OWNERSHIP   What Does This Mean?, p. 58

1. Google Investor Relations, "Financial Tables, 2008." http://investor.google.com/fin_data.html.

2. Information Aesthetics, "Number of Google Employees," February 8, 2008 http://infosthetics.com/archives/2008/02/number_of_google_employees_visualized.html.

3. Jon Fine, "Google and Other People's Content: It Sticks Ads All Over. But to Maintain Growth, It May Need to Own the Places It Puts Them," *Business Week*, December 3, 2007, 75.

4. Catherine Rampell, "Google's Profit Jumps 46 Percent, Sets Record." *Washington Post*, October 19, 2007, p. D3.

5. Dominic White, "Internet Google's Rapid Growth Facing Slowdown. Despite Profits Rising, the Internet Search Engine's Full-Year Results Beg the Question: How Long Can This Continue? *Daily Telegraph* (London), February 1, 2008, p. 4.

6. Gary Rivlin, "After Months of Hoopla, Google Debut Fits the Norm," *New York Times*, August 20, 2004, http://www.nytimes.com/2004/08/20/technology/20google.html?ex=1250740800&en=856f04ed73aef6fd&ei=5090&partner=rssuserland.

7. "Giants in Combat: Microsoft, Yahoo and Google." *Economist*, February 7, 2008, http://www.economist.com/opinion/displaystory.cfm?story_id=10651824#top.

8. Jon Swartz and Byron Acohido, "Deal Could Turn Up the Heat on Google to Do Likewise; AOL Could Make an Attractive Target, *USA TODAY*, February 4, 2008, p. B2.

9. Ibid.

10. John Foley, "Google in Oregon: Mother Nature Meets The Data Center," Information Week, August 24, 2007, http://www.informationweek.com/blog/main/archives/2007/08/google_in_orego.html.

11. John Markoff and Saul Hansell, "Hiding in Plain Sight, Google Seeks More Power," *New York Times*, June 14, 2006, http://www.nytimes.com/2006/06/14/technology/14search.html.

12. Chris Mellor, "Does Google Have The Biggest IT Carbon Footprint On The Planet?" Techworld, June 26, 2007, http://www.techworld.com/green-it/features/index.cfm?featureid=3487.

◢ **GLOBAL VILLAGE   China's Great Firewall, p. 61**

1. Pat Kane, "Media: Saint of the Superhighway," *Independent* (London), April 28, 1997, p. 8.

2. Martin Walker, "Keyboard Whiz-Kid; William Gibson, the Novelist Who Created Cyberspace, Has Sony's Corporate Millions Riding on His Talent," *Guardian* (London), May 29, 1995, p. T8.

3. Bill Gates, "Shaping the Internet Age," speech to the Internet Policy Institute, December 2000, http://www.microsoft.com/billgates/shapingtheinternet.asp.

4. Philip P. Pan, "Reference Tool on Web Finds Fans, Censors," *Washington Post*, February 20, 2006, http://www.washingtonpost.com/wp-dyn/content/article/2006/ 02/19/AR2006021901335.html.

5. See the Open Net Initiative, http://www.opennctinitiative.net/. Also see Rebecca Mackinnon, RConversation, http://rconversation.blogs.com/rconversation/.

③ **Sound Recording and Popular Music**

1. Thom Yorke, "David Byrne and Thom Yorke on the Real Value of Music," *Wired*, December 18, 2007, http://www.wired.com/entertainment/music/magazine/16-01/ff_yorke (accessed March 8, 2008).

2. Greg Kot, "1.2 Million Downloads Reported for Radiohead's 'In Rainbows,' a Collection of Chilling Love Songs," ChicagoTribune.com, October 12, 2007, http://leisureblogs.chicagotribune.com/turn_it_up/2007/10/12-million-down.html (accessed March 8, 2008).

3. Andrew Lipsman, ComScore, "Radiohead Redux," February 12, 2008, http://www.comscore.com/mt/mt-search.cgi?tag=Radiohead&blog_id=2 (accessed March 8, 2008).

4. ComScore, "For Radiohead Fans, Does 'Free' + 'Download' = 'Freeload'?" November 5, 2007, http://www.comscore.com/press/release.asp?press=1883.

5. Thomas Edison, quoted in Marshall McLuhan, *Understanding Media* (New York: McGraw-Hill, 1964), 276.

6. Mark Coleman, *Playback: From the Victrola to MP3* (Cambridge, Mass.: Da Capo Press, 2003).

7. IFPI Digital Music Report 2008, http://www.ifpi.org/content/section_resources/dmr2008.html (accessed March 10, 2008).

8. See Bruce Tucker, " 'Tell Tchaikovsky the News': Postmodernism, Popular Culture and the Emergence of Rock 'n' Roll," *Black Music Research Journal* 9, no. 2 (Fall 1989): 280.

9. Robert Palmer, *Deep Blues: A Musical and Cultural History of the Mississippi Delta* (New York: Penguin, 1982), 15.

10. LeRoi Jones, *Blues People* (New York: Morrow Quill, 1963), 168.

11. Mick Jagger, quoted in Jann S. Wenner, "Jagger Remembers," *Rolling Stone*, December 14, 1995, 66.

12. See Mac Rebennack (Dr. John) with Jack Rummel, *Under a Hoodoo Moon* (New York: St. Martin's Press, 1994), 58.

13. Little Richard, quoted in Charles White, *The Life and Times of Little Richard: The Quasar of Rock* (New York: Harmony Books, 1984), 65-66.

14. Quoted in Dave Marsh and James Bernard, *The New Book of Rock Lists* (New York: Fireside, 1994), 15.

15. Tucker, "'Tell Tchaikovsky the News,'" 287.

16. Ed Ward, quoted in Ward, Geoffrey Stokes, and Ken Tucker, *Rock of Ages: The Rolling Stone History of Rock & Roll* (New York: Rolling Stone Press, 1986), 89.

17. See Gerri Hershey, *Nowhere to Run: The Story of Soul Music* (New York: Penguin Books, 1984).

18. K. Tucker, in Ward, Stokes, and Tucker, *Rock of Ages,* 521.

19. Stephen Thomas Erlewine, "Nirvana," in Michael Erlewine, ed., *All Music Guide: The Best CDs, Albums, & Tapes,* 2nd ed. (San Francisco: Miller Freeman Books, 1994), 233.

20. IFPI Digital Music Report 2008. http://www.ifpi.org/content/section_ resources/dmr2008.html.

21. Steven Winograsky, "Artist Royalties From iTunes: New Media, Same Old Battle," The Royalty Report, 2007, http://www.royaltyreport.com/ article/Artist-Royalties-From-iTunes-New-Media--Same-Old--60.html (accessed March 8, 2008).

22. Jeff Leeds, "The Net Is a Boon for Indie Labels," *New York Times,* December 27, 2005, p. E1.

23. Josh Belzman, "Bands and Fans Singing a New Tune on MySpace," MSNBC.com, February 13, 2006, http://www.msnbc.msn.com/ id/11114166/ (accessed March 10, 2008).

24. Nat Hentoff, "Many Dreams Fueled Long Development of U.S. Music," *Milwaukee Journal/*United Press International, February 26, 1978, p. 2.

SONY OWNERSHIP   What Does This Mean?, p. 98

1. Sony Corporation of America, "Corporate Fact Sheet," http://www.sony .com/SCA/corporate.shtml (accessed March 11, 2008).

2. Ibid.

3. Sony Annual Report 2007, http://www.sony.net/SonyInfo/IR/ financial/ar/2007/index.html. All other sources are from the Sony Annual Report, unless otherwise noted.

4. See Sony Corporation of America, "Corporate Fact Sheet."

5. Sony Pictures, "Corporate Fact Sheet," http://www.sonypictures.com/ corp/corporatefact.html.

◢ TRACKING TECHNOLOGY   The Rise of MP3s and Digital Downloading, p. 78

1. "Instant Gratification," David Hajdu, *New Republic,* March 6, 2006; "Tila Tequila for President," Jonah Weiner, *Salon,* April 11, 2006.

2. "Official: My Space to Form Joint Venture with Major Record Labels," Steve O'Hear, ZDNet.com, April 3, 2008.

④ Popular Radio and the Origins of Broadcasting

1. See Peter DiCola, "False Premises, False Promises: A Quantitative History of Ownership Consolidation in the Radio Industry," Future of Music Coalition, December 2006, http://www.futureofmusic.org/ research/radiostudy06.cfm.

2. Derek Turner, "Off the Dial: Female and Minority Radio Station Ownership in the United States," Free Press, June 2007, http://www .stopbigmedia.com/files/off_the_dial.pdf.

3. In Michelle Chen, "Reclaiming Radio," *ColorLines,* March/April 2008, http://www.colorlines.com/article.php?ID=278.

4. Tom Lewis, *Empire of the Air: The Men Who Made Radio* (New York: HarperCollins, 1991), 181.

5. Captain Linwood S. Howeth, USN (Retired), *History of Communications-Electronics in the United States Navy* (Washington: Government Printing Office, 1963), http://earlyradiohistory.us/1963hw.htm.

6. Margaret Cheney, *Tesla: Man out of Time* (New York: Touchstone, 2001).

7. William J. Broad, "Tesla, a Bizarre Genius, Regains Aura of Greatness," *New York Times,* August 28, 1984, http://query.nytimes.com/gst/fullpage .html?res=9400E4DD1038F93BA1575BC0A962948260&sec=health&spon= &partner=permalink&exprod=permalink.

8. Michael Pupin, "Objections Entered to Court's Decision," *New York Times,* June 10, 1934, E5.

9. Lewis, *Empire of the Air,* 73.

10. For a full discussion of early broadcast history and the formation of RCA, see Eric Barnouw, *Tube of Plenty* (New York: Oxford University Press, 1982); Susan Douglas, *Inventing American Broadcasting, 1899-1922* (Baltimore: Johns Hopkins University Press, 1987); and Christopher Sterling and John Kitross, *Stay Tuned: A Concise History of American Broadcasting* (Belmont, Calif.: Wadsworth, 1990).

11. See Jefferson Cowie, *Capital Moves: RCA's Seventy-Year Quest for Cheap Labor* (New York: New Press, 2001).

12. Robert W. McChesney, *Telecommunications, Mass Media & Democracy: The Battle for Control of U.S. Broadcasting, 1928-1935* (New York: Oxford University Press, 1994).

13. Michele Hilmes, *Radio Voices: American Broadcasting, 1922-1952* (Minneapolis: University of Minnesota Press, 1997).

14. "Amos 'n' Andy Show," Museum of Broadcast Communications, http://www.museum.tv/archives/etv/A/htmlA/amosnandy/amosnandy .htm (accessed April 1, 2008).

15. "Media Monopoly Made Simple: Corporate Ownership & the Problem with U.S. Media," http://www.freepress .net/media/tenthings.php (accessed May 25, 2004).

16. Shaun Assael, "Online and on the Edge," *New York Times,* September 23, 2007, http://www.nytimes.com/2007/09/23/arts/music/23assa.html.

17. Radio Advertising Bureau, *Radio Marketing Guide & Fact Book, 2007-2008,* http://www.rab.com/public/MediaFacts/2007RMGFB-150-10-11.pdf.

18. See Joe Mahoney, "Warner OKs 5M Payout for Payola," *Daily News* (New York), November 23, 2005, p. 6; and Jeff Leeds, "Spitzer Alleges Payola in Lawsuit," *New York Times,* March 9, 2006, p. C1.

19. Neil Strauss, "Pay-for-Play on the Air but This Rendition Is Legal," *New York Times,* March 31, 1998, pp. A1, A21.

20. DiCola, "False Premises, False Promises."

21. "Statement of FCC Chairman William E. Kennard on Low Power FM Radio Initiative," March 27, 2000, www.fee.gov/Speeches/Kennard/ Statements/2000/stwek024.html.

CLEAR CHANNEL OWNERSHIP   What Does This Mean?, p. 138

1. Clear Channel, Form 10-K for 2007 (Annual Report to the Securities and Exchange Commission), http://www.clearchannel.com/Investors/ Documents/291.pdf. All Clear Channel ownership information from this source unless otherwise noted.

2. Clear Channel, "International Radio," http://www.clearchannel.com/ IntRadio/PressRelease.aspx?PressReleaseID=1489&p=hidden (accessed April 2, 2008).

⑤ Television and the Power of Visual Culture

1. David Blum, "Sitcoms Are Dead! Long Live Sitcoms!" *New York Times,* May 14, 2007, p. A19.

2. Ibid.

3. J. Fred MacDonald, *One Nation under Television: The Rise and Decline of Network TV* (Chicago: Nelson-Hall Publishers, 1994), 132.

4. Ibid., 70.

5. Quoted in MacDonald, *One Nation under Television,* 78.

6. See Horace Newcomb, *TV: The Most Popular Art* (Garden City, N.Y.: Anchor Books, 1974), 31, 39.

7. Ibid., 35.

8. Eric Barnouw, *Tube of Plenty: The Evolution of American Television,* rev. ed. (New York: Oxford University Press, 1982), 163.

9. Quoted in Barnouw, *Tube of Plenty,* 163.

10. See Sydney Head and Christopher Sterling, *Broadcasting in America,* 4th ed. (Boston: Houghton Mifflin, 1982), 258.

11. Quoted in B. J. Bullert, "Public Television: Safe Programming and Faustian Bargains," *Chronicle of Higher Education,* September 19, 1998, p. B7.

12. See Charles McGrath, "Is PBS Still Necessary?" *New York Times,* February 17, 2008, pp. 1, 23.

13. Louise Story, "Every Move You Make; Nielsen Looks beyond TV, and Hits Roadblocks," *New York Times,* February 26, 2008, pp. C1, C4.

14. Head and Sterling, *Broadcasting in America,* 206.

15. MacDonald, *One Nation under Television,* 181.

16. Quoted in Timothy McNulty and Rob Owen, "Brave New Worlds: When TV Viewers Decide What's Prime Time," *Pittsburgh Post-Gazette,* November 13, 2005, p. A-1.

17. See Richard Campbell, "Don Hewitt's Durable Hour," *Columbia Journalism Review* (September-October 1993): 25.

18. Stuart Elliott, "How to Value Ratings with DVR Delay," *New York Times,* February 13, 2006, p. C15.

19. Bill Carter, "NBC Acquires 'Quarterlife'; Internet Series Will Run First Online," *New York Times,* November 19, 2007, www.nytimes.com.

20. Ibid.

◢ TRACKING TECHNOLOGY   Digital Television Takes Over, p. 149

1. Jacques Steinberg, "Converters Signal a New Era for TVs," *New York Times,* June 7, 2007, p. C3.

2. Ibid.

NEWS CORP. OWNERSHIP   What Does This Mean?, p. 168

1. All data was obtained from Hoover's Company Records, April 22, 2008, at Hoover's Online, premium.hoovers.com.

⑥ Cable: A Wired versus Wireless World

1. The Pew Research Center for the People & the Press, "Cable and Internet Loom Large in Fragmented Political News Universe," January 11, 2004, http://people-press.org/reports.

2. The Pew Research Center for the People & the Press, "Public Knowledge of Current Affairs Little Changed by News and Information Revolutions: What Americans Know: 1989-2007," April 15, 2007, http://people-press.org/reports.

3. *United States v. Midwest Video Corp.,* 440 U.S. 689 (1979).

4. Federal Communications Commission, "Report on Cable Industry Prices," February 4, 2005, http://hraunfoss.fcc.gov/edocs_public/attachmatch/FCC-05-12A1.pdf.

5. National Cable & Telecommunications Association, "Industry Statistics," April 2008, http://www.ncta.com/statistics.

6. Ibid.

7. See "Tom Freston: The Pied Piper of Television," *Broadcasting & Cable,* September 19, 1994, 40.

8. William J. Ray, "Private Enterprise, Privileged Enterprise, or Free Enterprise," January 28, 2003, www.glasgow-ky.com/papers/#PrivateEnterprise.

9. Ibid.

◢ CASE STUDY   ESPN: Sports and Stories, p. 196

1. See Linda Haugsted, "ESPN's First-Place Finish," *Multichannel News,* March 3, 2008, p. 21.

VIACOM OWNERSHIP   What Does This Mean?, p. 206

1. Data in this section was obtained from Hoover's Company Records, April 22, 2008.

⑦ Movies and the Impact of Images

1. John Cawelti, *Adventure, Mystery, and Romance: Formula Stories as Art and Popular Culture* (Chicago: University of Chicago Press, 1976), 35.

2. See Charles Musser, *The Emergence of Cinema: The American Screen to 1907* (New York: Scribner's, 1991).

3. Douglas Gomery, *Shared Pleasures: A History of Movie Presentation in the United States* (Madison: University of Wisconsin Press, 1992), 18.

4. Douglas Gomery, *Movie History: A Survey* (Belmont, Calif.: Wadsworth, 1991), 167.

5. See Cawelti, *Adventure, Mystery, and Romance,* 80-98.

6. See Barbara Koenig Quart, *Women Directors: The Emergence of a New Cinema* (New York: Praeger, 1988).

7. See Gomery, *Shared Pleasures,* 171-80.

8. Ismail Merchant, "Kitschy as Ever, Hollywood Is Branching Out," *New York Times,* November 22, 1998, sec. 2, pp. 15, 30.

9. See Eric Barnouw, *Tube of Plenty: The Evolution of American Television,* rev. ed. (New York: Oxford University Press, 1975, 1982), 108-9.

10. See Douglas Gomery, "Who Killed Hollywood?" *Wilson Quarterly* (Summer 1991): 106-12.

11. Ken Belson, "A Star May Be Fading: As DVD Sales Slow, the Hunt Is on for a New Cash Cow," *New York Times,* June 13, 2006, pp. C1, C10. Also see Jason Turbow, "After Winning the Format War, Blu-ray's Future Looks Bright," *New York Times,* March 13, 2008, p. C6.

12. National Association of Theater Owners, "Total U.S. & Canada Admissions," http://www.natoonline.org/statisticsadmissions.htm.

13. Motion Picture Association of America, "Theatrical Market Statistics 2007," http://www.mpaa.org/researchstatistics.asp.

14. Jennifer Mann, "AMC Makes Surprise Bid for Rival Theater Chain," *Kansas City Star,* July 12, 2001, p. A1.

15. Carolyn Giardina, "Fithian: Next Year Pivotal for 3-D," *Hollywood Reporter,* April 13, 2008, http://www.hollywoodreporter.com/hr/content_display/film/news/e3i841febf193b81360e8ddc311c1254dff.

16. David S. Cohen, "Academy to Preserve Digital Content," *Variety,* August 3, 2007, http://www.variety.com/article/VR1117969687.html.

17. David Thorburn, "Television as an Aesthetic Medium," *Critical Studies in Mass Communication* (June 1987): 168.

◢ CASE STUDY   Breaking through Hollywood's Race Barrier, p. 228

1. Douglas Gomery, *Shared Pleasures: A History of Movie Presentation in the United States* (Madison: University of Wisconsin Press, 1992), 155-70.

DISNEY OWNERSHIP   What Does This Mean?, p. 242

1. Hoover's.com, "The Walt Disney Company," http://www.hoovers.com/disney/--ID__11603--/free-co-factsheet.xhtml (accessed April 30, 2008).

2. All sources come from *The Walt Disney Company Fact Book 2007*, http://corporate.disney.go.com/investors/fact_books/2007/index.html, or the Walt Disney Company, Form 10-K for 2007, Annual Report to the Securities and Exchange Commission, https://clients.moultoncommerce .com/disney/pdfs/200710K.pdf, unless otherwise noted.

8 Newspapers: The Rise and Decline of Modern Journalism

1. See Brooke Kroeger, *Nellie Bly: Daredevil, Reporter, Feminist* (New York: Times Books/Random House, 1994).

2. James Janega, "Tribune Toy-Safety Investigation Honored: Stories on Unsafe Toys, Cribs Lead to Major Changes," *Chicago Tribune*, www.chicagotribune.com, April 7, 2008.

3. Project for Excellence in Journalism, "The State of the News Media 2008: Executive Summary," p. 9, www.journalism.org.

4. See Kay Mills, *A Place in the News: From the Women's Pages to the Front Page* (New York: Dodd, Mead, 1988).

5. Piers Brendon, *The Life and Death of the Press Barons* (New York: Atheneum, 1983), 136.

6. William Randolph Hearst, quoted in Brendon, *The Life and Death of the Press Barons*, 134.

7. Michael Schudson, *Discovering the News: A Social History of American Newspapers* (New York: Basic Books, 1978), 23.

8. See David T. Z. Mindich, "Edwin M. Stanton, the Inverted Pyramid, and Information Control," *Journalism Monographs* 140 (August 1993).

9. John C. Merrill, "Objectivity: An Attitude," in Merrill and Ralph L. Lowenstein, eds., *Media, Messages and Men* (New York: David McKay, 1971), 240.

10. Roy Peter Clark, "A New Shape for the News," *Washington Journalism Review* (March 1984): 47.

11. Curtis D. MacDougall, *The Press and Its Problems* (Dubuque: Wm. C. Brown, 1964), 143, 189.

12. See Edwin Emery, *The Press and America: An Interpretive History of the Mass Media*, 3rd ed. (Englewood Cliffs, N.J.: Prentice-Hall, 1972), 562.

13. Walter Lippmann, *Liberty and the News* (New York: Harcourt, Brace and Howe, 1920), 92.

14. Lippmann, *Liberty and the News*, 64.

15. Tom Wolfe, quoted in Leonard W. Robinson, "The New Journalism: A Panel Discussion," in Ronald Weber, ed., *The Reporter as Artist: A Look at the New Journalism Controversy* (New York: Hastings House, 1974), 67. See also Tom Wolfe and E. E. Johnson, eds., *The New Journalism* (New York: Harper & Row, 1973).

16. Tom Wicker, *On Press* (New York: Viking, 1978), 3-5.

17. Jack Newfield, "The 'Truth' about Objectivity and the New Journalism," in Charles C. Flippen, ed., *Liberating the Media* (Washington, D.C.: Acropolis Books, 1973), 63-64.

18. See Newspaper Association of America, www.naa.org, April 25, 2006. For updates, see also Project for Excellence in Journalism, "State of the News Media 2008," www.journalism.org.

19. Ibid.

20. See Sreenath Sreenivasan, "As Mainstream Papers Struggle, the Ethnic Press Is Thriving," *New York Times*, July 22, 1996, p. C7.

21. See Phyl Garland, "The Black Press: Down but Not Out," *Columbia Journalism Review* (September-October 1982): 43-50.

22. American Society of Newspaper Editors, www.asne.org. See also Mark Fitzgerald, "ASNE Survey: Over Last Year, Dailies Shrank Their Newsrooms by the Biggest Margin in Three Decades," *Editor & Publisher*, April 13, 2008, www.editorandpublisher.com.

23. Dianiela Gevson, "Spanish-Language Dailies Expand a Bitter Battle," *New York Sun*, January 21, 2004, p. 2.

24. Project for Excellence in Journalism, "State of the News Media 2007," http://www.stateofthenewsmedia.org/2007/.

25. RTNDA/Ball State 2006 Women & Minorities Survey, http://www .rtnda.org/diversity/index.

26. Wil Cruz, "The New *New Yorker*: Ethnic Media Fill the Void," *Newsday*, June 26, 2002, p. A25.

27. See Fitzgerald, "ASNE Survey."

28. PR Newswire, "NAA Finds Newspaper Readership Steady in Top 50 Markets," May 3, 2004. See Newspaper Association of America, www .naa.org, for updates.

29. Project for Excellence in Journalism, "The State of the News Media 2008: Executive Summary," p. 8, www.journalism.org.

30. World Association of Newspapers, "World Press Trends: Global Newspaper Circulation, Advertising on the Upswing," June 4, 2007, www .wan-press.org.

31. Ibid.

32. *International Herald Tribune*, "As American Newspapers Flail, Indian Papers Are on the Rise," May 28, 2007, www.iht.com.

33. See Philip Meyer, "Learning to Love Lower Profits," *American Journalism Review* (December 1995): 40-44.

34. Project for Excellence in Journalism, "The State of the News Media 2008," www.journalism.org.

35. James Rainey, "L.A. Times Plans Job Cuts," *New York Times*, April 24, 2007, p. 3.

36. Nancy Cleeland, "Why I'm Leaving the *L.A. Times*," The Huffington Post, May 28, 2007, http://huffingtonpost.com/nancy-cleeland.

37. Quoted in Noam Cohen, "Blogger, Sans Pajamas, Rakes Muck and a Prize," *New York Times*, February 25, 2008, www.nytimes.com.

38. Brian Deagon, "You, Reporting Live: Citizen Journalism Relies on Audience; Now, Everyone's a Stringer . . .," *Investor's Business Daily*, March 31, 2008, p. A4.

39. See Noam Cohen, "Journalism in the Hands of the Neighborhood, *New York Times*, March 10, 2008, www.nytimes.com.

40. Committee to Protect Journalists, "Journalists Killed: Statistics and Background," www.cpj.org (accessed May 6, 2008).

41. Marc Santora and Bill Carter, "War in Iraq Becomes the Deadliest Assignment for Journalists in Modern Times," *New York Times*, May 30, 2006, www.nytimes.com.

42. John Carroll, "News War, Part 3," *Frontline*, PBS, February 27, 2007, http://www.pbs.org/wgbh/pages/frontline/ newswar/etc/script3.html.

CASE STUDY   Alternative Journalism: Dorothy Day and I. F. Stone, p. 267

1. Stone, quoted in Jack Lule, "I. F. Stone: Professional Excellence in Raising Hell," *QS News* (Summer 1989): 3.

CASE STUDY   Newspaper Circulation Is Up! (For Free Papers), p. 271

1. Kathleen P. Mahoney and James H. Collins, "Consumer Newspaper Choice in Markets with Free Print Options: Are Free Daily Newspapers Competition or Opportunity for Traditional Paid Products?" Scarborough Research, October 26, 2005, http://www.scarborough.com/ press.php.

2. Michael Stoll, "At Free Dailies, Advertisers Sometimes Call the Shots," Grade the News, July 27, 2005, http://www.gradethenews.org/2005/ freepapers1.htm.

GANNETT OWNERSHIP   **What Does This Mean?, p. 274**

1. Hoover's Company Records, May 13, 2008.
2. Gannett Company Profile, http://www.gannett.com/about/company_profile.htm (accessed May 14, 2008).

9 Magazines in the Age of Specialization

1. Jennifer Benjamin, "How Cosmo Changed the World," http://www.cosmopolitan.com/magazine/about-us_how-cosmo-changed-the-world (accessed April 27, 2008).
2. Sammye Johnson, "Promoting Easy Sex without the Intimacy: *Maxim* and *Cosmopolitan* Cover Lines and Cover Images," in Mary-Lou Galician and Debra L. Merskin, eds., *Critical Thinking about Sex, Love, and Romance in the Mass Media* (Mahwah, N.J.: Erlbaum, 2007), 55-74.
3. Karen S. H. Roggenkamp, "'Dignified Sensationalism': Elizabeth Bisland, *Cosmopolitan*, and Trips around the World," paper presented at "Writing the Journey: A Conference on American, British, and Anglophone Writers and Writing," University of Pennsylvania, June 10-13, 1999, http://faculty.tamu-commerce.edu/kroggenkamp/bisland.html.
4. John Tebbel and Mary Ellen Zuckerman, *The Magazine in America, 1741-1990* (New York: Oxford University Press, 1991), 116.
5. See Theodore Peterson, *Magazines in the Twentieth Century* (Urbana: University of Illinois Press, 1964), 5.
6. See Richard Ohmann, *Selling Culture: Magazines, Markets, and Class at the Turn of the Century* (New York: Verso, 1996).
7. See Peterson, *Magazines*, 5.
8. Generoso Pope, quoted in William H. Taft, *American Magazines for the 1980s* (New York: Hasting House, 1982), 226-27.
9. See S. Elizabeth Bird, *For Enquiring Minds: A Cultural Study of Supermarket Tabloids* (Knoxville: University of Tennessee Press, 1992), 24.
10. See Robin Pogrebin, "The Number of Ad Pages Does Not Make the Magazine," *New York Times,* August 26, 1996, p. C1.
11. See Gloria Steinem, "Sex, Lies and Advertising," *Ms.,* July-August 1990, 18-28.

◢ CASE STUDY   The Evolution of Photojournalism, p. 290

1. Andrew Adam Newman, "3 Magazines Are Accused of Retouching Celebrity Photos to Excess," *New York Times,* May 28, 2007, http://www.nytimes.com/2007/05/28/business/media/28fitness.html.
2. Jessica Bennett, "Picture Perfect," *Newsweek,* May 2, 2008, http://www.newsweek.com/id/135166/page/1.

◢ Media Literacy and the Critical Process   Uncovering American Beauty, p. 299

1. David Carr, "On Covers of Many Magazines, a Full Racial Palette Is Still Rare," *New York Times,* November 18, 2002, p. C1.
2. Academy for Eating Disorders, "Academy for Eating Disorders Guidelines for the Fashion Industry," http://www.aedweb.org/public/fashion_guidelines.cfm.

ADVANCE PUBLICATIONS OWNERSHIP   What Does This Mean?, p. 308

1. Center for Media and Democracy/SourceWatch, "Advance Publications," http://www.sourcewatch.org/index.php?title=Advance_Publications (accessed April 30, 2008); Forbes.com, "#65 Samuel Newhouse Jr.," http://www.forbes.com/lists/2006/10/7EWB.html; Forbes.com, "#100 Donald Newhouse," http:// www.forbes.com/lists/2007/10/07billionaires_Donald-Newhouse_LOKT .html.

2. Forbes.com, "#100 Donald Newhouse."
3. Julie Scelfo, "Condé Nast," *St. James Encyclopedia of Pop Culture,* http://findarticles.com/p/articles/mi_g1epc/is_tov/ai_2419100281.
4. Condé Nast Media Kit, "Circulation/Demographics," http://www.condenastmediakit.com/port/circulation.cfm, November 2007.

10 Books and the Power of Print

1. Caroline Horn, "Harry Potter and the Children's Publishing Boom," *Bookseller,* March 16, 2007, p. S6.
2. Jack Zipes, quoted in Henry Kisor, "Way Too Many Books . . . ," *Chicago Sun-Times,* December 25, 2005, p. 9B.
3. See Elizabeth Eisenstein, *The Printing Press as an Agent of Change* (Cambridge: Cambridge University Press, 1980).
4. See Quentin Reynolds, *The Fiction Factory: From Pulp Row to Quality Street* (New York: Street & Smith/Random House, 1955), 72-74.
5. For a comprehensive historical overview of the publishing industry and the rise of publishing houses, see John A. Tebbel, *A History of Book Publishing in the United States,* 4 vols. (New York: R. R. Bowker, 1972-81).
6. National Association of College Stores, "FAQ on College Textbooks," May 2008, http://nacs.org/common/research/faq_textbooks.pdf (accessed May 15, 2008).
7. National Association of College Stores, "FAQ on College Textbooks."
8. For a historical overview of paperbacks, see Kenneth Davis, *Two-Bit Culture: The Paperbacking of America* (Boston: Houghton Mifflin, 1984).
9. See John P. Dessauer, *Book Publishing: What It Is, What It Does* (New York: R. R. Bowker, 1974), 48.
10. Bibb Porter, "In Publishing, Bigger Is Better," *New York Times,* March 31, 1998, p. A27.
11. David D. Kirkpatrick, "Report to the Authors Guild Midlist Books Study Committee," 2000, http://www.authorsguild.org/prmidlist.html.
12. Jon Ortiz, "The Tale of the Little Guys . . . ," *Sacramento Bee,* September 1, 2005, p. D1. Also see Bridget Kinsella, "Study Shows Shopping Local Boosts Neighborhoods," *Publishers Weekly,* May 4, 2007, http://www.publishersweekly.com/article/CA6439417.html.
13. Jim Milliot, "As Amazon Soars, Bookstores Creep," *Publishers Weekly,* April 14, 2008, http://www.publishersweekly.com/article/CA6550867.html.
14. National Endowment for the Arts, *To Read or Not to Read: A Question of National Consequence,* November 2007, http:// www.nea.gov/research/ToRead.pdf.
15. Ezra Klein, "The Future of Reading," *Columbia Journalism Review,* May/June 2008, pp. 35-40.

◢ GLOBAL VILLAGE   Books: Cultural Status Defines Market, p. 333

1. Michael Kimmelman, "German Border Threat: Cheap Books," *New York Times, October 24, 2007, p. 1.*
2. Teri Tan, "A Land of Avid Readers: Scandinavians Are Buying up a Storm and Changing the Publishing Landscape," *Publishers Weekly,* September 18, 2006, http://www.publishers weekly.com/article/CA6372606.html.

BERTELSMANN OWNERSHIP   What Does This Mean?, p. 338

1. Bertelsmann 2007 Annual Report, http://www.bertelsmann.com/bertelsmann_corp/wms41/bm/index.php?ci=173&language=2.
2. Bertelsmann 2007 Annual Report.
3. Bertelsmann 2007 Annual Report.

4. Arianne Cohen, "A Publishing Company: Random House," *New York*, June 4, 2007, http://nymag.com/news/features/2007/profit/32906/.

5. Bertelsmann 2007 Annual Report.

6. Bertelsmann Corporate Web site, http://www.bertelsmann.com/bertelsmann_corp/wms41/bm/index.php?ci=26.

7. RTL Group, "About Us," http://www.rtlgroup.com/AboutUs_15.htm.

8. Bertelsmann Corporate Web site.

11 Advertising and Commercial Culture

1. "The Ultimate Network," *Adweek*, May 17, 1993.

2. Saul Hansell, "Google Wants to Dominate Madison Avenue, Too," *New York Times*, October 30, 2005, http://www.nytimes.com/2005/10/30/business/yourmoney/30google.html.

3. Google Annual Report 2007, http://investor.google.com/pdf/2008_additional_proxy_materials.pdf.

4. Eric Schmidt, address to the American Association of Advertising Agencies 2008 Leadership Conference, April 29, 2008, http://www.youtube.com/watch?v=Ph9MmzecrSo.

5. For a written and pictorial history of early advertising, see Charles Goodrum and Helen Dalrymple, *Advertising in America: The First 200 Years* (New York: Harry N. Abrams, 1990), 31.

6. Michael Schudson, *Advertising: The Uneasy Persuasion* (New York: Basic Books, 1984), 164.

7. Stuart Elliott, "Advertising's Big Four: It's Their World Now," *New York Times*, March 31, 2002, sec. 3 (Money and Business), p. 1.

8. Spotlight, "X-Ray Films Hits Target's Bull-Eye," *Shoot Magazine*, February 6, 2004.

9. Randall Rothenberg, *Where the Suckers Moon: An Advertising Story* (New York: Alfred A. Knopf, 1994), 20.

10. See Bettina Fabos, "The Commercialized Web: Challenges for Libraries and Democracy," *Library Trends* 53(4) (Spring 2005): 519-23.

11. Miguel Helft, "Internet Giants Vie to Snap Up Web Ad Firms," *New York Times*, May 19, 2007, p. A1.

12. Robert Guth et al., "Web Wars: With Big Buy, Microsoft Joins Online-Ad Flurry," *Wall Street Journal*, May 19, 2007, p. A1.

13. Leslie Savan, "Op Ad: Sneakers and Nothingness," *Village Voice*, April 2, 1991, p. 43.

14. See Mary Kuntz and Joseph Weber, "The New Hucksterism," *Business Week*, July 1, 1999, 79.

15. Ibid.

16. Schudson, *Advertising*, 210.

17. Vance Packard, *The Hidden Persuaders* (New York: Basic Books, 1957, 1978), 229.

18. See Eileen Dempsey, "Auld Lang Syne," *Columbus Dispatch*, December 28, 2000, p. 1G; and John Reinan, "The End of the Good Old Days," *Minneapolis Star Tribune*, August 31, 2004, p. 1D.

19. See Schudson, *Advertising*, 36-43; and Andrew Robertson, *The Lessons of Failure* (London: MacDonald, 1974).

20. Kim Campbell and Kent Davis-Packard, "How Ads Get Kids to Say, I Want It!" *Christian Science Monitor*, September 18, 2000, p. 1.

21. See Jay Mathews, "Channel One: Classroom Coup or a 'Sham'?" *Washington Post*, December 26, 1994, p. A1+.

22. See Michael F. Jacobson and Laurie Ann Mazur, *Marketing Madness: A Survival Guide for a Consumer Society* (Boulder, Colo.: Westview Press, 1995), 29-31.

23. "Ads Beat News on School TVs," *Pittsburgh Post-Gazette*, March 6, 2006, p. A7.

24. Hilary Waldman, "Study Links Advertising, Youth Drinking," *Hartford Courant*, January 3, 2006, p. A1.

25. Robert Weissman, "Commercial Alert Asks Book Reviewers Not to Review Ad-Laden Children's Series 'Mackenzie Blue,'" Commercial Alert, March 12, 2008, http://www.commercialalert.org/issues/culture/product-placement/commercial-alert-asks-book-reviewers-not-to-review-ad-laden-childrens-series-mackenzie-blue.

26. Douglas J. Wood, "Ad Issues to Watch For in '06," *Advertising Age*, December 19, 2005, p. 10.

27. Associated Press, "Two Ephedra Sellers Fined for False Ads," *Washington Post*, July 2, 2003, p. A7.

28. Beth Harskovits, "Corporate Profile: Legacy's Truth Finds Receptive Audience," *PR Week*, June 12, 2006, 9.

29. See Stephen Ansolabehere and Shanto Iyengar, *Going Negative: How Attack Ads Shrink and Polarize the Electorate* (New York: Free Press, 1996).

30. Leslie Wayne, "Political Spending Not Benefitting TV Stations Yet," *New York Times*, May 1, 2008, http://thecaucus.blogs.nytimes.com/2008/05/01/political-spending-not-benefitting-tv-stations-yet/.

◢ GLOBAL VILLAGE   Smoking Up the Global Market, p. 371

1. Mark O'Neill, "Weeding Out the Profits," *South China Morning Post*, August 1, 2002, p. 1; and Rina Omar, "Light Up, Lights Out?" *New Strait Times* (Malaysia), May 31, 2002, p. 1

12 Public Relations and Framing the Message

1. Matthew J. Culligan and Dolph Greene, *Getting Back to the Basics of Public Relations and Publicity* (New York: Crown Publishers, 1982), 90.

2. Ibid., 100.

3. See Stuart Ewen, *PR! A Social History of Spin* (New York: Basic Books, 1996).

4. Marvin N. Olasky, "The Development of Corporate Public Relations, 1850-1930," *Journalism Monographs*, no. 102 (April 1987): 14.

5. Ibid., 15.

6. Edward Bernays, "The Theory and Practice of Public Relations: A Résumé." In E. L. Bernays, ed., *The Engineering of Consent* (Norman: University of Oklahoma Press, 1955), 3-25.

7. Edward Bernays, *Crystallizing Public Opinion* (New York: Horace Liveright, 1923), 217.

8. Michael Schudson, *Discovering the News: A Social History of American Newspapers* (New York: Basic Books, 1978), 136.

9. PRSA, 2006 Silver Anvil Awards, "Teaching Teens Love Is Not Abuse," http://www.prsa.org/_Awards/silver/index.asp. Also see National Teen Dating Abuse Helpline, http://www.loveisrespect.org/index.html.

10. The author of this book, Richard Campbell, worked briefly as the assistant PR director for Milwaukee's Summerfest in the early 1980s.

11. Fareed Zakaria, ABC News, *This Week*, November 19, 2006.

12. Philip Shenon, "3 Partners Quit Firm Handling Saudis' P.R.," *New York Times*, December 6, 2002, http://www.nytimes.com/2002/12/06/international/middleeast/06SAUD.html?ex=1040199544&ei=1&en=c061b2d98376e7ba.

13. David S. Cloud, "Quick Rise for Purveyors of Propaganda in Iraq," *New York Times*, February 15, 2006, pp. A1, A10.

14. William Small, "Exxon Valdez: How to Spend Billions and Still Get a Black Eye," *Public Relations Review*, vol. 17, no. 1, pp. 9-25 (1991).

15. Stanley Walker, "Playing the Deep Bassoons," *Harper's*, February 1932, 365.

16. Ibid., 370.

17. Ivy Lee, *Publicity* (New York: Industries Publishing, 1925), 21.

18. Schudson, *Discovering the News*, 136.

19. Ivy Lee, quoted in Ray Eldon Hiebert, *Courtier to the Crowd: The Story of Ivy Lee and the Development of Public Relations* (Ames: Iowa State University Press, 1966), 114.

20. See Walter Lippmann, *Public Opinion* (New York: Free Press, 1922, 1949), 221.

21. See Jonathan Tasini, "Lost in the Margins: Labor and the Media," *Extra!* (Summer 1992): 2-11.

22. John Stauber and Sheldon Rampton, "Flack Attack," *PRWatch* 4(1) (1997), http://www.prwatch.org/prw_issues/1997-Q1/index.html.

23. John Stauber, "Corporate PR: A Threat to Journalism?" *Background Briefing: Radio National,* March 30, 1997, http://www.abc.net.au/rn/talks/bbing/stories/s10602.htm.

24. See Alicia Mundy, "Is the Press Any Match for Powerhouse PR?" in Ray Eldon Hiebert, ed., *Impact of Mass Media* (White Plains, N.Y.: Longman, 1995), 179-88.

25. Elisabeth Bumiller, "In Ex-Spokesman's Book, Harsh Words for Bush," *New York Times*, May 28, 2008, http://www.nytimes.com/2008/05/28/washington/28mcclellan.html.

◢ **CASE STUDY** **Video News Releases: Manufacturing the News, p. 392**

1. Center for Media and Democracy, "Know Fake News," October 11, 2007, http://www.prwatch.org/fakenews3/summary.

◢ **EXAMINING ETHICS** **Improving the Credibility Gap, p. 396**

1. Paul Pressler, "Executive Summary," Gap Inc. 2003 Social Responsibility Report, http://www.gapinc.com/social_resp/social_resp.htm.

2. Nia Elizabeth Shepherd et al., "Who's Who: The Eco-Guide," *Time*, April 20, 2006, http://www.time.com/time/magazine/article/0,9171,1185518,00.html.

◢ **Media Literacy and the Critical Process** **The Invisible Hand of PR, p. 403**

1. John Stauber, "Corporate PR: A Threat to Journalism?" *Background Briefing: Radio National,* March 30, 1997, http://www.abc.net.au/rn/talks/bbing/stories/s10602.htm.

⑬ Media Economics and the Global Marketplace

1. Kenneth Li, "MySpaceTV Lands Global TV Distribution Deal," EWeek.com, April 10, 2008, and Brian Stelter, "MySpace Makes a Deal to Reach a Bigger Screen," *International Herald Tribune*, April 12, 2008, finance section, p. 11.

2. See Howard Kurtz, "Journal's Publisher Moves to Top Newsroom Job; Company Apologizes in Ouster of Previous Editor," *Washington Post*, May 21, 2008, p. C7.

3. For this section the authors are indebted to the ideas and scholarship of Douglas Gomery, a media economist and historian, formerly from the University of Maryland.

4. Douglas Gomery, "The Centrality of Media Economics," in Mark R. Levy and Michael Gurevitch, eds., *Defining Media Studies* (New York: Oxford University Press, 1994), 202.

5. Ibid., 200.

6. Ibid., 203-4.

7. Larry Neumeister, "YouTube Suit Called Threat to Online Communication," Associated Press Financial Wire, May 27, 2008.

8. Ibid.

9. David Harvey, *The Condition of Postmodernity: An Enquiry into the Origins of Cultural Change* (Oxford: Basil Blackwell, 1989), 171.

10. Ibid., 158.

11. Thomas Geoghegan, "How Pink Slips Hurt More Than Workers," *New York Times,* March 29, 2006, p. B8.

12. Louis Uchitelle, *The Disposable American: Layoffs and Their Consequences* (New York: Alfred A. Knopf, 2006).

13. Paul Krugman, "For Richer," *New York Times Magazine,* October 20, 2002, pp. 62ff.

14. Antonio Gramsci, *Selections from the Prison Notebooks* (New York: International Publishers, 1971), 12-13.

15. Richard J. Barnet and John Cavanagh, *Global Dreams: Imperial Corporations and the New World Order* (New York: Simon & Schuster, 1994), 131.

16. James Stewart, *Disney War* (New York: Simon & Schuster, 2005).

17. Ben Bagdikian, *The Media Monopoly,* 6th ed. (Boston: Beacon Press, 2000), 222.

18. Harry First, "Bring Back Antitrust!" *Nation*, June 2, 2008, 7-8.

19. William Paley, quoted in Robert W. McChesney, *Telecommunications, Mass Media and Democracy: The Battle for Control of U.S. Broadcasting, 1928-1935* (New York: Oxford University Press, 1993), 251.

20. McChesney, *Telecommunications, Mass Media and Democracy*, 264.

21. Edward Herman, "Democratic Media," *Z Papers* (January-March 1992): 23.

22. Barnet and Cavanagh, *Global Dreams*, 38.

23. Richard J. Barnet and Ronald E. Muller, *Global Reach: The Power of Multinational Corporations* (New York: Simon & Schuster, 1974), 175.

24. The Lear Center Local News Archive, "Local News Coverage of the 2004 Campaigns," http://www.localnewsarchive.org/pdf/LCLNAFinal2004.pdf.

25. Robert McChesney and John Nichols, "Who'll Unplug Big Media? Stay Tuned," *Nation*, May 29, 2008, www.thenation.com/doc/20080616/mcchesney. This article also appeared in the June 16, 2008 print version of the *Nation*.

26. Jeffrey H. Birnbaum, "The Road to Riches Is Called K Street: Lobbying Firms Hire More, Pay More, Charge More to Influence Government," *Washington Post*, June 22, 2005, p. A1.

TIME WARNER OWNERSHIP **What Does This Mean?, p. 418**

1. Hoover's Company Fact Sheet for Time Warner: http://www.hoovers.com/time-warner/--ID__102518--/free-co-factsheet.xhtml.

2. Ibid.

3. All further information from Time Warner's corporate Fact Sheets, http://www.timewarner.com/corp/aboutus/fact_sheet.html.

⑭ The Culture of Journalism: Values, Ethics, and Democracy

1. Scott McClellan, *What Happened: Inside the Bush White House and Washington's Culture of Deception* (Public Affairs/Perseus Books: Philadelphia, 2008), preface.

2. See Helen Thomas, "Lap Dogs of the Press," *Nation*, March 27, 2006, 18-20.

3. Dean Baquet and Bill Keller, "When Do We Publish a Secret?" *New York Times*, July 1, 2006, p. A27; and see Frank Rich, "Can't Win the War? Bomb the Press!" *New York Times*, July 2, 2006, sec. 4, p. 10.

4. Scott Sherman, "Chilling the Press," *Nation*, July 17/24, 2006, 4-5.

5. Neil Postman, "Currents," *Utne Reader* (July-August 1995): 35.

6. Reuven Frank, "Memorandum from a Television Newsman," reprinted as Appendix 2 in A. William Bluem, *Documentary in American Television* (New York: Hastings House, 1965), 276.

7. For another list and an alternative analysis of news criteria, see Brian S. Brooks et al., *The Missouri Group: News Reporting and Writing* (New York: St. Martin's Press, 1996), 2-4.

8. Horace Greeley, quoted in Christopher Lasch, "Journalism, Publicity and the Lost Art of Argument," *Gannett Center Journal* 4(2) (Spring 1990): 2.

9. David Eason, "Telling Stories and Making Sense," *Journal of Popular Culture* 15(2) (Fall 1981): 125.

10. Jon Katz, "AIDS and the Media: Shifting out of Neutral," *Rolling Stone*, May 27, 1993, 32.

11. Herbert Gans, *Deciding What's News* (New York: Pantheon, 1979), 42-48.

12. Ibid.

13. Ibid., 48-51.

14. See Michael Schudson, *Discovering the News: A Social History of American Newspapers* (New York: Basic Books, 1978), 3-11.

15. Evan Thomas (with Suzanne Smalley), "The Myth of Objectivity: Is the Mainstream Press Unbiased?" *Newsweek*, March 10, 2008, 36.

16. Ibid.

17. Baquet and Keller, "When Do We Publish a Secret?"

18. Code of Ethics, reprinted in Melvin Mencher, *News Reporting and Writing*, 3rd ed. (Dubuque, Iowa: William C. Brown, 1984), 443-44.

19. Ibid.

20. For reference and guidance on media ethics, see Clifford Christians, Mark Fackler, and Kim Rotzoll, *Media Ethics: Cases and Moral Reasoning*, 4th ed. (White Plains, N.Y.: Longman, 1995); and Thomas H. Bivins, "A Worksheet for Ethics Instruction and Exercises in Reason," *Journalism Educator* (Summer 1993): 4-16.

21. Christians, Fackler, and Rotzoll, *Media Ethics*, 15.

22. See Jimmie Reeves and Richard Campbell, *Cracked Coverage: Television News, the Anti-Cocaine Crusade, and the Reagan Legacy* (Durham, N.C.: Duke University Press, 1994).

23. See David Eason, "On Journalistic Authority: The Janet Cooke Scandal," *Critical Studies in Mass Communications* 3(4) (December 1986): 429-47.

24. Mike Royko, quoted in "News Media: A Searching of Conscience," *Newsweek*, May 4, 1981, 53.

25. Don Hewitt, interview conducted at *60 Minutes*, CBS News, New York, February 21, 1989.

26. Jonathan Alter, "News Media: Round Up the Usual Suspects," *Newsweek*, March 25, 1985, 69.

27. Fairness and Accuracy in Reporting, "Power Sources: On Party, Gender, Race, and Class, TV News Looks to the Most Powerful Groups," *Extra!* (May-June 2002), www.fair.org.

28. William Greider, quoted in Mark Hertsgaard, *On Bended Knee: The Press and the Reagan Presidency* (New York: Farrar, Straus & Giroux, 1988), 78.

29. Bluem, *Documentary in American Television*, 94.

30. See Joe Holley, "Should the Coverage Fit the Crime?" *Columbia Journalism Review* (May-June 1996), www.cjr.org/year/96/coverage.asp.

31. Based on notes made by the author's wife, Dianna Campbell, after a visit to Warsaw and discussions with a number of journalists working for *Gazeta Wyborcza* in 1990.

32. Davis "Buzz" Merritt, *Public Journalism and Public Life: Why Telling the News Is Not Enough* (Hillsdale, N.J.: Lawrence Erlbaum, 1995), 113-14.

33. Jay Rosen, "Politics, Vision, and the Press: Toward a Public Agenda for Journalism," in Jay Rosen and Paul Taylor, *The New News v. the Old News: The Press and Politics in the 1990s* (New York: Twentieth Century Fund, 1992), 14.

34. See Jonathan Cohn, "Should Journalists Do Community Service?" *American Prospect* (Summer 1995): 15.

35. Davis Merritt and Jay Rosen, "Imagining Public Journalism: An Editor and a Scholar Reflect on the Birth of an Idea," *Roy W. Howard Public Lecture* (Bloomington: Indiana University), no. 5, April 13, 1995, p. 12.

36. Poll statistics cited in Merritt, *Public Journalism and Public Life*, xv-xvi; see Philip Meyer, "Raising Trust in Newspapers," *USA Today*, January 11, 1999, p. 15A; and Project for Excellence in Journalism, www.journalism.org, and the Pew Research Center, www.people-press.org/reports, for current research data.

37. See "State of the News Media 2006," Project for Excellence in Journalism, www.journalism.org.

38. See "Extreme Prejudice," *Investor's Business Daily*, June 22, 2007, p. A14.

39. James Agee and Walker Evans, *Let Us Now Praise Famous Men* (Boston: Houghton Mifflin, 1960), xiv.

40. David Broder, quoted in "Squaring with the Reader: A Seminar on Journalism," *Kettering Review* (Winter 1992): 48.

41. Christopher Lasch, "Journalism, Publicity and the Lost Art of Argument," *Gannett Center Journal* 4(2) (Spring 1990): 1.

42. Jay Rosen, "Forming and Informing the Public," *Kettering Review* (Winter 1992): 69-70.

◢ CASE STUDY **Bias in the News, p. 442**

1. Harris Poll #52, "News Reporting Perceived as Biased . . . ," June 30, 2006, www.harrisinteractive.com/harris_poll/ index .asp? PID=679.

2. Pew Research Center for the People and the Press, "Bottom-Line Pressures Now Hurting Coverage, Say Journalists," May 23, 2004, www.people-press.org/reports/display.php3?PageID=829.

3. *Random House Webster's Unabridged Dictionary*, 2nd ed., S.V.V. "conservative," "liberal."

4. Herbert Gans, *Deciding What's News* (New York: Vintage, 1980).

5. See Bernard Goldberg, *Bias: A CBS Insider Exposes How the Media Distort the News* (New York: Perennial, 2003).

6. See Eric Alterman, *What Liberal Media? The Truth about Bias and the News* (New York: Basic Books, 2003).

7. M. D. Watts et al., "Elite Cues and Media Bias in Presidential Campaigns: Explaining Public Perceptions of a Liberal Press," *Communications Research* 26 (1999): 144-75.

◢ EXAMINING ETHICS **Reporting Violence on Campus, p. 462**

1. Steve Capus, quoted in Chris Cobb, "The Killer and the Networks," *Ottawa Citizen*, April 21, 2007, p. B4.

2. See Cobb, "The Killer and the Networks."

3. Capus, quoted in Cobb, "The Killer and the Networks."

4. Harry Smith, quoted in Ben Grossman, "NBC's Internal Debate–and the Fallout," *Broadcasting & Cable*, April 23, 2007, 14.

5. Bob Steele, quoted in Cobb, "The Killer and the Networks."

6. Brian Williams, quoted in Matea Gold, "Massacre at Virginia Tech . . . ," *Los Angeles Times,* April 20, 2007, p. 1A.

7. Tony Burman, quoted in Cobb, "The Killer and the Networks."

8. Kevin Cameron, quoted in Cobb, "The Killer and the Networks."

9. Al Tompkins, quoted in Gold, "Massacre at Virginia Tech . . . ."

10. See Gold, "Massacre at Virginia Tech . . . ."

15 Media Effects and Cultural Approaches to Research

1. Alexis de Tocqueville, *Democracy in America* (New York: Modern Library, 1835, 1840, 1945, 1981), 96-97.

2. Steve Fore, "Lost in Translation: The Social Uses of Mass Communications Research," *Afterimage,* no. 20 (April 1993): 10.

3. James Carey, *Communication as Culture: Essays on Media and Society* (Boston: Unwin Hyman, 1989), 75.

4. Daniel Czitrom, *Media and the American Mind: From Morse to McLuhan* (Chapel Hill: University of North Carolina Press, 1982), 122-25.

5. Ibid., 123.

6. Harold Lasswell, *Propaganda Technique in the World War* (New York: Alfred A. Knopf, 1927), 9.

7. Walter Lippmann, *Public Opinion* (New York: Macmillan, 1922), 18.

8. Sheldon R. Gawiser and G. Evans Witt, "20 Questions a Journalist Should Ask about Poll Results," 2nd ed., http:// www.ncpp.org/qajsa.htm (accessed July 11, 2004).

9. See W. W. Charters, *Motion Pictures and Youth: A Summary* (New York: Macmillan, 1934); and Garth Jowett, *Film: The Democratic Art* (Boston: Little, Brown, 1976), 220-29.

10. Czitrom, *Media and the American Mind,* 132. See also Harold Lasswell, "The Structure and Function of Communication in Society," in Lyman Bryson, ed., *The Communication of Ideas* (New York: Harper and Brothers, 1948), 37-51.

11. Wilbur Schramm, Jack Lyle, and Edwin Parker, *Television in the Lives of Our Children* (Stanford, Calif.: Stanford University Press, 1961), 1.

12. See Joseph Klapper, *The Effects of Mass Communication* (New York: Free Press, 1960).

13. Schramm, Lyle, and Parker, *Television,* 1.

14. For an early overview of uses and gratifications, see Jay Blumler and Elihu Katz, *The Uses of Mass Communication* (Beverly Hills, Calif.: Sage, 1974).

15. National Public Radio, "Death-Penalty Option Varies Depending on Question," *Weekend Edition,* July 2, 2006.

16. See George Gerbner et al., "The Demonstration of Power: Violence Profile No. 10," *Journal of Communication* 29, no. 3 (1979): 177-96.

17. Kaiser Family Foundation, *Sex on TV 4* (Menlo Park, Calif.: Henry C. Kaiser Family Foundation, 2005).

18. Robert P. Snow, *Creating Media Culture* (Beverly Hills, Calif.: Sage, 1983), 47.

19. See Maxwell McCombs and Donald Shaw, "The Agenda-Setting Function of Mass Media," *Public Opinion Quarterly* 36, no. 2 (1972): 176-87.

20. See Nancy Signorielli and Michael Morgan, *Cultivation Analysis: New Directions in Media Effects Research* (Newbury Park, Calif.: Sage, 1990).

21. Em Griffin, "Spiral of Silence of Elisabeth Noelle-Neumann," from *A First Look at Communication Theory* (New York: McGraw-Hill, 1997), http://www.afirstlook.com/archive/spiral.cfm?source=archther.

22. Robert Lynd, *Knowledge for What? The Place of Social Science in American Culture* (Princeton, N.J.: Princeton University Press, 1939), 120.

23. Czitrom, *Media and the American Mind,* 143; and Leo Lowenthal, "Historical Perspectives of Popular Culture," in Bernard Rosenberg and David White, eds., *Mass Culture: The Popular Arts in America* (Glencoe, Ill.: Free Press, 1957), 52.

24. See Stuart Hall et al., *Policing the Crisis: Mugging, the State, and Law and Order* (London: Macmillan, 1978).

25. Horace Newcomb, *TV: The Most Popular Art* (Garden City, N.Y.: Anchor Books, 1974), 19, 23.

26. See Janice Radway, *Reading the Romance: Women, Patriarchy and Popular Literature* (Chapel Hill: University of North Carolina Press, 1984).

27. James Carey, "Mass Communication Research and Cultural Studies: An American View," in James Curran, Michael Gurevitch, and Janet Woollacott, eds., *Mass Communication and Society* (London: Edward Arnold, 1977), 418, 421.

28. Scott Janny, "Postmodern Gravity Deconstructed, Slyly," *New York Times,* May 18, 1996, p. 1. See also The Editors of Lingua Franca, eds., *The Sokal Hoax: The Sham That Shook the Academy* (Lincoln, Neb.: Bison Press, 2000).

◢ **EXAMINING ETHICS** What to Do about Television Violence? p. 473

1. Federal Communications Commission, "Violent Television Programming and Its Impact on Children," April 25, 2007, http://hraunfoss.fcc.gov/edocs_public/attachmatch/FCC-07-50A1.pdf.

◢ **Media Literacy and the Critical Process** Counting Sexual Scenes on TV, p. 479

1. Kaiser Family Foundation, *Sex on TV 4* (Menlo Park, Calif.: Henry C. Kaiser Family Foundation, 2005).

◢ **CASE STUDY** Labor Gets Framed, p. 485

1. Christopher Martin, *Framed! Labor and the Corporate Media* (Ithaca, N.Y.: Cornell University Press, 2003).

2. Richard B. Freeman and Joel Rogers, *What Workers Want* (Ithaca, N.Y.: Cornell University Press, 1999).

16 Legal Controls and Freedom of Expression

1. DJ Drama, "The History and Legality of Mix Tapes," *News & Notes,* NPR, June 15, 2007.

2. Kelefa Sanneh, "With Arrest of DJ Drama, the Law Takes Aim at Mixtapes," *New York Times,* January 18, 2007, http://www.nytimes.com/2007/01/18/arts/music/18dram.html.

3. Kembrew McLeod, *Freedom of Expression®: Overzealous Copyright Bozos and Other Enemies of Creativity* (New York: Doubleday, 2005), 67-68.

4. Ibid.

5. Michael D. Ayers, "White Noise: Girl Talk," *Billboard,* June 14, 2008.

6. Committee to Protect Journalists, "Journalists Killed: Statistics and Backgrounds January 1, 1992-June 30, 2008," http://www.cpj.org/deadly/index.html (accessed July 10, 2008).

7. Fred Siebert, Theodore Peterson, and Wilbur Schramm, *Four Theories of the Press* (Urbana: University of Illinois Press, 1956).

8. See Douglas M. Fraleigh and Joseph S. Tuman, *Freedom of Speech in the Marketplace of Ideas* (New York: St. Martin's Press, 1997), 71-73.

9. Michael Schudson, *The Good Citizen: A History of American Civic Life* (Cambridge: Harvard University Press, 1998), 77.

10. See Fraleigh and Tuman, *Freedom of Speech,* 125.

11. Hugo Black, quoted in "New York Times Company v. U.S.: 1971," in Edward W. Knappman, ed., *Great American Trials: From Salem Witchcraft to Rodney King* (Detroit: Visible Ink Press, 1994), 609.

12. Robert Warren, quoted in "U.S. v. The Progressive: 1979," in Knappman, ed., *Great American Trials,* 684.

13. See Eric Alterman, "The Liberal Media: The *Times* Is Us," *Nation,* July 31/August 7, 2006.

14. Lawrence Lessig, "Opening Plenary–Media at a Critical Juncture: Politics, Technology and Culture," National Conference on Media Reform, Minneapolis, Minnesota, June 7, 2008, http://www.freepress.net/conference/video.

15. See Knappman, ed., *Great American Trials,* 517-19.

16. Ibid., 741-43.

17. Douglas Gomery, *Movie History: A Survey* (Belmont, Calif.: Wadsworth, 1991), 57.

18. See Eric Barnouw, *Tube of Plenty: The Evolution of American Television,* rev. ed. (New York: Oxford University Press, 1982), 118-30.

19. See "Dummy and Dame Arouse the Nation," *Broadcasting-Telecasting,* October 15, 1956, p. 258; and Lawrence Lichty and Malachi Topping, *American Broadcasting: A Source Book on the History of Radio and Television* (New York: Hastings House, 1975), 530.

20. Dean Burch, quoted in Peter Fornatale and Joshua Mills, *Radio in the Television Age* (Woodstock, N.Y.: Overlook Press, 1980), 85.

21. Human Rights Watch, "Become a Blogger for Human Rights," http://hrw.org/blogs.htm (accessed June 17, 2008).

22. Bill Kovach, "Big Deals, with Journalism Thrown In," *New York Times,* August 3, 1995, p. A17.

23. Herbert J. Gans, *Democracy and the News* (Oxford: Oxford University Press, 2003).

Glossary

A&R (artist & repertoire) agents talent scouts of the music business who discover, develop, and sometimes manage performers.

access channels in cable television, a tier of nonbroadcast channels dedicated to local education, government, and the public.

account executives in advertising, client liaisons responsible for bringing in new business and managing the accounts of established clients.

account reviews in advertising, the process of evaluating or reinvigorating an ad campaign, which results in either renewing the contract with the original ad agency or hiring a new agency.

acquisitions editors in the book industry, editors who seek out and sign authors to contracts.

actual malice in libel law, a reckless disregard for the truth, such as when a reporter or an editor knows that a statement is false and prints or airs it anyway.

adult contemporary (AC) one of the oldest and most popular radio music formats, typically featuring a mix of news, talk, oldies, and soft rock.

affiliate station radio or TV station that, though independently owned, signs a contract to be part of a network and receives money to carry the network's programs; in exchange, the network reserves time slots, which it sells to national advertisers.

agenda-setting a media-research argument that says that when the mass media pay attention to particular events or issues, they determine–that is, set the agenda for–the major topics of discussion for individuals and society.

album-oriented rock (AOR) the radio music format that features album cuts from mainstream rock bands.

alternative rock nonmainstream rock music, which includes many types of experimental music and some forms of punk and grunge.

AM amplitude modulation; a type of radio and sound transmission that stresses the volume or height of radio waves.

analog in television, broadcast signals made of radio waves used before 2009.

analog recording a recording that is made by capturing the fluctuations of the original sound waves and storing those signals on records or cassettes as a continuous stream of magnetism–analogous to the actual sound.

analysis the second step in the critical process, it involves discovering significant patterns that emerge from the description stage.

anthology drama a popular form of early TV programming that brought live dramatic theater to television; influenced by stage plays, anthologies offered new teleplays, casts, directors, writers, and sets from week to week.

ARPAnet the original Internet, designed by the U.S. Defense Department's Advanced Research Projects Agency (ARPA).

association principle in advertising, a persuasive technique that associates a product with some cultural value or image that has a positive connotation but may have little connection to the actual product.

astroturf lobbying phony grassroots public affairs campaigns engineered by public relations firms; coined by U.S. Senator Lloyd Bentsen of Texas (named after AstroTurf, the artificial grass athletic field surface).

audience studies cultural studies research that focuses on how people use and interpret cultural content. Also known as reader-response research.

audiotape lightweight magnetized strands of ribbon that make possible sound editing and multiple-track mixing; instrumentals or vocals can be recorded at one location and later mixed onto a master recording in another studio.

authoritarian model a model for journalism and speech that tolerates little criticism of government or public dissent; it holds that the general public needs guidance from an elite and educated ruling class.

avatar an identity created by an Internet user in order to participate in a form of online entertainment, such as *World of Warcraft* or *Second Life*.

bandwagon effect an advertising strategy that incorporates exaggerated claims that everyone is using a particular product, so you should, too.

basic cable in cable programming, a tier of channels composed of local broadcast signals, nonbroadcast access channels (for local government, education, and general public use), a few regional PBS stations, and a variety of popular channels downlinked from communication satellites.

Big Five/Little Three from the late 1920s through the late 1940s, the major movie studios that were vertically integrated and that dominated the industry. The Big Five were Paramount, MGM, Warner Brothers, Twentieth Century Fox, and RKO. The Little Three were those studios that did not own theaters: Columbia, Universal, and United Artists.

Big Six the six major Hollywood studios that currently rule the commercial film business: Warner Brothers, Paramount, Twentieth Century Fox, Universal, Columbia Pictures, and Disney.

block booking an early tactic of movie studios to control exhibition involving pressuring theater operators to accept marginal films with no stars in order to get access to films with the most popular stars.

blockbuster the type of big-budget special effects films that typically have summer or holiday release dates, heavy promotion, and lucrative merchandising tie-ins.

block printing a printing technique developed by early Chinese printers, who hand-carved characters and illustrations into a block of wood, applied ink to the block, and then printed copies on multiple sheets of paper.

bloggers individuals who post or publish an ongoing personal or opinion journal or log online.

blogs sites that contain articles in chronological journal-like form, often with reader comments and links to other articles on the Web (from the term *Web log*).

blues originally a kind of black folk music, this music emerged as a distinct category in the early 1900s; it was influenced by African American spirituals, ballads, and work songs in the rural South, and by urban guitar and vocal solos from the 1930s and 1940s.

book challenge a formal complaint to have a book removed from a public or school library's collection.

bootlegging the illegal counterfeiting or pirating of CDs, cassettes, and videos that are produced and/or sold without official permission from the original songwriter, performer, or copyright holder.

boutique agencies in advertising, small regional ad agencies that offer personalized services.

broadband data transmission over a fiber-optic cable—a signaling method that handles a wide range of frequencies.

broadcasting the transmission of radio waves or TV signals to a broad public audience.

browsers information-search services, such as Netscape's Navigator and Microsoft's Internet Explorer, that offer detailed organizational maps to the Internet.

CATV (community antenna television) an early cable system that originated where mountains or tall buildings blocked TV signals; because of early technical and regulatory limits, CATV contained only twelve channels.

celluloid a transparent and pliable film that can hold a coating of chemicals sensitive to light.

chapter show in television production, any situation comedy or dramatic program whose narrative structure includes self-contained stories that feature a problem, a series of conflicts, and a resolution from week to week (for contrast, see **serial programs** and **episodic series**).

cinema verité French term for *truth film,* a documentary style that records fragments of everyday life unobtrusively; it often features a rough, grainy look and shaky, handheld camera work.

citizen journalism a grassroots movement wherein activist amateurs and concerned citizens, not professional journalists, use the Internet and blogs to disseminate news and information.

codex an early type of book in which paperlike sheets were cut and sewed together along the edge, then bound with thin pieces of wood and covered with leather.

commercial speech any print or broadcast expression for which a fee is charged to the organization or individual buying time or space in the mass media.

common carriers a communication or transportation business, such as a phone company or a taxi service, that is required by law to offer service on a first-come, first-served basis to whoever can pay the rate; such companies do not get involved in content.

communication the process of creating symbol systems that convey information and meaning (for example, language, Morse code, film, and computer codes).

communist or state model a model for journalism and speech that places control in the hands of an enlightened government, which speaks for ordinary citizens and workers in order to serve the common goals of the state.

compact discs (CDs) playback-only storage discs for music that incorporate pure and very precise digital techniques, thus eliminating noise during recording and editing sessions.

conflict of interest considered unethical, a compromising situation in which a journalist stands to benefit personally from the news report he or she produces.

conflict-oriented journalism found in metropolitan areas, newspapers that define news primarily as events, issues, or experiences that deviate from social norms; journalists see their role as observers who monitor their city's institutions and problems.

consensus narratives cultural products that become popular and command wide attention, providing shared cultural experiences.

consensus-oriented journalism found in small communities, newspapers that promote social and economic harmony by providing community calendars and meeting notices and carrying articles on local schools, social events, town government, property crimes, and zoning issues.

contemporary hit radio (CHR) originally called Top 40 radio, this radio format encompasses everything from hip-hop to children's songs; it remains the most popular format in radio for people ages eighteen to twenty-four.

content analysis in social science research, a method for studying and coding media texts and programs.

cookies information profiles about a user that are usually automatically accepted by the Web browser and stored on the user's own computer hard drive.

copy editors the people in magazine, newspaper, and book publishing who attend to specific problems in writing such as style, content, and length.

copyright the legal right of authors and producers to own and control the use of their published or unpublished writing, music, and lyrics; TV programs and movies; or graphic art designs.

Corporation for Public Broadcasting (CPB) a private, nonprofit corporation created by Congress in 1967 to funnel federal funds to nonprofit radio and public television.

correlation an observed association between two variables.

counterfeiting the unauthorized copying of CDs, cassettes, and their packaging.

country claiming the largest number of radio stations in the United States, this radio format includes such subdivisions as old-time, progressive, country-rock, western swing, and country-gospel.

cover music songs recorded or performed by musicians who did not originally write or perform the music; in the 1950s, cover music was an attempt by white producers and artists to capitalize on popular songs by blacks.

critical process the process whereby a media-literate person or student studying mass communication forms and practices employs the techniques of description, analysis, interpretation, evaluation, and engagement.

cross platform what media marketers often call convergence; a particular business model that involves a consolidation of various media holdings–such as cable connection, phone service, television transmission, and Internet access–under one corporate umbrella.

cultivation effect in media research, the idea that heavy television viewing leads individuals to perceive reality in ways that are consistent with the portrayals they see on television.

cultural imperialism the phenomenon of American media, fashion, and food dominating the global market and shaping the cultures and identities of other nations.

cultural studies in media research, the approaches that try to understand how the media and culture are tied to the actual patterns of communication used in daily life; these studies focus on how people make meanings, apprehend reality, and order experience through the use of stories and symbols.

culture the symbols of expression that individuals, groups, and societies use to make sense of daily life and to articulate their values; a process that delivers the values of a society through products or other meaning-making forms.

deficit financing in television, the process whereby a TV production company leases its programs to a network for a license fee that is actually less than the cost of production; the company hopes to recoup this loss later in rerun syndication.

demographic editions national magazines whose advertising is tailored to subscribers and readers according to occupation, class, and zip-code address.

demographics in market research, the study of audiences or consumers by age, gender, occupation, ethnicity, education, and income.

description the first step in the critical process, it involves paying close attention, taking notes, and researching the cultural product to be studied.

design managers publishing industry personnel who work on the look of a book, making decisions about type style, paper, cover design, and layout.

desktop publishing a computer technology that enables an aspiring publisher/editor to inexpensively write, design, lay out, and even print a small newsletter or magazine.

developmental editor in book publishing, the editor who provides authors with feedback, makes suggestions for improvements, and obtains advice from knowledgeable members of the academic community.

digital in television, signals that are transmitted as binary code.

digital communication images, texts, and sounds that use pulses of electric current or flashes of laser lights and are converted (or encoded) into electronic signals represented as varied combinations of binary numbers, usually ones and zeros; these signals are then reassembled (decoded) as a precise reproduction of a TV picture, a magazine article, or a telephone voice.

digital divide the socioeconomic disparity between those who do and those who do not have access to digital technology and media, such as the Internet.

digital recording music recorded and played back by laser beam rather than by needle or magnetic tape.

digital video the production format that is replacing celluloid film and revolutionizing filmmaking because the cameras are more portable and production costs are much less expensive.

dime novels sometimes identified as pulp fiction, these cheaply produced and low-priced novels were popular in the United States beginning in the 1860s.

direct broadcast satellite (DBS) a satellite-based service that for a monthly fee downlinks hundreds of satellite channels and services; they began distributing video programming directly to households in 1994.

directories review and cataloguing services that group Web sites under particular categories (e.g., Arts & Humanities, News & Media, Entertainment).

direct payment in media economics, the payment of money, primarily by consumers, for a book, a music CD, a movie, an online computer service, or a cable TV subscription.

documentary a movie or TV news genre that documents reality by recording actual characters and settings.

domestic comedy a TV hybrid of the sitcom in which characters and settings are usually more important than complicated situations; it generally features a domestic problem or work issue that characters have to solve.

drive time in radio programming, the periods between 6 and 10 A.M. and 4 and 7 P.M., when people are commuting to and from work or school; these periods constitute the largest listening audiences of the day.

DVR (digital video recorder) a device that enables users to find and record specific television shows (and movies) and store them in a computer memory to be played back at a later time or recorded onto a DVD.

e-books digital books read on a computer or electronic reading device.

e-commerce electronic commerce, or commercial activity, on the Web.

economies of scale the economic process of increasing production levels so as to reduce the overall cost per unit.

electromagnetic waves invisible electronic impulses similar to visible light; electricity, magnetism, light, broadcast signals, and heat are part of such waves, which radiate in space at the speed of light, about 186,000 miles per second.

electronic publishers communication businesses, such as broadcasters or cable TV companies, that are entitled to choose what channels or content to carry.

e-mail electronic mail messages sent by the Internet; developed by computer engineer Ray Tomlinson in 1971.

engagement to actively work to create a media world that best serves democracy.

episodic series a narrative form well suited to television because main characters appear every week, sets and locales remain the same, and technical crews stay with the program; episodic series feature new adventures each week, but a handful of characters emerge with whom viewers can regularly identify (for contrast, see **chapter shows**).

e-publishing Internet-based publishing houses that design and distribute books for comparatively low prices for authors who want to self-publish a title.

ethnocentrism an underlying value held by many U.S. journalists and citizens, it involves judging other countries and cultures according to how they live up to or imitate American practices and ideals.

evaluation the fourth step in the critical process, it involves arriving at a judgment about whether a cultural product is good, bad, or mediocre; this requires subordinating one's personal taste to the critical assessment resulting from the first three stages (description, analysis, and interpretation).

evergreens in TV syndication, popular, lucrative, and enduring network reruns, such as the *Andy Griffith Show* or *I Love Lucy*.

evergreen subscriptions magazine subscriptions that automatically renew on the subscriber's credit card.

experiments in regard to the mass media, research that isolates some aspect of content, suggests a hypothesis, and manipulates variables to discover a particular medium's impact on attitudes, emotions, or behavior.

Fairness Doctrine repealed in 1987, this FCC rule required broadcast stations to both air and engage in controversial-issue programs that affected their communities and, when offering such programming, to provide competing points of view.

famous-person testimonial an advertising strategy that associates a product with the endorsement of a well-known person.

feature syndicates commercial outlets or brokers, such as United Features and King Features, that contract with newspapers to provide work from well-known political writers, editorial cartoonists, comic-strip artists, and self-help columnists.

Federal Communications Act of 1934 the far-reaching act that established the FCC and the federal regulatory structure for U.S. broadcasting.

Federal Communications Commission (FCC) an independent U.S. government agency charged with regulating interstate and international communications by radio, television, wire, satellite, and cable.

Federal Radio Commission (FRC) established in 1927 to oversee radio licenses and negotiate channel problems.

feedback responses from receivers to the senders of messages.

fiber-optic cable thin glass bundles of fiber capable of transmitting thousands of messages converted to shooting pulses of light along cable wires; these bundles of fiber can carry broadcast channels, telephone signals, and all sorts of digital codes.

fin-syn (Financial Interest and Syndication Rules) FCC rules that prohibited the major networks from running their own syndication companies or from charging production companies additional fees after shows had completed their prime-time runs; most fin-syn rules were rescinded in the mid-1990s.

first-run syndication in television, the process whereby new programs are specifically produced for sale in syndication markets rather than for network television.

flack a derogatory term that journalists use to refer to a public relations agent.

FM frequency modulation; a type of radio and sound transmission that offers static-less reception and greater fidelity and clarity than AM radio by accentuating the pitch or distance between radio waves.

focus groups a common research method in psychographic analysis in which moderators lead small-group discussions about a product or an issue, usually with six to twelve people.

folk music music performed by untrained musicians and passed down through oral traditions; it encompasses a wide range of music, from Appalachian fiddle tunes to the accordion-led zydeco of Louisiana.

folk-rock amplified folk music, often featuring politically overt lyrics; influenced by rock and roll.

format radio the concept of radio stations developing and playing specific styles (or formats) geared to listeners' age, race, or gender; in format radio, management, rather than deejays, controls programming choices.

Fourth Estate the notion that the press operates as an unofficial branch of government, monitoring the legislative, judicial, and executive branches for abuses of power.

fringe time in television, the time slot either immediately before the evening's prime-time schedule (called *early fringe*) or immediately following the local evening news or the network's late-night talk shows (called *late fringe*).

gag orders legal restrictions prohibiting the press from releasing preliminary information that might prejudice jury selection.

gangster rap a style of rap music that depicts the hardships of urban life and sometimes glorifies the violent style of street gangs.

gatekeepers editors, producers, and other media managers who function as message filters, making decisions about what types of messages actually get produced for particular audiences.

general-interest magazines types of magazines that address a wide variety of topics and are aimed at a broad national audience.

genre a narrative category in which conventions regarding similar characters, scenes, structures, and themes recur in combination.

geosynchronous orbit the orbit in space, 22,300 miles above the earth, where communication satellites traveling at about 6,800 miles per hour can maintain the same position (or "footprint") above the earth as the planet rotates on its axis.

grunge rock music that takes the spirit of punk and infuses it with more attention to melody.

HD radio a digital technology that enables AM and FM radio broadcasters to multicast two to three additional compressed digital signals within their traditional analog frequency.

headend a cable TV system's computerized nerve center, where TV signals from local broadcast stations and satellites are received, processed, and distributed to area homes.

hegemony the acceptance of the dominant values in a culture by those who are subordinate to those who hold economic and political power.

herd journalism a situation in which reporters stake out a house or follow a story in such large groups that the entire profession comes under attack for invading people's privacy or exploiting their personal tragedies.

hidden-fear appeal an advertising strategy that plays on a sense of insecurity, trying to persuade consumers that only a specific product can offer relief.

high culture a symbolic expression that has come to mean "good taste"; often supported by wealthy patrons and corporate donors, it is associated with fine art (such as ballet, the symphony, painting, and classical literature), which is available primarily in theaters or museums.

high-definition a new digital standard for U.S. television sets that has more than twice the resolution of the system that served as the standard from the 1940s through the 1990s.

hip-hop music music that combines spoken street dialect with cuts (or samples) from older records and bears the influences of social politics, male boasting, and comic lyrics carried forward from blues, R&B, soul, and rock and roll.

Hollywood Ten the nine screenwriters and one film director subpoenaed by the House Un-American Activities Committee (HUAC) who were sent to prison in the late 1940s for refusing to discuss their memberships or to identify communist sympathizers.

HTML (HyperText Markup Language) the written code that creates Web pages and links; a language all computers can read.

human-interest stories news accounts that focus on the trials and tribulations of the human condition, often featuring ordinary individuals facing extraordinary challenges.

hypodermic-needle model an early model in mass communication research that attempted to explain media effects by arguing that the media shoot their powerful effects directly into unsuspecting or weak audiences; sometimes called the *bullet theory* or *direct effects model*.

hypotheses in social science research, tentative general statements that predict a relationship between a dependent variable and an independent variable.

illuminated manuscripts books from the Middle Ages that featured decorative, colorful designs and illustrations on each page.

indecency the government may punish broadcasters for indecency or profanity after the fact, and over the years a handful of radio stations have had their licenses suspended or denied over indecent programming.

independent station a TV station, such as WGN in Chicago or WTBS in Atlanta, that finds its own original and syndicated programming and is not affiliated with any of the major networks.

indies independent music and film production houses that work outside industry oligopolies; they often produce less mainstream music and film.

indirect payment in media economics, the financial support of media products by advertisers, who pay for the quantity or quality of audience members that a particular medium attracts.

individualism an underlying value held by most U.S. journalists and citizens, it favors individual rights and responsibilities over group needs or institutional mandates.

infotainment a type of television program that packages human-interest and celebrity stories in TV news style.

instant book in the book industry, a marketing strategy that involves publishing a topical book quickly after a major event occurs.

instant messaging a Web feature that enables users to chat with buddies in real time via pop-up windows assigned to each conversation.

Internet the vast central network of high-speed telephone lines designed to link and carry computer information worldwide.

Internet radio online radio stations that either "stream" simulcast versions of on-air radio broadcasts over the Web or are created exclusively for the Internet.

Internet service provider (ISP) a company that provides Internet access to homes and businesses for a fee.

interpretation the third step in the critical process, it asks and answers the "What does that mean?" and "So what?" questions about one's findings.

interpretive journalism a type of journalism that involves analyzing and explaining key issues or events and placing them in a broader historical or social context.

interstitials advertisements that pop up in a new screen window as a user attempts to access a new Web page.

inverted-pyramid style a style of journalism in which news reports begin with the most dramatic or newsworthy information—answering *who, what, where,* and *when* (and less frequently *why* or *how*) questions at the top of the story—and then tail off with less significant details.

irritation advertising an advertising strategy that tries to create product-name recognition by being annoying or obnoxious.

jazz an improvisational and mostly instrumental musical form that absorbs and integrates a diverse body of musical styles, including African rhythms, blues, big band, and gospel.

joint operating agreement (JOA) in the newspaper industry, an economic arrangement, sanctioned by the government, that permits competing newspapers to operate separate editorial divisions while merging business and production operations.

kinescope before the days of videotape, a 1950s technique for preserving television broadcasts by using a film camera to record a live TV show off a studio monitor.

kinetograph an early movie camera developed by Thomas Edison's assistant in the 1890s.

kinetoscope an early film projection system that served as a kind of peep show in which viewers looked through a hole and saw images moving on a tiny plate.

leased channels in cable television, channels that allow citizens to buy time for producing programs or presenting their own viewpoints.

libel in media law, the defamation of character in written expression.

libertarian model a model for journalism and speech that encourages vigorous government criticism and supports the highest degree of freedom for individual speech and news operations.

limited competition in media economics, a market with many producers and sellers but only a few differentiable products within a particular category; sometimes called *monopolistic competition.*

linotype a technology introduced in the nineteenth century that enabled printers to set type mechanically using a typewriter-style keyboard.

literary journalism news reports that adapt fictional storytelling techniques to nonfictional material; sometimes called *new journalism.*

lobbying in government public relations, the process of attempting to influence the voting of lawmakers to support a client's or an organization's best interests.

longitudinal studies a term used for research studies that are conducted over long periods of time and often rely on large government and academic survey databases.

low culture a symbolic expression allegedly aligned with the questionable tastes of the "masses," who enjoy the commercial "junk" circulated by the mass media, such as soap operas, rock music, talk radio, comic books, and monster truck pulls.

low-power FM (LPFM) a new class of noncommercial radio stations approved by the FCC in 2000 to give voice to local groups lacking access to the public airwaves; the 10-watt and 100-watt stations broadcast to a small, community-based area.

magalogs a combination of a glossy magazine and retail catalog that is often used to market goods or services to customers or employees.

magazine a nondaily periodical that comprises a collection of articles, stories, and ads.

manuscript culture a period during the Middle Ages when priests and monks advanced the art of bookmaking.

market research in advertising and public relations agencies, the department that uses social science techniques to assess the behaviors and attitudes of consumers toward particular products before any ads are created.

mass communication the process of designing and delivering cultural messages and stories to diverse audiences through media channels as old as the book and as new as the Internet.

mass customization the process whereby product companies and content providers customize a Web page, print ad, or other media form for an individual consumer.

mass market paperbacks low-priced paperback books sold mostly on racks in drugstores, supermarkets, and airports, as well as in bookstores.

mass media the cultural industries—the channels of communication—that produce and distribute songs, novels, news, movies, online computer services, and other cultural products to a large number of people.

mass media channel newspapers, books, magazines, radio, television, or the Internet.

media buyers in advertising, the individuals who choose and purchase the types of media that are best suited to carry a client's ads and reach the targeted audience.

media convergence the process whereby old and new media are available via the integration of personal computers and high-speed satellite-based phone or cable links.

media effects research the mainstream tradition in mass communication research, it attempts to understand, explain, and predict the impact—or effects—of the mass media on individuals and society.

media literacy an understanding of the mass communication process through the development of critical-thinking tools—description, analysis, interpretation, evaluation, engagement—that enable a person to become more engaged as a citizen and more discerning as a consumer of mass media products.

mega-agencies in advertising, large firms or holding companies that are formed by merging several individual agencies and that maintain worldwide regional offices; they provide both advertising and public relations services and operate in-house radio and TV production studios.

megaplexes movie theater facilities with fourteen or more screens.

messages the texts, images, and sounds transmitted from senders to receivers.

microprocessors miniature circuits that process and store electronic signals, integrating thousands of electronic components into thin strands of silicon along which binary codes travel.

minimal-effects model a mass communication research model based on tightly controlled experiments and survey findings; it argues that the mass media have limited effects on audiences, reinforcing existing behaviors and attitudes rather than changing them.

modern term describing a historical era spanning the time from the rise of the Industrial Revolution in the eighteenth and nineteenth centuries to the present; its social values include celebrating the individual, believing in rational order, working efficiently, and rejecting tradition.

monopoly in media economics, an organizational structure that occurs when a single firm dominates production and distribution in a particular industry, either nationally or locally.

Morse code a system of sending electrical impulses from a transmitter through a cable to a reception point; developed by the American inventor Samuel Morse.

movie palaces ornate, lavish single-screen movie theaters that emerged in the 1910s in the United States.

MP3 short for MPEG-1 Layer 3, an advanced type of audio compression that reduces file size, enabling audio to be easily distributed over the Internet and to be digitally transmitted in real time.

muckrakers reporters who used a style of early-twentieth-century investigative journalism that emphasized a willingness to crawl around in society's muck to uncover a story.

multiple-system operators (MSOs) large corporations that own numerous cable television systems.

multiplexes contemporary movie theaters that exhibit many movies at the same time on multiple screens.

must-carry rules rules established by the FCC requiring all cable operators to assign channels to and carry all local TV broadcasts on their systems, thereby ensuring that local network affiliates, independent stations (those not carrying network programs), and public television channels would benefit from cable's clearer reception.

myth analysis a strategy for critiquing advertising that provides insights into how ads work on a cultural level; according to this strategy, ads are narratives with stories to tell and social conflicts to resolve.

narrative the structure underlying most media products, it includes two components: the story (what happens to whom) and the discourse (how the story is told).

narrative films movies that tell a story, with dramatic action and conflict emerging mainly from individual characters.

narrowcasting any specialized electronic programming or media channel aimed at a target audience.

National Public Radio (NPR) noncommercial radio established in 1967 by the U.S. Congress to provide an alternative to commercial radio.

network a broadcast process that links, through special phone lines or satellite transmissions, groups of radio or TV stations that share programming produced at a central location.

network era the period in television history, roughly from the mid-1950s to the late 1970s, that refers to the dominance of the Big Three networks–ABC, CBS, and NBC–over programming and prime-time viewing habits; the era began eroding with a decline in viewing and with the development of VCRs, cable, and new TV networks.

news the process of gathering information and making narrative reports–edited by individuals in a news organization–that create selected frames of reference and help the public make sense of prominent people, important events, and unusual happenings in everyday life.

newshole the space left over in a newspaper for news content after all the ads are placed.

newspaper chain a large company that owns several papers throughout the country.

newsreels weekly ten-minute magazine-style compilations of filmed news events from around the world organized in a sequence of short reports; prominent in movie theaters between the 1920s and the 1950s.

news/talk format the fastest-growing radio format in the 1990s.

newsworthiness the often unstated criteria that journalists use to determine which events and issues should become news reports, including timeliness, proximity, conflict, prominence, human interest, consequence, usefulness, novelty, and deviance.

nickelodeons the first small makeshift movie theaters, which were often converted cigar stores, pawnshops, or restaurants redecorated to mimic vaudeville theaters.

O & Os TV stations "owned and operated" by networks.

objective journalism a modern style of journalism that distinguishes factual reports from opinion columns; reporters strive to remain neutral toward the issue or event they cover, searching out competing points of view among the sources for a story.

obscenity expression that is not protected as speech if these three legal tests are all met: (1) the average person, applying contemporary community standards, would find that the material as a whole appeals to prurient interest; (2) the material depicts or describes sexual conduct in a patently offensive way; (3) the material, as a whole, lacks serious literary, artistic, political, or scientific value.

off-network syndication in television, the process whereby older programs that no longer run during prime time are made available for reruns to local stations, cable operators, online services, and foreign markets.

offset lithography a technology that enabled books to be printed from photographic plates rather than metal casts, reducing the cost of color and illustrations and eventually permitting computers to perform typesetting.

oligopoly in media economics, an organizational structure in which a few firms control most of an industry's production and distribution resources.

open-source software noncommercial software shared freely and developed collectively on the Internet.

opinion and fair comment a defense against libel which states that libel applies only to intentional misstatements of factual information rather than opinion, and which therefore protects said opinion.

opt-in or **opt-out policies** controversial Web site policies over personal data gathering: *opt in* means Web sites must gain explicit permission from online consumers before the site can collect their personal data; *opt out* means that Web sites can automatically collect personal data unless the consumer goes to the trouble of filling out a specific form to restrict the practice.

option time now considered illegal, a procedure whereby a radio network paid an affiliate station a set fee per hour for an option to control programming and advertising on that station.

Pacifica Foundation a radio broadcasting foundation established in Berkeley, California, by journalist and World War II pacifist Lewis Hill; he established KPFA, the first nonprofit community radio station, in 1949.

paperback books books made with cheap paper covers, introduced in the United States in the mid-1800s.

papyrus one of the first substances to hold written language and symbols; obtained from plant reeds found along the Nile River.

Paramount decision the 1948 Supreme Court decision that ended vertical integration in the film industry by forcing the studios to divest themselves of their theaters.

parchment treated animal skin that replaced papyrus as an early pre-paper substance on which to document written language.

participatory media messages that individuals produce and distribute, allowing them to become producers rather than just consumers of media content; the Internet is particularly conducive to participatory media.

partisan press an early dominant style of American journalism distinguished by opinion newspapers, which generally argued one political point of view or pushed the plan of the particular party that subsidized the paper.

pass-along readership the total number of people who come into contact with a single copy of a magazine.

pay-for-play up-front payments from record companies to radio stations to play a song a specific number of times.

payola the unethical (but not always illegal) practice of record promoters paying deejays or radio programmers to favor particular songs over others.

pay-per-view (PPV) a cable-television service that allows customers to select a particular movie for a fee, or to pay $25 to $40 for a special onetime event.

penny papers (also *penny press*) refers to newspapers that, because of technological innovations in printing, were able to drop their price to one cent beginning in the 1830s, thereby making papers affordable to working and emerging middle classes and enabling newspapers to become a genuine mass medium.

phishing an Internet scam that begins with phony e-mail messages that pretend to be from an official site and request that customers send their credit card numbers and other personal information to update the account.

photojournalism the use of photos to document events and people's lives.

piracy the illegal uploading, downloading, or streaming of copyrighted material, such as music.

plain-folks pitch an advertising strategy that associates a product with simplicity and the common person.

podcasting enables listeners to download audio program files from the Internet for playback on computers or digital music players.

political advertising the use of ad techniques to promote a candidate's image and persuade the public to adopt a particular viewpoint.

political economy studies an area of academic study that specifically examines interconnections among economic interests, political power, and how that power is used.

pop music popular music that appeals either to a wide cross section of the public or to sizable subdivisions within the larger public based on age, region, or ethnic background; the word *pop* has also been used as a label to distinguish popular music from classical music.

populism a political idea that tries to appeal to ordinary people by contrasting "the people" with "the elite."

portal an entry point to the Internet, such as a search engine.

postmodern term describing a contemporary historical era spanning the 1960s to the present; its social values include opposing hierarchy, diversifying and recycling culture, questioning scientific reasoning, and embracing paradox.

premium channels in cable programming, a tier of channels that subscribers can order at an additional monthly fee over their basic cable service; these may include movie channels and interactive services.

press agent the earliest type of public relations practitioner, who sought to advance a client's image through media exposure.

press releases in public relations, announcements–written in the style of news reports–that give new information about an individual, a company, or an organization and pitch a story idea to the news media.

prime time in television programming, the hours between 8 and 11 P.M. (or 7 and 10 P.M. in the Midwest), when networks have traditionally drawn their largest audiences and charged their highest advertising rates.

printing press a fifteenth-century invention whose movable metallic type technology spawned modern mass communication by creating the first method for mass production; it reduced the size and cost of books, made them the first mass medium affordable to less affluent people, and provided the impetus for the Industrial Revolution, assembly-line production, modern capitalism, and the rise of consumer culture.

prior restraint the legal definition of censorship in the United States, which prohibits courts and governments from blocking any publication or speech before it actually occurs.

product placement the advertising practice of strategically placing products in movies, TV shows, comic books, and video games so the products appear as part of a story's set environment.

professional books technical books that target various occupational groups and are not intended for the general consumer market.

Progressive Era a period of political and social reform that lasted from the 1890s to the 1920s.

progressive rock alternative music format that developed as a backlash to the popularity of Top 40.

propaganda in advertising and public relations, a communication strategy that tries to manipulate public opinion to gain support for a special issue, program, or policy, such as a nation's war effort.

propaganda analysis the study of propaganda's effectiveness in influencing and mobilizing public opinion.

pseudo-events in public relations, circumstances or events created solely for the purpose of obtaining coverage in the media.

psychographics in market research, the study of audience or consumer attitudes, beliefs, interests, and motivations.

Public Broadcasting Act of 1967 the act by the U.S. Congress that established the Corporation for Public Broadcasting, which oversees the Public Broadcasting Service (PBS) and National Public Radio (NPR).

Public Broadcasting Service (PBS) the noncommercial television network established in 1967 as an alternative to commercial television.

public domain the end of the copyright period for a work, at which point the public may begin to access it for free.

publicity in public relations, the positive and negative messages that spread controlled and uncontrolled information about a person, a corporation, an issue, or a policy in various media.

public journalism a type of journalism, driven by citizen forums, that goes beyond telling the news to embrace a broader mission of improving the quality of public life; also called *civic journalism*.

public relations the total communication strategy conducted by a person, a government, or an organization attempting to reach and persuade its audiences to adopt a point of view.

public service announcements (PSAs) reports or announcements, carried free by radio and TV stations, that promote government programs, educational projects, voluntary agencies, or social reform.

pulp fiction a term used to describe many late-nineteenth-century popular paperbacks and dime novels, which were constructed of cheap machine-made pulp material.

punk rock rock music that challenges the orthodoxy and commercialism of the recording business; it is characterized by loud, unpolished qualities, a jackhammer beat, primal vocal screams, crude aggression, and defiant or comic lyrics.

qualified privilege a legal right allowing journalists to report judicial or legislative proceedings even though the public statements being reported may be libelous.

Radio Act of 1912 the first radio legislation passed by Congress, it addressed the problem of amateur radio operators increasingly cramming the airwaves.

Radio Act of 1927 the second radio legislation passed by Congress; in an attempt to restore order to the airwaves, it stated that licensees did not own their channels but could license them as long as they operated in order to serve the "public interest, convenience, or necessity."

Radio Corporation of America (RCA) a company developed during World War I that was designed, with government approval, to pool radio patents; the formation of RCA gave the United States almost total control over the emerging mass medium of broadcasting.

radio waves a portion of the electromagnetic wave spectrum that was harnessed so that signals could be sent from a transmission point and obtained at a reception point.

random assignment a social science research method for assigning research subjects; it ensures that every subject has an equal chance of being placed in either the experimental group or the control group.

rating in TV audience measurement, a statistical estimate expressed as a percentage of households tuned to a program in the local or national market being sampled.

receivers the target of messages crafted by a sender.

reference books dictionaries, encyclopedias, atlases, and other reference manuals related to particular professions or trades.

regional editions national magazines whose content is tailored to the interests of different geographic areas.

rerun syndication in television, the process whereby programs that stay in a network's lineup long enough to build up a certain number of episodes (usually four seasons' worth) are sold, or syndicated, to hundreds of TV markets in the United States and abroad.

responsible capitalism an underlying value held by many U.S. journalists and citizens, it assumes that businesspeople compete with one another not primarily to maximize profits but to increase prosperity for all.

rhythm and blues (or **R&B)** music that merged urban blues with big-band sounds.

right to privacy addresses a person's right to be left alone, without his or her name, image, or daily activities becoming public property.

rockabilly music that mixed bluegrass and country influences with those of black folk music and early amplified blues.

rock and roll music that mixed the vocal and instrumental traditions of popular music; it merged the black influences of urban blues, gospel, and R&B with the white influences of country, folk, and pop vocals.

rotation in format radio programming, the practice of playing the most popular or best-selling songs many times throughout the day.

satellite radio pay radio services that deliver various radio formats nationally via satellite.

saturation advertising the strategy of inundating a variety of print and visual media with ads aimed at target audiences.

scientific method a widely used research method that studies phenomena in systematic stages; it includes identifying the research problem, reviewing existing research, developing working hypotheses, determining appropriate research design, collecting information, analyzing results to see if the hypotheses have been verified, and interpreting the implications of the study.

search engines computer programs that allow users to enter key words or queries to find related sites on the Internet.

Section 315 part of the 1934 Communications Act; it mandates that during elections, broadcast stations must provide equal opportunities and response time for qualified political candidates.

selective exposure the phenomenon whereby audiences seek messages and meanings that correspond to their preexisting beliefs and values.

selective retention the phenomenon whereby audiences remember or retain messages and meanings that correspond to their preexisting beliefs and values.

senders the authors, producers, agencies, and organizations that transmit messages to receivers.

serial program a radio or TV program, such as a soap opera, that features continuing story lines from day to day or week to week (for contrast, see **chapter shows**).

share in TV audience measurement, a statistical estimate of the percentage of homes tuned to a certain program, compared with those simply using their sets at the time of a sample.

shield laws laws protecting the confidentiality of key interview subjects and reporters' rights not to reveal the sources of controversial information used in news stories.

situation comedy a type of comedy series that features a recurring cast and set as well as several narrative scenes; each episode establishes a situation, complicates it, develops increasing confusion among its characters, and then resolves the complications.

sketch comedy short television comedy skits that are usually segments of TV variety shows; sometimes known as *vaudeo*, the marriage of vaudeville and video.

slander in law, spoken language that defames a person's character.

slogan in advertising, a catchy phrase that attempts to promote or sell a product by capturing its essence in words.

small-town pastoralism an underlying value held by many U.S. journalists and citizens, it favors the small over the large and the rural over the urban.

snob-appeal approach an advertising strategy that attempts to convince consumers that using a product will enable them to maintain or elevate their social station.

social learning theory a theory within media effects research that suggests a link between the mass media and behavior.

social networking Internet Web sites that allow users to create personal profiles, upload photos, create lists of favorite things, and post messages to connect with old friends and to meet new ones.

social responsibility model a model for journalism and speech, influenced by the libertarian model, that encourages the free flow of information to citizens so they can make wise decisions regarding political and social issues.

soul music that mixes gospel, blues, and urban and southern black styles with slower, more emotional, and melancholic lyrics.

sound bite in TV journalism, the equivalent of a quote in print; the part of a news report in which an expert, a celebrity, a victim, or a person on the street is interviewed about some aspect of an event or issue.

space brokers in the days before modern advertising, individuals who purchased space in newspapers and sold it to various merchants.

spam a computer term referring to unsolicited e-mail.

spiral of silence a theory that links the mass media, social psychology, and the formation of public opinion; it proposes that people who find their views on controversial issues in the minority tend to keep these views silent.

split-run editions editions of national magazines that tailor ads to different geographic areas.

spyware software with secretive codes that enable commercial firms to "spy" on users and gain access to their computers.

stereo the recording of two separate channels or tracks of sound.

storyboard in advertising, a blueprint or roughly drawn comic-strip version of a proposed advertisement.

stripped [syndicated rerun] in TV syndication, the showing of programs–either older network reruns or programs made for syndication–five days a week.

studio system an early film production system that constituted a sort of assembly-line process for moviemaking; major film studios controlled not only actors but also directors, editors, writers, and other employees, all of whom worked under exclusive contracts.

subliminal advertising a 1950s term that refers to hidden or disguised print and visual messages that allegedly register on the unconscious, creating false needs and seducing people into buying products.

subsidiary rights in the book industry, selling the rights to a book for use in other media forms, such as a mass market paperback, a CD-ROM, or the basis for a movie screenplay.

supermarket tabloids newspapers that feature bizarre human-interest stories, gruesome murder tales, violent accident accounts, unexplained phenomena stories, and malicious celebrity gossip.

superstations local independent TV stations, such as WTBS in Atlanta or WGN in Chicago, that have uplinked their signals onto a communication satellite to make themselves available nationwide.

survey research in social science research, a method of collecting and measuring data taken from a group of respondents.

synergy in media economics, the promotion and sale of a product (and all its versions) throughout the various subsidiaries of a media conglomerate.

talkies movies with sound, beginning in 1927.

Telecommunications Act of 1996 the sweeping update of telecommunications law that led to a wave of media consolidation.

telegraph invented in the 1840s, it sent electrical impulses through a cable from a transmitter to a reception point, transmitting Morse code.

textbooks books made for the el-hi (elementary and high school) and college markets.

textual analysis in media research, a method for closely and critically examining and interpreting the meanings of culture, including architecture, fashion, books, movies, and TV programs.

time shifting the process whereby television viewers tape shows and watch them later, when it is convenient for them.

Top 40 format the first radio format, in which stations played the forty most popular hits in a given week as measured by record sales.

trade books the most visible book industry segment, featuring hardbound and paperback books aimed at general readers and sold at bookstores and other retail outlets.

transistors invented by Bell Laboratories in 1947, these tiny pieces of technology, which receive and amplify radio signals, make portable radios possible.

transponders the relay points on a communication satellite that receive and transmit telephone and TV signals.

TV newsmagazine a TV news program format, pioneered by CBS's *60 Minutes* in the late 1960s, that features multiple segments in an hour-long episode, usually ranging from a celebrity or political feature story to a hard-hitting investigative report.

underground press radical newspapers, run on shoestring budgets, that question mainstream political policies and conventional values; the term usually refers to a journalism movement of the 1960s.

university press the segment of the book industry that publishes scholarly books in specialized areas.

urban one of radio's more popular formats, primarily targeting African American listeners in urban areas with dance, R&B, and hip-hop music.

uses and gratifications model a mass communication research model, usually employing in-depth interviews and survey questionnaires, that argues that people use the media to satisfy various emotional desires or intellectual needs.

Values and Lifestyles (VALS) a market-research strategy that divides consumers into types and measures psychological factors, including how consumers think and feel about products and how they achieve (or do not achieve) the lifestyles to which they aspire.

vellum a handmade paper made from treated animal skin, used in the Gutenberg Bibles.

vertical integration in media economics, the phenomenon of controlling a mass media industry at its three essential levels: production, distribution, and exhibition; the term is most frequently used in reference to the film industry.

videocassette recorders (VCRs) recorders that use a half-inch video format known as VHS (video home system), which enables viewers to record and play back programs from television or to watch movies rented from video stores.

video news releases (VNRs) in public relations, the visual counterparts to press releases; pitch story ideas to the TV news media by mimicking the style of a broadcast news report.

video-on-demand (VOD) cable television technology that enables viewers to instantly order programming such as movies to be digitally delivered to their sets.

viral marketing short videos or other content which marketers hope will quickly gain widespread attention as users share it with friends online, or by word of mouth.

vitascope a large-screen movie projection system developed by Thomas Edison.

Webzines magazines that publish on the Internet.

Wi-Fi a standard for short-distance wireless networking, enabling users of notebook computers and other devices to connect to the Internet in cafés, hotels, airports, and parks.

wiki Web sites Internet Web sites that are capable of being edited by any user, the most famous of which is Wikipedia.

WiMax a communication technology that provides data over long distances in multiple ways, from traditional cell phone connections to services that link mobile phones to traditional mass media.

wireless telegraphy the forerunner of radio, a form of voiceless point-to-point communication; it preceded the voice and sound transmissions of one-to-many mass communication that became known as broadcasting.

wireless telephony early experiments in wireless voice and music transmissions, which later developed into modern radio.

wire services commercial organizations, such as the Associated Press, that share news stories and information by relaying them around the country and the world, originally via telegraph and now via satellite transmission.

World Wide Web (WWW) a free and open data-linking system for organizing and standardizing information on the Internet; the WWW enables computer-accessed information to associate with–or link to–other information no matter where it is on the Internet.

yellow journalism a newspaper style or era that peaked in the 1890s, it emphasized high-interest stories, sensational crime news, large headlines, and serious reports that exposed corruption, particularly in business and government.

zines self-published magazines produced on personal computer programs or on the Internet.

Credits

Used with permission of Millward Brown Optimor. **365,** "Dynamic and 'Baked-in' Ads Hit Video Games," by Abbey Klaassen. From "Game-ad boom looms as Sony opens up PS3," *Advertising Age,* February 25, 2008, p.1. Reprinted with permission of *Advertising Age,* a Crain Communications Inc. publication. **388,** Figure 12.1: "The Top 6 Holding Firms, with Public Relations Subsidiaries, 2008 (by worldwide revenue in U.S. dollars, revenue in $ billions)," from "Agency Family Tree 2008," Advertising Age, May 5, 2008. http://adage.com/datacenter. Reprinted with permission of *Advertising Age,* a Crain Communications Inc. publication. **400,** Table 12.1: Public Relations Society of America, Member Code of Ethics. Reprinted with permission of The Public Relations Society of America (www.prsa.org). **421,** Makani Themba-Nixon, "Co-Opting Consumers of Color." Reprinted from the July 3, 2006 issue of *The Nation.* For subscription information, call 1-800-333-8536. Portion of each week's *Nation* magazine can be accessed at http://www.thenation.com. Used with permission. **426,** "Top 10 U.S. Media Companies, 1981, 1997, 2007" from Ad Age's 100 Leading Media Companies Report, published Dec. 7, 1981; *Advertising Age,* 100 companies by media revenue, Aug. 18, 1997; *Advertising Age,* 100 leading media companies, Oct. 2007. Reprinted with permission of *Advertising Age,* a Crain Communications Inc. publication. **442,** Is There a Bias in Reporting of News? From http://www.harrisinteractive.com/harris_poll. The Harris Poll ® #52, June 30, 2006. Reprinted with permission. **444,** Figure 14.1: "Code of Ethics," Society of Professional Journalists, www.spj.org. Copyright © 2006 by the Society of Professional Journalists. Reprinted with permission. **457,** "Falling Short: Olympic Promises Go Unfulfilled As China Falters on Press Freedoms," Chapter 5, "Censorship at Work: The Newsroom in China." Posted June 5, 2008. Used with permission of the Committee to Protect Journalists. http://cpj.org/Briefings/2007/Falling_Short/China/5_2.html. **503,** John Siegenthaler, excerpt from "A False Wikipedia 'Biography.'" First published in *USA TODAY,* November 30, 2006, p. 11A. Used with permission of John Siegenthaler. **509,** Gene Policinski, "Cartoons, T-shirts and more: why we must protect what offends," First Amendment Center, May 18, 2008. Reprinted with permission of the author. http://www.firstamendmentcenter.org/commentary.aspx?id=20058.

Photo Credits

Key: AP-WW = Associated Press/Wide World Photos, CO = Corbis Pictures, CO-BA = Corbis/Bettmann Archive, CO-SY = Corbis/Sygma, GI = Getty Images, PF = Photofest.

"Praise" Spread CO-BA; **xv,** AP-WW/Carolyn McGoldrick; **xvi,** Jose Luis Pelaez/Blend/Robertstock; **xvii,** AP-WW/Steve Parsons; **xviii,** AP-WW/Lawrence Jackson; **xix,** NBC/PF; **xx,** Scott Gries/GI for MTV Networks; **xxi,** Lucasfilm Ltd./Twentieth Century Fox Film Corp./PF; **xxii,** AP-WW/Ted S. Warren; **xxiii,** Santi Visalli/GI; **xxiv,** Marcus Brandt/AFP/GI; **xxv,** AP-WW/Paul Sakuma; **xxvi,** Columbia Pictures/PF; **xxvii,** William West/AFP/GI; **Media Ownership Insert** (from l. to r.), FAMOUS-ACE PICTURES.Ace Pictures, Inc./Newscom, © Atlantide Phototravel/CO, © 20th Century Fox Film Corp. All rights reserved, Courtesy Everett Collection, Lluis Gene/AFP/GI/Newscom, Courtesy of hulu.com. Reprinted by permission, Scott Gries/GI; **Timeline Insert,** (from l. to r.) CO-BA, NYPL, NYPL, CO-BA, CO, CO-

BA, CO-BA, PF, Shannon Stapleton/Reuters-CO, Franck Robichon/epa/CO, Courtesy of Apple, Inc.; **2–3,** AP-WW/Carolyn McGoldrick; **6,** GI; **7,** Bibliotetheque Nationale, Paris/Scala-Art Resource; **9,** (l.) The Art Archive / Culver Pictures; (r.) Kimberly White/Landov; **11,** CO-BA; **14,** Greg Whitesell/Reuters-CO; **18,** (l.) PF; (cent.) PF; (r.) 20th Century Fox / PF; **19,** © 20th Century Fox Film Corp. All rights reserved; **20,** ABC/PF; **21,** PF; **26,** (l.) Chaplin/Zuma Press; (r.) PF; **30,** Wayman Richard/CO-SY; **34–35,** AP-WW/ Aaron Harris; **37,** (bot.) © Franck Robichon/epa/CO; (r.) MCT/Newscom; **38,** (l.) Courtesy Rockstar Games/Zuma Press; (cent.) *Halo 2* screenshot reprinted with permission from Microsoft Corporation/Courtesy Microsoft Corporation and Bungie Studios; (r.) *The Sims* 2 images © 2007 Electronic Arts Inc. All rights reserved. Used with permission; **40,** (l.) Courtesy Paramount Pictures/ZUMA Press; (r.) © Screen Gems/courtesy Everett Collection; **41,** Courtesy of Red Octane; **42–43,** Jose Luis, Pelaez/Blend/Robertstock; **45,** Courtesy of Eric Faden and Youtube.com; **46,** (l.) Image courtesy of The Advertising Archives; (r.) Courtesy of the National Center for Supercomputing Applications and the Board of Trustees of the University of Illinois; **47,** John Lund/Marc Romanelli/Blend Images/GI; **48,** Image courtesy of The Advertising Archives; **49,** Courtesy of the National Center for Supercomputing Applications and the Board of Trustees of the University of Illinois; **50,** Lou Brooks; **51,** John Lund/Marc Romanelli/Blend Images/GI; **52,** Courtesy of talkingpointsmemo.com. Reprinted by permission; **53,** www.facebook.com; **54,** KRT/News.com; **56,** AP-WW/Paul Sakuma; **58,** Lluis Gene/AFP/GI/Newscom; **61,** Kevin Lee/Bloomberg News/Landov; **64,** Dimitri Negroponte; **65,** Jonathan Ernst/Reuters/Landov; **67,** Courtesy of Apple, Inc.; **70–71,** AP-WW/Steve Parsons; **72,** © David Brabyn/CO; **74,** (top) Russell Knight/BIPs/GI; (l.) Russell Knight/BIPs/GI; (r.) © CO-BA; **75,** (top) Justin Sullivan/GI; (l.) CBS/Landov; (r.) Courtesy of Apple, Inc.; **78,** Inti St Clair / Blend Images/Jupiter Images; **79,** Courtesy of Apple, Inc.; **80,** © CO-BA; **81,** Robert Johnson, photo booth self-portrait, early 1930s, © 1986 Delta Haze Corporation. All Rights Reserved. Used by Permission; **82,** © CO-BA; **83,** © CO-BA; **84,** Evening Standard/GI; **85,** © CO-BA; **86,** CBS Photo Archive/GI; **87,** (top) © CO-BA; (bot.) © CO-BA; **89,** (l.) AP-WW; (r.) AP-WW/David J. Phillip; **90,** (top) CBS/Landov; (l.) AP-WW; **91,** Andrew DeLory/Hulton Archive/GI; **92,** Sire Records/GI; **93,** Robert Roberton/Retna; **95,** (l.) Donald Bowers/GI; (r.) Michael Tran/FilmMagic/GI; **98,** GI; **99,** AP-WW; **100,** Naashon Falk/Full Frame; **102,** Bryan Bedder/GI; **106–107,** AP-WW/Lawrence Jackson; **110,** (l.) © CO-BA; (r.) SSPL-The Image Works; **111,** (top) SSPL-The Image Works; (cent.) Courtesy WOR radio; (bot.) Getty Images for Meet the Press; **112,** © CO-BA; **113,** GI; **114,** GI; **115,** (l.) Minnesota Historical Society/CO; (r.) © CO-BA; **117,** Courtesy WOR radio; **118,** © CO-BA; **119,** © CO-BA; **122,** © CO-BA; **123,** Schenectady Museum Archives; **124,** (l.) Hulton Archive/GI; (r.) © CO-BA; **125,** Petrified Collection/GI; **128,** Rodney Oman Bradley/Oman Studios; **129,** Lenny Moore/REACH Media Inc.; **131,** Marissa Roth/The New York Times/Redux; **132,** Getty Images for Meet the Press; **134,** Shannon Stapleton/ Reuters-CO; **135,** Sam Diaz, "HD Radio Grabs the Ears of Satellite Rivals," *Washington Post,* July 3, 2007, p. D04; **138,** Colin Young-Wolff/PhotoEdit, Inc.; **139,** Anthony Souffle/*Naples Daily News*; **142–143,** NBC/PF; **145,** Daniel Berehulak/GI; **146,** (top) CBS Photo Archive/GI; (bot.) © CO-BA; **147,** (top) PF; (bot.) © 20th Century Fox Film Corp. All rights reserved, Courtesy Everett Collection; **148,** © CO-BA; **149,** U.S. Department of Commerce; **150,** Newhouse News Service /Landov; **151,** CHUM Television Photo/

Index

information superhighway, as
term, 45
infotainment, 26, 167
Ingraham, Laura, 130
Inktomi, 51
In Living Color (television
program), 168
innovations, media, 10
In Policing the Crisis (Hall), 483
In Rainbows (Radiohead), 71-72
Insight, 308
Insight Communications, 204
instant books, 325-26
instant messaging (IM), 27, 47, 52
InStyle, 307
integration, racial, 82
interest films, 230
International Telephone &
Telegraph (ITT), 415
Internet
  advertising on, 343-44, 358-59
  alternative music and, 93, 102
  broadcasting of television
    shows on, 169-70
  democracy and, 66-67
  evolution of
    commercial structure, 49-51
    development stage, 46-47
    entrepreneurial stage, 48
    overview, 45, 46-47
    Web 1.0, 49
    Web 2.0, 51-55
    Web 3.0, 54-55
  evolution of Information Age
    and, 8
  freedom of expression and,
    519-20
  issues
    access, 63-66
    appropriateness, 62-63
    overview, 59
    security, 60-62
  journalism and, 454-55
  media economics and, 412-13
  mob psychology and, 103
  as music retailer, 97
  as news source, 279
  ownership issues
    advertising, 57, 59
    alternative voices, 57-58
    leading companies, 55-57
  print journalism and, 261-62
  public relations and, 391, 393
  revival of conversational and
    letter-writing skills with, 27
  as source of television
    programming, 177
  user statistics, 13

Internet Archive, 58
Internet Explorer, 50, 56, 61
Internet radio, 133-34
Internet service providers
  (ISPs), 49-50
Interpol (rock and roll group), 93
interpretation
  in critical process, 28-29
interpretive journalism, 258-59
Interpublic Group, 353, 359
Interpublic Group of Cos., 388
Interstate Commerce Act, 384
interstitials, 358
Interview with a Vampire
  (Rice), 334
In the Heat of the Night (motion
  picture), 228
In These Times, 308
Into the Wild (Krakauer), 260
In Touch Weekly, 296
Invasion from Mars, The
  (Cantril), 475
Invasion of the Body Snatchers
  (motion picture), 225
inverted-pyramid style, 257
investigative journalism, 250
  Nellie Bly and, 246-48
  use of deception in, 443
  Veronica Guerin and, 248
  yellow press and, 254
iPhone, 67
iPod, 79, 105
Iraq war
  distrust of media and govern-
    ment and, 27
  ethics of media coverage of, 14-15
  support for, 12
  television coverage of, 146
Iron Man (motion picture), 328
Ironside (television program), 161
irritation advertising, 360
Irving, Washington, 286
ISPs (Internet service providers),
  49-50
"It Don't Mean a Thing (If It Ain't
  Got that Swing)," 82
It Happened One Night (motion
  picture), 223, 224
It's Perfectly Normal (Harris), 330
iTunes
  as adaptation to MP3 format, 79
  Digital Rights Management
    software used by, 78
  displaces Wal-Mart as music
    retailer, 72
  launching of, 97
  popularity of, 77
  profits from, 99

success of, 78
Time magazine on, 103
See also online music stores
iUniverse, 337
Ivins, Molly, 375
Ivory Soap, 348

J. B. Lippincott, 320
Jack Benny Show (television
  program), 157
Jackson, Janet, 518
Jackson, Michael, 93, 94, 198
Jackson, Peter, 328
Jackson 5, 89
Jacobson, Michael F., 355
Japanese cinema, 231
Jaws (motion picture), 226, 237, 481
Jay-Z, 95
jazz, 73, 80
Jazz Singer, The (motion picture),
  214, 222
Jefferson, Thomas, 436, 498,
  501, 523
Jefferson Airplane, 91
Jeffersons, The (television
  program), 157
Jeffries, Jim, 511
Jennings, Peter, 155
Jeopardy! (television program),
  153, 162, 173
"Jerry and David's Guide to the
  World Wide Web" (Yang
  and Filo), 50
Jesus Christ Superstar (motion
  picture), 225
Jet, 300
Jett, Joan, 93
Jewell, Richard, 446-47
Jewish Currents, 308
JFK (motion picture), 12
Jimi Hendrix Experience, 91
Jim Rome Show, The (radio
  program), 138
JOAs (joint operating agree-
  ments), 272-73
Jobs, Steve, 105, 424
Jodhaa Akbar (motion picture),
  231
Joe Camel advertising campaign,
  347, 369, 370
John, Elton, 84, 91
John Adams (television
  program), 165
John Hancock Financial, 393-94
"Johnny B. Goode," 83
Johnson, Jack, 511, 512
Johnson, Jeffrey, 273
Johnson, John H., 300

Johnson, Lyndon, 154, 155, 162
Johnson, Robert, 81
Johnson, Samuel, 284, 327
Johnson, Steven, 20-21, 36
Johnson & Johnson, 349, 397-98
joint operating agreements
  (JOAs), 272-73
Joker's Wild, The (television
  program), 152
Jolie, Angelina, 26
Jolson, Al, 80, 214, 222
Jones, Grace, 84
Jones, Jason, 183
Jones, Larry W., 170
Jones, LeRoi, 266
Jones, Mary Harris, 308
Joplin, Janis, 90, 91
Joplin, Scott, 80
Jordan, Michael, 360
journalism
  alternative models
    overview, 456, 457
    public journalism, 456,
      458-59
    satiric journalism, 459-60
  democracy and, 461-63
  ethics and
    ethical predicaments, 443-45
    overview, 443
    resolving ethical problems,
      445-47
  historical trends, 25
  in modern age
    Internet, 454-55
    print vs. television news,
      452-54
    visual language, 455
  overview
    definition of news, 437-39
    values, 439-41
  public relations and
    alternative voices, 401-2
    elements of professional
      friction, 399-400
    image enhancing strategies,
      400-401
    overview, 398
  reporting rituals
    adversarial stance, 451-52
    balancing conflict, 451
    focusing on the present,
      447-50
    use of experts, 450-51
Joyce, James, 22, 330, 505
Joyce, William ("Lord Haw
  Haw"), 474
Joyner, Tom, 129
Judas Priest, 467